MARBLED PAPER

A Publication of the

A. S. W. ROSENBACH FELLOWSHIP

IN BIBLIOGRAPHY

MARBLED PAPER

ITS HISTORY, TECHNIQUES, AND PATTERNS

With Special Reference to the Relationship of

Marbling to Bookbinding in Europe and

the Western World

RICHARD J. WOLFE

upp

UNIVERSITY OF PENNSYLVANIA PRESS

Philadelphia

Library of Congress Cataloging-in-Publication Data

Wolfe, Richard J.
    Marbled paper: its history, techniques, and patterns: with special references to
the relationship of marbling to bookbinding in Europe and the Western world /
Richard J. Wolfe.
    p.   cm.—(A Publication of the A. S. W. Rosenbach fellowship
in bibliography)
    Bibliography: p.
    Includes index.
    ISBN 0-8122-8188-8
    1. Marbled papers.   2. Marbling (Bookbinding)   3. Bookbinding.
I. Title.   II. Series.
Z271.W638   1989
686.3'6—dc20   89-14614
                                                                   CIP

Designed by Carl Gross

For
RALPH T. ESTERQUEST
AND
HARALD OSTVOLD

CONTENTS

ILLUSTRATIONS

PREFACE

THE work that follows is the outcome of research begun more than twenty-five years ago when I was completing a bibliography of early secular American music at the New York Public Library. It started casually—almost by accident. Having become curious about the marbled papers decorating many of the book bindings in the stacks adjacent to my office, I naively set out one day in the early 1960s to determine just how and when these papers had come into existence, and who had been responsible for making them. My initial searches informed me that great confusion existed on all these points, and great gaps in the available literature as well. None of the sources consulted could answer my questions with any degree of assuredness. I next sought out whatever technical literature I could find on the subject of paper marbling and in several cases translated it, for most of the available marbling manuals I soon learned, had been written in German. Using this material as a guide, I succeeded in the following years in training myself in the methods and mysteries of marbling paper.

During the quarter century since the outset of my research, I have marbled more than 20,000 sheets of paper, reproducing almost all of the patterns that are known. I reinforced this practical experience by accumulating along the way a substantial collection of literature on marbling and paper decoration—over thirty linear feet of manuals, and other books, pamphlets, and related materials—as well as thousands of sheets of early and original marbled papers obtained from bookbinders and restorers, booksellers, and other pertinent sources. Moreover, because I was continually in contact with marbled papers in old bindings in my daily work as a curator of rare books, I was able constantly to observe original specimens and interpret them through my practical experience and large store of literature and gradually build up a fund of knowledge that eventually enabled me to answer some of the questions that had provoked my initial quest.

Early in my search, I learned that a veritable Bedlam of misinformation existed on this seemingly simple craft, for many of the facts that had been put on the record over the years controverted and were at variance with one another. Little information of a professional nature had been made available until the craft had run most of its course and had begun to wane. And it seemed that later commentators on marbling had developed pet theories about how marbling had arisen and had come to be practiced over the ages, with many of their ideas seemingly snatched out of thin air. While the more reliable commentators either explored the initial practice of the craft in the Eastern world or concentrated on its introduction into the Western one, others were content merely to comment on this or that aspect of the subject or to describe events that had occurred in recent times. No one, it appeared, had ever attempted to trace the course of this craft through the long stream of history; no one, it was obvious, had ever tried in a serious way to fill in the middle period of the craft's existence, which constituted its largest and most important phase; nor had anyone tried to trace its practice in all of the various locations throughout the world. The confusion, noted before, and the fragmentary, dispersed, and difficult-to-find literature on the subject had obviously discouraged the undertaking and completion of any such task—and indeed, not very many years ago it had seemed beyond the realm of possibility to me as well. However, as I point out in the text which follows, persistence is the key to overcoming the difficulties in learning and accomplishing this art, and the same sort of persistence has resulted in the book which follows.

An invitation from the University of Pennsylvania authorities to serve as the A. S. W. Rosenbach Fellow in Bibliography for the year 1981 and to deliver two lectures on the subject of marbling paper provided me with an excuse to begin putting onto paper some of the ideas that I had been formulating about marbling during the previous fifteen years or more. Afterwards, when Maurice English, then Editor of the University of Pennsylvania Press, asked me to expand my lectures into a book, an ideal opportunity arose to bring into reality a bona fide history of paper marbling—a matter that I had been contemplating almost from the time that I had commenced my investigations on this art. The enormity of the project and its attendant problems, however, required the better part of an additional decade of investigation and writing, and several trips abroad, before that objective was finally attained.

As shall be noted many times over in the pages that follow, much of the information I rely on when tracing the practice of the marbling art in the various regions of the Western world is based on the marbling remnants that survive within the covers of old books. In order to interpret correctly what those fragments can tell us, one must be cognizant of the changes in bookbinding methods and styles developed over the ages—an important element that has been lacking from prior research on the history of marbling. Marbled papers in ancient bindings can serve the same function as the tracks and bony fragments of prehistoric fossils; when studied in a careful systematic way, and when correlated with their environment, they can provide form and substance to a way of life that has become all but extinct. The material contained in the pages that follow, then, does not derive from book-learning or historical research alone; it is the re-evaluation of all data through the eyes of a practicing marbler of many years' experience and of a rare books librarian who for many years has been in constant contact with marbled papers that are preserved in ancient tomes surviving from the very time of their making.

This work is divided into three parts. The longest part, the first eleven chapters, reconstructs the history of marbling as it probably began and came to be practiced in the Eastern world and subsequently in the West. At the same time, I follow its course through the various lands where its conduct became substantial or at least significant; and I take into account and discuss all of the important literature bearing on this subject. The second part (Chapters 12, 13, and 14) discusses the technical aspects of the craft. Here is described the marbling technique and how it is carried out; what materials are necessary for its conduct; and the physics and chemistry underlying the process and its constituents. The last chapter constitutes the final part. Here I endeavor to explain and illustrate the best-known patterns that have come into existence and usage during the craft's life in Europe and the Western world. I have attempted, thus, in the pages that follow to place every aspect of this subject in its proper perspective and to provide in a definitive way an overall view of paper marbling as the art has unfolded throughout the course of time.

ACKNOWLEDGMENTS

As I complete a work that has taken more than a quarter of a century to compile and bring to fruition, it is difficult to remember and acknowledge everyone who has made some contribution along the way. During this time, librarians, archivists, museum curators, bookbinders, book restorers, booksellers, friends, and even casual contacts have assisted me in one way or another in gaining the necessary information and materials to form this volume. Some of the data provided and gathered sometimes seemed inconsequential at the outset; however, reevaluated in the light of other or later evidence, minute information often proved more important and eventually became strong threads that were woven into the finished fabric which follows.

Two individuals stand out as especially important in the development of this work—and, paradoxically, neither of them had any direct contact with marbling or its history. One was the late Dr. Mark D. Altschule—physician and physiologist *supérieur,* medical historian and art connoisseur, unique philosopher, and my friend and counselor for a period of more than twenty years. Through his wide knowledge, imparted in innumerable conversations and discussions and grounded in a keen sensibility and appreciation of fine and applied art, he contributed much to this work as it took shape in my mind. Dr. Altschule also helped make possible, through a grant from the Eleanor Naylor Dana Charitable Trust of New York, the many color illustrations so necessary to an undertaking of this sort. The other person to whom I owe a special debt is Rollo G. Silver, also of Boston, who, like Mark Altschule, formed standards and models to be emulated. His guidance and constructive criticism, and, in several cases, the special information he provided, form a significant part of this book. His affable friendship over several decades has been important in shaping my thinking as well. Mr. Silver read the manuscript through several drafts and, with his usual eaglelike perspicacity, offered many suggestions which vastly improved the final version.

I must also acknowledge the extraordinary aid and almost unparalleled resources of the Harvard University libraries and particularly the Rosamond B. Loring collection on paper decoration that is contained in the university's Houghton Library. Because information on this subject is scattered in difficult-to-obtain books around the world, the resources of the Harvard libraries and the Loring collection, combined with the significant collection of literature that I had assembled, formed a wide base on which I could construct this work. In addition, William H. Bond, formerly Librarian of the Houghton Library, supplied me with several important pieces of information relative to early English marbling, and Roger Stoddard, its Curator of Rare Books, allowed me to examine the masses of books that had been grouped by national origin in the Houghton Library's bookstacks so that I could inspect marbled decoration in them. The Kress Library of economics and business history in the Baker Library of the Harvard Business School also provided many eighteenth- and nineteenth-century dictionaries and economic texts containing information on marbling; Ruth R. Rogers, Curator of the Kress Library, and her staff were most helpful to me in the use of these resources.

Over the past quarter century I have corresponded with individuals all over the world in an attempt to locate literature and gain information on the conduct of marbling through the centuries and in various locations. I have also visited libraries and museums throughout Europe and America to inspect such literature and to examine original examples of marbled paper, particularly in bookbindings. In doing so, I came into contact with many people who made it possible or at least easier for me to gain access to such materials; sometimes they even contributed special information that otherwise would have passed unnoticed.

Henck Voorn, formerly curator of the significant paper collection preserved in the Koninklijke Bibliotheek in the Hague, was especially helpful and cooperative. The large collection on paper and paper decoration that he has assembled there, comprising one of the most important resources for the study of these fields not only in Europe but worldwide, stands as a monument to his resourcefulness; Drs. Albert J. Elin, who succeeded him at the Royal Dutch Library, continues Mr. Voorn's enlightened policy of allowing researchers to make use of that library's materials. J. Toulet of the Bibliothèque Nationale and his staff, and particularly Geneviève Guilleminot-Chrétien, have also been extremely helpful to me in compiling part of this volume. Mme. Chrétien recently completed an important study of early French marbling which resulted in a major exhibition on the subject; she also helped me obtain from the exhibition catalog some of the important color illustrations for reprinting here (with the kind permission of Adriaan Verburg of Middleburg, the Netherlands, who holds the copyright on the catalog and to whom I am also grateful). Another curator of an important collection of materials on marbling, Dr. Wolfgang Schlieder, Leiter der Papierhistorische Sammlung of the Deutsche Bücherei in Leipzig, and Frau Schneiderhinze of his staff, must especially be thanked for services rendered to me by mail and during a recent visit to Leipzig. The Deutsche Bücherei holds key materials on German marbling and upholds the finest scholarly traditions of the past as well.

In Scandinavia, Dr. Sten V. Lindberg, formerly of the Kungliga Biblioteket, and Dr. Jonas Bey of the Nordiska Museet in Stockholm assisted me in obtaining information on marbling in Sweden in earlier times; Erland Kolding Nielsen, Chief Librarian of Det Kongelige Bibliotek in Copenhagen, through his many courtesies and through the special assistance of two members of his staff, Ingrid Ilsøe and Ruth Benzen, provided similar assistance with regard to Danish marbling. Mme. G. Bonté of the Musée des Arts Décoratifs in Paris gave me similar help and courtesies during my visits there. Mirjam M. Foot of the British Library assisted me in using the resources of that institution, especially the Olga Hirsch collection of books and other materials relating to paper decoration, as did Jeanne D. Hamilton when I visited the Victoria and Albert Museum in London. Jack Baldwin and his successor, Nigel Thorp, of the library of Glasgow University were exceedingly helpful in assisting me by mail and during a visit there. Mr. Thorp aided me further by transcribing the difficult-to-read seventeenth-century French manuscript account of marbling discussed in Chapter 4 so that I could eventually translate and publish it. And Professor Tsuen-hsuin Tsien, Curator Emeritus of the Far Eastern Library of the University of Chicago, and Jixing Pan of the Institute for the History of Natural Science of the Academia Sinica in Beijing, China, greatly assisted me in obtaining some idea of the marbling activity that likely existed in China in antiquity.

Other library and museum curators lent assistance that must be acknowledged as well. They include Marcus A. McCorison, Director and Librarian of the American Antiquarian Society, and Joanne D. Chaison, Sidney Berger, and other members of his staff; William Matheson, late of the Library of Congress; Dorothy T. Hanks, formerly with the National Library of Medicine; Susan Alon of the Yale University Medical Library; Austin McLean of the Princeton University Library; Paolo Veneziani of the Biblioteca Centrale Nationale in Rome; Dr. R. Heinrich of the Deutsches Museum von Meisterwerken der Naturwissenschaften und Technik in Munich; Dr. Ruth

Malhotra of the Museum für Kunst und Gewerbe in Hamburg; Daniel W. Woodward and Thomas V. Lange of the Huntington Library in San Marino; Woodman Taylor, formerly of the Islamic Department of the Harvard University Museums; R. Russell Maylone of the Northwestern University Library; Jerilynn Marshall of the Newberry Library in Chicago; Helen S. Butz of the University of Michigan Libraries; Dr. R. Bansa of the Bayerische Staatsbibliothek in Munich; Walter A. Frankel of the Free Library of Philadelphia; Alice N. Loranth of the Cleveland Public Library; Charles Mann of the Pennsylvania State University Libraries; Christa Sammons of the Beinecke Rare Book and Manuscript Library of Yale University; Linda A. Naru of the Center for Research Libraries, Chicago; Judith J. Ho of the National Agricultural Library; Mark Dimunation of the Stanford University Libraries; Libby Chenault of the University of North Carolina Libraries; librarians and archivists at the Franklin Institute of Philadelphia, the Rhode Island Historical Society, the University of Wisconsin Libraries, the Boston Public Library, and the Boston Athenaeum; and numerous others whose kindnesses are reflected in letters dispersed throughout my files.

A number of institutions kindly allowed reproduction of materials in their collections: the Germanisches Nationalmuseum in Nürnberg; the Houghton Library, the Widener Library, and the Fogg Art Museum of Harvard University; the Free Library of Philadelphia; the Koninklijke Bibliotheek in the Hague; Det Kongelige Bibliotek in Copenhagen; the Musée des Arts Décoratifs and the Bibliothèque Nationale in Paris; the Bayerische Staatsbibliothek in Munich; the Toshiyo Miyazawa Paper Museum in Tokyo; the British Library; the Boston Public Library; the Boston Medical Library in the Francis A. Countway Library of Medicine; the Kunstbibliothek, Berlin; the Bryn Mawr College Library; and the American Antiquarian Society.

Many bookbinders and book restorers provided information and marbled papers over the years. Bernard Middleton, dean of British bookbinding historians and an internationally known book restorer, lent help, advice, and encouragement and sent me photocopies of rare materials in his collection of bookbinding literature (which is now owned by the Rochester Institute of Technology); along with Mirjam Foot of the British Library, he also read the manuscript in its next to final form and made suggestions to improve it. C. Allan Carpenter, Jr., of Shrewsbury, Massachusetts, provided, over the years, many unusual marbled papers that he had removed from old bindings and in this way helped me learn much about pattern development; some of the materials he supplied appear as illustrations at the conclusion of Chapter 15. Fred C. Shihadeh, a bookbinder and book restorer of Ardmore, Pennsylvania, sent photocopies of some of the rare bookbinding and marbling manuals he owns. And

Willman Spawn, a former book restorer at the American Philosophical Society who is now cataloging the outstanding bookbinding collection at Bryn Mawr College, provided information, advice, criticism, and materials as well.

A number of booksellers also contributed significantly to this effort. Herman Cohen, proprietor of the Chiswick Book Shop, formerly of New York City and recently of Sandy Hook, Connecticut, sold me my first piece of literature relating to marbling more than twenty-five years ago (a copy of the 1881 edition of James Nicholson's bookbinding manual) and later provided many more important pieces. Oscar Shreyer of New York, a dealer specializing in Portuguese literature, sent me a number of early Portuguese pamphlets containing marbled and decorated paper and marbled paper removed from early Portuguese books; he also sent me several important pieces of information. Bernard Gordon of Chestnut Hill, Massachusetts, and Watch Hill, Rhode Island, referred interesting bindings to me as well as other materials containing unusual examples of marbling; Ron Lieberman, proprietor of The Family Album bookshop in Glen Rock, Pennsylvania, supplied several important pieces of marbling literature, as did Samuel Murray of Wilbraham, Massachusetts, Charles B. Wood III of Boston, Emil Offenbacher of Kew Gardens, Queens, New York, Jeremy Norman of San Francisco, and Gerhard Zaehringer of Kreuzlingen, Switzerland.

Among private individuals and friends who assisted me in organizing and compiling this work were the late Hans Schmoller of Windsor, England, who brought to my attention and copied information on marbling from the archival records of the Royal Society of the Arts in London, and his wife, Tatiana, who has been a collector of decorated paper for many years. Dr. Helen C. Brock, now living in Cambridge, England, performed similar services while on the staff of Glasgow University. Estrellita Karsh of Ottawa, Canada, searched the archives of Venice to unearth information on the Remondini family and their activities there and in nearby Bassano. Dr. Martin C. Carey of the Brigham and Women's Hospital in Boston, an expert on bile metabolism, increased my knowledge of bile fluid and its use in marbling through many discussions, memoranda, and criticisms of my manuscript, and he also helped me solve some of the problems concerning colloidality and surface tension that are inherent in the marbling process. Hannah D. French of Rye, New Hampshire, dean of American bookbinding historians, gave me several important tips leading to information that was integrated into this work, as did Sue Allen of New Haven. Dr. Peter Wagner of the Sprach- und Literaturwissenschaftliche Fakultät of the Katolische Universität Eichstatt provided invaluable assistance by searching in German libraries for rare manuals and pieces of literature so I could examine them in the limited time available during my foreign travel. Diana Patterson of Toronto, a Laurence Sterne scholar and enthusiast, helped me with some of the problems relating to the initial editions of *Tristram Shandy.*

Other individuals who provided information and special assistance were Edward A. Artesani of Wellesley Hills, Massachusetts; John R. Gannett of the Geo. D. Barnard Company of St. Louis; Eric P. Newman, also of St. Louis; the late Dard Hunter of Chillicothe, Ohio, and his son, Dard Hunter II; Pauline Johnson, formerly Professor of Art at the University of Washington in Seattle; Mary B. Higgins of Forest Hills, New York; Henry Morris of Newtown, Pennsylvania; Morrison Haviland of Stanford, California; Corinne Blakeslee of Boston; Michael Hutchins of the Camberwell School of Arts and Crafts in London; Walter Krepl of Ulm, West Germany; E. Furch of Hannover, West Germany; S. Moessner of Weilheim, West Germany; the late Gerhard Hesse of Leipzig, East Germany; and Semsa Yegin of Istanbul, Turkey.

From the ranks of marblers, marbling historians, and marbling enthusiasts I must cite first and foremost Stéphane Ipert, who is presently working as a book and paper restorer in Arles, France. M. Ipert passed on to me many valuable facts about marbling which appear in this book. Norma Rubovits of Chicago, a marbler and long-time correspondent, also divulged some facts that appear in the pages which follow. And Ilsa Mühlbacher, an Austrian bookbinder and paper decorator, helped me search out information on marbling in museums and institutions in Vienna.

Robert Arndt, Editor of *Aramco World Magazine,* allowed me to reproduce here some of the photographs he took many years ago while compiling an article on Mustaffa Düzgünman, Turkey's leading marbler; Isik Yazan and Nusret Hepgul of Istanbul (the latter a marbler) kindly furnished reproductions of early Turkish marbling with calligraphy that appear among the color illustrations here; and Hiraku Kido of the Takao Paper Company's Toshiyo Miyazawa Paper Museum in Tokyo provided the pictures on *suminagashi* marbling. Leonard Finn of West Roxbury, Massachusetts, a collector of numismatic materials, loaned me some of his rare marbled money so that I could have it photographed for reproduction here, and Joseph Rubinfine, now of Miami Beach, Florida, allowed me to reproduce the Benjamin Franklin marbled document that appears along with the marbled money. Walter Tower of the Nimrod Press in Boston provided technical assistance with regard to the layout and production of the color illustrations in this book.

I must thank Richard DeGennaro, now of the New York Public Library but formerly Director of the University of Pennsylvania Libraries, and his Rosenbach board, for extending to me an invitation to become the Rosenbach Lecturer in Bibliography for the year 1981. It was in the preparation for the two Rosenbach lectures that I commenced formal writing on this book. My wife Elin spent many hours and long evenings reading the next to final draft of the manuscript, editing and improving it and making many valid suggestions that were worked into the final version. I must also acknowledge the very professional assistance of the staff of the University of Pennsylvania Press, especially Arthur B. Evans, its Associate Director, with whom I chiefly interacted in the publication of this work; Carl Gross, who supervised its design; and Alison Anderson, who attended to the copy editing of the final manuscript.

I also am grateful to the American Council of Learned Societies for granting funds for my travel to Europe in the fall of 1982, where I did important research on marbling in many of the lands where it flourished. And I must acknowledge once more the valuable assistance of the Eleanor Naylor Dana Charitable Trust of New York for helping fund the color illustrations in the chapters which follow.

Steven Borack of Randolph, Massachusetts, did most of the black and white photography and many of the color illustrations as well; Nicholas Bakalis of Watertown, Massachusetts, photographed the three-dimensional objects that are illustrated in this work.

Richard J. Wolfe

1

The Nature and Origin of Marbling; Marbling in the Far and Near East

Few people today are aware of the considerable role that marbled paper played in the everyday life of Europe and the Western world from late in the seventeenth century until late in the nineteenth. And even fewer—mainly those who work in or have had a great deal of contact with large research libraries or the antiquarian book trade—are in a position to appreciate the enormous contribution that marbling has made to the overall history of the book.[1]

Until after the middle of the nineteenth century, when the development of mechanized bookbinding methods first diminished and afterward virtually did away with the need for their services, hand bookbinders utilized marbled paper and the marbler's craft to embellish many of the books that were bound during the previous several centuries.[2] Marbled papers were employed outside the book trade as well to adorn a great many products of everyday use. They served, for example, as wall coverings;[3] as linings for the interiors of trunks, boxes, wallets, musical instrument cases and other containers;[4] for covering boxes and other receptacles; as ornamentation in the panels of cabinets, furniture, and even harpsichords; as wrappings for toys, drug powders, and other consumer goods; for enclosing blank books used for writing, and for many stationery purposes; and as shelf papers for lining cupboards and cabinets and for many home-decorating purposes (Plate I).[5]

Despite their prior popularity and extensive employment, marbled papers and the marbler's craft have remained the most obscure, and least investigated and understood, of all aspects of the book arts. This situation resulted mainly because of the restrictive manner in which the trade was carried on in former times and because of the guarded and limited literature resulting therefrom.[6] By and large, the very nature of the product has worked against a better understanding of it. The work of the marbler was almost never signed and is encountered today only in piecemeal form. When used as adornment on books, marbled papers were cut up and pasted onto binder's boards to serve as cover papers without or as

decorative lining papers within. When employed in the course of everyday life, as wrappers or for other ornamental yet utilitarian purposes, they usually wore out or were discarded after use. Moreover, the large number and variety of patterns evolving over the centuries and the complications arising from the multiplicity or seeming multiplicity of forms caused by color variation and the intermixture of designs have resulted in near total confusion. Such factors have combined to frustrate the identification, classification, and dating of the earlier marblers' output and have inhibited accurate historical research that would lead to a better understanding and appreciation of this once popular yet arcane craft.[7]

For about two and a half centuries after its introduction into Europe about the year 1600, marbling was one of the chief means available for producing the colored papers used in bookbinding and other decorative work. It performed a similarly important role in the day-to-day life of the Near East, where the art was brought to perfection even earlier and used in conjunction with Islamic bookbinding, calligraphy, iconography, fine arts, and even administrative uses. In both the East and the West, large numbers and many generations of people spent their working lives in the production of marbled papers needed for these varied purposes. But the relentless changes brought about by the Industrial Revolution in the nineteenth century, which caused a diminution in hand bookbinding, also resulted in the decline and near extinction of the marbler's art. It was continued thereafter (as it is today) by a small number of artisans who catered to the needs of the surviving hand bookbinders, in a mere semblance of its prior form.

In the pages that follow I shall attempt to describe and reconstruct from the proverbial ashes the rise and fall of this charming craft, which in its heyday comprised an appreciable industry. At the same time, I will strive to document a much overlooked area, in the field of hand bookbinding in particular and the book arts in general. Hopefully, these pages will give form and substance to an under-appreciated group of artisans who, often intrigued with the possibilities of this particular art, worked to continue and perfect it and nursed it into its most glorious moments of flowering.

Definition of the Marbling Process

The description which over the years has come to be accepted as the standard definition of marbling is the one provided by the celebrated English marbling master Charles Woolnough just after the middle of the nineteenth century, in his *The Art of Marbling*, the first really comprehensive manual of this heretofore mostly secret method of decorating paper.[8] Shortly thereafter it was reprinted in the first comprehensive American work on bookbinding, James B. Nicholson's *A Manual of the Art of Bookbinding* (for which reason that book or author has sometimes been cited as its source).[9] "Marbling," Woolnough tells us,

> is an art which consists in the production of certain patterns and effects, by means of colors so prepared as to float upon a preparation of mucillaginous liquid, possessing certain antagonistic properties to the colors prepared for the purpose, and which colors when so prepared, floated, and formed into patterns upon the surface of the liquid, are taken off by laying thereon a piece or sheet of paper, or dipping therein the smoothly cut edges of a book.

While this overly long sentence does indeed describe the marbling process, perhaps as well and as accurately as can be done, it tells us only part of the matter. Another definition, which takes into consideration the chemical and technological aspects of the subject, might explain marbling as a method for producing colored designs on paper or on the edges of books in which liquid colors are first suspended upon a liquid surface-tension medium. The colors are manipulated into patterns or configurations by physical or chemical means and then transferred by absorption onto paper or onto book edges by bringing the paper or book into contact with the medium. The surface tension effects, the most important and most complicated parts of the process, are controlled by adding to water appropriate quantities of starch derived from a starch-bearing plant; the action of the colors is governed by the addition to them of chemical substances which promote their buoyancy and enhance their expansion. But more on this later. Finally, definitions of the marbling technique may be reduced to the most simplistic terms by quoting a recent commentator, who stated that "paper marbling may be defined simply as the floating of colors on a liquid to form a pattern, which may be lifted by placing a sheet of paper on the floating colors and then removing it."[10]

Marbling is a handcraft invented or discovered in antiquity to fulfill the need for decorated paper in a simple and practical way. Although elementary in conception, it is extremely difficult to execute, for many of the components in the process are unstable and antagonistic to one another. Furthermore, success or failure often depends on external forces over which the marbler has little or no control, such as temperature and humidity of the outside environment, the fluidity or viscosity of the size (i.e., the glutinous consistency of the surface-tension medium), the subtle changes that take place in the colors as chemical agents are added to them, and the like. Also involved are some of the most complex and least controllable chemical and physical phenomena known, such as colloidality, capillarity, and Brownian movement, for the size or surface-tension medium is, in effect, a colloidal system.[11] It should come as no surprise that most beginners soon become discouraged, and success in the technique is almost always achieved only after years of hard work, frequent disappointments, and dogged persistence.[12]

The process was called "marbling" and the papers "marbled" because the earliest examples seen by Europeans resembled the appearance of marble, that is, they were veined like marble stone. And while its later forms often took on different appearances, the method has continued to be designated in this primal way. Like many of the hand processes that have come down through the ages, the beginnings and early history of this craft are clouded in the mists and haze of time. As the late Franz Weisse pointed out in his 1940 manual on this art form, the last major marbling manual to issue from the hands of a marbling master and teacher,

> The history of marbling has not really been written yet. What appears on it in books is based more on conjecture than on certainty. We know only for sure that marbled papers have existed for some centuries now. This is known to us through imprints in old books which indicate the years of their origin. In such books colored papers are commonly present in the form of end-papers, providing evidence of these remarkably charming, lovely papers. But who were the manufacturers, who were the inventors, this the gods alone know. Up till now they have divulged their identities to no investigator.[13]

One might conjecture that the art arose in very early times when an artist or calligrapher discarded his stale colors that contained bile or urine, for these organic substances often were added to colors to brighten them or to better disperse them. Afterward, noticing the colors floating intermixed upon a pool of water, he had the good sense to lay a piece of paper on the surface and absorb the marblelike pattern onto it.

Early European Notice of Marbling;
and the Album Amicorum

By the end of the fifteenth century, both the Ottoman Empire and Islam reigned supreme in the Near East and throughout much of the Mediterranean world and threatened central Europe. Their territorial expansion westward early in the next century brought the Ottomans into direct conflict with the Habsburgs and the Holy Roman Empire. In furtherance of his goals, the Ottoman emperor Süleyman I (referred to in Europe as "the Magnificent") made alliances with a number of European states. One such accommodation was made with France, the enemy of Austria, early in the sixteenth century, and Süleyman also incited the Protestant princes of Germany against the pope and the Holy Roman Emperor. As a result of these actions, the French received important trading concessions in the eastern Mediterranean, and after 1580 England and Holland were granted special status and important trading positions as well. Additionally, the Fuggers, banker princes of Augsburg, and other astute European merchants and traders moved wherever and whenever possible to exploit the opening that had been made. In the aftermath of these developments, the territories of Islam, which previously had been severely restricted in access to Christians, came to be visited by increasing numbers of them. These visitors brought Europe into direct contact with the exotic culture and traditions of the East and in time they discovered marbling, which had already existed there for several centuries.

The craft of marbling paper, as we understand it today, first became known to European travelers to Turkey, Persia, and adjacent regions of the Near East after the middle of the sixteenth and early in the seventeenth centuries. These travelers observed marbled papers there and began to send home samples of these and other newly encountered curiosities. Some of them also came to write about the novel customs and objects they were discovering. In 1553, the Frenchman Pierre Belon du Man published a description of his travels through the Mediterranean and the regions to its east, and made reference to the curious way in which the Turks polished their paper.[14] In time, actual notices of marbled paper and of marbling were made by Englishmen who also had visited these regions. George Sandys in 1610 reported the use of such colored and veined papers by the Turks,[15] and Sir Thomas Herbert mentioned them twice in an account of his travels in Persia in the years 1627–1629.[16] The first report in Western literature of the actual technique of marbling paper and of the workings of the craft was made by the Jesuit mathematician, physicist, chemist, and teacher of oriental languages, Athanasius Kircher in his *Ars Magna Lucis et Umbrae,* published at Rome in 1646.[17] A number of literary allusions to marbling followed over the next half century, many of which were made by scientists and natural

historians: the process seemed to possess mysterious and even magical qualities that placed it within the realm of alchemy, and thus, it aroused their curiosity.[18]

European, English, and American libraries preserve many manuscript books and albums containing marbled papers of Turkish and Persian manufacture that can be dated through manuscript entries and other internal evidence to late sixteenth-century origin, proving beyond all doubt that such papers were being sent or brought home. Their employment in the "Album Amicorum" was particularly popular. The Album Amicorum, which originated in Germany around the middle of the sixteenth century and continued in vogue there into the eighteenth, consisted initially of a number of blank leaves bound into the fronts and backs of printed volumes. These leaves were intended to receive the signatures and armorial bearings of the owner's friends and acquaintances. The signatory often added his motto or device, a few classical or biblical quotations or sentences, some good advice, and a dedication. While this custom was restricted mostly to Germany and Switzerland, a few of these forerunners of the modern autograph album are known to have originated in France, the Low Countries, and Italy. The Germans referred to such an album as a "Stammbuch" and the French called it a "livre d'amis."

These albums were particularly popular with students and scholars, who in the sixteenth and seventeenth centuries did not restrict their studies to one university alone. Max Rosenheim, who has compiled the best general account of the subject,[19] points out that it was the custom, after attending one or more universities at home, to travel (although, admittedly, travel was then risky and no easy task) to foreign seats of learning and to attend lectures at French, Netherlandish, and Italian universities; many of the surviving Album Amicorum contain manuscript entries from the prevailing seats of learning of those early times. Disagreement exists as to the origin of these albums. Two other investigators, Robert and Richard Keil, suggest that they were the offspring of the medieval tourney books, or the documentary proofs of noble descent and coat-armor required by the heralds from the knights when entering the list of a tournament, or the outcome of the *Wappenbuch,* the *liber gentilitii* kept by many noble families.[20] Rosenheim discounts this theory and proposes instead that the origin of the custom can be attributed to the fact that students who were scions of noble families remembered the old *Wappenbuch* or *Stammbuch* (genealogical album) at home and wanted to possess and treasure something of the same kind while traveling to universities throughout the world.

The popularity of these Album Amicorum is proved by the considerable number of them that have survived the ravages of many centuries. Rosenheim reports locating nearly five hundred of them alone, and adds that they were particularly popular among the rich patrons of Augsburg and Nürnberg. In the first half of the sixteenth century the merchants of Augsburg and Nürnberg were the most important in the world. Having accumulated enormous fortunes, the Fuggers and Welsers—the Rothschilds and Morgans of their time—often supplied the monarchs of Europe with the cash to purchase their weapons of war. It is no wonder, Rosenheim theorizes, that their scions of the second half of the century, when visiting universities and traveling over the world, should adopt this form of remembrance. He points out that one album in the British Museum (now Library) contains no less than seven inscriptions with the arms of different Fuggers, and that there are only a few in this period that do not contain the arms and inscriptions of a Fugger, a Welser, or a member of another of the patrician families of Augsburg or Nürnberg.

The Album Amicorum changed somewhat as time advanced. First, it came to serve as a place for recording notes and memoranda and sometimes even for making diary entries. Then, as travelers and merchants more frequently came into contact with the regions between Europe and China, they began to include in their albums some of the marvelously colored papers that they were discovering. Further, as the practice of adding blank leaves to the fronts and backs of printed books became less frequent, the custom arose of binding into albums blank leaves that could be inscribed and decorated at will. Besides the coats of arms that had been included almost from the beginning, signatories also began to pay artists to embellish pages with scenes of student life and other subjects. Accordingly, late in the sixteenth century and through much of the next, artists and publishers came forward to supply albums designed especially for this purpose. They included in these volumes woodcut prints of religious and mythical subjects and emblems or coats of arms of celebrated personages, as well as blank sheets of paper for writing purposes.

The practice of adding sheets of marbled and other types of decorated paper from the East began in the mid-1570s, and the custom became more common by the first half of the seventeenth century as such papers became increasingly available. Nevertheless, albums displaying colored papers make up a small percentage of the large corpus of Album Amicorum that survives today. In addition to blank leaves, these albums might contain an intermixture of Turkish or Persian marbled papers, Turkish silhouette papers (Plate II), white papers ornamented with wash drawings and coats of arms, and woodcut prints of the type mentioned above. I have examined many of the Album Amicorum that contain decorated papers in libraries in Europe and America. They can be found in the Houghton Library of Harvard University, the Olga Hirsch collection in the British Library and the Victoria and Albert Museum in London, the Bibliothèque Nationale in Paris, the Koninklijke Bibliotheek in the Hague, the Deutsche Barockgalerie of the Schaezler-

palais in Augsburg, the Germanisches Nationalmuseum in Nürnberg, and in several other locations. Many more are mentioned and sometimes partially pictured in bookbinding and related literature.[21]

Turkish Silhouette Papers

In his classic work on decorated paper, *Buntpapier, Herkommen, Geschichte, Techniken; Beziehung zur Kunst,* Albert Haemmerle tells us that silhouette papers (Plate II) allegedly were made by artists in the palace of the Turkish Sultan and thus were especially prized by European travelers in the sixteenth and seventeenth centuries. Because one or more sheets of silhouette paper can frequently be found in the Album Amicorum along with marbled papers (another rarity and prized possession of this early time) and because little information has actually appeared about them in print (virtually none of it in English), I will devote a number of the following paragraphs to the subject.[22]

Haemmerle states that silhouette papers were Persian in origin but became a special branch of the crafts of Turkey, many of which, including marbling, were adapted from earlier Iranian art forms. He also mentions that, in the seventeenth century, a Turkish master by the name of Fahri zu Bursa brought this art to a very highly developed form; about ten works containing his silhouette papers are preserved in the Topkapi Seray Museum in Istanbul. Undoubtedly, European travelers received the inspiration for including these papers, as well as marbled ones, in their albums after seeing them bound in Turkish costume books and other exotic works. Such a conclusion is suggested by the reproduction on page 40 of Haemmerle's *Buntpapier* of an illustration in a Turkish costume book dating to about 1580 that depicts (from among many similar illustrations) sultan Murad III in watercolors; the book contains a large number of silhouette papers as well.[23]

Haemmerle explains that the colored effects of this particular type of decorated paper were achieved through patterns; that is, by employing stereotype designs that were cut in outline with a knife. The pattern was cut from thin leather in as many individual pieces as the artist might choose. These pieces of leather would be separated according to the colors that had been selected for each of them; they were soaked in their corresponding colors, and the surplus colors on their surfaces were stripped off. Next, the pattern was assembled on the side of the paper that was intended for printing, the other half of the sheet was brought down over it, and the whole assembly was subjected to great pressure. The paper, which was always thin, was moistened beforehand with strong alum water to prevent the colors from running and insure better permeation throughout. The colored design on the overall pattern was imparted to the paper through a process that the letterpress printer would call "offset" or "setoff." This method of transferring designs to paper could only produce faint images, that is, mere outlines that were best perceived when the sheets were held up and exposed to light.

After printing, the opened sheet was brushed on both sides with "Aher" solution (a preparation containing beaten egg whites that had been stirred together with alum and strained), then polished with a smooth stone to give it a washed appearance. Now and then the outlines of the silhouettes were traced over in gold by hand before polishing. In order to avoid monotony, the outlines of the images in the pattern were arranged so that they repeated only at great intervals. Another method of making silhouette paper corresponded to the technique of the stenciler or silhouettist. The pattern was cut out of paper that had been oiled or washed, and the stencil laid upon unpolished paper treated with Aher solution. It was then painted over with very strong Aher solution impregnated with earth colors.

Although silhouette papers were not very artistic, they were rich both in forms and in colors. Their everrepeating motifs indicate their common source, a pattern or stencil. The designs most frequently seen in extant examples are flowers, foliage, ornamental latticework, mosques, first quarter moons (the symbol of several Islamic countries), and other easily reproducible images. The colors most popularly employed were bright—flesh pink, green, and yellow. These penetrated the paper while allowing the designs to be visibly stronger on one side of the paper than on the other. Frequently, according to Haemmerle, one encounters a pattern that has been put down twice. While such papers often appear charming to Western eyes they were not so highly esteemed by Eastern cultures as were marbled papers, most likely due to the religious restrictions and traditions of Islam which placed less importance on (and sometimes even prohibited) pictures and imagery.

Marbling in the Far East
MARBLING IN CHINA
While the quality of the marbled papers that European travelers encountered in Turkey and Persia in the sixteenth and seventeenth centuries was very high, and even surprisingly advanced, we know very little today about the origins and early history of the art or of its antecedents in these regions. Albert Haemmerle, our greatest authority on early decorated paper, merely reports, without documentation, that precedents for marbling were already known in China during the Ming dynasty, at which time writing paper that had been colored by hand was in use; and that a little later a true marbling technique, one employing a tank or bath (a method that later became known in Japan as "suminagashi") replaced it.[24] For-

tunately, historical research in recent years has produced some evidence to back up Haemmerle's vague report and thus give more substance to this matter.

Tsuen-hsuin Tsien, Professor of Chinese Literature and Curator Emeritus of the Far Eastern Library at the University of Chicago, has recently published a volume on paper and printing in China that not only provides information on the use of colored papers in that country in early times but also identifies marbling as part of that tradition.[25] Tsien's conclusions are somewhat sketchy, as are the documents he depends on, but they seem to tell enough.

The process of dyeing paper to a yellowish color apparently was used very early in China and was common when paper began to be employed extensively for books in the second and third centuries. According to Tsien, it was a practice at that time to have ordinary paper dyed in order to prevent damage from insects and to give it a glossy surface. The dyestuff was a liquid, obtained from the inner bark of the Amur cork tree, which is yellow and bitter and is toxic to insects. Many papers dyed with this preparation are found in manuscripts today dating from the sixth, seventh, and eighth centuries; manuscripts treated in this way are found in better condition than those which were not. Tsien notes that in some cases the name of the dyer is given in the colophon, indicating the importance of such artisans in producing books.

Another method of treating paper with insecticides involved the use of litharge, or red lead (a mixture of lead, sulfur, and saltpeter). Paper treated with these chemicals turns a bright orange and is toxic to bookworms. Many books printed in the Ming and Ch'ing periods and bound with such papers have been preserved in perfect condition without insect damage. Initially, paper dyeing was undertaken primarily for insecticidal reasons and for permanency, but in time color was added for artistic purposes, possibly because users came to expect the tinted appearance in their paper. The earliest known colored paper in China was a silk paper, dyed red for writing, which developed in the first century and was first described in the third century. At the court of the later Han (25–220 AD), princes were given a hundred sheets each of maroon and bright red hemp papers when they were invested.

The use of yellow paper continued in the following centuries and probably reached a peak in the Tang dynasty (618–907) when official documents were ordered written on them. Papers in a variety of colors also were used and became plentiful and popular in the Tang dynasty. In the fourth and fifth centuries, writing papers were dyed in ten different colors, with bright green, blue, and red in use in Szechuan. Fancy varieties of artistic papers in different patterns and colors were made specifically for writing and decoration on various occasions, and even for imitating aged paper (especially for forgeries of old paintings and for calligraphy). From early times, paper was the most popular artistic medium of the Chinese as well as peoples of other nations in East Asia; it was adapted not only for writing and calligraphy but for making rubbings from inscriptions and for many different kinds of decorative art. Notepaper with multicolored pictures was developed early and was probably used for writing poetry and other artistic purposes.

Tsien relates that "apparently, paper with embossed designs, with watermarks, and even a marbled paper was also developed at this time" (circa 940 AD).[26] He bases his information about early Chinese marbling on the book *Wen Fang Ssu Phu* (Four Implements for Writing in a Scholar's Studio) by Su-I-chien (953–996), who in turn based his sources mostly on the Tang dynasty. Tsien quotes the following passage from the *Wen Fang Ssu Phu*:

> Sometimes, paste was prepared from honey locust pods (*Gleditschia sinensis*) mixed with croton oil and water, with black and coloured inks on its surface. Colours were scattered when ginger was added and gathered if dandruff was applied with a hair brush. The various designs which looked like human figures, clouds, or flying birds were transferred from the surface of the liquid to the paper, and in this way a marbled paper was made.[27]

Tsien, because of the nature of his sources, admits to being sketchy on this matter, but it seems likely from this description that the Chinese did carry on some form of paper marbling from the tenth century on—perhaps as a natural extension of the practice, begun centuries before, of dyeing papers for insecticidal purposes. It must be emphasized, however, that we have a paucity of information and no samples or reproductions of samples to help us make more refined judgments.[28] Tsien concludes his discussion of coloring paper with the following statement: "Western authorities have set the origin of watermarks in +1282 in Europe and of marbled paper in 1550 as 'a Persian invention,' but the literary record as well as existing specimens show that the Chinese made such papers at least three to five hundred years earlier."[29]

MARBLING IN JAPAN

When Haemmerle published his *Buntpapier* in 1961 and made the above-mentioned reference to the manufacture of suminagashi paper in Japan in early times, he used as his authority material that only a few years earlier had been made known to the world by Kiyofusa Narita (1887–1979), Director of the Paper Museum in Tokyo. For thirty years a member of the staff of the Oji Paper Company (the largest manufacturer of paper in Japan), Narita was responsible in his later years for the establishment of its Paper Making Memorial Museum and Library, and he carried on a great deal of research on the history of papermaking in Japan. Narita originally had thought that the marbled papers, which were used extensively in Japanese

bookbinding when he was a small boy, had been imported from England. He later discovered, however, that authentic and carefully preserved examples are extant that prove that this sort of paper, suminagashi, was produced in Japan from the twelfth century; he included a chapter on this unique form of marbling in his book, *Japanese Paper-Making*, published at Tokyo in 1954.[30] Suminagashi marbling became better known to the Western world through an article which Narita published in *The Paper Maker* (a house organ of the Hercules Powder Company) a year later,[31] and since the early 1970s several additional publications have brought this Oriental form to an even larger circle of readers interested in paper decoration.[32]

As Narita initially pointed out, the manufacture of marbled paper in Japan in this early period is proved through a number of samples preserved as national treasures in the National Museum in Tokyo. Specifically, he cites a leaflet entitled (in translation) *Poetical Works of Thirty-Six Men*, published in the year 1118, which contains four sheets of suminagashi paper. Narita relates that suminagashi paper decoration appeared at the end of the Heian-Cho era (794–1185), one of the most illustrious periods of Japanese history, during which art, sculpture, and architecture, originally influenced by Chinese culture, began to show a national character. At present, however, there is no way of knowing whether this art form was adapted from a Chinese example or originated spontaneously as part of Japan's emerging nationalism.

Suminagashi (sumi means ink, and nagashi means floating, thus "a pattern formed by floating ink") was exceedingly attractive to members of Japan's upper classes, who especially employed sheets of it for writing *tanka*, short poems of thirty-one syllables. For more than four hundred years this product was not available to the general public, but was used exclusively by the Imperial Household and by the nobility. In 1582, Toyotomi Hideyoshi became head of the shogunate and as a way of encouraging industry—including papermaking—allowed commoners to use suminagashi paper. The Hiroba family of Takefu, Echizan Prefecture, became famous producers of the paper, and later a family bearing the name of Uchida came to be recognized as their equal. This Japanese form of paper coloring continues to be practiced today in its original way by a few families and individuals who carry on its centuries-old tradition.

The technique of suminagashi marbling consists of letting down successive rings of thin, liquid vegetable color (usually carmine or black or blue) onto a bath of clear water. After these rings have formed a series of concentric lines, they are manipulated into wavy, moiré-like configurations by a stylus or a human hair stiffened with oil. They are then taken off onto paper in the usual way (Figure 1; Plate III).

FIGURE 1. Reproductions of suminagashi marbling from Kiyofusa Narita's article "Suminagashi." The top scene depicts a marbler making his pattern on the colors floating on the surface of the liquid bath. Below, he is shown inspecting the design that has been transferred to paper. (Courtesy of the Paper Museum, Takeo Paper Company, Tokyo).

Marbling in the Middle and Near East

It is not known whether there was a connection between the early Oriental forms of marbling and the method that later flourished among the Persians and the Turks and, eventually, in the Western world. There are reports, however, that a form of our modern marbling was being practiced in Turkestan in the thirteenth century and in Samarkand, Herat, and other regions east of Persia in the early decades of the fourteenth century. So it does not seem unlikely that the technique worked its way westward from the Orient, following the silk trade routes much in the same way as paper, another Oriental invention, had, and that it was modified, improved, and further developed along the way. In the transition, which occurred over several centuries, the simple forms carried out in the Far East (illustrated by the method practiced in Japan even in modern times) took on more elaborate proportions and evolved into the sophisticated medium we recognize as marbling in the Western world today.[33]

While very little is known about the origins and early history of marbling in Persia, Turkey, and other eastern and adjoining areas, it is evident that the Seljuk and Ottoman empires provided fertile soil for this form of paper decoration to germinate and flower. In time, marbling came to play a significant role in the diplomatic and administrative practices of these regions. More importantly, the marbler's craft provided the Persians and the Turks with a fitting medium for their greatest artistic expression and development.

As early as the fifteenth century the regions of the Near East produced a number of proficient makers of *ebrû,* as marbling and marbled paper came to be termed there. It is uncertain whether the word "ebrû" derives from the Persian (Farsi) word "ebr," meaning cloud (connoting a "cloud-art" or paper distinguished by the appearance of a cloud), or whether, as M. Uğur Derman has speculated, it originated from the term "ab-ru," meaning water surface, because marbling is created on water in a vessel.[34]

In any event, ebrû came to serve several important functions in the Seljuk and Ottoman empires. Initially, marbled paper was employed for pure decoration, as many papers that emanated from the shops of great marbling masters (or *ebrucus*) were put on display in lieu of pictures in the homes of the rich, or served as gifts from one king or noble to another. Eventually, when the ebrucu's work resulted in beautiful sheets of pale patterns, the papers were used for writing government documents and official communications. *Aher* paper, the common writing paper of these regions, was prohibited by Ottoman law for use in official documents, because it facilitated forgery.[35] Ebrû paper represented a check against forgery and alteration since any erasure in the writing would be betrayed by a break in the color pattern of the ebrû background. And in cases where a particular pattern or design was made by a particular marbler who alone had knowledge of pro-

ducing it, the use of his paper afforded an additional check against forgery and misrepresentation. This was especially true because Persian and Turkish marblers, like their brethren in the West, maintained their art and the advanced patterns they developed in strict secrecy.

As I have mentioned previously, marbling also played an important role in the artistic expression of the Persians and the Turks and the peoples they influenced. Mehmed Ali Kâğitçi, the historian of Turkish papermaking, observed: "Whereas in Europe art has found expression in pictorial representation, in the East it has developed in ornament and script, which are of equal standing with each other and with pictorial illustration. Ornamentation seems to grow naturally from the written hand, the script itself taking on an ornamental character."[36] Thus the marbling technique provided the peoples of the Middle and Near East with both pure ornament and an art form that blended with and enhanced their calligraphy and script. Furthermore, it filled a void created by the prohibition of pictorial representation under Mohammedan law. Like most prophetic religions, Islam was not conducive to the fine arts. Because representation of living things was forbidden (not in the Koran but in the prophetic tradition), Islamic tradition centered around calligraphy, for the word was the medium of divine revelation. Nevertheless, after the thirteenth century a highly refined art of miniature painting did develop, primarily in Persia and the non-Arabic countries, though it rarely dwelt on religious subjects and much of it was devoted to book illustration.[37]

In 1977, M. Uğur Derman published the first book devoted solely to the history of marbling in Turkey.[38] His slender volume, and a later article excerpted from it,[39] emphasize the point that Islam devoted all of its art to the most beautiful expression of the divine. Its music, literature, and architecture (which centered around the mosque), as well as its calligraphy, textile weaving, tile making, glassmaking, metalworking, wood carving, mother-of-pearl inlaying, and other arts and crafts, focused primarily on what was mystical. Islam did not develop an "absolute" fine art along European lines, but counted among its masterpieces not only architecture and painting but the creations of weavers, potters, metalworkers, and other artisans as well. The Turks accepted the Arabic alphabet (which had gained importance with the Koran) as yet another branch of the arts; they developed six separate styles of writing that made up the art of calligraphy. Holy verses and traditions were worked into all media—from paper to cardboard, from large cloth panels to marble, wood, tile, and metal. In this manner, subsidiary branches of art arose that embellished calligraphy, headed by the arts of illumination, ornamentation, marbling, and bookbinding.

Arabic script is compatible with great calligraphy, becoming itself a form of artistic expression; ebrû served either as a beautiful and fitting background to complement and enhance the calligraphy or as an ornamental framing border around it. On occasion, writing was done directly on papers showing pale marbled patterns, and papers intended for writing purposes often were marbled with their centers blocked out by a solid stencil. When the stencil was removed, the calligrapher obtained a writing sheet with a beautiful marbled border around its outer edges. When so used, the script within took on an additional ornamental character, one in which the rich manuscripts of the Koran and the Persian poets as well as all of the imagination and grace and glory of this culture could find its ultimate expression (Plate IV).[40] (Pale marbled papers that were produced for writing were called "Yazali-ebrû" by Turkish marblers and calligraphers, and those with white center panels "Akkâse-ebrû.")

Frequently, whole manuscript books were made up of these sheets containing calligraphy; and, as one source has noted, bits of marbled paper were sometimes mounted as découpage on paintings inserted into Turkish manuscripts and books to enhance their colorful designs.[41] It was no accident that many of the great marbling masters of Persia and Turkey worked also as calligraphers or bookbinders or gilders, that is, in related fields that permitted and even encouraged great artistry.

It is evident that the cultural, political, and social structures of the Seljuk and Ottoman empires provided a fitting medium for the blossoming of this "cloud-art," and that this development lasted over an extended period of time, for beautiful and highly advanced examples remain from early in the sixteenth century. Kâğitçi mentions a Turkish manuscript dating to the year 1646 that gives a detailed account of the making of ebrû.[42] The specifications call for a gum tragacanth medium for the size, the use of earth and mineral colors, and for ox-gall to be used as the expanding agent; in short, it lists all the constituents of the marbling technique practiced today in the Near East and in the West as well. Kâğitçi further enumerates some of the types of patterns that over the centuries have become standard in Turkish marbling (Plate V).[43]

For a five-hundred-year period a large trade flourished in Persia, Turkey, and contiguous regions in the manufacture of ebrû papers required for both official documents and artistic purposes. The craft produced a succession of fine masters, many of whom elevated the art to greater heights through the invention and manufacture of new designs and even floral patterns, in the designation of which their names survive some centuries later. According to M. Uğur Derman, the earliest known marbler was an artist named "Sebak," who is mentioned in the "Tertib-i Risale-i Ebri" ("Organized Treatise on Marbling," written in 1608), the oldest document relating to the techniques of marbling. The first person whose name is associated with his particular style of marbling was Hatip Mehmed Efendi, a preacher of the Aya Sofya (St. Sophia) Mosque in Istanbul, who died in 1773 and whose father was also a gifted marbler (Plate V).

The technique of marbling, like all classical Ottoman arts, was not taught by writing or systematic instruction; rather, it was transferred from one generation to the next through the master-apprenticeship system, and it has survived to the present day through this unbroken chain. Derman's recent history, Kâğitçi's contributions to Turkish papermaking and marbling, and Phoebe Jane Easton's generalized account of marbling provide lists and a chronology of outstanding Turkish marblers whose names and patterns have come down from the distant past or are known through local legend.[44] Additional information may be contained in other sources which were unavailable to me during my research.[45] It must be emphasized, however, that most of the work carried on in this field remains anonymous, and the vast majority of Turkish marbling masters named and described in the literature were active in the nineteenth century and afterwards.

Mrs. Easton cites as examples of the popularity of marbling as an adjunct to Turkish calligraphy the resources at the library of the Suleymaniye Mosque in Istanbul, which contains more than 100,000 manuscripts, many enriched with ebrû decoration. Kâğitçi mentions a magnificent collection of early marbled papers preserved in the Topkapi Seray Museum in Istanbul, with one example dating to the year 1447.[46] Without doubt, the output of the ebrucus was considerable, and it continued uninterrupted until relatively recent times. As late as the 1920s, it has been said, whole streets of Bayazit, Istanbul's printing and paper quarter, were lined with ebrucus' workshops. Their creations were employed as endpapers in books, mats for decorative calligraphy, and decorative panels on fine woodwork and the like. Kâğitçi reports that, as in the Western world, marbled papers were also used for lining the interiors of chests and trunks, and for playthings.

In recent times, however, as cheap, machine-made papers imported from Europe replaced the works of the living marbler, the Eastern craft (and its related practice in the West) declined, to the extent that what once was a flourishing industry is represented in Turkey today by one master. Mustaffa Düzgünman continues to produce sheets for connoisseurs and for those who honor the culture and traditions of the past (Plates IV and V). Fortunately, there appears to be a revival of interest in marbling in Turkey today, and Düzgünman has been giving instruction in the methods of this ancient and venerable craft to a number of people there.[47]

As a concluding comment on this account of the art in the Middle and Near East, I must point out that while many Persian and Turkish papers, and perhaps papers from nearby regions, were sent or brought back to Europe in the sixteenth and seventeenth centuries, little seems to have found its way westward after the establishment of the marbling trades in Germany and France. The industries that were established in these countries by the middle or end of the seventeenth century were soon able to satisfy the desires and requirements of their own societies and cultures; by that time, and in that contemporary scene, marbled paper was no longer a curiosity but was fast becoming a staple item in the home as well as in the bookbinder's shop.

Deccani Marbled Paintings

One more observation on early Eastern marbling needs to be set forth here, concerning a group of early Eastern wash drawings that contain marbling as part of their general decoration (Plate IV). It is something of a side issue, however, and not nearly as important to the overall history of this craft as present-day commentators would have us believe. Probably more meaningful is the example these paintings provide of the likely dispersal of the craft throughout the East and eventually into Europe.

The first printed report of these mixed-media works appeared in 1912 when the British art historian F. R. Martin reproduced three of them in his work on miniature painting in Persia, India, and Turkey and attributed them to Ottoman Turkey.[48] His examples were depictions of a *Cow and Calf* (in his own collection), an *Ascetic Riding a Nag* (then privately owned but now in the Pierpont Morgan Library), and a *Nag* (formerly in the Victor Goloubew collection in Paris but now in the Boston Museum of Fine Arts).[49] Slight attention seems to have been paid to Martin's observation, possibly because these partially marbled paintings were little understood by the art world of his time and were considered interesting but minor curiosities. In recent years, however, these mixed-media representations have begun to attract considerable interest. This new focus seems to date from about 1973, with the first of a series of exhibitions of Indian miniature paintings in the collection of Edward Binney III.[50]

In 1976, the British art historian Basil W. Robinson described another of these unusual paintings,[51] and an exhibition of Indian drawings and painted sketches at the Asia House Gallery in New York included two others.[52] Phoebe Easton discusses these partially marbled pictures in her *Marbling: a History and a Bibliography,* and the late Christopher Weimann, a contemporary marbler, made them the subject of a recent article.[53] Almost simultaneously, two works devoted to Indian art, which will be referred to below, also took notice of these special paintings, and the subject finally seems now to be in proper perspective.

According to Easton, these pictures had marbled decoration added to them through a resist technique and/or through the use of stencils, and do not represent collage (or découpage). She reports that only about twenty examples are known and that they were created during a limited period, possibly from the mid-sixteenth to the mid-seventeenth centuries, and probably in an area far removed from the usual centers of Eastern marbling. She relates that Persian, Turkish, and Indian styles and motifs

are represented, but that since artists moved about frequently in this period, actual places of origin remain uncertain. She notes that Robinson believed that a case could be made for attributing them to the Deccan region of south-central India, following a Turkish tradition. Turkey had sultanates in Malwa and the Deccan, and a distinct style of painting, incorporating indigenous art forms with Persian and Turkish motifs, flourished in several population centers and courts in the Deccan from the sixteenth century.

A variety of subjects are represented in these miniatures: forage and riding animals, elephants and tigers, court scenes, and human figures, including even a female at prayer. To enhance them, traditional styles of so-called Turkish marbling then in use were applied to them, including combed and sprinkled types. Weimann, who checklists eighteen of these unusual representations, believes that they were produced in the Deccan around 1650; because of the similarities of marbling in the paintings, he ventures a guess that they could have been produced by one artist or in one workshop.[54]

Weimann devotes most of his article on these miniatures to showing how the marbled decoration could have been effected, either through a resist method or by the use of stencils. In the resist method, the artist may have first sketched his subject on paper and brushed a solution of gum arabic or gum tragacanth onto those areas which were not to receive color. After the gum had dried, the paper was marbled; the areas blocked out by the gum would not take the marbling. Finally, the gummed areas were rinsed clear and the resulting blank spaces could be painted to complete the scene. When stencils were used, the areas to be marbled were cut out from the stencils, with those to be painted left in place. One side of the stencil was covered with a water-soluble glue and positioned on a sheet of paper, which was then marbled. The stencil was afterward soaked away, and the paper could be painted after it had dried.

I have marbled several hundred figures of animals and other subjects, including some of the actual Deccani scenes, by duplicating and sometimes even enlarging illustrations of them on a photocopying machine and then using these reproductions to cut multiple stencils and patterns. My own experiments make me doubt that resist methods were much used. I believe that these works were accomplished mainly with stencils; in some cases the artists simply overpainted the marbling or scraped it off and painted in the resulting blank spaces, for remnants of marbling can sometimes be seen beneath their painting. For example, Figure 35 of Stuart Cary Welch's catalog, *Indian Drawings and Painted Sketches, 16th through 19th Centuries,* illustrating "a Begum," which I have photocopied and marbled in an imitative manner, shows faint traces of marbling in the face and raised hand of the figure, indicating that most, but not all, of the marbling in these areas had been removed.

In 1981 Toby Falk and Mildred Archer published a catalog of the Indian miniatures in the India Office Library in which they provided descriptions of fourteen representations containing marbled decoration.[55] The majority of these display either marbled borders or marbled background for calligraphy, but a few show marbling incorporated directly into the pictures themselves. (Some of these had been described previously by B. W. Robinson in his catalog of Persian paintings in the India Office Library.) This collection was begun in 1801 by officers of the East India Company who desired to learn more about Indian art and culture; it was augmented by sympathetic donors throughout the nineteenth century.

In their section on the art of the Deccan, Falk and Archer note not only that the Deccani court had direct trade routes to the Middle East and Africa (regions they looked to for cultural examples), but also that the population of the court in the seventeenth century was mixed, including Turks, Persians, and Abyssinians, some of whom were artists and calligraphers. They observe too, that it is sometimes difficult to distinguish between Persian pictures painted in Iran and pictures by Persian artists who had moved to the Deccan; and they suggest that the practice of using marbled decoration for pictures and calligraphy appears to have reached the Deccan from Turkey.

In a subsequent work devoted to Deccani painting, Mark Zebrowski has listed or illustrated some of the miniatures accounted for by Weimann and others.[56] As evidence that these surviving drawings were executed in the Deccan (not in Persia or Turkey), probably during the reigns of Sultan Ibrahim Adil Shah II (1579–1627) and his successor, Sultan Muhammad Adil Shah (1627–1656), Zebrowski argues that some of the best examples are in Deccani collections, while others were acquired from the Deccan. Furthermore, where human figures occur, faces and costumes are distinctly Bijapuri; the paintings resemble those done in Bijapur in technique as well. Finally, he contends, there is a close resemblance between the styles of marbling in these paintings and those found in the bindings of Deccani manuscripts and the decorative borders or margins of Deccani paintings. Welch, in his 1976 exhibition catalog of Indian drawings and painted sketches, observes that "marbling was a Bijapuri specialty, often employed in the margins of calligraphy and miniatures as well to create complete pictures."[57]

It appears that the consensus of recent opinion has solidified around the conclusion that these uniquely marbleized paintings were indeed produced in the Deccan in the period just before or around 1650; further, in all likelihood they were the products of a single workshop, or of a marbler or more likely a group of marblers who worked there at the time. These workmen probably also marbled for bookbinding and calligraphic purposes and carried on all of the usual tasks alloted to the marbler. Unlike most such craftsmen, however, they extended their repertoire to include these artistic curiosities that, with their

unique charm, arouse our special interest many centuries later. Although these miniatures might well have been produced by Turks or Persians or both, it seems to me that the marbling in them shows a strong Persian flavor. It is known that large numbers of Persians lived in India in this period and that they exerted great influence on that country's general life and culture.[58] One piece of evidence in support of this view is an eighteenth-century Indian manuscript account of marbling that Stéphane Ipert recently brought to my attention and sent to me in both photocopy form and in translation. This account, found in the India Office Library in London, was written entirely in Persian, thus corroborating an especially strong Persian connection with marbling in India.[58]

Mughal or Mongolian rule over a large part of India was established in 1526 and held sway for two centuries. Mughal civilization in India fused indigenous artistic traditions with new inspirations from Persia and central Asia and achieved great and distinctive influence in painting, architecture, literature, and other artistic forms. Robinson notes in regard to miniature painting in central Asia at this time that wars and raids in Persia and neighboring regions by Ottomans, Uzbeks, and other peoples scattered the art throughout a wide area as painters were carried off by conquerors. When an enlightened prince with a taste for painting came to power, painters and artists flocked to his court. On the other hand, when royal patronage shrank, production of pictures and illustrated manuscripts on a commercial level increased, popularizing and expanding these arts even more.[59]

Some of Robinson's observations about painting can be applied to marbling and marblers as well, for in the Middle and Near East this cloud-art not only was on an equal plane with pictorial representation but was probably more widespread because of its use in government work and its close association with bookbinding and calligraphy. Robinson's comments about miniature painting are also relevant to the spread of marbling throughout central and western Asia and into India; they account for its wide dissemination and its practice in far-off places where it previously had not been recognized and has been little understood. Thus the charming Deccani paintings help fill a gap in our knowledge and appreciation of how this art diffused as they focus our attention on its early practice in India.

Concluding Remarks

In recent decades there has occurred a worldwide revival of interest in marbling, especially among craftspeople, some of whom have narrowly centered their attention on Eastern marbling, attracted perhaps by its mystical aspects and by the sophisticated floral patterns its Turkish masters have developed. The literature that a number of these commentators have produced may therefore give the impression that the art reached its pinnacle and fulfilled its potential in Turkey and the East. Being restricted to modern workshops and having limited access to the riches of the research libraries of Europe and America, these commentators have been little exposed to the immense amount of beautifully marbled paper that survives in European and Western books and thus have paid little (or at least less) attention to European and Western marbling. For this reason, a few concluding remarks are called for.

Suminagashi marbling, which has received a good deal of attention lately, represents marbling in its initial and simplest form. While attractive and pleasing, it lacks the intricacy and richness evident in the patterns developed after the craft's journey westward. Turkish marbling, which justifiably likewise has been receiving much recent notice, also has about it many simple and rudimentary aspects. Some of its rough, unfinished features have been obscured by depictions in recent literature of the dramatic floral patterns developed in this century by Necmeddin Okyay and perfected by Mustaffa Düzgünman. But when one compares sheets or samples or even reproductions of simpler Turkish designs (such as the "Battal-ebrû" or "Somaki-ebrû" spot patterns, or the combed "Terakli-ebrû") with highly finished European sheets, one cannot but be impressed with the lack of finesse of the former. With regard to technique and overall finish, Turkish papers do not stand up well under scrutiny alongside the combed and many other patterns developed in Europe and the West.

Moreover, the subject of marbling in Persia or Iran has practically been ignored, both in the literature of marbling and in histories of Iran's arts. Yet marbling was practiced in Iran well before it was transferred to Turkey. Indeed, the art probably was highly developed even before that transfer took place, for I have observed examples of early Persian marbling in museum collections that show higher technical excellence than appear in papers later produced in Turkey. Such observations form the basis of my opinion that the Deccani miniatures were likely either produced by Persian marblers or strongly influenced by Persian marbling, for many that I have seen exhibit the same technical proficiency usually found in early marbled papers containing Persian calligraphy.[60] Of course, we should like to know more about Persian marbling—and about marbling in India—in its everyday applications to calligraphy and bookbinding and not just its employment as an adjunct to miniature painting. Political events in Iran make this impossible at present, however, and we can only hope that in the future research will develop along this line.

It was in the hands of its Western practitioners that the art of marbling was brought to technical perfection, especially in the production of delicately combed forms. The industry that developed in the West, we shall soon see, ran a wider course than the industry in the East, with many more people employed in its practice in Europe and undoubtedly many more papers produced there as well. Nevertheless, it would be a mistake to compare Eastern marbling with the type that came to exist in Europe and the West. We should accept both for what they are and recognize that, although similar, they represent very different expressions of this simple yet delightful form of paper decoration.

With this in mind, we now turn òur attention to the industry and trade in marbled paper that evolved in Europe, devoting the remainder of this work to marbling there and the techniques, supplies, equipment, and patterns that were associated with its practice in the West.

2

The European Cradle Period

Aｆｔｅｒ European travelers first encountered the "cloud-art" in the East and began to send news of it home, it took only about a quarter of a century for the art itself to be transferred to the West. In his classic work on "Buntpapier," the German generic term encompassing all types and forms of colored and decorated papers, Albert Haemmerle tells us that the actual technique of marbling paper became known in Germany around 1600, for several albums dating to the early years of the seventeenth century are extant that contain marbleized paper of German manufacture, and their places of origin are attributed to southern Germany.

Haemmerle cites an album that can be dated through internal and physical evidence to the year 1604; others are traced to the interval between 1608 and 1612, the year 1618, and the period 1626–40. Indisputable proof of German manufacture of the so-called Turkish or marbled patterns in these albums is afforded by watermarks in the papers; both the white and colored papers show European watermarks and other obvious signs of European manufacture, indicating that their marbling took place not in the East but in the West. And in the few cases where stencils were employed to produce scenes or designs in these papers, the subjects of these representations are European and not Oriental in character.

Haemmerle's *Buntpapier* illustrates a page from the album of 1604 (his figure 40) and another from the album of 1618 (his figure 41), both of which are now in the Olga Hirsch collection in the British Library.[1] Bound into the 1618 album are a number of marbled papers with stenciled designs. Two of the simpler types of these designs were illustrated by Mirjam M. Foot, then assistant keeper in the Library's Department of Printed Books, in her description of the Hirsch collection.[2] Two more elaborate examples are illustrated here in Plate VII.

During a visit to the British Library in 1982 I was shown the 1618 volume by Mrs. Foot. Having arrived directly from the Continent, where I had observed a number of Album Amicorum containing Turkish and Eastern marbled papers as well as plain and silhouetted ones, I thought at first glance that I was looking at still another Near Eastern work, in spite of the obvious European motifs on some of the stenciled sheets. A closer inspection of the paper, however, immediately convinced me

that I was looking at very early seventeenth-century German marbling, indeed the earliest European marbling that I had ever seen. Both the white and marbled paper in this 1618 volume consisted of thick European sheets containing mould marks and watermark configurations that were visible when the book was held up to the light; and contrary to Eastern practice, the paper had been left unpolished and untreated.

The European-style designs in the stenciled sheets were applied in about the same manner as the Deccani marbleized patterns. The cut-out portions of the stencils, however, were mounted on white paper before marbling took place, for the designs show as white and marbling makes up the background. In this earliest European marbling, the exotic decoration was used for the same purpose as it often was in the East, to create pictorial designs that became part of the inner contents of a book rather than plain marbled sheets that served as a part of its binding.

Despite this evidence of European manufacture, Haemmerle concedes that we do not know how or by whom the craft of marbling was transferred to Germany, for he notes that the few people who had learned to do it guarded their knowledge carefully and maintained it as a trade secret, a custom that still prevails. The speculative observation made by the German master bookbinder and marbler Paul Kersten in his 1922 marbling manual, *Die Marmorierkunst*, is perhaps as reasonable as any. Kersten theorized that knowledge of marbling possibly entered Germany through the port of Venice, where Oriental objects and ideas were first brought to the West by German traders frequenting the East; and that additional interest in these curiosities, as well as knowledge of their making, may have spread across Germany and perhaps into France by way of the Frankfurt Fair.[3]

It is also possible that the craft could have been introduced into Europe from a number of other entry points. In the seventeenth century, in their continual wars with the Habsburgs, the Ottomans extended their domain over present-day Hungary and Rumania and advanced into central Europe to the very outskirts of Vienna, not far from the part of southern Germany where the art of marbling allegedly first took root in Western soil.

France is identified as the other European country

where the early, continuous, and prolific production of marbled paper occurred. The introduction of the art into this region coincided with the golden age of French bookbinding. Without doubt, the French were the first in Europe to use marbled paper as endpapers in order to lend their highly decorated or "extra" bindings an air of elegance and sumptuousness. Sometimes they even applied marbled decorations to the edges of the books themselves. Various authorities have tended to follow nationalistic biases when crediting either France or Germany with the introduction of this craft into Europe. Although the interval between the beginnings of the practice of marbling in the two countries is very slight, all evidence points to German priority, and even the great French encyclopedia of Diderot and D'Alembert states in its description of the marbler and his work that "ce petit art a pris naissance en Allemagne."[4]

Some of the marbled paper produced in France early in the seventeenth century was purchased by rich connoisseurs who prized it not only as a curiosity but also as a rare possession to be displayed in their homes. Much, perhaps even most, marbled paper, however, was used in bookbinding, for as we shall see in a later chapter, in France the bookbinders were the first to marble. Marbled paper was scarce and expensive during this early time, and French binders restricted its use to their very finest productions, employing it on bindings commissioned by royalty, nobility, and merchant princes, and even then only by the most discriminating connoisseurs and collectors among them.

Circumstances in Germany were entirely different, for there bookbinding had not yet attained the refinement it had in France. German books were not especially prized for their fine bindings, nor were German royalty and nobility accustomed to adorning their library shelves with ornately decorated books. The use of marbled paper in German bookbinding did not occur until about the middle of the seventeenth century, or perhaps even later, possibly because marbled paper was initially made not by bookbinders, as in France, but by artists who specialized in the decoration of all sorts of paper. As the seventeenth century progressed, German marbling continued to be looked upon as a rare and expensive curiosity. For the most part, marbled papers were used for decorating albums, or, in the home, as substitutes for pictures.

A splendid example of marbling in wall decoration in Germany during this period is preserved in the Germanisches Nationalmuseum in Nürnberg, which possesses a choice collection of Buntpapier, including marbled papers. (Its collection of damask and calico and paste papers is especially fine, with some of the most interesting and charming examples of the latter to be seen.) Box number 701, containing marbled papers only, has a sheet of the "Turkish" variety dating from the later seventeenth century with pictorial matter mounted on it in the form of a collage (Plate VII). The mountings consist of cut-

out wash drawings of birds, men bearing grapes, and a dog chasing a hare; the entire production, with its marbled background, conveys a simple yet charming scene. In this instance, marbling evidently served the function it sometimes fulfilled in the East, for clearly this work was created as a picture that could be hung on a wall to be observed and enjoyed. Although the passage of time has made such examples rare today, it seems likely that the use of marbled paper in this manner may have been relatively common during this early period.

By the final decades of the seventeenth century, however, German binders had come to follow the French example and had begun to add marbled endpapers to their higher-quality works, so that from about the 1670s or 1680s marbled decoration became as closely associated with bookbinding in Germany as it was in France (the practice soon came to be imitated by better bookbinders in other countries as well). Indeed, in both countries, but particularly in France, by the end of the seventeenth century the lack of marbled endpapers in good calf gilt bindings is reason for commentary. The years from about the 1630s to the 1680s constituted marbling's formative period in both Germany and France: not only did knowledge of the art spread in both countries during this time, but the use of such decoration in bookbinding increased as well. The manufacture of marbled paper in both areas had grown to such an extent in the later decades of the century that traders began to export it to other countries and overseas.

I have encountered European marbled papers in fine English bindings dating from the 1660s. Graham Pollard records in his survey of bookbinding decoration between 1550 and 1830 that the earliest English binding he had seen containing marbled endpapers was a volume of tracts (now in St. John's College, Oxford) that Charles Mearne bound for Cornelius Pigeon in 1655; he notes that such marbleized decoration had become a common feature in bookbindings by the 1670s.[5] Charles Adams, whose contribution to the history of early marbling will be discussed shortly, has pointed out that the diary of Samuel Sewall of Boston (one of the judges at the Salem witchcraft trials of 1692) contains references in 1683 and 1685 to having his books stitched in marbled paper.[6] Hannah D. French has reported in her classic essay on "Early American Bookbinding by Hand" that Judge Sewall left memoranda for the importation of marbled papers from Amsterdam in 1698, indicating that export was in fact taking place.[7]

Evidence also shows that decorated papers were being exported from Germany to France in the late seventeenth century. In manuscript letters sent by a citizen of Paris named Collinet to a citizen of Strasbourg named Colbart de Villermont and now preserved in the Bibliothèque Nationale, Stéphane Ipert has found a number of references that discuss the importation of German decorated papers into France in the late 1690s.[8] Ipert reports that in one message (a letter dated 20 November 1698), Collinet informed Monsieur de Villermont that one could find as large a quantity as one could want of "papier marbré doré" in Paris. These could be obtained from a bookseller named Boucher, who had his son ship them from Germany; Collinet mentions papers made in Frankfurt, Augsburg, and Nürnberg. Ipert rightfully questions the meaning of the phrase "marbled gilded papers" employed by Collinet, for we soon shall see that in this early period marbled papers were referred to not as "marbled" but as "Turkish," with other types designated as "marbled." Thus it seems likely that Collinet was referring to the brocade or "Dutch gilt" papers that were commonly made in Augsburg and in other German locations.[9] Nonetheless, his reference is important evidence that the trade in such commodities was going on in Europe at that time.

In her monograph on decorated book papers,[10] Rosamond B. Loring observes (correctly, I believe) that the custom of using marbled papers in finer bookbindings was disseminated throughout Europe by fairs and over the inland waterways connecting north Germany with the heartland of Europe. The Rhine, Danube, and Elbe, with smaller connecting rivers and canals, formed a natural network for trading in the days when road travel was difficult and perilous. The Leipzig and Frankfurt fairs played an important role in the exchange of manufactured wares among Italy, France, Germany, Belgium, and Holland; many items displayed and exchanged in Leipzig later found their way north and into England through Dutch trading ports, with the Dutch acting as commission merchants for the Germans, buying and selling German commodities for reexport.

In his classic 1853 work *The Art of Marbling,* Charles Woolnough noted, with regard to one of the most popular patterns of the seventeenth century:

Many years ago this old Dutch Paper, in the size of foolscap, used to be imported from that country [Holland] and in order to evade payment of the duty, some of it (I do not mean to say all,) was wrapped round small parcels of Dutch toys, and thus passed free; and when it was taken off, was carefully smoothed and sold to bookbinders, fetching a good price, being used only on the better kinds of work; indeed so choice was it, that in some old books you may see pieces joined together for the inside linings.[11]

According to Mrs. Loring, the "Dutch" toys were among the great variety of goods, manufactured in the industrious city of Nürnberg, which found their way into England by way of Holland.[12] The designation "Dutch" was possibly a corruption of the German "Deutsch" or Dutch "Duits," both meaning "German." It seems more likely, however, that the term arose because of the English habit of referring colloquially to all German peoples and things as "Dutch." We shall see later that indeed the well-known German marbled pattern to which Woolnough was referring received its "Dutch" name in this way.[13]

The Earliest Literature of Marbling

Confirmation of the growing interest throughout the seventeenth century in marbling and in marbled papers for book decoration and other purposes is afforded by the expanding literature on the subject that appeared in Europe at that time. Such literature, it should be pointed out, did not reflect the exchange of information by professional marblers in the day-to-day pursuit of their new calling; on the contrary, these sedulously guarded their knowledge and would have deemed it a disadvantage to impart it to outsiders. Recipes and information needed for their craft undoubtedly were maintained in private manuscript records that, for the most part, have disappeared with the passing of time. (The few surviving bits and pieces of professional literature will be discussed as this study unfolds.) In actuality the marbling literature and commentary reflect the curiosity that this novel method was provoking in scientific circles and among the literati of that era.

Charles M. Adams published the first detailed study of seventeenth-century European paper marbling in 1947; he surveyed the earliest literature and discussed all the references he could find that had been printed on the conduct of the craft during its cradle period in the West.[14] Adams's information, although supplemented to some degree by subsequent investigators and commentators, remains the key contribution to the early history of paper marbling. What follows is a recapitulation of the information assembled by Adams and other commentators that will serve to document the growing interest in this method at the time when its magical qualities brought it within the pseudo-science of alchemy and the nascent science of chemistry. This information also sets the stage for my subsequent discussions of early marbling in Germany, France, England, and other countries.

As I have pointed out earlier, the first description of the marbling process to appear in print in Europe was published at Rome in 1646 by the Jesuit priest and natural historian Athanasius Kircher (who also invented the magic lantern). Kircher (1602–1680), originally a teacher of philosophy, mathematics, and Oriental languages, was driven from Würzburg in 1631 by the Thirty Years War. He settled first in Avignon and afterwards in Rome, where he taught mathematics and Hebrew at the Collegio Romano, resigning in 1643 to study archaeology and to write. His *Ars Magna Lucis et Umbrae,* which appeared three years later, was a large work both in size and scope, for it summarized his investigations and ideas in the fields of physics, optics, mathematics, natural history, and related subjects. While discussing such topics as optics, artificial colors, and the refraction of light rays in water and vitreous bodies, Kircher provided a short account—five paragraphs, amounting to about 500 words—of the method of coloring paper in the Turkish style: 500 words in a 935-page volume containing in excess of 350,000 words! Kircher's description, as well as allusions made by later commentators, implies that the Jesuit included marbling among the many experimental sciences he studied. We may assume that he actually did practice marbling and that he sometimes demonstrated the process for interested onlookers as a new scientific curiosity, just as a modern-day teacher might demonstrate for students an experiment in chemistry or physics.

Although Kircher's description was the first to be published in Western literature, it was not the first to be made by a European. Sometime before 1636, the year of his death, Daniel Schwenter, who, like Kircher, was a mathematician and teacher of Oriental languages, wrote out a detailed account of marbling, "Turckisches Papyr zu Machen und zu Figuieren," which remained unpublished until 1677, when the Nürnberg poet and historian Georg Philip Harsdorfer included it in the second part of his *Deliciae Physico-Mathematicae und Philosophische Erquickstunden*.[15] Schwenter's account of the marbling technique, although brief, is an authentic one that explains the nature of the process, the colors that may be used, and the designs that may be created. It also mentions the making of a floral pattern, which, as Adams points out, is characteristic of Turkish papers and is described by Taherzade Behzad in the recent *Survey of Persian Art* as one typical of Persian motifs.[16]

Much space in Adams's study is devoeted to a lecture on marbling delivered by the English country gentleman and author John Evelyn to the Royal Society in London on the evening of 8 January 1662. Evelyn's description of the craft was so exact, especially for his time, that Adams speculates that he may well have observed marbled papers and possibly even a demonstration of the process during his travels to the Continent as a young man. In a diary entry made during his visit to Rome on 8 November 1644,[17] Evelyn recorded that

> Here Father Kircher (professor of Mathematics and the Oriental tongues) shew'd us many singular courtesies, leading us into their refractory, dispensatory, laboratory, gardens, and finally (through an hall hung round with pictures of such of their order as had been executed for their pragmatical and buisy adventures) into his own study; where, with Dutch patience,[18] he shew'd us his perpetual motions, catoptrics, magnetical experiments, modells, and a thousand other crotchets and devices, most of them since published by himselfe or his industrious scholar Schotti.

As Adams reports, John Houghton first printed Evelyn's Royal Society lecture almost verbatim in his weekly folio number of *Husbandry and Trade Improv'd* in 1699, approximately thirty-seven years after its actual delivery.[19] This was the earliest detailed description of the craft to be published in English, although Francis Bacon had made a very brief reference to marbling in his *Sylva Sylvarum* as early as 1627.[20] The manuscript of Evelyn's lecture, which Adams reprinted, is preserved in the collection of Sir Hans Sloane in the British Library. Like the other literature on marbling during this period, it must be considered as a report of a learned man to a learned society on a current scientific curiosity.

In addition to the publications above, which constituted the most important of the early discussions, several descriptions of paper marbling were incorporated into European literature during the second half of the seventeenth century. Some of them, admittedly, derived from Kircher's description of the process or were influenced by it. Gaspar Schott, whom Adams describes as a favorite and diligent pupil of Kircher, included a section on marbling (entitled "Chartam Variis Coloribus More Turcico Pingere") in his *Magia Universalis Naturae et Artis, Sive Recondita Naturalium et Artificialium Rerum Scientia*, published at Würzburg in 1657.[21] And in the early 1660s that great English scientist and "sceptical chemist" Robert Boyle took brief notice of marbling and marbled papers and of Kircher's curiosity about them.[22]

In 1665, Antonio Neri, a citizen of Florence, devoted a few pages (chapter 42) of his theoretical and practical treatise on glassmaking, *De Arte Vitraria Libri VII*, to chalcedony, jaspers, and agates, that is, stones with a variegated or marbled appearance. His allusion to ornamental stones prompted comments on marbling by two subsequent observers, who likened the process to Neri's chalcedony, jaspers, and agates. The first such commentary appeared in Johann Kunckel von Löwenstein's *Ars Vitraria Experimentalis*. Published initially at Frankfurt in 1679, this work, like Neri's treatise, was devoted mainly to the art of making and decorating glass; because optical aspects of color play a large role in glassmaking, a discussion of that other optical curiosity, marbling, was included.[23] The English scholar Christopher Merrett, when preparing and editing a second edition of Neri's work, issued at Amsterdam in 1686, made a brief reference to marbling in his notes, commenting on the similarities in appearance of Neri's "marbled" stones and marbled paper.[24]

Merrett's attention may have been drawn to marbling by the publication in the previous year of a book entitled *Modern Curiosities of Art and Nature*, which included a brief description of how to marble and jasper paper. This work, according to its title page, had been composed by the Sieur Lemery, apothecary to the French king. It was a translation of a book issued originally at Paris in 1674 and reissued there ten years later, with several more French editions following; two other English editions would appear as well.[25] All of these will be discussed at some

1

2

3 a

4 a

3 b

4 b

5 a

5 b

6

PLATE I

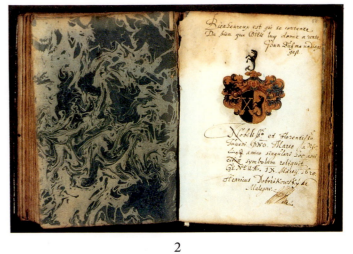

1

2

3

4

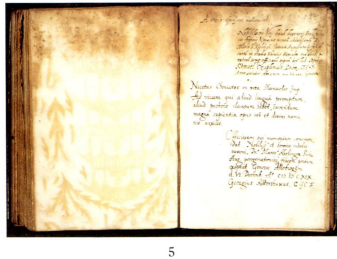

5

6

PLATE II

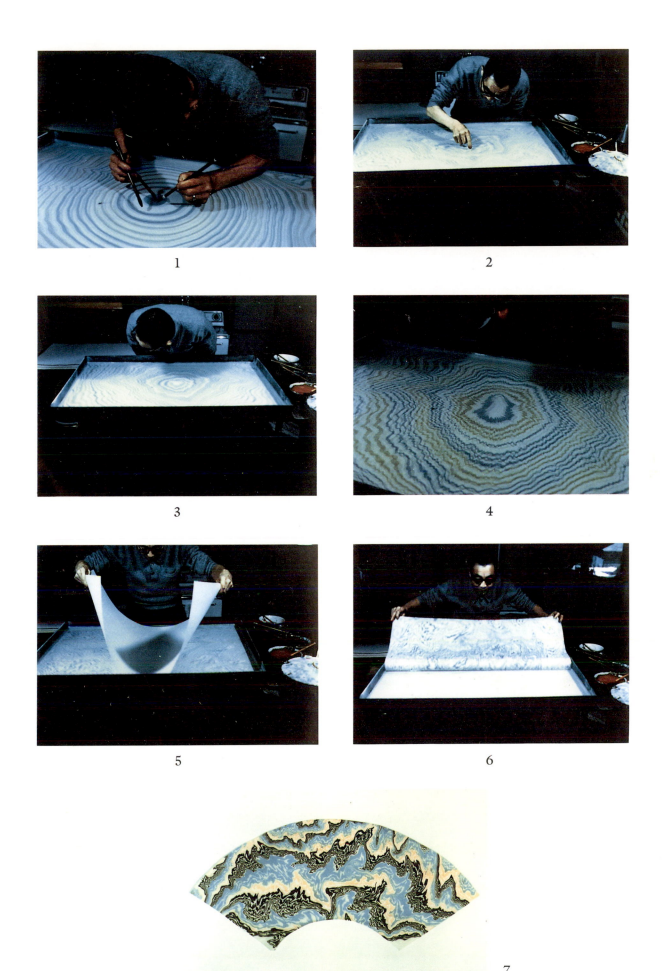

1

2

3

4

5

6

7

PLATE III

1

2

3

4

5

6

PLATE IV

PLATE V

1

4

2

5

3

6

PLATE VI

Captions for Plates I–VI

PLATE I: 1. Piece of marbled paper, badly faded, said to have been used as wallpaper in the poet Goethe's study. Formerly in the Dessauer-Aschaffenburg collection, now in the Koninklijke Bibliotheek, the Hague; 2. Marbled paper of the so-called "Dutch" pattern, used to package Dr. James's fever powders. London, 1760–1780. Author's collection; 3. Chest or casket lined with marbled paper of the "Stormont" variety. Such chests were used to store valuables such as jewels and papers. America, first or second decade of the 19th century. Author's collection; 4. Chest or casket lined with marbled paper of the "shell" or "mottled" variety. America, 1830 period. Author's collection; 5. English wallet or pocket secretary, made of crimson morocco leather and lined with marbled paper of the "Stormont" variety. First decade of the 19th century. Author's collection; 6. Large box, approximately 20 inches high, built in the shape of a book and intended to hold dried and mounted botanical specimens (i.e., a herbarium). The marbled paper covering it is the familiar "shell" design. America, 1830–1840. Author's collection.

PLATE II, marbled and silhouette papers in old Album Amicorum: 1. Marbled leaf and silhouette leaf on facing pages in the album of Antoniem Duits, the Reichshofrat of Kaiser Rudolf II, ca. 1580. Koninklijke Bibliotheek, the Hague; 2–4. Marbled leaves in the Album Amicorum of Marcus Conrad von Rehlingen, Augsburg and Geneva, 1618–1620. Houghton Library, Harvard University; 5–6. Silhouette papers of Turkish origin in the Album Amicorum of Johannes Jentsch, 1628–1643. The album contains 92 silhouetted leaves in all and approximately 170 engravings by Flemish artists; it belongs to the late type of such albums that were commercially produced. Houghton Library, Harvard University.

PLATE III, modern Japanese manufacture of suminagashi paper (courtesy of Hiraku Kido and the Toshiyo Miyazawa Paper Museum, Tokyo): 1. Putting rings of color onto the bath; 2. Manipulating the rings into broken configurations with the finger; 3. Blowing onto the size to further manipulate the configurations; 4. The pattern formed on the size; 5. Laying a sheet of blank paper onto the pattern to absorb it; 6. Removing the marbled sheet from the bath; 7. An old fan made with suminagashi paper.

PLATE IV: 1–4. Early Turkish calligraphy employing marbling as a background or a border. 1–2, Fogg Art Museum, Harvard University; 3–4, Courtesy of Işik Yazan and *Antika* magazine, and Nusret Nepgul, Istanbul; 5–6. Scenes showing Mustaffa Düzgünman, Turkey's leading marbler of the present day, at work making one of the patterns for which he is famous (Necmeddin-ebrû) (Courtesy of Robert Arndt and *Aramco World* magazine).

PLATE V, modern Turkish marbled paper: 1–5, Patterns made by Necmeddin Okyay and mounted into Mehmed Ali Kâ-ğitçi's *Kâğitçilik Tarihçesi* (1936). Author's collection. 1. Battal-ebrusu; 2. Tarakli-ebrû; 3. Somaki-ebrû; 4. Hatip-ebrusu; 5. Necmeddin-ebrusu. (6–9 Patterns made by Mustaffa Düzgünman. Author's collection.) 6. Tarakli-ebrû; 7–9. Floral patterns for which Düzgünman has become celebrated.

PLATE VI, Deccani marbled paintings: 1. A starving horse harassed by birds; 2. Two camels fighting; 3. Cow and calf; 4. Two figures and landscape; 5. Princess carrying peacock; 6. Rider on elephant fighting rider on horse. (1–4 courtesy of the Fogg Art Museum, Harvard University; numbers 5–6 courtesy of The Free Library of Philadelphia.)

length in subsequent accounts of the early French and English literatures of marbling.

Two other English publications of the late seventeenth century contained short resumes of paper marbling. The first, William Salmon's *Polygraphice, or The Art of Drawing, Engraving, Etching, Limning, Painting, Washing, Varnishing, Colouring and Dyeing in Three Books,* was issued initially at London in 1672 and was republished six or more times until 1701, when the final edition appeared.[26] Salmon devoted only a few sentences to an exposition of this subject; however, John White, in his *Arts Treasury: or, A Profitable and Pleasing Invitation to the Lovers of Ingenuity. Contained in Many Extraordinary Experiments, Rarities and Curious Inventions,* was not so succinct. His description of the marbling process amounted to about 200 words and would remain the standard English definition until 1740. White's book was first printed at London in 1688. It appeared in at least two more editions before 1696, with another issued in 1710 and, surprisingly, additional editions reprinted at Glasgow in 1771 and 1773.[27]

In the mid-1680s a Dutch work containing a description of marbling was published at Amsterdam. (This book actually dealt with conjuring and other magical processes, but it also reported many secret recipes.) It was entitled *Het Natuurlyk Tover-Boek, of, 't Nieuw Speeltoneel der Konsten,* and its author or compiler masked his identity with the pseudonym Simon Witgeest. Although fairly good for this period, the information it contained on marbling was not on a par with that provided in Kunckel's book. *Het Natuurlyk Tover-Boek* went through at least three more Amsterdam editions by the end of the seventeenth century, and eight more Dutch editions would appear before the conclusion of the eighteenth; as further evidence of its great popularity it was translated into German and issued at Nürnberg in 1700, with more than fifteen German editions following by 1796, when the last one that I have observed came into print.[28]

In the third volume of his *Oculis Artificialis,* issued at Würzburg in 1685–1686, Johannes Zahn contributed further to the early literature of paper marbling,[29] as, reportedly, did another German, Johann Zieger, in his *Kunst- und Werck-schule,* published at Nürnberg in 1696.[30] This work, we soon shall see, contained a very important contribution to the early literature of this field. Its material on this subject, however, is contained in a second volume dating to the early eighteenth century; thus, it will be discussed in Chapter 3 on marbling in Germany.

Charles Adams in 1947 speculated that there might be other books published at this early time that showed an interest in marbling and thus contributed to its spread throughout Europe in this, its cradle period. In fact, several such works have turned up in recent years that had not been previously described in the literature; a few have already been mentioned, and still others will be cited as our survey unfolds. In addition, we shall discuss an important early French manuscript account that has escaped attention until now, and an early Italian manuscript recipe that was noticed in the literature nearly a century and a half ago and has been virtually ignored since. Their recent unearthing suggests that there may still exist in library collections and archival repositories other sources that document the conduct of this craft during its early stages in the West.

In the three chapters which follow we shall observe the development of the marbling industry and trade in Europe: first in Germany and France and then in the other countries where the craft took root. Reconstructing and accurately describing much of this activity will prove a difficult task, for the scientific curiosity that the technique provoked during the early and middle decades of the seventeenth century appears to have subsided as this infant left its cradle and began to attain maturity. As a result, we do not have many reports about marbling activity in these countries before the later eighteenth century. Fortunately, some fragmentary evidence does exist and Albert Haemmerle and a few others have undertaken pioneering researches that provide us with insights into the activity of the late-seventeenth and early eighteenth centuries. And we can learn a great deal more from the marbled papers themselves, which seem to have been produced in enormous quantities at this time and which survive today in hundreds of thousands of bookbindings in European and American libraries. This documentation is substantial enough, I believe, and illuminating enough, to form a coherent picture of the industry and the trade that existed in the late seventeenth century onward. Let us now look at the images and features that we can identify in this view.

3

Marbling in Germany

Looking at the development of marbling in Germany, we shall see that in this land, unlike most other European countries where the process came into use, the production of marbled paper was inextricably entwined with the overall manufacture of colored and decorated paper. This fact makes it impossible to identify a separate German marbling industry; thus, it is necessary to examine the development and structure of the entire colored-paper industry in Germany in order to determine where and how the craft of marbling fit into its scheme.

Augsburg and the Fugger Connection

Evidence marshaled by Albert Haemmerle on the subject of German colored and decorated paper—Buntpapier—indicates that the initial manufacture of colored papers in Germany occurred in or around the Swabian (now Bavarian) town of Augsburg after the middle of the sixteenth century. The establishment of the industry in this south German town was no accident; indeed, it may be considered a natural outgrowth of the book-related and printing industries for which this place was already well known, as well as a branch of its later textile industry.

During the fifteenth and sixteenth centuries, Augsburg was one of Europe's leading banking and commercial towns, becoming, after Nürnberg, the center of the trade carried on between Italy and northern Europe. Its business houses, headed by the Fugger and Welser merchant families, rivaled the Medici of Florence not only in power and splendor but also in their encouragement of the arts and sciences. (Munich, about thirty-five miles to the south, was still a sleepy town with a population of 20,000 or less; it would develop slowly and not outstrip Augsburg until the late seventeenth or eighteenth century.)

Before the invention of printing, Augsburg had been a center for the copying and illumination of manuscripts, as well as for the manufacture and coloring of playing cards. It supported a well-organized guild of woodblock cutters who became responsible for some of the earliest book illustration in the decades immediately following the invention of printing. Later, the town developed a trade in the engraving and printing of copperplates and fostered an extensive textile and tapestry industry; in fact, Augsburg became the textile center of Germany.

Woodblocks, metal plates, and the techniques associated with them were common to all of these activities, and the further transfer of these media and methods to the industry of colored and decorated paper was a natural development. The woodcut illustration, popular in Germany for several centuries previously, declined in the late sixteenth century, and it seems likely that many individuals engaging in this craft turned their skills to making blocks and plates for imprinting the calicoes and other textiles that were becoming increasingly popular. Consequently, many calico printers eventually combined their manufacture of textiles with the printing of colorful designs on paper, and some artists may also have turned their attention to decorating paper in this way.

Haemmerle speculates that the printing of colored paper by means of woodblocks began in Germany in the period around 1570; he cites (from the state archives of Baden in Karlsruhe) a privilege for its manufacture granted to the court painter, Heinrich Trorbach of Heidelburg, on 21 April 1589, the first such German patent known. This document informs us that Trorbach had partly inherited from his father-in-law, Johann Pesserer, and partly purchased from his co-heirs the necessary blocks that enabled him to stamp and color paper in all sorts of designs.[1] Thus, there was already production and trade in colored papers in south Germany by the time that the Eastern art of marbling arrived there at about the beginning of the seventeenth century.

It is impossible to ignore the Fugger family's importance to the development of Augsburg's textile trade or their probable influence on the rise of a decorated paper industry there, which within a short time had incorporated marbling into its production. No one possessing a sense of history can fail to appreciate the important role that the Fuggers exerted on that town's early economic, social, and cultural life. Members of the richest family in Europe in the sixteenth century, these astute businessmen were both generous patrons of the arts and learning and outstanding philanthropists, particularly in Augsburg, their place of residence. (Remains of the famous Fuggerei, the oldest housing development for the poor in the world, dating from 1519, can still be viewed there.)

Armed with merchant fleets, the powerful Fuggers built their vast fortune with a virtual monopoly in the mining and trading of silver, copper, and mercury, and they increased it through banking and moneylending. Along with the Welsers, another local family of merchants and bankers, they made Augsburg into a center of worldwide importance in the fifteenth and sixteenth centuries. As the residence of emperors and a meeting place for imperial diets, the town attracted and fostered many famed painters, sculptors, and musicians. (Hans Holbein, the Elder and the Younger, and Hans Burgkmair were natives of Augsburg; Mozart's father, Leopold, was born and raised there.) The Fuggers reached the height of their power under Jakob Fugger (known as Jakob the Rich), who died in 1525, and Anton Fugger, who died in 1560. Thereafter, their firm began a gradual decline which continued until its final dissolution after the end of the Thirty Years War in 1648.

The decline of the Fugger enterprise paralleled that of the Habsburgs, to whom the Fuggers had loaned enormous sums of money and from whom they had in turn received the status of nobility, sovereign rights over vast estates, and the privilege of coining their own money. Jakob and Anton's descendants showed little inclination toward commerce. After acquiring humanistic educations at European universities and marrying into their own class, they spent most of their lives on their estates, where they built magnificent residences and established valuable libraries, preserving some part of the large wealth once held by their family.

Hans Fugger, who had established the family in Augsburg in 1367 and who was the founding father of the firm, began as a weaver and afterward conducted a successful textile business there; and, as noted, his descendants were active in Augsburg's later development as the textile center of Germany. There is good reason to conclude that the Fuggers may well have been involved in transferring marbling from the Near East to Germany, for the technique became one of the several methods carried on in the colored paper industry that they presumably helped to establish in Augsburg.

Indeed, there is some evidence to indicate that the Fuggers had an appreciation of marbled paper at a very early time, and they may have engaged in importing marbled papers from Turkey and the East; we know this in part from their penchant for including marbled and other Eastern papers in the many Album Amicorum maintained by members of the family. In addition, in 1946 Gabriel Magnien, city librarian of Lyon and collector of decorated paper, published an article entitled "L'Exotisme dans les vieux papier dominos" in which he described and partly illustrated an early art album that further proves the Fuggers' connection with this commodity.[2] Some years later he provided additional details in a tripartite series of articles published on "Vieux papiers de garde et de couverture de livres"—old endpapers and cover papers for books.[3]

In the first article of this series Magnien discussed the art album he had described and partly illustrated in 1946: a bound, octavo volume containing sixteen plates of Albrecht Dürer's *Little Passions* (sometimes also referred to as his *Small Passions*). The volume not only contained a seventeenth-century manuscript notation on a flyleaf identifying the Fuggers as its owners, but it included, as interleaves between Dürer's plates of the different scenes of the passion of Christ, fifty-six colored and decorated leaves of Eastern manufacture, *of which twenty-two were marbled.* Thirty-four of these interleaves are papers colored and decorated in the silhouette style, showing vases, Turkish crescents, mosques, and other Eastern subjects. Magnien describes the twenty-two marbled sheets as being either pale or lively but tastefully colored, with most stained blue on a ground that is tinged lighter blue; some show other colors and tones such as white, gray, yellow, and rose, and some are flecked with gold.

Magnien also describes the seventeenth-century manuscript note on one of the book's flyleaves that reads, *Rarissimam hanc Imaginum Passionis Christi ab Albrecht Dürer, ex oppido Hungariae Gyula oriendo collectionem, suo aevo charta in Oriente diversis cum coloribus elaborata intermixtam adornarunt Augustae Vindelicorum Comites ditissimi Fuggeri;* or, translated, "The very rich Fuggers, Associates of the Imperial Court of Augsburg, have ornamented this very rare representation of the passion of Christ by Albrecht Dürer, acquired from the Hungarian town of Gyula, where it was created, by intermingling into it colored papers of their own era from the Orient that have been embellished with colors of various sorts." Magnien also reports that one of the colored leaves contains a watermark in the form of an angel, indicating that this sheet of paper was not made in the East (where watermarks were not used), but in Italy, probably at Venice, where the angel watermark was standard after the fifteenth century.[4]

According to Magnien, the Fuggers engaged in the sale of books and prints at the beginning of the sixteenth century and in Italy they sold the scenes and prints of Albrecht Dürer. (The Fuggers obviously had a fondness for the art of Dürer, for Magnien mentions that Dürer painted a portrait of Jakob Fugger which now is preserved in an art gallery in Munich.) Magnien also writes that the Fuggers owned a bank and a store in Venice in the vicinity of the old Rialto bridge, where they sold objects of art and valuable books and where they maintained a very large warehouse containing commodities of all sorts. This establishment, known as "il fondaco de Tedeschi"—the German warehouse—served for the traffic of merchandise either from the Levant or destined for exportation there or (through Venetian traders) to Constantinople.[5]

It is well known that even at this early time the Turks were fond of using European paper, for their own quality often was poor; they gave it the appearance of Aher paper by treating it with Aher solution or polishing it to ready it for use. This fact not only explains the presence of a Western watermark in an Eastern colored paper but suggests that other, unwatermarked sheets in the Fugger volume may have originated in the West.

Magnien proposes several possibilities regarding the origin of the colored papers in this volume. He speculates, first, that either these decorated sheets originated in Hungary, for Dürer worked on his *Little Passions* at Gyula in 1508–1513, when Hungary was part of the Turkish Empire (along with the Balkans, Asia Minor, Persia, and the coast of North Africa from Egypt to Gibraltar); or, alternatively, that the marbled decoration could have been applied to the paper in Italy, where Venetian art was influenced by Oriental styles. While the first of Magnien's speculations seems reasonable, his second hypothesis does not. There is no evidence indicating that any sort of marbling took place in Venice (or Europe, for that matter) in the decades prior to 1600, when the volume containing Dürer's *Little Passions* apparently was assembled; furthermore, the incorporation of silhouette papers and the presence of gold flecks on its marbled sheets seem to provide absolute proof of Eastern manufacture.

Thus, these German men of commerce and patrons of art and learning (for Magnien also mentions that the Fuggers established an important library which they gave to the University of Heidelberg in 1584) were in a position to appreciate and acquire marbled paper at a very early time. A "Fugger connection" in the transfer of the marbling method from the East to the West and in its subsequent incorporation into the overall production of German decorated and colored paper seems likely, for it would account for the fact that marbling first took root in or around Augsburg—their town.

Early Augsburg Activity

Information on marbling in Germany during all of the first and much of the second half of the seventeenth century simply does not exist. That such activity went on, however, is proved by the existence of German marbled paper made during this time: the early sheets in some of the Album Amicorum mentioned above, and by the collage in the Germanisches Nationalmuseum in Nürnberg that shows evidence of an advanced technique (Plate VII). There are many more early German marbled papers in the Nürnberg and other collections, and in books bound in the second half of the seventeenth century, that furnish additional and indisputable proof of such activity. But exactly who was responsible for making these papers remains unknown, although we may assume that they

must have been made in south German workshops. It is only when we come to the last quarter of the seventeenth century that we begin to sense the activity inside the Augsburg workshops.

Albert Haemmerle, who spent more than twenty years researching the early history of the colored paper industry in Augsburg mainly through archival sources, tells us that a demand for ornamental papers arose from bookbinders and others after the middle of the seventeenth century; by the beginning of the eighteenth century, Augsburg was at the center of this burgeoning trade. According to Haemmerle, many people can be associated with the production of colored paper in Augsburg, including more than forty people involved in making Turkish or marbled papers between 1700 and 1800.[6] However, as he points out, it is difficult to determine who did what within a given workshop, for the titles the workmen bestowed on themselves are often confusing. Several sorts of colored and decorated paper were produced concurrently in these small factories or workshops, with the specialty of marbling just one activity among them; thus the workmen so employed often identified themselves with more than one particular specialty.

In an early and important study on this subject, entitled "Augsburger Buntpapier," Haemmerle provided a thirty-five-page alphabetical register of all of the makers of colored paper in Augsburg during the late seventeenth and entire eighteenth centuries whom he had identified through his searches in archival and other records.[7] The ranks of such workmen included makers of decorated papers that had been stamped with wood or metal blocks or through the use of stencils (i.e., damask, calico, and pattern papers); of paste papers; of brocade or gold or silver papers (types that later came to be designated collectively as "Dutch gilt"); and of Turkish or marbled papers. Also included were general paper merchants who were in business in Augsburg during this time.

By reading through this list entry by entry, it is possible to count a total of sixty people described by the term "Türckisch-Papiermacher," the contemporary designation of a true marbler, or by some variant, recognizable form. Ten individuals so identified were active in the period before 1700. The earliest of them, one Franziskus Fuchs, was identified as a maker of Turkish paper in the year 1675. Three others, Christoph Ainmiller (1676), Hans Ludwig Stumpp (1678), and Hans Georg Scheppich (1679), were so designated before 1680; two more individuals were identified during the 1680s, and four others in the 1690s.

Marbled paper, when it first came to be manufactured in Germany, must have been as much a rarity as was the Oriental product beforehand; an expensive curio, it was affordable only by the noble and wealthy mercantile classes, who used it to embellish their precious albums and for special decorative purposes at home. Despite its early introduction in Germany, the art developed slowly. Its technique, always difficult to learn properly, was probably known initially by only a handful of artists and professional paper colorists who worked in strict secrecy. Moreover, gum and other necessary ingredients must have been expensive and difficult to obtain. In time, however, the demand arose for such papers on the part of German bookbinders who, following the French example, wished to dress up their better class of work. This increasing demand, in turn, resulted in the establishment of a group of artisans who, like Fuchs and Ainmiller, began to specialize in, and eventually came to identify themselves almost exclusively with, the manufacture of Turkish paper. Nonetheless, in Germany the art remained primarily in the workshops and small factories of general paper colorists, where many types of colored and decorated papers were also produced.

The ever-increasing requirements of bookbinders, and the widening manufacture and cheapening of the product in response to their demands, made the marbling trade a "growth industry" throughout the eighteenth and into the nineteenth centuries. As Pollard and Polter have noted, the use of marbled paper in bookbinding had already become a more common feature by the 1670s. And before the end of the seventeenth century, marbled paper began to be used as limp wrappers on pamphlets, theses, and legal documents; for covering royal privileges; and for dressing up bound books of blank leaves used as diaries and for home and business purposes. Its manufacture was especially stimulated by changing bookbinding styles.

In the early 1800s French, German and other binders developed what became known in the trade as "half" and "quarter" leather bindings. These served as substitutes for full leather covers, which heretofore had been the rule in bookbinding. Half bindings incorporated leather at the book's spine and corners (or tips), with marbled or other types of colored and decorated paper being employed elsewhere on the covers; quarter bindings called for leather only on the spine. This innovation freed up precious leather, needed to shoe and clothe an ever-growing population. At the same time, it lowered the cost of bookbinding while still allowing books when shelved upright to appear like traditionally bound leather volumes. The smallness of its patterns, its simple yet colorful and often charming designs, its increasing production—all of these factors made marbled paper ideal for book decoration, and it has reigned supreme in bookbinding to this day. Marbled paper also became increasingly employed in the home and in industry for some of the purposes cited earlier. Time, however, and mechanization have taken their relentless toll and have all but obliterated the larger role that marbled paper played in the everyday life of this era.

The Enlarging Augsburg Trade

Once the craft of paper marbling established itself as an important industry by the final decades of the seventeenth century, it became more firmly entrenched in Augsburg with each succeeding decade. As Haemmerle's registers show, more and more people went into the business of decorating paper in the Turkish style after 1700, so that the subspecialty came to be an important part of Augsburg's paper-coloring industry. While some of these artisans are identified by Haemmerle solely as makers of Turkish or marbled paper, most of them also engaged in making other decorated types in the workshops of the general paper colorists. If they marbled privately, or exclusively, they marketed their paper through distributors who handled and sold all sorts of colored and decorated papers in their centralized emporiums.

Several illustrations in Haemmerle's *Buntpapier* and in collateral sources give us glimpses into the early eighteenth-century Augsburg trade and indicate how marbling fit into its overall scheme. Reproduced in *Buntpapier* (page 18) are two pertinent prints, published by the important Augsburg engraver and print seller Martin Engelbrecht between 1720 and 1750 (Plate VIII), which depict a male *dominotier* and a female *dominotière*, the contemporary French designations for makers of colored papers. Each is represented together with one or more aspects of colored paper production. The dominotier stands before a copperplate or rolling press with which he had imprinted damask, calico, and pattern papers with colorful designs, using registering woodblocks or metal plates. The dominotière occupies the center stage of a scene in which other women are engaged in decorating paper. Both the dominotier and the dominotière have fancy papers suspended from their clothing as symbols of their trade and as advertisements of their wares—damask and brocade papers, paste papers, and others. The legend that describes the female colorist refers to a utensil suspended from her waist as a "trough for marbled papers" (*Der Trog zum Türckisch-Papier*, or *auge au papier marbré*), indicating that marbled papers were among the types she apparently produced or sold.

These two prints are part of a series of nearly 150 or more that Engelbrecht produced to illustrate the trades and professions of his age.[8] Their inclusion demonstrates that the making of colored and fancy papers had achieved both importance and the status of a large and identifiable trade in Augsburg (as well as in other places) by the early decades of the eighteenth century.

Two other illustrations reproduced by Haemmerle reveal the variety of papers produced and offered for sale, including the marbled type (Plate IX). These show pattern cards of the Augsburg manufacturer and seller of decorated paper, Georg Christoph Stoy. These rare examples of early advertising literature which, Haemmerle believes, were published in the period around 1730, indicate, both through printed text and actual mounted samples, what types of fancy and decorated papers could be obtained from Stoy at this time. Described and illustrated on his cards are stained or monochrome papers, sprinkled papers, paste papers, "Kattun" or calico papers, brocade or gilt papers (in which Stoy is said to have specialized), and papers of the Turkish or truly marbled variety.

The word "marbled" as it was used in this period did not denote the type of paper we class in that category today, but referred to several other varieties, including paste papers and brocade papers. Papers that we designate today as "marbled" were described on Stoy's cards as "Turkish."[9] The limited range of marbled patterns being produced in Germany in the early eighteenth century is proved by the few Turkish patterns Stoy illustrated on his cards and offered for sale: simple spot and combed designs.

Haemmerle describes Stoy as one of the most prolific and important makers of damask and brocade papers in Augsburg of his day, but he doubts that Stoy produced all of the papers exhibited on these pattern cards. Many, Haemmerle felt, were supplied to him by small, independent makers in Augsburg. Stoy (1669–1750) was active in Augsburg from 1703 until his death. In his "Augsburger Buntpapier" article, Haemmerle writes that in 1703 Stoy married Maria Barbara Enderlin, widow of oil painter and Turkish papermaker Mathias Frölich, whereupon he assumed Frölich's privilege and took charge of his colored paper factory.[10]

Hans Enderli, a more recent commentator on marbling and its history, points out that Frölich, who in 1698 received the privilege of making brocade papers, had himself switched over from oil painting to the manufacture of colored papers.[11] And Haemmerle speculates in his article that Frölich was perhaps the first in Augsburg to manufacture Turkish papers on an extensive scale. Frölich's previous occupation as a painter reinforces the point that many of the early German marblers rose out of the ranks of artists and, unlike French marblers, were not at all connected with the bookbinding trade. The craft's early association with artists and professional paper colorists accounts for the fact that marbled papers in early seventeenth-century Germany did not serve as decorations for bookbindings but filled artistic and ornamental functions in the home.

Calico and Gilt Papers

A discussion of the several types of stamped papers that were being made in Augsburg in Stoy's era will provide a better understanding of the contemporary German paper coloring trade and clear up any confusion about their nature, for they were referred to loosely and variantly and often even as "marbled." The term "Kattunpapier" meant decorated papers produced with woodblocks and stencils. They usually were produced in two or more colors and often displayed simple yet charming designs. The German description of this type as *Kattunpapier* or calico paper is indicative of its origin in the textile industry; for

the blocks or plates that were used in its manufacture originally had been employed for imprinting *Kattun*, or calico cloth. Thus, the transition of the *Kattunmacher*, or calico maker, to the *Kattunpapiermacher*, or calico paper maker, seems an obvious and natural one. Damask papers were of the same variety, but usually showed larger designs that imitated the patterns of damask cloth of the early type that was imported from Damascus and frequently used as tablecloths.[12] All of these papers were known simply as "dominotier" paper in France, as "Kattun" or calico paper in Germany, and as "chintz" papers in Holland and Belgium. I have found it convenient over the years to group them under the general designation "pattern papers."

Brocade or gilt papers were produced in just about the same way, but formed a separate and distinct class because they were highly embellished with a metallic finish. A useful account of this brocade or gilded type appears in an unpublished paper by Henck Voorn, the Dutch paper historian.[13] He points out that this particular kind of colored paper was called brocade paper, or, alternatively, Augsburg paper, or paper of Augsburg, after its most important place of origin; he also notes that Mrs. Loring referred to it as "Dutch gilt paper" or "Dutch flowered paper."[14] Voorn too distinguishes this variety from the plainly decorated (by means of woodblocks, metal plates, and stencils) and ungilded types mentioned above.

Voorn relates that the first attempts to make gilt paper at Augsburg occurred in approximately 1690, when Jeremias Neuhofer, working in conjunction with Jacob Enderlin, an engraver from Isny, experimented with printing cotton with a varnish mixed with bronze powder. Enderlin, who began working independently just before 1700, was the first to produce gold-bronze and silver-bronze papers—that is, papers printed with bronze varnish through the raised surfaces of engraved wooden blocks. Enderlin's example was followed by Abraham Mieser (or Meser) and his son Leopold, Georg Christoph Stoy, Simon Haichele, and others.

Mieser also began to produce such papers in about 1690, using a copperplate press, and was the first in Europe to do so. He covered the paper first with thin sheets of gold or silver leaf and then with a heated plate containing a design on its surface; by submitting the whole to the pressure of the press, he transferred in gilt the image in relief on the plate to the paper. The type of gilt paper embossed in this way did not immediately oust the bronze varnished paper from the market, but it soon surpassed it in beauty, so that after about 1735 the bronze varnished paper showed a rapid decline. Often stencils were employed to color the paper in various ways before it was gilded, with the result that several colors and images appeared underneath or in conjunction with the gilt decoration, and sheets of great beauty resulted.[15] Voorn notes that Dutch gilt paper was primarily a German product, made from about 1700 in Augsburg, from about 1720 in

Fürth and Nördlingen, and from about 1730 in Nürnberg and Leipzig.

Paul von Stetten's 1779 *Kunst- Gewerb- und Handwerks Geschichte der Reichs-Stadt Augsburg* includes a two-page description of "gefärbtes und gedrucktes Papier." Von Stetten names Abraham Mieser, the Younger, who was active from about 1690 until his death in 1742, as the person who developed the trade, and states also that Stoy's factory had been long in existence. (Haemmerle's brief biographical sketch of Mieser identifies him as a maker of colored paper and of Turkish paper as well.)[16] Von Stetten further asserts that the business of paper decoration in Augsburg was related to textile printing there and presumably arose from it.[17] Examples of German eighteenth-century calico and brocade papers may be seen on Plate X.

The Spread of Marbling Throughout Germany and the Industrial Manufacture of Colored Paper

Available sources, both old and new, indicate that it did not take long for other centers of colored paper making to develop throughout Germany. Haemmerle relates that workshops were established at Fürth, on the outskirts of Nürnberg, around 1720 and in Nürnberg itself by 1730, with the founding of others at Nördlingen and Frankfurt-am-Main in the following years.[18] From information that will be introduced below, however, it seems obvious that the beginning of activity at Fürth may have occurred in 1715, or earlier, and at Nürnberg even before that time.

It is possible that manufacture of colored paper could have reached Saxony also as early as 1718. In that year, the young bookbinder David Liscovius (who had been established in Leipzig since 1715) and his associates petitioned the revenue office in Dresden for the privilege of making brocade, Turkish, and other types of fancy papers. Whether Liscovius and his cohorts were successful in obtaining their patent is uncertain, but it seems likely that they were. Two accounts, both published prior to World War II, reported that Liscovius's petition was preserved in the Leipzig city archives.[19] In his petition, Liscovius mentioned that in his journeyman years he had observed the making of colored and decorated papers in Augsburg and Fürth and wished to establish at Leipzig the same sort of factory as existed in Augsburg and Nürnberg, which, he pointed out, distributed many fancy papers throughout the Saxon countryside.

The period between 1750 and the early 1800s witnessed ever-increasing activity in the production of colored and decorated papers in Germany. Regardless of the outcome of Liscovius's petition early in the century, we know that a factory definitely was established in Leipzig by 1755. As the Leipzig historian Arno Knapp reported, it was located in the Petersstrasse in the inn "Zum Weinstock,"

where all sorts of decorated papers were made, including marbled ones.[20] Leipzig by this date stood alongside Augsburg, Nürnberg, and Frankfurt as a leading center of book production in Germany, and there arose both a demand for colored paper and the means of satisfying it. Haemmerle recounts that in 1776 another such factory was opened in Leipzig by J. C. Breitkopf, who carried on the manufacture of colored papers in connection with a factory he had previously established for the making of playing cards.[21]

Johann Beckmann began a nine-page account of the manufacture of colored papers in Germany in the period around 1780 by stating that although the art of making colored paper had been carried on in Nürnberg and Augsburg for many years, it was Herr Breitkopf who brought it to perfection.[22] Beckmann enumerated the various kinds of colored and decorated papers produced in Breitkopf's newly erected factory in Leipzig and provided an accompanying price list. Types of paper advertised were paste paper, monochrome paper, sprinkled paper, and the Turkish variety (truly marbled paper), both fine and ordinary types. Beckmann also provided a brief description—covering about three-fourths of an octavo page—of the marbling process, stating that Herr Breitkopf had given him a lesson and was allowing him to publish an account of it.

Additional production was begun at Leipzig by a marbler named Graul about 1799 and by Johann Heinrich Gräff at about the same time.[23] In 1804 Gräff published in the *Journal für Fabrik, Manufaktur, Handlung und Mode* a short account of the latest happenings in the manufacture of fancy papers in Saxony.[24] He began by reporting on the activity of Graul, who for some years previously had made colored papers for bookbinders in Leipzig and neighboring towns, and who, with state approval, stood at the forefront of the business there. Gräff then told about his own manufacture of Buntpapier, relating that although he had failed in his petition for a similar privilege, obtaining only an excise stamp, he nonetheless had commenced his business and was endeavoring to make it known. Now, with five years' experience, he was able to offer all sorts of colored paper to the public, including brocade, marbled, and many other papers listed at the conclusion of his article with their prices. His work also included French, English, and German-style paper hangings and the fancy borders for their trim.

The last quarter of the eighteenth century appears to have been a period of great expansion in the making of marbled and other types of fancy papers in Germany, with workshops and factories springing up in many places throughout the countryside. The Weimar *Journal des Luxus und der Moden,* which was devoted to feminine fashion and decoration in the home, reported in its September 1787 issue that marbled paper was being produced at the paperhanging factory of Carl Friedrich Eggebrecht in Weimar. At the conclusion of this account were displayed eight mounted samples of marbled paper Eggebrecht made for the purpose of wall decoration, showing, for the most part, pale Turkish or spot patterns.[25] And in its issue of the following June, the same journal reported the manufacture of colored paper, including marbled paper, by Johann Georg Zeller in the south Bavarian town of Kempten. Zeller was said to produce all sorts of colored paper, including English marbled paper, "new-fangled" marble paper, streaked and spotted types, and extra fine Turkish paper, as well as monochrome, calico, and other decorated paper.[26]

In 1803 an important factory was established at Schneeberg by Gottfried Heinrich Wilisch, and in the same year another Saxon plant opened in Dresden. Wilisch (1771–1837) was probably the first maker to actually mass-produce colored papers, at least in the modern sense. Trained as a bookbinder at Leipzig, he learned during his apprenticeship to make decorated papers for use in his own work. After attaining the rank of master bookbinder, he settled in Schneeberg, a small town south of Zwickau, not far from the present Czechoslovakian border. The high quality of his bindings soon resulted in a demand for his colored papers, and Wilisch began to manufacture them in quantity. In 1805 his continuing success led him to initiate factory production and he established a firm bearing his name.

In Wilisch's first years of business, the strong demand for his papers necessitated the employment of from fifty to seventy-five workers, a rather large labor force in those times. But because of difficulties with his Leipzig agents, who had exclusive rights to the sale of his wares, he suffered a business reversal and in 1809 was forced to sell part of his establishment to meet the demands of creditors. He was, however, able to hold onto the remainder. About this time he was approached by a businessman from Aschaffenburg by the name of Alois Dessauer, who had begun to take an interest in the production of colored paper, although he had no previous experience in this business. Dessauer purchased some of Wilisch's production with the condition that the Saxon maker come to Aschaffenburg, arrange for its disposition, and bring Dessauer's factory into production. (This event, as we shall see, later had important ramifications in the manufacture of colored paper in Germany.) While Wilisch was overseeing the installation of his equipment and methods in Dessauer's new factory, reportedly in 1810 and 1811, his wife Dorothea remained at Schneeberg and continued his diminished business. Upon his return to Saxony, Wilisch once more assumed control of his firm and directed it until his death. His wife then conducted the business until 1849, when their sons Franz Friedrich and Julius Robert Wilisch assumed control and renamed it the "Gebrüder Wilisch" (Wilisch Brothers), eventually adding a second factory at Oberschlema. This information on the Wilisch family's activity was provided by the founder's grandson, Gottfried Julius Alexander Wilisch, in 1938, at which time the firm was still in existence.[27]

Paste Papers

Although paste papers have been frequently mentioned in this account as a principal type of early decorated paper, I have thus far not described them in detail. There can, however, be no serious discussion of the subject of colored papermaking in Germany without some detail on their background and making. Often referred to in the early literature as "marbled," paste papers actually were not made on a tank or bath and thus are not marbled papers at all; however, these charming papers probably originated in the same workshops of the Augsburg and south German paper colorists. Essentially a German method of paper decoration, the manufacture of paste papers with few exceptions remained so. Haemmerle tells us that paste colors were known and used from about 1600, and were being employed then and afterward by craftsmen who were in the business of manufacturing playing cards; however, papers decorated in paste colors are not known before about 1650.[28] Paste papers nevertheless had attained a high level of production by the end of the seventeenth century and in the early years of the eighteenth, as is indicated by their frequent use as covers for estate inventories of Nürnberg citizens at this time (Plate XI).

In order to produce paste papers, makers coated paper with one or more applications of colored paste made from flour and then stamped or otherwise worked designs into the colored sheet. The method was relatively simple, quick, and inexpensive. When properly executed, it resulted in a pleasing and tasteful product, one that could be achieved by anyone with a modicum of technique and taste. Next to marbled papers, paste papers came to be most adaptable to bookbinding and the kind most often associated with it. Their employment in Germany along with marbled paper, especially for book decoration, is reflected in the term most frequently used to describe them in both ancient and modern times, "Kleistermarmorieren," or paste marbling—despite the fact, as we have noticed, that they are not marbled at all.

The existence of at least half a dozen samples of paste papers on Georg Christoph Stoy's pattern cards indicates how popular they had become by about the 1730s. Yet they seem not to have been used in bookbindings before the middle of the eighteenth century, and we may assume from the largeness of the patterns found on early examples extant that they were more frequently utilized for domestic or other purposes. After mid-century, however, German bookbinders came to employ them more frequently, as did binders in adjacent lands who had traveled to Germany to improve their techniques and observe the new and different work methods carried on there. And from about 1750 some of these binders, both in Germany and elsewhere, also came to apply paste paper decoration occasionally on the edges of their bindings also.

The production of paste paper was begun in the Saxon town of Herrnhut at about 1765, and it was there, during the next fifty years or more, that this form of paper decoration attained its highest level of perfection.[29] "Herrnhut papers," as they came to be popularly known (Plate XI), achieved their superior quality through the bright yet tasteful colors employed in their making and the symmetrical yet charming repeat patterns they contained. These designs were applied by means of wood blocks, wooden rollers with patterns cut into them in relief, and wooden combs and rakes.

Herrnhut had been founded in 1722 by Count Nikolaus Zinzendorff as a refuge for persecuted members of the Moravian Church, which was reconstructed there in the decades that followed. Linen and wool milling, along with other trades and handicrafts, came to be taught and carried on there. In 1764 the decision was made to begin the production of paste papers in the house of the community's sisterhood. For some time, a number of unemployed women had proposed undertaking the manufacture of paste papers, and the tradespeople with whom the community dealt had a desire for such materials.[30] By the mid-seventies, Herrnhut papers were distributed throughout Germany where they were quite popular for bookbinding and for uses in the home; large numbers of them were even exported and used abroad.

Many missionaries at the end of the eighteenth century set out from Herrnhut, some of them locating in Moravian settlements in eastern and central Pennsylvania or in North Carolina. The method of decorating paper through the paste technique and through simple blocks and plates emigrated with them, for many examples can be found in German-American bookbindings of the late eighteenth and early nineteenth centuries.[31] Nevertheless, except for their employment among the Moravian settlers and by German emigrant bookbinders, the use of paste papers is mostly alien to American bookbinding practice; they are only infrequently encountered on a better American binding. John Roulstone of Boston was an exception to this rule. One of the leading American bookbinders of the early nineteenth century (he died in 1826), he sometimes covered his half leather bindings with paste paper perhaps not only to achieve variation in his work, but also to lessen expense.

As has been pointed out, the making of paste papers was mainly a German technique, although the French also manufactured some in the late eighteenth century. The article on the marbler of paper in the Diderot-D'Alembert *Encyclopédie* outlined the method, and now and then paste papers are encountered on French bindings of that era and in the decades following. In addition to their manufacture in the workshops and factories of professional paper colorists, paste papers came to be made by individual bookbinders who could not obtain or afford the marbled or more sophisticated varieties of decorated paper. The method of making them, we have observed, was simple.[32] Such knowledge usually was imparted to German bookbinders during their apprenticeship years and migrated with them to wherever these trainees journeyed. Conversely, itinerant craftsmen who wandered to Germany in search of additional training and experience observed their manufacture and use in German shops and carried the knowledge back to their native lands. Thus, one sometimes encounters paste-coloring methods on the cover papers and even on the edges of Swedish, Danish, Dutch, and Bohemian books and on volumes bound in the eighteenth and early nineteenth centuries in nearby lands.

The practice of making paste papers has been passed down into modern times. The master bookbinder Paul Kersten explained the paste coloring method in his 1922 marbling manual *Die Marmorierkunst,* recounting that in his early childhood he had observed their manufacture by his grandfather, who was also a bookbinder.[33] And they continue to be made today, sometimes by professionals and sometimes by bookbinders themselves.

The Dessauer-Aschaffenburg Enterprise

In 1810 in the north Bavarian city of Aschaffenburg, located a short distance southeast of Frankfurt and about an equal distance from Darmstadt to the west, a business was established that was destined to become the largest and best known in the world for the manufacture of colored and decorated papers, one that would give Germany mastery of this industry. Initially founded by a bookbinder named Johann Daniel Knode (or Knothe) for the production of colored and fancy papers on the industrial level, it soon encountered financial difficulties and then fell into bankruptcy due to poor planning and undercapitalization. Late in the same year, Knode's factory was taken over by Alois Dessauer, a banker and trader who had a special interest in the stationery business.

Dessauer, as we have previously seen, then purchased part of Gottfried Heinrich Wilisch's Saxon plant and enlisted his expertise to get his Aschaffenburg plant into stable operation. Dessauer's production force, which amounted to twenty workers when he commenced operation in 1812, grew steadily along with his business. The Aschaffenburg plant in 1815 employed fifty workers; in 1826, following the construction of a second building, 140; and in 1832, 200. The colored papers turned out were produced entirely by hand, in four or five locations throughout the city, and in all varieties.

An 1820 article in the *Allgemeiner Anzeiger der Deutschen* provides some measure of Dessauer's early activity and of the dimensions and output of his operation.[34] As reported there, in the space of but a few years after he had taken hold, his factory employed more than 100 workers and produced every kind of colored paper, of which the Turkish or marbled type was but one. Furthermore, it shipped products not only throughout Germany, but to neighboring countries and regions as well, including Switzerland, Holland, the Brabant, the Hanseatic cities, Prussia, Saxony, Poland, Denmark, Russia,

Italy, and Spain. In 1816 and 1817—miserable years of famine in Germany in the aftermath of the Napoleonic campaigns, during which factories of all sorts lost or laid off large numbers of workers due to the high cost of food—all the labor force in Dessauer's plants remained in employment. In fact, Dessauer obtained so large an amount of business that he had to increase the working hours of his employees, increasing their wages significantly and making it possible for them to get through this severe time.

L. W. Schertel, in his 1836 commentary on the condition of the Bavarian economy and industries since the beginning of the reign of Ludwig I (1825), devoted several paragraphs to the Dessauer operation at Aschaffenburg, praising its success and acknowledging its economic and national value to Bavaria.[35] Schertel claimed that it employed 500 workers at that time and had opened up markets with the north German states as well as with Denmark, Sweden, Poland, and Russia. Schertel also referred to the manufacture of fine colored paper by J. N. Schönecker and Company at Würzburg, Johann Friedrich Lodter at Augsburg, Christian Schleich at Schwabach, Johann Leonhard Zertahelly at Fürth, Sebastian Egger at Munich, and G. A. Aurnheimer, Jr., at Regensburg. Schertel asserted that many of these companies had issued beautiful pattern cards that attested to the quality of their products.

Dessauer early introduced mechanical methods for the production and finishing of his papers, beginning in 1820 with the construction of a polishing machine that did away with the tedious hand polishing (by means of an agate stone) of colored papers. In 1840 new buildings were erected and Dessauer's first steam engine came into operation. Dessauer continued to introduce machinery into his business as soon as it was developed, and he was quick to bring in other innovations—lithography, for example—whenever possible. Nonetheless, he maintained in his total output the traditional marbled and paste papers that were made in the old ways, although by this time he had come to produce "pseudo" types as well. While these were designated as "marbled," they were made through chemical processes and, consequently, were not true "Tunkpapiere," as the Germans called papers made on a bath.

Some idea of the extent of the Aschaffenburg enterprise can be obtained from examples of its pattern books that have survived. Enderli speaks of one such pattern book in his possession that contains a total of 4,552 original samples of colored papers and includes all of the designs and types that this firm manufactured.[36] I myself have examined a large number of pattern books, including earlier ones, at the Dutch Royal Library in the Hague and in the Rosamond B. Loring collection at Harvard. Although apparently not quite so extensive as Enderli's, the Loring copy contains between 3,500 and 4,000 small mounted samples, representing the various kinds of papers and patterns made at about mid-century. Among

them are wallpapers, pattern or calico papers, brocade papers and monochrome papers, as well as paste papers and marbled papers, both true and false types (Plates XII and XIII).[37]

Alois Dessauer died on 11 April, 1850, at the age of eighty-seven, and his firm was continued by his sons Joseph and Franz, who soon erected a new factory. At that time, their work force amounted to about 500. In 1859, when the firm went public and issued stock on the exchange, its production doubled. By 1900 fifty percent of its output was exported, mainly in large rolls consisting mostly of wallpaper. During the second half of the nineteenth century, Dessauer's sons increased their business appreciably by opening or taking over other businesses and plants. Colored paper firms gradually absorbed by the Dessauer enterprise included, among others, Franz Dahlem & Co. and Nees & Co. of Aschaffenburg; E. T. Kretschmar, Dresden; the Bunt- und Luxuspapierfabrik, Goldbach; Gebrüder Wilisch, Schneeberg; P. Schnell, Kassel; Oswald Enterlein, Niedersedlitz (near Dresden); W. Stern & Co., Fürth; the firm of Sell at Stuttgart; Ludwig Bahr, Kassel; and A. Dittberner, Breslau. Obviously, there was money to be made in this business.

Such was the success of the Dessauer operation that it survived two cataclysmic world wars and continued in production until a short time ago (under the name Buntpapierfabrik A. G. Aschaffenburg), making wallpapers and papers for household and industrial use.[38] I have in my collection a set of the firm's pattern books from the 1960–61 period. These include samples of only a handful of the "Marmor-Papiere" designs that have become traditional in book decoration; none of the true hand-marbled papers appear among them, however, only the so-called "Achat" and "Gustav" marbles, which were made outside of the bath. These and other non-marbled papers were developed early in the nineteenth century in order to more quickly, easily, and cheaply produce quasi-marbled designs for the book trade; to a large degree these contributed to the eventual demise of true hand marbling, at least at the factory level.

It was for the celebration of the sesquicentennial of the founding of the Dessauer-Aschaffenburg enterprise in 1961 that Albert Haemmerle (with the assistance of Olga Hirsch) compiled his classic *Buntpapier*.[39] When the directors of the company began to consider ways of observing its 150th anniversary, they decided not to put their resources into banquets and celebrations but to underwrite the compilation and publication of Haemmerle's book, a decision for which those interested in the book arts in general and Buntpapier in particular will be eternally grateful.[40] Sad to relate, the firm did not survive long after its 150th anniversary. While apparently solvent, it was not making a sufficient profit to satisfy its stockholders; liquidation began in 1968 and its factories were torn down in 1971.

At the time of its closing, the firm was the oldest sur-

Nᵒ.	Marmorpapiere.		Format	Im fl. 24 Fuss. pr. Ries	
				fl.	kr.
1	Fein türkisch Marmor	⎫ Gleiche Preise	Staab	8	—
2	» » dᵒ auf Irisgrund		Median	11	—
3	» » dᵒ Flussmarmor	⎬	grand raisin	14	—
100	» Pfauen – Marmor				
5	» Tiger – Marmor	Gleiche Preise	Löwen	11	—
101	» Pariser Marmor		Median	14	—
4	» Schrottel- und Corallenmarmor . .		grand raisin	18	—
6	» Griechisch Marmor auf Patent Velin	⎭			
*76	Feinst Agath– oder Chinesisch – Marmor . auf Patent Velin		Löwen	18	—
	» dᵒ » dᵒ dᵒ . . . . » »		Median	24	—
	» dᵒ » dᵒ dᵒ . . . . » »		grand raisin	30	—
11	» Polnisch– und Sultan - Marmor . . . . » »		Löwen	15	—
	» dᵒ » dᵒ dᵒ . . . » »		Median	20	—
	» dᵒ » dᵒ dᵒ . . . » »		grand raisin	25	—
*14	» Glanzfeuermarmor zum Vergolden appretirt		Löwen	28	—
	» dᵒ » » » . .		grand raisin	42	—
*13	Fein Ledermarmor		Löwen	15	—
	» dᵒ		Median	18	—
	» dᵒ		grand raisin	24	—

FIGURE 2. Title page and first page (providing current prices for various marbled papers) of the separate price list of Alois Dessauer's Aschaffenburg colored paper factory. Dating to about 1850, these pages accompany the pattern book in the Rosamond B. Loring collection in the Houghton Library of Harvard University.

viving industry in Aschaffenburg. Sometime later, the large collection of books, colored papers, and other pertinent materials accumulated during the firm's long existence were disposed of. Its valuable collection of books, including many rare manuals and some manuscript recipe books, were sold to the Dutch Royal Library in the Hague, which, under the direction of Henck Voorn, has assembled one of the best historical collections on Buntpapier in Europe.[41] A very large collection of colored papers manufactured by the Aschaffenburg and other, mostly German, firms in the nineteenth and twentieth centuries was sent to the Gutenberg Museum in Mainz; later this collection was redeposited in the Deutsches Museum von Meisterwerken der Naturwissenschaft und Technik in Munich, where, along with similar materials collected from other sources, it represents the largest and most important assembly of colored papers to be seen.[42]

The Industry at Mid-Century

Additional insights into the status and production of colored papers in Germany at the middle of the nineteenth century may be obtained from M. Fichtenberg's *Nouveau manuel complet du fabricant de papiers de fantaisie*, issued at Paris in 1852.[43] Little is known about Fichtenberg, although his name and the nature of his information suggest that he was German or German-trained and had a familiarity with the German colored-paper industry. Fichtenberg mentions that marbled papers were made in many countries, but notably in Germany, France, and England; he notes that the papers designated "German" have always merited preference, owing to their variety of patterns, beautiful finish, and brilliant gloss. (One highly polished paper in the Dessauer pattern book at Harvard is designated as "fire gloss.")

Fichtenberg informs us that in 1852 many factories existed in Germany, Prussia, and Saxony, and at Offenbach, Darmstadt, and Aschaffenburg. Messrs. G. Wuste at Darmstadt and Dessauer at Aschaffenburg had the reputation of being expert makers, especially the latter, who possessed one of the largest factories in existence. In the area of Neustadt on the Harte, he continues, nearly all of the inhabitants owed their existence to the fabrication of common, single-colored, and printed papers (termed "Indian") that sold considerably well in the colonies. At Nürnberg and Augsburg in Bavaria, many papers were covered with imitation gold; here also papers were produced printed with the images of saints, birds, and the like (that is, Kattun papers). While many of these impressions and patterns were gross, Fichtenberg asserted, they were cheap, and their manufacture was large, particularly at Augsburg, which shipped huge amounts to all parts of the world. (Augsburg's fame by this time was such that many of the brocade and other types of stamped papers were referred to commonly as "Augsburg papers,"

whether they were made there or not.) As regards marbling in particular, he stated, the Germans were also renowned for the manufacture of Turkish papers, to which they knew how to impart a pleasing surface and brilliant finish. In Saxony, and particularly in Dresden, highly finished marbled papers were made that exhibited a great variety of patterns and colors.

The above information from Fichtenberg's manual concludes this survey of the early development of marbling and of colored papermaking in Germany. A subsequent chapter will tell more about the making of marbled paper in Germany, especially with regard to increasing mechanization in the colored paper industry there as well as to an eventual renewal of interest in the old hand methods. Before concluding, one task remains: to review the literature on marbling that appeared in print in Germany during the eighteenth and early nineteenth centuries.

The Growing German Literature on Marbling

While the early marbling trade in Germany carefully restricted knowledge of techniques and processes to its own groups of workers, curiosity and interest in this still somewhat-novel craft resulted in its description in a number of dictionaries, encyclopedias, and reference works published in Germany in the eighteenth and early nineteenth centuries. Brief and, for the most part, explanatory in nature, these accounts were usually insufficient to instruct novices in the proper workings of the art. Nonetheless, a few substantial, more informative, accounts did appear in print, and thus the foundation of a solid marbling literature began to take form.

In the period after 1679, the short (approximately 750 words) but adequate description of marbling that appeared in the several editions of Johann Kunckel von Löwenstein's *Ars Vitraria Experimentalis* (discussed in Chapter 2) could be read by any German who wished to know something about the subject. At the beginning of the eighteenth century, a more important and informative account became available, one which has been overlooked or underappreciated in recent times by those few who might have come across its citation in the literature, for the work in which it appears is extremely difficult to locate today. Thus, it is not easy to judge how influential it may have been in its time.

At the end of Chapter 2, I mentioned a book entitled *Kunst- und Werckschule*, issued by Johann Zieger at Nürnberg in 1696. Emil Kretz's *Dreihundert Jahre Marmorpapier* is the source for this information, as he reports that Zieger's "Kunst und Werckschule, anderer Theil" contains an extensive and detailed section on marbling that provides a richly informative, impressive sketch and diagram of the technique. It was with the utmost difficulty that I was able to locate a copy of the initial part of this work, published reportedly in 1696. It was somewhat easier to find its second half, issued a decade later, which does indeed contain an extensive and impressive section on marbling—in fact, several accounts of the process.[44] These accounts were certainly detailed and informative enough to have enabled any interested and persistent reader to overcome initial difficulties and learn to marble—at least in the manner that accorded with the simple patterns and standards of the day. Indeed, the several descriptions of the making of Turkish paper that are contained in this second part of the *Kunst- und Werck-Schul* (as it is properly titled) constitute collectively the largest and most detailed description of marbling to appear in Western literature before the year 1765, when the extensive and highly informative account of the marbler of paper was published by Diderot and D'Alembert in their famous *Encyclopédie*.

Zieger's *Kunst- und Werck-Schul* is a highly complex and bibliographically frustrating work. Its second part, which can be found in the Houghton Library at Harvard University, has a long and convoluted title:

Der neu-aufgerichteten und Vergrösserten In Sechs Bücher oder Theilen verfassten curieusen Kunst- und Werck-Schul, sehr verlangter nunmehr erfolgter Anderer Theil, darinnen jedes Theils oder Buches Innhalt, auf folgendem Blat zu ersehen: Ein werck so vielen Kunst-begierigen und curieusen Liebhabern sehr dienlich und nutzlich, dergleichen auch noch nie also beysamm heraus kommen, mit überaus grosser Müh und Fleiss, und vielen angewanden Unkosten von vielen Jahren her meistens an grossen und hohen Orten zusammen getragen, und selbsten viel daran experimentirt und experimentiren helffen, nun aber aus Christlicher Liebe und Zuredung grosser Liebhaber treuhertzig und ohne einigen Vorbehalt mitgetheilet und an Tage gesehen von J. K. Chymiae ac àliarum Artium Cultore. Nürnberg, in Verlegung Johann Ziegers anno 1707.

Roughly translated, the above title tells us that this is the newly established and enlarged Curious Arts and Crafts School, which has been written in six books or parts, and that its very much required second part now follows; that it is a work which is useful and necessary for those who are eager and curious admirers of the arts; that it is the sort of book that has never been issued before; that the information it contains has been collected over many years with great toil and diligence and at much expense from a variety of sources, as well as through personal experimentation; and that it is now through Christian love, through the encouragement of a great admirer, and without reservation issued by J. K., a cultivator of chemistry and other arts. Its author, identified by initials alone, is unknown. In his preface he acknowledges that much of his information derives from the earlier works of Fathers Kircher and Schott, and an examination of his text reveals an indebtedness as well to Johann Kunckel,

the well-known court chemist and apothecary who later directed the laboratory of the Brandenburg glassworks. (One is tempted to infer from the initials "J. K." that this could be a partly posthumous work of Johann Kunckel himself; however, no biographical sketch and no catalog or bibliography of early chemical literature associates him with it.) This work is just what its anonymous producer promises, a compilation of data and recipes from many sources and from personal experience.

Both volumes of this work are huge; each numbers about 1,500 pages. The first is devoted to the making of metals—gold, silver, steel, and iron—as well as plaster, glass, and porcelain; the second discusses the decoration of metals and glass, the decoration and lacquering of wood, the preparation of colors, the decoration of paper, and other subjects of chemical, alchemical, and artistic interest. It contains two separate sections devoted to marbling, with several varied discussions of the subject in each. One, entitled "Vom türckischen Papier-Machen" (on the making of Turkish paper), appears on pages 1010–1015, and the other, "Von schönen Papier Arbeiten" (on pretty paper works), on pages 1365–1373.

The first discussion of marbling "Vom türckischen Papier-Machen," encompasses the "usual" description of the craft. The details presented include the utensils to be used; how the size is prepared from gum tragacanth and how its viscosity is tested; how the colors (red lake, indigo blue, vermillion yellow, white lead, etc.) are prepared and how they are dropped and controlled on the size through the addition of fish- or ox-gall; and, finally, how the resultant pattern is removed from the size onto paper. The making of spot (or Turkish) and combed patterns is also discussed, and there is even a brief description of how figures and images—a rose and other flowers—may be placed in the pattern. A second section describes another way of making Turkish paper; much of the same information appears, though more extensive and varied. A third section gives details on sprinkling paper; and a fourth provides yet another method for making beautiful Turkish paper. While these sections are somewhat repetitive, they supplement one another and widen the possibilities for achieving the desired patterns. A final, short discussion in this initial treatment describes the process of staining paper with colored flour, stamping images into the paper with woodblocks and metal plates, and decorating these images with "Augsburg metal"—that is, by sprinkling metallic powder over the paper and imprinting gilded designs into it by means of relief plates.

The second treatment of paper decoration "Von schönen Papier Arbeiten," begins with a word-for-word reprinting of the description of Turkish papermaking that appeared in editions of Johann Kunckel's *Ars Vitraria Experimentalis* from 1679 onward. The sections that follow include: new and original directions for another method of making Turkish paper; a section discussing how to marble paper so that it will resemble jasper stone; and yet another large and mainly repetitive description for making an exceedingly beautiful sort of Turkish paper. Concluding these discussions are a number of recipes for other types of specialty paper: paper with a cloudlike appearance; transparent or clear paper for covering windows and shutters; paper that can be written on with a metal point (that is, without ink); and monochrome or stained papers in several colors. A few paragraphs in these last descriptions are also word-for-word from Kunckel's text. Close examination of this second part of the *Kunst- und Werck-Schul* leaves one with the impression that its author derived the first treatment from his own experiences and from information he had gathered at an early time; then, once he found Kunckel's work, he added a second section to both include Kunckel's explanation and supplement it with his most recent information.

The *Kunst- und Werck-Schul* is an amazing compilation: it provides a large amount of esoteric information in varied, albeit repetitive, ways that was otherwise unavailable at the time. Its excellent descriptions of paper marbling amount to nearly 4,000 words, comprising the largest store of information to be published on this subject in Europe up to that time. When one considers that the work appeared when the art of marbling in Germany was presumably restricted to the Augsburg workshops, it becomes apparent what a truly splendid offering it must have been in its day. To reiterate a point made earlier, however, we have no way of knowing what influence it exerted on the spread of this craft, for the work is extremely rare today and may have been difficult to obtain in its own time. It is also impossible to gain a true bibliographical sense of this extraordinary compilation or to take full measure of its importance. Kayser's *Vollständiges Bücher-Lexicon* refers to a fifth edition of the "Kunst u. Werckschul" published by Bauer and Raspe at Nürnberg in 1785, but I have been unable to locate either this or any earlier editions that may have been issued after the initial 1696–1707 edition.[45]

No other marbling literature of this sort appeared in Germany for the remainder of the eighteenth century, although two further accounts of marbling were included in art compilations published at Nürnberg at about the same time. I found these bound together into a single, thick volume that is now preserved in the Loring collection at Harvard. The first work in this "Sammelband" is entitled *Neu Eröffnete Kunst- und Schatz-Kammer Rarer und Neuer Curiositaeten*, and was issued in 1707.[46] Extending to many hundreds of pages, it provides the equivalent of only a one-page account of "Türckisch Papier zu machen" (pp. 580 and 581). The work bound in after it, bearing the title *Grund-Mässige und Sehr Deutliche Anweisung, zu der Schönen Laccir- und Schildkrotten-Arbeit*, was issued in two parts, the first appearing in 1706 and the second in 1707.[47] In the initial part of its chapter 20 (pages 234 to 240) there is a rather good, detailed account of "Wie Man das Türckische Papier machen soll," though it is far less extensive and informative than the treatment of this sub-

ject in the *Kunst- und Werck-Schul*. Still another relatively long and detailed early account—over 1,000 words—appeared in the comprehensive dictionary, *Grosses Vollständiges Universal Lexicon*, which Johann Friedrich Zedler of Leipzig and Halle published in a total of 68 volumes between 1732 and 1750. The account of "Türckisch Papier" covers almost a complete folio page in double columns, and there are also brief descriptions for making gold paper and edge coloring.[48]

More typical of the information available in this period are the accounts published by Johann Hübner in 1712 (and in 1746, 1766, and 1792); J. T. Jablonski in 1721 (and again in 1748 and 1767); J. C. Adelung's *Kurtze Begriff Menschlicher Fertigkeiten und Kentnisse* of the 1770s; Johann Beckmanns' 1780 *Beyträge zur Oekonomie, Technologie, Polizey- und Generalwissenschaft* (see notes 9 and 22); Johann Friedrich von Pfeiffer's *Die Manufacturen und Fabriken Deutschlands*, published in the same year;[49] and Carl Gottlob Roessig's *Lehrbuch der Technologie* published ten years later.[50] Brief but accurate outlines of the process, they gave more information than dictionary definitions, but again far less than the detailed accounts appearing in the *Kunst- und Werck-Schul*.

In 1741 Christoph Ernst Prediger, a bookbinder of Anspach (now Ansbach), Bavaria, brought out the first volume of his comprehensive four-volume manual, *Accurate Buchbinder und Futteralmacher*, devoting approximately three and a half pages to "Schnitt wie Türkisch Pappier zu machen," or how to decorate the edges of books in the manner of Turkish paper. Not only are Prediger's directions on marbling the first to appear in a bookbinding manual, but they also constitute the first printed attempt to instruct bookbinders in this manner of decorating book edges. (Prediger's manual is also remarkable as the first exhaustive and technical work on bookbinding and slipcase making to appear anywhere in the world.) Taking into consideration their appearance at a time when it was taboo for bookbinders and other craftsmen and artisans to reveal the secrets of their trades, Prediger's instructions on edge marbling are extremely thorough, and he even mentions how to add gold and silver veins to Turkish patterns by mixing gold and silver powder with gum arabic or with the colors carmine or ultramarine.[51]

For some time now it has been known (through an entry in C. G. Kayser's *Vollständiges Bucher-Lexicon*) that there may have been a work issued at Leipzig in 1808 that could qualify as the first handbook devoted solely to the making of colored and decorated papers (and to the marbling of paper as well). I use the phrases "may have been issued" and "could qualify" because this work has hitherto been only fabled in marbling literature and no copy has been located.[52] Kayser reports its title as *Vollständige Anweisung Bunte Papier als Tuerkisch, Kattunpapiere und Andere zu Machen*, and indicates that its author or publisher was one W. A. Schuder. On a recent visit to Leipzig, however, I observed in the excellent collection of books on marbling and paper decoration in the Deutsche Bücherei a pamphlet which may well qualify as the long-lost (or long unrecognized) Schuder work.

This pamphlet has no author's name on its title page, nor is it dated (thus explaining why it has gone unrecognized for so long). Its title identifies it as *Der Vollkommene Papierfärber, oder Anweisung, mit Wenigen Kosten Alle Sorten Gefärbtes, Gedrucktes, Maroquin-, Gold-, Silber-, und Tapetenpapier zu Verfertigen. Aus Eigner Erfahrung und Nach den Besten Quellen Bearbeitet* (translated, *The Accomplished Paper Colorer, or Directions for the Making at Little Cost of all Sorts of Colored, Printed, Morocco, Gold, Silver and Wall Papers. Adapted from Personal Experience and from the Best Sources*. According to its imprint, it was published at Leipzig by the Literalisches Central-Comptoir. The pamphlet extends to sixty pages, the last describing an accompanying plate—"Erklärung des Kupfers, Fig. 1–4"—which, unfortunately, is lacking from the seemingly unique copy in the Deutsche Bücherei.

Anyone familiar with eighteenth- and early nineteenth-century printing and paper would recognize this as a production of the period; and it certainly dates many, many decades before the 1875 date assigned to it in the catalog of the Deutsche Bücherei. The paper on which it is printed is the standard "laid" kind that was in use in Europe from early times but which began to give way to the "wove" type late in the eighteenth century, and was supplanted by it by the early decades of the following century. As its title indicates, the pamphlet was printed in the old-style German of the eighteenth century and earlier, with the superscript "e" used in place of the umlaut to indicate vowel assimilation or modification. In fact, to any eye familiar with German printings of the eighteenth and early nineteenth centuries, this work shows every indication of having been issued at the time that the Schuder title supposedly was published. It also does what the title of the Schuder work promises to do, namely, it describes the making of all sorts of decorated papers in use in Germany at this time, not the marbled type exclusively. It appears to be the first of a series of German manuals on the making of colored and fancy papers, including those of C. F. G. Thon and Johann Roehberg to be discussed later.

The officials of the Deutsche Bücherei have kindly allowed me to obtain a photocopy of this rare and important piece, which I plan one day to publish in translation. This work describes all the types of Buntpapier made in Germany early in the nineteenth century, including printed and calico paper, marbled paper, sprinkled paper, maroquin or morocco paper, damask, and wallpaper. The notation in the pamphlet that maroquin paper (to be discussed in some detail at a later time), is a new discovery or invention, is another clue pointing to the early publication of this manual, for that type of paper developed no later than the 1830s and, more likely, some twenty years before. Pages 12 to 33 of the work provide descriptions of the colors used in these processes, together with details for their preparation; the section dealing with marbled paper extends from pages 36 to 44 and follows the well-established format, with good information and clear directions.

In 1806 J. G. Krünitz had published in his *Encyklopädie* another brief account of the marbling process,[53] and in a subsequent volume, issued in 1818, he provided additional information in a general article on coloring and decorating paper which mentioned that Turkish paper was being made in large quantities.[54] In 1807 another discussion of marbling intended to assist bookbinders was provided by J. J. H. Bücking of Wolfenbüttel. His *Die Kunst des Buchbinders* contained brief and modest directions for marbling book edges and paper.[55] Additional and more substantial accounts of this process appeared in manuals that were produced by German bookbinders Christian F. G. Thon and Ernst Wilhelm Greve in 1820 and 1822, respectively. Thon devoted nearly nine pages to techniques for marbling book edges and paper in his *Die Kunst Bücher zu Binden*.[56] Greve's *Hand- und Lehrbuch der Buchbinde- und Futteralmacht-Kunde*, issued in two volumes,[57] also gives a good account of how to marble paper as well as make other sorts of decorated paper then in use, such as Herrnhut, calico, and brocade paper. His section on the making of Turkish paper is the largest of these accounts.

When considering this flow of literature, we cannot discern a growth pattern or orderly trend in one direction or another. The subject of marbling, noted initially in scientific and technical works later in the seventeenth century, seems then to have passed early in the next century into books dealing mostly with artistic processes, of which the *Kunst- und Werck-Schul* is an extraordinary and exceptional example. Information about this process next appeared in a number of dictionaries and general reference works; later in the eighteenth century marbling appeared in economic treatises that intended, in true German fashion, to put every subject into its proper order.

Beginning with the publication of Christoph Ernst Prediger's manual of 1741, we notice the incorporation of marbling information in an incipient bookbinding literature. Prediger's bold and groundbreaking effort was not soon matched, for it would not be until the early 1800s that other German bookbinding manuals would include details on marbling, particularly edge marbling, a subject of growing interest to binders.[58] Finally, in the first quarter of the nineteenth century, we encounter in Germany the establishment of a separate and distinct literature devoted to Buntpapier—one that would increase with time. Eventually, works devoted to marbling alone would also appear; however, this occurred at a later time and will be discussed in a subsequent chapter. The following chapters provide a background to that development by reviewing the establishment of marbling trades in other regions of Europe, beginning with France.

4

Marbling in France

ITTLE is known about marbling or a marbling industry and trade in France during the seventeenth,
eighteenth, and nineteenth centuries. Although the scant
information and documentation available initially suggest a pattern somewhat similar to that observed in Germany, careful consideration of the bits and pieces leads
to an entirely different conclusion. The approximate nature of early French marbling can be determined largely
through an analysis of marbled endpapers, cover papers,
and edges on extant French bookbindings of the time.
Additional knowledge can be gained from the scattered
and fragmented facts that have survived and the descriptions of various aspects of color papermaking printed in
the ever useful Diderot-D'Alembert *Encyclopédie* of the
late eighteenth century. Under such scrutiny, the traditional view of the trade that has come down over the
years—that the craft originated in the shops of bookbinders about the third decade of the seventeenth century
and gradually came to be absorbed into the workshops of
professional paper stainers and colorists classed generally
as *dominotiers*—simply does not hold up. As we soon
shall see from a review of all the evidence, the matter progressed in quite a different direction.

The confusion has arisen in part from the fact that the
Diderot work and other pertinent literature have classed
the *marbreur,* or marbler, as one of the dominotiers. In
fact, the marbler was a dominotier in name only, and
considered so only because he colored paper, as they did.
Our examination of all of these sources will show that the
French marbler was independent of the larger paper-
coloring trade, maintaining a separate identity and an individual workshop character.

The few works that have referred to French marbling
in the past fall mainly within the category of general
histories of wallpaper. As a result, later works on the coloring of paper, and, specifically, marbling and the relationship of marbled paper to bookbinding and book
decoration—for example, Rosamond Loring's *Decorated
Book Papers* and, more recently, Marie-Ange Doizy and
Stéphane Ipert's *Le Papier marbré*—have largely depended
on this general wallpaper literature for their information.
No one, it seems, has worked out the actual relationship
of the marbreur with regard to the general categorization
"dominotier" or defined the marbler's specific role in the
overall production of French colored paper in the seventeenth, eighteenth, and nineteenth centuries. Thus, our
first task in reviewing the development of French marbling will be to untangle the knotted threads of the existing literature on the French marbreur and dominotier
and trace each strand back to its original skein.

The Dominotier and the Marbreur

The roles of the dominotier and of the subspecialists such
as the *tapissier en papier, dominotier-imagier, marbreur,* and
others in the production of colored paper in France at
this early time can best be determined by considering
their descriptions in the Diderot-D'Alembert encyclopedia. As I have noted elsewhere,[1] Denis Diderot (1713–
1784), man of letters and philosopher-friend of Jean-
Jacques Rousseau, commenced work on his famous *Encyclopédie* in 1745, with Jean Le Rond d'Alembert acting as
co-editor. A product of the French Enlightenment, this
ambitious enterprise enlisted many important writers
and specialists of its day to produce the most remarkable
compendium of information existing up to that time. The
articles on colored papermaking were contributed by experienced artisans, for example, the one on pattern paper
and on wallpaper by Jean-Baptiste-Michel Papillon, already an acknowledged master in the manufacture of these
wares and soon-to-be author of an important work on
wood engraving.[2] The views expressed in the *Encyclopédie*
provide a good overview of the fancy papermaking industry in France and also insight into its development.

The French dominotiers, like their German counterparts, had their origins in the groups of professional
woodblock cutters who were responsible at an earlier
time for making prints (most holy pictures), playing
cards, broadside proclamations, advertisements, and kin-
dred objects. Later, when the advent of the printing press
forced their profession to reorganize, they executed book
illustrations as well. The dominotiers also had some relationship with the craftsmen in the *"Indiennage"* business:
the *tapissiers* or tapestry makers who, like those involved
in the German textile industry, eventually turned the
woodblock (and later metal-block) techniques they used

to imprint cloth and calico to the production of similar designs on paper. In this latter capacity they came to be known more specifically as *tapissiers en papier* or *dominotiers-imagiers*. Classed within the generic group of dominotiers, according to Diderot, were also the marbreurs with whom we are specifically concerned.

The making of fancy papers or *dominos,* as they initially were called, was already underway in France in a primitive way late in the sixteenth century. A diaper pattern of this period, illustrated in black and white but described as being in its original form black on yellow paper, is reproduced on page 64 of Albert Haemmerle's *Buntpapier.*[3] And Haemmerle shows later ·productions of the French dominotiers, including more developed and even floriated designs of the polychrome pattern paper or calico paper variety that date to the late eighteenth century. Both Nancy McClelland, in her *Historic Wall-papers, from Their Inception to the Introduction of Machinery,*[4] and Rosamond Loring[5] mention a Guild of Dominotiers, Tapissiers, et Imagiers formed at Paris in 1586. They also allude to the legislation and restrictions imposed on these craftsmen in that year and again in 1618 and 1649 mainly through the Guild of Printers, whose jealousy had been aroused because of infringements on their privilege. As a result, the printers were empowered to visit the workshops of the dominotiers and confiscate any work that trespassed on their domain; also, the dominotiers were not permitted to use presses of any kind employed in the letterpress printing, that is, in printing metal type. Both McClelland and Loring confuse the role of the marbler in all of this, disregarding the fact that the marbreur actually entered the picture somewhat later; for, as in Germany, the dominotier was active well before the marbreur was even on the scene.[6]

The priority of the dominotiers is demonstrated not only by the early papers they left behind but also by the actual meaning of "dominotier," the etymology of which suggests that they were artisans who printed by methods that antedated European marbling. The Diderot-D'Alembert encyclopedia defines a *domino* as a paper on which the tracings, designs, or figures were first printed with a clumsily made wooden block; colors were then applied by means of one or more *patrons,* or stencils, as was the practice in the manufacture of playing cards. The same source further states that (in the 1760 period) such papers were made particularly at Rouen and in other provincial towns, and were used by the peasants who purchased them to decorate the upper parts of their fireplaces. Furthermore, the encyclopedia notes that they were inartistic, badly drawn, and still more poorly decorated in harsh colors.

Mrs. Loring speculates that the dominotiers derived their name from the Italian word "domino," meaning little cloak or hood, and therefore refers to part of the costume worn by men who did marbling. Her theory, however, appears to me to be farfetched. A check through innumerable French dictionaries, both of the eighteenth century and today, shows that a domino was a headdress or piece of drapery covering the head that was worn by women in earlier times, sometimes as part of a religious costume.[7] A more plausible explanation might well be that the word "domino" referred in earlier times to a paper prepared from a master form (a *dominus*) or a stencil or a "patron." *Webster's New International Dictionary of the English Language* defines "patron" as an earlier though now obsolete form of the word "pattern," and the French word "patron" has a similar meaning. The Germans employed the word "Patron" in exactly the same way. Thus, the French "domino" (or "dominus," to use the original Latin word) and the German "Patron" were synonymous, as is implied in the Diderot-D'Alembert definition. Both words mean "master" in every sense, including "master pattern." Note, for example, the German "Patronist" (i.e., the maker of fancy colored papers by means of a "Patron") who is pictured on page 80 of Haemmerle's *Buntpapier,* reproduced there (and as Figure 3 here) from a copperplate engraving executed about 1690 by Christoph Weigel of Nürnberg.

FIGURE 3. The Patronist. Copperplate engraving by Christoph Weigel, Nürnberg, ca. 1690. (Bayerische Staatsbibliothek, Munich.)

The French marbler did not spring from the same soil as the dominotier, but entered the field through bookbinding, a separate trade. As a result, the factories that made all sorts of colored paper in Germany, including Turkish or marbled paper, did not have counterparts in France. And while the *marbreur* came to be classed among the dominotiers, he actually worked apart from them, with the products of his labor destined for a different clientele. This is evidenced by the Diderot-D'Alembert encyclopedia, which describes the two occupations in separate articles written by separate authorities or based on separate sources. The dominotiers worked in their shops decorating paper by using wooden blocks, metal plates or stencils (or from blocks and stencils in combination), producing papers for home and industrial use, and eventually specializing in the manufacture of wallpapers. (Dominotiers are shown making wallpaper in plates accompanying the dominotier article in the Diderot-D'Alembert *Encyclopédie*.) The French marbler, on the other hand, remained aloof from this activity, producing papers (predominantly marbled, but sometimes paste papers as well) for the use of the hand bookbinder, at least until the Industrial Revolution diminished both roles.

It must be emphasized that the French marbler, though classed among the dominotiers, never employed a dominus, *patron,* or stencil in his work; this is also true of European marblers in general. A rare exception occurred in the earliest period of marbling in the West, the years after 1600, when German artists or colorists employed marbling in combination with stencils for pictorial purposes, such as those illustrated on Plate VII. Indeed, one might conjecture that the German Patronists, who used stencils in their everyday work, turned to marbling initially at the turn of the seventeenth century in order to use it as a novel background for their stencil work, having seen examples of stenciled and silhouette designs on the Persian and Turkish papers that had found their way to Germany. Marbling with stencils is not at all difficult, and only a certain amount of experience in the proper cutting, mounting, and laying of the sheet is necessary in order to turn out fairly advanced work; the German Patronists certainly did have that know-how.

Transfer of the Art to France

Entries in the diary of Pierre de L'Estoile in 1608 and afterward indicate that a sheet of marbled paper was a prized possession in the early seventeenth century. As Charles Adams has commented, at the beginning of the seventeenth century these papers were viewed as curiosities in Europe.[8] And yet, L'Estoile's diary also shows that marbled paper was readily available to him and other Parisians who collected and prized it. My own observations over many years of French imprints from the first half of the seventeenth century indicated to me that by about 1630, or perhaps a little earlier, French bookbinders

had begun to add marbled endpapers of French manufacture to many of their finest gilt bindings, with the small combed design being especially favored. There was no evidence, however, showing how the makers of such paper had acquired their knowledge or attained the ability to marble well, for most of these combed papers showed excellent technique and proficiency.

When I visited the Bibliothèque Nationale in 1982 to examine volumes that contained marbled endpapers from the collections of the French kings, there seemed to be little interest in the subject of marbling among modern researchers, but this soon changed. After taking charge of the Library's Département des Imprimés Réserve a few years later, M. J. Toulet, himself an expert on French bookbinding, put a young researcher on his staff, Mme. Geneviève Guilleminot-Chrétien, to work on the problem of early French marbling. Mme. Guilleminot-Chrétien examined many early manuscript and printed volumes with the goal of determining just how early and in what manner marbled decoration began to appear in French bookbindings. Her researches resulted in a pair of exhibitions held in 1987 and in an important color-illustrated catalog that enlarges our perspective of this matter.[9] Thanks to this effort, which supplements earlier evidence, we can now make some reasonable and fairly safe judgments about the beginning and early development of marbling in France. This evidence indicates that the French were becoming interested in marbled paper and were beginning to marble at about the same time as the Germans.

Mme. Guilleminot-Chrétien points out near the beginning of her catalog that the Album Amicorum, so favored in German lands, was not much in use among the French (although one splendid French example, dating to the year 1686, is described and partly illustrated in Doizy and Ipert's *Le Papier marbré.*)[10] The earliest known use of marbled paper for book decoration in France, she states, occurred in a manuscript collection of twenty-three sonnets, "Les Oeuvres Poetiques" of Henri d'Angoulême, dating to about the same year. Cased in a Turkish binding, the book contains 106 sheets of Turkish marbled paper. Angoulême, the natural son of King Henry II, served as admiral in the Levant and later as governor of Provence, where he maintained a brilliant court at Aix.

A number of paragraphs in Mme. Guilleminot-Chrétien's catalog are devoted to the well-known diary of Pierre de L'Estoile, a well-connected chancellery official and collector of curious objects, who maintained it until his death in 1611. L'Estoile, she points out, when not handling revenues and conducting other business, devoted every spare moment to his personal passion, the collection of information and "curiosities" kept in his cabinet for display and to attract eminent visitors. (By the early sixteenth century, cabinets were popularly used in France; originally a small room for displaying precious objects, some cabinets later came to be exquisitely carved, sumptuous pieces of furniture with a network of small drawers that were enclosed by a pair of doors. Within these, china, coins, shells, and many other objects then curious and rare were preserved and treasured.) During the last years of his life, L'Estoile became friendly with a young man named Pierre Dupuy, to whom he first loaned then later gave many of the treasures he maintained in his cabinet, among them sheets of marbled paper and books covered with it.

Mme. Guilleminot-Chrétien's catalog quotes several passages from L'Estoile's diary in which marbled paper is the subject. On 15 December 1608, L'Estoile recorded that he had given his friend Dupuy a small book of Chinese paper covered with beautiful marbled paper, which he had preserved in his cabinet for a very long time. And on May 13 of the following year, he noted that he had given Dupuy six sheets of marbled paper, a curious item of which he always maintained a reserve in his cabinet. On 14 July 1609, L'Estoile's diary tells us, Monsieur Guittart, valet in the king's chamber and his neighbor and good friend, had just sent L'Estoile a book from his own cabinet, owed him due to Guittart's loss in a wager the two had made. The book had been exquisitely bound in Turkey and contained all sorts of beautiful papers. (Whether these were marbled papers or silhouette papers or both remains unknown; we do know, however, that L'Estoile gave Guittart's volume to Dupuy on 16 April 1610.)

As Mme. Guilleminot-Chrétien relates, Guittart, with whom L'Estoile had been in contact since 1598, had traveled to Turkey and throughout the Mediterranean basin; he was sent in 1596 by Henry IV to establish contact with François Savary de Brèves, the French ambassador to Constantinople. Guittart had charge of the diplomatic courier as well as subsidies and clocks, the latter making up traditional gifts to the grand Turkish court. His own cabinet contained an infinite number of beautiful and rare objects brought from the Levant and was well known enough to attract a visit from Queen Marie de Medici herself in 1601. L'Estoile, Mme. Guilleminot-Chrétien observes, had available a large amount of marbled paper; and, although he viewed it as a great curiosity and prize, he did not place a high monetary value on it.

Much space in the recent French exhibition catalog is devoted to a superb album of watercolors of Turkish scenes put together at Paris in about 1607 as a present for the dauphin, the future King Louis XIII. These forty-eight scenes of different Eastern motifs had been painted by the geographer Nicolas de Nicolay during a visit to Turkey in the years 1551–1552. More than fifty years later, they were mounted on Turkish marbled paper and bound in red morocco leather, with the dauphin's crown as a centerpiece, and with marbled endpapers. Mme. Guilleminot-Chrétien suggests that Savary de Brèves may have been behind the making of this album. Savary de Brèves had served as Turkish ambassador to Constantinople from 1591 until 1605, and not only spoke Turkish and Arabic but also was intimately acquainted with Ot-

toman culture and civilization. He could have brought these scenes back or acquired them when he returned to France in 1605 and had them mounted into this album for his future king before taking up his ambassadorship to Rome in 1607. Savary de Brèves was close to the royal family and to Jacques-Auguste de Thou, grand master of the king's library and an enthusiastic book collector. The album, Guilleminot-Chrétien speculates, might well have been a present to the dauphin during a visit of the ambassador and his entourage to Fontainebleau on June 27, 1607.

Guilleminot-Chrétien suggests that the first use of marbled paper in French bookbindings dates to the same era. She identifies as the earliest known example a volume of the *Epistolae Familiares* of Cicero in the Bibliothèque Nationale's collection that was bound for Henry IV and contains his crown and fleur-de-lis as well as marbled paste-down endpapers. Eighteen more such examples in the library's holdings are cited in her catalog, with a number of them illustrated here on Plates XIV and XV. Dating to the 1610–1630 period, these were either presented or dedicated to the king or the grand lords. Guilleminot-Chrétien also poses an important possibility: although marbled papers contained in these works closely resemble papers executed at Constantinople at the beginning of the seventeenth century, some of them appear to be different, and may have been marbled in France instead. Indeed, the abundance of marbled paper in France at this time is proved by its use in the early albums, by L'Estoile's many references to it, and by its frequent use by French bookbinders; while much or perhaps most of this probably was of Turkish manufacture, some appears to be of French making, she believes.

Because of their crudeness, Guilleminot-Chrétien contends that one can see in the initial six examples illustrated in her catalog (and on Plate XIV here) the first attempts at marbling in France. Turkish marbled papers in circulation there could have served as models or inspiration for the French artisans; and, she questions, could not individuals who had traveled in Turkey and the East have given oral observations to those who first tried to marble paper in France? One binding in particular, on a copy of *Les Oeuvres de Feu M. Claude Fauchet*, printed at Paris in 1610 and bound for Henry II de Bourbon-Conde, has a rather intriguing feature about it, one that is unique among these early French marbled bindings. It not only contains marbled flyleaves before the title page and bound in after white ones (with a similar arrangement at the end of the text), but the watermark in these marbled sheets is that of Nicolas Le Bé, a papermaker of Troyes, a city not far southeast of Paris. If paper used at Constantinople was readily imported from Italy, Guilleminot-Chrétien asks, would not direct transport of papers from Troyes to Paris be a plausible indication that the decorated papers in this volume had been marbled in France?

The catalog also discusses and illustrates early French

combed marbles, which date to the period from 1625 to the 1640s. Guilleminot-Chrétien gives particular attention to the first illustration: it shows French combing in its earliest form, she theorizes, because of the clumsiness of its execution and its harsh tones, and because it appears on an imprint of 1625. The small-combed designs she illustrates are just the kinds of marbled papers that I have observed over the years in bindings (particularly of small format) on French imprints of 1625–1650 (and sometimes later), which I had previously considered among the earliest examples known of French marbled paper. While some aspects of Mme. Guilleminot-Chrétien's argument are, by her own admission, speculative, it seems that her evidence not only has much substance but also constitutes an important leap forward—over terrain previously uncharted. Almost all of the combed patterns she illustrates (four of which appear here on Plate XV) display a high level of technique, in spite of the fact that small combing is difficult to execute evenly and well. Surely, early French marblers did not have this proficiency at the start but, as is customary for this troublesome craft, attained it only after a lengthy period of work and much experience. We must let the matter rest at this point and reserve further opinion until more evidence is produced to build on this; nevertheless, I believe that we now have a solid foundation.

The Early French Trade

The first name traditionally associated with marbling in France is that of Macé Ruette, royal binder from 1635 to 1644 (but active much earlier). The source for this attribution is Jean La Caille, who made the association in 1689, nearly half a century after Ruette's period of activity.[11] La Caille also claimed that Ruette was the inventor of marbling, which, with regard to France alone, might have some validity, for the first half of the seventeenth century—the cradle period of French marbling—was also Ruette's era. Others often associated with early French marbling, either as makers, or as users of marbled paper in their bindings, or as both, include Le Gascon, Pasdeloup (or Padeloup), Derome, and Le Breton, whose names have cropped up in bookbinding and marbling literature for a century or more.[12]

The binder who is known as "Le Gascon" is otherwise unidentified, but was one of the leading craftsmen of his age. A gilder and finisher of the highest order, he is credited with the introduction of the "fanfare" binding—a highly ornamented binding on which the gilt decoration spreads out on the book cover in a series of repeated fanfare patterns effected by pointillé tooling, all bordered and interconnected by strapped configurations that were effected mainly by curved gouges.[13] Le Gascon was active from the 1620s to the 1640s, and many specimens of his work have been preserved that do indeed contain marbled decoration.

While the family of binders named Pasdeloup (or Padeloup) was active from the 1620s as well, its members' association with marbling and the making of marbled papers probably dates from the latter half of the seventeenth century, at the earliest. Mrs. Easton refers to the marbled papers of Antoine-Michel Pasdeloup, who was known as "le jeune," and identifies him as court binder from 1653 to 1669, but she is obviously confused on this matter.[14] Roger Devauchelle devotes a section of his book to this important bookbinder whose line extended to five generations of binders, some of them outstanding craftsmen of the eighteenth century, and also provides a genealogical table of their lineage and biographical resumes for some of the family members.[15] According to Devauchelle and other sources on French bookbinding, Antoine-Michel Pasdeloup, one of the greatest craftsmen of his age, was born in 1685 and died in 1758.

The family of Derome also turns up frequently in literature that refers to marbling. This name too was of significance to French bookbinding, and again Devauchelle devotes a chapter and a genealogical table to the family.[16] The table shows a succession of binders from the 1660s until the late eighteenth century. Mrs. Easton mentions that Derome (otherwise unidentified, but assumedly Claude) was court binder from 1673 to 1677 and used the snail pattern to great effect, but does not document her source. During my visit to the Bibliothèque Nationale half a dozen years ago, I had the opportunity to examine bookbindings in the library of Louis XVI (who appears to have lost his head over fine bindings and marbled paper as well as matters of state). The marbled decoration in most of these, consisting of a common Turkish-style pattern with green as the predominating or "ground" color, was attributed by M. Toulet to a member of the last generation of the Derome family, specifically Nicolas-Denis Derome, called Derome "le jeune" (1731–ca. 1788), who attained the rank of master in 1761.[17]

Two others often associated with early French marbling are the Le Bretons, *père et fils*. The Diderot-D'Alembert *Encyclopédie* relates that both father and son worked at the end of the seventeenth and well into the eighteenth centuries (but mainly in the latter), producing in this genre little masterpieces; further, they had a secret process for intermingling in their papers small filaments of gold and silver within waves of colored veins.[18] This work points out, however, that the gilt decoration was not part of the actual marbling, but was applied after marbling and after the paper had dried, by gilding or silvering with stencils. As Mrs. Loring indicates, "Papillon tells us that the Le Bretons had so perfected their art that they imitated real stone more exactly with their marbled papers than an artist with his brush. Some other lovely papers that they made were stenciled with figures of flowers on a highly calendered surface."[19]

Roger Devauchelle mentions a few bookbinders named Breton who worked at the end of the sixteenth century and at the beginnings of the seventeenth, but makes no reference to later binders of that name. He does, however, cite the Le Bretons, *père et fils,* as marblers who were active from the end of the seventeenth century.[20] There can be little doubt that these two craftsmen were marbling specialists rather than bookbinders; they are the first Frenchmen identified as professional marblers, although it is probable that other unnamed and unidentified individuals may have preceded them.

Evidence shows that some of the families that produced several generations of bookbinders also became associated with marbling, with some members in time devoting themselves exclusively to this activity. In this way, undoubtedly, specialized marbling workshops arose in France, where workmen produced marbled papers (and later, paste papers) mainly for the book trade. Although some of their products filtered down through stationers' shops to be used for industrial and household purposes (as papers for drug powders, for wrapping toys and other consumer goods, and for general decoration in the home), these marbling specialists existed mainly to service bookbinders, from whose ranks they had sprung and with whom they remained interrelated.

The fact that Martin Engelbrecht of Augsburg used both German and French terminology in his 1720–1750 prints depicting contemporary makers of colored paper indicates that marbling was then taking place in both countries. These prints, however, refer only to German marbling, for the nature of the activity that went on in France, as we have seen, was somewhat different. In France, a number of the larger workshops were undoubtedly located in Paris and the larger cities, with smaller establishments located throughout the countryside wherever bookbinding took place in any appreciable form, for marblers depended on bookbinders for their existence.

Several arguments can be made to reinforce the conclusion that the French marbling industry was made up of specialized workshops quite separate from the ateliers of the dominotiers. First, nowhere in the earlier literature is there any mention of the existence of French counterparts to the factories that were typical of the German trade. Nor do we have the pattern cards or advertising literature (as in the case of the German maker Georg Christoph Stoy) of French makers to suggest a large, multifaceted production and a wide distribution. Finally, with regard to French marbling, there is the additional evidence of edge marbling. Add to this evidence the fact that the French tradition has historically emphasized the independent worker who produces on his own and is little attracted to the efficient, large-scale production that typifies his German counterpart. As a result, one can scarcely expect to encounter an exact copy of the German experience transplanted to the soil of France.

Marbled papers preserved in large numbers of early French bookbindings indicate that the golden age of marbling in France—typified by high production levels and beautifully executed patterns—extended roughly from about 1670 or 1680 to about 1730 or 1740. (Another

noteworthy era—not gold this time, but silver—would occur toward the end of the eighteenth century, perhaps fueled by the new spirit of the French Revolution and extending into the first decade or two of the following century.) Some of the freshest and most beautiful papers ever made came from French marblers during this golden era, in a range of patterns surpassing anything done elsewhere, then and for many decades afterward. By the second half of the eighteenth century, however, these excellent techniques and patterns had mostly faded. One particularly notices this decline when one looks at long runs of French periodicals in libraries, where marbled papers often are found in successive volumes of sets that encompass, sometimes, a period of fifty or more years. The freshness and vividness of color and the overall technical superiority that mark the marbled papers in the volumes from the early 1700s are not seen in the later ones, where the colors often are pale or muddy and the patterns less finely executed by comparison. Nor is the same pattern always continued throughout the period, indicating that some of the earlier designs were no longer being made, probably because ancient methods and standards were forgotten as older workpeople passed from the scene. Even in cases where early patterns are continued, the quality has not been sustained. It would be wrong to say that good marbled papers were never made after the 1740s or 1750s—they were; but the fine product is seen less frequently, and the great variety of patterns typical of the pre-1740 trade is no longer present. Usually one encounters in French decorated bindings of the later eighteenth century only two patterns: the simple "spot" or Turkish design, and the type referred to as "curl," "snail," or, to use the French term, "commun." Encountering any other patterns would be highly unusual.

Edge Marbling

Early in the seventeenth century, not long after they had learned to marble well, French binders began to marble the edges of their finest bookbinding productions as a way of complementing and enhancing the marbled endpapers. This novel technique consisted of dipping the smooth book edges, usually clamped between wooden boards so that they overlapped slightly, onto the colors on the bath, one edge after the other. Sometimes the binders went one step further, gilding over the marbled decoration so that it emerged magically when the foreedge was fanned. This practice was employed only for the finest bookbinding productions, those commissioned by royalty and nobility, and it was expensive. As time passed, however, edge marbling became more affordable; two centuries later, by the early decades of the nineteenth century, it became quite common, at least in France, and in England, America, and many other countries.

In *The French Bookbinders of the Eighteenth Century,*[21] Octave Uzanne refers to the practice of edge marbling in the early 1700s in his discussion of the price of decorated bindings prepared for the king's library. He quotes a memorandum, dated 16 July 1723, from the binder Boyet (i.e., Boyer), signed by Anisson-Duperron and de Cotte, the latter the architect of the Bibliothèque Royale, as follows:

1.   Bound for the King in Levant morocco, violet outside, the inside red, with deep borders of gold outside and in . . . 90 livres

1.   Idem for Monseigneur the Duc d'Orleans, bound the same, for which he furnished me the skin of violet morocco   1 l.

321.   In red Levant morocco, gilt with three border filets and a border, arms and monogram of the King at 35 livres per volume, price fixed with the late M. Rigaut and M. Anisson, now Director of the Imprimerie Royale . . . . 11340 l.

     Bound in calf, gilt and marbled on the edges, and with the outside like those in morocco, at 15 l. . . . . 2115 l.

Edge marbling is little associated with German bookbinding, at least before the nineteenth century. The Germans, remember, were producing masses of marbled and other types of decorated paper in workshops and factories and had little time or concern for the individual needs of bookbinders who used their papers in locations far removed from their source. French marblers, on the other hand, carried on their trade in local workshops to which bookbinders had access when they wished to have marbled decoration added to the edges of books they were binding. When one encounters edge decoration on early German imprints, even those dating to the early nineteenth century, it usually is the non-marbled variety, achieved primarily by sprinkling color through a sieve or with paste colors. Infrequently, one encounters exceptions that indicate that now and then a German bookbinder may have tried his hand at edge marbling (possibly following Prediger's instructions); or, alternately, that depots were established here and there where binders could leave their productions before covering and have them forwarded to a nearby workshop or factory to have their edges marbled according to instructions. This was a practice, I have noted elsewhere, that took place in early nineteenth-century America.[22]

The simple paste color design that was added to the edges of the medical book shown as the final illustration on Plate XI is an example of one of the alternatives to edge marbling used in Germany (and in Holland and other countries). This book was published at Nürnberg in 1750 and bound at about the same time. While it contains professionally marbled endpapers of the "Dutch" variety, its binder could not turn to a marbling shop for edge decoration and had to decorate his edges himself as best he could. In this case, his best means was to resort to the paste-color

technique, covering his edges with a blue paste and then imposing a design on them. Paste-paper methods, or *Kleistermarmor,* as previously noted, were known to and employed by many German binders, though only infrequently for edge decoration. Similar practices were carried on in Holland and in other Germanic and Nordic regions at this time (Plate XVI).

As we have been observing and will further observe in succeeding chapters, a bona fide marbling literature finally developed because edge marbling had become extremely popular early in the nineteenth century; and bookbinders and marblers sympathetic to the needs of the bookbinding community began to issue small marbling manuals out of a desire to help their brethren apply marbled decoration to their productions themselves. These manuals gave rise to an extensive nineteenth-century German literature on marbling and to a fairly extensive French and English literature of the same type, which began early in the nineteenth century and continued into the beginning of the next.

A final observation about edge marbling is in order, because it is an important one. Edge marbling presents us with a "control" condition for proving whether or not marbling activity took place in a given region at a given time. Even though marbled papers were frequently used by bookbinders hundreds of miles away from their points of origin (for example, German and French papers often were employed as endpapers by Danish, Swedish, Italian and English binders in the eighteenth century) the presence of marbled decoration on the edges of Danish, Swedish, Italian and English bindings, as we soon shall see, gives positive proof of marbling activity in these regions, for it would be absurd to think that foreign bookbinders shipped their still-unbound volumes to Germany and France to have marbled decoration applied to their edges before their covers were laced in. And we have irrefutable proof of local manufacture when the endpapers and edges are marbled in the same design: such decoration had to be placed there locally.

French Literature on Marbling in the Late Seventeenth and Early Eighteenth Centuries

The paucity of French literature on paper marbling in the seventeenth century has always been something of a puzzle, despite the fact that the method was practiced in secret by professional workpeople who guarded their knowledge jealously. We also cannot explain why marbling did not arouse the scientific curiosity in France that it had elsewhere. Brief and general descriptions of the technique did appear in French dictionaries from the late seventeenth century on, but at best these provided only terse definitions and descriptions. With but one exception, as far as I have been able to determine, an account published by Jacques Gautier d'Agoty in 1752, no printed marbling literature of any substance appeared in France before 1758, when the *Journal Oeconomique* published a reasonably complete and useful description of the marbling process; this was followed several years later by a more detailed account in the Diderot-D'Alembert *Encyclopédie*.

One description of the marbling technique in the printed literature of France in the late seventeenth century was, though brief, reprinted often, both in French and in translation, and became a standard description throughout the eighteenth century. This work first appeared at Paris in 1674 under the title *Recueil de Curiositez rares et nouvelles de plus admirables effets de la nature,* with the name of its author given as Sieur d'Emery.[23] On pages 348–350, at the end of its chapter XVI, a short description of slightly less than 150 words was printed, entitled "Pour marbrer & jasper le papier." Later editions were issued at Lyon in 1684 and at Paris in 1686 with this same title. Others, retitled *Nouveau recueil de secrets et curiositez les plus rares & admirables de tous le effets que l'Art & la nature sont capables de producir,* came out at Paris in 1685 and 1737; at Lyon in 1688; at Amsterdam in 1697 and again in the early 1700s.[24]

As previously noted, this book was translated into English and issued as *Modern Curiosities of Art and Nature* in 1685; its extended title further detailed that the volume's contents had been extracted from the cabinets of the most eminent personnages of the French court, together with the choicest secrets in mechanics, communicated by the most approved artists of France, and had been composed by the Sieur Lemery, apothecary to the French King. In 1711 there appeared two English editions, one with the title *New Curiosities of Art & Nature,* and the other entitled *Curiosa Arcana: Being Curious Secrets, Artificial and Natural.*[25] The marbling recipe in the *Recueil de curiositez rares et nouvelles* was the basis for instructions provided in many eighteenth-century editions of a popular French book of secrets published under the title *Secrets concernent les arts et métiers;* it also appeared in translation in numerous British eighteenth-century books of secrets and from there found its way into similar American works of the early nineteenth century.

The original French work has in the past been attributed to Nicolas Lemery (1645–1715), a French apothecary and physician who published a number of early works on pharmacy and chemistry. (Lemery is perhaps best remembered for having composed a popular *Cours de chymie* that went through more than thirty French and translated editions after its original publication in 1675.) In the recent *Dictionary of Scientific Biography,* however, Lemery's biographer states that these earlier attributions are inaccurate, and that this work is not likely to have been authored by Lemery.[26] We cannot, of course, think of this "bagatelle" of marbling literature as highly significant in detail and content; nonetheless, it indicates that the subject of marbling was noticed in the French popular literature of the late seventeenth century; the fact that it continued to appear thereafter, both in France and abroad, is also significant.

In recent years, I have been fortunate to unearth, with the help of others, a mid-seventeenth-century French manuscript account that establishes the existence of a more important, albeit private, marbling literature in France in very early times. (Photofacsimiles of this account and the details of how it was uncovered may be found in *Three Early French Essays on Paper Marbling, 1642–1765,* along with my translations of the manuscript and the marbling articles that appeared in the 1757 *Journal Oeconomique* and in the Diderot-D'Alembert encyclopedia.)[27] This newly discovered manuscript description dates to the period after 1642 and constitutes possibly the earliest and fullest account yet known, for both France and elsewhere. Furthermore, it indicates that knowledge of the method had progressed beyond the walls of seventeenth-century French marbling shops and may have been disseminated on a wider basis and at an earlier time than heretofore believed. We must admit, however, that it is not possible to determine the actual impact, if any, of this manuscript recipe.

The early French account, part of the Ferguson alchemical collection acquired by the University of Glasgow in 1921, is contained in a seventeenth-century book of recipes (a type of compendium often referred to as a "book of secrets").[28] This book, in turn, appears to be the second half of a larger, unidentified work, for its pages are marked (after eight preliminary leaves) "175–353," with three additional unmarked pages following. It is written in one hand in both French and Italian, but mainly in French, and contains a few pages of drawings (none related to marbling). Among the subjects discussed are fireworks; firearms, general weaponry, and recipes for gunpowder; miscellaneous household recipes on dyes, dyeing, wax modeling, horticulture, and the like; medicine and the compounding of medicines; writing materials (especially for secret writing) and invisible ink; and hunting and fishing. On pages 199–205, is a section entitled, "Pour le papier marbre, appelé papier de Turquie," and on page 205, outside and in the margin of the nonmarbling article that follows, is written the note, "F. Joseph de St. Antoine Carmé, à Lyon le 14ᵉ Janvier 1642" (see Figure 4).

There is no need to go into detail about the marbling information reported in the manuscript, as it appears in translation in my *Three Early French Essays on Paper Marbling, 1642–1765.* Suffice it to say, however, that the discussion is a fairly detailed one (in fact, as noted previously, the most complete description of marbling extant from the seventeenth century), amounting to over fifteen hundred words. (It would be surpassed only by the descriptions included in the *Kunst- und Werck-Schul* published early in the next century.) After the preparation of the colors are discussed, there follows a step-by-step description of how the marbling technique is accomplished, in-

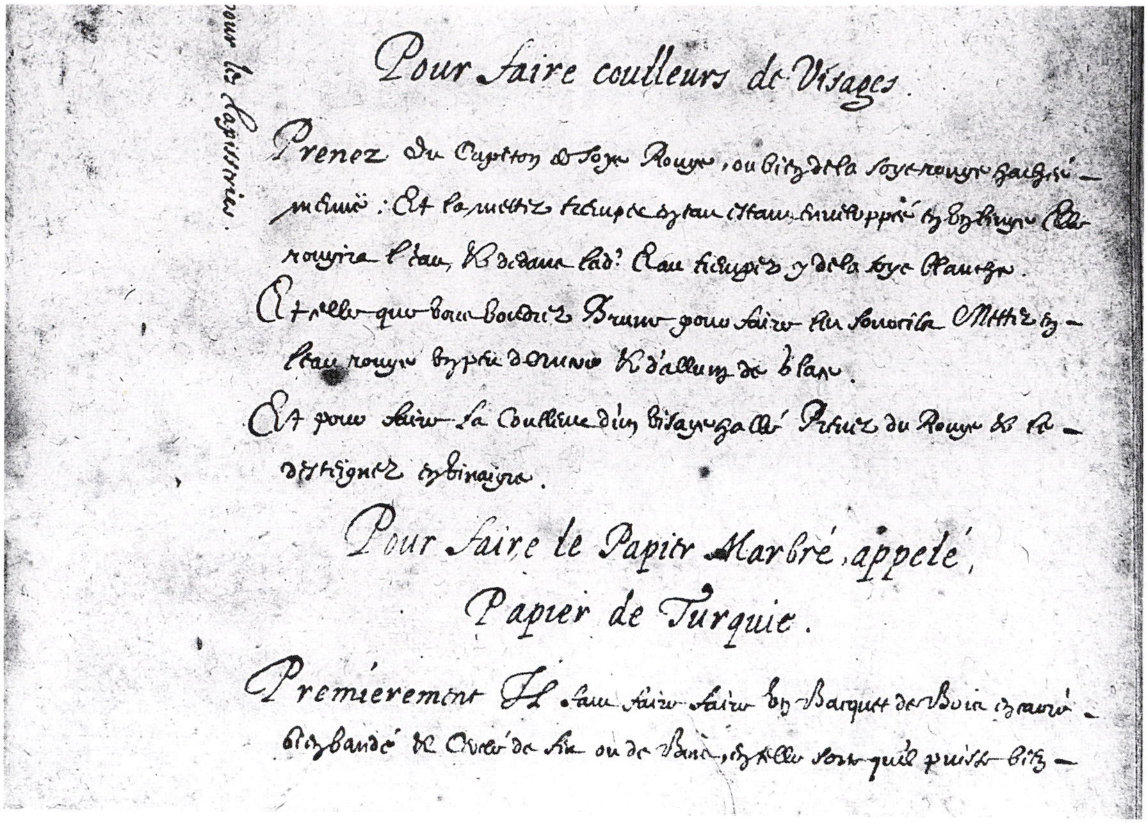

Pour faire coulleurs de Visages

Pour faire le Papier Marbré, appelé
Papier de Turquie.

Premièrement [handwritten text, partially legible]

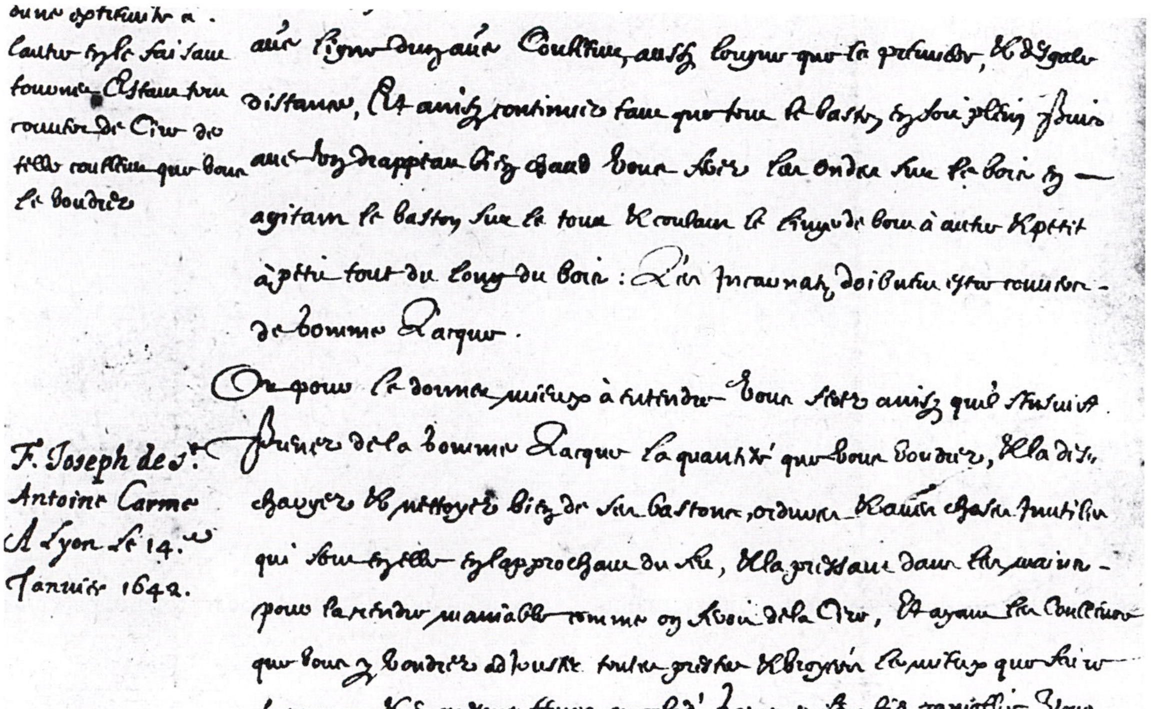

F. Joseph des.
Antoine Carme
A Lyon le 14.
Janvier 1642.

FIGURE 4. The first and last pages of the marbling account in MS. Ferguson 50.

cluding directions for the making of two patterns: a "spot" or Turkish design, and a combed one. The directions conclude with instructions for burnishing or polishing the marbled sheet to give it a proper finish and keep the colors from smearing. The information provided in this early manuscript is sufficiently detailed and clear to enable any experienced binder or competent craftsperson to marble on his or her own—and we may assume that some did.

Secrets concernant les arts et métiers (which, we have noticed, contained a slight rewriting and modernization of the process outline that first appeared in the 1674 *Recueil de curiositez rares et nouvelles,* attributed to Dr. Lemery), remained in print in France throughout the eighteenth century, thereby making its limited description available on a continuous basis.[29] A more extensive and detailed description, however, appeared early in the eighteenth century in the large dictionary of Jacques Savary des Bruslons,[30] to be followed just after mid-century by an even more informative account published in a quaint and highly illustrated work devoted to "new discoveries." In 1752, Jacques Gautier d'Agoty, master of the process of color printing by registering engraved plates, began to issue a collection of essays and observations on natural history, medicine, and the fine arts, illustrated with plates both colored by hand and color-printed through his own special process.[31] This interesting and beautifully produced work appeared in eighteen parts and comprised six volumes before its completion in 1755. In the second part of the initial volume, in a section entitled "Les Secrets des arts et les nouvelles découvertes," a description of the "Manière de marbrer le papier" was printed. This account of about eight hundred words extended over three columns of its quarto-size volume and gave its readers a fairly good outline of the paper-marbling technique.

The Accounts in the Journal Oeconomique and the Diderot-D'Alembert Encyclopédie

The previously mentioned account that appeared in the *Journal Oeconomique* in 1758 offers us our first really worthwhile printed encounter with French marbling,[32] but this roughly 3,500-word article is devoted largely to the technical aspects of the craft. The details it provides on the marbling process are more numerous but little different from those reported in the seventeenth-century manuscript now in the Ferguson collection. Nevertheless, it does divulge a few facts about the status and background of the contemporary French craft which require our attention.

The anonymous author of this piece may have been an actual craftsman, for obviously he was well acquainted with the mysteries of the art; or he may simply have been allowed to witness the process in action. He begins his discussion by observing that the wide employment of marbled paper at that time proved how useful this commodity was; therefore, he reasoned, its making should not be considered unimportant. Although marbled paper had become very common, he continued, there were not many people who knew how to make it, and those who did treated its manufacture as a secret they were unwilling to communicate to others. Yet, even among these workmen very few possessed the skill to make it really well. "Foreigners, above all the Germans," he complained, "surpass us considerably in this and compel us to purchase from them the most perfect examples in this genre. This results in a great disadvantage to our trade."

By publishing this article, the author wanted to make the general public aware of the nature of this secret, in such a way that a better marbled paper would result. While it is true that private individuals have not attempted to make this commodity themselves in larger cities where it can be obtained at a moderate price, he goes on, a knowledge of its making would enable them to better judge its quality and make wiser choices when purchasing it. Such knowledge could be put to even better use in provincial towns, or in the country, where marbled papers frequently cannot be procured or cost double the price charged elsewhere because of the added cost of transportation and the tradesmen's profit. The author concludes his introductory remarks by noting that not only could one amuse one's self by making large quantities personally at small cost, for the colors ordinarily employed were not expensive, and few of them are needed; one could derive great satisfaction from creating such figures of fantasy, without it costing too much.

The instructions that follow in the article discuss only a single pattern, the so-called Turkish or spot design, which involves merely throwing colors onto the marbling size and afterward taking them off onto paper. The only variation in this pattern mentioned is a method for making waves, swirls or streaks in the colors by twirling a comb around in them; such a comb being four or five inches wide, with projecting teeth distributed on it somewhat in the configuration of a chess board (that is, staggering them or placing them on alternate sides of all the comb). Overall, the unknown author's opinions, as well as the information he provides, confirm the low estate to which French marbling had sunk by the end of the 1750s.

We get a far more detailed view of French eighteenth-century marbling from the anonymous article on the "Marbreur de papier"—the marbler of paper—published in the Diderot-D'Alembert encyclopedia in 1765. Not only does this account represent the fullest eighteenth-century description of the contemporary status and workings of the craft, but it also includes two illustrations that depict marblers at work and some of their tools. This long (about 7,000 words) and detailed article is authoritative, as anyone knowledgeable of the craft can readily discern. Equally important, the patterns discussed are those of the earlier, golden age of French marbling.

Significantly, while the editors of the *Encyclopédie* seemingly had little trouble enlisting experts in many fields to write authoritative articles for this ambitious work, the subject of marbling presented something of a problem for them. The craft was known only to a limited number of professional makers, who conducted it in private and were not inclined to divulge its workings to others who might use that knowledge to compete against them. This was also the time of the apprenticeship system, which dictated that such knowledge be divulged only for gain, and then on a limited and regulated basis. The editors of the encyclopedia circumvented this obstacle, they tell us early in their marbling discussion, by locating "the widow of one of these workmen who was in extreme poverty." It was she who provided them with the details needed to make their description authoritative, and only because of her plight was she induced to cooperate in this way.

We can postulate, given the life expectancy of that period, that our widow was probably from fifty to sixty years old at the time, having been born in the first decade of the eighteenth century or shortly thereafter, and that she married, thereby beginning her association with the craft, in the 1720s or early 1730s at the latest. The Diderot-D'Alembert article thus gives us a glimpse not of marbling techniques and patterns in the mid-1760s, when the volume was published, but rather in 1720–1740 when it was still in its prime and when the methods and patterns of old still prevailed. In fact, the patterns discussed were no longer in vogue after the middle of the eighteenth century, and even had disappeared long before the publication of the 1758 *Journal Oeconomique* article.

The Diderot-D'Alembert article begins with a short definition of what the marbler of paper does, noting that if he is skillful, has a little taste, and employs fine paper and becoming colors, an effect results that is most pleasing to the eye. As to its purposes, marbled paper is used chiefly for covering paperbound books and serves as ornamental endpapers in the most highly finished bindings. Then follows a résumé of the types of patterns that are made, after which we are told that

> This small art first took root in Germany. The Swedes, and Norwegians and the peoples of the northern countries call it *officina gentium*. The Germans refer to it as *officina artium*.

A year or two after translating the Diderot-D'Alembert article, I discovered that others had recently completed this same task and had even published a translation.[33] In rendering the above passage into English, they had translated the two Latin phrases to mean "workshops of the people" and "workshops of the arts." While these translations are literally correct, they require further interpretation and explanation if we are to sense the real meaning of the words. Indeed, the other translators and editor noted in their brief introductory remarks that a few tech-

nical terms in the original article had remained obscure and could not be identified with confidence, and they indicated that this passage fell within that very category.[34]

When properly analyzed in the light of our knowledge of the divergent French and German systems, this passage is reflective of the individual workshop character of the French marbler and marblers in most other countries also, in contrast to the larger general production that was going on at the same time in the German factories. I translated *officina gentium* as "workshops of families," that is, workshops conducted by families or small related groups, while I interpreted *officina artium* as "workshops of trades," that is, of tradesmen or professionals. It seems evident that the first phrase refers to a workshop in the hands of individuals or groups of individuals, and the latter to a workshop conducted by professional paper colorists, as was the case with the German trade.

The "Marbler of Paper" article also devotes much space to the technical aspects of the craft and discusses the materials and utensils used in the process. In addition, there are lengthy discussions concerning making several specific patterns. These, I have pointed out earlier, are actually patterns of an earlier time and are not representative of designs of the period around 1765; the information provided here instead corresponds to marbled-paper designs preserved in bindings dating from the early eighteenth century. *Commun*, or ordinary paper, the first type discussed, was produced simply by throwing down colors and forming curled configurations in them before the pattern absorbed onto paper; curling (the pattern came to be known among later English marblers as "French curl" or "snail") was achieved with a comb with only a few teeth, or with an implement known as a "Dutch apparatus," a wide board with many rows of widely spaced teeth. The second pattern discussed was one called *placard*; the third, *persillé* or parsley; and, finally, we are given instructions on how to make the "small-comb" design. Three more patterns, *montfaucon*, *Lyonese*, and large *montfaucon*, are mentioned in passing, but we are told only that a comb was employed in their making. As several varieties of combed paper were being made in France in this period, we can only guess what these patterns might have looked like.

The term "montfaucon" apparently also designated a size of paper manufactured in France at that time (of undetermined dimensions), and the montfaucon comb had eighteen teeth.[35] The pattern designated as *Lyonese* suggests that a specific pattern had become associated with the manufacture of marbled paper at Lyon. I shall have more to say about early French patterns in the final section of this book. It should be mentioned, however, that the Diderot-D'Alembert article also discusses edge marbling and the making of paste papers.

The two marbling scenes provided in one of the encyclopedia's volumes of plates (Figures 5–6) will also be discussed in greater detail later on; for now we must de-

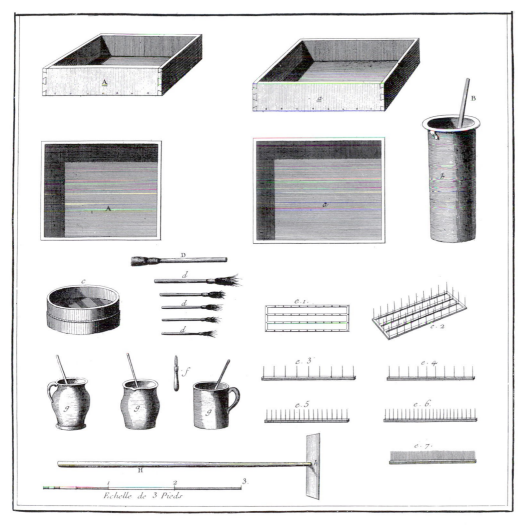

FIGURE 5. First marbling plate in the Diderot-D'Alembert *Encyclopédie*.

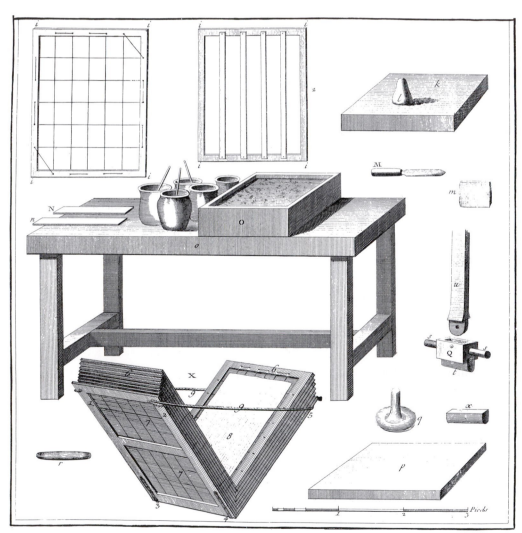

FIGURE 6. Second marbling plate in the Diderot-D'Alembert *Encyclopédie*.

termine how representative they are of a French marbling workshop of the eighteenth century. Franz Weisse speculated that such a large work force was depicted in these prints in order to illustrate all the stages of marbling; in reality, he believed, not that many people would have been engaged together in marbling at this time.[36] He was, however, speaking with his own experience and period in mind, that is, the twentieth century, when large-scale production was no longer undertaken and when marbling was practiced mainly by individuals working alone. In my view, the Diderot-D'Alembert plates might well typify a French atelier of the early eighteenth century, for marbled paper was being used extensively by bookbinders at this time and large work forces were required to satisfy their demands. These plates seemingly do preserve the appearance and flavor of French marbling workshops of this vital period and give us further evidence of its separate, specialized character.

The last notable description of marbling technique in French literature of the eighteenth century appeared in Henri Duchesne's *Dictionnaire de l'industrie, ou collection raisonnée des procédés utiles dans les sciences et dans les arts.* Initially published at Paris in 1776 in three volumes, the work was reissued in 1795 and again in 1801 in six volumes; an Italian translation was published at Turin in 1792–1793 in four volumes under the title *Dizionario dell'Industria Ossia Collezione Ragionata de' Processi Utili nelle Arte, e nelle Scienze.* The description, under the title "Papier marbré. Procédé simple & facile pour faire de très beau papier marbré," in Duchesne's original account amounted to about 1,300 words and gave an adequate explanation of how this craft was carried out.[37]

The Enlarged French Trade

It would be incorrect to assume that French marbling was restricted to a few families and makers alone in the eighteenth century and afterward. The massive amount of marbled paper that survives in untold numbers of volumes in national and research libraries throughout Europe and America bespeaks a very large production and trade, and a multiplicity of workshops, not only in Paris but also in other French cities and towns where printing and bookbinding flourished. Several lists have recently been compiled of French makers of colored paper from the seventeenth into the nineteenth century. While, I suspect, many if not most of the craftsmen named in these lists belonged to the ranks of the dominotiers, who were a more identified and identifiable class, the lists are still worth noting here.

We may assume that marblers servicing the bookbinding trade were well known to bookbinders who used them to supply decorative papers and to marble the edges of their books. As a result, there was little need for marblers to advertise, and few did. Those who needed their services knew where to find them and knew what they had to offer. But there were marblers and makers of fancy papers who also supplied the stationery trade with decorative papers, and the names of a few of these have become known. In 1913 John Grand-Carteret published an important work on the French stationery trade and described stationers who were located not only in Paris but also throughout the country. This very interesting and useful book discusses those tradesmen who from the seventeenth century on dealt in the manufacture and sale of merchandise for everyday use: writing and other types of paper, quills, pens, inks, music paper, printed certificates and forms, blank books, sealing wax, playing cards, calendars, decorative boxes, wallets, pocket books, portfolios, calling cards and other types of cards, colored and fancy paper (for lining shelves and other decorative purposes), wallpaper, globes, and similar materials. The list also includes materials introduced later on, such as bags, envelopes and glues for sealing these, and pencils—in effect, all the materials needed for correspondence, literary and educational purposes, and home use.[38]

Grand-Carteret provides a list extending over a hundred pages to include merchants and those connected with the stationery business, in addition to manufacturers or suppliers; he has even reproduced some of their quaint trade cards that he found in archival and other sources. Among these appear the names of a few individuals who actually marbled or seem to have marbled (and in some cases made other types of decorative paper, too), and the names of stationers who advertised marbled paper among their many products. Often it is difficult to distinguish who actually were makers and who merely were merchants; in cases where individuals advertised that they made or sold every type of decorated paper, we can only speculate that their inventory may have included the marbled kind.

As for those who actually or probably made marbled paper, Grand-Carteret's very first entry provides us with a likely prospect. At the head of the list is a firm by the name of Angrand, identified as a maker and merchant of decorated papers (papiers de fantaisie). This house had been in existence from the end of the eighteenth century, and continued in trade for a very long time. Grand-Carteret relates that Angrand's firm received honorable mention at the exposition of 1802, and in 1812 *Le Bazar Parisien* reported that its wares encompassed all sorts of decorated papers including gilt, silver and bronze, satin and gauffered, morocco and marbled. Little by little, Grand-Carteret states, this house abandoned the stationery trade and devoted itself in large part to making fancy and colored papers; it also had a box factory.

Another firm that appears to have produced marbled paper from the late eighteenth century was that of Carpentier. According to a literary notice of 1810, Carpentier manufactured all sorts of fancy papers (including morocco and marbled paper), and music paper as well. The firm Chagniat, "fabricant de papiers de fantaisie," which went into the business of producing fancy papers in 1838 and which, after 1881, was continued by Georges Putois (to whom Grand-Carteret dedicated his book, and who was its publisher), in all likelihood also made marbled papers. While marbled papers were not specifically listed among the many kinds that Chagniat advertised, later sample books of Putois reveal a wide array of marbled papers among the many types he produced.[39]

M. Fichtenberg, the author of the extremely fine and valuable 1852 treatise on the making of fancy papers, appears in the list as a maker of decorative papers, including marbled papers, at 34, rue de Bernardins (later rue de la Vieille-Monnaie). Grand-Carteret reports that Fichtenberg's business began early in the nineteenth century; thus, we may assume that he was probably in his sixties and a seasoned maker at the time that his treatise came out. The firm Prévost *père* (later Prévost-Wenzel), listed as makers of fancy papers from the early nineteenth century until succeeded by Batardy in 1841, counted marbled papers among the many types it produced. A Parisian paper merchant named Fournier, who was active from about 1760, advertised that he manufactured every sort of colored paper; and Melchior Tacussel, an early nineteenth-century tradesman, had a store specializing in colored paper and sold every article related to stationery in general. In Lyon, Antoine Girard, a manufacturer and merchant of paper in the nineteenth century, also listed marbled paper among his productions and wares.

Many of those on Grand-Carteret's list were stationers who advertised in one way or another that they sold marbled paper among their general merchandise. The paper merchant Declaron, who was in business in Paris in the eighteenth century, did so, as did another stationer named Delermoy. Delermoy's trade card, reproduced by Grand-Carteret on his page 223, locates him "à la bonne foi, rue Dauphine, à Versailles," and shows that he sold marbled paper (papier marbré) as well as German marbled paper (découpures venant d'Allemagne, papier marbré). The eighteenth-century Parisian stationer Lefebre advertised that the types of colored paper he offered for sale also included the marbled kind, which he described as being very beautiful, and which could be used in dining-rooms, wardrobes, and for dressing up compartments. The house of Petit, successor of M. Guérard after 1760, also sold marbled paper, according to the eighteenth-century trade card that Grand-Carteret illustrates. And the paper merchant Voison, who conducted his business in Paris during the second part of the eighteenth century, likewise listed the marbled variety among the many different papers and products he handled. Outside Paris, the merchant Bouvet of Troyes specifically singled out marbled paper among his wares, and the firm of Daudet and Joubert of Lyon advertised that they handled "papiers peints fins et communs." Finally, Pierre Pavie, "merchant-cartier" and "papetier-dominotier," who was located at Troyes in the later eighteenth century, also advertised marbled paper among the various kinds of paper he provided.

In 1950, Gabriel Magnien published an article which listed about sixty French makers who, he believed, turned out ornamental papers for bookbinders in the seventeenth, eighteenth, and early nineteenth centuries, as well as similar makers in Germany and Italy.[40] His French makers range geographically from Paris and Lyon, where large numbers are recorded (but perhaps only a fraction of those who may have been thus occupied), to other localities throughout France, including Orléans, Chartres, le Mans, Alençon, Amiens, Rouen, Caen, Nantes, Épinal, Troyes, Dijon, Besançon, Avignon, Montauban, Mende, Toulouse, and Bourg-en-Bresse. Magnien's list presents us with something of a puzzle. Since French bookbinders rarely used decorated papers other than the marbled kind to embellish their bindings, until the nineteenth century, at least, one suspects that the majority of makers he names were dominotiers and not marblers.

In 1967, the Musée des Arts Décoratifs in Paris sponsored an exhibition of early French decorated papers entitled "Trois Siècles du Papiers Peints" and issued an accompanying catalog that provided a list of early makers.[41] While this exhibition related mainly to French pattern papers, and especially wallpapers (that is, papers produced by dominotiers), its catalog and the Magnien list give some idea of the extent and geographical range of the French decorated paper industry in former times; and although marblers did not really partake of that activity, I believe we may assume that there were likewise large numbers distributed in about the same areas, silently plying their craft in support of the bookbinding trade.

The Decline of the French Trade

French marbling, which had commenced on a bright note early in the seventeenth century, gained strength and maturity by the 1670s or 1680s, and surged vigorously for six or seven decades thereafter, began to taper off in the period around 1740. It seems likely that the early generations of marbling masters who had injected life into this trade were then passing from the scene, and their vigor and high standards were not being sustained. The beautiful and rather formal patterns they had introduced and made in enormous numbers during their golden era now began to give way to just a few simple designs, and the quality and vividness of colors showed a decline also. This deterioration may have been due also to a lessening of interest in fine bookbinding in general, which possibly was influenced by political and economic events of the time. By the 1760s the low standards that were described in the *Journal Oeconomique* had replaced those detailed in the Diderot-D'Alembert article, which recalled the high standards of the pre-1740 era.

This decline continued through the final years of the

monarchy, although bright spots did glimmer here and there. By the 1790s, however, perhaps influenced by the establishment of the Republic and the new enthusiasm and freedom it and other political events inspired, a revival occurred. New marbled patterns and new methods for producing them were introduced (to be discussed later), and with these innovations French marbling took on a fresh vigor and regeneration that sustained it for several decades more.[42] But even while this upward surge was taking place, the seeds of its decline were once more being sown, for the burgeoning Industrial Revolution was beginning to exert its relentless pressures.

The first inroads made in the manufacture of traditional marbled paper came just after the beginning of the nineteenth century, when a decorated paper called "maroquin," or morocco, was introduced. Produced not on the traditional marbling bath but through engraved plates, in imitation of the tree marbling that had become a popular decoration on leather (mainly sheepskin) bindings, maroquin paper was soon adopted by bookbinders as a covering material, especially on blank books produced for stationery purposes; in this way, it replaced much marbled paper that previously had been utilized for this purpose.[43] Around the third decade of the nineteenth century, the French and Germans introduced a pseudo-marbled paper under the names "agathe" and "Achat" (or agate). Because of its cheapness and novelty, this type too, made inroads on the marbles of old wherever it was imported and sold. Additionally, pressure was already being exerted on the French industry by the growing German factory industry and trade in marbled and other decorated papers, beginning early in the nineteenth century. Indeed, the pamphlet which I have identified as the possible Schuder work of 1808 relates that large amounts of German marbled papers were being exported to France and Switzerland.[44]

In France, an especially harsh blow was dealt to the marbling trade by innovations that M. Montgolfier and others introduced in the late 1820s and afterward. Montgolfier began to produce fancy papers in his factory at Annonay (and it may have been just that, a factory approximating contemporary German standards) which, while called "marbled," actually were made by means of caustic and other types of chemicals, outside of the bath. Both the German and French "pseudo" papers were made more easily and in greater numbers; thus, they sold more cheaply than the old marbled ones and soon began to replace many of them. The "papiers d'Annonay," as Montgolfier's papers were called, had a fresh charm and appeal about them that brought them into wide use and vogue. Indeed, it must be admitted that many examples dating from the 1820s, 1830s and beyond are a delight to behold even today, when encountered on the covers of old French books.

By the time that Fichtenberg issued his important manual on the making of fancy and colored papers at Paris in 1852, the old-style French marbling industry was all but gone. Those patterns he described and in some cases illustrated with small bits of actual colored paper were mainly the non-marbled kinds—monochrome paper, lithographed, and pseudo-marbled types. Of the thirty-two patterns illustrated in his manual, only eight, one-fourth of them, were true marbles, produced on a bath; and of these the majority were of the newer and more simple designs. Thereafter, the authentic hand-marbling of old was carried on, as today, in the workshops of a very few specialists (such as Chagniac and Putois) who worked alone or with only a few others to supply limited amounts of these papers to professional and amateur hand bookbinders; to restorers; and to connoisseurs who strived to maintain the standards and traditions of the past. Thus in France marbling had come full circle, ending where it had originated, in the workshops of a few.

5

The Further Spread
of the Craft in Europe

ARBLED papers found in European bookbindings of the seventeenth and early eighteenth centuries invariably prove to be German or French in origin. Clearly, the abundance of high-quality German and French marbles and the restricted use of such decoration (limited to the finer work of leading craftsmen) made production in other countries unnecessary. By the middle of the eighteenth century, however, more and more binders throughout Europe were beginning to employ marbled decoration, and often in less fine works; at the same time, marbled paper was becoming less available to them because the French trade had begun its initial decline. It was at this time that a few bookbinders and paper colorists in Italy, Spain, Denmark, Sweden, and other European lands turned their attention to decorating paper, and sometimes even the edges of their books, in the Turkish style. Thus, the craft gradually began to migrate beyond the two European countries in which it had first taken hold and gained eminence.

The spread of marbling to some of these lands can be ascribed to political and economic events. In other areas, it can be attributed to changing customs in bookbinding that required marbled decoration as part of the "new wave." Early in the eighteenth century, German binders began to migrate throughout Europe, taking with them their methods and styles, including marbled decoration. Later on, binders in neighboring regions traveled to Germany and France in search of additional training and new methods and fashions. Here they increasingly came into contact with marbled decoration and an incipient marbling literature. While the early emigrant binders had depended on imported German and French marbled paper to line the covers of their books, some of the later binders who had traveled to France and Germany and gained exposure to the modern workshop practices there began to experiment with marbling themselves after returning home; in particular they sought methods for decorating the outer edges as well as the insides of their books. Some of these people eventually did learn to marble, as evidence of surviving edge decoration proves; a few of these

binders not only carried on the craft during their careers but taught it to others who continued it after their teachers had passed from the scene. In all the European countries outside France and Germany, however, the activity that developed never resulted in the large production or the high quality achieved in these two lands. And the competition from enormous factory production in Germany in the nineteenth century would overwhelm the activities that had commenced in many if not most of these countries and bring them to a standstill.

The pigments and colors available in these various regions resulted in distinctly individual or nationalistic appearances in the marbled papers. The same can be said for the patterns; these characteristics aid greatly in identification and historical reconstruction.

Though it is not known in what sequence the craft actually migrated to these adjacent lands, both for convenience's sake and because in all probability it was the next country after Germany to receive this art, we shall begin our discussion with Italy.

Marbling in Italy

Marbled decoration, as well as other types of colored decoration, never became an extensive or integral part of bookmaking and bookbinding in Italy. Such ornamentation simply did not develop as a characteristic of hand bookbinding there. As a rule, full-leather bindings had white endpapers, while pale monochrome paper over soft pasteboard formed the covering material on most half and quarter bindings. Only infrequently does one encounter marbled and other types of decorated endpapers in Italian leather bindings of the late seventeenth and early eighteenth centuries; when they occasionally do appear, such papers can be identified as French or German in origin. I have examined large collections of early Italian imprints in a number of research libraries, opening cover after cover for hours on end, and this observation has universally held true. Although Italian bookbinders of the earlier period often resorted to non-marbled edge decoration—daubing spots and configurations of red and green and yellow and blue onto the edges of their volumes or sprinkling them red or blue, giving their bindings a distinctly Italian flavor—they rarely inserted anything but white endpapers inside the covers of books. Exterior appearance seems to have been all that concerned these early Italian bookbinders.

On imprints dating from the third, fourth, or fifth decades of the eighteenth century, but even more after the middle of the century, however, endpapers containing marbled decoration of indisputable Italian origin began to appear in Italian leather bindings. That these papers were manufactured in Italy is proved by their distinctly Italian colors and often by the individualistic pattern on them, a pattern that later came to be labeled "Italian." Yet, I must emphasize, such decoration did not become typical of Italian bookmaking but remained an occasional practice, employed only now and then, almost whimsically, out of what motive or for what reason I cannot say.

While we know precious little about the origin of marbling in the Italian states and regions in the eighteenth century, the available evidence points toward a connection between the rise of marbling in Italy and the making of fancy papers there, somewhat as was the case in Germany, but on a much smaller scale. (The decorated papers produced in Italy in early times through the use of wood and metal blocks and plates were intended mainly for use in the home; like the marbled variety, they did not become greatly identified with Italian bookmaking, although they were often employed as wrappers or cover papers on pamphlets and printed music.) The occasional appearance of marbled papers in extant eighteenth-century Italian bindings indicates that sometime around the middle of the century (more probably after mid-century and not before)[1] marbling came to be carried on in the workshops of craftsmen who decorated paper by stamping it with wooden blocks and metal plates. Most notable among these practitioners was the firm of Remondini, located in the Italian town of Bassano del Grappa (Venice province) in the Venuto region of northern Italy. (Bassano is situated directly north of Padua and about an equal distance northwest of Venice.)

The family of Remondini was connected with publishing and the manufacture of prints and colored and decorated paper for a period of more than two hundred years. "Remondini papers," as the firm's pattern papers came to be known, enjoyed an extensive reputation and popularity throughout Italy and Europe, even though they were not very frequently used in bookmaking. A little of the history of the Remondini enterprise has been reported by Rosamond Loring,[2] but many additional details can be found in the state archives and in other sources in Venice and at Bassano, where a Remondini museum now exists.

The firm was established by Giovanni Antonio Remondini (b. 1634), an ironware dealer who, upon moving from his home town in the Po valley to Bassano, purchased a printing press and some woodcuts from a bankrupt printer. Giovanni's strategy was to publish a large number of prints, mainly small representations of religious scenes, as cheaply as possible and with little attention to quality. His success was such that by 1670 he had four wooden printing presses in operation and had begun to work with copperplates as well. His prints were sold not only in the shops of Bassano, but also by traveling salesmen throughout Europe.

Giovanni, the founding father of this dynasty of *stampatori*, died in 1711 and left a large fortune to his son Giuseppe, who proceeded to make the Remondini establishment one of the most important in Europe. Giuseppe completely reorganized the printing shop and brought in his own papermakers to insure a supply of paper and other raw materials; in 1732 he instituted a school for teaching wood carving in order to meet the demands of the factory. Records show that he employed over a thousand persons and thirty-eight printing presses, and his enterprise eventually included a paper mill with ten vats and a dye works. Through his diplomatic skills, Giuseppe gained the protection of the Venetian republic, securing exemptions from taxes and obtaining privileges that quashed competition. As a result, his business continued to prosper and grow.

Giuseppe died in 1773, but his sons Giovanni Antonio and Giovan Battista had long before succeeded to management of the firm; the former attended to matters in the factory while the latter concentrated on sales and on expanding the range of products. By the middle of the eighteenth century, the business had become so large and important that it was one of the leading firms of not only Bassano, but the entire Venetian republic, and a branch was opened in Venice proper.

While the firm engaged in printing books and decorating paper, its bedrock activity was the mass production of popular prints, including the pirating of engravings made by foreign craftsmen—a matter that brought the Remondinis into legal suits and exposed them to scrutiny by the Five Inspectors of Commerce of Venice. The most famous in a succession of legal incidents occurred in 1772 when Charles III of Spain took them to court on the charge of producing an insulting print. The Remondini workshop had copied for a Marseilles merchant the scene of the "Last Judgment" by the French artist Poilly, replacing the original coat of arms with those of the king of Spain. The insult arose from the fact that the Spanish crest had been placed on the side of the picture populated with devils. An international incident ensued, and the Jesuits were expelled from Spain in protest. The Pope made his indignation known to the Venetian authorities, who followed through with an investigation by the Council of Ten. Further legal disputes arose due to the strong resentment of other Venetian printers who suffered because of the unfair competition of the Remondinis.

Original documents in the Venetian state archives relate that in 1738 the authorities issued an executive decree granting Giovanni and Giovan Battista Remondini a concession to manufacture prints and gilded and other types of decorated papers for the course of their natural lives.[3] Subsequently, in 1755, the Five Inspectors of Commerce published a broadside decree of the Senate granting the Remondini firm additional privileges with respect to its new factory at Bassano, among which was the right to make damask paper.[4] Finally, in 1764 the Five Inspectors issued still another decree of the Senate, greatly enlarging the scope of the concessions made to the Remondinis. In this decree, reproduced as Figure 7 here, the Venetian Senate empowered the Remondinis to manufacture and sell gilded and other types of decorated paper.[5] In the first line of the second paragraph, which describes the various types of prints and products the firm was privileged to make and distribute, reference is made to "carte marmorate," or marbled papers, indicating that the firm had brought this particular type into production by that time.

Reference to the manufacture of marbled paper by the Remondinis was also made, as Phoebe Jane Easton noted in her *Marbling, a History and a Bibliography,* on page 14 of their catalog issued in 1784, *Catalogo delle Stampe in Rame, in Legno ec. delle Varie Qualitá de Carte Privilegiate, le Quale Di Lavorano in Bassano Presso la Dita di Giuseppe Remondini e Figli de Venezia, Con I Suoi Pressi Fissati a Moneta Venetia.*[6] I have not been able to locate a copy in America, but a subsequent catalog, published by the same firm in 1791, is now in the National Library of Medicine in Bethesda, Maryland, and, indeed, the sale of marbled paper is outlined in it.

The catalog in the National Library of Medicine carries the identical title, and while its imprint is dated 1791, its final pages include materials added in July of 1793. According to the preface ("Avviso"), this catalog was the sixth to be issued, the first appearing in 1766 and others following in 1770, 1778, 1784, and 1789. It is evident that the decorating of paper was but one aspect of that firm's overall business, and a lesser one at that. Most of the Remondini effort continued to be directed toward the manufacture of prints: pictures of saints, reproductions of Italian and other masters, and similar materials printed from copperplates and woodblocks and intended probably to be displayed in contemporary Italian homes. The 1791 catalog mentions (p. III) several types of paper designated "marmorata." The first categories include papers marbled in one color only—red, yellow, green, indigo, sky blue, and "the color of night"—followed by a listing of papers classed as "marmorata reale." The latter group comprised papers that were marbled in many colors and were the best that the firm produced; they appeared in the same colors as the others, but at nearly double the price. We may surmise from this series of catalogs that

ambitious production followed the granting of the privilege of 1764 and that they were subsequently issued to advertise and exploit it. But we cannot be sure whether true marbling was carried on in the Remondini factories before 1764 or whether it was introduced about then as part of the firm's increased activity.

Further evidence of paper marbling at the Remondini works, as well as actual samples of the firm's range of colored and decorated papers, are provided by one of its pattern books preserved in the Loring collection in the Houghton Library at Harvard.[7] Dating to the year 1808 and bearing the title *Campione delle Carte Colorata delle Fabbrica Giuseppe Remondini e Figli, Bassano,* this book contains in all thirty-six leaves, with eight to sixteen small samples of colored paper mounted on the recto of each. Displayed there are mainly papers of the stamped variety (designs printed from copperplates and woodblocks), but there are also two pages of sprinkled, monochrome, and paste papers (the latter of inferior quality, as might be expected of papers produced by a method that was distinctly "un-Italian"). One leaf, the twenty-fourth, contains nine samples of Turkish paper, which not only illustrate the simplicity of the patterns that the firm produced and offered, but also emphasize that marbling represented a very limited part of the firm's overall production (Plate XVI). This finding accords with my observations on the limited status of marbling in Italy.

Early in the nineteenth century, the Remondini firm began a slow decline. The failure of this printing dynasty's later descendants to keep abreast of the new production processes being developed in France and England, coupled with tardy and ill-considered decisions, and changing political, economic, and social conditions, reduced the firm more and more; in 1861 it closed its doors altogether.

"Remondini papers," the pattern papers for which the firm became famous, had been printed on hand presses by means of artistically carved woodblocks and metal plates, one for each design or color, with several often employed to effect a colored pattern. Each color was printed separately and the plates were made to register so that the resulting product showed a variety of designs printed in a variety of colors. The colors used were permutable vegetable dyes, and thus subtle variations in color often were achieved. With the closing of the Remondini enterprise in 1861, thousands of Remondini woodblocks (some inlaid with metal) and copperplates lay scattered about and forgotten. Subsequently, a large number of these were traced and acquired by later owners, who eventually united with another paper decorating firm that had been established at Varese. In this way, some of the Remondini papers of old were reissued under the Remondini name, although they also came to be known as Varese papers.

The Loring collection also contains pattern books of other colored paper makers located in Bassano in the nineteenth century, specifically those of Giovanni Menegassi and Borgo Angarano. Their pattern books date to the period around the middle of the century and display

1

2

3

PLATE VII

1

2

PLATE VIII

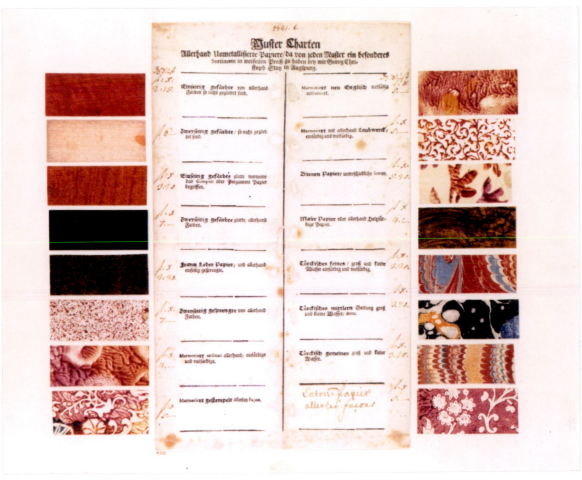

1

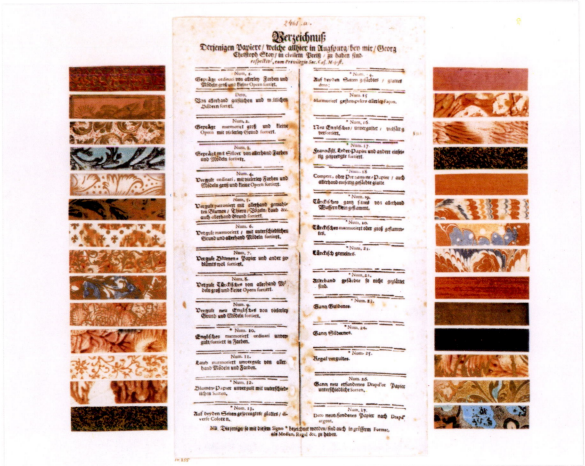

2

PLATE IX

1

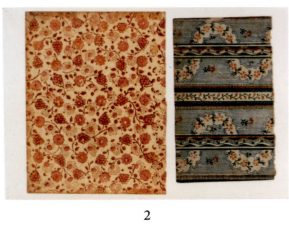

2

3

4

5

6

PLATE X

1   2   3

4   5

6   7

PLATE XI

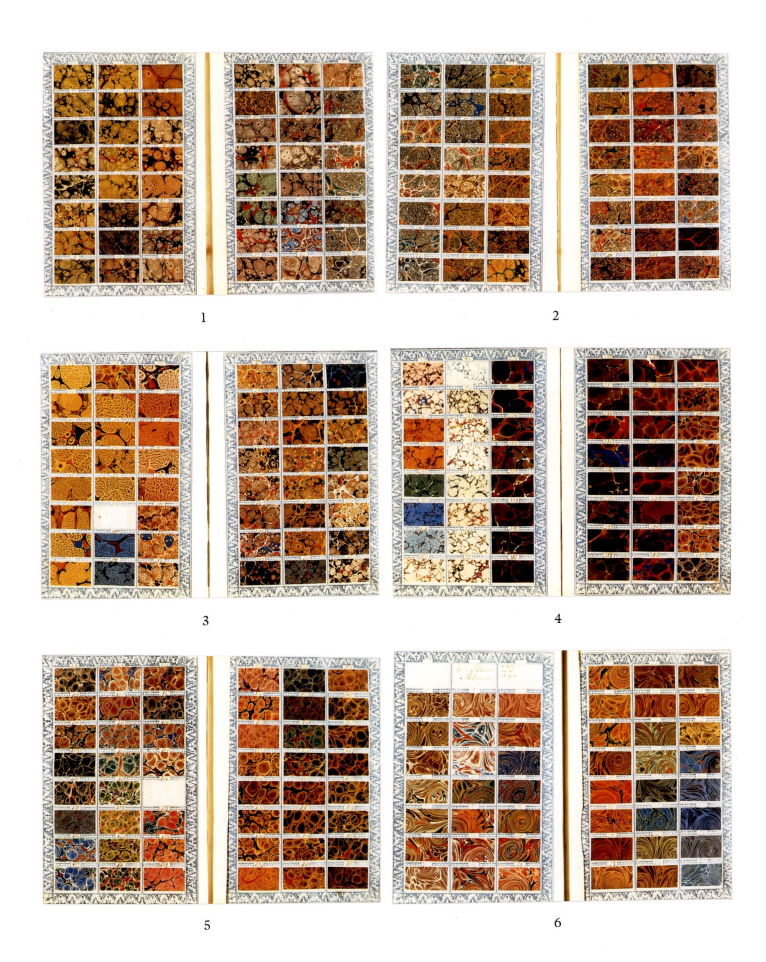

1

2

3

4

5

6

PLATE XII

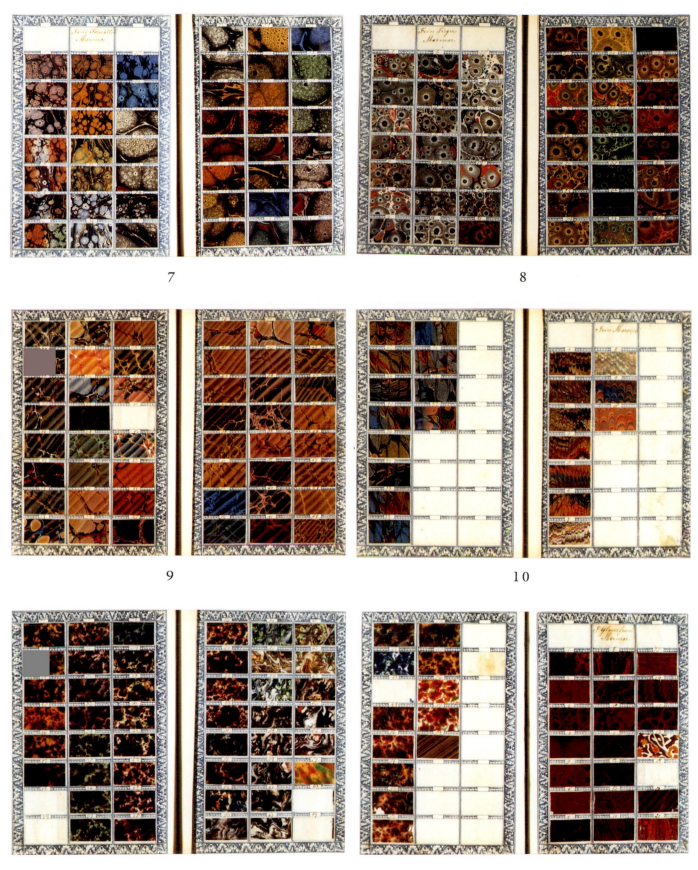

7

8

9

10

11

12

PLATE XIII

1

2

3

4

5

6

PLATE XIV

1

2

3

4

5

6

PLATE XV

1

2

3

4

5

6

PLATE XVI

Captions for Plates VII–XVI

PLATE VII: 1–2. Marbled papers containing stenciled patterns, made in Germany early in the 17th century. These are among the earliest examples of European marbling yet known. From the Album Amicorum of I. Pfinzing von Helfenfeld of Nürnberg, 1618. Now in the Olga Hirsch collection in the British Library; 3. Wash drawings of birds, a hunter, dogs, and grapes, cut out and mounted onto a piece of German marbled paper to make up a pictorial representation. This may represent a frequent use for marbled paper in Germany at this early time. Germany, later seventeenth century. Germanisches Nationalmuseum, Nürnberg.

PLATE VIII: 1–2. Hand-colored prints of the Augsburg engraver and printseller Martin Engelbrecht. These depict male and female makers of colored paper at this time. Augsburg, 1720–1750 period. Musée des Arts Décoratif, Paris.

PLATE IX: 1–2 Pattern cards of Georg Christoph Stoy, ca. 1730. Stoy was a major manufacturer and distributor of colored paper in Augsburg during the first half of the eighteenth century. Kunstgewerbemuseum, Berlin.

PLATE X, calico, damask, and brocade or gilded papers: 1. Damask or calico paper. Nürnberg, late 17th or early 18th century. Germanisches Nationalmuseum, Nürnberg; 2–3. Calico papers. Germany, 18th century. Loring Collection, Houghton Library, Harvard University; 4. Brocade or Dutch gilt paper. Augsburg or Nürnberg, 18th century. Author's collection; 5. Brocade paper. Augsburg or Nürnberg, 18th century. Loring Collection, Houghton Library, Harvard University; 6. Brocade paper made by Johann Michael Munck. Augsburg, ca. 1750. Loring Collection, Houghton Library, Harvard University.

PLATE XI, paste papers: 1–3. Paste papers used as cover papers or wrappers on inventories of estates of Nürnberg citizens, late 17th and early 18th centuries. Germanisches Nationalmuseum, Nürnberg; 4. Paste paper, gilded over with a stencil. Germany, probably Augsburg, 18th century. Loring Collection, Houghton Library, Harvard University; 5–6. Red and blue Herrnhut papers, mid- to late 18th century. Loring Collection, Houghton Library, Harvard University; 7. German marbled endpapers, and paste color decoration on the edges, on a copy of Matthiäs Georg Pfann's *Sammlung Verschiedener Merkwürdiger Fälle,* published at Nürnberg by A. Stein and G. N. Raspe in 1750. The binding is original sheepskin, gilt. The marbled papers were made professionally in one of the contemporary factories or workshops, while the edge decoration was applied locally, possibly by the binder. Author's collection.

PLATES XII and XIII: Pages containing samples of marbled paper in the pattern book of the factory of Alois Dessauer at Aschaffenburg am Main, 1848–1852 period. Loring Collection, Houghton Library, Harvard University.

PLATE XIV, marbled endpapers, possibly of French manufacture, in French royal bindings and presentation bindings of the early seventeenth century in the Bibliothèque Nationale, Paris, and illustrated in Geneviève Guilleminot-Chrétien's *Papiers marbrés Français* in 1987 (courtesy of the Bibliothèque Nationale and Adriaan Verberg, Middelberg, the Netherlands): 1. Turkish pattern, light blue and rose, in a copy of Cicero's *Epistolae Familiares* (Paris, Mamert Pattison, 1578). Bound for King Henry IV; 2. Turkish pattern, dark blue, with traces of rose and pale yellow, in a copy of René de Sainct-Clement's [Projet d'un College], dating to about 1620. The binding contains the coat of arms of King Louis XIII; 3. Turkish pattern, pale blue with traces of red, in a copy of a manuscript manual of the Prières du Roy au Sainct Esprit, dating to 1614. The binding was executed for King Louis XIII; 4. Combed Turkish design, blue, rose, yellow, and green, in a copy of J. Morin de la Masserie's *Les Armes et blasons des chevaliers de l'ordre du Saint-Esprit* (Paris: Pierre Firens, 1623). The binding contains the coat of arms of King Louis XIII, who created this order; 5. Combed Turkish pattern, dark blue, pale blue, rose, and green, in a copy of Claude Antoine de Valles's *Le Théâtre d'honneur de plusieurs princes anciens et modernes* (Paris, 1618). This copy was presented to Gaston d'Orléans, the brother of King Louis XIII, and is dated April 20, 1620; 6. Turkish pattern, pale blue with traces of rose, in a copy of Claude Fauchet's *Oeuvres* (Paris: Jean de Heuqueville, 1610). The binding contains the coat of arms of King Henry II.

PLATE XV, early French combed patterns (numbers 1–4 are reproduced from endpapers in bindings in the Bibliothèque Nationale and also were illustrated in Mme Guilleminot-Chrétien's catalog): 1. Small comb pattern, swirled; black, pale blue, blue-green, green, yellow, and rose, in a copy of François Harlay de Champvallon's *Apologia Evangelii Pro Catholicis ad Jacobum Majoris Britanniae Regem* (Paris: Antoine Estienne, 1625); 2. Small-comb pattern, slightly swirled; red, black, green, and yellow, in a copy of Jean Jaubert de Barrault's *Bouclier de la foy Catholique, contre le bouclier de la réligion prétendue, du ministre du moulin* (Paris: Antoine Estienne, 1626). The binding contains the coat of arms of King Louis XIII; 3. Small-comb pattern, red, black, yellow, and green, in a copy of Philippe de Gamaches's *Summa Theologica* (Paris: Regnaud Chaudière, 1627). The binding contains the coat of arms of King Louis XIII; 4. Small-comb pattern, curled; red, orange, green, yellow, black, and blue, in a copy of Charles de Noailles *L'Empire du juste selon l'institution de la vraye vertu* (Paris: Sébastien Cramoisy, 1632). The binding contains the coat of arms of King Louis XIII; 5. Front cover of a binding by Le Gascon of Paris on a copy of the *Auctores Latinae Linguae in Unum Redacti Corpus* (Paris: Johannes Vignon, 1622), with the notes of Dionysius Gothofredus. Richardson bookbinding collection, Houghton Library, Harvard University; 6. Endpapers at the back of the same volume, showing a contemporary French combed design on the paste-down endpaper. Because of scarcity and cost of marbled paper at this time, bookbinders often used white paper for the other endpaper.

PLATE XVI: 1. Title page of the first of a series of sample books of decorated papers made by the Remondini firm at Bassano, Italy, 1806. Loring Collection, Houghton Library, Harvard University; 2. Page from the above sample book, showing the only marbled papers made by the Remondini firm at that time. The remaining hundreds of samples in these volumes show pattern papers only; 3. Italian binding of the late eighteenth century with Remondini-style pattern paper on its covers. On Domenico Cotugno's *De Ischiade Nervosa Commentarius* (Naples, 1789), in the Boston Medical Library in the Francis A. Countway Library of Medicine, Boston; 4. The usual edge decoration on Dutch bindings of the eighteenth century—paste color decoration and not marbled decoration—although edge decoration on Dutch bindings of this period is uncommon. On four volumes in the Harvard College Library, as follows: *Het Leven van Willem de* I. (Leyden: S. Luchtmans; Middelburg; L. Bakker, 1732); Pieter Langendijk, *Gedichten* (Haarlem: J. Bosch [1721–1740]; Lukas Rotgan, *Poezy, van Verscheide Mengelstoffen* (Amsterdam: A Schoonenburg, 1735); and Cornelius Van Gestel, *Historia Sacra et Profana Archieposcopatus Mechliniensis* (The Hague: C. Van Lom, 1725); 5. Dutch binding of the mid-eighteenth century, containing French or German marbled endpapers of the "Dutch" variety, and a rare example of edge marbling by its Dutch binder. On a copy of Lorenz Heister's *Institutiones Chirurgriae*, printed at Amsterdam in 1739, and now in the Boston Medical Library; 6. Volume bound by Georg Julius Liebe of Copenhagen in the 1760 period, opened to show his marbled paper on one of its endpapers and his edge decoration. On a copy of *Den Neu Psalm Bok*, 1745. Det Kongelige Bibliotek, Copenhagen.

TERMINAZIONE

DEGL' ILLUSTRISSIMI, ED ECCELLENTISSIMI SIGNORI

CINQUE SAVJ ALLA MERCANZIA

Esecutiva di Decreto dell' Eccellentiʃʃimo Senato de dì 9. Febbraro 1764.

CONCERNENTE LA FABBRICA DELLE CARTE DORATE, MINIATE, ED IN VARIE ALTRE MANIERE CONFIGURATE, DELLA DITA GIUSEPPE REMONDINI, E FIGLI DI BASSANO.

Imarcata dall' Eccellentiʃʃimo Senato nel ʃuo Decreto 9. Febbraro paʃʃato l'utilità, che ne deriva al Veneto Commerzio dall' Invenzione già introdotta di Carte Dorate, Miniate, e Nere, Colorate, Stampate, e Stampate in Rame a varj uʃi inʃervienti, ad onta di gravoʃe ʃpeʃe, con benemerita induʃtria dalla Dita Remondini di Baʃʃano, ritrovò per conʃeguenza oneʃto il ricorʃo della Dita predetta, e li motivi per i quali degna ʃi rende del Pubblico favore per racchiudere il Ricorʃo ʃteʃʃo oggetti di facilitare lo ʃpazzo della nuova Manifattura, a fronte degli Eʃteri conʃimili Lavori con vantaggio dei Sudditi, e delle Arti pur Suddite.

Quindi volendo gl' Illuʃtriʃʃimi, ed Eccellentiʃʃimi Signori Cinque Savj alla Mercanzia preʃtare la dovuta eʃecuzione alla Pubblica decretata Volontà, all'effetto che queʃta nota ʃia ad ogn' uno per la reʃpettiva immancabile oʃʃervanza, terminano, e comandano.

I. Che tutte le Carte Dorate, Colorate, Stampate, e Stampate pure in Rame, Figurate, Miniate, e Nere, Indiane, Marmorate, Sbrufate, ed in varj altri modi Configurate, e a varj uʃi inʃervienti, fabbricate dalla Dita Remondini in Baʃʃano, quali la Dita medeʃima ʃarà per iʃpedire in Venezia per tranʃito, per eʃʃer ʃuʃʃeguentemente traʃmeʃʃe per via di Mare, e poʃcia diffuʃe nel Levante, Ponente, e principalmente nell' America, ove in iʃpeziale maniera con molto ʃuo merito introduʃʃe un nuovo ragguardevole Commerzio, ʃiano, e s' intendano eʃenti dai Dazj d'Ingreʃʃo, e d' Uʃcita dalla Dominante, ʃalva l' oʃʃervanza dei metodi, che quì ʃotto ʃaranno dichiariti, dovendo rapporto alla Terra Ferma, continuar a goder di quelle Facilità, ed Eʃenzioni, che gli furono già dal Decreto 13. Gennaro 1739. accordate.

II. Doveranno queʃte Carte come ʃopra, che per tranʃito dirette foʃʃero alla Dominante, per quindi eʃʃer ʃpedite per via di Mare, eʃʃer accompagnate dal Mandato a ʃtampa di queʃto Magiʃtrato, il di cui Formulario ʃarà pure ʃtampato, ed il quale in più eʃemplari numerati ʃarà conʃegnato alla Dita predetta, nel qual Mandato avrà ad eʃʃer ʃpecificato il numero de' Colli, che tranʃiʃtaʃʃero, dovendo nella più proʃʃima Cancellaria della Dominante eʃʃere annotato il giorno del Carico per lettera, ed abbaco, per eʃʃer direttamente tradotti alla Dogana Intrada da Terra.

III. Arrivati li Colli ʃteʃʃi nella Dogana predetta, quali dovranno in appreʃʃo eʃʃere accompagnati da Bolletta d'Intrada da Terra, e da due Fedi della ʃteʃʃa Dita Remondini, con una delle quali atteʃti eʃʃere li Colli, o Involgi compoʃti di Carte, delle qualità ʃopra deʃcritte, e con altra connoti il luogo preciʃo della direzione, dovranno alla preʃenza del Governatore, dall' Agente, o altro Miniʃtro d' eʃʃa Dita Remondini, eʃʃer riconoʃciuti li Colli, ʃicchè ʃi rilevi eʃʃer ʃoltanto compoʃti di eʃʃe Carte, per eʃʃer quindi ʃpediti per nulla rapporto all' Ingreʃʃo.

IV. E perchè è della Sovrana benefica Pubblica intenzione, che le Carte compoʃte di varj generi ʃuddetti, quali s' introduceʃʃero nella Dominante per tranʃito, e ʃi deʃtribuiʃʃero per la via di Mare, abbiano pure a godere eʃenzione di Uʃcita; perciò aʃʃicurato, che ʃi farà il ʃunominato Governatore dell' Intrada da Terra, che li Colli, o Involgi, come ʃopra ʃiano compoʃti ʃoltanto di eʃʃe Carte, dovrà all' Agente, o Miniʃtro della Dita ʃteʃʃa rilaʃciare Atteʃtato, che aʃʃicuri non contener eʃʃi Colli, che Carte come ʃopra, con la qual Fede unita all' altra della Dita predetta, che individuerà il luoco preciʃo della loro deʃtinazione, paʃʃerà l' Agente, o Miniʃtro predetto alla Dogana d' Uʃcida, ove riʃcontrati da quel Governatore, e l' Atteʃtato, e la Fede, quali a Pubblica cauzione dovrà tener in Filza ʃeparata per gli opportuni riʃcontri, che occorreʃʃero, avrà a rilaʃciargli Bolletta Gratis d' Uʃcida per li ʃuddetti Colli di Carte, all' effetto che poʃʃano eʃʃer ʃenza moleʃtia, ritardo, o impedimento d' Uffiziali di Barca, o di altre perʃone, caricati ʃopra il Baʃtimento, a cui foʃʃero addrizzati.

V. Coll' oggetto poi, che in ogni tempo conoʃcer poʃʃa il Magiʃtrato, e particolarmente il N. H. Deputato alle Fabbriche pro tempore, a lui per ʃpeziale Decreto è commeʃʃo d' invigilare ʃempre mai ʃopra l' andamento delle Fabbriche interne, ed eʃterne dello Stato; ʃe tutti li Colli di Carte, che per tranʃito capitaʃʃero nella Dominante, ʃaranno in fatto ʃtati ʃpediti, nè convertiti ʃi ʃiano con danno dei Pubblici Dazj in Conʃumo; perciò ʃarà debito del Miniʃtro, o Agente della Dita predetta il produrre al Fedel Nodaro del Magiʃtrato il Mandato a ʃtampa numerato, che avrà ʃervito di ʃcorta per la traduzione de' Colli in Venezia deʃtinati per la via del Mare, qual Mandato dovrà il ʃuddetto Fedel Nodaro pur tener in Filza ʃeparata, onde confrontar ʃi poʃʃa colle Bollette d' Uʃcita.

VI. Quelle Carte però Dorate, Miniate, e Nere, Colorate, Stampate, e Stampate pure in Rame, Indiane, Marmorate, Sbrufate, ed in varj altri modi Configurate, e a varj uʃi inʃervienti, fabbricate dalla Dita ʃuddetta, quali rimarranno per Conʃumo della Dominante, dovranno corriʃpondere il Dazio d' Ingreʃʃo ʃtabilito dalla corrente ʃtampata Tariffa 1751.

VII. Relativamente al Decreto 7. Aprile 1763. s' intenderanno diʃaggravate dai Dazj della Terra Ferma tutte quelle Carte di varia ʃpezie, e lavoro, che dopo tal tempo foʃʃero nuovamente dalla ʃopraddetta Dita inventate, ed introdotte; La quale eʃenzione per altro non dovrà aver effetto, ʃe non ʃe dopo ʃpirate le correnti Condotte; quando nel fratempo la Dita ʃuddetta col conoʃcimento di queʃto Magiʃtrato non conveniʃʃe Accordo colli reʃpettivi Impreʃʃarj de' Dazj, in modo che per tal conto non abbia ad eʃʃere eʃpoʃta la Pubblica Caʃʃa ad alcuna, benchè menoma, bonificazione. E la preʃente dovrà eʃʃere ʃtampata, e circolarmente traʃmeʃʃa per tutta la Terra Ferma, nonche intimata, e conʃegnata in eʃemplare al Fedel Nodaro di queʃto Magiʃtrato, alli Governatori dell' Intrada da Terra, ed Uʃcida, ed a chiunque altro occorreʃʃe per la pronta inviolabile ʃua eʃecuzione.

Dat. dal Magiʃtrato ʃuddetto li primo Marzo 1765.

    { SEBASTIAN ZUSTINIAN SAVIO ALLA MERCANZIA.
    { ANTONIO CAPPELLO 1.° SAVIO ALLA MERCANZIA.
    { PROSPERO VALMARANA SAVIO ALLA MERCANZIA.

Michel Moʃcopulo Nod.

STAMPATA PER LI FIGLIUOLI DEL QU. Z. ANTONIO PINELLI STAMPATORI DUCALI.

FIGURE 7. The decree of the Venetian Senate of 9 February 1764, empowering the Remondinis to manufacture marbled and other types of colored paper. Reproduced from the copy in the Loring collection in the Houghton Library of Harvard University.

morocco papers and a few of the later "pseudo-marbled" types, but no samples of the true marbling of old.

Today, opposite the main entrance of the Pitti Palace in Florence, strategically located to catch the tourist trade, is the marbling store "Il Papiro" of Giulio Giannini & Figlio. Here can be purchased newly marbled papers, books of blank white paper in bindings covered with marbled paper, marbled pencils, marbled pill boxes, marbled napkin rings, and other household items decorated in this ancient manner. The Gianninis have established similar outlets in Venice and in other Italian cities, throughout Europe, and recently in America as well; they thereby exploit a product that, while centuries old, appears novel and intriguing, for until recently marbling has been little seen outside of large research libraries. In my opinion, the Gianninis' marbling is far from first-rate, but it is colorful and appealing to a public that has been exposed to little classical marbling and thus lacks the means for comparison. The Giannini firm, according to its advertising literature, was established in Florence in 1856 when a bookbinder by that name began to marble. He eventually deserted bookbinding for the marbling occupation alone, and the business has been carried on by his descendants into the present time. No bookbinding activities are done at their establishment except for the making of blank books with marbled covers.

While in Florence a few years ago, I purchased a number of marbled papers, some marbled pencils, and other marbled objects sold at "Il Papiro." Later that day and the next, I encountered three other retail establishments where marbled papers were being made and sold. Alas, with each new discovery, the product was one additional step down in quality. It is clear that the success and popularity of the Giannini enterprise had induced others to try to cash in on the market. In the same way, probably, earlier Italian bookbinders and paper colorists attempted marbling now and then, perhaps from the eighteenth century on, for it is unlikely that all the marbled papers made in Italy came out of the Remondini works. As probably was the case in several other countries, some of these people were successful in mastering the craft and produced papers for a number of years. But when they ceased marbling, or died, their special kind of marbled decoration appeared no more. (The Gianninis are an obvious exception in this regard.) All told, their efforts mattered little, for marbled paper never achieved the same popularity among Italian bookbinders as among French, German, and other ones. Nor could Italian marbled paper rival for home and industrial use the "Remondini papers" and other stamped papers that were more easily and more cheaply mass-produced.

There did not arise in Italy any appreciable marbling literature, as the foregoing discussion would lead us to expect. While the earliest European description of the technique did appear in a book issued at Rome, this was written not in vernacular Italian but in Latin, the language of the erudite, and, moreover, in a scientific book that would be read and appreciated only by a few. Subsequently, no marbling manual or extensive explanation of the technique has ever been published in Italy or in Italian. The only pertinent information has come in the form of limited descriptions in such works as the previously mentioned Italian translation of H. G. Duchesne's industrial dictionary published at Turin in 1792 and 1793.

Recently, Stéphane Ipert, who has a special talent for unearthing information on this craft in obscure sources, brought to my attention another account which, although written in Italy perhaps as early as the late seventeenth century and published nearly one hundred and forty years ago, has been overlooked in recent times. This early Italian manuscript is devoted mostly to the making of colors, but it contains, near its conclusion, brief directions on how "To make the Turkish paper waved with diverse colors"—"Per fare la carta turchesca ondada di diversi colori." Ipert not only generously shared this information with me and sent me photocopies of pertinent pages of the manuscript, but also informed me that it had previously been located, translated, and published in 1849 in a collection by Mrs. Mary Philadelphia Merrifield entitled *Original Treatises, Dating from the XIIth to the XVIIIth Centuries, on the Arts of Painting*.[8] As this account is somewhat important as well as interesting, it requires more than mere mention in our survey of marbling on the Italian peninsula.

In the preface to the initial volume of her two-volume work, Mrs. Merrifield relates that she was commissioned by the British government in the autumn of 1845 to proceed to the north of Italy to collect manuscripts relating to the technical aspects of painting, principally the processes and methods of oil painting that had been adopted by the Italians. In addition, she was instructed to attempt to procure traditional and practical information on this subject from other sources; thus, her collection contains transcriptions of Italian manuscripts found also in libraries outside of Italy. In carrying out this task, she uncovered in the library of the University of Padua the manuscript (numbered 992) under discussion here.

Mrs. Merrifield, in her preliminary comments, describes this particular work as a quarto-size manuscript written on paper, without a date or the name of its author, but certainly Venetian. The handwriting, she notes, is of the seventeenth century, but from internal evidence could have been written in the latter part of the sixteenth. "However," she adds, "I think it is more probable that it was composed during the middle, or latter part, of the seventeenth century." While parts of the early sections of this work bear strong resemblance to the third book of Lomazzo's *Treatise on Painting*, published in 1584, many differences from earlier manuscripts appear with regard to the kinds of pigments, varnishes, essential oils, and other ingredients employed in painting, indicating that it was composed at a later time. She particularly observes that articles of South American and Mexican produce are mentioned, such as cochineal lac and the dyewoods of brazilwood and "campeachy wood."

Almost all of the manuscript is devoted to "Recipes for all Kinds of Colours," as its title translates. At the very end of the manuscript (the next to last of approximately a dozen in her collection that range chronologically from the twelfth to the eighteenth centuries) there are a few pages on Turkish marbling, consisting of about seven hundred words. The description contains two drawings: one depicts how a feather should be conducted through the size in a zigzag fashion to test its thickness or viscosity, and the other illustrates a double comb with points consisting of hog bristles. The colors used in the process are described as orpiment, common lake, or cinnabar for red; indigo for dark blue; indigo and white lead for sky blue; indigo and lake for purple; orpiment and indigo for green; orpiment and cinnabar for gold; and black mixed with ivory that had been calcined: "These then alone are the colors which succeed; they must be well ground up with simple water and be moderately liquid." Other directions provided here on marbling are fairly standard for the seventeenth and eighteenth centuries: the use of gum water and a trough; the addition of gall and spirits of wine to the colors; the dropping of the colors from a pencil or pointed stick; and their subsequent combing. The manuscript concludes by advising that "if you choose, you may make with the feather, circles, snakes, labyrinths, and similar things."

At first, I was skeptical that this interesting account could have dated to the late seventeenth century, as Ipert claimed, and I was even more suspicious when I examined the photocopy he sent me.[9] The handwriting in it appeared more typical of the eighteenth century than earlier. However, after close examination of the photocopy and Mrs. Merrifield's text and introduction, I am inclined to believe that it may date to the latter part of the seventeenth century, as she alleges. Still, there are a few aspects that, I confess, leave me in doubt. Handwriting in Italy changed less than in the north of Europe; because of this, it is often difficult to assign a date to an Italian manuscript based on the evidence of handwriting alone. Admittedly, there are details that suggest an earlier rather than a later origin, particularly some of the terminology used to describe colors and the process of etching, to which it also devotes a few paragraphs. For example, it mentions turnsole, a color source not noticed after the seventeenth century (and one referred to in the French manuscript account of about 1642); it also refers to etching on copper *or iron plates,* the latter being employed only very early in the history of etching. On the other hand, its reference to the dyes imported from America—cochineal, brazil and campeachy wood—imply that it was probably written after the middle of the seventeenth century, at the earliest.[10]

It is difficult to assess exactly where this account might

fit into the overall literature of marbling; nor can we even guess what impact it might have had on the exercise of the craft in Italy—most probably, it had little or none. Mrs. Merrifield relates that most of the manuscripts in her collection were monastic ones, having been compiled by monks who preserved the fine arts during the Dark Ages and promoted them in the Middle Ages that followed. Many of the early works on paintings were the work of ecclesiastics, as were the paintings themselves. She relates that the materials she extracted from one of the manuscripts (the sixteenth-century "Marciana Manuscript" in the Library of San Marco at Venice) relative to painting and the composition of varnishes were removed from a collection of recipes that the professors used in medicine, surgery, farriery, chemistry, painting, illuminating, gilding, stucco working, varnishing, and similar fields. These various recipes indicated to Merrifield that the manuscript, like many others, was compiled for convent use by some monk or lay brother, who presided over the infirmary, compounded the medicaments, and procured them.

While the evidence (or lack of evidence) of marbled paper in extant Italian bindings indicates that marbling did not exist on any appreciable scale on the Italian peninsula in early times—at least before the early or mid-eighteenth century—this manuscript shows that the craft might well have been conducted intermittently by interested individuals who met the local demand for decorated paper without any intention of sustaining production. But the manuscript may suggest even more. As previously noted, there is good reason to suspect that, around 1600, marbling entered Europe and Germany through Venice, where the Fuggers and other Europeans maintained trading contacts with the Islamic world. Thus, the discovery (or, more accurately, the rediscovery) of a manuscript such as this not only is another instance of early European interest in this art but, because of its Venetian origin, also provides us with a possible link in the transmission of the art from the Eastern to the Western world.

Marbling in Spain

The early eighteenth century witnessed profound changes in Europe, arising from what has been described as the first world conflict in modern history, the War of the Spanish Succession (1701–1714). The conflict was precipitated by the will of Charles II (who died childless on 1 November 1700), which decreed that the Duc d'Anjou, grandson of Louis XIV of France, become Philip V of Spain. As a result, Spain came under the rule of a Bourbon king and under the influence of French civil servants; with them came French ways. If this French influence had any bearing on the beginning of marbling in Spain such an influence exerted itself only at a later date. I have seen no evidence to indicate that marbling came to Spain before the middle of the eighteenth century, although, as was the case with Italy, it could have occurred slightly earlier. Spain, of all of the regions of continental Europe, was probably most important after France and Germany in support of marbling activity and the production of marbled paper (although by comparison, the effort was slight). Not only did it produce the famous "Spanish" pattern that continued to be made in other countries long after it had ceased to be made at home, but the Spanish, next to the French and Germans, most frequently came to employ marbled papers as endpapers in bookbindings.

As in Italy, marbling did not become part of the early bookbinding tradition of Spain; Spanish binders, unlike their Italian counterparts, almost never added French or German marbles as endpapers to books bound before the middle of the eighteenth century. Despite the assertion of Mrs. Loring and others that marbled papers of Spanish manufacture were used to decorate Spanish books from early in the seventeenth century, my own observations of Spanish bookbindings for many years have convinced me that the technique of marbling was unknown in that country in the seventeenth century.[11] As a matter of fact, Spanish marbling could not have begun much earlier than the middle of the eighteenth century. The later binding and rebinding of older books and the addition of marbled endpapers to these works upon their restoration fifty and even a hundred years or more after publication have led to dating errors and resulted in misattributions by those not fully versed in the traditions of the craft or in the history of bookbinding practice and design.[12]

Spanish marbled paper is most frequently found in bindings on Spanish imprints of the 1770s, 1780s, and later decades. The pattern invariably encountered prior to the early 1800s (and sometimes for a decade or two afterward) is the familiar Turkish one, but its appearance is quite different from that pattern made elsewhere. The colors used to decorate these papers have a distinctly Spanish flavor—light green, rose, a soft reddish brown or fawn, and blue. Papers so colored were inserted into bindings that also have a characteristic appearance and flavor—calf or sheepskin tooled in a typically Spanish manner, and toward the end of the eighteenth century, frequently with tree marbling on the covers as well.

The most distinctive and remarkable feature of Spanish marbling, in addition to the characteristic soft colors, is the appearance of a "waved" effect in the pattern; hence its name "Spanish." This distinctive effect was achieved through the method of laying the paper on the size. In authentic Spanish papers—that is, those made in Spain in the later eighteenth century and in the early years of the nineteenth—the waving is irregular and in wide bands, approaching, but not quite achieving, a moiré-like appearance. The waves almost seem to have been placed in a careless manner, without purpose or intent. But this aspect, instead of being a defect, along with the soft colors, gives Spanish paper its special charm. In the early decades of the nineteenth century, when the waved effect was going out of vogue in Spain itself, the Spanish pattern was taken up and imitated in Germany and England, where it became one of the most popular patterns for many decades. In these countries, however, and later in America as well, the waves lost their casual appearance, and were placed in the pattern in a regular, almost mechanical way. While one can appreciate these later "Spanish" papers for their perfection and skillful execution, they lack the spontaneity and charm of the authentic Spanish article, which can be a pure delight.

In the final edition of his classic marbling manual, *The Whole Art of Marbling,* Charles Woolnough provides us with two accounts of the possible origin of the traditional Spanish pattern.[13] The first supposes that a workman, after all of the colors had been thrown onto the size, got under the trough and shook it to produce an undulating surface. The second hypothesizes that a marbler who had been indulging too freely in strong drink came to work one morning with a trembling hand and unsteady nerves:

He could not hold a joint still, and alas! had neither money nor credit to get a drop more (just to steady him); so to work he must go as he was. But when he came to lay the paper down, his poor palsied hand shook so much that he spoiled (as he admitted) every sheet he tried. Some of this attracted the notice of the master, to whom the cause was explained, and the light thus thrown on the subject gave rise to further investigations and improvement, till at last the perfect development was obtained, and it became exceedingly popular, and brought in a very liberal remuneration.

Rosamond Loring retells both of these stories, the first with a slightly different twist.[14] Her account supposes that a man working at his marbling trough was about to lower a sheet of paper onto the gum when a fellow workman knocked against the trough with such force that the whole surface of the size was set in motion, bringing about the waved or moiré effect; the master of the establishment was so interested in this chance development that further study and experiments were made to perfect it.

All these accounts and versions strike me as contrived and romanticized. Many times in my own experience as a marbler, especially when working with thin paper, I have accidentally put irregular waves into a sheet when it slipped from my fingers and fell to the size in a helter-skelter fashion, or when the partly damp paper buckled and fell uncontrollably onto the colors. This kind of chance occurrence seems a far more likely explanation for the origin of the Spanish pattern than the imaginative stories carried down through oral tradition to Woolnough's time. And I believe that the use of thin paper played an important role in the development of the authentic Spanish design.[15] Regardless of its actual origin, the Spanish pattern became a popular one and continued to be made in Spain until the 1820s, when it was displaced by another pattern that was becoming popular in Europe, known as shell, or French shell.

I know of no literature on the origin or practice of marbling in Spain; nor has any technical literature developed there. The history outlined above, however, may be inferred from extant papers in old bindings. Such evidence also indicates that the art of marbling in Spain did not arise from the making of colored or fancy papers, or in concert with a paper coloring industry, for there is little evidence of the existence of such an industry in Spain. It seems more likely that Spanish marbling flourished solely for the benefit of the Spanish bookbinding community and that Spanish marblers came from the ranks of bookbinders, as in France. Enough craftsmen entered the profession and labored in sufficient numbers in the various centers of fine bookbinding (Madrid, Barcelona, Seville, etc.) to satisfy the demand for this product for perhaps a hundred years or so. This activity could not have been too extensive, however, for edge marbling is never seen on early Spanish bookbindings.

With the translation into Spanish of Louis Sébastian LeNormand's classic French bookbinding manual (to be discussed in detail later) and its publication in 1840 under the title *Manual del Encuadernador,* Spanish binders and other interested parties were provided with printed, though very basic, instructions, which would enable them to learn to decorate book edges and to make paper on their own.[16]

Portugal

Before leaving the Iberian peninsula, a few words about marbling in Portugal are in order, although this trade undoubtedly was not large and was late in its arrival. What slight knowledge I have on this topic was gained by examining Portuguese books and pamphlets in a few research libraries and from papers sent to me by a bookseller who deals mainly in Portuguese imprints. These Portuguese marbled papers were removed from their bindings in recent times and show distinct colors not identifiable as Spanish or other national types. Since they reappear time and again in Portuguese bindings from the last few decades of the eighteenth century and into the nineteenth, we may conclude that marbling was indeed carried on in Portugal at this time, but on a very small scale, for the frequency of their appearance overall was not great. I have also noticed in Portuguese books Portuguese papers that were decorated by means of stamp-

ing with metal plates or wooden blocks in the early nineteenth century. I have even collected a few samples In one example, block printing was done on a sheet of printer's waste with Portuguese text still visible. Apparently, then, some sort of colored-paper industry existed in this small country. Undoubtedly it was a very limited one; whether it had any connection with the Portuguese marbling trade, with regard to both output and size, is unknown.

The Netherlands

The history of marbling in the Netherlands has been placed later in this survey than would be expected because I have found no direct evidence that the craft actually was carried on in the Low Countries of Western Europe as early as 1675, as has been claimed. On the contrary, extant Dutch bookbindings indicate that the real beginnings of marbling in the Netherlands occurred more than a hundred years later, just after the turn of the nineteenth century. In any event, marbling in the regions populated by the Dutch never became important or considerable; and, if it was practiced at all in Holland in the seventeenth and eighteenth centuries, it was on a far more limited scale than in Italy or Spain. Even in the nineteenth century, as we shall see, the same holds true.

W. H. J. Weale and derivative commentators have claimed that the Dutch were the first people known to marble the edges of books—"an application of marbling that dates from about 1675," according to Mrs. Loring.[17] But, as we know from material introduced in the preceding chapter, the French had attended to this specialty long before that date and thus can claim priority. The sources that Weale, Loring, and, more recently, Doizy and Ipert, Easton, and others have relied on when attributing marbling in Holland to the late seventeenth century are twofold: one is a reference to the contemporaneous marbling of book edges in Holland in a work published in 1675; the other consists of a few documents discovered in the city archives of Amsterdam identifying two individuals of that period as "marblers." These two pieces of evidence must be scrutinized closely in order to determine exactly what they contribute to our understanding of early marbling in the Netherlands.

Weale, in his 1898 *Bookbindings and Rubbings in the Victoria and Albert Museum,* affirmed that the Dutch were the first to marble the edges of books (beginning in about 1675), and that they sometimes gilded or silvered the edges before marbling them;[18] he based his claim on information provided in the first edition of Johann Kunckel von Löwenstein's *Ars Vitraria Experimentalis.* Considering the time and place, the chemist Kunckel furnished an excellent description of the craft and its workings, discussing ten points in all. He talked first about the trough needed, then the combs, the gum tragacanth, and how to mix it properly. Next he discussed the use and handling of combs, and afterwards the colors, mainly what they were and how to mix them (his fifth, sixth, and seventh points). His eighth concern took notice of paper and how to handle it in the process, while the ninth described how it was finally coated with soap and polished. Kunckel's final point told how gold and silver could be applied to book edges by mixing in gum arabic—not too thick and not too thin (the metals assumedly were in powdered form). After commenting that one could not go wrong if he followed the foregoing directions, for he had done it many times himself, he ends his discussion with the statement that is critical to the matter under examination, namely:

Die Buchbinder können auch auff solche Art ihre Bücher auff den Schnitt bemahlen/ (gleich wie ich in Holland gesehen) ist was neues/ und siehet/ wañ sonderlich Gold un Silber drunter komt/ überaus anmuthig aus[,]

which may be translated as:

Bookbinders can also paint over the edges of their books in such a way (just as I have seen done in Holland), it is the latest thing, and in cases where gold and silver are applied underneath, it is exceedingly charming.

One hesitates to challenge an authority such as Kunckel, but his assertion presents us with a puzzle, for, as I have maintained, late-seventeenth-century Dutch bindings with marbled edge decoration simply are not in evidence, at least in my experience. Good Dutch books of that period are bound sturdily but plainly, usually (the better ones) in white tawed vellum over thick pasteboards, with minimal ornamental stamping, usually in blind, and without ornamental endpapers and other gaudy decoration. Later, when calf- and sheepskin came more to be used and the spines (but less often the covers), were elaborately gilded, binders occasionally inserted marbled endpapers. The combed pattern, however, with or without curls, almost invariably was used (the type that came from German and French shops), and the edges were almost always left blank. When edge decoration did infrequently occur, it took the form of solid red or blue staining, of sprinkling, of simply decorating the edges by the paste-color method (see Plate XVI, example 5), or sometimes through gauffering or gilding.

Phoebe Jane Easton apparently was the first to take notice in print of the pertinent marbling-related documents in the Amsterdam city archives; she perhaps was led to them by an abstract in the Dutch Royal Library regarding one Sijmon Egbertsz Visscher.[19] This document noted that Visscher had received the possessions of his mother as her only heir, and it listed his occupation as "marbled papermaker."[20] Easton also reports that the Amsterdam archives contained the 1682 betrothal record of Abraham Cajeweile, who was similarly described. At first glance these documents seem to offer proof that marbling took place in Holland at this time, but we must recall that in this early period the term "marbler" was used in Germany and nearby regions to describe not the artisan who marbled paper in the classical manner, but the maker of decorated papers that were produced through the use of stencils and stamping devices made of wood and metal. "Real" marblers preferred to call themselves makers of Turkish paper. Thus, it seems reasonable to believe, Visscher and Cajeweile were the kind of craftsmen who would have been classed in France as "dominotiers" rather than "marbreurs."

We must acknowledge, nonetheless, the possibility that marbling activity could have been going on in Amsterdam or perhaps elsewhere in Holland during this period. Whatever may have occurred, however, was short-lived or self-limiting, for my research indicates that marbling trade or industry did not exist in the Netherlands even in the eighteenth century. (Sometimes the marbling activity in a given area, or even in an entire country, was the effort of one individual; when he stopped marbling, activity in that region ceased as well.) We must also concede that there was a Dutch literature on marbling at this time, albeit a minuscule one. Such information was available in the *Naturrlyk Tover-Boek* (published under the pseudonym Simon Witgeest), a work that was in print from 1684 on, and also in the 1686 Amsterdam edition of Antonio Neri's *De Arte Vitraria,* within Christopher Merrett's notes.

Again, I must emphasize that a great deal of the confusion regarding early marbling in the Netherlands results from the loose use of the term "Dutch" by the English in their marbling literature. For instance, in a review article of Charles Woolnough's classic manual that appeared in the *Journal of the [Royal] Society of Arts* in 1853, it was reported (based on Woolnough's account) that "the art of marbling is believed to date from the beginning of the seventeenth century, and its discovery is attributed to the Dutch."[21] Of course, it was the Germans and not their neighbors in Holland or other Netherlandish regions who introduced marbling into Western Europe around the year 1600. As for another of Woolnough's statements, to the effect that marbled paper first came into England wrapped around Dutch toys, we have already noticed Loring's observation that these "Dutch" toys in reality had originated in Nürnberg and other German locations.

My examination of several large research collections of Dutch printings of the seventeenth, eighteenth, and nineteenth centuries, as well as general observation of such materials on a long-term basis turned up no evidence that the Dutch made marbled papers before the beginning of the nineteenth century, and that even then they did so on a rather casual basis. When marbled paper is found in

Dutch bindings of the seventeenth and eighteenth century and, more frequently, afterward, it proves to be German or French in origin. The fact that the Dutch served as traders of German and French manufactured goods indicates how readily available this commodity must have been to any Dutch binder who chose to use it. In addition to availability, the high quality and reasonable price of the German and French marbles undoubtedly stifled efforts on the part of the Netherlanders to produce their own marbled paper—a situation, we have seen, not uncommon in Europe in these early times.

Only on nineteenth-century Dutch imprints do we encounter marbled decoration that can be judged as Dutch in origin. When one does see an occasional edge decoration on Dutch imprints and bookbindings before that time, it is almost invariably of the paste-color variety, similar to the example of the Nürnberg printing shown on Plate XI. Eighteenth-century Dutch bindings with marbled edges are not entirely unknown, as the recent discovery of one such example demonstrates (Plate XVI), but they are so unusual that it causes one's head to turn not twice but three or four times. Although the marbled decoration on these infrequent finds is usually inferior and often primitive, it demonstrates that every now and then a Dutch binder of this period did try his hand at dressing up the edges of some of his better work in the most traditional manner.[22]

From the middle of the eighteenth century, and more frequently in the nineteenth century, bookbinders and other craftsmen began to divulge the secrets of their trades in manuals and similar publications. Some of the information in this literature included details on marbling to assist bookbinders in decorating the edges of their work. Graham Pollard and Esther Potter's list of early bookbinding manuals indicates that in as early as 1790 a Dutch bookbinding manual appeared in Holland: M. van Loopik's *Volkomen Handleiding tot de Boekbind-konst*, published at Gouda.[23] Since I have been unable to locate a copy of this work, I cannot say what information, if any, it contained on marbling. But in 1806 Hendrik de Haas of Dordrecht issued a Dutch manual on bookbinding, *De Boekbinder, of Volledige Beschrijving van Al het Gene Wat Tot Deze Konst Betrekking Heeft*, which does tell us something about the contemporary state of marbling in the Low Countries.[24]

De Haas devotes four and a half pages to "het marmeren on de snede"—marbling on the edges. The information he provides strongly reinforces my impression about the infrequent conduct of the marbler's craft in the Netherlands in early times and even in de Haas's day. De Haas begins by noting that edge decoration is not used in his country as much as it could be, mainly because it is considered more a fad than a necessity. If Dutch binders had local access to workshops where marbled paper was made, they simply could send their books out to be marbled, as was done in France. As an alternative, de

Haas goes on to provide directions for useful ways to color book edges. His discussion summarizes two methods: one, for covering book edges with paste and color, with designs worked onto them with the finger or in other ways, and the other, for sprinkling. De Haas says nothing in his book on the subject of classical marbling or on dipping books onto a bath.

The Pollard-Potter checklist records two other Dutch bookbinding works, probably published in the period between 1820 and 1840, that contained information on marbling. Neither is dated, and Pollard merely assigns them to the early nineteenth century. One (known only through a catalog listing, no copy having been found) is a Dutch translation of Ernst Wilhelm Greve's manual of 1822, and if it actually was printed, its publication would date after that time.[25] The other, entitled *Geheimen der Boekbinderij*, or "secrets of bookbinding," is a fifteen-page pamphlet located by Pollard and Potter only in the private collection of English bookbinder and bookbinding historian Bernard Middleton, who has kindly sent me a photocopy. This anonymous work (its author merely identifies himself as "B . . . .") does indeed contain a section devoted to the marbling of book edges, providing about two pages of rather standard directions.[26] These call for adding linseed oil and stale beer to the four colors (indigo, yellow, green, and black), and, of course, gall. Because it is similar to other manuals that date later in the first half of the nineteenth century, it seems likely that this work was issued in the 1830s or 1840s; this conclusion is reinforced by the appearance of its type and the layout and form of its title page.

In this same period, another book was published that revealed the techniques of marbling to Dutch bookbinders so that they could color their book edges and, perhaps, decorate paper as well. This was a Dutch translation of Louis Sébastien LeNormand's popular French bookbinding manual that had initially appeared fifteen years earlier.[27] In 1861 another such work followed: a Dutch translation of Ludwig Brade and E. Winkler's *Illustriertes Buchbinderbuch*, issued just a year after the first edition had been published at Stuttgart. This book contained a much fuller account of the marbling process than had any other work appearing previously in the Netherlands.[28]

As for the actual conduct of marbling in Holland and the Low Countries, the scant information we have comes from a much later time. At the end of the nineteenth century, Josef Halfer of Budapest (whom we shall meet again later in this work) began to experiment and publish information on the classical form of marbling, but along new lines that he had introduced. Before long, his efforts revived interest in the technique that had been on the wane for some decades; he and his agents abroad arranged to manufacture marbling colors and the other materials needed to carry on his new style of marbling. At the same time, they published a number of small instruction booklets to assist beginners in using these colors and learning to marble. One such publication was issued in England by the Hostmann Printing Ink Company under the title *The Art of Marbling and the Treatment of the New Bronze Colors. A Practical Guide to Marbling by Halfer's Method.*[29] In a section of this pamphlet entitled "History of the Art of Marbling," Halfer was quoted:

According to the "Journal für Buchbinderei," the cradle of the art of marbling was apparently in France. But during my journey to France, undertaken in 1898, I was much disappointed. I went there full of expectation, but found marbling in such a neglected state that it scarcely seemed possible that that country saw its beginnings. In Belgium it received more attention; but, unfortunately, the colors there are very bad. In Holland, however, where I lectured for several months, marbling is exceptionally well cultivated.

Halfer's comment on the cultivation of marbling in Holland at the turn of the twentieth century undoubtedly referred to the new activity that his own efforts had sparked among enthusiasts and amateurs rather than to any prolonged or professional industry carried over from an earlier time. This new interest and enthusiasm resulted in the publication in 1899 (or 1900) of a Dutch translation of a marbling manual by Halfer's leading exponent, Josef Hauptmann,[30] and, later, the publication of another manual based on Halferian principles, J. Van Wingerden's *Geschiedenis der Marmerkunst.*[31] Van Wingerden's undated pamphlet, which constitutes the first real Dutch manual on the art and which, doubtless, appeared early in the present century, is imbued with pure Halferian methods and principles. Not only does it closely follow the style and substance of the Hostmann Printing Ink Company's 1906 instructional booklet on marbling—even discussing the use of the new bronze colors, it also makes reference to the work of Josef Halfer of Budapest (p. 6) and Josef Hauptmann of Gera (p. 18).

Belgium

According to Paul Kersten's survey article on the history of colored paper, the colored-paper industry in Belgium was established at Turnhout by workers from the Aschaffenburg factory, presumably in the 1830s.[32] Turnhout, a village about twenty miles northeast of Antwerp, became well known for the manufacture of lace and, in the eighteenth century, for wallpaper and other kinds of colored paper. But here the manufacture of colored paper, including probably the production of some marbled paper, never approximated the proportions of the enormous industry that was established in Germany.

In their brief discussion of the mass-production of colored paper in Germany and Belgium, Marie-Ange

Doizy and Stéphane Ipert have also observed the activity that went on at Turnhout; they mention the firm of Brepols, a producer of fancy papers, which obtained a silver medal at the Brussels exhibition in 1835 and which by 1850 was exporting decorated papers throughout the world.[33] In his history of bookbinding in Belgium, H. Dubois D'Enghien discusses marbled paper briefly and in passing, mentioning styles that were used by Flemish and Belgian binders in the eighteenth and nineteenth centuries.[34] (Undoubtedly, before the early nineteenth century they had used French or German productions.) With regard to the making of colored paper in Belgium, he reports that production was carried on long before the early nineteenth century, but that its manufacture became more and more extensive from that time on.[35] Producers D'Enghien names include Brepols and Dierkx, and Glenisson and Van Genechten of Turnhout; Gambard de Courval of Coutrai; and Hemeleers and Vandelaer of Brussels. He singles out M. Glenisson et fils as displaying fine examples of papier d'Annonay as well as agate and shaded types at the Brussels exposition of 1862, and relates that M. Van Genechten also showed fine agate papers on that occasion.

Much of the fancy-paper production that occurred in Belgium focused on the manufacture of non-marbled colored papers and, after 1840, on the production of wallpaper printed on large rolls of paper. While most of the output of the Belgian colored-paper industry was destined for home and industrial purposes rather than for use by the hand bookbinder (as was increasingly the case with materials that came from the Aschaffenburg empire), a very small part of its production nonetheless was paper of the marbled and pseudo-marbled variety that was produced specifically for bookbinding decoration. This fact is confirmed by D'Enghien's notice above, and from a small pattern book of the Brepols and Dierkx firm now preserved in the Royal Library in the Hague, which shows marbled patterns corresponding to some of those produced at Aschaffenburg and seemingly dates to the late nineteenth or early twentieth century.

Denmark

Toward or after the middle of the eighteenth century, the art of marbling migrated to the great Scandinavian peninsula of northern Europe and came to be practiced in Denmark and Sweden, in what order we cannot say. Illustrations in Sofus Larsen and Anker Kyster's 1930 treatise, *Danish Eighteenth Century Bindings,* show that marbling was indeed carried on in the more southerly country, Denmark, after the middle of the eighteenth century, for they reproduce on one of their plates some Danish bindings with marbling on their edges, a sure indication of native manufacture.[36] While these authors doubt the existence of an industry in Denmark in the eighteenth century that could have paralleled those in

France and Germany for the making of colored papers in general and marbled ones in particular, the evidence of marbling on the edges of some of their productions indicates that some Danish binders did apply themselves to marbling. Larsen and Kyster note that the styles of some of these early craftsmen—the binder G. J. Liebe, for example—were so individualistic that various marbled endpapers sometimes allowed them to determine who had produced various unsigned bindings in question.

Plate IX of *Danish Eighteenth Century Bindings* illustrates, as examples of decorative papers found in such bindings, three Herrnhut paste papers; the first figure on Plate X of that volume shows a marbled paper that is of German origin. Two more decorated papers, French or German, are shown beneath it, and other foreign papers appear on succeeding plates. These illustrations are proof of the Danes' strong dependence on foreign products for high quality book decoration during this time. Some Danish binders of the eighteenth century were emigrant Germans; later, a number of Danish binders drifted south during their learning and apprenticeship years to acquire new techniques, widen their experience, and improve their skills. In so doing, they obviously encountered the use of marbling in book decoration and, in a few cases, acquired knowledge of the marbling technique or taught themselves after their return home. Plates VII and VIII of Larsen and Kyster's book show native bookbindings with edge marbling as well as paste-paper decoration, which indicate attempts by local craftsmen to dress up their better work and prove beyond doubt that marbling and the making of paste papers occurred in Denmark at this time.

Not long ago, I viewed some of the bookbindings preserved in the Royal Library in Copenhagen, where curators over the years, building on Larsen and Kyster's pioneering efforts, have identified additional works of prominent Danish bookbinders of the eighteenth century. As a result, I had access to many shelves full of such bindings, ranging from those done early in the eighteenth century to work executed in the early decades of the following century. The first bookbinder in Denmark to use marbled paper in his work was Johann Boppenhausen, who was born about 1666, obtained his master's certificate in 1703, and died in 1740. Boppenhausen, a German craftsman who migrated to Denmark, produced some beautiful work during his long residence there, and was succeeded by Johan Christoph Boppenhausen (1708–1751) who achieved the rank of master in 1732, and Jacob Wilhelm Boppenhausen (1710–1761) who obtained his master's in 1733. The bindings of the Boppenhausens show the influence of contemporary German and English styles. Although all these binders used German and French marbled paper and Dutch gilt paper for endpapers, there is no evidence that they were directly involved in marbling.

The Lymens were another early Danish family of good bookbinders, including Andreas, the father (who achieved the rank of master about 1690 and died about 1728) and his sons Peter (1695–1768) and Andreas F. (1700–1767). The work of these craftsmen is often indistinguishable from that of the Boppenhausens, for they all used the same tools and styles, as well as many of the same kinds of decorated paper. The Lymens most often used the French "commun" paper, with small curls and with the color blue predominating (the dominant pattern produced in France from about the 1730s on.)

It is in the work of Georg Julius Liebe (who was born in 1710, obtained his master's certificate in 1734, and died in 1778) that we begin to notice the presence of native marbling, for many of his bindings not only display edge decoration but also contain endpapers of the same marbled design, indicating that Liebe had learned the techniques for marbling paper and book edges. Liebe, who Larsen and Kyster note "travelled abroad on behalf of his trade," appears to have executed his marbling in the 1750s and 1760s, producing beautiful, often brilliant, imitations of Turkish-style papers than being made in great numbers in Germany, as well as the old French "placard" pattern, which at that time was no longer manufactured in France itself (see plate X.1 in the Larsen-Kyster history and Plate XVI, number 6 in this volume). While at the Royal Library, I examined more than two dozen of Liebe's bookbindings, not only with marbling on their edges but with his marbled paper in many as well.

Another of the Danish binders of this period who apparently made his own marbled paper was August Heinrich Helmuth (born 1714, master's certificate 1740). Helmuth worked for Liebe; he produced the same German pattern as Liebe and also French combed and placard patterns; some of his bindings show edge marbling as well. Helmuth's colors are softer or lighter than Liebe's, and his combed patterns show a tendency to drift; that is, the combed colors did not hold their original position but moved to the left or to the right on the size (which usually occurs when the size is too thin). Helmuth died in 1777, but another binder who cannot be identified (but who was probably trained by Helmuth) continued to produce marbled decoration until the end of the century. With this anonymous craftsman's passing, marbling in the Danish realm ended for a very long time.

In the period before 1800 other good binders at work in Denmark used imported French marbled papers in their work. Jørgen Piper (who obtained his master's certificate in 1761 and died in 1765) and Johan Tobias Wilhelmi (1713–1798) were two such craftsmen. In the period after 1800, Danish binders employed mainly German marbled paper, which, with the growth of the German factories, was becoming common throughout all of the European regions. Anker Kyster, who taught himself to marble (and to make paste and other decorated papers as well), reintroduced the art of marbling into Denmark in the 1890s; his efforts will be noted later in this survey.

Sweden

Sweden is yet another country where marbling came into being at or about the middle of the eighteenth century. This is indicated in its bookbinding literature, as put forth in Avarvid Hedberg's 1960 publication, *Stockholms Bokbindare, 1460–1880*,[37] and expanded in Sten G. Lindberg's 1980 catalog of an exhibition of eighty-nine master binders, which was issued in conjunction with the 350th anniversary of the guild of master binders in Sweden.[38] Dr. Lindberg devoted a few of the 270 pages in this catalog to marbled and decorated endpapers, and in a letter sent to me in 1982 he elaborated on the information he had provided there.[39]

It is evident that when foreign bindings containing marbled and other types of decorated papers came to their attention, leading binders in Sweden were as quick as those in Denmark and elsewhere to make use of them to enhance the quality of their work; this is especially true of binders working for the royalty and nobility. And, as Lindberg notes, such binders especially employed marbled paper to cover the patents and privileges granted to their noble and upper-class patrons.

As was the case in Denmark, much of this paper, particularly in early times, came from the south. Lindberg's catalog tells of the use of the combed pattern by Christoffer Schneidler in the early eighteenth century, and he conjectures that in time Schneidler may have manufactured his own marbled paper. He says the same of Fredrik Wilhelm Statlander, who worked in Stockholm at the end of the eighteenth and in the early part of the nineteenth centuries, for his bindings show papers with varied Turkish patterns.

In his 1982 letter, Lindberg (who afterwards retired from the Swedish Royal Library) wrote of newly discovered information about the manufacture of marbled papers by the "gold-hammer-smith" (goldbeater) Johan Holgren at Stockholm in the 1774 period: "I have been quite certain that our most prominent binders in earlier times have made their own endpaper [sic.], such as Chr. Schneidler and Statlander in the 18th century and many more in the 19th." Both his 1980 catalog and the Hedberg history contain information that positively establishes the manufacture of marbled paper in Sweden by M. F. Åkerdahl, who in the year 1831 published a sheet or pattern card of twenty-four samples of marbled and decorated papers; Lindberg indicates that his range soon expanded. Of the samples on the pattern card, four were of the paste paper variety and five were marbled. In a recent conversation, Lindberg informed me that this pattern card is known in but a single copy, owned by one of the binder's descendants, and he was not able to obtain a photograph for reproduction.

On the occasion that I visited the Danish Royal Library in Copenhagen, I also went to the Swedish Royal Library in Stockholm, where I was permitted to examine its large collection of Swedish printings of the seventeenth and eighteenth centuries. While none dating from the earlier period contained edge decoration, I removed from the shelves for closer examination more than a dozen eighteenth-century volumes that were so decorated. The imprints on seven of these works dated to the 1740s and 1750s, with one earlier (but undoubtedly bound later) and the remainder of the 1760–1780 decades. All, presumably, had been bound by Christoffer (or Christoph) Schneidler, whose career spanned the 1746–1787 period, and all contained similar edge decoration: swirls of red and dark blue with the swirls overlapping, indicating that these colors had been applied in non-marbled ways, possibly by stamping or some other method. All these volumes contained marbled endpapers, most of them Dutch or combed patterns, but two showed a version of the old French placard pattern combed in a rather odd way. (The placard pattern, as noted before, was not made in France after the 1730s or 1740s.) Although it is possible that Schneidler could have effected the marbled decoration in these volumes, I found no definite evidence that this was the case.

Afterward I examined a number of bindings on the *Svenska Akademiens Handlinger* (which had been published at the end of the eighteenth and early in the nineteenth centuries) that were said to be the work of Fredrik Wilhelm Statlander (active from 1780 to 1830). Nicely bound in beautiful red morocco, they contained marbled endpapers that gave every indication of being produced by Statlander. They were mostly spot patterns in the contemporary English style, with red, yellow, and black vein colors, sometimes drawn into streaks, and with blue or green spots serving as the ground colors. The marbling was not nearly so well done as in England, with the spots often too large or the colors cloyed. And yet these papers had a certain originality about them that indicated Swedish manufacture, unlike anything being produced elsewhere in Europe at approximately the same time.

I also visited the Nordiska Museet, the museum of Swedish folk arts, in an attempt to locate papers decorated by the goldbeater Johan Holgren which were said to be there. The collection of Holgren's papers, unfortunately, could not be located; but Mr. Lindberg subsequently informed me that Holgren did not marble and only made brocade or Dutch gilt papers—a more likely occupation for an artisan who hammered gold into thin leaves for gilding. While there, however, I was able to confirm that marbling actually had taken place in Sweden after the middle of the eighteenth century. In the museum's Anders Berch collection of proof papers dating from about the middle of the eighteenth century was a small collection of marbled and other types of decorated papers made by Lorns Walter Rothof dating to 1754 and described in a contemporary note as having been made at Alingsås (near Göteborg). Rothof is identified as a "magister," or teacher, in a local account of Alingsås, but I could find no other information about him.

The Swedish East India Company, which was established in the 1730s, erected factories at Alingsås for the manufacture of products to trade and sell. Called "mixed factories," they produced all sorts of useful products—furniture, clothes, household items and so on, and likewise decorated paper. The length and extent of Rothof's activity of this kind, and the nature of his connection to the company's factories, is unknown. Among the papers that he made or decorated, according to those now preserved in the Berch collection, were marbled, Dutch gilt, paste, sprinkled, and stained or monochrome papers—in fact, most of the types being turned out in Germany at that time. Among proofs of his marbled papers were found the standard eighteenth-century combed "Dutch" pattern, both with and without curls; spot patterns that were not well executed; and the placard design, approximately the same pattern observed in the Schneidler bindings in the Royal Library. Because of this similarity, it is certainly within the realm of possibility that Schneidler used paper made by Rothof or by another Swedish marbler and did not actually engage in marbling himself. As a matter of fact, the lack of true marbling on the edges of his creations lends credence to this supposition. It is not possible to be authoritative about this, however, for Lindberg's belief that Schneidler actually did marble cannot be discounted. His opinion as a library curator, coming from many years of observation and experience, will have to be respected until absolute proof to the contrary is found.

Elsewhere in Europe

When we look elsewhere in Europe to establish where marbling might have been practiced, we are less fortunate in attempts to find the kind of evidence that exists in Scandinavia and other countries. We can instead only hypothesize about the presence in indigenous bindings of marbled paper that also appears to be native. To take but one example, the idiosyncratic appearance of marbled papers in many Swiss imprints in the period between 1750 and 1800 leads me to suspect that marbling was carried on in at least one of the cantons at that time. For when one looks at works printed at Basel, Lucerne, or other Swiss locations and sees marbled papers with a certain coloration reappearing again and again (but not in volumes published elsewhere), suspicions are indeed aroused. Because Swiss books were printed for the most part in French or German, they usually appear on library shelves with French or German volumes, grouped according to language rather than geographical origin. Thus, one does not find in the large European and American research libraries Swiss imprints conveniently located in one area for examination. Nor was I able to gain access to book stacks in Swiss libraries, where I might have examined large numbers of Swiss imprints and bindings that had

not been scattered or disturbed; and so we must let the matter rest for the time being. We can only hope that one day this subject will be considered by future historians of paper and Buntpapier and be settled once and for all. On the other hand, we must not discount the possibility that Switzerland's proximity to both France and Germany discouraged native production of marbled and decorated papers, at least to any appreciable extent. Indeed, I have already quoted the *Vollkommene Papierfärber* to the effect that large amounts of marbled paper were being exported from Germany to Switzerland early in the nineteenth century.

Proximity to major sources of supply flowing out of the Bavarian factories also played a role in discouraging marbling by bookbinders and others in Austria in the eighteenth and early nineteenth centuries; there simply was little need for anyone in Austria to marble. An examination of part of the 15,000-volume library of Prince Eugene of Saxony (1663–1736), preserved intact in the Austrian National Library in Vienna, proves that Austrian as well as German bookbinders availed themselves of a superior product. Here can be found beautifully bound volumes decorated in the "extra" style, with marbled papers in them that show distinctly German manufacture. (Such libraries are exceptions to the lack of interest in fine bookbindings that most German book collectors and large libraries at this early time display.) I have seen no evidence of native marbling in Austria proper in the eighteenth century or before.

In the nineteenth century, however, almost imperceptible changes took place. The existence of factory production (approximating the Aschaffenburg model) at about the middle of the nineteenth century is demonstrated by the Koninklijke Bibliotheek's large pattern book (again equivalent to similar Aschaffenburg productions) from the Knepper'schen Buntpapier und Oberwaltersdorfer Maschinen Papier Fabrik at Vienna. It contains 306 pages and thousands of samples of Buntpapier, including all sorts of printed and decorated papers, paste papers (referred to therein as "Herrnhut papers," see Chapter 3), and marbled papers. Turkish, combed, "Stormont" and shell patterns—the types most popular in the early nineteenth century—appear here, along with "pseudo-marbled" papers that were developed over succeeding decades, lending the volume an overall appearance that places its publication date at about the middle of the century, or perhaps the 1840s, at earliest. The copy in the Dutch Royal Library, the only one that I have ever seen, contains Albert Haemmerle's manuscript note that it was issued before 1860.

Recent attempts to locate information about this Viennese factory in the Austrian National Library in Vienna and elsewhere have proved unsuccessful. We might well speculate, however, that because this so-far unique volume found its way into the collection preserved at the Royal Library in the Hague, along with many marbling manuals, pattern books, and original marbled papers from the Aschaffenburg works, the Viennese factory may have been part of or had some connection with the Dessauer empire. The great number and variety of samples mounted into this volume, and the fact that the firm was listed on the stock exchange, as its title implies,[40] suggests that it probably employed hundreds of workers whose production was sufficient to supply the needs of most Austrian homes, industries, and bookbinders.

There may have been (and probably were) other areas of Europe where the craft was carried on in the eighteenth and especially the nineteenth centuries; however, such activity remains unrecorded or, at least, has passed unnoticed. Norway could be one such place, as well as Hungary (especially Prague), and it is possible that the craft was attempted even in Russia, probably by emigrant German bookbinders who had relocated beyond sources of supply. With regard to Russia, I have noticed now and then St. Petersburg imprints of the late eighteenth or early nineteenth centuries containing crudely marbled papers, mostly of the combed variety, indicating that marbling activity in Russia was more than a mere possibility. All available evidence, however, tends to argue that the large amount of decorated paper exported by the German factories throughout Europe made such attempts only occasional or sporadic. We can only hope future researchers will attempt to seek out any such activity and put their findings on the record.

6

The Initial British Experience

E shall now follow the migration of the craft across the English Channel. The beginning of a marbling industry in the British Isles was probably an expression of the same momentum that was responsible for the introduction of the technique into Italy, Spain, and other European countries. Indeed, the events that we shall be reviewing next might be considered as a microcosm of what was going on in other parts of Europe. However, we shall see that the English experience with marbling was also very different from that of the rest of Europe. first of all, it took fifty years or so for marbling to reach production level in England after the first serious attempts had been undertaken. Secondly, once achieved, marbling became a far more important industry in Britain than it did in these other countries. It may even be said that in English book circles marbling attained something of the status of a mania, for after Germany and France, Britain came to be the region most prolific and most important to the production of marbled paper in the world, with a special fascination for marbled decoration. Moreover, marbling continued to be carried on industrially in the British Isles long after its popularity had peaked in the two lands that had been responsible for its birth in Europe.

Although the technique of marbling had attracted the attention of Francis Bacon as early as 1627, as well as John Evelyn in 1662 and Robert Boyle before 1664, there is little evidence that marbling was attempted in Great Britain in the seventeenth century except on an experimental or trial basis. Notices of marbling in the early literature, including Evelyn's actual demonstration of the process to the Royal Society in 1662, were largely attempts to satisfy scientific curiosity or explanations of this new and mysterious phenomenon in the light of current interest in alchemy or protochemistry. Again, marbled papers preserved in English bindings of the late 1700s and early 1800s give no indication of native production; they show that English binders used German and French papers to dress up the insides of their "extra" bindings—those executed mainly for royalty and nobility—or as cover papers on half calf or even cheaper half sheepskin bindings. And while edge marbling has been noticed infrequently on the edges of English bindings of the later seventeenth century, its poor, watery quality is indicative of failed attempts rather than successful conclusions.

Fortunately, Great Britain, unlike the countries previously reviewed, has a fairly extensive literature on the subject of marbling, a wealth of information that cannot be attributed solely to the fact that we are dealing with a language that is more familiar to us. Because the art arrived in Britain at a later date, it coincided with the development of a marbling literature that had begun in the later eighteenth century and matured in the nineteenth, especially with regard to helping bookbinders learn to marble for the purpose of edge decoration. Indeed, with respect to later developments, it was the English who led the way and thus gave us more information on what was happening in their land. Additionally, the British looked on the establishment of a marbling industry and trade as a desirable goal, one worthy of promotion; some individuals actively did promote it, and a number of their records have survived.

Attempts to marble paper continuously and for practical purposes—that is, for use in bookbinding and not just on an experimental basis or as a curiosity—can be said to have begun in England in 1731, when, on 20 May, Samuel Pope was granted patent number 530 for marbling. This privilege related to the use of marbled decoration to prevent forgery; as Pope alone would be empowered to marble, only bank notes and other paper instruments containing his special ornamentation could be considered authentic. Pope's petition, first printed in the *Abridgements of Specifications Relating to Printing, Etc.* in 1859, is of such interest that it requires quotation here in full.[1] In his petition Pope explained

> that the practice of counterfeiting of bank and other notes, &c. at this time appears very notorious, to the great detriment of the trade and comerce of this kingdom, and that the making use of paper marbled with a margent for merchants notes, bills of exchange, companys notes or bonds, receipts for subscripcons, or any other instruments that admit of a cheque, being generally allowed to be the most effectual remedy to prevent so great an evil, he [the patentee] has, by long study and great industry, invented and brought to perfection

a new art of marbling paper with a margent,[2] never practised by any person whatsoever before he invented it, which is performed by a method entirely new by taking off the colours from a body of water prepared after a particular manner, with a proper strength for supporting the said colours and make them flow upon the surface [of] it, whereby the said colours are more easily taken off upon paper, which will be of very great service to the publick by preventing the counterfeiting of all such notes, bills, bonds, &c.

Phoebe Jane Easton refers to Pope's patent as something of a curiosity because, she points out, there is no record of anybody actually caught forging or tampering with English bank notes until 1758, when the Stafford linen draper Richard William Vaughan was found guilty and executed at Tyburn for his crime amid much publicity, and because Pope's scheme was never used in England due to its expense.[3] Nevertheless, the wording of Pope's petition, and even the fact that he presented it and received his patent, is indication enough that something foul was going on in the realm. The passing of false money and commercial instruments, it would seem, was a constant problem in the English monetary and financial systems. There are many extant documents signed by Sir Isaac Newton relating to the coining of counterfeit money, and imprisonment for doing so, during his term as warden and then master of the mint (a sinecure granted to him after his second nervous breakdown in 1693 and which left him a rich man upon his death in 1727). Pope's patent only makes mention of commercial instruments—bills of exchange, company notes and bonds, subscription receipts, and the notes of private banks. By "bank note," Pope assumedly did not imply money as the term later came to be used when national and central banking developed, but a promissary note given by a banker, as the *Oxford English Dictionary* defines the term, and illustrates it with early literary allusions.

In 1978 Geoffrey Wakeman published, from his small private press in Leicestershire, a little work entitled *English Marbled Paper, a Documentary History*, in which he described a large number of the publications and documents relating to English marbling from its formative period until modern times. "By the eighteenth century," Wakeman wrote, "marbling was undoubtedly being practiced in England," and while we shall see that this statement is true, it requires qualification.[4] It must be emphasized that marbling was not achieved in England over night; it took nearly half a century after Pope's patent was issued for marbling to come to fruition, for the art really did not fully blossom in Britain until the 1770s, at which time large and continuous production was finally achieved. Prior attempts to marble—and there were more than a few—can be categorized as sporadic and experimental. Before considering events leading up to final achievement, we must first examine the scant literature that appeared in England between 1700 and 1755; specifically, those works that were available to help a ready and willing Englishman learn how to marble.

English Literature on Marbling in the Early Eighteenth Century

Brief descriptions of the marbling process were available in England early in the eighteenth century from reissued editions of William Salmon's *Polygraphice*, in the *Modern Curiosities of Nature* and the *Curiosa Arcana* attributed to Nicolas Lemery, and in John White's *Art Treasury*, as well as through John Evelyn's more extensive account republished in the 1727 edition of John Houghton's *Husbandry and Trade Improv'd*. White's outline was circulated further through its reprinting in two publications that came out in the year 1735, John Barrow's *Dictionarium Polygraphicum: or, The Whole Body of Arts Regularly Digested*[5] and a small work with an overly large title (typical of that period), abbreviated here as *The Gentleman's Companion; or, Tradesman's Delight*, issued anonymously at London.[6]

A somewhat original description appeared in the second (1738) edition of Ephraim Chambers's *Cyclopaedia; or, An Universal Dictionary of Arts and Sciences*.[7] The unknown individual who assembled the succinct, but reasonably thorough, description of marbling that appears in this and several successive editions gave as his source Kircher, Merrett, and Houghton (i.e., Evelyn). When Abraham Rees took over the complete revision of Chambers's encyclopedia and reissued it in five volumes in 1778–1788, the description was slightly rewritten and extensively enlarged, but it retained some of the originality of the earlier version.[8]

It was with the publication in 1738 of another book, entitled *The Laboratory, or School of Arts*, that the first really worthwhile description of the marbling technique was made known to Englishmen, though in all it amounted to only about 800 words and was barely longer than the account printed in Chambers's work. *The Laboratory, or School of Arts* also had a lengthy subtitle, and its title page related that it was "translated from the high Dutch" (i.e., German) and illustrated with copperplates.[9] One, depicting the marbling process and some of its actual implements and reprinted as Figure 8 here, was the first illustration relating to marbling to appear anywhere in the world. *The Laboratory, or School of Arts* went through at least nine editions between 1738 and 1810, appearing in reprintings in 1739, 1740, 1750, 1755, 1756 (twice, by different publishers), 1770, 1799, and 1800, which attests to its popularity.[10]

Little is known about the author of this work, the "G. Smith" whose name appears on later editions. (The British Library catalog records his first name as "Godfrey," while the American *National Union Catalogue* and some

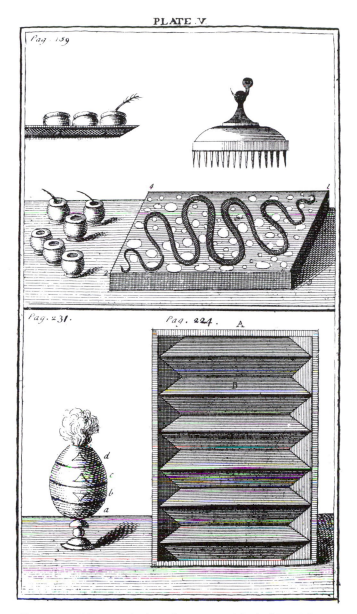

FIGURE 8. Plate V of *The Laboratory, or School of Arts*. The upper half, illustrating the discussion on marbling, is the first illustration of marbling to appear in print. Reproduced from the 1740 edition.

Werck-Schul of 1705 (and perhaps later) first comes to mind, as there was only a limited amount of material available in German at this early time; and, as a matter of fact, some of Smith's text is strikingly similar to a rough translation I made of the marbling sections of that work. Smith's instructions, however, do not follow those of the *Kunst- und Werck-Schul* literally—far from it—so that if he did use it as a source, he wandered away from its text and rewrote freely. It seems a logical conclusion that Smith may have observed marbling in action during his years on the Continent, and the plate that accompanied his text is a further indication that this assumption is reasonable. Smith's text was later reprinted in several English dictionaries and other works, and for a while it served as the standard description of marbling.

Only about twelve years passed before these useful instructions were twice reprinted, word for word, in *The Universal Dictionary of Trade and Commerce*, edited by Malachy Postlethwayt and issued by John and Paul Knapton at London in two folio volumes in 1751.[12] This work, according to its title page, was translated from the French of the celebrated Monsieur Savary (i.e., Savary des Bruslons), but with additions and improvements throughout to adapt the information to the trade and navigation, laws, customs, and usages of the British kingdom.[13] It contained two identical articles on marbling, reprintings of the text that had appeared earlier in G. Smith's *Laboratory, or School of Arts* rather than the short definition in the original French work. The Smith account appears in the first volume under "Bookbinding" (p. 319), and in the second under "Paper" and the subheading "Marbled Paper" (p. 401).

The above works, then, represent the literature that an aspiring marbler might find available to guide him in his fledgling efforts in England before 1756. Without doubt, during these years and, as we shall see, in the several decades that followed, a number of individuals did avail themselves of it in attempts to learn to marble, for there was money to be made in its accomplishment.

Robert Dossie and the Society for the Encouragement of Arts, Manufactures, and Commerce

bibliographies record it as "George"; that it was Godfrey is proved by the fact that he signed the dedication in the first and some of the later editions of *The Laboratory* with the name "Godfrey Smith.") It seems evident that he had lived and worked in Germany and knew its language well.[11] The instructions he provided on marbling undoubtedly were sufficient to instruct even a novice in how to marble according to the simple standard of the day. Since the author announced that his text was derived from a German source, we may wonder what original work it could have been taken from. The *Kunst- und*

Because the British Isles lagged behind Germany and other European countries in various aspects of agriculture, commerce, and industry, a number of enlightened and philanthropic individuals interested in rectifying this situation in 1754 formed a Society for the Encouragement of Arts, Manufactures, and Commerce. The aim of this group was to cultivate experimental research within the realm, to collect information, to promote industrial production and bring its fruits to the public, and to reward those who had helped achieve these goals. One of the methods the Society soon adopted was to offer annual premiums or prizes for the fulfillment of certain tasks or the development of certain inventions it deemed necessary or at least desirable for the well-being and commercial independence of the country. Some of these improvements were in the field of agriculture, while others related to scientific, industrial, commercial, and artistic goals. For instance, the Society offered premiums for introducing sawmills into England; improving methods of iron and steel manufacturing; drawing gold, silver, and brass wire; improving the cider mill and press; refining the copper-plate printing press; improving wheel carriages, compasses, and protractors; producing a machine for boring auger holes; and even developing a better method for hanging doors.

In 1759 the Society, which later became the Royal Society for the Arts, adopted as one of its particular objectives the introduction of marbled-paper manufacturing in England. This article, it was pointed out, was one for which the English paid great sums to foreigners; making it had been frequently attempted in England, but without real success, in supplying a considerable part of the demand.[14] To accomplish this objective, the Society offered the first of several premiums to individuals who would produce marbled paper according to certain standards and in quantities to assure that this goal finally had been achieved. The person most influential in assisting the Society in this task was Robert Dossie, who might today be called an industrial chemist; in 1758 Dossie had published an important work similar to G. Smith's *Laboratory*.

Dossie's book, entitled *The Handmaid to the Arts,* has been described by a recent commentator as "by far the best treatise on the practice of the industrial arts that had yet appeared in the language and addressed specifically to that class of progressive tradesmen through whom the Society was aiming to effect country-wide improvements in order to promote commerce."[15] In this work, published anonymously by J. Nourse in two volumes at London in 1758, and reprinted in 1764, Dossie provided detailed information on most of the arts and decorative trades known and exercised at that time.[16] These included painting and the preparation of colors, gilding, bronzing, japanning (his account of this method ran to one hundred pages and remained one of the best treatises on the subject throughout the eighteenth century), engraving, glass- and porcelain-making, and many others. In an appendix on pages 377–381 of volume two, Dossie provided a description "of the method of preparing and colouring marbled paper."

Although Dossie's account is not especially long or detailed, amounting to just over one thousand words (nowhere near the length of the seven-thousand-word article that would appear in the Diderot-D'Alembert *Encyclopédie* eight years later), it represents the definitive description of the marbling process published in English during the eighteenth century. There can be no doubt that it was influential, even into the following century.

Equally important was Dossie's connection with the Society, which, with his help, did much to promote the development of marbling in Great Britain. Before considering this collaboration, I must devote a few paragraphs to Dossie and his background and work, for clearly he was not only one of the most important and influential scientists in England in his day, but also a prime mover in the advancement of many industrial and artistic processes throughout the realm.

Born in Sheffield in 1717, the son of a Cambridge-educated vicar, Dossie was apprenticed at an early age to an apothecary, and in consequence acquired a considerable knowledge of pharmacy, chemistry, and the industrial arts that were practiced in the busy towns of north England. In addition to study and experiments in chemistry, he applied himself to the study of physics and the construction of machines. Until the fortieth year of his life, he appears to have earned his living first by practicing pharmacy and then as a consulting chemist in the large manufacturing towns of Manchester, Warrington, Macclesfield, Halifax, Leeds, Wakefield, Sheffield, and Birmingham—all within easy reach of one another. The books he later published indicate that he was a well-read man, familiar with the works of British and Continental authors alike, with an extensive practical knowledge of both factory and laboratory procedures and a considerable capacity for research and inventiveness. By 1757, at the latest, Dossie had moved to London, where he quickly established a reputation based primarily on his literary, scientific, and industrial talents. A crucial event that proved a turning point in his career was doubtless the formation, in May of 1754, of the Society for the Encouragement of Arts, Manufactures, and Commerce, to which he dedicated his *Handmaid to the Arts*.

During his residence in London, Dossie soon became acquainted with Samuel Johnson, who also was deeply interested in chemistry, medicine, and the overall aims of the Society. Johnson, in fact, thought enough of Dossie's chemical ability to help him become a member of the Society in 1760. According to James Boswell, Johnson said of Dossie, "Sir, of the objects which the Society of Arts have chiefly in view, the chymical effects of bodies operating on other bodies, he knows more than any man." Boswell also records that Johnson, in order to give Dossie his vote to become a member of the Society, paid an arrear that he had run for two years. Dr. Johnson's high esteem for Dossie was based in part upon his *Handmaid to the Arts* and another important work which he published in 1758, *The Elaboratory Laid Open*. Republished in French and German in 1759 and 1760, this work gained Dossie a European reputation as a practical chemist, as did another, *Institutes of Experimental Chemistry,* which was issued at about the same time.

Dossie published, or translated from Latin and French, more than three dozen articles and books, which are listed in his bibliography (appended to the recent biographical article by F. W. Gibbs) and in another article supplementing it (see note 15). Before his death in 1777 at the age of sixty, Dossie had experimented on a wide range of industrial and chemical processes and published on a diversity of subjects, including, to mention but a few, chemistry, pharmacy, agriculture, the making of silk, and insecticides. He even wrote a play, *The Statesman Foil'd,* which was performed at the Theatre Royal in the Hay-Market in 1768. Dossie sat regularly on the Society's committee on chemistry, and served with equal energy on its committees for agriculture and for trades and the colonies. In 1767 the Society awarded him a gold medal for his chemical work in establishing the manufacture of potash in North America, a project for which, at an earlier time, he had shared an interest with a fellow member of the Society, Benjamin Franklin.[17]

It was as a writer and as a popularizer of the ideas and goals of the Society—namely, for improving the arts, manufactures, agriculture and commerce of Great Britain—that Robert Dossie appears to have devoted the later years of his life. His most important literary effort of these years was the periodic issue of the chief papers of the Society, together with several new articles of his own, which he published under the title *Memoirs of Agriculture & Other Oeconomical Arts* (see note 14). From Dossie's description (vol. 1, pp. 122–123) of the early work of the Society and from the Society's extant Guard Books, as well as other sources, we are able to obtain a clear view of the activity that was taking place to encourage the manufacture of marbled paper in England from about 1760— activity that helped to achieve this desired goal once and for all.

Because, as Dossie noted in his *Memoirs of Agriculture,* large sums of money were paid to foreigners for marbled paper, and because Englishmen had previously failed to manufacture much of their own, the Society in 1759 offered ten pounds to the person who should marble the greatest quantity of paper, not less than one ream, equal in quality to the best foreign imported kind. The following letter, still preserved in the Society's Guard Book for this period,[18] records one applicant's disappointed reaction to the Society's initial offer:

Gentlemen,

Either I am greatly mistaken as to the Difficulty and the Excellence of the art of Marbling, or else the Premium of Ten pounds *only,* offered by the Society was a great deal too small—yet, so I conceived it; and any great part of my necessary Business in the Marbling way to comply with your Advertisement as to quantity—However, I was willing to shew you by a small Specimen that I valued your Approbation more than the Premium. That the four sheets accompanying this may meet with the former (however you may dispose of the latter) is the hearty desire of your

> very Humble Servt.
> J. Cole
> Papermakers' Alley
> Little Moorefields

12 Feby. 1760.

The Society's officers' reaction to Cole's letter can be found in its records as well:[19]

Marbled Papers & Drugges
    Strand April 2d 1760
    Mr. Charles Lowth in the Chair
Mr. R. H. Chester   Mr. Grignion   Mr. Blake
Mr. Stephenson   Mr. Wm. Bailey Mr. Bridgen
Mr. Bathurst
Marbled Paper.

The Committee on reconsidering the two samples of Marbled Paper delivered in for the Premiums offered for that Article, and referred to them and mark'd No. 1 and No. 2 are in the Opinion, That the Maker of No. 1 be paid the Premium offered for this article being £10.

N.B. This paper was made by Mr. John Baskerville of Birmingham.

A Quire of Marbled Paper made by Mr. John Cole was delivered in to & examined by the Committee; but that not being the Quantity directed by the Society's Advertismt, [sic] he could not be admitted a Candidate for the Premium offered for this Article; but as his Paper is much superior to the other Samples delivered in, they recommend it to the Society to reward the said Mr. Cole with a Bounty of five Guineas.

The Committee recommended it to the Society to give a further Premium the next Year for Making Paper.

The minutes of this committee not only give us an answer to Cole's petition, they also affirm that the illustrious English type designer and printer John Baskerville was engaged in making marbled paper at this time; equally interesting, he had earned the approbation and premium of the Society for his efforts. Although it is unfortunate that the Society's manuscript records do not contain any samples that were submitted in the competition for a premium in the year 1759/60—or, for that matter, in later years—we can obtain some idea of what Baskerville and his cohorts were turning out from the marbled decoration on one of his works, reproduced here on Plate XVII, number 3. Marbled endpapers which are pasted inside the covers of Baskerville's printing of Milton's *Poetical Works*[20] (the book's edges are marbled as well) indicate that his attainment was not high and that there was some way to go before marbling on the European standard was to be achieved in England. Except for this reference, heretofore hidden in the Society's minute books, we would have no actual proof of Baskerville's marbling and his receipt of a premium for it, although I was convinced of his activity the second I opened up the Milton binding several years earlier and correlated its "un-European" marbled endpapers with the Baskerville imprint it contained. Because of the mediocre quality of Baskerville's marbled paper, one is tempted to wonder if he may not have been awarded a prize because of his reputation as a printer and type designer and because his own aims and efforts coincided with those of the Society, that is, the upgrading of British industry, and also because he was a gentleman.

We may also wonder whether the poor response to the committee's initial proposal or the argumentation of J. Cole had some effect, for in a meeting held on 1 April 1760, the previous day, with Dr. William Watson in the chair and Benjamin Franklin in attendance, the members voted to raise the premium to £100 for the following year. They also raised the number of reams required to one hundred, foolscap size, and ordered that the next contest be closed on Tuesday, the first day of February, 1761.[21]

Some insight into the low status of paper marbling in Great Britain at this time is furnished by a 1761 publication designed to aid parents in the choice of a profession for their offspring: Joseph Collyer's *The Parent's and Guardian's Directory, and the Youth's Guide in the Choice of a Profession or Trade.*[22] In his description "Of the Paper-Marbler," Collyer wrote:

> This art is yet but in its infancy in England; Marbled-Paper having been made in London only a very short time. . . . This business is yet but in few hands; and it is possible they have not yet taken apprentices. Though there is sufficient room for extending and improving this branch of trade; as most of the Marble Paper used here is still imported from Holland.

Such paper, of course, would have been German or French in origin, coming into the realm by way of Dutch ports.

In his *Memoirs of Agriculture & Other Oeconomical Arts*, Robert Dossie reviewed the chronology of the Society's efforts to promote indigenous manufacture of marbled paper in Great Britain. The Society's records indicate that in 1760 the premium offered was set at £100 (although Dossie says £50)[23] for one hundred reams not to be inferior to the best imported marbled paper; but this proved too difficult a requirement and understandably produced no winners. As a result, the premium was lowered in 1761 to £25 and the task to fifty reams. In 1762 the committee raised its premium to £100 and reduced the ream requirement to forty for the first premium and twenty for the second, but once more did not obtain the desired results. In 1763 a claim was made for which the premium of £50 was adjudged; it was with the success of this experiment that the Society decided to offer no more inducements for marbled paper. Dossie reports that the specimen was equal, if not superior, to the best foreign marbled paper; furthermore, it appeared that "the candidate was actually setting on foot a considerably manufactory."[24] Dossie concluded in his review that the public owed the Society a considerable debt, "for we have now got this article, as far as regards our own consumption, wholly in our own hands; and supply ourselves with paper, of this kind, more elegant and beautiful than the foreign." Furthermore, he added, obtaining this manufacture "makes a very considerable national saving."

Although Dossie does not divulge the names of the candidates who obtained the Society's approval and premium in 1763, they are recorded in William Bailey's 1772 compilation, which chronicled the Society's efforts and achievements to that time: *The Advancement of Arts, Manufactures, and Commerce.*[25] In a chapter titled "*Premiums for making* MARBLE PAPER," Bailey states:

> An account having been laid before the Society of the great quantity of paper, commonly called Marble Paper, imported into this kingdom, from foreign countries, the Society came to a resolution to offer a Premium of Fifty Pounds to the Candidate who should produce Forty Ream of the best, and nearest in quality to foreign, Marble Paper; and a Premium of Twenty-five Pounds to the Candidate who should produce Twenty Reams of ditto, manufactured in England.
>
> The Candidates, who obtained these Premiums, were, Mr. Henry Houseman, of Endfield, and Mr. Samuel Hervey, June 29, 1763

Little else is recorded about Hervey, but Geoffrey Wakeman informs us[26] that in 1762 Houseman had been granted Patent 770 for a "Method of gilding, colouring and marbling of paper," and that he employed gum tragacanth, alum and all of the colors and pigments associated with the marbling of that era.[27]

Despite Dossie's enthusiasm (or unbridled overoptimism) it appears that it took another decade or so before the Society's goals were achieved once and for all. While it is true that there was good progress, the evidence afforded by English marbled papers in contemporary English bindings indicates that there really was not extensive and continuous production until the early to mid-1770s. But, apparently, the Society's interest in promoting marbled paper manufacture was not entirely dormant after 1763. In their history of the Royal Society of Arts, Derek Hudson and Kenneth W. Lockhurst state that, with regard to the manufacture of marbled paper, "the Society's offers resulted in the establishment of 'a considerable manufactory,' sufficient to meet all internal requirements, and for this the proprietors, Messrs. Portbury & Smith, received the advertised prize of £50 in 1765."[28]

Robert Dossie notwithstanding, the efforts of the Society for the Encouragement of the Arts, Manufactures, and Commerce to promote the production of marbled paper in England continued long after the events just reviewed. This is clearly demonstrated by a letter on the subject, published in the Society's *Transactions* in 1789,[29] which was preceded by an explanation that it was an early objective of the Society to establish the manufacture of marbled paper in England and that that goal had been attended to with happy results. The letter that followed was proof of this success. It was written by one John Davis, who had just been awarded the Society's silver medal for the several samples of marbled paper he had submitted that were found superior in elegance of pattern and variety of color to those commonly made at the time. Davis's letter, transmitting his samples, which, it was noted, were reserved in the Society's Repository (but unfortunately cannot be located there today), is an interesting one. In it, he addressed the officers and members of the Society:

> My Lords and Gentlemen,
> The manufacture of Marbled Paper having some years since been thought worthy the countenance and support of your most useful and public-spirited Society, I hope I may be permitted to address you thereon, and lay some specimens of Marbled Paper of my own invention and manufacture before your very valuable Institution: the utmost of my wishes is to merit your countenance and support; and the present application, if so fortunate as to be considered worthy of your attention, is only to sollicit [sic] the sanction of the Society, which I should esteem as the highest honour I can obtain, and would prove the greatest encouragement to my assiduity in the improvement of this manufacture, and considerably increase my endeavours to bring the same to the greatest degree of perfection. The principal consumption of this paper is by the Book-binders, and the common Marbled Paper, from the coarseness of its figure and glare of colours is as little used as possible. The perfect specimens (many of which are imitations of foreign marbles), from the delicacy of the figures, and beauty of the patterns and colours, will, as the inventor flatters himself, if approved of by the Society, extend its manufacture, and prevent the importation of Marbled Paper from abroad.
> I am,
> My Lords and Gentlemen
> Your most obedient humble servant,
> John Davis
> Salisbury-court, Fleet-street

In my opinion, John Davis can be considered the first English marbler of note. We have observed many others who attempted marbling long before he arrived on the scene, but he was the first individual to whom we can impute a long and undoubtedly productive manufacture. The marbling paper business that he carried on in Fleet Street in 1788, and probably even before, continued into the early years of the next century, for, as Wakeman notes, he is recorded as a manufacturer of marbled paper at Herne Hill, Dulwich, as late as 1802.[30] The large number of marbled papers of English manufacture surviving in contemporary bindings indicates beyond any reasonable doubt that full production had been achieved by Davis's time, and not only by him. The increasing use of

marbled paper by English binders after 1800 and as the new century advanced indicates that other, still unidentified marblers had joined the ranks and were now at work as well.

Some Side Issues

Bits and pieces of evidence that have been placed on the record over the years or have gone unnoticed until now indicate that while these events were transpiring, other marbling activities were taking place independently. Rosamond Loring, for example, quotes the advertisement of a little-known English bookbinder named Richard Dymott (died 1788 or 1789), who apparently marbled paper, and also made curious marbles on leather, and did bindings in embroidered velvet.[31] At the end of a pamphlet published in 1766, entitled *Examination of the Rights of the Colonies upon Principles of Law*, Dymott printed an advertisement that he had brought to perfection the making of French and Dutch (i.e., German) marbled paper in England. And Geoffrey Wakeman records that the *Bath Chronicle* for 13 September 1770 contains an advertisement by William Wever of Holborn, London, relating that he was the inventor of "Curious Marbled Paper" in imitation of real variegated marble such as had never been exposed to sale in any shop in Great Britain.[32] Another proof that marbling occasionally took place in England at this time appears in the first edition of Laurence Sterne's *Tristram Shandy* in a curious and intriguing development that has about it some of the mysterious elements of a modern spy thriller—a sort of "Tristram Shandy caper."

In London in 1759 two small duodecimo volumes appeared with no publisher or city of origin but with the title *The Life and Opinions of Tristram Shandy, Gentleman*. These were the first installments of a witty and somewhat complicated novel that immediately brought its author, Laurence Stern, into London's most fashionable society.[33] This discursive work which, when completed, extended to nine volumes, is full of curiosities, and has been described as combining sentiment, whimsy, indecency, and novelty, all with comic effect. And what, one may ask, does the novel *Tristram Shandy* have to do with marbling? Just this: near the middle of volume 3, making up its pages 169–170, Sterne arranged to have inserted a sheet of paper that had been marbled on both sides.

Many opinions have been expressed over the years about Sterne's motive for inserting this marbled leaf into his work. One commentator recently told me that the author of *Tristram Shandy* included this seemingly extraneous piece of Turkish paper into the work symbolically, because in real life his father was a turkey merchant.[34] Psychobiography and literary criticism aside, Sterne's inclusion of a sheet of marbled paper is a clear indication that in 1761—at a time when the Collyer book claimed that marbling was yet in its infancy in England, and when it was still practiced mainly on an experimental or at least developing basis—the author of *Tristram Shandy* found a local marbler who could supply him with a sufficient quantity of decorated paper to illustrate this work. The marbling on the leaf in *Tristram Shandy* is a modest effort, not like anything made abroad at the time, and not very handsome or well-executed at that. It is a simple Turkish pattern made up of small green, yellow, and white spots on a red Turkish ground, with white veins. Certainly it qualifies mainly as a curiosity, and it seems likely that Sterne placed the sheet in his novel (personal motives aside) just for its "novel" effect; for English marbling at this critical time in its development was exactly that—a curiosity and a novelty. I have not made a concentrated attempt to check all editions of volume 3 of *Tristram Shandy* in order to determine how long and in what manner marbled paper continued to be inserted into this work. However, I have noticed that the same pattern, but with much larger white margins, appeared in the second edition of this volume, issued by R. and J. Dodsley in 1761 also. In later editions, published by the Dodsleys in 1771 and 1773, the marbled sheets contained entirely different coloration and the pattern was much more sophisticated—the veins were much smaller, with yellow standing out among them, and the predominating ground color was green or blue. Indeed, progress had been made in British marbling during the interim.

Proof that marbling was being carried on in certain localities in early times often requires the condition of a "controlled environment." Edge marbling, as indicated earlier, provides just such a condition and control. The marbled paper found in many early bindings might be made in areas other than where the binding took place, even in other countries, but edge marbling had to be executed locally, in or near the actual shop where the binding was being done, with the marbled decoration put onto the edges before the boards of its covers were finally attached. An opportune and somewhat rare example of such a "controlled condition" is afforded by a number of books which the English gentleman Thomas Hollis had bound in England between the late 1750s and the 1770s and then sent to Harvard University for its library. Not only do some of these volumes contain edge marbling, but evidence shows that many of them were bound before 1764, thus giving further proof of marbling activity in Britain at an early date.

Before I discuss some of these books, a few words about Thomas Hollis and the background of this "controlled condition" are in order. The grandnephew of another Thomas Hollis, who had been an earlier benefactor to the Harvard College Library,[35] Thomas Hollis (1720–1774) was born in London to a successful merchant family and, after completing schooling, spent a year in Amsterdam in 1732 with the intention of learning Dutch and French for commercial purposes. In 1735 he inherited

his father's property as well as that of his great-uncle, the elder Thomas Hollis, and abandoned his commercial pursuits, spending much of the following decade touring various countries on the Continent. Hollis had been strongly opposed to Tory principles from early childhood, and had declined to enter parliament for that reason; eventually, he found a way to propagate his republican principles through literature. He spent hundreds of pounds yearly on the production and purchase of books and medals, large numbers of which he gave to libraries all over the world, those of Harvard, Berne, and Zürich being especially favored. His fondness for seventeenth-century republican literature led him to have the covers of his books decorated with daggers, caps of Liberty, and similar designs. He lived the life of a recluse, and in 1770 left London and retired to the seclusion of an old farmhouse on his property at Corscombe in Dorsetshire, where he continued collecting and dispensing books until his death.

Harvard College records indicate that this republican bibliophile made his first gift to its library in 1754 and, after most of the college library was destroyed by a disastrous fire in 1764, he doubled his efforts to favor Harvard with books, many of them especially decorated with symbols of freedom. It has been estimated that in all Hollis sent Harvard 1,200 books, but the figure may be much higher.[36] He had "liberty prints" designed and executed by Cipriani, Bartolozzi, and other artists and designers from portraits he often sought from far afield; and he had his bookbinders stamp such decoration onto the covers of his books, both those he kept and those he gave away. At times these binders bound or rebound books anew, but often they "vamped" them to refashion them in accordance with Hollis's tastes. Sometimes such vamping included, in addition to stamping with symbols of liberty, the addition of newly made marbled paper for endpapers; and sometimes Hollis had his binders arrange for the addition of edge marbling. Early on he employed the services of a London binder named Mathewman, who worked for this eccentric bibliophile mainly between 1762 and 1764.[37] Mathewman's shop burned down in 1764, and Hollis's tools with it, causing the binder to flee his creditors. Afterward, Hollis utilized the services of John Shove, who had appeared as a bookbinder in London about 1756 and who worked from 1763 at Maiden Lane in Covent Garden.[38]

Plate XVII illustrates one of two volumes (of the same title) which Hollis sent to Harvard, copies of William Sheppard's *Englands Balme*, issued at London in 1657. This was a particular favorite of Hollis's, who purchased every copy he could get and had them bound identically. According to William H. Bond, who has made a study of Hollis's Harvard bindings,[39] these were bound by Mathewman before 1764, probably in 1761 or 1762–1764, for the stamps were destroyed in Mathewman's fire of 1764. The edges of both volumes have been dressed up with marbled decoration, and the marbled papers they contain also give indication of English manufacture, showing once more the activity that was going on in London and perhaps elsewhere in this early and formative period.

Other examples of sporadic marbling taking place in England at this time are afforded by advertisements published by two emigrant English bookbinders, T. Anderton and George Leedell, in New York City in 1764 and 1773 respectively. Both were recent arrivals from abroad and advertised edge marbling among the services they offered (more will be written about these binders later). While it might appear that in 1764 and 1773 there were enough marblers in England to permit the export of some of them, that appearance is misleading. These advertisements indicate, undoubtedly, that many bookbinders were trying their hands at edge marbling (as the Baskerville and Hollis books clearly indicate), and some binders who had achieved some success in this area happened to emigrate. It was not until the middle of the 1770s that marbling specialists existed in sufficient numbers and with sufficient skills to insure the British Isles an ample and continuous supply of marbled paper and marbled decoration.

A case in point is provided by a recent publication about two Scottish bookbinders of this period, James Scott and his disciple, William Scott. As James H. Loudon, the author of this work indicates, the Scotts were actively engaged in bookbinding in Edinburgh in 1770–1790. Their work was of the highest quality, so much better than others in that period and location that Loudon has described them as rising "like a landmark in the anonymous plain of eighteenth-century Scottish bookbinding."[40] He provides what scant details he could assemble on the lives and activities of these two outstanding craftsmen, and then reproduces and documents all the extant bindings that can be shown to be theirs, basing his conclusions on the evidence of style, tooling, archival records, and the like. His research was aided by the fact that James Scott sometimes inserted his identifying ticket or label into the volumes he bound, a rare occurrence in those times when, as Loudon notes, gentle patrons were reluctant to have their books defaced by advertising. Loudon adds a description for each known or identifiable James Scott or William Scott binding, giving dates, the type of skin used as covering material, rolls and stamps employed to decorate it, the type of endpapers inserted, and the nature of any edge decoration. Finally, he illustrates each work (in black and white) and provides rubbings and reproductions of tools so that we can gain first-hand knowledge of the overall design.

Loudon arranges his work chronologically, beginning with 1770, the year in which James Scott completed his earliest known binding. When examining Loudon's initial descriptions (which should serve as models for all future historians and bibliographers working in the field of bookbinding), we note that for the first fifteen works listed, produced in 1770–1775, James Scott employed only plain white paper as endpapers. In 1776, however, as Loudon's description of the sixteenth entry indicates, Scott used marbled papers of the large spot or Turkish variety as endpapers; Loudon notes that this was "probably Scott's first use of this paper." Successive entries tell us that Scott continued to use marbled paper for endpaper decoration, mainly of this Turkish design. In sum, this well-organized descriptive catalog provides additional evidence that full production of marbled paper did not occur in Britain until the mid-1770s, but proves as well full and lasting production thereafter. Scott's marbled papers were doubtless imported from London, where they were available a bit earlier; however, news of recent developments, and the developments themselves, traveled quickly, even in those days.

When examining the illustrations in Loudon's book soon after its publication, I recognized in several cases (where Scott had mounted presentation labels on his marbled endpapers) a pattern that I had observed in many London bindings of this early period. This design shows red, yellow, and black veins, with dark green spots predominating, and pink spots, or a shower of white spots, thrown about on them. Thereupon I resolved to visit Scotland when next abroad and examine as many of these early Scott bindings as I could find, which, thanks to Loudon's work, proved not difficult. Afterward, when I was in Glasgow searching out the French marbling recipe of the 1642 period (mentioned previously), I encountered my first two Scott bindings (on books bound by William Scott, Loudon's WS 4 and WS 5). These confirmed my suspicion that this indeed was the early spot pattern that I had seen lining the bindings of a great many contemporary London imprints. In Edinburgh I examined a number of James Scott bindings in the National Library of Scotland (JS 24, JS 25, JS 26, JS 27, and JS 32); finally, in London I viewed in the British Library the very first volume into which James Scott is known to have inserted marbled paper (JS 16), a copy of James Beattie's *Essays,* printed for William Creech at Edinburgh in 1776. The marbled papers in this and in the earliest of the Scotts' bindings, where they used them, were more primitive than those in their later ones, showing the marblers' initial lack of experience and their improving technique thereafter.

Significantly, this spot pattern continued to be made in England until the early years of the nineteenth century, indicating, possibly, the constant production of a single shop throughout this period. Thus, just as the study of bookbinding can aid us in proving early developments in marbling and in the history of decorated paper, so too can the study of marbling assist materially in the identification and dating of bindings, a matter that has been employed hitherto on only a very limited basis.

Dossie's Widening Influence

Robert Dossie's influence on the spread and popularization of marbling in Britain has not hitherto been sufficiently recognized. The eighteenth century was the century of the encyclopedist; many large compends of knowledge appeared throughout the century, each containing some material on this marvel, marbling. In the period after 1758, when Dossie's *Handmaid to the Arts* first appeared, almost all of the large dictionaries and encyclopedias published in England reprinted his description verbatim or nearly so.

The first such work known was Temple Henry Croker's *The Complete Dictionary of Arts and Sciences,* issued at London in 1764–1766. Its second volume reprinted Dossie's description in full.[41] About half a dozen years later another large compendium, entitled *A New Royal and Universal Dictionary of Arts and Sciences,* issued for the London bookseller J. Cooke in 1771 and 1772, followed suit. In this instance, however, the Dossie description was accompanied by two plates freshly re-engraved from the Diderot-D'Alembert encyclopedia, with material added to explain the activities and processes depicted in the illustrations. This was the first reprinting of the famous Diderot illustrations that has come to my attention.[42]

Approximately seven years later, in 1778, the Reverend Erasmus Middleton and several of his coworkers issued yet another large dictionary at London, containing an explanation of marbling based on Dossie's account and also including copies of the two Diderot-D'Alembert illustrations. This work, with a lengthy title that began *The New and Complete Dictionary of Arts and Sciences; or, An Universal System of Useful Knowledge,*[43] covered a wide range of subjects, from Agriculture and Algebra in the As to Theology and Trigonometry in the Ts (oddly, it didn't discuss subjects later in the alphabet); particular attention was given to including everything of value in Chambers's encyclopedia, as well as the encyclopedia that had been issued by Diderot and D'Alembert in Paris, the newly published *Encyclopaedia Britannica,*[44] and similar works. The passage on marbling from Dossie's *Handmaid to the Arts* was also reprinted in the 1788 *New Royal Encyclopaedia, and Cyclopaedia: or, Complete Modern and Universal Dictionary of Arts and Sciences,* edited by George Selby Howard, but without the illustrations.[45] Dossie's description was published in another such work that I know of,[46] and it may have appeared in others that have yet to be discovered; it became the standard of its day, replacing the description provided in G. Smith's *The Laboratory, or School of Arts.*

When Abraham Rees revised and reissued Ephraim Chambers's *Cyclopaedia* in 1778–1786, it contained a fairly comprehensive article on marbling that was not derived from Dossie or other contemporary accounts, but was an enlarged version of the reasonably good description that had appeared in the second and later editions of the Chambers work (1738, and later). When Rees issued his own *New Cyclopaedia; or Universal Dictionary of Arts and Sciences,* a large, multi-volume work that commenced publication in London in 1802 and was reprinted in Philadelphia in the second and third decades of the century,[47] this enlarged definition was included.

Additionally, a short description of how to marble paper, approximating the earlier instructions attributed to Nicolas Lemery, appeared in a succession of books of secrets issued in England from about the 1750s. These carried the title *Valuable Secrets Concerning Arts and Trades* or *Valuable Secrets in Arts and Trades,* and reprintings of them across the Atlantic would be the means by which information on marbling first appeared in American publications. They are often said, though I have not verified this, to be translations of the popular book of secrets that first appeared in France in 1716 and was reprinted repeatedly thereafter under the title *Sécrets Concernant les Arts et Métiers,* a work which incorporated Lemery's marbling instructions in a modernized form.[48]

Finally, we have from this early period a short quotation which, although not directly applicable to marbling, is indicative of the widening interest both in paper decoration in Great Britain and in the professional exploitation of it. Priscilla Wakefield offered to the public in 1798 a volume of *Reflections on the Present Condition of the Female Sex; with Suggestions for Its Improvement* and discussed what sorts of employment, usually conducted by men, might also be appropriate for women.[49] After explaining that needlework, miniature painting, and painting in enamel—which hitherto had been performed mostly by men—were occupations that could more properly be assumed by the female sex, she noted that "patterns for calico-printers and paper stainers are lower departments of the same art, which might surely be allowed as sources of subsistence to one sex with equal propriety to the other."

We might infer, both from the description of marbling in the Diderot-D'Alembert encyclopedia contributed by the widow who may have assisted in a marbling workshop (see pp. 000–000) and from the Engelbrecht print of the 1720–1750 period, that France and Germany were ahead of England in permitting women the right to work in those times.

7

The Matured British Trade

BRITISH marbling, we have seen, reached maturity in the mid-1770s after a prolonged infancy that lasted nearly fifty years. While John Davis, working as a marbler in London from the mid- or late 1780s into the early years of the nineteenth century, has been identified as one of its early and principal exponents, one should not assume that he was the only such craftsman in London at this time. Geoffrey Wakeman has gleaned from London directories and other sources the names of additional craftsmen who plied this trade at about the same time: William Heath, recorded as a marbler in London from 1790 until 1830; John Poole, who marbled in London from 1799 to 1817; and John Sheeler, who was so engaged from 1799 to 1811.[1] Established tradesmen paid to have their names entered in city directories, so we may surmise that there were others working as marblers in London in this early period who did not choose to pay the entry fee and who probably made up the less-established ranks of the trade. Then, too, there were the apprentices, some of whom later would leave their masters and venture into business on their own.

Now that this fledgling marbling industry had become fully entrenched, and was growing and producing increasing amounts of paper colored by its special technique, the demand for marbled paper grew apace. Denied for so long an affordable and readily available supply, British bookbinders turned more and more to marbled paper to embellish their work, employing it as endpapers not only in their finest productions (as the two Scotts had previously), but with increasing frequency in more common bindings and for partly covering the outsides of books, ledgers, and periodicals of the everyday variety. Edge marbling, once restricted to fine bookbinding productions, similarly came to be applied to less fine bindings and sometimes even to plain ones. Once caught up in this trade and smitten with it, the English began to seek out books with the "right" appearance, and propriety decreed that marbled decoration was an important component in the formula.

"Oswestry 1811"

Although edge marbling was practiced in Britain from the last years of the 1750s and in the decades following,

when experimentation in marbling was conducted by bookbinders and others, the practice did not become common until after 1800, at which time it was more likely carried on by the newly entrenched marbling specialists than by the bookbinders themselves. But having the edges of his books marbled by a professional caused some difficulty for a binder, because transport to and from marbling shops and bottlenecks in production there brought delays and inconveniences. An attempt to help binders learn to marble on their own through printed instructions (mainly to enable them to decorate their book edges) came in 1811 with the publication of the first English bookbinding manual, *The Whole Art of Bookbinding, Containing Valuable Recipes for Sprinkling, Marbling and Colouring.*

Bernard Middleton, the expert on English craft bookbinding, has referred to this work in a recent reprinting of it[2] as "Oswestry 1811" after its place of origin. He speculates that the author of this anonymous pamphlet, published in that Shropshire market town close to the border of Wales, was one of three persons (Middleton is inclined to believe it was the third): (1) W. Price, an Oswestry binder, whose earliest date in the directories seems to be 1828; (2) Nathaniel Minshall, the printer of the manual; (3) Henry Parry, in whose name the book was registered at Stationers' Hall and who may have been the same Henry Parry who wrote another manual, *The Art of Bookbinding,* published at London in 1818. (According to Pollard and Potter's *Early Bookbinding Manuals,* Parry died in 1814, but his business was conducted by his widow until 1819.)[3] Oswestry 1811 does not appear to have been reprinted in England; it was reprinted at Richmond, Virginia, in 1824, however, in an edition that constituted the first bookbinding manual to be published in America.[4]

The Whole Art of Bookbinding contains directions for coloring the leather covers of a book and for sprinkling its edges; it also has two small sections (really the first and second parts of one section) with a few paragraphs on marbling. These were incorporated into the manual to help binders learn to marble their book edges, or, as the directions indicate, for ornamenting fire screens and other objects. The first section, "Soap marble," directs the reader to mix various colors, such as Prussian blue, king's yellow, or brown, with either brown or white soap.

(Soap, we shall see later in our discussion of the methods and materials of marbling, has a close chemical affinity to ox-gall and is still used in marbling in addition to or in place of gall as a dispersing agent, causing the colors to float and expand on the size.)

The second part of the instructions, which mostly relates to marbling the edges of books, is entitled simply "Marbling" and advises the reader to use hard water as the surface medium, onto which the aforesaid colors mixed with soap are thrown from a brush. The use of water as a surface medium in marbling does not permit pattern development or control, for water has little surface tension; the colors will drift or move about in an unrestrained manner as successive colors are thrown down or under any sort of combing. This method, therefore, is an imperfect one and does not constitute true marbling. Nonetheless, this first English bookbinding manual was a step forward, intended to help English binders accomplish some sort of edge marbling and marblelike paper decoration.

Hugh Sinclair, and the Beginning of an Independent Marbling Literature

As "Oswestry 1811" shows, the restrictive trade and apprenticeship system that had prevailed for some centuries was beginning to ease. Here and there craftsmen were coming forward to divulge some of their specialized knowledge in print, though few yet were bold enough to place their names on the title pages of these early technical books. Another step forward in this easing process occurred within a few years of the publication of *The Whole Art of Bookbinding* with the appearance about 1815 (or possibly 1820), of the first known manual devoted exclusively to marbling (although it contained a few concluding pages on staining paper). Whereas the previously noted 1808 publication attributed to Schuder encompassed the making of all varieties of colored and decorated paper, the work I will now discuss is remarkable not only as the first English publication devoted mainly to marbling, but as the first bona fide manual to appear on the subject worldwide as well.

The Whole Process of Marbling Paper and Book-Edges: To Which Is Added the Art of Staining Paper, Including Yellow, Green, Pink, &c., as this small book of approximately fifty pages is entitled, is known today in but five copies, three containing title-pages dated 1820 and two lacking title pages.[5] Its author, as indicated on the three with title-pages, was one Hugh Sinclair, "marble papermaker, Glasgow." In the recent reprinting of this rarity, along with "Oswestry 1811," Bernard Middleton speculates that the book was issued initially at Glasgow about 1815, and certainly no earlier than 1813; the two copies without a title-page being from a first edition and the three with a title-page bearing a London, 1820, imprint representing

a second. He appears to base his conclusion on three facts: its final page contains a colophon note that the work was printed by T. Duncan, 149 Saltmarket, the name and address of a contemporary Scottish printer; its paper has an 1813 watermark date; and its author worked in Glasgow during the second decade of the nineteenth century.

On the three copies with title pages, however, there appears the imprint "London, Printed for R. N. Rose, 45 Holborn Hill, and Sold by T. and J. Allman, Prince's Street, Hanover Square, 1820," while everything else, including its colophon, is identical to the two copies without title-pages. Thus, it is entirely possible—I believe even likely—that all five copies are one and the same edition, and that the title-pages were simply removed from two of the copies, with the fly-titles or half-titles preceding them allowed to serve as substitutes. In my view, it seems likely that Sinclair composed and had his pamphlet printed at Glasgow, perhaps because it was cheaper and because he lived there and had contacts there; but it may well have been issued in London in 1820, instead of in Glasgow before that date. I have had the opportunity to examine carefully only one of the five extant copies. There is no watermark date in the wove paper on which it was printed, although part of one is visible in one of the endpapers making up its binding. Unfortunately, the last two numbers of the date are not discernible, being on the part of the sheet that was pasted onto the inside of the covers. There are a number of reasons to explain the removal of the title pages from two of these copies. One might argue that in an era when it still was taboo—or at least unpopular or unwise—for workmen to reveal the secrets of their trades, Sinclair may have feared that his name on the work's title would expose him to the scorn and opprobrium of his fellow craftsmen, so he removed it from copies initially distributed; the copies with a title page could represent those sold or disposed of at a much later date, when Sinclair no longer feared or cared about this possibility.[6]

Thus far we have considered mainly the marbling activity that went on in London, but this pamphlet shows its extension to other locales. According to Sinclair, the art of marbling paper and book edges heretofore had been confined chiefly to London; he boasts of being the first to attempt to introduce the craft into Scotland: "As all my Predecessors in the art, in this Country, have failed in success, I may claim the honour of being the original manufacturer of Marble Paper, having produced nearly two thousand Reams, the greater part of which has been reckoned superior to London paper at the same price." In exactly what year Sinclair introduced the art to the northern country is unclear; it could have been as early as 1804, when "Hugh Sinclair, bookbinder" at 11 Bell Street first was entered in a Glasgow city directory, but this is questionable. His name did not reappear in Glasgow directories until 1810 (and again in 1811), when he was listed as a marble papermaker at 31 Bell Street. His final listing came in 1817, when "H. Sinclair & Co., Booksellers, 21 Salt-Market" was entered.[7] The only additional information we have about him comes from the title page of his manual and from details he provides within.

Sinclair, in his introduction, reveals his motives in bringing out this little work. Instructions previously published on marbling, he began, were imperfect and likely to lead beginners astray; moreover, Glasgow binders had previously paid for instructions from persons traveling about the country who pretended to teach marbling but knew nothing about it, and whose only aim was to procure money at the expense of others who trusted them. His text aimed to alter that situation. "As the want of knowledge," he pointed out, "in the Art of Marbling Edges has been found to be a considerable Disadvantage to Book-binders in Country Towns, both in England and Scotland, the author is confident that the following Treatise will fully remove this Difficulty, and put the means of attaining complete Success in the power of every person who may choose to practice the Art, as it will be found to convey, in the clearest and most simple manner, a thorough idea of the whole process of Marbling." He concluded his introduction with the claim that the lessons he was laying down were derived from observations made during a period of nearly seven years of constant practice as a marble papermaker.

Sinclair's instructions follow the usual format adopted in the earliest writings on this subject, but differ in that they are more complete and are accompanied by actual samples of marbled paper illustrating the end results and the actual patterns that can be obtained. After reviewing the implements and supplies needed and discussing the colors to be employed, Sinclair devoted the major part of his manual to specific directions for marbling three patterns: the simple spot or Turkish design, which he referred to as the "common French marble," another pattern which would later be known in England as "Stormont," and, the pattern that came to be called "shell" or sometimes "mottled."

Bernard Middleton, in his brief foreword to the 1987 reprinting of Sinclair's manual, provides a vivid picture of the conditions in Glasgow under which bookbinders and craftsmen like Sinclair had to labor:

Glasgow, at the time of Sinclair's writing, was not known for its salubrity. J. C. Symons, writing in 1839, stated, "It is my firm belief that penury, dirt, misery, drunkenness, disease and crime culminate in Glasgow to a pitch unparalleled in Great Britain."[8] He alluded particularly "to the dense and motley community which inhabit the low districts of Glasgow, consisting chiefly of the alleys leading out of the High-street, the lanes to the Calton, but particularly the closes and wynds which lie between the Trongate and the Bridegate, the salt-market and Maxwell-street. These districts contain a motley population, consisting in almost all the lower branches of occupation; but chiefly of a community whose sole means of subsistence consists in plunder and prostitution."

As for Britain in general Middleton points out that conditions in binderies, "though not so piratical, were likewise 'insanitary, dark and dismal' according to Henry Aston, who apprenticed in the 1830s. 'Incredible as it may seem now,' Aston reminisced many decades later, 'when I first went to the trade candles were in common use in our workshops. Finishers were allowed two candles each, a poor and miserable light they gave'."[9]

Little is known about the conditions under which marblers labored in those days. They always considered themselves to be the elite of the bookbinding community, but their situation may not have been much different than the lowly lot of their fellow binders. As Middleton relates in another work,[10] the standard working day for bookbinders in 1805 was 6 A.M. to 6 P.M., six days a week, but owing to the great quantity of work to be done by a small labor force (about 200 men in London) many binders were unable to finish before 9 or even as late as 11 P.M. Wages varied, but probably did not allow many master binders to make more than a bare living. Although coal gas was introduced for street lighting in the 1820s, many years passed before it was made available in workshops, so binders and others continued to work by candlelight. Supplies of water (so necessary in marbling) had to be obtained from wells and pumps in the streets, or from rain barrels placed on roofs and elsewhere. Sanitary conditions and food also were poor, bringing Middleton to conclude from obituary notices that there was a high incidence of tuberculosis among the binders, with many deaths occurring before the age of forty.

Exactly how much influence Sinclair's little pamphlet exerted in increasing the amount of marbling, or in improving its quality, we cannot gauge. The samples that he mounted in his manual indicate that he himself had indeed attained professional competency, and they may have helped others to follow suit. It would appear, however, that the pamphlet's circulation was limited, and that it went far beyond what bookbinders needed to help them attain their simple goals. We cannot determine what may have happened to Sinclair after 1820. He may have died, retired, or left the trade; or perhaps he was driven from London by the insults and ostracism of his fellow workmen and lived out his existence in peaceful anonymity.

In the introduction to his work, Sinclair claims to have marbled 2,000 reams of paper, which translates into a million sheets! Based on my own marbling experience, I initially attributed this figure to exaggeration, or at least over-enthusiasm. With time for set-up and the minutes required to throw down even a simple spot pattern, absorb it onto paper, and rake the size clean for each sheet, simple mathematics seemed to argue against Sinclair's claims, which call for the production of a ream of paper a day in the seven-year period of his marbling activity. It would seem to be a stupendous feat even with assistants working with him. But then again, my experience, for the most part, has been with modern, Halferian marbling and with the recreation or duplication of ancient patterns, both of which take considerable time to accomplish. For example, intricate combing, one of the mainstays of Halferian marbling, takes at least twice as long to accomplish as does throwing down a simple spot pattern. Nonetheless, an article that appeared in 1951 and described and illustrated spot or Turkish marbling being done in contemporary France [11] informs us that "an efficient marbler can pull fifty sheets an hour, size 19 × 25." (In contrast, my own norm when combing, is about twelve sheets per hour.) In an eight-hour day, this French production would amount to four hundred sheets, or the better part of a ream, and we must keep in mind the fact (as Middleton points out) that the work day in Sinclair's era extended to twelve hours and sometimes even more. Thus, on reflection, Sinclair's boast does not appear to be without substance, especially when one considers that he probably had help, or worked in tandem with another marbler, and worked a twelve-hour day.

Marbling in the Bookbinding Literature

Some thirty years passed between the publication of Sinclair's manual and the appearance of the next English work devoted exclusively to marbling, Charles W. Woolnough's *The Art of Marbling, as Applied to Book Edges and Paper*, issued at London in 1853. During this interval, a number of bookbinding manuals were published in England that followed the format of the Oswestry 1811 *Whole Art of Bookbinding*, and all of them contained instructions, more or less, on marbling, for by this time it was deemed imprudent to publish such a manual without devoting at least a few paragraphs to a subject of keen interest to every bookbinder.

In 1817 a work of some 90 pages appeared in London, entitled *The Art of Bookbinding: Containing a Description of the Tools, Forwarding, Gilding and Finishing, Stationary Binding, Edge-Colouring, Marbling, Sprinkling, &c., &c.* Its author, although not cited on its title page, was identified on its printed boards (which were intended eventually to be discarded and replaced by a more solid and tasteful leather binding) as Henry Parry, mentioned previously as the possible author of "Oswestry 1811." But the 1817 *Art of Bookbinding* was a giant step forward from the 1811 *Whole Art of Bookbinding*, and the information it contained on marbling was also more advanced. This manual provided information on marbling leather, on sprinkling, and on other methods for coloring paper and, especially, book edges. While it provided instruction on soap marbling and marbling on hard water (both seemingly derived from "Oswestry 1811," but with slight variations),

its most specific information appears under the heading "French Marbling," on pages 57–60. Here are provided four pages of rather good instructions on classical marbling to help binders accomplish good edge work. According to Easton's bibliography, the Baumgartner Buchhandlung in Leipzig issued a German translation of this work under the title *Die Englische Buchbinderkunst* in 1819, with a second German edition following in 1821.[12]

It is of interest to note—with some reflection on the printing of Hugh Sinclair's manual—that though the imprint on the 1817 *Art of Bookbinding* indicates that it was published by Messrs. Baldwin, Cradock, & Joy of Paternoster Row in London, a brief colophon statement tells that its actual printing took place in the provincial town of Burton-upon-Trent, located north of Birmingham and due east of Oswestry. I have not had the opportunity to examine a copy of another English work in this genre, G. Martin's *The Bookbinder's Complete Instructor*, issued at Peterhead in 1823; but Geoffrey Wakeman indicates that its section on marbling consists of a description of soap and water marbling taken word for word from "Oswestry 1811," and the few passages he quotes confirm this view.[13]

The Bookbinder's Manual: Containing a Full Description of Leather and Vellum Binding; Also, Directions for Gilding of Paper & Book-Edges: and Numerous Valuable Receipts for Sprinkling, Colouring, & Marbling: Together with a Scale of Bookbinders' Charges; a List of All the Book and Vellum Binders in London, &c. &c., issued in 1828 at London by Cowie and Strange, Paternoster Row and Fetter Lane, is yet another in this group of manuals under discussion. Published anonymously, but often attributed to George Cowie, its printer, it was undoubtedly written by a practicing bookbinder. Its section on marbling, however, is mainly derivative. The description it provides on classical marbling, which extends over a full five pages,[14] is a reprinting, with some slight alterations and modernizations, of Robert Dossie's discussion of more than seventy years earlier. Then follows a section on "Soap Marbling," much of it a rewrite of the instructions provided in the 1817 *Art of Bookbinding*. Next are directions on "Vein Marbling," another medium altogether, which describe the painting of marble or stone slabs with paste impregnated with color and alum; a plate of strong glass was then placed on the colors and lifted from them, whereupon the colors were found veined on the glass in all directions. Paper was then pressed onto the glass to absorb its colored image. The making of splash papers, also a non-marbled variety, concluded the subject of paper decoration in the manual attributed to Cowie, a popular one, reissued in seven editions by 1860.[15]

The last significant example of these manuals to appear in print before mid-century was entitled *Bibliopegia: or, The Art of Bookbinding, in All Its Branches*. Its first edition came out in London in 1835, with successive editions issued in 1836, 1842, 1848, and 1865; a German translation, *Bibliopegia oder die Buchbinderkunst in Allen Ihren Zweigen*, appeared at Stuttgart in 1837. This manual—the best by far to appear in England before the end of the nineteenth century, with the most up-to-date information on the mechanization that was developing for bookbinding—was the work of John Hannett (1803–1893), who initially had been apprenticed to a printer and bookbinder and who set up as a printer and bookbinder in 1837. Not daring to print his real name on the title of the early editions, Hannett used the pseudonym John Andrews Arnett instead; it was not until the fourth edition of 1848 that he ventured to reveal his true identity after its title.[16]

On pages 42–49 of the first edition of *Bibliopegia: or, The Art of Bookbinding in All Its Branches,* in a section headed "Marbled Edges," Hannett not only provided binders with the best information on marbling to date, but also identified and gave directions for the making of three specific patterns: shell, Spanish, and Anglo-Dutch. Although Wakeman says that Parry's *Art of Bookbinding* was the first manual to give names to marbled patterns, I could find none in the copy I examined, and I believe that the credit actually belongs to Hannett. From his descriptions for making shell, Spanish, and Anglo-Dutch (this last was the pattern that later became better known as "nonpareil") we may surmise that these designs had become sufficiently popular by 1835 to be commonly designated by these names; and the enormous numbers of papers surviving on the bindings of British nineteenth-century imprints indicates that they were being produced in very substantial quantities.

Technical and descriptive information on marbling may be found in many English dictionaries and other works issued during the first half of the nineteenth century. For example, Thomas Martin's (i.e., John Farey's) *Circle of the Mechanical Arts,* which was devoted to the various arts and trades being practiced in Britain in 1813 (the year it was issued), contains three brief paragraphs on the subjects of water marble, soap marble, and classical marbling, this material deriving from the work issued at Oswestry just a few years before.[17] Of all the various English dictionaries and encyclopedias containing definitions or descriptions of this process, Alexander Jamieson's 1827 *Dictionary of Mechanical Sciences, Arts, Manufactures and Miscellaneous Knowledge* can be singled out as fairly representative of the group.[18] Finally, one of the best discussions of marbling to appear before mid-century appeared in 1829 when *Gill's Technological Repository* printed a translation of a substantial article that had recently appeared in France. Entitled "On Improvements in Marbling the Edges of Books and Papers," it provided a fairly detailed résumé of the art as practiced early in the nineteenth century.[19]

Charles Woolnough: Marbler Par Excellence

A major event in British marbling, and surely one of the prime events in the entire history of marbling, occurred in 1853 with the publication of Charles W. Woolnough's *The Art of Marbling, as Applied to Book Edges and Paper, Containing Full Instructions for Executing British, French, Spanish, Italian, Nonpareil, Etc., Etc. Illustrated with Specimens. With a Brief Notice of Its Recent Application to the Cloths So Extensively Used by Bookbinders.* According to the imprint on this work, it could be obtained from Alexander Heylin at 28 Paternoster Row, and from the author as well, described here as "Manager of the Patent Marbled Cloth Manufactory, 51, Bunhill Row." As a matter of fact, this initial edition of Woolnough's manual was bound in marbled cloth that had been produced at his plant; the copy in the Olga Hirsch collection at the British Library is the finest example in its original binding that I have seen.

Woolnough's preface is quite revealing of conditions prevailing at this time; it also divulges some of his background and tells us what finally induced him to publish many of the secrets of his trade:

I have been repeatedly solicited during the last few years, and especially by Binders in provincial and remote country-towns, where there is no possibility of getting a book marbled but by sending it up to London at considerable expense and inconvenience, to publish some work on the Art of Marbling; but hitherto I have refused to do so, because I considered that by so doing I should militate against the general interests of the trade. But I now find that most of those houses who did any amount of business in book-edges worthy of a marbler's notice, have obtained, or are endeavouring to obtain some one to do it on their own premises, and which, though frequently executed in a style not equal to that of a professional marbler, yet is sufficiently tolerable to answer their purpose: the convenience of having it done on the spot is more than compensating for the inferiority of the work.

Then (in a moralizing tone that would be iterated by James Sumner when he compiled a manual on marbling a year or so later and had been expressed by Sinclair forty years earlier) Woolnough mentioned yet another reason that induced him to bring out this important work. It seems that some individuals were going about the country who, though having a slight knowledge of one part of the craft, had been obtaining sums of money from credulous beginners, pretending to teach them a subject which, to a great extent, they were ignorant of themselves. Furthermore, they produced just enough to astonish novices and lead them to believe that the communication of a very few simple secrets was sufficient to enable them to become good marblers. Continuing, Woolnough declared,

I also consider the art is open to very great improvement and as most of those now engaged in it have very limited ideas, and think merely of getting a livelihood by it, it is not unlikely that it will make much advancement. Could the light of Chemistry, with its various agencies and combinations be brought to bear upon the knowledge at present possessed, some very novel and perhaps beautiful results might be produced, and I should not be very sorry to see it taken up by some one competent to investigate it.

I, therefore, now come forward with a work, which, could I have obtained twenty-five years ago, would have saved me an amount of not less than one hundred pounds, which at various times has been expended in fruitless experiments or worse than useless information.

After relating that what he now was providing was the result of actual experience, and that he was prepared to perform all of the descriptions and instructions stated in his book, he concluded by saying,

I have no doubt that I shall experience the ill-will and opposition of some who may fancy their interests are at stake, but let us consider that every thing is making advances, and why should not this curious and simple art, which has been kept back so long, and which so few have ever heard of, be brought into notice, that, if possible, its capabilities may be tested, and its powers brought into active and useful operation.[20]

In a lecture on "The Art of Marbling" delivered to the Royal Society of Arts in 1878,[21] Woolnough reminisced about his introduction to marbling and his early attempts to master this simple-appearing yet complex craft. In so doing, he provided us with a vivid description of his initial experience. "Fifty years ago," he reported to the Society,

It was almost as difficult to get a sight of the inside of a marbling establishment as it would be to get into the presence of Royalty; every crack and aperture, nay even the very keyholes, were stopped up or obscured, to prevent any glimpse being obtained as to the method by which it was accomplished; and, as comparatively few were in possession of its secrets, it was a very remunerative craft.

When I was about 13 years of age, I accompanied an individual who was going to fetch some books which had been sent out to be marbled; when we arrived they were not all finished, and your humble servant was admitted into the sanctum to wait for the remainder. I was so stricken with wonder and admiration at the sight, that I determined not to rest till I had found out how to do it.

Not wishing to take up the audience's time by telling of all the failures and disappointments he had encountered, Woolnough went on to relate that, by unremitting toil and perseverance, he was finally rewarded with success. Although his efforts for a long time were imperfect,

he had "got hold of the root of the matter" and after much practice approached nearer to a perfect result.

And as I was indebted to no one for the knowledge I had obtained, in the year 1853 I published a small work on the subject, which gave great offense to the fraternity, on account of its truthfulness, and the way in which the various kinds of marbling were set forth, and the manner of their accomplishment explained.

Thus, Charles Woolnough has told us that he was self-trained, learning his marbling through the trial-and-error method, driven on by a curiosity and doggedness inspired by his first fascinating encounter with the magic-like qualities of the art. Unlike similar artisans of his day, he did not approach the subject by way of the apprentice system but through an overwhelming attraction; nor did he see fit to withhold from others the important lessons he had learned at the expense of much time, money, and effort.

Except for his own revelations, we know pitifully little about this extraordinary man. In his brief survey of English marbling, Geoffrey Wakeman has thrown us a few crumbs of information derived from local directory listings and similar sources.[22] According to Wakeman, Charles Woolnough's name first was entered in London directories in 1822, at 18 Hill Street, Finsbury; from 1826 until 1863 such listings located him at 6 Bateman's Row, Shoreditch; he was not listed thereafter. Wakeman also reports that a second Charles Woolnough appeared in the directory for 1860, listed at 12 Upper Marlborough Row, Golden Square. This other Charles Woolnough moved in 1866 to 1 George Yard, Princess Street, Soho, and was listed at that location until 1885.

The obvious inconsistencies between Wakeman's directory information and some of the statements made by Woolnough himself have always puzzled me and made me feel uneasy about the reliability of Wakeman's identifications. For example, in the introduction to the initial 1853 edition of *The Art of Marbling*, Woolnough mentioned having twenty-five years' experience, and in the 1878 lecture he stated that his first encounter with the art came at the age of thirteen. This information would indicate that he was born about 1815, or perhaps a year or two earlier, and not about 1805, as Wakeman has speculated. His birth at this later time would be inconsistent with a directory listing as early as 1822, at which time he would have been less than ten years old. Clearly, there appeared to have been two Charles Woolnoughs at work in London in the same period. In a recent trip to that city, I searched for the name through many local and postal directories with some interesting and revealing results. In all fairness to Wakeman, I must add that the matter is not so easy to research as one might initially suppose, for a number of competing directories were published in those days; moreover, it is difficult to obtain long or near-complete runs of them, even in sophisticated research libraries; nor could I locate duplicate copies of the issues that Wakeman used, because, unfortunately, he did not cite the specific sources of his information.

In the London directories that I consulted,[23] I did not find any listing for Charles Woolnough in the 1820s; it was in a copy of *Robson's London Directory, Street Key and Conveyance List* for 1833 that I first encountered an entry for "Woolnough, C., bookbinder, 6 Batem[a]ns r[o]w, Shor[e]d[itch]." The same directory listed an S. Woolnough, also a bookbinder, at 51 Marshall Street, and 7 Upper James Street, Golden Square. Both of these Woolnoughs continued to be listed in subsequent directories,[24] but in the *Post Office London Directory* for 1846, I found the following listings as well:

Woolnough, Charles, bookbinder, 6 Bateman's row, Shoreditch
Woolnough, Charles Wingham, marbler, 24 Fleet lane
Woolnough, Edwd. Graham, surgeon, 15 St. Thomas st., Boro'

These, in fact, were all the Woolnoughs listed in the 1846 issue. I could locate no directories between 1842 and 1846; accordingly, the issue for 1846 was the first one in which I could find the other Charles Woolnough—that is, our marbler, Charles Wingham Woolnough. This second Charles Woolnough was entered also in the *Post Office London Directory* for 1847, but in 1856, the next directory that I was able to locate, his name was omitted, never, so far as I could tell, to appear in such a source again. From the information Woolnough provided, we can deduce that he was involved in the production of marbled paper and perhaps cloth during the last two or three decades of his life and spent much time traveling about the country soliciting orders for it; this could account, perhaps, for the lack of directory listings in the 1850s and afterwards.

Now aware that the Charles Woolnough who was noticed by Wakeman was not our marbling master, we must ask ourselves *who* was the earlier listed Charles Woolnough? We may postulate that if, as I have suggested, our marbler Charles Wingham Woolnough was born about 1815 and first appeared in London city directories in the mid-1840s when he was about thirty years old, he would have been about sixty-six in 1881, when the final edition of his classic marbling manual came into print. His advanced age at that time is supported by his statement in its preface that "this is probably the last time the author will intrude upon the notice of the public." Therefore, it seems not unlikely that the first Charles Woolnough, listed in directories from the 1820s on, was his father; moreover, it is not illogical to stretch the presumption further and wonder if the bookbinder S. Woolnough, who disappeared from London directories about 1842, might have been his grandfather, or perhaps an uncle. And to carry the matter a little further, it seems possible that the surgeon Edward Graham Woolnough could have been our marbling master's brother.[25] In summary, it appears that Charles Wingham Woolnough came from a family of bookbinders and was in the company of one of them or an agent on an errand to fetch books that had been sent out to be marbled when he was put on a collision course with his life's calling.

It was probably about 1828 when Woolnough's initial encounter with the wondrous aspects of marbling took place, and it was in the early or mid-1830s that he finally achieved success in mastering the art, as he mentioned in his lecture of 1878. By the time that the Great Exhibition of London opened at the Crystal Palace in 1851, he would have been in the marbling business for two decades or more and, as the title page of his manual tells us, he had risen to head the Patent Marbled Cloth Manufactory. This firm, he relates in his manual, was then in the hands of Mr. R. Ruding (late a partner in the firm that had been established in the name of Cussons & Co.) and manufactured cloths for bookbinders under a patent.

Cloth had been introduced as a material for covering books in about the third decade of the nineteenth century. With the arrival of mechanization and edition binding in the 1830s, cloth had begun to supplant leather and marbled paper as the chief book covering material in the same way that edition binding began to make the work of the hand bookbinder obsolete. In a section headed "Patent Marbled Cloth," at the end of his 1853 manual, Woolnough related how it was discovered (at the time of the Exhibition) after numerous experiments that marbling could be applied to the woven or textile fabrics used in bookbinding. Marbled cloth, however, never seriously challenged dyed and printed fabrics as a covering material for books, for I have noticed only a few trade bindings of that period with marbled cloth coverings.[26]

There is no denying that Charles Wingham Woolnough's *The Art of Marbling* was the most remarkable contribution to the literature up to that time, and it remains, together with a handful of other manuals, an essential work. In 1854, Woolnough issued his manual in a second printing that was almost identical to the first. In these initial editions he not only provided for all posterity the most intimate and detailed information on the actual materials and methods of the craft then in use, but also gave precise instructions for making approximately thirty patterns—the complete armamentarium of the English marbler at mid-nineteenth century—including both older designs and those that recently had become popular.

Woolnough's new and slightly enlarged edition of his manual, issued in 1881, incorporated a few more patterns that had been introduced in the intervening years. His preface to this edition, which he retitled *The Whole Art of Marbling, As Applied to Paper, Book-Edges, Etc.*, reveals even more of the conditions that prevailed in his time, and he gives some important historical facts about marbling as well. Once more, this master mentions the hostility and bitterness of those in the trade who, thinking that he had revealed their secrets, heaped on him "a variety of abuse, contumely, annoyance, and persecution." Woolnough apparently had little respect for many of those who bore the name "Master," for he felt that they had a very limited knowledge of the principles and practice of the art, and still less ability to impart it to others. According to Woolnough, some of these masters had even attempted to obstruct the progress of the art and discourage its development: "Masters take lads as apprentices," he recounted,

> engaging to teach them the Art and Mystery of Marbling, to whom it is a perfect mystery in every respect; these masters, in fact, possessing little or no knowledge of the practical or experimental working of the various and intricate processes connected with the successful carrying out of their object, and, as a rule, these lads are handed over to the tender mercies of the men employed, and, unless they are gifted with a little more than ordinary acuteness and penetration, will be kept in the dark as much as possible with regard to many things essential to their advancement and ultimate perfection in their calling.

Woolnough then introduced a case in point, stating that in the beginning of the century

> a person possessing a general knowledge of the art as it was practiced in those days, devised a plan by which he acquired a moderate competency and retired in comfortable circumstances. The course adopted by him was the following. He took some half-dozen or more boys from the parish workhouse, and selecting such as appeared likely to suit his purposes, had them bound as apprentices. These lads he carefully trained, each to a separate class of work; for instance, he would keep one upon large French or Shell, another on the small, another on Italian, another to certain patterns of Spanish, and so on, bringing each to excel in a few patterns, but not making them perfect in all, with the exception of one, whom he required to do book edges, and for him it was necessary he should be taught the whole, he, as a matter of course, having higher wages than the others. Although at first there was a good deal of imperfect work produced, yet at that time prices were such as would amply remunerate for disposing of the produce of these embryo workers at a reduced price, and as they improved every week, while the cost of labour was so small, he soon found that his speculation was successful, and by the time these youths were out of their time he was able to command one of the most successful and best paying concerns going.

Woolnough added that if any dispute arose and any of the men left, he found difficulty in obtaining work elsewhere since his knowledge of the art was incomplete; thus he was forced to return to his old place. These conditions continued for many years, but when the master died and the business was divided among the men, who had been taken from the humble and illiterate class, none of them was equal to the responsibility of running it and the business declined.

When Woolnough issued the final edition of his classic work, he was in his middle or late sixties. He probably died a few years later and almost certainly before the end of the 1880s. The final section of his marbling manual bore as its frontispiece a facsimile of a letter from Michael Faraday, the great experimental physicist and chemist, thanking the marbling master for sending him a copy of his book. Faraday, having begun his working life as a bookbinder and bookseller, was particularly touched by Woolnough's presentation and was in a position to appreciate his significant contribution.

A final note here on Charles Wingham Woolnough is in order. The Charles Woolnough noticed by Wakeman in the London directories of 1860–1865 most likely was a son of Charles Wingham Woolnough who worked as a bookbinder and perhaps as an edge gilder and marbler. Approximately twenty-five years ago, when attempting to purchase a copy of Woolnough's manual in the hands of a woman in New Jersey, I learned that she was the great-granddaughter of our marbling master. Her father, she informed me, Charles Wingham Woolnough's grandson, had come to New York and had made his living as a bookbinder there; in time he specialized in gilding and became known as the best gilding craftsman in the city.[27]

The Mysterious Marbler: James Sumner

In 1854—just a year after the initial publication of Woolnough's *Art of Marbling* and coincidental with the issue of its second edition—James Sumner, a self-described "bookbinder and practical marbler," published the third British marbling manual to appear in the nineteenth century. The elongated title of Sumner's work, a small pamphlet of twenty-four pages, leaves little room to doubt either his viewpoint or his motive for issuing it. It reads, *The Mysterious Marbler; or, The Mystery Unfolded: Shewing How Every Bookbinder May Become a Marbler, to Establish and Defend the Rights of His Trade; For It Is His Definite Right That He Should Marble.* Dedicated to all connected with the trade of bookbinding, Sumner's work was distributed by T. J. Dunning and W. Bockett in London, and it could be obtained as well from any secretary of the Bookbinder's Consolidated Union throughout the country or from Sumner himself at Messrs. Lamberts in Newcastle-upon-Tyne. Assumedly, Sumner was working as a binder and perhaps as a marbler with the Lamberts in 1854, and his pamphlet provides directions for making the various marbles popular at that time. The copy in my possession is illustrated with small samples of original marbled paper, thirteen in all, which are mounted into the inner margins of its pages. These samples, showing the large and small Dutch, zebra, nonpareil, Spanish, shell, "French" (or Stormont), antique spot, west end, and Italian patterns, correlate with text directions for their manufacture.

In 1976, when I arranged for the reprinting of James Sumner's *Mysterious Marbler,* I marbled samples to illustrate it in imitation of those tipped into my own copy—the only copy of this rare manual that I had seen up to that time.[28] I have since examined the Olga Hirsch copy, now in the British Library, which does not have samples, and it became apparent to me that the original edition lacked samples altogether, those in my copy having been added by a contemporary owner. As I noted in my historical introduction to the 1976 reprint, my copy, its binder's title on the front cover implies, was owned by one John Hargreaves, who identified himself as a bookbinder of Rochdale. Bound in before Sumner's pamphlet is a copy of the fourth edition of John Hannett's *Bibliopegia; or, The Art of Bookbinding,* and at the end of the volume are several pages containing manuscript notes on marbling and an original mounted sample of Stormont paper. Among the notes are two recipes, one headed "How to Prepare Wax, by J. Sumner," and the other "Marbling Calf," each bearing dates in the year 1858 and accompanied by what appear to be authentic signatures of James Sumner, indicating that this copy once was in his hands. It is entirely possible that Sumner himself pasted in these samples, for they are uniformly and neatly cut and carefully chosen to illustrate the directions; they are also carefully mounted, and the marbling contained on them is well done and professional in every way.

At the beginning of his manual, Sumner pointed out that marbling had always been shrouded in mystery and that others, particularly bookbinders, had been denied a view of it; further, the information in the published literature was inadequate to teach the craft well. As a result, few bookbinders knew how to marble; their lack of marbling ability was detrimental to their interests and often caused them to lose good positions. Sumner argued that marblers had no right to restrict knowledge of their craft, for every bookbinder had a right to marble. In place of the monopolistic marbling shops that existed in many of the larger towns of Britain, he advocated a more democratic system whereby marbling would be done directly by bookbinders in bookbinding shops. Such a situation, he reasoned, would be beneficial to employers and proprietors of bookbinding establishments because it would not only eliminate their delays when books were sent out to have their edges decorated, but also challenge the independent status of the marbler who selfishly caused delays and other inconveniences. Sumner's introductory remarks concluded by noting that the observations he provided were based upon the experience and experiments of eight years. By learning and following his directions, bookbinders could do their own marbling, even in towns like London, Edinburgh, Dublin, Glasgow, Liverpool, Manchester and elsewhere where separate and independent marbling shops already were in existence.

Charles Woolnough, who provided us with information on marbling in Britain in his own time as well as glimpses of German and Spanish marbling, has also given us an additional view of James Sumner. From the circumstances to be related below, there is little doubt that Woolnough's venture into marbling cloth was not altogether successful and that he went back to decorating paper and book edges for bookbinders, often traveling around the countryside to solicit orders.

In the preface to the 1881 edition of his *Whole Art of Marbling,* Woolnough recounted that once, as he entered a business house in one of the larger manufacturing towns, his attention was directed to an individual who was just leaving. "Do you know that man?" the proprietor asked. Upon answering in the negative, Woolnough was told, "Why he is one of your fraternity, a most clever fellow, according to his own account he can do everything, and he has published a book which tells you all about it for the small charge of sixpence; we shall soon be able to do without you altogether and be 'Every man his own Marbler'." Woolnough met the visitor by chance the following day, and noticing that he did not appear too well off, felt a little sympathy for him. "Well, friend," he asked,

> "Were you not in such a place yesterday?" "Indeed I was," said he, putting the tip of his little finger into the bowl of his pipe, and tapping it on the palm of the other hand, "but I don't remember seeing you there." "Never mind," was the reply, "I saw you, and was informed what a clever fellow you were. Now I sometimes do a little in that way myself; have you met with any success?" "Ah no," said he, "I have been on the tramp these ten days, worn the shoes off my feet walking from place to place in search of employment; but no luck anywhere; shall leave here tonight and push on towards Liverpool." On a trifle being slipped into his hand, his countenance brightened, and with an exclamation of surprise, "Gad," said he, "but you are the best fellow I've met in many a day," and thrusting his hand into his coat pocket, he drew therefrom a small pamphlet of a few pages, saying, "Here, take this, there's something in it worth trying, I've tried it, and proved it myself, and I can confidently recommend it to you; it's first-rate. I took it out of a half-guinea book published by one Woolnough of London; and it's worth all the money."

Woolnough related that he never again saw the poor fellow, who never knew that it was Woolnough himself to whom he had confessed his delinquency and to whom he had strongly recommended his own production. Sumner's name is not mentioned in Woolnough's account, but it seems irrefutable from the circumstances that he was the man Woolnough had encountered: no one else had produced a marbling pamphlet in Britain at this time, and no one else had advocated that every man be his own marbler. No more is known of James Sumner, and it is likely that he passed his days at a journeyman bookbinder and sometime marbler, working in the Newcastle-upon-Tyne region and in the country to the south.

Other Doings

Because they are known to us through the literature they handed down, we tend to think of Charles Woolnough and James Sumner as the chief marblers in Britain of their time. Yet they are but two principals of a much larger trade that remains unrecognized because, guarding their secrets as they did, the vast majority of the craftsmen have left no notice of themselves other than their unsigned papers. We only know from these remnants, and through Woolnough, and Sumner, and other small bits of literature, that such a trade did exist. That it was substantial is attested to by the vast quantity of marbled paper that survives today in British imprints and publications of the late eighteenth and throughout the nineteenth century.

British marbling, which finally attained full and continuous production in the 1770s, grew vigorously and had a strong and energetic existence over the next fifty to seventy-five years. But in the 1830–1880 period the introduction of mechanization into bookbinding and the consequent decline in hand binding brought about a decrease in the use and production of marbled paper. This situation was hastened by a growing trend among publishers calling for the mechanized binding of whole editions of given works in uniform cloth cases, in which marbling was to have no role. These practices were beginning to sound the death knell for marbling even as Woolnough was preparing the first edition of his famous manual; indeed, it may well be that he was experimenting with the marbling of cloth as a means of countering the new technology and surviving it. By the end of the nineteenth century, marbling went out of vogue as decoration for all but specially hand-bound books, where ancient traditions were still practiced. Almost simultaneously, the numbers of hand binders decreased proportionately until their ranks had become severely diminished; mechanization brought new methods and materials into the book world at the expense of those employed in earlier times.

When *The British Bookmaker*, a journal for printers, illustrators, book designers, and bookbinders, ran, in its September 1890 and July 1892 supplements, pages containing six samples each of gold-veined English marbles and other new marbled papers manufactured by the firm of Berry & Roberts of Ludgate Circus, London, none of these were hand marbles of old. All were produced through mechanical or photomechanical methods, as were most other marbled papers that I have seen in a few Berry & Roberts sample books of this period that have come to my attention.[29] As a matter of fact, the 1890/91

volume of *The British Bookmaker* also contained an article describing "A Machine for Marbling Paper."[30]

According to a full-page advertisement that appeared in the July 1891 issue of *The British Bookmaker*,[31] the firm of Berry & Roberts had succeeded Joseph Corfield, who had established the business in 1832. The firm manufactured and sold bookbinding papers and similar materials of every description, such as gold vein and wood grain marbles and all sorts of imported marbles. Berry & Roberts also sold marbling supplies, including colors and gum tragacanth—"exactly the same as used by the firm in their marbling shops"—and it executed edge marbling and gilding for the trade. Berry & Roberts, then, was a marbling shop that serviced the bookbinding trade. Over the years it had expanded its activities, and by the 1890s it supplied the trade with a wide range of bookbinder's papers, including those manufactured on its premises and, as advertised, the company sold imported papers as well. Several small sample books that have come to my attention indicate that Berry & Roberts still executed hand marbling at this late date; but handwork must have constituted a lesser part of the overall business, for the majority of papers in its sample books show mechanically produced designs.

The reference to Joseph Corfield in the advertisement of Berry & Roberts suggested to me that he had been one of those anonymous marblers who plied their craft in London during Charles Woolnough's time. Consequently, while tracking Woolnough through the various local directories, I searched for Corfield as well, and my suspicions were confirmed: Joseph Corfield did indeed marble paper there, and for a very long time at that. Fortuitously, the *Post Office London Directory*, in its issues from the late 1830s on, included in its contents a "Trades' Directory," which served to index by occupation those listed in its main alphabetical register. Less fortuitously, however, marblers were not listed separately, but were grouped together with "Book & Card Edge Gilders & Marblers" or with "Book Edge Gilders & Marblers," making it necessary to check all individuals so described in the alphabetical section in order to ascertain their specific occupations.

Joseph Corfield was listed in the *Post Office London Directory* for 1846 and 1847 as a "book edge gilder," just as he had been designated in *Robson's London Directory, Street Key and Conveyance List* for 1837. But in the 1856 issue of the post office directory his occupation was described as "Corfield, J. W., book edge gilder & marble paper maker," and throughout the 1860s and into the early 1870s he was listed with the description, "Corfield, Joseph William & Son, dealers in bookbinders materials, manufacturers of marbled & colored papers, head bands, &c., agents for foreign marble paper &c., book edge gilders & marblers."[32] Directories from about 1878 until 1883 listed Joseph Corfield in approximately the same way, but without his son William Henry, who was listed separately as a "book edge gilder." Though the 1884 issue describes him in the same manner, he is listed as "Corfield, Joseph (now Berry & Roberts)," and Berry & Roberts is entered as "(late Joseph Corfield), wholesale stationers, dealers in bookbinders' materials, marble and colored paper manufacturers, millboard warehouse, foreign marble paper & straw board importers."

One source relates that J. Corfield and his son were commended at the 1862 London exposition for their finely combed papers. Reporting them to be of great beauty, the source also states that their colors were well distributed and that they were lively, distinctive, and left nothing to be desired, except that the red was a little too dominant. Further, their combed papers with swirls or curls in them, while a little pale, were judged to be good imitations of those made in the sixteenth and seventeenth centuries.[33]

While searching the London directories, I also checked in selected issues all of the names under the combined category "Book Edge Gilders & Marblers" to determine which among these craftsmen were specifically identified with marbling. Among those categorized thus in the 1847 postal directory, for instance, four of the thirteen were described in the main section as marblers, the remainder (including Corfield) being designated as book edge gilders. Only the following individuals were connected directly with the marbling trade:

Harley, John, book edge marbler, marble & colored
    paper maker & dlr in bookbinders' materials
Page, William, book marbler
Sanford, Wm., book edge &c. marbler
Woolnough, Charles Wingham, marbler

The *Post Office London Directory* for 1856 listed twenty individuals in this combined category, with the majority once more connected with edge gilding alone. Those appearing additionally as marblers, or as marblers alone, were:

Corfield, Joseph, book edge gilder and marbled
    papermaker
Crawford, John, book edge marbler
Hall, James, book marbler & gilder
Harley, Mrs. Mary, book edge marbler, marbler & col-
    ored papermaker, & dlr in bookbinders' materials
Page, Mary Hannah (Mrs.), book marbler
Powell, Wm., book clasp & edge ma [marbler?]
Ruding, Rogers, manufacturer of bookbinder's cloth,
    marbled coth, ultramarine cloth & marble paper,
    cotton, linen & wool dyer, calenderer, embosser &
    packer

Although Charles W. Woolnough's name is lacking from this list and no longer appears in any sections of the *Post Office London* directories thereafter, it is likely that he

continued as manager of the marbled paper and cloth manufacturing activities of the Rogers Ruding firm, which continued to be listed at 51 Bunhill Row.

The 1862 issue listed as marblers only Corfield, Mrs. Mary Harley, Samuel Page (as "account book marbler"), and Ruding & Co. And in the 1878 directory, the last one examined, the following individuals were connected with book or paper marbling:

Caudle, William & Chas., book edge marblers
Corfield, Joseph, wholesale stationer, marble & col-
    ored paper manufacturer & millboard & foreign
    marbled paper warehouse
Hall & Crawford, book marblers
Stevens, Henry & Co., book edge marblers

Some, if not many, of the book-edge gilders in these directories could also have marbled book edges and even paper, as Joseph Corfield did, but edge and paper gilding appears to have remained their primary occupation. There appears to have existed a closer connection between edge gilding and marbling than we can now determine, perhaps well beyond the common grouping of these occupations as related to the decoration of book edges. Finally, it should be noted that the marbling community, even in the British metropolis, was made up of only a small number of craftspeople. However, these limited numbers were sufficient to attend to edge decoration as well as turn out all of the marbled paper that, along with imported stock, was needed by their brethren in the bookbinding community to cover and embellish their bindings.

Several contemporary publications indicate that hand marbling, of both paper and book edges, was still going on in Britain in the 1890s.[34] The process doubtless continued into the present century, but on a diminished scale, being maintained now by individuals rather than shops. Here and there in London a few craftsmen remained to execute edge gilding and marbling for the trade on a specialty basis, and at extremely large printing houses a marbler was sometimes employed to do the edges of special editions and special productions or to marble the edges of ledgers and cash books to give them the comfortable appearance of old. Nevertheless, with regard to the larger trade that had existed earlier in the nineteenth century for the production of large amounts of decorated paper for hand bookbinders, time had all but run out. The marbling of paper would continue to be carried on in Great Britain in the present century, but not to the great extent or on the same basis as before, and not by the same type of artisan. More about these developments will be discussed in a later chapter.

Grace Notes

Just as in Europe, the mystique that marbling had possessed in earlier times diminished in nineteenth-century Britain as technology and the Industrial Revolution advanced. Accordingly, the dictionary and encyclopedia literature noticed it less and less, and in time either dropped the subject altogether or mentioned it only in passing. There were a few exceptions, however, which are worthy of notice. Just after mid-century, a fairly detailed account of this process appeared in Charles Tomlinson's *Cyclopaedia of the Useful Arts, Mechanical and Chemical, Manufactures, Mining, and Engineering*.[35] The editor referred to the 1829 account in *Gill's Technological Repository*, stating that he had extracted that description and embellished it with details of the art based on a demonstration he had witnessed in the shop of one of the most skillful marblers in London, the particulars of which did not necessarily agree with the earlier published account. He described how the marbler produced with five or six colors a pattern he named the "Battle of Waterloo" because of "some fanciful resemblance in the patterns to the colours of the uniforms of the opposing forces at the battle"; and he apologized for not giving more precise details respecting the mixing of colors, because they had purposely been withheld.

In the Olga Hirsch collection in the British Library, I examined another minor contribution to the English literature of marbling that seems to have been largely ignored by prior commentators, although Dard Hunter recorded its title in his early bibliography of marbling[36] and Mrs. Easton reprinted his citation.[37] Issued at London in 1873 under the title *Prepared Papers And How To Make Them*, this small pamphlet deals with the manufacture of all sorts of specialty papers, such as lens paper, filtering papers, paper for water color painting, and other esoteric types, and describes, in a three-page résumé, how marbled varieties were produced.[38]

The last worthwhile notice of this art in Britain in the nineteenth century occurred in 1880, when Joseph W. Zaehnsdorf, a leading London specialty binder, included a few pages on "Marbled Edges" in his manual on *The Art of Bookbinding*, of which a sixth edition had appeared by 1903.[39] In his initial description, Zaehnsdorf provided a brief history of the art, derived in part from Woolnough's 1878 address on the subject (which he may have heard); he added that marbled papers could be purchased from Messrs. Eadie & Son of Queen Street, London, who had succeeded in getting a gold vein intermixed with the colors, which had a most curious but excellent effect. Beginning with the second edition, Zaehnsdorf reproduced the illustration from G. Smith's *The Laboratory, or School of Arts* (1750 edition) and also illustrated a complete marbling apparatus, containing colors in bottles, gall, cups, combs, and so forth, which the Leo firm of Stuttgart had put up and placed on the market.[40] Zaehnsdorf's volume was intended especially for the use of the hand bookbinder who occasionally might wish or have need to add edge decoration to his works, for hardly any professional marblers existed anymore; it was also meant for the interested amateur.

Bookbinders could obtain information on marbling, mainly to assist them in edge decoration, from several other English publications that were issued at the end of the nineteenth century and in the early years of the succeeding one. Of these, W. J. E. Crane's *Bookbinding for Amateurs*[41] and Paul N. Hasluck's *Bookbinding*[42] can be cited, for both contained ample instructions on how to marble and both remained in print for a long time. Each of these works espoused the classical English type of marbling that was epitomized in the writings of Charles Woolnough. Crane's account, in fact, derived directly from Woolnough's manual, although among Hasluck's directions can be perceived some of the "new marbling" that had been introduced in the meantime by Josef Halfer. This, however, will be a subject to be considered in a later chapter.

8

Marbling in the New World, I

IN America, as in Britain, attempts at marbling were going on as early as 1764–1773, but overall the development of the craft in the New World lagged behind that in England by twenty-five to fifty years. In contrast to the British experience, however, we have little evidence documenting the embryonic stage of the craft in America, and so we are once again forced to piece together scraps of information in order to gain some sense of the activity that apparently took place in these early times.

In her ever-useful compilation of newspaper advertisements of early New York craftsmen and tradesmen, published in three volumes under the collective title *The Arts and Crafts in New York,* Rita Susswein Gottesman provides our first "two bits." Her initial volume (covering the years from 1726 to 1776) includes an advertisement from *The New York Mercury* of 24 December 1764 of one T. Anderton, "Book-Binder, Letter Case, and Pocket Book-Maker," lately arrived from England, who gave notice that he "performs book-binding in its full perfection, in all sorts of plain and rich bindings," and "marbles and gilds the edges of books," and carried out similar functions. One of Anderton's functions, according to the advertisement, was making note cases, pocketbooks, and wallets of the type illustrated on Plate I.[1] Anderton's name appears in George McKay's register of the early New York book trades in a listing for the year 1764 only, at "The Sign of the Orange Tree, in Cannon's Wharf";[2] little else is known about him beyond the fact that he soon moved on to Philadelphia where Hannah French locates him in 1768.[3]

In the same volume, Mrs. Gottesman republished the advertisement of another itinerant bookbinder, George Leedell, "late of London." When giving notice in *The New-York Gazette and the Weekly Mercury* of 3 May 1773 that he had moved his business to another location, he also advertised the various services that he was prepared to render, including "books marbled on the edges, as in London."[4] Leedell, like Anderton before him, seems to have worked in New York City but briefly, for he too is known only through this single advertisement. We can only surmise from these two notices that some marbling was going on in New York as well as in London at that time, although we must acknowledge, the edge marbling

they professed to carry out may have had little resemblance to the true marbling discussed in these pages. It may have been decoration applied to book edges through sprinkling, rubbing, or in some other process. It may also have been the simple water marbling that came to be discussed in English bookbinding manuals early in the nineteenth century.

Benjamin Franklin and the Marbling of Money and Documents

Within two years of Leedell's advertising, the American colonies revolted from their mother country. While such an occurrence usually results in a slowdown or temporary stoppage of many domestic affairs (particularly the production of luxury items such as fine bookbindings), events associated with the Revolution provide us with a further clue that marbling indeed was going on in the American colonies; interestingly enough, we get a sense that Benjamin Franklin was somehow mixed up in the business.

When we last noticed Ben Franklin, he was present at the committees of the Society for the Encouragement of Arts, Manufactures, and Commerce meeting in London in 1760–1762, including the committee that voted a premium of £100 to promote the manufacture of marbled paper. He spent the next dozen years shuttling between England and America, trying his best to reconcile the widening breach between the two countries and to present the American case to his British friends and the British public, even as he watched the crisis grow. In 1775, when the break finally came, Franklin took an active part in forging the new republic, serving on one committee for the organization of a postal system, another for drafting the Declaration of Independence, and on a third that failed in its attempt to bring Canada into the war as an American ally. Still another matter in which he became deeply involved was the design and printing of Continental paper money.

In June and November of 1775 and early 1776, Congress authorized the issuance of $7,000,000 in Continental currency to pay the initial expenses of the American Revolution, and Franklin was appointed to the committee superintending its printing. Entries in his extant papers suggest that he was involved in adapting designs from older paper bills, as well as designing new ones.[5] Further, the $20 bills printed individually by Hall & Sellers, the printing firm that had succeeded Franklin's own, were printed on white paper supplied by Franklin; and its reverse side was polychromed by the marbling process, no doubt as a means for checking counterfeiting. Plate XVIII illustrates the reverse side of one of these $20 bills, to which the marbled decoration had to be added locally, possibly at Franklin's instigation.[6]

This was not the only instance in which Benjamin Franklin was connected with a marbled document. In 1776 he was sent by Congress to France to seek economic and military aid, although such assistance was not immediately forthcoming. Only after the defeat of General Burgoyne at Saratoga early in 1778 did the French authorities finally see fit to lend support: they agreed to sign a treaty with the American revolutionaries and advance them substantial loans. Some of the loan agreements and promissory notes with Franklin's signature were printed by Franklin on the private press he set up at Passy to serve the needs of the American mission. The edges of these documents were marbled, no doubt, as a means of assuring their authenticity. On these occasions, the marbled decoration was put there by an unknown French marbler whose technique was far superior to that of his American counterpart. Printed presumably in duplicate, with one copy retained by the French government and the other by Franklin himself, several of these notes are preserved by the American Philosophical Society, the highest number of their series being no. 20, dated 12 March 1782. The note illustrated here on Plate XVIII, numbered 18 and dated 4 December 1781, is now in a private collection.[7]

The use of marbling to authenticate early American paper currency is in evidence again in 1789; and while Benjamin Franklin probably was not directly involved in this undertaking—he was at home, in bed, and died within the year—one source relates that once more he furnished the paper for it. Moreover, this currency was printed by Benjamin Franklin Bache, his grandson.[8] When a "copper panic" occurred in July of that year, after banks refused to accept copper coins, the Bank of North America in Philadelphia issued small bills payable in specie. Some of the bills contained marbled borders (put there with the aid of a stencil or perhaps the "margent" that Samuel Pope spoke of fifty years earlier) and others, like the one illustrated here (Plate XVIII), were marbled across their reverse sides.

These curiosities of early American printing and numismatics are not only interesting because they connect Benjamin Franklin with early American marbling and show the ingenuity and pragmatism of the man, but they are also important because they indicate once again that a knowledge of marbling was present and the process in use in late eighteenth-century America. It is likely, however, that the skill was restricted at this time to less than a handful of individuals, perhaps even to only one or two; if this were not so, marbling would not have constituted an additional check on counterfeiting paper money. But, one may ask, who was the individual or individuals responsible for applying such decoration to these bills? Who were the marblers? The answer, in the words of Franz Weisse, is "this the Gods alone know. Up till now they have divulged their identities to no investigator."

Misty Beginnings

To those of us who work in large research libraries with extensive collections of early American printings and bookbindings, it is evident that the real beginning of marbling in America extends from the last decade of the eighteenth century into the first and second decades of the next. It is true that considerable numbers of foreign marbles—British, German, and French—continued to arrive into American ports and subsequently appeared as endpapers or cover papers on American bookbindings; at the same time one also sees marbled paper that exhibits color and pattern configurations distinctly dissimilar from European sheets, and in which the techniques of their makers were not nearly so highly developed. This situation is especially apparent in the period just after 1800, and becomes more evident with each succeeding year. It is obvious that individuals in several locations in America where extensive printing and bookbinding activities existed were beginning to apply themselves to marbling for their livelihood (or at least to supplement their circumstances). Such activity can be associated with Philadelphia, New York, and Boston, with Worcester, Massachusetts, where Isaiah Thomas oversaw a large printing and bookselling enterprise, and perhaps with a few other locations, too. Some of these activities may have been undertaken by stationers, who in those times not only sold products associated with their trade but also published, sold, and bound books as well.

As to the identities of these craftsmen and the makers actually involved in this activity, admittedly, we are once more in the dark. This much, however, we do know or can surmise: most if not all of these marblers probably were self-taught, slowly groping their way toward mastering a difficult and capricious medium. The sheets that they turned out provide evidence of the hurdles that they had to overcome and their lack of experience along the way. That it took a long time to surmount all the difficulties is reflected in the crude and imperfect appearance of many of the sheets of this time, especially when compared with the superior finish of contemporary English and European papers. Additionally, no authentic American bookbindings before about 1804 are known to contain marbled decoration on their edges, and edge marbling would remain an extremely rare occurrence for a decade or two to come.[9] As in Britain, these American craftsmen sensed that there was money to be made in the business of marbling. Unlike their British counterparts, however, they had no munificent society of learned and enlightened men to encourage them; probably only the perennial American quest to make a dollar spurred them on.

Some insight into the state of marbling at the end of the eighteenth century is afforded by entries in Isaiah Thomas's ledger books, which are preserved in the archives of the American Antiquarian Society that he founded in 1812. Although consideration of this matter will leave us with more questions than answers, it should nonetheless be mentioned. Specifically, there are a number of entries in Thomas's "Paper Mill Account" of 1794 for the procurement and purchase of marbled paper from Caleb and Elijah Burbank, papermakers of nearby Sutton, Massachusetts. Hannah French cites one such entry in her "Early American Bookbinding by Hand," recording that on 13 August Thomas ordered from the Burbanks five quires of marbled paper (120 to 150 sheets) for the sum of twelve shillings.[10] (Much to our regret, Thomas himself does not mention marbled paper in his *History of Printing in America,* issued in 1810.) The Burbanks were papermakers, and normally marbling was never connected with the process of making paper but was carried on independently, after the paper was made, and by a different sort of craftsman. However, it is not impossible that the Burbanks engaged in marbling as an adjunct to their papermaking activities, and perhaps they employed a specialist to do it for them. Paper was in short supply in America in the 1790s, and a marbler or someone interested in supplying marbled paper was best advised to connect himself with a paper mill to assure a steady supply of his most basic material.

The always useful and reliable directories of the early American book trades, compiled for New York City by George McKay, and for Philadelphia by the husband and wife team of H. Glenn and Maude O. Brown,[11] provide us with our first identifications of marblers who were working in early America. Even in these publications, however, the situation is somewhat confused by the broad and imprecise occupation titles with which many of these artisans were identified and by the fact that some were engaged in collateral pursuits, such as making and hanging wallpaper, staining paper, and decorating paper for purposes other than bookbinding and stationery use.

McKay's *Register of Artists, Engravers, Booksellers, Bookbinders, Printers & Publishers in New York City, 1633–1820* includes a number of individuals in these categories, a few of whom are called marblers. Moses Valentine, probably a member of a family of local paper merchants, appears as a "marble paper manufacturer" in 1805; David Carvallo is designated "marble paper manufactory" in the following year; and Francis Lippens is described with the all-encompassing term "paper colorer" in 1820. Other names appear in McKay's *Register* with the description "paper stainer," a designation most often associated with the coloring of monochrome papers, although it sometimes was used to describe makers of wallpaper as well.

The Browns' *Directory of the Book-Arts and Book Trade in Philadelphia to 1820, Including Painters and Engravers* provides similar listings of individuals whose names were culled from local directories as well as other contemporary sources. The name of John Shease (or Shiese) was picked up from local directories for the years 1802–1806 as a "marble papermaker." Francis Germon appears as "paper hanger, marble papermaker" in the period from 1814 through 1820 and is further listed with this designation in Philadelphia directories through 1825, finally appearing in the issue for 1825 as "paperhanger." Henry Young is also designated in the Browns' directory as a "paperhanger and marble papermaker" in 1819 and 1820. He continued to be included in Philadelphia directories through 1843, with the descriptions "paperhanger" or "gilder." Finally, William Swain is identified as a "marble papermaker" in 1820.

All attempts to learn more about the specific activities of these artisans and craftsmen have so far proved unsuccessful, and thus the exact nature of their work remains unclear, although it seems certain that some of them must have marbled. Fortunately, a major breakthrough in our understanding of the marbling trade in New England, and in America, for that matter, came a few years ago with the discovery of the manuscript papers of a family in the book trades named Mann, whose members marbled paper during the first half of the nineteenth century in Boston, Providence, and, for the most part, in Dedham, a small Massachusetts town between those two locations. By examining the role of the Mann family in paper marbling, we may obtain a remarkably detailed view of the early American paper marbler at work.

The Mann Family, and Marbling in the Boston Area

We begin this discussion of marbling in nineteenth-century America with the city of Boston—not because it was the first American locale to receive the art, for we know clearly that it was not, but because it is the area for which the most information exists, thanks to the fortuitous discovery of the Mann family's papers. In essence, these papers provide the most intimate view of a group of working marblers that exists for any place in the world.

Herman Mann, the patriarch who began the family's connection with the book trades and with marbling, was a pedantic, somewhat romantic, and overly optimistic individual—traits that would lead him into business disappointments and financial crises throughout most of his publishing and bookselling career.[12] Mann came from good New England stock and had received a better than average education for his time. In June of 1797, when he was nearly twenty-seven years old and was working in nearby Walpole as a school teacher, he came to Dedham, a town seven miles south of Boston, in search of a printer to set into type the manuscript journal of a young Massachusetts woman who had served in disguise in the American army during the Revolutionary War. The young idealist had, a few years earlier, discovered this account and edited it; he now wished to have it published in honor of his bride. The upshot was that he not only got his manuscript published, but also purchased half an interest in the *Minerva,* the Dedham weekly newspaper. Within a year he purchased the other half and became solely responsible for printing it, beginning at the same time a lifelong career in printing, bookselling, bookbinding, and all the other activities that were necessary for the survival of those engaging in the book trade of that time.

In addition to his newspaper publishing, Herman Mann began to issue what amounted, over the years, to a considerable number of books and pamphlets on a variety of subjects, with a strong peppering of sermons and religious tracts among them, and schoolbooks as well. (In a letter to a son, whom he had trained to set type and print, he advised the printing of sermons as a source of good and steady income.) In 1804, because of his interest in music, he purchased a font of music type and became one of the most active publishers of music books of early nineteenth-century America—a specialty, he felt, that was necessary at that time in America and one likely to bring him a good income. Never idle or without a scheme to make money, he also tried his hand at papermaking and other ventures.

In September 1809 Herman Mann informed the readers of his newspaper, now the *Columbian Minerva,* that he had established a marble paper manufactory, "having obtained the apparatus and art of Marbling Paper, at much trouble and expense." He had thus launched himself and his family on a path that was to lead through this rough terrain for the next fifty or more years, for most of the ten surviving Mann children would become engaged in this activity in one way or another, with sons Daniel, Samuel, Edward, and Franklin (named after one of Herman's favorite authors and philosophers, Benjamin Franklin) becoming especially proficient and active.

The wording of Herman's announcement strongly implies that he had paid someone for the necessary marbling equipment and for training in the technique of the craft, and this leads us to a matter that has provoked my curiosity for many years. It became apparent to me that some individual, who still remains unidentified, was marbling paper in the Boston and Cambridge area from about 1800 on. Many extant books and pamphlets published in these locations around 1800 and for half a decade or more afterward are covered with marbled paper of a pattern that continually turns up on these imprints, but not on ones published elsewhere, leading to the conclusion that someone was producing these papers locally.

In 1800 and for a year or two afterward, the pattern is a very individualistic one, showing black and orange veins (actually, rather thick blobs of black and orange color) that are broken up by blue lacy spots characteristic of the Stormont pattern. While Stormont seems the only pattern this marbler produced (remember, this was the period of the pattern's greatest popularity worldwide), he later used red color in place of orange, and yellow was introduced into the pattern as well. An example of this maker's early pattern appears as sample 85 on Plate XXX here.

Just who produced these papers we do not know, nor can we determine where or how he had learned to marble. Sometime around 1808 or 1809, or perhaps even earlier, our unidentified marbler apparently ceased working. At least those early sheets we associate with him are not seen after that period, and it may be that he sold his equipment, supplies, and knowledge to Herman Mann, who succeeded him, for it is only the Mann's marbling that we notice later. What may have caused this earlier artisan's departure from marbling and perhaps from the Boston area remains a mystery.[13]

Herman Mann ceased publishing his newspaper in late 1809, concurrent with his entry into the marbling field, and for some unknown reason he moved his family and his printing business to nearby Providence, Rhode Island, late in 1812. However, the house in Dedham was retained and family letters indicate that there was much coming and going between the two places during the family's three-year residence in Providence. By this time he was assisted by his sons, who had grown or were growing to manhood.

As I have described in my book on the Mann family, the letters the family exchanged at this time give us glimpses of Herman's oldest son Daniel marbling in Dedham in 1812 and of Daniel and the family conducting the process in Providence as well, where most of the Manns lived during the War of 1812 and where some of the sons worked intermittently as printers and in other phases of the book arts in the late teens and early twenties. In 1821, and also in 1825, Herman Mann, who had opened up his Norfolk Bookstore in Dedham following his return from Providence in 1815, advertised that the shop manufactured marbled paper of various qualities and in all sizes, polished or unpolished. All Herman's sons were at one time or another involved in the various aspects of his business, including printing, marbling, bookselling, and probably bookbinding; the younger sons, Samuel C. and Edward, later became major exponents of marbling in the Boston area.

Early in 1827, Samuel Mann decided to begin a career in marbling. He had worked in his father's bookstore for about seven years, where he undoubtedly learned his marbling, and was now contemplating marriage, which necessitated a private income. Establishing his workshop initially at Dedham, he soon moved his field of activity to

Boston in order to be accessible to a larger clientele and connected himself in some sort of business relationship first with Lemuel Blake, a local paper merchant, and later with Josiah Loring, a long-established Boston bookseller, stationer, and bookbinder. In September of 1829 he enlarged his business, opening the "Boston Marble-Paper Manufactory" on Bromfield Street, where he boasted of making a marbled paper superior to anything previously offered, and at a low price. About two and a half years later he was joined in partnership by Edward Mann, who, according to a letter from Samuel of July 5, 1830, was then living in Dedham and learning to marble. In November of 1831 Samuel sent Edward, still living in Dedham, a long letter in which he outlined plans for their partnership. He mentioned, as an important consideration, settling the question of where they would permanently locate, and he urged expediency lest a person named Mitton get ahead of them by opening up another manufactory.

R. C. Mitton (his Christian names are unknown) had advertised in the *Boston Daily Advertiser* of October 28, 1831 that he was recently from England, and would instruct for a moderate price any person wanting information on the art of fancy paper coloring and the marbling of book edges in a style superior to any made in the United States. He would also teach papermakers how to color paper in the pulp and would instruct paperhangers as to how to make a superior type of French green. The only other information we have about Mitton comes from Samuel Mann's November 12, 1831 letter to his brother Edward. Attempting to work out an equitable financial arrangement for their partnership—with himself, as senior partner, to receive a larger share of the profits—Samuel related that he had paid Mitton the then considerable sum of $300 for instruction, undoubtedly in the latest and best techniques, for making the newest patterns in vogue. Mitton, it appears, fell into the category, referred to earlier by Hugh Sinclair and later by Charles Woolnough, of the itinerant craftsman (and perhaps bookbinder), who traveled about imparting some of his marbling knowledge for a fee. But in this case, he had obviously moved even further afield than did his British brethren in the trade. We hear no more of Mitton after this time. He apparently did not enter into competition with the Manns in manufacturing marbled paper in Boston, and it may be assumed that, having earned so large a fee there, he went on to other green fields, or perhaps even returned to England.

Samuel and Edward Mann threw themselves into manufacturing marbled paper in Boston with tremendous energy. This is indicated by contemporary advertisements and a few letters and documents that reveal that they had a seemingly insatiable need for paper on which to apply their decoration. By the end of 1832 they advertised that they had on hand, and for sale, 300 reams of marbled and colored paper of various qualities and sizes, including

40 to 50 reams Medium and Foolscap, Spanish shaded, a superior article. Also, 30 reams Medium Mottled, a good article for *Blank Books, Trunks, Fancy Boxes,* &c. The Papers are generally superior to those heretofore offered, and are manufactured on paper made expressly for that purpose, and put up with *20 perfect quires to the ream.*

It was the Mann's voracious appetite for paper (as indicated in my book on this family, Samuel and Edward evidently acquired nearly 350,000 sheets in 1832 alone) that brought them into financial difficulties. Their dilemma was probably caused by what we call today a "cash flow problem," caused by too many purchases on credit and not enough cash coming in to pay for them or at least to keep their creditors at bay. At the rate the Manns appear to have been marbling in this period, Hugh Sinclair's boast of having produced 2,000 reams or nearly a million sheets of marbled paper in a seven-year period does not seem absurd at all. Early in 1834, the Manns' creditors, chiefly the Boston paper-merchant firm of Carter & Hendee, called their notes, attached their property, gained judgment, and liquidated their assets. In the meantime, Samuel and Edward had transferred their operation back to Dedham, and here they spent the remainder of their business careers, employing a Boston agent to handle the sale and distribution of their wares in the city. Their output included marbled and fancy papers and enameled and other types of business cards, a sideline that brother Daniel had started while working in Providence and New York in the late teens and early twenties. By the time that Herman Mann, Jr., compiled and published his *Historical Annals of Dedham* in 1847, things seem to have been going quite well, for he described his brothers' factory thus, when summing up the business activities of the town:[14]

Establishment for Marble and Fancy Colored Papers, 1. Gross Value of marble and fancy paper, $10,000; of enamelled and other business cards, $8000. Capital invested in said business, $7500. Males employed, 5, females, 10.

Clearly brother Franklin, the baby of the family, worked in the factory and learned his marbling there. In the mid-1840s, however, for some obscure reason, he moved to New York City; his activities there will be discussed in a later section. Some, and perhaps all, of the Mann sisters also worked in the Dedham plant, probably embossing and gilding business cards, folding, wrapping, and performing accounting and clerical duties. In mid-1848, Edward, who, like his father, was a poetic and somewhat romantic man, was seized with a fit of melancholy following the death of his wife and died about three months later, leaving Samuel to carry on the business alone. Samuel and his sisters continued operating the factory into the late 1850s or early 1860s, when he too became ill.

After Samuel's illness, the business seems to have ceased. Daniel, the eldest of the brothers, had died in 1830; Herman Sr., the father, had died in 1833; and William and Herman had deserted marbling in favor of other pursuits.

All evidence seems to indicate that the Manns were the only marblers—or at least the only significant ones—in or around Boston in the 1810–1860 period. While stationers and a few others may have engaged in marbling on a much smaller scale during this time, the Manns probably produced most of the product that was needed to satisfy local demand, and they shipped their surplus stock all over New England, especially to Hartford, and further south to New York, two cities which, by the 1840s, had become large publishing centers. In this same period, however, with the increasing employment of cloth as a bookbinding material and the concurrent growth of edition binding (in which marbling played little or no role), the demand for marbled paper diminished, making it easier for the Manns to keep abreast of business as it too began to dwindle. Various advertisements of the Manns, including the broadside catalog of the wares they manufactured and sold (Figure 9), indicate that they had come to make all or at least most of the patterns popular in their day, although, from the viewpoint of technique, their products were a step down from the best European and English sheets and papers being manufactured in Philadelphia at the same time. (This broadside also shows that in the 1850s Samuel Mann had an agent in Baltimore.) Nonetheless, their quality was considered excellent by their users, and the Manns deserve recognition for developing and fostering the art in America. In the final analysis, they measured up to the rigid standard that separates the veteran marbler from the novice or amateur: long and extensive production on a level that meets the requirements of master bookbinders.

In 1837, when they were back at Dedham and working in their factory there, Samuel and Edward Mann entered a sampling of their marbled paper into competition in the first exhibition and trade fair sponsored by the Massachusetts Charitable Mechanic Association in Boston. The printed catalog of this event noted, under the category "Bookbinding, Binders' Tools, and Blank Books," the judges' approval of the samples that the Manns had submitted:

> S. C. & E. Mann, *Dedham, Mass.* Various specimens of marbled paper, showing a wonderful improvement in the art, both in common form of patterns, and in some very difficult imitations of stones, marbles and wood. They should be highly appreciated.
>
> *A silver medal*[15]

Before leaving the Mann family and the Boston area to consider marblers and marbling activities elsewhere, I feel it would be appropriate to examine another subject which has been heretofore little observed and all but ignored in the literature of marbling: the overmarbling of printed sheets early in the nineteenth century. This appears to be another activity in which the Manns were deeply involved, and, with regard to its practice in America, possibly to the exclusion of all other craftsmen.

The Overmarbling of Printed Sheets—and the Fanny Hill Affair

It was not unusual for paper to be in short supply in early America, and this situation persisted into the first decades of the nineteenth century.[16] At the same time, poor economic conditions in the new republic and the scarcity

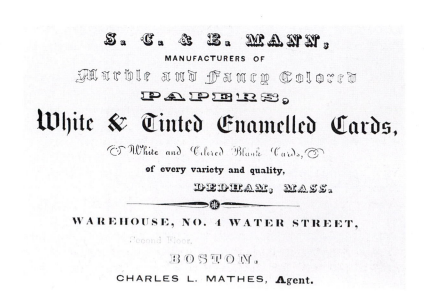

FIGURE 9. *Left,* trade card of Samuel C. and Edward Mann (1840), indicating that Charles L. Mathes acted as their Boston agent; *right,* broadside advertisement of Samuel C. Mann (1850s), indicating sizes and sorts of marbled paper offered.

Samuel C. Mann,

—— MANUFACTURER OF ——

MARBLE AND FANCY COLORED PAPERS,

WHITE AND TINTED ENAMELLED CARDS,

PEARL SURFACE, WHITE AND COLORED BLANK CARDS,

OF EVERY VARIETY AND QUALITY,

DEDHAM,...MS.

Agent.

~ WHOLESALE PRICE CATALOGUE. ~

MARBLE PAPERS....ASSORTED.

Medium, Common,	-	No. 1,	$14 00 per Ream.	Medium, Nonpareil,	-	No. 2,	$16 00 per Ream.
Do. "		" 2,	11 50 "	Old Dutch,			16 00 "
Do. "		" 3,	10 00 "	Double Crown,			13 50 "
Do. Span. Shaded,		" 1,	16 00 "	Cap, Common,		No. 1,	7 50 "
Do. "		" 2,	12 50 "	Do. "		" 2,	6 50 "
Do. " Crimpled	-		18 00 "	Double Cap, Common,			12 00 "
Do. Nonpareil,	-	" 1,	20 00 "	Italian Waved, same price as No. 2, Common Marble.			

COLORED PAPERS....ASSORTED AND SEPARATE.

Medium.	-	No. 1,	$14 00	Medium, Black, Glazed,	$15 00 to 20 00
Do.	-	" 2,	11 50	Extra Qualities, Colored Papers,	$15 00 to 30 00
Do.	-	" 3,	10 00	Common,	$9 00

COLORED, AND OTHER STOCK....FOR TICKETS....Constantly on Hand.

SECOND QUALITY ENAMELLED CARDS.....Half Price.

SCALE OF SIZES AND PRICES of Pearl Surface and Colored Cards, MANUFACTURED BY SAMUEL C. MANN, DEDHAM...MASS.

No. 8	—3.25 per dozen.
" 7	—2.75 "
" 6	—2.25 "
" 5¾	—1.75 "
" 5	—1.33 "
" 4	—1.25 "
" 3	—1.15 "
" 2	—1.08 "
" 1	—1.00 "

SCALE OF SIZES AND PRICES of White and Tinted ENAMELLED CARDS, MANUFACTURED BY SAMUEL C. MANN, DEDHAM...MASS.

No. 10, WHITE OR TINTED.	—$7.00 per dozen.
" 9, "	6.00 "
" 8½, "	5.00 "
" 8, "	4.75 "
" 7½, "	4.00 "
" 7, "	3.75 "
" 6½, "	3.50 "
" 6, "	3.00 "
" 5, "	2.50 "
" 4, "	2.37½ "
" 3, "	2.25 "
" 2, "	2.12½ "
" 1, "	2.00 "

of hard money often forced printers, bookbinders, and others in the book trades to operate marginally, procuring supplies as best they could and stretching their resources to the utmost. Accordingly, it should come as no surprise to learn that some early American marblers (as well as a few English and German marblers of the same time) occasionally obtained whole sheets of paper that already had been printed for editions of books but were left unsold after interest in such works had subsided; they then applied marbled decoration to the sheets and offered them for sale. Similarly, whole sheets printed for editions that were abandoned before completion or otherwise left unfinished were grist for the overmarbler's mill. Sometimes marblers acquired sheets printed on one side only and could decorate the unprinted side; more often, however, waste sheets were printed on both sides, so the marbler had to apply decoration over printed text. Undoubtedly, such waste sheets were bought and subsequently sold by their marblers more cheaply than the plain white sheets that they marbled concurrently.

Although not restricted to American marbling,[17] the practice was especially prevalent here because of frequent shortages of paper and hard cash. It seems likely that overmarbling was mostly practiced in the New England area and that it may have been carried on exclusively, or almost exclusively, by the Mann family, for in almost every case where I have been able to make an identification (mainly through the printing underneath the marbling), such sheets can, in one way or another, be traced to them. As is the case with edge marbling, these overmarbled printed sheets provide us once again with a set of "controlled conditions," and reveal something of special interest about the early American marbling trade. Almost all the printed sheets with marbling on them date to the first three decades of the nineteenth century; this applies to English and German as well as American sheets. Only rarely do we discover that the marbling was executed at an earlier or later time.[18]

Before the third or fourth decades of the nineteenth century, when modern publishing houses began to come into existence in America along with edition binding, printers and booksellers sponsoring editions frequently put parts of the editions in cheap sheepskin bindings ready for use; these were sold at a low price. Other parts were often put into even cheaper, temporary pasteboard covers to be rebound more elaborately later according to their purchasers' wishes. Still other parts of these editions were often left in whole sheets, unsewn and unbound, their bookseller-publishers putting no further investment in them until demand justified such expense. In many instances, the loose sheets remained unsold for years, as anticipated interest in their printed matter did not come about. These out-of-date and remaining whole sheets, as well as sheets left over from editions that were never completed, provided materials that marblers were able to acquire cheaply and decorate in their special way. The practice was not uncommon in the early nineteenth cen-

tury, and such overmarbled papers were used most often to cover periodicals, account books, and other cheap work. With regard to this practice in America, in almost every example I have encountered where the texts can be identified, there is some association with New England or some connection between their marbling and the Mann family of Dedham.

Plates XVIII and XIX reproduce several examples of marbling over sheets printed in America during this early period. The last two illustrations on Plate XVIII show this type of overmarbled paper on the endpapers of a beautiful gilt morocco binding that was executed in Boston in the period after 1808 and is now preserved in the Bryn Mawr College Library, which possesses an outstanding collection of early American bookbindings. Two works are contained in this volume: a copy of the Protestant Episcopal Church's *Book of Common Prayer*, printed at Boston in 1794 by Manning and Loring for Isaiah Thomas and E. T. Andrews, and a copy of the *Hymns, Selected from the Most Approved Authors, for the Use of the Trinity Church, Boston*, issued by Munroe, Francis, & Parker at Boston in 1808. (The latter contained printed music to which the texts in both works could be sung.) The printing underneath the marbling has been identified as a sheet from *The Monthly Anthology, and Boston Review* for 1804 as the title and date of this magazine clearly show through the color on top, as does the pseudonym of its editor, "Sylvanus Per-Se" (D. P. Adams).[19] The marbled pattern is the popular and ubiquitous Stormont that appears on many contemporary Boston bindings or serves as wrappers on many local pamphlets. Thus, the marbling was executed locally, no earlier than 1808, the year of the printing of the *Hymns* contained in this volume, and probably within a few years later.

The initial illustration on Plate XIX reproduces part of the binding and one of the overmarbled endpapers in a copy (in the author's collection) of Washington Irving's *Salmagundi* that was reprinted in two volumes by David Longworth at New York in 1814. The presence of these overmarbled waste sheets in the *Salmagundi* binding would seem to indicate, at first glance, that their marbled decoration had been executed in New York City, where this work was printed. Furthermore, I have identified the printing beneath as part of a deluxe edition of James Foxe's *The New and Complete Book of Martyrs* that had been printed and sold by the New York printer and stationer William Durrell at his shop in Pearl Street, near the Fly Market, in 1794; the location thus seems even more likely.[20] But also in my collection is the exact overmarbled text on the cheap pasteboard covers of a copy of Dr. James Mann's *Medical Sketches of the Campaigns of 1812, 13, 14*, which the Mann family printed at Dedham in 1816.[21] And, further, my collection of early overmarbled papers contains several other overmarbled sheets from this same edition of *The New and Complete Book of Martyrs*, and they have been observed or reported on books and periodicals in a number of New England libraries, including many at the American Antiquarian Society; their abundance indicates that the marbling was done in the New England area, and in all likelihood, by the Manns.[22] It should be pointed out that the use of printed papers with overmarbling as endpapers in finer bindings (such as *The Book of Common Prayer* and *Salmagundi*) is unusual, for more often than not they were employed for paper covers on cheap work. And the fact that twenty years elapsed between the printing of the Durell sheets of the *Book of Martyrs* and their employment as marbled endpapers in the *Salmagundi* binding (which, based on style and tooling, appears to have been done in New England) also seems unusual. According to the Manns' preserved correspondence, however, they were selling and trading marbled papers and printed books in New York City at this time and it seems probable that they acquired out-of-date printed sheets for overmarbling wherever they encountered them.

Several other examples of overmarbling can be associated with the Mann family (see Plate XIX). In my collection are three overmarbled sheets with visible running heads reading "Militia Laws," and some of the accompanying text refers to the laws of Massachusetts. Evidence indicates that these sheets probably were printed around the time of the War of 1812, and as the Manns were active in the Dedham area and in nearby Providence at this time, it was not difficult to find an edition of the *Militia Laws of the United States and of the Commonwealth of Massachusetts* that had been printed at the office of the *Gazette* in Dedham in 1815.[23] Not only is it likely that the Manns did the printing, but, as the text of the volume matches perfectly with the one on my disbound sheets, there is not much doubt that they also executed the marbling (Plate XIX, number 3); the shell pattern is one of theirs as well. Illustration 2 on Plate XIX shows another example of overmarbling that can be identified positively as the work of the Manns. This time their decoration was applied to waste sheets of their own printed music; the overmarbling partly covers a copy of Elias Smith's *The Age of Enquiry, Christian Pocket Companion and Daily Assistant*, issued at Exeter, New Hampshire, by Abel Brown in 1825 and, as its imprint relates, sold also by the booksellers in Boston. Through deductive reasoning and some "shoe leather" detective work, it was possible eventually to identify the music and text on this cover sheet as coming from the Oliver Shaw, Amos Albee, and Herman Mann psalmbook, *The Columbian Sacred Harmony*, that Herman Mann had printed in Dedham in 1808—specifically from the whole sheet containing its page 29. The reemployment of some of the printed sheets of this edition, now overmarbled, as cover papers on an imprint issued seventeen years later is a further indication that such remnants were used when they were long unsold or hopelessly out of date.

One of the most interesting examples of overmarbling relates to a supposed American edition of that most famous of all English pornographic or libertine books,

John Cleland's *Memoirs of a Woman of Pleasure*, more familiarly referred to after the name of its heroine, Fanny Hill. This publication has become something of a cause célèbre in recent years but has never been discussed from the viewpoint of its marbling; therefore, a few details of its history and printing are appropriate here.

In a 1935 issue of *The Colophon*, Ralph Thompson reported the partial printing in America of an edition of "Fanny Hill" with the false imprint, "London: Printed for G. Felton, in the Strand, 1787"; and he attributed it to the shop of Isaiah Thomas between the years 1786 and 1814.[24] After its first twenty-four pages had been printed (that is, one whole sheet had been perfected), the edition was stopped, and the aborted sheets later were decorated by a marbler who then sold them widely. Thompson based his attribution of the printing to Thomas's shop during this wide span of time largely on the fact that in the period around 1814 Thomas had a hundred or more volumes of newspapers, dating to the first decades of the nineteenth century but mainly to the years 1809–1813, bound with these overmarbled waste sheets. Thompson also related that there is evidence in the form of a holograph letter, written to Thomas in 1786 by one of Thomas's English suppliers, to the effect that this bold and imaginative Massachusetts printer was then attempting to acquire an edition of the surreptitious Cleland work, and Thompson presumed that Thomas's intention was to publish it.

More recently, a number of articles have appeared that embellish or alter Thompson's account. Marcus McCorison of the American Antiquarian Society initially argued that if this "Fanny Hill" had been started into print at the Thomas Shop in Worcester, it would have been by Isaiah Thomas, Jr., who in 1802 assumed responsibility for the printing done there, and not by his father, as indicated by Thompson.[25] According to John Alden, formerly of the Boston Public Library, the type font making up the printing of these sheets was never used by the Thomas firm at all; he identified it as the Binny & Ronaldson face that was introduced only in Philadelphia from 1798, and observed that this face was used in Boston by the firm of Munroe & Francis, which was active there throughout the first quarter of the nineteenth century.[26] McCorison has since speculated that the clandestine "Fanny Hill" sheets were printed at the office of Munroe & Francis, probably by a couple of apprentices or journeymen who were caught in the process and had their sheets confiscated by the owners of the shop. Afterward, he reasoned, the sheets were sold by their thrifty owners to a marbler who decorated and resold them.[27]

That Isaiah Thomas or his firm probably had no involvement in this affair, other than as thrifty purchasers of a large lot of these overmarbled sheets,[28] is indicated by the appearance of "Fanny Hill" sheets on imprints and bindings found all over New England: from Boston to Vermont and in such locations as Portland, Maine, Albany, New York and many places in between. The staff of the American Antiquarian Society has, over the years, compiled a list of printings in its collection with these clandestine sheets on their covers, and that list has grown to considerable size.[29] The titles cover a wide range of subjects in addition to newspapers, among them laws and statutes, religious tracts, schoolbooks, and an edition of George Washington's farewell address. There are, in addition, two publications of the Boston printing firm of Munroe & Francis: Jonas Hanway's *Advice from Father Trueman, to His Daughter Mary* (1810) and the Rev. Dr. Jones's *Sermon on Botany and Natural History* (1813). These overmarbled sheets have also been observed on account and manuscript books, some even in Isaiah Thomas's own papers; clearly they were manufactured in large numbers and distributed widely.

It seems likely that the marbling on these "Fanny Hill" sheets was executed in the Boston area, probably in the years 1809–1814. The pattern on them, as Illustrations 4 and 5 on Plate XIX indicate, is always the Stormont design, and a fairly early one at that, with black and red most often making up the vein colors, but sometimes with yellow or golden yellow appearing as a third vein color; at other times, only one vein color is present, usually either black or red. Because the Manns were the principal (and perhaps only) craftsmen marbling in New England in the 1809–1815 period, one would be tempted to conclude that it must have been one of the Manns who applied the marbled decoration to these "Fanny Hill" sheets; indeed, one could even go so far as to conclude that, assuming that Alden's observation has some validity, they had printed them as well, for I have noticed that fonts of the Binny & Ronaldson types were available to them in Dedham from early 1814,[30] and, as we shall see, in even earlier Providence.

This overmarbling business, however, is not a simple matter to resolve. In fact, it is complicated enough to have engaged my attention for several years and to have drawn me into numerous frustrating investigations. In addition to American overmarbled sheets, I have collected, over the years, several that were removed from Boston and New England bindings of the early nineteenth century, as well as several such bindings themselves, containing the texts of English and Irish documents (tax lists, customs forms, bank and commercial note forms, parliamentary and court proceedings) and other identifiable English printings beneath their Stormont decoration. Thus, we must ask, were such overmarbled sheets also being imported from abroad, or, alternatively, were the Manns or other unidentified marblers somehow obtaining imported waste sheets and then applying marbled decoration to them?

Furthermore, many of the hundred or so (there actually may be many more) volumes of newspapers in the American Antiquarian Society that I have examined and that Isaiah Thomas had covered with these overmarbled sheets date to the eighteenth century and even to the mid- or late 1820s, and there are several texts beneath their colored decoration other than that of "Fanny Hill." Although some of these volumes are covered with the overmarbled *Book of Martyrs* text which we have associated with the Manns, others are covered with the initial pages of a medical text and with a printing of the Psalms; and at least one is covered with printed sheets containing running heads that read "Strictures on Correspondence Concerning Russia" (see below).

The New-England Weekly Journal of 1740, the *Massachusetts Sentinel* of 1786, the *Boston Gazette* of 1807, the *New England Palladium* of 1808, and possibly other early American newspapers in the Antiquarian Society contain the aforementioned medical text beneath their layer of paint. I have identified this text as the beginning section of an octavo edition of Thomas Denman's *Introduction to the Practice of Midwifery*, which initially appeared at London in 1788 and went through half a dozen English editions by 1820. However, the printing of the overmarbled sheets does not match any of these, nor does it accord stylistically with the two early American editions of this work: neither the one published at Philadelphia by William Falconer and Evert Duyckinck in 1802 nor the other issued at Brattleboro, Vermont, by William Fessenden in 1807, both of which were also composed in slightly different types or in slightly different measures.

The only inference that can be drawn from this fact is that these overmarbled Denman sheets represent an edition that was begun but soon aborted, and that the abandoned sheets eventually came into the hands of their marbler. Such a conclusion is supported by the fact that in every case so far observed it is only the first quire that appears under the marbled design. The Denman work is a large one, and we can reasonably conclude that in this case an ambitious printer soon became aware of the enormity of the job and of its unlikely success and abandoned the project. Because this Denman text has thus far been observed on newspapers dating no later than 1808, we may assume that its printing was undertaken in the first decade of the nineteenth century. The type is a smallish one, and the printer tried to squeeze as many words into a line as possible, probably to save paper over the long run. This is the same sort of type and layout that I have observed on many Mann printings, and it is not impossible that these sheets could have been worked off in the Mann's printing shop and then reused in their marbling shop after the edition had been abandoned. On the other hand, these Denman sheets could have been produced by a great many other printers as well.

While I was attempting to identify the edition of the Psalms appearing on some of these overmarbled sheets, I was able to satisfy myself that Herman Mann or members of his family were not only overmarbling these waste sheets that had been brought in from abroad, but were responsible as well for decorating the "Fanny Hill" sheets. Specifically, I encountered in the American Antiquarian Society an edition of Isaac Watts's *Hymns and Spiritual Songs* that Herman Mann had printed at Dedham in 1811. Though its text did not match the one of the Psalms that had been overmarbled, which still remains to be identified, the work was contained in an early American hand-binding that, by all indications, was executed by Herman Mann himself, and in his best manner as well. We know through advertisements that Herman Mann also did bookbinding, although elaborate examples of his work had not previously been identified.[31] The binding on the Watts *Hymns,* shown on Plate XIX, not only exemplifies his simple and limited, yet charming, style and method of decoration (probably the best that he was capable of, and, appropriately enough, done on a psalmbook or sacred text),[32] but, more importantly, contains his marbled papers as endpapers; their pattern and coloration match or nearly approximate several of the "Fanny Hill" sheets, the overmarbling on a number of Boston 1814–1817 imprints, and the decoration on several of the overmarbled foreign sheets as well. From this evidence, we may conclude—and, I believe, with confidence—that the Manns definitely did overmarble the "Fanny Hill" sheets as well as foreign printed sheets, although we cannot determine from what sources they may have obtained these various waste sheets.

It is difficult to determine whether the Manns were the only ones doing overmarbling in early America, but it is hard to imagine anyone else doing as much. In my quest to solve this puzzle, I located imprints from Philadelphia, New York City, Albany, and other areas that have overmarbled sheets making up part of their bindings, and sometimes the texts beneath appear to be printings from Philadelphia, New York, and other locales. Thus, it is possible that the practice was carried on elsewhere in America, perhaps by stationers, but this cannot now be determined with any degree of certainty.

To be sure, a number of questions remain to be answered, or at least better explicated. The problem is a complex one, for the Manns appear to have acquired waste sheets for overmarbling from all around eastern America and even from abroad; additionally, they sent such papers that they overmarbled all over the East, where they were placed on imprints in many locations. Furthermore, volumes bound in New England containing these papers have migrated all over the country in the intervening years. Willman Spawn, an authority on early American bookbinding who has collected more than 14,000 rubbings of early American bindings, confirms my impression that the overmarbling of printed sheets in early America was mainly—or even exclusively—a New England phenomenon. He has observed large numbers of overmarbled printings in New England libraries, on New England imprints, and on bookbindings identified as or suspected to be the work on early nineteenth-century New England binders; conversely, he can recall seeing only a few examples of this practice elsewhere.[33]

Overmarbled sheets found on early American imprints and manuscripts dating to the mid- and even later 1820s indicate that the Mann Family continued to carry on this practice. I have in my collection an account or ledger book from this period (sent to me through the good graces of Mr. Spawn) that is covered with such overmarbled sheets, put there when the volume was made up as a blank book. Manuscript entries within it date from 1823 and mention Mt. Pleasant, Leverett, Pelham, and Sunderland—all Massachusetts communities. Not only does the text (which contains the running heads, "Report of Cases in the" on one page and "Supreme Judicial Court" on the other) refer to Massachusetts, but its shell-type marbling is unmistakably that of Samuel C. Mann, who, then in his mid-twenties, was still in Dedham, working with his father.

On a volume in the American Antiquarian Society containing a run of the *Boston Weekly Messenger* from June 1824 to the end of 1825, overmarbled sheets appear with running heads reading "Strictures on the" on one page and "Correspondence Concerning Russia" on the other. The pattern over the text is predominantly a brown shell, thrown onto a blue Stormont and driving the Stormont into veins. This same design appears in a pattern book of the Manns, now preserved in the Dedham Historical Society, that was unavailable to me some years ago when I was researching and completing my study of this interesting family, and which has only recently turned up. This pattern book, containing sixty-six samples of Stormont and shell patterns, and patterns showing shell with Stormont veins, was originally titled in ink, "Made in Dedham by Herman Mann," but the name "Herman" was crossed out and "Samuel" substituted. These patterns undoubtedly date to the early or mid-1820s and indicate that Samuel was then attaining proficiency.[34]

I have been unable to locate any American imprint of the pre-1825 period entitled "Strictures on the Correspondence Concerning Russia," but I have ascertained that in 1813 William Fry of Philadelphia printed a volume entitled *Correspondence Respecting Russia between Robert Goodloe Harper, Esq., and Robert Walsh, Jr.* In the text beneath the marbled decoration on the 1824–1825 *Boston Weekly Messenger* can be discerned the names of these two individuals, indicating either that an edition of the "Strictures" may have been attempted and subsequently aborted, or that the sheets emanated from an as yet unidentified periodical, for they contain page numbers in the 80s and 90s.[35]

The only reference I have noticed in the Mann records that divulges the sources of the paper they employed in marbling comes too late to help us in the "Fanny Hill" problem, but it does show that they were marbling printed sheets. When setting up their partnership, Samuel and Edward Mann drew up a "Statement of Paper Purchased by S. C. & E. Mann for marbling and colouring, Boston, 1831."[36] This records lots of paper they were then purchasing from a variety of sources, mainly in Boston but also from as far away as New York, as well as paper that both of the brothers had owned and were bringing into the firm and crediting to one or the other. While nothing is recorded here about the acquisition of the kind of waste sheets that we have been discussing—

indeed, it is doubtful that Samuel and Edward would have marbled waste sheets at this late date that had been printed on *both* sides—there is, nonetheless, one notation of special interest to us. Among entries of paper that were being acquired from Samuel and credited to him appear "9 [reams] Pot [writing paper] one side printed @1—[$]9.00." Other entries show that the Manns were purchasing paper for about $2.50 per ream to nearly $5.00, depending on size and quality. Sheets printed on one side only, to be marbled on their unprinted sides, obviously could be purchased quite cheaply. We can only imagine how much more cheaply the Manns had acquired the earlier sheets that had been printed on both sides; these must have been had for a pittance.

Let us now reconsider the "Fanny Hill" problem. While it still is impossible to determine who exactly was responsible for printing these "Fanny Hill" sheets which came to be overmarbled and subsequently applied to a great many early American bookbindings, I must put into the record a considerable amount of pertinent information that I have gathered in the process of trying to discover who was responsible for decorating them. This information should contribute to a better understanding of the matter and could be useful to future historians and bibliographers. One point pertains to the type face used in printing these sheets and what it reveals about where the types may have originated; another concerns how this attempted printing fits into the overall bibliography of "Fanny Hill" editions and into the overall "Fanny Hill" literature; a third relates to the Manns' possible involvement in this episode; and a fourth to another early American edition of this most notorious of all English libertine books.

John Cleland's *Memoirs of a Woman of Pleasure* was first published in two volumes in late November 1748 and February 1749 under the imprint "London: Printed for G. Fenton in the Strand. M.DCC.LXIX." "G. Fenton" is thought by some to be a cover for Fenton Griffiths, the brother of Ralph Griffiths, who was active as a bookseller and publisher in London from 1747 until 1803 and who became famous for having founded the *Monthly Review* and for harshly treating Oliver Goldsmith, whom he had engaged to write for it. After a considerable period of silence, the government officials, apparently stirred by the bishops, in November of 1749 issued warrants for the author, printer, and publisher. Fenton Griffiths apparently could not be found, and in his place Ralph Griffiths—who, one commentator has pointed out, may not have been as detached an observer as he made himself out to be—furnished the authorities with the background and printing of the book, as Cleland himself did later. For whatever reason, the matter seems not to have been strongly pursued and no subsequent legal action was taken against those involved.[37]

According to a number of bibliographical and literary sources, an abridgment—actually, a somewhat expurgated version, recast as an epistolary novel—appeared in

1750, and subsequently two-volume editions were published (most of them under the G. Fenton imprint) in 1755, 1760, 1777, 1779, 1781, and 1784. There also appeared a number of pirated editions, with French translations coming out from 1751 on. No source records a British edition between 1784 and 1829 and 1831, when subsequent English editions were published, making it seem probable that for some unknown reason action was taken about 1784 to quash further printings. This might explain, as Ralph Thompson has pointed out, why Isaiah Thomas's London contact could not find a copy when attempting to locate one for Thomas in 1786.[38]

Obviously, there was money to be made for anyone who dared publish such a work, for pornographic books usually fetch many times the price of an ordinary book, particularly illustrated editions. But there also were risks. In a memorandum written many years ago, Clarence Brigham, then Director of the American Antiquarian Society, pointed out that Peter Holmes of West Boylston, Massachusetts, had been arrested in 1818 for having sold copies of and illustrations from the *Memoirs of a Woman of Pleasure,* and was indicted at the July 1819 Session of the Court of Common Pleas and subsequently fined $300 plus court costs. And in April 1820 Stillman Howe, a wheelwright of Holden, Massachusetts, was accused of having sold copies of the Cleland work and a picture from it to six residents of Holden in 1818 and 1819. According to records of the Supreme Judicial Court for April 1820, he was sentenced on two of these counts to one day's solitary imprisonment and six month's hard labor in the House of Correction. "It is rather an irony," Brigham commented, "that records of the Court of Common Pleas, Volume 36, for 1812–1813, has its Index bound in the same marbled oversheets of the *Memoirs of a Woman of Pleasure.*"[39] More recently, McCorison has written about the possible publication of two editions of "Fanny Hill" in Vermont, one at Brattleboro and one at Windsor, in 1816–1818, which were said to be circulating then in all parts of the state and in adjoining states.[40]

After a considerable amount of time examining in detail the overmarbled "Fanny Hill" waste sheets that initially provoked all this commotion, I have no doubt whatsoever that John Alden was correct in observing that they were printed with Binny & Ronaldson types. In 1796 two emigrant Scotsmen, Archibald Binny and James Ronaldson, established at Philadelphia the first United States type foundry that was to achieve permanency; apparently, they were quite successful in doing so, and eventually acquired sizable fortunes for their efforts. In 1809 they issued a specimen book of metal ornaments cast at their foundry,[41] and in 1812 they brought out the first specimen book of type to be issued in America.[42] Their specimen of "Pica Roman No. 1" printed in this first book accords exactly with the types used to print the aborted "Fanny Hill" whole sheets, establishing beyond doubt, I believe, that these were composed and printed in America and most likely in New England, probably

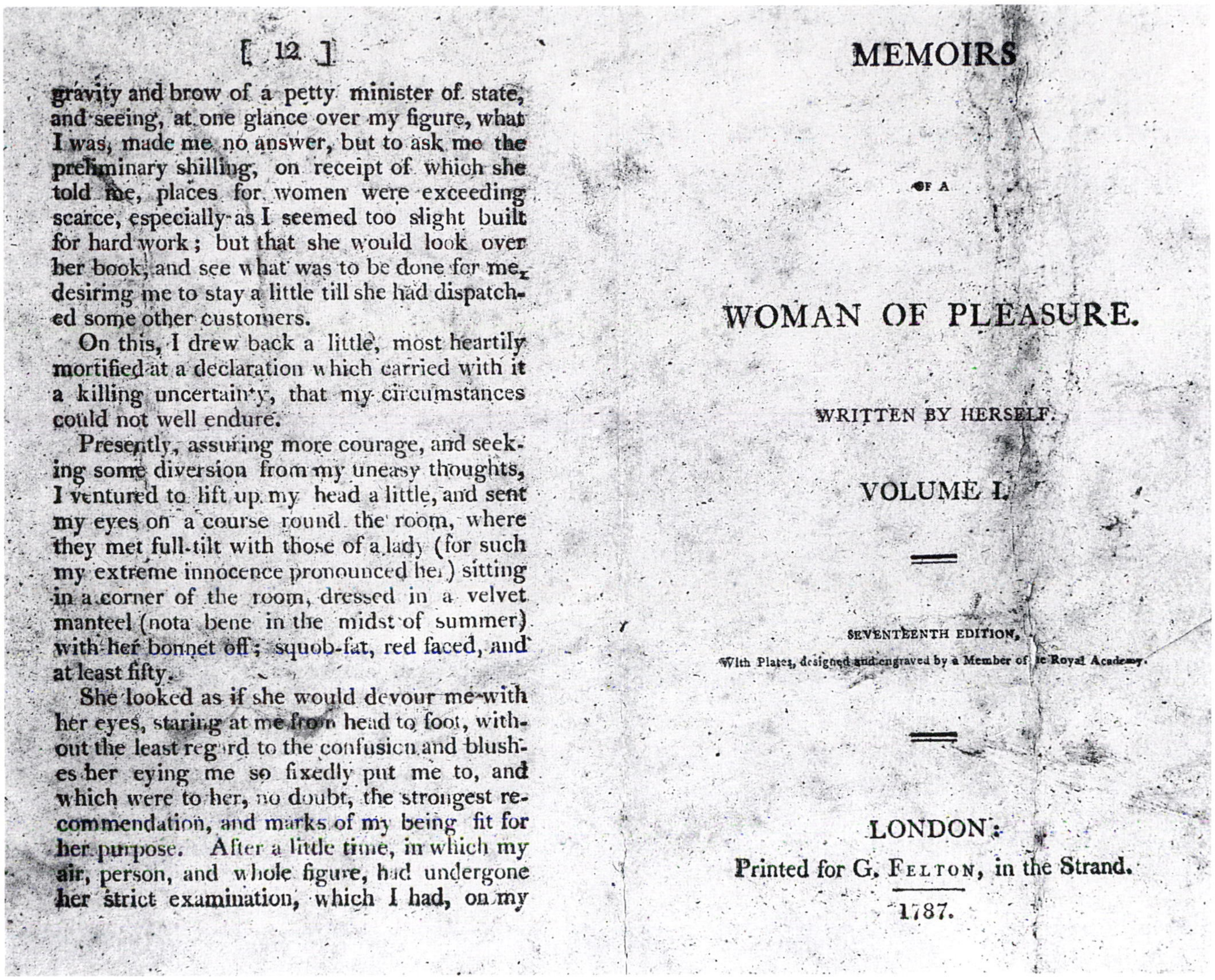

[12]

gravity and brow of a petty minister of state, and seeing, at one glance over my figure, what I was, made me no answer, but to ask me the preliminary shilling, on receipt of which she told me, places for women were exceeding scarce, especially as I seemed too slight built for hard work; but that she would look over her book, and see what was to be done for me, desiring me to stay a little till she had dispatched some other customers.

On this, I drew back a little, most heartily mortified at a declaration which carried with it a killing uncertainty, that my circumstances could not well endure.

Presently, assuming more courage, and seeking some diversion from my uneasy thoughts, I ventured to lift up my head a little, and sent my eyes on a course round the room, where they met full-tilt with those of a lady (for such my extreme innocence pronounced her) sitting in a corner of the room, dressed in a velvet manteel (nota bene in the midst of summer) with her bonnet off; squob-fat, red faced, and at least fifty.

She looked as if she would devour me with her eyes, staring at me from head to foot, without the least regard to the confusion and blushes her eying me so fixedly put me to, and which were to her, no doubt, the strongest recommendation, and marks of my being fit for her purpose. After a little time, in which my air, person, and whole figure, had undergone her strict examination, which I had, on my

MEMOIRS

OF A

WOMAN OF PLEASURE.

WRITTEN BY HERSELF.

VOLUME I.

SEVENTEENTH EDITION,

With Plates, designed and engraved by a Member of the Royal Academy.

LONDON:
Printed for G. FELTON, in the Strand.
1787.

FIGURE 10. Title page and another page from the un-marbled, verso side of a "Fanny Hill" sheet in the American Antiquarian Society.

late in the first decade of the nineteenth century or early in the following decade, but certainly by 1814 at the latest. (It must be pointed out that, however, as Figure 10 shows, this title page was set in a different type face, one that did not belong to the Binny & Ronaldson family; this might confuse anyone initially looking at this problem from the standpoint of typography.) Carl Purington Rollins, who contributed an introduction to the facsimile reprinting of these two specimen books in 1936,[43] pointed out that the Binny & Ronaldson types marked a complete divorce from the Caslon old-style influence; he particularly (and rightfully) singled out the "Roman No. 1" as being "a delicate and friendly type." It must have appeared as something of a revelation to many American printers when it was introduced in the early years of the nineteenth century, and I would guess that it ushered in the new era of the modern Romans.

As I have related before, a complete set of the Binny & Ronaldson fonts was acquired by the *Dedham Gazette* early in 1814; such an acquisition was representative of the "new wave" that was sweeping printing circles throughout the country, and many printers, I am sure, felt that they could not compete without these new types. Thus it is entirely possible that the Manns could have been involved in the printing of the aborted "Fanny Hill" waste sheets as well as in their marbling since they had access to such type at that time. Furthermore, when I looked into Herman Mann printings of a slightly earlier time—those dating to the years when he was engaged in printing in Providence—I discovered an 1813 edition printed by him, *Formulas and Prescriptions, and Various Instructions, for the Service and Guidance of Those Who Have Applied, Are Applying, or Shall Apply to the Enemy of Human Disease*, "by Sylvan, Enemy to Human Disease," that also has special interest for me. This edition was not only composed in the same Binny & Ronaldson "Pica Roman No. 1" types, but also contained on its title page one of the identical "English dashes" (the second one) depicted in Binny & Ronaldson's 1812 specimen book as well as a headpiece on its initial page of text, the last (no. 13) of the "English Flowers" displayed in the volume.[44]

Despite the fact that these bits of evidence strongly point in the direction of the Manns' involvement in the "Fanny Hill" episode, we should not at this time feel obliged to attribute the printing of these whole sheets to them. The Binny & Ronaldson types were widely available, and such a project could have been undertaken by any number of printers in any number of locations. (I believe, however, that the printer and publisher Isaiah Thomas can be excluded from this group.) Because of the delicate nature of this printing, one which could lead to fine and imprisonment if caught, we should not expect to find evidence revealing the identities of those who perpetrated it; they would have taken great pains to cover their tracks. If the Manns actually did play a role in this aborted printing, however, I would guess that it was one of the maturing Mann boys—most probably Daniel, the oldest—and not Herman, the father. Daniel, as I pointed out in my book on this Dedham family of printers and marblers, was a somewhat impractical dreamer and schemer who was perpetually on the lookout to make a quick fortune; family letters indicate that such yearnings got him involved in a number of disappointing business ventures in the very period under discussion—some of them embroiling him in legal troubles with creditors.[45]

The Beinecke Library at Yale University preserves an early edition of "Fanny Hill" that, in my opinion, is of certain American origin. Identified on its title page also as the "seventeenth edition," and containing as its imprint, "London: Printed for G. Felton, in the Strand, 1813," this issue was produced in a different format and composed in a different typeface than was the aborted edition under discussion; thus, it formed a different edition altogether.[46] The Yale copy, the only one now known, was printed on a coarse paper having a grayish cast that is also undisputably American; additionally, it contains three rather obscene plates that were crudely or naively drawn and cut on wood, these obviously being of American origin as well. The Yale copy is incomplete, however, lacking a large block of pages, and it is possible that more

plates were originally present.[47] When I examined this copy recently, I was immediately struck with the thought that it could easily qualify as one of the editions Brigham and McCorison described as circulating in Massachusetts, Vermont, and nearby states in 1816–1820; indeed, I believe that it must be one of these.[48]

Another interesting fact can be deduced from this reissue. In the same way that the title page appears on the aborted sheets, this edition also contains the misspelled publisher's name, "G. Felton" on its imprint. Because the "Fanny Hill" sheets under discussion were unavailable to the printer of the Beinecke copy, we can conclude that he must have been following a copy of still another edition when setting type—one common to both of these editions—for the printing of "seventeenth edition" and "G. Felton" on both seems more than mere coincidence. The compositors in both instances must have had access to an earlier, common text; since it seems there were no editions issued in Britain after 1784 or before about 1829 and because British editions only listed "G. Fenton" as publisher, this earlier, common edition was probably another American version which thus far has not become known or which did not survive the ravages of time. Salacious and pornographic literature is usually kept hidden and eventually disposed of in order to avoid embarrassment; indeed, were it not for these "Fanny Hill" waste sheets and for the single copy at Yale, we would be without any physical evidence at all of the existence of early American printings of this most libertine of all English novels, *The Memoirs of a Woman of Pleasure. Written by Herself.*

One more comment seems in order. Alden and McCorison have speculated that the edition did not progress beyond its initial whole sheet because, being of a salacious nature and unlawful, it was stopped. I have searched court records in Norfolk County, of which Dedham is the seat, and in Suffolk County also to determine if any legal proceedings eventuated in this case, but without success. While Alden and McCorison could be correct in their reasoning, there could be other explanations as to why the edition did not progress beyond the completion of its initial quire, the principal one being that its printers soon realized that effecting the plates advertised on its title page would be a major impediment in completing the task. To me, this seems the best explanation as to why the edition is represented only by its initial quire and remained unfulfilled.

9

Marbling in the New World, II

Philadelphia

THE marbled money described earlier indicates that the process of paper marbling was carried on in Philadelphia two and perhaps three decades prior to the close of the eighteenth century, but on an extremely limited basis. The presence of crudely marbled paper on Philadelphia imprints of the late 1790s and early 1800s is additional proof of the development of such a manufacture and trade. Philadelphia in the 1790s was the nation's largest city, and its capital as well, and the place where many ideas were being generated with respect to America's new political, economic, social, cultural, and intellectual life, especially by immigrants coming from Europe. It stands to reason that primacy and leadership in this field of paper marbling also took place there.

In spite of this, and despite the fact that we have the names of a few individuals described in local sources as marblers (Shease, Germon, Young, and Swain), as well as the names of a few others who could fit into this category, we have no actual information that marbling was carried on in Philadelphia before the year 1825, although we know that it was. Even then, our knowledge—like that gained about the activities of the Mann family of Dedham—is due to a benign nod from "Lady Luck"; indeed, the circumstances surrounding this piece of good fortune provide another interesting story.

One of the prime factors contributing to the Industrial Revolution was the development of steam power, which allowed heat energy to be converted into mechanical energy, with the generation of steam occurring by means of a boiler. The Industrial Revolution is said to have begun about 1765, when James Watt, an instrument maker of Glasgow, modified and brought into practical use an earlier and somewhat different engine, developed by Thomas Newcomen of Dartmouth, Devon, and his assistant Thomas Calley. Newcomen and Calley had developed in 1712 the first piston-operated steam engine, but it required Watt's later refinements and changes to make it practicable.

After 1800, steam engines, and boilers to fuel them, came into wide use in England and elsewhere, and they proliferated as the years advanced. By the third and fourth decades of the nineteenth century, they were becoming common in America, as were accidents related to them, for a great many explosions occurred with their use that resulted in loss of life and injuries to persons or property. The situation reached such proportions that in 1838 Congress instructed the Secretary of the Treasury to make a census of steam engines in America in order to pass legislation and set standards that would reduce the carnage. In 1838, the Secretary of the Treasury presented Congress with his report.[1] On page 167 of this lengthy document, in a list of such machinery used in Philadelphia in 1838, we learn that there was a steam engine in "Dohnert's marble-paper manufactory." From other data supplied in the document we also learn that this engine was owned by one Kates, that it was used for the making of marbled paper, that it was a high-pressure apparatus erected in 1836 by one Rowland, and that it was the vibrating type, based on Rowland's patent. Using this information, I was able to track Dohnert through city directories of early Philadelphia and learn more about its marbling trade than has hitherto been known.

While various individuals named Dohnert appear in Philadelphia directories from the early 1800s on, none of those so named had any visible connection with the book trades until the name John H. Dohnert appeared with the description "marble paper manufac." in the 1825 issue. At the same time, J. "Katez" was identified as a bookbinder there. (The name "Katez" was corrected in the 1829 directory and given its proper spelling, "Kates," as it appeared thereafter.) Dohnert's name again appeared in the 1828 directory, the next one available, with his occupation described as "marble paper manufacturer," and he continued to be listed in subsequent directories in this way until the end of the 1840s, proving long and continuous activity in this line. In the issues for 1846 and 1847, Dohnert was listed as "County treas. & marble paper manufac.," and one assumes that he had been appointed or elected to local political office for those two years. The 1848 Philadelphia directory was the last in which he was described as a marbler; those from 1849 to 1854 enter his name without an accompanying occupation or description. His name is altogether absent from the issue for 1855, and those from 1856 through 1863 designated him as "gentleman & pres. Sp[ring] Garden Fire Insurance Co." He continued to be listed, sometimes as "gentleman" and sometimes as "pres." but mostly without any indication of occupation, in Philadelphia directories through 1888. There is no listing for him in the issue for 1889, and the one for 1890 lists his estate at the Girald Building.

Based on the above information, we may postulate that John H. Dohnert's life was a long and prosperous one. If we assume that he was about twenty years old when he was first listed as a marbler in 1825, he would have been eighty-three or more at the time of his death. His presidency of an insurance company, his appointment or election to public office, his listing as "gentleman"; all these indicate substance, popularity, and success. We might conclude that he made enough money from his early marbling activities between approximately 1825 and 1848 to enable him to give up this strenuous line of business and engage in occupations that promised more ease and comfort. It is possible that he continued to marble paper between 1848 and 1854 or 1856, but listings after 1856 indicate that he no longer did so. The important fact is that he did work as a professional marbler for twenty-five years or so before 1850, and this information adds substantially to our knowledge of the marbling trade in Philadelphia at this early time.

The "Kates" named in the 1839 government report has been identified through contemporary directory listings as Jacob J. Kates, who worked as a bookbinder from about 1825, when his name first appeared in a city directory (in its misspelled version) along with the initial listing of Dohnert. Jacob J. Kates continued to be included in directory issues through 1846. His name did not appear in the annual number for 1847, but inasmuch as the name of Sarah Ann Kates, his widow, appeared in the succeeding number, he obviously had died in one of the two preceding years. The fact that Kates is listed as owner of the steam engine Dohnert was using in 1836 reveals a relationship between the two artisans, and we might speculate that they started in business as partners in bookbinding, with Dohnert later branching out into marbling. Directory listings show that Kates lived on the same street, North Ninth, as did a bookbinder named George Dohnert. Perhaps the three men were related either by blood or by marriage. George Dohnert, probably a brother of John, was described as a bookbinder in directories between 1837 and 1845, while a William Dohnert was listed as a paperhanger in 1835 and 1836. One of Kates's ornate bindings is illustrated on plate 34 and described on page 13 of the catalog *Early American Bookbindings from the Collection of Michael Papantonio,* issued originally by the Pierpont Morgan Library and other libraries in 1972 and reissued by the American Antiquarian Society (now owner of the Papantonio collection) in

1985. Kates bound the book for Mrs. Julia Rush (probably of Philadelphia); it contains his identifying ticket, on which his name is spelled "Katez."

As to what purpose John Dohnert put Kates's steam engine, we can only guess. Most likely it drove an apparatus for polishing his marbled sheets, but it could have been used for providing hot water for blending large amounts of color, or for other purposes now unknown. The records of the Mann family refer to the addition of a steam engine to the marbling works that Samuel and Edward conducted on Bromfield Street in Boston in 1831, indicating, once more, that the Industrial Revolution was beginning to have an association with this craft.

The Philadelphia directory for 1845 suggests the existence of two other marbling concerns in that city: it associates a firm named Gilbrith & Frost and an individual by the name of Joseph Dietrichs with marbled paper and possibly its manufacture. These two listings appear only in that year, and nothing more has been learned about either of them or their involvement with marbled paper. It is in James B. Nicholson's 1856 publication, *A Manual of the Art of Bookbinding,* that we obtain our next insight into the status of paper marbling in Philadelphia—and our most important one at that. Not only did Nicholson (who from 1849 was associated in business with an English binder named James Pawson) derive much of his information for this work from John Hannett's *Bibliopegia,* he also reprinted in toto Charles Woolnough's landmark manual on the art of marbling paper; it occupies pages 83–130 in Nicholson's work and includes seven marbled sheets as illustrative exhibits. While a pirate, Nicholson was not an out-and-out buccaneer, for in his introduction he acknowledged the source of his marbling information. Nonetheless, this did not deter Woolnough from mentioning in the London 1883 reprinting of his own work that "the author was also honoured (though with what motives he will leave others to guess) by our worthy transatlantic brethren, who reprinted it in Philadelphia, and published it there in conjunction with some work on bookbinding." Woolnough complained that the Philadelphia publishers, not being content with the benefits accruing to them in their own territory, exported a quantity of the manuals into England and began to circulate copies in London, which obliged him to institute proceedings for infringement of copyright.[2]

The marbled sheets added as illustrations to Nicholson's work were manufactured locally, for near the end of the discussion of marbling (p. 126), he advised:

Should there be any difficulty in obtaining any of the articles described, they may be procured from Mr. Charles Williams, No. 213 Arch St., Philadelphia. The specimens of marbled paper accompanying these pages, illustrate the prominent classes of patterns of marbling. They were executed by him and show his mastery of the art.

Williams's proficiency, which is attested to by the quality of the samples bound into copies of the Nicholson 1856 manual, was further noticed a few years later by Edwin T. Freedley, a compiler of business and legal treatises. In his *Philadelphia and Its Manufacturers: a Hand-Book Exhibiting the Development, Variety and Statistics of the Manufacturing Industry of Philadelphia in 1857*, Freedley referred to the manufacture of marbled paper that Williams was carrying on in Philadelphia at that time:

Of *Marble Paper*, Philadelphia has the Principal Manufactory in this country, that of Mr. CHARLES WILLIAMS. He claims to have been the first in the Union who has made the Antique Dutch and Drawn patterns, and also the one that has succeeded in matching the celebrated "Papier de Annonay," of France; and still is the only manufacturer in the United States of all of the English, Dutch and French patterns. He supplies Boston, New York and the chief cities of the whole Union with nine-tenths of the fine papers that are used on extra work, and go by the name of English and French paper. "There is no manufacturer in this country," he says, "that has equaled my style of work, and none that has even matched my common papers for durability and finish." [3]

In 1871, 1882, 1887, and again in 1902, Henry Carey Baird & Co. reissued editions of the Nicholson manual. These editions were reprinted from stereotype plates made by L. Johnson & Co. of Philadelphia from the type of the original edition and, as would be expected, they contained the same information about Williams as the marbler of their samples. Although we have no actual knowledge that Williams marbled the samples for the 1871 and 1882 editions, I believe that he probably did. The samples in these editions are nearly identical in form and fashion to those of the first edition, and Williams was still actively engaged in marbling in Philadelphia in these years. Even more, the samples in these two editions are more expertly made and display a finer finish overall, as would be expected of a marbler who had gained much experience and greatly improved his technique during the intervening years. The samples in the 1887 edition are similar to those in the earlier three, indicating that they also may have emanated from Williams's workshop, perhaps being obtained earlier and set aside for the eventuality of a later reprinting. However, the seven samples added to the final edition that was printed in 1902 differ greatly in quality and color configurations from those included in the earlier editions, and a few of the patterns are not even the same as the ones originally described; in fact, they appear to be German and machine-made. Williams had died before the publication of the 1902 edition, and the publishers must have looked around for whatever paper they could find to illustrate it, resorting to imported, machine-made specimens in lieu of authentic ones, which no longer were being produced locally.

Who was Charles Williams and what can be learned about him and his career in the paper marbling trade? To answer these questions, we turn once more to contemporary Philadelphia city and business directories, which indicate that he was originally trained as a bookbinder—or so the 1852 city directory lists him. In the directory issued in the following year, he is described as a marble paper-maker, and he continued to be so identified until 1861. His name is missing from directories published in 1862 and 1863, and we may wonder if his disappearance from them at this time had a connection with the ongoing Civil War. His name reappears in the 1864 directory, and it continues to reappear with a hodgepodge of descriptions—marble paper manufacturer, papermaker, marbleizer, wallpaperer, paper edger, and the like—until 1891 when it disappears altogether.

In the period around 1866, Williams's name appears in directories in conjunction with those of his sons, Charles E. and Roswell E. Williams, who are described as makers of slate mantels. In January through April of 1988 the Vermont Historical Society sponsored an exhibition devoted to marbleized slate. Barbara Knapp Hamblett, who was responsible for this presentation, has written that in 1840 an Englishman adapted paper-marbling techniques to transform slate to appear as marble. Like paper craftsmen, these slate marbleizers jealously guarded their formulas, which they brought to the United States from England. A marbleized slate industry flourished in the slate-producing regions of Rutland County, Vermont, and Washington County, New York, as well as in Pennsylvania. [4] We can infer from this information that the Williamses were somehow involved with the industry that was being carried on in eastern Pennsylvania. (Actually, as discussed elsewhere, wood, cloth, leather and other objects will accept marbled decoration done in the classical way, with only minimal adjustments in the process needed.) Mrs. Hamblett has noted that marbleized slate was popular in interior decor during the last half of the nineteenth century, used mainly for mantels, tabletops, wainscoting, and altars.

Probate court records and newspaper obituaries show that Charles Williams died on 8 April 1895, at the age of seventy. This would place his birth at about the year 1825 and his age when his name first appeared in Philadelphia directories at about twenty-seven. (Williams died about six years after John H. Dohnert, but was born nearly a generation after that octogenarian.) Additional information about Williams, and about his proficiency as a marbler of paper, may be found in the archival records of the Franklin Institute in Philadelphia, which, around the middle of the nineteenth century, sponsored competitions in the manufacturing trades, much the same as did the Massachusetts Charitable Mechanics Association in Boston. In 1852, the first year that he emerged as a binder and marbler in Philadelphia, Williams won first prize for his manufacture of marbled paper under the category of "Bookbinding." According to the Committee on Marbleized Paper's report, which still exists in holograph form among the Institute's archival records,

> The judges appointed by the Franklin Institute of Pennsylvania to examine and report on Bookbinding, Stationary, et. cet., after having carefully examined No. 2602, Marble paper manufactured by Charles Williams, report that the said marble paper is better than anything of the kind ever seen by this Committee manufactured in this Country; and is fully equal to the foreign article manufactured in England and France and better than is generally imported from Germany. The Committee would therefore suggest the propriety of awarding a premium of the First Class to Charles Williams for skill in the manufacture of Marble paper.[5]

Charles Williams became Franklin Institute member no. 5095 in 1852/53, paying dues of $3.00, and continued to be carried on its membership rolls (with the description "marble paper manufacturer") until 1860/61. In 1874 he was awarded the Institute's bronze medal for "a very large display and fine imitation of Green marble" and for the manufacture of marbleized slate mantels.[6] No further personal information has turned up about Charles Williams, nor have any marbled papers that can specifically be associated with his manufacture (other than those in the initial editions of the Nicholson manual) been identified. I have seen, over the years, countless marbled papers that seemingly originated in Philadelphia during Williams's period of activity. Many of these were very professionally executed, and their Philadelphia origin is often proved by the printed waste sheets used as lining papers between the marbled endpapers and the boards of the bindings in which they ultimately appeared, for many of these sheets turn out to be Philadelphia legal and commercial forms. While we might strongly suspect that Williams marbled many of the cover and endpapers in these volumes, we have no positive evidence that allows us to ascribe them directly to his manufacture. There can be no doubt that he marbled an immense amount of paper during his long and active career; much of it is still preserved on bindings of the second half of the nineteenth century. Similarly, we cannot deny that his boast about supplying much of the country's need for this product has valid foundation, even with respect to Boston, where the Manns held sway, for his period of greatest activity coincided with their downturn in the manufacture of marbled paper.

One of the more interesting facts that I have been able to discover about Williams relates to his invention of a marbling machine. In 1858, the records of the U.S. Patent Office indicate, he was awarded a patent for his invention of an apparatus for coloring paper, and his actual drawings of it are reproduced as Figure 11 here.[7] (His patent specification, which is a lengthy one, will be discussed

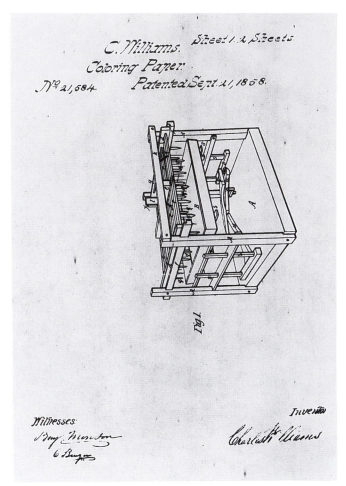

FIGURE 11. Drawings accompanying Charles Williams's 1858 application for a patent on his apparatus for coloring paper.

in some detail later.) Significantly, his invention was not the total marbling machine described in the discussion of British marbling, but an apparatus for distributing colors evenly on the bath, thus solving one of the most difficult problems that confront even highly experienced and highly advanced marblers.

All of the information we have on Charles Williams indicates that he was indeed an extraordinary marbler—probably the best this country ever produced—who was responsible for a large output of decorated paper over his long career. It seems likely that he was the only person marbling in Philadelphia during most, if not all, of the period in which he was active. Boyd's Philadelphia directory for 1859/60, for instance, which listed the various trades and professions carried on in Philadelphia at that time and the individuals engaged in them, entered Charles Williams and no other person under the category of "Marbled Paper Makers"; and, of course, we have the evidence of Edwin Freedley supporting his primacy. During Williams's later career the trade was slowing down, and with his death would virtually cease as compared to the level of fifty or seventy-five years earlier.

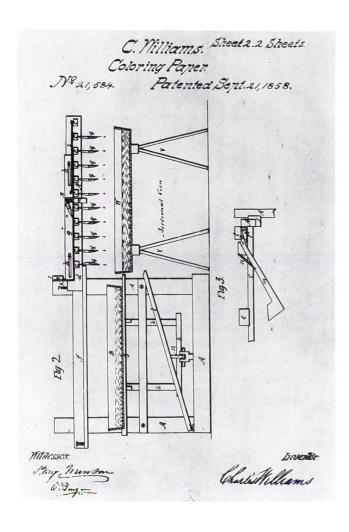

New York

Any attempt to assess the level of activity in New York City with respect to the marbling of paper and book edges presents us with a new and different set of problems. One might suppose that New York would become the focal point for such paper decoration, just as it became, by the middle of the nineteenth century, the center of the printing and bookbinding trades and the heart of the publishing industry in America. But this does not appear to have been the case; by the time New York achieved primacy in these areas, the book trade of old had altered its status markedly. By then, hand bookbinding, in which marbling played an important role, was scarcely part of the picture. Modern publishing was based on industrial production methods, with large factories and mechanized edition binding occupying an important part of that base. The only use for marbling in the new scheme was in the application of ancient decoration to the edges of some of the factories' cheaper editions, or to supply decorated papers that sometimes were added to special or deluxe editions. Consequently, marbling survived in New York after the 1830s and 1840s in the large mechanized binderies that were established independently to service the growing publishing industry or, less often, in bind-

eries maintained by a few publishing houses directly, where a small number of hand bookbinders were employed in their specialty departments along with one or more marblers. This was the situation with regard to the New York marbling trade from the middle of the nineteenth century and beyond.

Except for the presence of crudely marbled sheets on the bindings of many New York imprints, and the few directory references previously noticed, we have little hard evidence that marbling flourished in New York in the early part of the nineteenth century. Nor have we been able to discover, as in the cases of the Mann family in the Boston area or John H. Dohnert in Philadelphia, the names of any marblers who can be credited with long and continuous production there. All evidence indicates that in this early period no highly professional marblers emerged in New York; instead, the marbling that went on seems to have been performed by stationers and others connected with that line of business. The final volume of the New York City trade advertising history, which Mrs. Gottesman was working on at the time of her death, gives us a clue to the situation in these early days. She reprints from the *New York Commercial Advertiser* of 10 February 1804 the following advertisement of Thomas B. Jansen, who, McKay's *Register* indicates, was established as a bookbinder, bookseller, and stationer in New York from 1798 until the 1820s:[8]

> To Book-binders. Pasteboard, a superior quality, Band-box Board, (for spelling-books), Marble Paper, extra and common, Colors, Calico Paper, Red Ink Powder, Cutting Knives, Ruling Pens, Clasps for receipt books, Agrate [sic] and Flint Burnishers, Fillets—Edge Rools [sic.]—Pallets. Ornamental Back-stamps, Corners and Ovals of a variety of patterns. For sale by T. B. Jansen, Bookseller, 243 Pearl-street.

While we have no knowledge that Jansen actually marbled, and while we can feel assured that he did not manufacture but merely distributed many of the items on the above advertisement (the bookbinder's rolls and stamps, for example), I think that we can infer from the circumstances that he may have done some marbling, following the tradition of stationers in France, and was not just advertising paper imported or made by another. Indeed, a few references in the Mann family papers indicate the interest and possible involvement of New York City stationers in marbling at this time.

Daniel, the eldest of the Mann children, migrated to New York City in 1823 to seek his fortune through the manufacture of fancy cards and spent most of the years up to his untimely death in 1830 working in Manhatten and living in Brooklyn. Although his main interest was not directed toward marbling, his letters contain a few references to the craft, showing that he was occupied with it some of this time, and they indicate as well that others were anxious to profit from his knowledge. In

May of 1823, for instance, he instructed his mother to send him an old coat with his brothers and sisters, who then were planning a visit to him, as "it will answer to marble in." Other letters refer to various stationers' and tradesmen's interest in having him teach them to marble, but, as he reported home, he thought "it would be disadvantageous to show them the art of marbling." He later reported that Caleb Bartlett, a bookseller and card manufacturer, had offered him the sum of twenty dollars per week for five weeks of instruction in marbling.[9]

More to the point is the information provided in letters that brother Samuel sent back to Dedham during visits to New York in 1826 and 1827. In May of 1826, while in New York apparently to assess the market for marbled papers, Samuel wrote that the booksellers had pronounced the paper he and his father had produced to be the best of American manufacture they had ever seen. "There is no paper made in this City," he reported, "that is at all equal to it, or even decent. Porter's seems to be the best of the American paper that they get here."[10]

The identity of this Porter remains obscure, but it is likely that Samuel was referring to John T. K. Porter, proprietor of a New York book and stationery store and reading library in the 1820s and 1830s. As the Mann letters indicate, there was much interest on the part of New York booksellers, stationers, and related tradesmen in learning to carry on the marbling art. Nothing more is known about Porter and his marbled paper, but he also could have been a professional maker of marbled papers, living, like the Manns, outside the metropolitan area he serviced.

Seeking to learn more about marbling in New York, I carefully went through several city directories of the 1830s line by line for names of individuals who might be associated with this craft. To take just one example, of the more than 22,000 names appearing in the 1836/7 directory, not a single entry was identified with marbling, although many artisans were described in very specific terms. Five names did emerge, however, described with the more general occupations of "paperstainer" or "paper colorer": Thomas Drew, Henry Durell, John Jones, James W. White, and Isaac Winans. Only Jones, White, and Winans had been listed as paper stainers or paper colorers in the 1830/1 edition, another of the directories I searched; Drew's name was lacking altogether, and Durell was listed as a bookseller and nothing more.

This last fact raises the possibility that Henry Durell may have stained his paper by marbling it, for marbling was the method of paper decoration most associated with the book trade and an important one in the stationery business. We have every reason to believe that he was related to the William Durell whose name appeared in New York directories from 1786 into the 1820s with the descriptions printer, bookseller, stationer, and papermaker, and whose printed sheets were later overmarbled by the Manns and mounted by a New England bookbinder into the 1814 reissue of Washington Irving's *Salmagundi*. Nei-

ther can we ignore the implication that some members of the Durell clan could have been marbling paper as part of their activities as stationers. Nevertheless, despite the glimpses of New York marbling activity that can be discerned during the earlier decades of the nineteenth century, no single important and long-continuing maker emerges in the mold of the Manns, John Dohnert, or Charles Williams. And, as was mentioned previously, the entire New York book publishing scene altered dramatically at about the fourth decade of the century, the situation vis-à-vis bookbinding and marbling changing right along with it.

In the 1790s and for a few decades after, books were still being issued in Europe and America according to the methods that had evolved over many centuries. For the most part, they were published by printers and booksellers in the same way that William Durell in 1798 had printed and published *The New and Complete Book of Martyrs,* and they were afterward hand bound in various ways by bookbinders who often doubled as stationers or booksellers. In the late 1820s, and especially in the 1830s, however, things began to change. A number of commercial houses, most of them begun in a small way as printing and bookselling establishments, began to grow into the large publishing houses that would come to dominate American publishing for decades to come, a few of which are still in existence today. These houses took publishing out of the hands of booksellers and printers and relegated them to serve as mere tools of the trade. The firms themselves became responsible for every aspect of the publishing experience as we know it today, from the solicitation of manuscripts to their development (through editing, printing, and binding processes) into books that are promoted and marketed. These publishing concerns, arising in an era of economic and social expansion, used mechanization in printing and binding, and thus earned fortunes that made them giants in their field. In New York, the decades of the twenties and the thirties witnessed the establishment of such houses by Daniel Appleton, John Wiley, John Palmer Putnam, and the Harper Brothers, to mention only the most important.[11]

The firm of Harper & Brothers will serve as a case in point, since there is documentation that relates them directly to our subject. J. & J. Harper first appeared in New York City directories as printers in 1817, but by the mid-1830s they and their two brothers had already transformed their business into a large publishing, printing, and binding enterprise that would be preeminent by mid-century. (James Harper, the principal founder, was even elected mayor of New York in 1844.) Then, adversity struck, for on the afternoon of 10 December 1853, the Harper & Brothers establishment was gutted by fire.[12] But, as Jacob Blanck observed, no wind is wholly ill.[13] The Harpers rebuilt, and in 1855 opened their new plant that—by standards of that day—was considered an architectural marvel, an edifice that would withstand similar ravages and was looked upon, as Blanck put it, as a sort of mid-

THE MARBLING-ROOM.

SPRINKLING THE COLORS.

FIGURE 12. *Top,* "The Marbling Room," and *bottom,* "Sprinkling the Colors," in Jacob Abbott's *The Harpers' Establishment* (1855), which show how marbling was executed in the Harpers' plant.

nineteenth-century Empire State Building. Their building incorporated all the functions identified with the modern publishing house: business and editing offices, type-founding, composition, electrotyping, engraving, printing, binding, and distribution—everything under one roof.

One of the Harpers' authors was the Reverend Jacob Abbott, a teacher, pastor, and writer, whose *Rollo* series books in twenty-eight volumes are perhaps the most famous of his 180 books designed to impart history, science, and ethics to juvenile readers through stories. Such

an edifice as the Harpers had erected was, in Blanck's words, grist for Abbott's mill, and in 1855 they published his descriptive tour through their new plant, entitled *The Harper Establishment; or, How the Story Books Are Made.*[14]

Insofar as it describes and illustrates much of the machinery that by then had come into use, Abbott's description of how the Harpers produced their books is important. It is especially pertinent for us because he devoted an entire chapter to marbling. Since marbling had come to be one of the many phases of bookmaking incorporated into the Harpers' establishment, we learn not only how paper was marbled to decorate some of their books, but also how edge decoration was applied to them. As a complement to Abbott's description, two woodcut illustrations were provided to show the marbling process in action (Figure 12). Next to the plates in the Diderot-D'Alembert *Encyclopédie* (and reprintings of them), these are the earliest illustrations showing a marbler at work. Although the information in Abbott's account is rudimentary (he actually does not reveal much about the techniques of the craft, for these, he admitted, were not made known to him), it is useful as evidence that marbling was one of the operations carried on in a large bookmaking plant at this time. That such plants had, by mid-century, come to be an integral part of contemporary bookmaking may be seen as yet another instance of expansion in this industry.

In 1832 Edward Walker, a bookbinder about twenty-eight years old, came over from England and began working in New York. Four years later he established his own bookbinding concern, which he called the New York Bindery (or New York Book-Bindery). Within a short time he had built up a flourishing business. By 1850, his concern filled a four-story building at 114 Fulton Street, and was now renamed E. Walker & Sons, for in the meantime he had trained his two sons and taken them into partnership. It was at this time that the firm issued a descriptive account of its business, entitled *The Art of Book-Binding*,[15] and later issued several broadside advertisements that provide us with pictorial views of the kinds of activities that went on there.[16] On January 2, 1852, the Walker plant, like the Harper one, burned down; Walker rebuilt on the ashes, as the Harpers did, but more quickly and more modestly, for the building was restored and the plant back in operation by the following May. Walker continued to do all sorts of binding and became involved in some publishing as well, but the main work of the firm catered to the needs of the large local publishers, especially the binding of whole editions of works they issued. According to an obituary,[17] Edward Walker became prosperous and retired with a competency to his home in Yonkers in the mid-1870s, leaving his sons to carry on the business.[18]

Walker's little advertising booklet, *The Art of Book-Binding,* is pertinent to our narrative. One of the distinguishing characteristics of the New York Book-Bindery was the many processes performed within the establishment. *The Art of Book-Binding* related that "every variety of plain and ornamental binding is here executed in muslin, sheep, roan, English, French, and American calf, russia, vellum, morocco, velvet, and the inlaid or illuminated styles, as well as those unique and economic styles in half calf and morocco." Pages 48 and 49 provided a list of bindings with prices annexed, placed there to assist out-of-town customers in estimating the prices of corresponding book sizes and the styles in which they might wish to have theirs bound. From this list of ten titles two examples are reprinted here to show that marbling was one of the several processes of bookbinding performed by the Walkers:

HARPER'S PICTORIAL BIBLE.
    1 vol. royal 4to, library style 3.00
    Strong calf, marbled edges 4.00
    Turkey morocco, gilt, gilt edges 6.50
        do   extra   do 8.00
GODEY'S AND GRAHAM'S MAGAZINES.
    Half morocco, gilt, marbled edges $1.00
    Neat calf, gilt,   do 2.00
    Turkey mor., extra, gilt edges 3.00

Based on this and other information, we can ascertain that marbling was carried on in the Walker bindery and was not only applied to the edges of books, for E. Walker advertised in the *New York Times* of 27 October 1855[19] that he manufactured the usual patterns of marbled paper and had a large assortment on hand that he was disposed to sell at reasonable prices. The Walker and Harper plants give us a good indication of the large proportions the New York publishing industry had attained. They also demonstrate that marbling was not an independent activity, as elsewhere, but was largely carried on as part of extensive publishing and bookbinding operations. The illustration of the Walker bindery interior at mid-century, reproduced here from one of its broadside advertising pieces as Figure 13, allows us to view its binders and other craftsmen at work. The listings in the Walkers' *Art of Book-Binding* pamphlet give prices and styles of books bound only in the old way (in animal skins), but this firm also executed a large number of trade bindings for editions issued by various publishers in New York at this time, which were covered with cloth and stamped with fancy gilt decoration, in the new manner.[20]

It is somewhat ironic and amusing that the first person who can positively be identified with marbling in New York City is Franklin Mann, the youngest member of the Dedham family.[21] Among the Mann family papers is a letter of February 22, 1847, written by Franklin in New York to his brother Samuel in Dedham, indicating that he was marbling there. Evidence is provided not only by the contents of the letter—Franklin told Samuel about a marbled pattern he had just made "that would best suit the New York folks"—but by the fact that it was penned on the verso of a sheet of that same marbled paper, the pattern being nonpareil and showing that Franklin indeed was a proficient marbler.

In my book on the Mann family I speculated as to the date of Franklin's arrival in New York, and what, specifically, he was doing as a marbler there. I conjectured that Franklin might have migrated to New York in as early as 1840, although it has not been possible to document his location there earlier than the year of this letter. Even so, his name did not appear in a contemporary New York City directory until 1852, when the issue of that year listed

FIGURE 13. *Top,* the exterior of E. Walker & Sons New York Book-Bindery (probably in the late 1840s); *bottom,* an illustration showing the kind of activities carried on there (the latter scene was pirated by Walker from an English publication on the subject of bookbinding that had appeared earlier).

him as living on Wycoff Street in Brooklyn and working at 114 Fulton Street in New York. Since 114 Fulton Street was the address of the Walkers' New York Book-Bindery, it seems reasonable to conclude that Franklin was working for the Walkers in 1852, applying marbled decoration to the edges of books bound at the Walker plant and probably decorating paper as well.[22] Later directory listings locate Franklin at other addresses, and it seems likely that he spent the later fifties away from the Walker operation. His name is absent from New York directories from approximately 1861 to 1871, and his activities and whereabouts during this interval are unknown. A letter written to a sister during a visit to Boston in 1865, however, suggests that Franklin interviewed for a position in Henry O. Houghton's newly established Riverside Press in Cambridge, Massachusetts, assumedly as a marbler, a position that Houghton then was trying to fill.[23] While Franklin Mann's name reappeared in New York directories between 1872 and 1878 with the description of "papermaker," we learn nothing more about him, except that he died at Brooklyn in October 1881 at the age of sixty-eight.

Accounts of the publishing operations at both Houghton's Riverside Press and at the Harper establishment were printed in the years 1871 and 1887. Not only do these give us résumés of the extensive book-production activities of these respective plants, but they also describe briefly the role of the marbler in decorating book edges in their binderies and even provide illustrations of marblers at work (Figure 14).[24]

There is not much more that can be said about marbling activity in New York, for little else is known. Records show that Thomas Carson of Brooklyn received a patent in 1871 for his invention of a marbleized paper that could be used on walls, on fronts of counters, and for other purposes. Carson's process utilized the true marbling method, using a bath containing gum tragacanth, but he employed oil colors with Demar varnish, and the paper was varnished again after drying.[25] Although this information fits into the notion that here and there a marbler worked independently, the center of activity in New York was located in the large binderies and in plants maintained by the Harpers and other large publishing firms.

Marbling in Other Localities

From time to time I have noticed references suggesting that marbling was carried on in other American cities in the nineteenth century. Few of these can be followed sufficiently to prove any great depth of activity, but they are recorded here because they do indicate an involvement or interest in marbling and perhaps, with the help of additional evidence, will show more in the future. One such reference appears in an 1819 letter from Herman Mann, Sr., in Dedham, to his son Daniel, in Providence.[26] Writing about the procurement of gums and colors, Herman

FIGURE 14. *Left,* marbling book edges at the Riverside Press, Cambridge, Mass., 1871; *right,* at the Harper establishment, New York City, 1887.

advised his son, "If Mr. Kendall should be making marbled paper, you can perhaps get some new information." He evidently was referring to Oliver Kendall, a bookseller, publisher, and music seller in Providence. Born in Sterling, Rhode Island, in 1776, Kendall moved to Providence in 1805 and found work with the bookseller William Wilkinson, whose business he assumed in 1817 and continued until a few years before his death in 1843.[27] Laid into the back of one of the firm's account books (now preserved in the Rhode Island Historical Society), which details bookbinding and other work performed in the 1805–1813 period, is a sheet of paper containing a handwritten recipe entitled "Method of Preparing and Colouring Marbled Paper."[28] This account is essentially a word-for-word copy of Robert Dossie's classic description, and Kendall undoubtedly copied it from an encyclopedia or dictionary when he contemplated adding this line to his business. Booksellers and stationers, we have noted, had a particular interest in marbled paper, and we may presume that Kendall undertook its manufacture at about the time that he was establishing himself in business. How long or extensive his production of this article was cannot now be determined.

Another reference came to my attention through Sue Allen of New Haven, Connecticut, by way of a thesis written by Francis Gagliardi about John and Sidney

MARBLING BOOKS.

Babcock, printers and booksellers of New Haven in the 1795–1885 period.[29] Daniel Mann worked for John Babcock in 1812 as a printer of music, and it is possible that Babcock then learned something of marbling from him. Mrs. Allen has reported that an 1840 inventory of the Babcock printing shop (at that time Sidney Babcock had fallen into financial straits following the 1837 depression), contained the following items of interest:

1 marbling trough	$1
12 pots for marbling	$0.50
15 qrs. Cap marble paper, cost $6.50 per ream	$5.20
23 " double cap do $10.00	$11.50
5 " broken imperial do inferior	$1.25
12 " Mama's medium do cost $14.50	$7.62

The first two entries on the inventory provide a fairly good indication that marbling had been carried on, at least by the 1830s, as part of Babcock's overall activities. Many of the firm's imprints checklisted by Gagliardi have marbled paper in or on their bindings, and it is likely that Babcock used his paper in his own bookbinding work and sold some of it to others. It appears also that he had on hand paper produced by the Manns in Dedham, inasmuch as "Mama's medium" on the inventory might reasonably be interpreted as an illegibly written "Mann's medium."

A further reference to marbling in Rhode Island in the nineteenth century appears in a published report of the first exhibition of the Worcester County Mechanics Association, held at the Nashua Hall in September of 1848:[30]

937. SPECIMENS OF COLORED PAPER, Bliss, Potter & Co., Pawtucket, R. I. Of good material, bright colors, and exceedingly well finished. They reflect much credit upon the manufacturers. The patterns of marbled paper were of a more common quality, and would more properly stand as number two.

Diploma.

And evidence that yet another printing and binding house had added marbling to its total operation comes from the advertisement which George Wilson published in the Springfield, Massachusetts, city directory of 1853/4.[31] Wilson, having recently moved from Boston, where he had worked in the printing office of the late Samuel N. Dickinson, reported that job binding of every description was executed at his Steam, Book, Job, and Card Printing Office, Book Bindery, and Patent Blank Book Manufactory, "including the most elaborate Gilding and Marbling, done in our own Bindery, and under our personal supervision."[32]

Still another clue to the conduct of marbling in nineteenth-century America is provided in a book that Horace Greeley compiled and titled *The Great Industries of the United States,* issued at Hartford in 1872. Containing articles on political, social, economic, and industrial aspects of American life, this compilation is similar in character and intent to Edwin Freedley's previously discussed book on Philadelphia and its manufactures, but is national in scope. In a section describing "Book-Making," the following brief description of marbling appeared: [33]

> In marbling the artist—for a skilled artisan in this department is an artist—sprinkles his colors upon a preparation of mucilaginous liquid in a wooden trough, and then with "combs" makes the "comb-work," which is the pattern usual for edges. With various colors, and by skillful sprinkling, he makes the different patterns known as shell,—of various colors and differently veined,—blue stormont, light Italian, west end, curl, Spanish of all colors, antique, wave, British, Dutch, and so on, in great variety, for marbling paper used for the sides of books.

At the conclusion of this section, its unidentified author cited as the source of his information the printing and binding establishment of Case, Lockwood & Brainard of Hartford, Connecticut. This firm was somewhat similar in size and scope to Harper's, which had been the subject of Jacob Abbott's *Harper Establishment*. Although a printed description of the history and activities of the Case, Lockwood & Brainard firm does exist, it makes no mention of marbling.[34] Nevertheless, I believe we can safely infer that marbling facilities were there, for marbling was not always mentioned in these descriptive handbooks, as the case of E. Walker & Sons' *The Art of Book-Binding* shows. From the color and distinctive patterns on Hartford imprints dating from the early decades of the nineteenth century, we have reason to suspect that marbling went on in Hartford in these early times, as did fairly good hand bookbinding; however, virtually no worthwhile research has gone on with regard to early bookbinding in this Connecticut city, a field worthy of serious study in the future. By the 1840s, Hartford was a thriving publishing center, and it produced books by means of factories that were cast somewhat in the mold of those in New York City. Furthermore, a goodly number of books produced and presumably bound in these plants contain marbled paper as end- and cover papers, and many have edge decoration as well. I have seen enough over the years to have become convinced that the art was carried on in the Hartford factory-bookbinderies in a considerable way.

All of the above instances indicate that marbling migrated to several locations outside the major urban centers of Boston, Philadelphia, and New York, where the craft initially took root in America; and it is likely that it came to be carried on in still other locations yet unnoticed. Two other topics are worthy of mention in this survey of nineteenth-century American marbling: one concerns the marbling of book edges, and the other deals

briefly with the literature that appeared on this subject in the United States.

Marbled Edges on American Books

The practice of marbling the edges of books did not occur in America in its colonial and federal periods on the scale that it did at the same time in England or France. Despite those advertisements of 1764 and 1773, marbling has not been found on the edges of American bindings before the early nineteenth century, and it was effected only infrequently in the decades immediately following and then only on the finer productions of native bookbinders. We have observed that marbling went on in America from the early years of the nineteenth century and probably even before; however it remained in a developmental stage during this period, with few craftsmen attaining mastery and even fewer achieving large production over a long span of time. Apparently those who did have some success in this line directed their efforts toward decorating paper, which was profitable enough.

The first actual reference to edge marbling in America that has come to my attention and can be taken as certain appeared in an advertisement of Samuel and Edward Mann. This was published in the *Boston Daily Advertiser & Patriot* on May 14, 1834, after the Mann brothers had moved their place of business from Boston to Dedham, to give notice that

> The Marbling Works of the subscribers having been removed to the Manufactory in Dedham they respectfully inform Bookbinders Generally, that they have an Order Box at the Store of Mr. CHARLES A. WELLS, No. 7, Water street, Boston, where Books to be Marbled directed to them, will be received and punctually attended to—and returned to the city, free of expense and transportation.[35]

Whereas the practice of edge marbling may have been conducted by some of those marblers already named and discussed, it was primarily in the large publishing concerns and trade binderies that it came to be carried on in a considerable way, as in the Harper establishment, the Walkers' New York Book-Bindery, and probably the plant of Case, Lockwood & Brainard in Hartford.

Indeed, the practices of such establishments were so deeply rooted in these early times that they still continue to be used today. The George D. Barnard Company in St. Louis is a case in point. This firm has been in business for well over a hundred years, specializing in the production of blank books for business purposes, and is best known today for making the large, leather-bound and gold-lettered record books that are seen in county courthouses and other record centers. These volumes are produced even today with marbleized edges, continuing a tradition that was well established in the past. In 1975, John R. Gannett, the chairman of the Barnard company, contributed the following interesting facts about the marbling of book edges in his company's plant:

> Barnards for the past 100 years has been decorating the edges of record books apparently using the same procedure now as then. That is, we still use the Spanish moss for the vehicle on which we float the water colors mixed with varying degrees of ox-gaul [sic.].
>
> Really, we know very little about the why and wherefore of marbling. We have a certain set of procedures that if we follow we get good results—we know that on certain days such as when the humidity is high we can't marble. It been [sic.] a successful hit or miss procedure.[36]

As mentioned above, Franklin Mann probably visited the Riverside Press of Henry O. Houghton in 1865 to be interviewed for a position as a marbler. In December 1863 Houghton had contracted to print and bind the fourth edition of the Merriam-Webster *Unabridged Dictionary,* which had been compiled by Noah Webster and published at Springfield, Massachusetts by G. & C. Merriam since 1844. The memorandum of agreement with Webster's heirs, from whom Houghton had obtained the rights, obliged him to accomplish this work over a three-year period, with prices negotiated each year according to those estimated for 1863. These ranged from $1.10 for copies in "Rough Sheep marbled edge" to $4.75 for "Turkey Morocco gilt edged, the best style work." It is evident that Houghton was looking for a marbler when Franklin visited his press, and while the youngest of the Manns did not get or take the job, someone else did, for the contract was fulfilled. In fact, marbling has been employed for decorating the Webster *Unabridged Dictionary* even into moden times.[37]

In the late 1960s I conducted a library school class through the Riverside Press of the Houghton, Mifflin Company and observed marbled decoration being applied to the Webster dictionary in just about the same manner that had been used since 1864 or 1865, when the Houghton firm produced its first edition. A few years later, I interviewed Edward A. Artesani, who had been a marbler at Riverside, about his experiences there.[38] Artesani began working at the Riverside Press around 1921 as an apprentice in the general bookbinding department, and not long afterward was asked if he would like to try his hand at marbling, for it was traditionally used to decorate the edges of the Webster dictionary.

Up to that time, one Henry Lang had been doing the marbling at Riverside, having begun about 1880 after learning the process from an earlier marbler who had been brought over from Germany. In the later years of his life Lang became independent, as many marblers are prone to be. The method is capricious and variable according to the weather, and Artesani related that on hot days, when Lang didn't feel like working, he would try the gum and report that it would not work because of the heat. Then he went home. Over time this behavior interfered with the company's work routine and resulted in the temporary layoff of six forwarders, who had to wait for the completion of the marbling operation before undertaking their phase of the work. To remedy this situation, the Riverside managers proposed that if Lang would teach Artesani the art, he would be paid a salary for the rest of his life, whether he marbled or not. Several times the recalcitrant Lang backed off, but finally he agreed. Nevertheless, he was not overly communicative while training another man to work in his place and Artesani eventually had to learn to marble through the trial-and-error method. He worked for ten years at marbling the edges of the dictionary and then became a supervisor elsewhere in the plant, training others to assume his marbling operation before moving on.

This story about marbling in the twentieth century illustrates once again how the craft has been carried on throughout a good part of its existence: it has remained a secret and restricted method right to the present time. Additionally, marblers have been looked upon as the prima donnas of the book production world—consider, for example, the indignation and irritation that James Sumner expressed in 1854. The sheer difficulty of mastering and controlling this method, its seemingly magical qualities, and its consequent restriction to a limited few have embued the successful marbler with a special aura that is accorded to few others in the bookmaking and binding trades. In that realm, the marbler has continued to be, if not king, then a nobleman of unique character, proudly independent, and owing allegiance to none but himself and his art.

The Marbling Literature of Nineteenth-Century America

If one general observation may be made about the existence or production of a marbling literature in early America, it is this: there wasn't much of it. American craftsmen who marbled, it would seem, were content to rely on their English and European cousins for information needed to learn and exploit this technique. Such a situation is indicated by the transcription that Oliver Kendall made, in about 1817, of Robert Dossie's "Method of Preparing and Colouring Marbled Paper" when he attempted to learn the art. By and large, the literature printed in America on this subject was derivative, and, with but a few exceptions, it was slight.

The first publication this side of the Atlantic of a description of the marbling process that has come to my attention was the very brief and familiar one entitled "How to Marble and Jasper Paper," which had appeared in many British editions of the *Valuable Secrets Concerning*

Arts and Trades (or, under the alternative title *Valuable Secrets of Arts and Trades*). Inexplicably, two American editions of this work were issued in the same year, 1795, in locations far removed from one another: the first to appear in the New World. One was published in Philadelphia under the title *One Thousand Valuable Secrets in the Elegant and Useful Arts*, having been printed for the booksellers by B. Davies and T. Stephens;[39] the other was issued by the Norwich, Connecticut, printer Thomas Hubbard under the more familiar title *Valuable Secrets Concerning the Arts and Trades*. While each differed slightly in the arrangement of some material, they were reprintings of the familiar British work (which itself was said to have been a translation of a popular French work) and contained the succinct descriptions of marbling that had appeared before. In 1798 J. Bumstead of Boston published another edition under the title *Valuable Secrets of Arts and Trades*, and in 1809 and 1816 Evert Duyckinck of New York City reissued this work with the title *Valuable Secrets in Arts, Trades, &c.* Another edition appeared in 1814 under the title *Valuable Secrets in Arts and Trades, Containing Directions from the Best Artists for Calico Printing*, printed by E. G. House for J. Norman, a Boston artist and engraver, who listed himself as "Chartseller."[40]

In 1803 William Young Birch and Abraham Small of Philadelphia republished in five volumes a work of the English physician A. F. M. Willich entitled *The Domestic Encyclopaedia; or, A Dictionary of Facts, and Useful Knowledge*. In this compilation, half a page was devoted to explaining the marbling process,[41] which apparently was a rewriting and modernization of Robert Dossie's earlier explanation. In 1814 the American chemist James Cutbush published in the second volume of his *American Artist's Manual, or Dictionary of Practical Knowledge in the Application of Philosophy to the Arts and Manufactures*[42] yet another discussion of this subject, most of it taken, its author acknowledged, from Willich's *Domestic Encyclopaedia*. A few years later there appeared in the Philadelphia reprinting of Abraham Ree's *New Cyclopaedia, or Universal Dictionary of the Arts and Sciences* the first useful description of the process to be made available in this country.[43] (This was actually the account that Rees included in his revision of Ephraim Chamber's *Encyclopaedia*, which had been issued in the 1778–1788 period.) And in 1824, with the republication of "Oswestry 1811" at Richmond, Virginia, America was not only given its first bookbinding manual but also became acquainted with the method of soap marbling and various recipes for staining, sprinkling, and coloring paper.[44]

In 1829 the *Journal of the Franklin Institute of the State of Pennsylvania* reprinted the lengthy article that had been translated from its French original and published in *Gill's Technological Repository* earlier that year. This, I would judge, constitutes the best treatment of the subject to appear in an American publication before the middle of the century; in fact, this article is so good, that I recently re-

published it.[45] It will be seen that everything appearing in America up to this time was borrowed from an English or European source. Scraps of marbling information were included in a number of compilations of recipes and trade secrets that began to appear from the late 1820s on, most of these, too, emanating from foreign sources. For example, in 1829 *MacKenzie's Five Thousand Receipts in All the Useful and Domestic Arts*, which was published in its first American edition by James Kay of Philadelphia,[46] provided a brief outline of marbling, as did another English compilation, Joseph Guy's *Pocket Cyclopaedia, or Epitome of Universal Knowledge*, issued initially in America by E. and G. Merriam of Brookfield, Massachusetts, in 1831.[47] Again, in 1857 Mrs. Sarah Josepha Hale's *Receipts for the Millions*, put out by the Philadelphia publisher T. B. Peterson, contained a short section entitled "To Marble Books or Paper," and, undoubtedly, there were other American works in this genre.[48] The Mackenzie and Hale compilations included almost identical descriptions of marbling, each, seemingly, a slight rewriting of the one that had appeared in *The Gentleman's Companion: or, Trademan's Delight* in 1735. However, a much fuller and a rather good description of the process was published by M. LaFayette Byrn, a physician of New York, in his *Artist's and Tradesman's Companion* of 1855.[49]

In 1855, we have observed, Jacob Abbott published his description of the Harper establishment and, with its account of the marbling operation that was conducted in its bindery, contributed much to our historical perspective of how the craft was practiced in New York. However, it was with the reprinting of Charles Woolnough's classic instructions on the art of marbling paper in James B. Nicholson's bookbinding manual of 1856 that America received its first detailed information on this subject; specific directions for making both classical patterns and those which only recently had come into vogue. The seven full-page samples (made by Charles Williams) incorporated into this manual showed how well some of these patterns could be done. So successful was Nicholson's *Manual of the Art of Bookbinding* that it was reprinted four more times over the next thirty-odd years.

Lesser descriptions of marbling were printed in several American books of recipes of the late nineteenth century, of which R. Moore's *The Universal Assistant, and Complete Mechanic* of 1881 can be cited as but one example.[50] Near the century's end there appeared an American translation and edition—in fact, the first English version—of one of the classic European works on marbling and another cornerstone of the literature, Josef Halfer's *Die Fortschritte der Marmorierkunst*. It was issued at Buffalo under the title *The Progress of the Marbling Art* by Louis H. Kinder, an emigrant German binder who worked there. This important event, as well as Kinder's involvement and interest in marbling, can best be described in a later chapter.

10

The Decline of the Art in Europe: "Pseudo-Marbling" and Marbling by Machine

IN the late 1820s and early 1830s, at approximately the same time that Charles Woolnough was launching his long and extraordinary career in London and Samuel and Edward Mann were planning and setting up their Boston Marble-Paper Manufactory, the marbling trade on the continent of Europe was beginning to undergo dramatic and drastic changes. Whereas marbling had finally attained virility in Great Britain and was straining toward maturity in America, it had entered a stage akin to old age in Europe. Clearly, the craft had run most of its course there. Economic pressures and other considerations were forcing bookbinders to look for cheaper and different ways to dress their bindings; this, in turn, led paper colorers also to seek easier and alternative ways of producing fancy papers, which, though reducing cost, altered their work's appearance. And while the Industrial Revolution had not yet caught the binding and marbling trades tightly in its grasp—this would come a little later, with the growing improvements of bookbinding machinery, mainly in Britain and America—signs pointing toward industrialization were already beginning to appear; in time, it would relentlessly tighten its grip on both of these time-honored professions and clasp them in a virtual stranglehold by century's end.

The new trend in paper coloring and decoration began about the third decade of the nineteenth century and can most directly be traced to the innovations of F. M. Montgolfier of Annonay, France; but although Montgolfier is the first to be clearly identified with the development of "pseudo-marbling" (as I prefer to call these new forms), similar but less documented processes were going on in the factories of Germany at about the same time. (It is amazing, with reference to new developments and trends in the marbling business, how the French and the German marblers always seemed to know what the other country's developments were and how quickly one country's advances were emulated by the other.) Indeed, the decline of traditional marbled paper decoration can be traced to the earliest years of the nineteenth century, when "maroquin," or morocco paper, was developed. Effected quickly and easily through engraved plates, this type was more easily produced and cheaper than the old marbled variety; it would come to be used extensively in Europe, especially for covering blank books and half bindings, and for other inexpensive work.

In about 1830, the French and the Germans began to produce in their factories one of these pseudo-marbled papers, under the designation *agathe* or *Achat* ("agate"). While this came into popular use as a substitute for marbled paper in bookbinding, the design that is best known in association with the new methods went under the name of *papier d'Annonay*. Invented by F. M. Montgolfier at his family's paper mills at Annonay after 1820, this variety, like the agathe or Achat, was produced without the aid of a bath, the colors being sprinkled onto the paper directly and achieving their special appearance through their combination with caustic chemicals.[1] The papier d'Annonay was highly regarded in France and elsewhere, and came into wide use as a cheap substitute for the traditional marbled papers, thereby contributing much to their decline.

Annonay is a small town in the Ardeche department of southern France, about nineteen miles southeast of Saint-Étienne and still further south of Lyon. It had long been an important tanning and paper milling center; indeed, the Montgolfier family connection with papermaking in Annonay dated to the end of the fourteenth century. By the middle of the eighteenth century, with Pierre Montgolfier in control, the firm boasted the title of Royal Manufactory. (Two of Pierre's sons, Joseph and Étienne, made aviation history by taking part in the first balloon ascent, a spectacle witnessed by Benjamin Franklin and others at Annonay's Place des Cordeliers in 1783.)[2]

The papier d'Annonay was prepared on a table and hence was not a true "Tunkpapier," as the Germans designated marbled and other types of decorated papers produced on a tank or bath. The colors, containing starch and alum, were applied to sheets of paper with brushes, sponges, and other implements after the paper had first been treated with a solution of potassium hydroxide or caustic potash. In this way—chemically, or with caustic materials—the colored effects and tones of the papier d'Annonay were produced more quickly, more cheaply, and without the element of chance that always accompanied the classical marbling method.[3] Before long, both the French and the Germans were developing methods to produce patterns in similar yet still more diverse ways.

That such chemically produced papers were not available prior to 1830 is proved by the absence of information on any of them in the paper-coloring manuals produced by LeNormand, Thon, and others in the preceding years. The only patterns these manuals took notice of, in addition to the ancient calico (Kattun), gold or brocade, paste and marbled papers, were maroquin, or morocco, (also known as Saffian papers), lacquered (known in Germany as *Titelpapiere*), and guilloche papers. These last three were considered to be of the same genre because special surface effects were imparted to them by engraved plates after several coats of a single color had been applied. The plate gave the maroquin paper an overall appearance of morocco leather or tree marbling; the guilloche paper's effect was one of an unending series of interlaced, curved lines; the surface of the lacquered, or Titelpapiere, was a smooth, highly polished one. The guilloche paper was probably the oldest pattern of the three, for C. F. G. Thon, in the 1832 edition of his *Der Farbrikant Bunter Papier*, reported that it had come into fashion forty-nine years before (that is, in the 1780s). That the maroquin paper dates to at least the first decade of the nineteenth century is indicated, we have seen, by its description in the early Leipzig manual entitled *Der Vollkommene Papierfärber*, assumedly the long-lost (or long-unrecognized) work by Schuder said to have been issued in the year 1808. Maroquin paper is also described in L. S. LeNormand's 1828 manual, and all three are discussed in detail in the 1832 edition of Thon's work.

One has only to refer to M. Fichtenberg's *Nouveau manuel complet du fabricant de papiers de fantaisie*, issued at Paris in 1852, to see how far the making of colored and fancy papers had strayed from the pure marbling methods of old and how much experimentation with chemically made patterns had occurred in the previous twenty years. Of the different papers Fichtenberg discusses (and in some cases illustrates with tiny samples of original marbling mounted at the end of his work), eight are listed as German, all made on a bath; two true marbled types are denominated as English, "ombres" and "peignes" (these undoubtedly were the Spanish and nonpareil or small-comb or Anglo-Dutch patterns for which the English had become famous); and two pseudo-marbled types are

called French, the papier d'Annonay and the agathe, which were not made on a bath. A few of the eight German patterns represent the marbling of old: No. 1, "papiers Cailloutages ou Turcs," and No. 5, "Marbres Grosse Caillous," for example, were the classic shell and Turkish designs respectively. The remainder, such as the partridge eye, Tiger, Schroëtel, and Polish patterns, Gustav marbling (which was named after a very popular Swedish prince who was active as a composer of songs at the middle of the nineteenth century), and several other later designs were made on a bath but incorporated foreign substances to bring about their new effects. Potash was used in almost all these patterns, along with other ingredients, such as alum, soda, tartar, rosin, shellac, and soap. Every other paper described and illustrated by Fichtenberg is of the non-marbled variety. Interestingly, the French at this time duplicated some of the patterns developed by the Germans (which Fichtenberg listed as German), and the Germans, in turn, came to make their own version of the papier d'Annonay.

Reproduced here on Plates XX and XXI are some of the popular imitation and pseudo-marbled papers that came into production early in the nineteenth century. The first three examples on Plate XX are maroquin or morocco or Saffian papers—the French also called these "papiers racines"—which, I have noted, developed early in the nineteenth century in imitation of the tree-marbled bindings of the 1780s onward. The morocco papers were popular and were used mainly for covering cheap work such as blank books; now and then, however, they were used to decorate better work as well. Examples 4–9 on Plate XX and 1–3 on Plate XXI show the well-known papier d'Annonay in all three of its forms. Numbers 4–7 on Plate XX show the type of Annonay paper called "papier tourniquet" and made in the 1830s and 1840s. The seventh example on Plate XX, while of this group, was undoubtedly made by Charles Williams in Philadelphia, for it was removed from the covers of a plain cloth binding done by Samuel Moore and Son of Philadelphia, whose ticket was inserted in it. Williams's paper, which dates to the 1862–1864 period—while a good imitation—does not show nearly the accomplishment or finesse of the authentic French examples in this class. Samples 8–9 on Plate XX display the second of the Annonay types, those known as "papier coulé (sliding paper), while the first three samples on Plate XXI illustrate the third of the Annonay papers, those called "papier croisé (twilled paper)" because of the twists and turns in the design. All three were made in essentially the same way, their different effects resulting from the ways they were finished (that is, by splattering, sponging, and the like). The samples of the coulé paper date to the 1840s and 1860s respectively. The first two of the tourniquet papers were produced in the 1830s, while the last example dates probably to the 1850s or later.

Samples 4–7 on Plate XXI show agate papers. The first

ones are French and date to the 1840s, while the others are German and originated after mid-century. The final two examples on Plate XXI illustrate the German "Gustav Marmor," which was developed just after the middle of the century and remained a popular pattern into the twentieth century. This paper was produced by coating it with color and subsequently using acid to bring about the final effect.

Thus, while one finds truly marbled papers as binding decoration in or on French books published in the 1840s and into the 1860s, classical marbling is only infrequently seen after that time, even though hand bookbinding remained common in France long after it had ceased to be popular elsewhere. Those marbled patterns appearing in French books in the 1850s and beyond were few in number, and were mainly of the shell design, with very small spots, and the Turkish pattern, which had small spots and veins. At times, these two patterns appeared in the same binding, with one type serving for the endpapers and the other for cover papers; and, at times, one or the other might appear on endpapers within a binding that was covered partly with leather and partly with papier d'Annonay or agathe paper. It should be emphasized, however, that the papiers d'Annonay and agates and other artificial designs were never used as endpapers in books, *but as cover papers only.* When such "pseudo-marbles" served as cover papers, the endpapers most often were white; however, when a decorated paper was used, as sometimes occurred in French bookbinding, it usually was one of the aforementioned small shell or Turkish designs that served as the interior decoration.

Once the industrialization of the bookbinding industry took hold in the middle and late nineteenth century, the numbers of the hand bookbinders of old declined, and the marbling shops that had been located in many cities and towns throughout France began to disappear, until there were only a few left. Located mainly in Paris, these shops inherited the job of supplying the remaining hand bookbinders with the traditional marbled papers they required to decorate their works. Some of the pattern books of these surviving firms are preserved in the Musée des Arts Décoratifs in the Louvre. All these sample books, disbound and mounted into large scrapbooks now shelved in the museum's library, are undated, but some of the information printed on their covers and some of the patterns they contain give us a pretty fair indication of the industry.

Within this collection are several pattern books of the firm of Putois & J. Le Manie. George Putois, as previously noted, assumed the business of the earlier maker, Chagniat, after 1881; no information, however, has turned up so far on the period of his collaboration with Le Manie. These booklets of small, oblong format probably date to the later years of the nineteenth century or to the early years of the twentieth. One contains 125 samples dis-

playing many truly marbled patterns such as Spanish, comb, and curl; chemically produced patterns such as Schrottel, agate, and the Gustav design; as well as paste papers. Another, of slightly larger format and probably later in date, has seventy patterns, many of which appear in the presumably earlier book; it contains, in addition, peacock and double-combed designs. I have in my own collection a small pattern book issued by "Putois & P., Paris," probably early in the present century, which displays only samples of pseudo-marbled paper types such as agate, Gustav, imitation papier d'Annonay, and other chemically produced designs. On its cover is printed a notice that the Putois (i.e., the Chagniat) firm had been awarded bronze and silver medals at exhibitions in Paris in 1867 and 1876, and at Havre in 1868. The firm has been long-lived, for in the 1950s the Stevens-Nelson Paper Corporation of New York was importing marbled papers still being made by this house.[4]

The scrapbooks at the Musée des Arts Décoratifs contain sample books of other Parisian makers. One—of the "Ancienne maison Charles Jaugeon," successor to Auguste Lemoine, "fabricant de percalines gaufrées pour rélieurs, papetiers, gainerie, portefeuilles et visières, papiers de fantaisie et papiers marbrés"—contains 130 samples, many of them apparently machine-made. Another, issued by A. Vautier, the successor of Ch. Hersant, shows agate and Gustav patterns among the pseudo-marblers; "romantic" and "sunshine" patterns introduced early in the nineteenth century (these were produced on a bath, but also with caustic chemicals); and curl, Spanish, and other classical types. There is also a pattern book, dating to the late nineteenth or early twentieth century, from the firm of Germier & Scherf of Paris. Since none of these makers appear in Grand-Carteret's list of stationers, one might hypothesize that they belonged to the ranks of true marblers who catered mainly to bookbinders and had little connection with the French stationery trade.

Although the information in Fichtenberg's manual seems to indicate that all the German marbled papers of this period were authentic "Tunkpapiere," this is not the case. The large pattern books of the Dessauer firm (described in an earlier chapter) indicate that by mid-century marbling was only a small part of its total output; the larger part consisted of wallpaper and industrial papers. Only the first 35 of the 163 pages that make up the Aschaffenburg pattern book in the Houghton Library at Harvard University, for example, are devoted to illustrating the marbled papers that this firm produced and offered for sale in the period around 1850: the majority of the book's pages are given over to samples of lithographed papers, as well as paste, monochrome, gold and silver, pseudo-marbled, and all the other types then categorized as colored and decorated types. There are some true marbles of old displayed among the marbled designs, such as the Turkish, Spanish, shell, and curl patterns, but for the most part those designated as "marbled" were the newer patterns of "Schroëtel," "romantic" or "sunshine" marbling; while made on the bath, these had potash, rosin, and other ingredients incorporated into them to produce their novel effects.

The Nineteenth-Century German Literature

Despite the impression given by Fichtenberg that all the methods he discusses were carried on in factory fashion in France at the middle of the nineteenth century, such production was not typical of the French trade, even though pseudo-marbled papers were manufactured at Annonay and at Strasbourg (and from the 1830s at Turnhout, Belgium) along with other forms of colored paper. With respect to classical marbling, however, the workshops had broken down and little of the old paper was being made in France. Fichtenberg's Germanic name and his familiarity with German techniques lead us to suspect that he may have worked for a time in the factories in Germany, but his knowledge of French techniques suggests that he may have worked at Strasbourg as well before setting up in Paris. Still, we know next to nothing of the conditions of this changing trade and of the industrial production of Buntpapier, except for general facts of the Dessauer operation and what we can glean from the literature. Unfortunately, the literature allows us to view only the surface and leaves the depths below clouded and unplumbed.

As in England, there developed in Europe an ever-widening literature of marbling and even of Buntpapier as the nineteenth century advanced. Fichtenberg's important manual is but one rather late example, for such a literature began several decades before. In 1820 Christian Friedrich Gottlieb Thon had issued at Sonderhausen and Nordhausen the first edition of his manual, *Die Kunst Bücher zu Binden,* a work intended to allow binders to learn all methods of bookbinding as well as gilding, lacquering, and marbling. Initially, Thon's discussion of processes for making various colored papers, including marbled ones, occupied only a small portion of his work, but when the manual was reissued at Ilmenau in 1826, Thon had altered its form drastically. Material on bookbinding was incorporated in a single volume (Part I), and a second volume (Part II) was devoted entirely to "Der Fabrikant bunter Papier." Because of the uncertain status of the Schuder work of 1808, Thon's book constitutes possibly the first known attempt to explain comprehensively all of the methods and facets of coloring paper. Thon's work on Buntpapier was reissued in a second edition (along with a third edition of his bookbinding manual) at Ilmenau in 1832; a fourth (and a fifth edition of the bookbinding manual) appeared at Weimar in 1844; other editions followed.[5]

All of these works are rare and difficult to find; not surprisingly, they are costly when purchased on today's antiquarian book market. The description that follows is based on a copy of the second edition in my collection and supplemented by photoreproductions of parts of other editions.

Der Fabrikant Bunter Papier is a very thorough work. It opens with three chapters (nearly 150 pages) that explain in detail the colorer's workshop, the utensils he used, and his materials, with special attention to the nature and preparation of colors. Additionally, there is a small but excellent section on the gums used in some of the processes (gum arabic, gum Senegal,[6] and gum tragacanth). Subsequent chapters contain directions for the making of monochrome, sprinkled, gold and silver, and stamped papers, including calico papers, wallpapers, and other types. And, naturally, there is a chapter on marbled papers, encompassing both "Kleistermarmor" (paste papers) and those of the Turkish variety.

About twenty-five pages in Thon's manual deal with classical marbling; they provide detailed instructions on the utensils, materials, and methods in making and ultimately polishing the papers. All that is lacking is instruction on making specific patterns, although a few are generally described. Inasmuch as the Thon manual went through many editions, we may be sure that it found a ready audience and thus had some impact on the production of colored papers in Germany, despite the fact that most production was going on in the factories where such a literature was not likely to be greatly needed, except by beginners.

Two comparable works were L. Sébastien LeNormand's *Manuel du Fabricant d'étoffes imprimées et du fabricant de papiers peints* and Johann Roehberg's *Die Papierfarbekunst in Allen Ihren Theilen.* LeNormand's work first came out at Paris in 1830 and almost immediately was translated into German, with another French edition following in 1856.[7] In a speech before the Verein der Papier- und Schreibwaarenhändler at Leipzig in 1881,[8] Philipp Dessauer, director of the Aschaffenburg company and grandson of its founder, rated Roehberg's book to be on a par with Thon's. Its first edition appeared in 1839, with a second following in 1851.[9] I have been fortunate in locating the first editions of these works, as well as several subsequent ones, and can state unequivocally that both are excellent and important manuals, containing extensive and informative sections on marbling and also on the manufacture of other types of colored paper and some of the pseudo-marbled types of that period.

Several bookbinders contributed to the literature of marbling in Germany at this time, their efforts apparently intended to assist fellow craftsmen who might want to marble book edges and make occasional papers. Edge marbling was restricted in Germany because of the prevailing factory system, and binders were thrown back onto their own resources in order to satisfy such needs. Some of these manuals, by incorporating the most current information available, enabled binders to imitate a few of the novel designs that were becoming popular. One such manual is J. A. F. Schade's *Die Marmorir-Kunst, oder Anweisung den Kamm und Türkischen Marmor Anzufertigen für Buchbinder* ("The Marbling Art, or Directions to Bookbinders for the Making of Combed and Turkish Marbled Paper"), printed at Berlin in 1845.[10] Schade, identified on the title page as a "master bookbinder in Berlin," relates in his brief introduction that he and many of his colleagues had worked at paper marbling for a number of years with more or less success. The available literature, however, was not sufficient to help them achieve the production of good marbled paper; he singled out Thon's work as an example, stating that while its discussion of marbling was very satisfactory, it lacked details explaining the manufacture of established patterns.

Schade wrote his small manual—less than thirty pages in length—to show what he had learned about making marbled paper, and thereby help follow binders share in his success. His directions are classic and simple, and the patterns he describes are few. In addition to the combed pattern, there is an account of the Turkish or spot design (but with oil added to produce the shell effect); "French" and "Greek" marbles (the former being a Turkish pattern with very small spots, in imitation of the late French pattern, and the latter the Spanish design);[11] and two late patterns, the "Schroffel" (or Schroëtel), or broken marble, and another, unnamed pattern (effectively, the "sunshine" pattern) which, according to Schade's instructions, was effected through the use of hydrochloric acid in addition to other ingredients.[12]

Still other German manuals or treatises on this subject were issued in the latter half of the nineteenth century. In some cases, the citations that follow are from the literature, for I have not been able to find and personally examine all of them. In 1853 and 1855 Gustav Ulbricht issued at Leipzig two works dealing with edge marbling: *Die Enthüllten Geheimnisse des Schnittmarmorierens* and *Neueste Erfahrungen in der Kunst des Schnittmarmorierens für Buchbinder.*[13] In 1870 Herbert Honer published at Tuttlingen his *Geheimnisse der Marmorierkunst, Nebst einer Anleitung zur Farbenbereitung.*[14] A decade later, in 1880, three other pertinent works appeared: Josef P. Boeck's *Die Marmorierkunst,* issued at Vienna;[15] Otto Winckler's *Die Marmorierkunst,* issued at Leipzig as the initial volume of his "Aus der Buchbinderwerkstatt" series;[16] and Jacob Suchanek's *Das Marmorieren der Buchschnitte,* issued at Olmütz.[17] Finally, in 1884 Wilhelm Leo produced at Stuttgart his *Anleitung zum Marmorieren von Buchschnitten,*[18] an offering that came out on the eve of the "new marbling."

We cannot conclude this survey of German nineteenth-century marbling literature without taking notice of two accounts of marbling (reasonably good ones) that appeared in comprehensive works devoted mainly to the making of wallpapers but also touched on the production of other types of colored papers. Both were issued in the last decades of the century. Professor W. F. Exner's *Die Tapeten-und Buntpapier-Industrie,* a handbook put out at Weimar in 1869, contained information on everything that manufacturers and technical students would want to know about these subjects, and displayed examples of decorated papers in an accompanying atlas.[19] Theodore Seeman's 1882 treatise, *Die Tapete, Ihre Ästhetische Bedeutung und Technische Darstellung,* likewise provided a fairly good resume of marbling but mainly discussed the larger subject of Buntpapier and especially wallpaper.[20]

The Nineteenth-Century French Literature

By and large, literature on marbling in France developed in a similar fashion, although manuals specifically devoted to marbling did not originate there. In France, however, as in Germany, several published works were devoted to the making of colored paper overall, of which the LeNormand work of 1830 was the first. Another work that appears to belong to this genre, compiled by one Fleury-Chavant and issued at Paris in 1845 under the title *Le Dessinateur des papiers peints,* is listed in Gabriel Grünebaum's "Bibliographie der Buntpapier-Literatur," but I have not been able to locate a copy for examination and comment.[21] Also in this category is the important Fichtenberg manual of 1852.

Manuals on bookbinding and its sister arts published throughout the nineteenth century also contained instructions on marbling so that French binders could learn to decorate their books' edges. The earliest of these was the second edition of François-Ambrose Mairet's *Notice sur la lithographie,* which appeared in 1824. Mairet had issued his first edition in 1818 without a section on bookbinding, but to the subsequent one he added an "Essai sur la reliure" with eight of its pages devoted to "Tranche marbrée."[22] Three years later Louis Sébastien LeNormand brought out the first of the many editions of his *Manuel de relieur,* which dealt in passing with edge decoration in various contexts, classical marbling prominently described among them. LeNormand's was the standard French bookbinding manual for about a hundred years, until the second quarter of the present century.[23] Pollard and Potter comment that LeNormand used much of Mairet's information in his account of marbling the book edges, leaves, and leather covers.[24] I have compared the marbling texts in these two works and have not found any great evidence that points to Mairet as LeNormand's source, although both works cover the same ground and adhere to a similar general arrangement.

According to Doizy and Ipert's *Le Papier marbré,* an

1828 work entitled *Manuel de marchand papetier,* issued apparently for the use of stationers, contained a number of pages devoted to the subject of marbled paper.[25] So far I have been unsuccessful in locating a copy of this obscure work, but I have found and examined another manual dating to the same year which was published with the same intention in mind, Julia de Fontenelle and P. Poisson's *Manuel complet du marchand papetier et du régleur;* this work does indeed contain a section on "Papiers colorés, marbrés et maroquinés." The manual apparently was popular, for its publisher reissued it in 1853 and again in 1854.[26] Edmond Pelouze's *Sécrets modernes des arts et métiers,* issued in three volumes between 1831 and 1840, also provided an excellent essay devoted to marbling book edges and paper.[27]

The remaining French works touching on this subject date to the last part of the nineteenth century or later: Henri Bouchet's *De la Reliure* (1891),[28] H. L. A. Blanchon's *L'Art et pratique en reliure* (1898),[29] and Émile Bosquet's *Guide manuel théoretique et pratique de l'ouvrier ou praticien doreur sur cuir et sur tissus à la main et au balancier* (1903).[30] The Blanchon manual, which exists in two editions, is particularly well done from the standpoint of imparting practical information on how to marble. The instructions provided are ample and detailed, and there are mounted samples to illustrate what can be achieved.

Mechanical Marbling

The master bookbinder and marbler Paul Kersten divides the history of paper decoration into two distinct phases.[31] The first and older phase included coloring and decorating paper solely by hand methods of which classical marbling was one of the most important types and the one most closely allied to bookbinding. This phase, as we have repeatedly noted, extended from about the beginning of the seventeenth century into the early decades of the nineteenth, a period of between 200 and 250 years; it encompassed such hand methods as printing colored papers by simple wood and metal blocks or stencils; by marbling; by sprinkling; by the application of paste colors (with stamping or other decoration following); and, in the early decades of the nineteenth century, by the use of chemicals.

The second and later phase involved producing colored paper by machinery and in a modern factory setting. It began about 1840 in Germany, the country that had led the way in this field. Both Paul Kersten and Philipp Dessauer emphasize that the later growth and development of the modern colored-paper industry owed much to the invention of a number of specialized machines, the most important of which was the papermaking machine. They claim, in fact, that had it not been for the papermaking machine, the modern colored-paper industry could not

and would not have attained its ultimate size and stature.[32]

According to Kersten, only hand-made paper was available in Germany until about 1840. As a result, it was necessary to paste twenty-four sheets of a single pattern together in order to produce a roll of wallpaper. The paper machine, which produced paper in continuous rolls and allowed the production of colored and decorated paper in continuing patterns, obviated the earlier tedious and imperfect scheme and opened the door for the manufacture of modern wallpaper. At the same time, new machines and other necessary products, such as aniline dyes and alizarin colors and blanc fixe (barium sulfate) for filler, became available, so that in the second half of the nineteenth century the colored-paper trade was transformed dramatically into a mechanical marvel that typified the emerging industrial era.

As mass machine production of printed and other types of colored paper increased, there was a corresponding decrease in the production of marbled and other hand-produced types. As might be expected of a society that was increasingly dependent on machines for producing its goods, attempts were made to develop and perfect a machine that would actually marble paper. But once the means for marbling paper mechanically was developed, the result was an inferior product, causing a further decline of interest in this type of decorated paper on the part of bookbinders and others. In this way, though the marbling machine was successful from the viewpoint of modern engineering technology, it had a deleterious effect on the art itself, resulting in the monotonous and mechanical repetition of patterns, the employment of substandard paper, and, in the end, a product that lacked the artistry and charm of the traditional marbled papers.

We saw in Chapter 3 that as early as 1820 Alois Dessauer was looking around for a means to speed up and increase production in his plant. In that year he introduced polishing machinery into his operation and in 1840 installed steam engines in the new factory he had built. This trend toward mechanization incorporated each new method and invention as it arrived on the scene—lithography, rotary presses, devices for printing and coloring paper and for pressing and glazing it—until, toward the end of the century, it reached a high (or low) with the development of machinery for actually marbling paper.[33] In Germany, events had been moving toward such an apparatus from about 1875, with similar developments reportedly taking place at Turnhout in Belgium and perhaps in England. Although the apparatus was not actually invented until the latter decades of the nineteenth century (and has been little documented), it is obvious that developments aimed at speeding up the marbling process were occurring continually throughout the nineteenth century and, indeed, seem to have contributed to the final design of the machine.

One development that is documented is the piece of machinery invented by Charles Williams of Philadelphia and patented by him in 1858. A basic problem encountered by every hand marbler is how to distribute his or her colors evenly throughout the surface of the size and thus achieve an evenly colored pattern. Color laid down the traditional way, by means of brushes, cannot easily accomplish this; color falls where it pleases, sometimes in larger and sometimes in smaller spots. Accordingly, the resultant pattern will show concentrations of one color here, another there—anywhere they chanced to fall on the surface of the size. Williams confronted this difficulty when he was a young marbler and attempted to solve it mechanically. Although his efforts did not provide the final solution that the marbling machine did, it was a step in that direction.

Williams's drawings (Figure 11) and the specifications he filed with the United States Patent Office reveal his conception of a device for distributing colors evenly upon the gum-water in the marbling trough. He stated that heretofore it had been the practice to take a brush, dip it in the fluid color and, by a particular mode of handling, sprinkle or deposit the color upon the surface of the gum-water. It was not often possible, using this method, to produce a marbleized sheet showing perfect symmetry and uniformity in the arrangement of spots and configurations, even for the most skilled artist. Nevertheless, he felt assured that through the use of his apparatus such a sheet could result, not once but repeatedly.

Williams's invention was to be used in conjunction with the usual marbling trough; it consisted of a rectangular frame above the trough supporting a sliding apparatus at its top that could be moved back and forth. Within the frame was placed a pan or reservoir for holding color, which, in turn, was supported by a sliding frame adapted to work up and down by means of a treadle. The sliding apparatus above the trough was fashioned with crosspieces of metal, secured parallel to one another at small intervals. Color carriers, constructed to take up and hold a portion of the color to be distributed, were extended vertically from these metal crosspieces and arranged in relation to one another according to the marbled paper pattern to be produced. The usual gum trough was supported on trestles at one end of the frame so that the sliding apparatus could be moved directly over it and away from it as well.

The mode of operation was as follows: First, the fluid color was placed in the reservoir or pan; by an upward motion the reservoir frame was adjusted to immerse the color carriers to the depth required to supply them with the desired quantities of color. Next the treadle was depressed to lower the reservoir, and the sliding apparatus was brought directly over the trough containing the size. A level hammer supported between the two middle strips was then activated, striking the underside of the slide and causing the discharge of color from the carriers onto the surface of the trough. Finally, the slide was returned to its position over the color reservoir, and a sheet of paper was laid upon the trough (either immediately, for spot patterns, or after combing had taken place) to complete the process. In such a manner, perfect uniformity of color could be produced in a succession of sheets. Undoubtedly, Williams had worked out—but did not divulge in his patent application and specifications—methods for putting several colors onto the size concurrently, probably involving the use of channels or the prearrangement of a number of containers within the color reservoir.

Another insight into the development of mechanical marbling comes from the article "A Machine for Marbling Paper," published in *The British Bookmaker* in 1890. The machine discussed consisted of a stationary vat containing a color-supporting liquid (i.e., marbling size) and, stationed over it, a series of color receptacles with each color having a delivery orifice over the vat. By a vertical reciprocating movement, color was conveyed through the orifices to the surface of the size and evenly distributed. "Brushing" and "combing" devices were provided by the machine as well and operated to produce the pattern desired. The paper was then fed through a roll and carried forward to a cutting mechanism which detached a sheet equal to the size of the trough. Carrying devices equipped with grippers conveyed the severed sheet to the vat and deposited it on the surface of the gum solution (to which color had already been applied and manipulated into a pattern), then returned to their former position to secure another sheet. At the same time another carriage, traveling from the rear of the machine, approached the vat, and a "capsizing device" lifted and turned the sheet that had received its color, whereupon it was borne away. Finally, the sheet was conveyed mechanically from the machine, with the colors given time to dry during the course of the transmission.

Still another work that gives us a view of the emergence of mechanical marbling in the large paper-coloring factories of Germany and elsewhere is Louis Andés's *Papier-Specialitäten*, which first appeared six years before *The British Bookmaker* article[34] and subsequently was reissued in translation in two English editions entitled *The Treatment of Paper for Special Purposes*.[35] When reading Andés, one gets the impression that he is describing almost the same apparatus discussed in *The British Bookmaker* article but in greater detail and with diagrams, some of which are reproduced here (Figure 15). Such a marbling machine, Andés pointed out, contained a tank for the floating bath, a device for distributing color on its surface, another device for feeding successive sheets of paper onto the surface of the color, and yet another for lifting the colored sheets and moving them along after the process was completed.

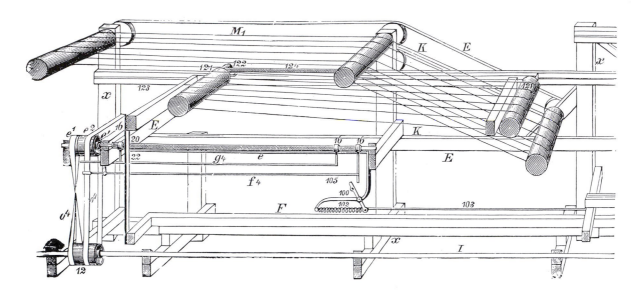

FIGURE 15A

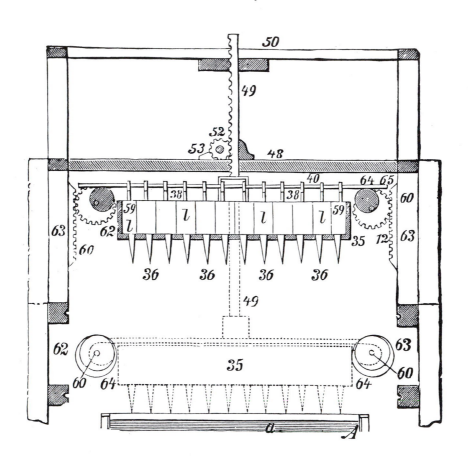

FIGURE 15B

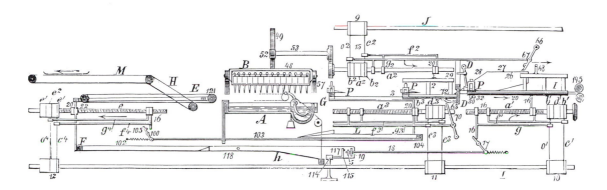

FIGURE 15C

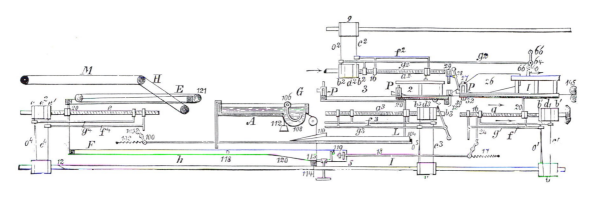

FIGURE 15D

FIGURE 15. Reproduced from L. E. Andés's *The Treatment of Paper for Special Purposes* (1907): *a,* front portion of the machine; *b,* vertical section through the color tank; *c,* discharge of a finished sheet; *d,* machine for marbling paper.

The paper was gripped by clips and moved by slides as it traveled along endless cords, all activated and controlled by machinery that incorporated spindles, pulleys, drive shafts, pinions, bearings, belting, and the like. Andés's machine also contained a cutting blade to sever paper from rolls. The device for distributing color consisted of a mounted box with color receptacles, each terminating in a tapered nozzle below the bottom of the box at one end and a wire in the form of a ring at the other. Color adhering to the wire was deposited onto the floating surface of the tank when brought into contact with it. The sheet was lifted and turned in about the manner outlined in *The British Bookmaker* article. To insure that the paper was laid properly on the surface of

the color on the bath so that its underside would be evenly coated, the machine was fitted with a brushing device. Additionally, there were special devices for producing a grained or cloudy appearance in the colors, for combing, and for bringing about other effects. Such a machine, Andés proudly claimed, could perform all the operations previously done by hand.

In 1896, the year of the first edition of Andés's work, another book that also detailed the mechanical production of marbled paper was published: the second edition of Josef Phileas Boeck's *Die Marmorierkunst.* When Boeck issued the first edition in 1880, it was a rather slim pamphlet of eighty pages devoted entirely to methods and patterns of hand marbling and to some developments that had occurred in the course of the nineteenth century. The second edition of 1896, however, was nearly twice as large and contained a lengthy section (pages 101 to 127) on the mechanical production of marbled paper, thus proving that great strides had been made in the interval in the development of machinery for producing imitations of marbled paper.

Both the Andés and the Boeck works were issued by W. Hartleben of Vienna, Budapest, and Leipzig; they contained not only essentially the same information on mechanical marbling but also the same illustrations of the new marbling machine—indicating, perhaps, some shared editing as well. Boeck, however, depicted a new machine that was not mentioned in the Andés work, a printing machine (his Figure 28) for producing marbled, veined, fantasy and other types of decorated papers. From the considerable amount of imitation marbled paper appearing in books produced from the 1890s it is apparent that mechanical methods for making such sheets (chiefly showing Spanish and Turkish designs) had been achieved and that such machinery had been put on the market.

Two further German works on papermaking or Buntpapier should be mentioned here; for while both describe machine methods for making color paper and refer to machine marbling, neither, strangely enough, discusses the making of actual marbled patterns other than through the hand methods. One, Egbert Hoyer's *Die Fabrikation des Papiers,* appeared in 1887, at a time when such machinery was being developed; that fact could account for its lack of information on mechanical marbling.[36] The other, however, August Weichelt's *Buntpapier-Fabrikation,* appeared initially in 1903, after such mechanization had been introduced, and reappeared in three other editions by 1932, so one would assume that it would contain the latest information on this subject. But it does not.[37] Hoyer's work is concerned mainly with making paper from wood, straw, and ersatz materials, but it also explains the making of pasteboard, colored paper, parchment papers, and other special types. It contains several pages on sprinkled and drawn marbled papers, but his discussion of these touches on only the hand methods.

The Weichelt work is devoted exclusively to the making of Buntpapier, in all of its varieties; it illustrates each kind with a generous number of original samples, and discusses and pictures existing machinery for making them, describing how it was used. Although Weichelt does speak of machine marbling, he relates that machinery was employed only for making the pseudo types, such as Achat, (a sprinkled variety), and Gustav-Marmor (produced, like the Achat, with acid). His discussion of classic marbled patterns is lengthy but it is devoted solely to the hand methods of earlier times, with no reference to their possible machine manufacture. Weichelt writes that hand marbles were cheap and were used on the commonest books in earlier times but that later on, when great numbers had to be produced and where greater costs were involved, it became necessary to seek cheaper alternatives such as the agates and other pseudo types. The only marbling machine that Weichelt refers to was one designed specifically to make these substitute types. When one observes the large amounts of mechanically produced marbled paper appearing from early in this century, along with the Andés book and other literature on the subject of mechanical marbling, it is difficult to account for the lack of information on mechanically produced marbled paper in Weichelt's large and presumably comprehensive treatise.

It is obvious from the evenness, repetition, and symmetry of the patterns on much of the marbled paper that serves as cover paper on hand-bound volumes of the last hundred years or so (see Plate XXXVII) that mechanized processes had been used. Some of the Berry and Roberts samples illustrated in *The British Bookmaker* in the early 1890s fall into this category. These papers, showing mostly Spanish or moiré patterns sometimes overprinted with gold veins, are too perfect in their appearance to have been produced by hand—only machines could have been responsible for such precise and orderly and repetitive productions. The papers do initially appear quite striking, but they quickly lose their appeal and become pedestrian and boring, for they lack the freshness and charm of the authentic article; neither do their colors seem to be quite "right."

One of my copies of Charles Woolnough's 1881 *Whole Art of Marbling* (containing the bookplate of book designer T. M. Cleland) has bound in at its front eight specimens of marbled paper of the Turkish and Spanish designs. These, a tipped-in printed note reported, were of recent manufacture and much used, and could be procured from W. Mansell, bookbinders, in Chancery Lane in London. Overprinted in gold, these papers were obviously machine-made, and undoubtedly they were added to this and assumedly other copies of Woolnough's manual that were bound and sold perhaps a decade or more after its appearance.[38]

Mechanical marbling appears to have reached its ultimate perfection within the last fifty years or so. In 1950, R. S. Bracewell described how a modern American manufacturer, the Marvellum Company, extended the process from a single-sheet operation to an operation that produced marbling on a continuous roll of paper.[39] By careful experimentation, Bracewell reported, pigment colors and metallic pigments were floated on the surface of a water bath and transferred to a continuously moving sheet of paper. Special cylindrical brushes mounted on revolving drums picked up color from receptacles on either side of the tank or bath and spattered color on the water or gum. Opposite a circular pan mounted on a circular monorail track, a set of contact rolls brought the roll of paper down onto the surface of the bath so that it would take up the pattern. Excess water was blown off by an air jet, and the paper was carried to drum driers. Continuous marbling was achieved by using half the machine on the approach to the contact rollers for the application of colors and the forming of the pattern, while the other half following the contact rolls was used for clearing the water surface before the application of new colors. Thus, the machine required a circular pan to rotate and allow one of its halves to be engaged in marbling while the other was being cleaned. Spot patterns were easily effected in this way and could be varied through the use of moving combs. Grain marbling was also done, but on a stationary inclined tank.

In the second half of the nineteenth century the deterioration of old ways and the search for substitutes also resulted in new and easy methods for giving book edges the appearance of combed and other types of marbled decoration without dipping the books themselves onto a bath. For the most part, simple wooden rollers—mounted on handles that allowed them to turn freely and covered with a rubber surface onto which a marbled pattern had been cast or incised—were dipped into a mixture of colors and applied to the edges of books. One such appa-

ratus, developed by Wilhelm Leo and reproduced in the second (1890) edition of Joseph Zaehnsdorf's *The Art of Bookbinding*,[40] is shown here in Figure 48. Although edge rollers (or "mechanical marblers") were quick and easy to use and allowed binders to undertake this operation themselves, they also produced an inferior article—yet another cheap substitute for the wonderfully marbled effect of the earlier method. Several of the descriptions in the second edition of the patent abridgements issued by the British Commissioners of Patents in 1879 indicate that inventors were at work adapting incised and otherwise prepared rollers for printing imitation marbled and other patterns on paper and book surfaces from about the middle of the nineteenth century.[41] It was only one simple step more for Leo (or whoever was originally responsible for this invention) to conceptualize the edge roller and perfect it.

Zaehnsdorf's manual also shows that a method had been devised for transferring the pattern from ordinary marbled paper to the edges of books by impregnating strips of marbled paper with hydrochloric acid after they had been laid, marble-side downward, on the edges of books. Once saturation had taken place the pattern could easily be blotted onto the edges themselves.[42]

11

The Revival and Later Events

It would be misleading to suggest that the ancient craft of hand marbling ceased to exist altogether as the old ways broke down and mechanization gained momentum. Instruction books and similar works by bookbinders such as Schade and Ulbricht—and, later, Boeck and others—indicate that interest in sustaining the traditions of the past continued, albeit on a diminished and less visible scale. And while the range of patterns being made available also was diminishing greatly as the German factories were turning to the manufacture of wallpaper and other products, a few of the entrenched designs, such as the shell and Spanish patterns, continued in production. These were not, however, much made at the factory level anymore, but by a few remaining marblers who continued to supply bookbinders with their traditionally made papers. Indeed, sometimes these craftsmen succeeded in refining some of the old designs and now and then even attempted to introduce new varieties.

This situation was not restricted to continental Europe. In England and America, changing methods of book production, led by mechanization in the bookbinding and publishing trades, were beginning to have the same effect. With the passing of the likes of Woolnough, Sumner, and Corfield in England and Williams in America, and the disappearance of the succeeding generation marblers who had sprung up around the middle of the nineteenth century, this industry would no longer exist in the ways and vigor of the past. Thenceforth, in England and America, as in Europe, only a few marblers would remain to sustain the art. Nonetheless, their limited production allowed hand binders—who also continued to operate on a greatly reduced level—to obtain the decorated papers they needed to embellish their best work in keeping with the traditions of the past. Some of the marblers and bookbinders who continued to carry on the art were given impetus by a revival in marbling which took place in the 1880s and which can be attributed to the efforts of an otherwise little known bookbinder of Budapest named Josef Halfer.

Josef Halfer and the Revival of the Art

As I noted in my introduction to the 1980 Bird & Bull edition of Franz Weisse's *The Art of Marbling,* the classi-

cal or traditional form of paper marbling was given new life late in the nineteenth century by Halfer's efforts to revitalize the craft through the introduction of new methods, new materials, and new patterns; in the process, he created the "new marbling." Although the craft was disappearing from the factories and was being carried on now mainly in a few remaining workshops, Halfer's methods and influence, based as they were on sound scientific research, resulted in the training of a new generation of marblers, many springing from the ranks of the bookbinding trade. These craftsmen not only were able to satisfy the need for fine, hand-marbled paper for a generation or two more, but, by adding to the marbling literature established by Halfer, contributed to the preservation of the art to the present time; further, they helped bring about the great improvements and the novel and beautiful results that Charles Woolnough had anticipated for marbling in the mid-1850s.

So great was Halfer's influence that we can now divide marbling into two distinct phases, before Halfer and after Halfer—just as physics is dichotomized as before and after Roentgen or anatomy as pre-Vesalian and post-Vesalian. The post-Halferian era is characterized not by large production in factories and workshops, but rather by a limited number of beautifully combed and exquisitely contrived patterns made, for the most part, by individuals working alone in a few locations around the world.

Not much has been written about Josef Halfer (Figure 17) to date; information about him and his so-called marbling revolution must be gathered from a variety of sources, including contemporary marbling and bookbinding literature, and his own writings. Careful scrutiny of these sources, however, provides ample and unimpeachable evidence of his supreme importance to the craft.[1]

Halfer was probably born in Budapest before the middle of the nineteenth century to parents who were part of the city's German-speaking community; he became a bookbinder and eventually turned his attention to marbling paper. His writings strongly indicate that he was a scientist at heart. After mastering the art of marbling as it was understood at that time, he spent several years attempting to establish a scientific basis for its methods, experimenting with the chemistry of colors and the physical nature of marbling sizes, and all the while trying to discover the why and wherefore of every ingredient. Out of his investigations flowed new methods and materials that solved old problems and heightened the level of accomplishment in this craft; Halfer was thus, in a sense, the messiah that Charles Woolnough predicted or hoped for in the initial edition of his marbling manual.

Halfer's earliest research, which he must have begun in the early or mid-1870s, was aimed at determining what colors were best suited to the craft. Finding that every manufactory then had its own system for producing colors and that no uniformity existed, he resorted to chemistry; from thousands of experiments and testing raw products such as earths, metals, acids, and bases, Halfer was able to determine what compositions were best as marbling colors. (A great deal of the work he reported in his own literature was devoted to this color preparation, for which Paul Kersten later would criticize him.)[2]

Halfer devoted equal attention to marbling size and the various gums suited to it, although his experiments were conducted over many years and were continuously reconsidered and refined. Before Halfer's time, gum tragacanth, a derivative of a starch-bearing plant of the Middle East, had served as the staple for making marbling size; for centuries it had been used in Turkey and the Near East, and it continues to be used there today in the few places where marbling is carried on. Ultimately, Halfer's experiments resulted in his adoption of carragheen moss (*Chondrus crispus*)—a seaweed known alternatively as Irish moss or Icelandic moss—as the best medium for the process. These algae grow near the shores of the North Sea, on the cliffs of the Atlantic Ocean and parts of the North American coast, and in many other oceans and seas around the world. The excellence of carragheen for marbling size had long been known and it had sometimes been used,[3] but because of the moss's tendency to spoil quickly, it was employed only sparingly and then usually in combination with another gum. Once mixed with water, carragheen size remained usable for only about eight days. The starch and sugar it contained soon broke down into lactic acid, turning the substance acidic, watery, and foul-smelling in the process.

Halfer's efforts to overcome this impediment succeeded after many years of experimentation and toil. He determined that adding borax would assure preserving the size for up to sixty days—a breakthrough of considerable importance both to the professional marbler who had to keep large quantities of size on hand, as well as to the occasional marbler who needed to have it available for a period of many weeks. As a result of Halfer's efforts, carragheen size came to be adopted as the "universal size" (the "Universalgrund," he called it) for marbling. Indeed, it is the best medium for this purpose, for its fine colloidal properties allow the formation of the most delicate patterns, particularly beautifully combed ones. Today carragheen is used almost exclusively in marbling in the Western world.

Before his death in 1916, Josef Halfer spent a great deal of time improving upon the methods and materials of marbling as well as passing along his knowledge to students. His researches into the nature and properties of colors resulted in the eventual production of a line of colors designed especially for marbling and marketed around the Western world under the name "Halfer's Marbling Colors." Wilhelm Leo of Stuttgart became a major manufacturer of these and other marbling materials, distributing them through agents and franchises in Germany, America, and elsewhere; other manufacturers, such as Paul Szigrist in Leipzig[4] and the Hostman Printing Ink Company in London, were also licensed to manufacture and sell them. Sometimes Halfer's colors were put up in sets or kits, along with other materials and implements such as gall, combs, and pans, and offered for sale. Such a kit, marketed as Josef Halfer's marbling apparatus, is reproduced in Figure 16.

!Für Buchbinder und Geschäftsbuchfabriken!

Marmorierapparat für Kleinbetrieb.

Komplett . . . . *M.* 15.—
Gedruckte Gebrauchsanweisung . . . . " 1.—
   Enthält in einem praktischen Kasten 6 Flacons echte Pester Farben. 1 Flacon präpar. Ochsengalle, 6 Farbennäpfe, 1 Blechbassin, 45×20 cm. 1 Marmorierkamm, 1 Stäbchen, 1 Abstreichbrettchen, 1 Seihtuch, 1 Paket ausgesuchtes Carragheenmoos und 6 Farbenpinsel;

Marmorierapparate für Grossbetrieb.

Bassingrösse 65×35 cm.
ca. *M.* 46—48.—.

   Anordnung im wesentlichen wie oben, jedoch mit ¹/₂ Liter Füllungen und entsprechend grösseren Farbtöpfen, Pinseln etc.
   Als weitere Beigabe enthalten die Apparate 2 Marmorierkämme verschiedener Breite, Einrichtung für Pfauen- und Boukettmarmor, 1 Flasche Sprengwasser für Aderschnitte.

Wilhelm Leo, Stuttgart.

Fabrik u. Lager von Buchbinderei-Materialien,
Werkzeugen und Maschinen.

FIGURE 16. Josef Halfer's marbling apparatus for the use of bookbinders and small marbling workshops. From an advertisement at the end of the 1891 edition of Halfer's *Fortschritte der Marmorierkunst*. This set was distributed by Wilhelm Leo of Stuttgart.

Halfer's discoveries, first published in his marbling manual issued at Budapest in 1885, *Die Fortschritte der Marmorierkunst,*[5] made an impact that revolutionized the craft. Whereas the old style of marbling allowed reasonably finely combed patterns, the results achieved through Halfer's methods are so far superior that his technique has predominated ever since. Carragheen size and other Halferian innovations, which are easier to work with and result in more delicate and brilliantly colored patterns, all but put shell, Spanish, and other thrown-on, traditional designs on the shelf, so that they are rarely produced today, except by those marblers employed by book restorers to simulate old-style effects.

In fact, the methods of making many of the old patterns were entirely forgotten in the aftermath of Halfer's "new wave," and one must turn to the manuals of Sinclair, Woolnough, Sumner, and the old bookbinding literature to rediscover them. Halfer's innovative manual, *Die Fortschritte der Marmorierkunst,* was issued in a second German edition by Wilhelm Leo at Stuttgart in 1891 (it was the first edition to contain original exhibits and marbled samples),[6] and an edition in French appeared at Geneva in 1893, translated by Joseph Grillet and Emile Schultze, who described themselves as binders and marblers.[7] This followed by about one year the publication of an American edition, translated by Herman Dieck of Philadelphia and issued at Buffalo by Louis H. Kinder under the title *The Progress of the Marbling Art.*[8] Kinder,

who had studied bookbinding at Leipzig at about the time that Halfer was carrying on some of his classic experiments, eventually assumed the position of head bookbinder in Elbert Hubbard's Roycroft Shop in East Aurora, New York. Kinder also served as an American agent for the sale of Halfer's marbling colors and produced some of his own bookbinding literature that contained instructions on marbling.[9] In 1904 the Hostman Printing Ink Company of London brought out an abridged and slightly rewritten form of the Halfer work under the title *The Art of Marbling and the Treatment of New Bronze Colours*: this was a small instruction booklet intended to promote the marbling colors the firm sold.

We cannot overestimate the importance of Josef Halfer and his influence in bringing marbling and marbled papers back into vogue, albeit within a limited orbit. His famous manual, as well as a series of little pamphlets he issued under the collective title "Meisterwerke der Marmorierkunst,"[10] attracted the attention of other bookbinders, and before long, others were learning his methods and using the special materials he produced. In this way a number of highly advanced masters took up this new form and style of marbling, which is based in large part on the production of clean, bright, and detailed comb work. In a short time, a school of marblers developed in accordance with the principles and techniques expounded by Halfer.

The Halferian School of Marbling

Halfer's innovations were adopted by a number of advanced German bookbinders and marblers, some of whom were also teachers; they, in turn, instructed their pupils in his methods or published manuals and other significant literature based on his principles, much of it embellished with samples of beautiful and delicately combed patterns. As a result Halfer's methods not only became widely accepted, but brought about renewed interest in marbling and maintained its continuity (but now at the small workshop level). It was in this way that a "Halferian school" of marbling became established, not a school in the formal sense but more a movement for universal acceptance of his methods to the exclusion of all others, and a desire to pass these new, superior ways along to succeeding generations of marblers.

Next in importance in this new wave was Josef Hauptmann of Gera and Berlin (1867–1917), who, in Paul Kersten's opinion, was Halfer's best pupil.[11] According to Kersten, the manual Hauptmann produced was second only to that of the master himself. Hauptmann's manual first appeared in 1895 under the title *Die Marmorierkunst. Ein Leitfaden zum Praktischen Erlernen des Marmorierens nach Halfer'schen Methode,* and it was reissued in 1901 and 1906,[12] with a Dutch translation appearing in 1899.[13] All of these editions contained original samples. It is from

the second, 1901 edition (though it is actually undated), that the portrait of Josef Halfer has been reproduced in Figure 17. Kersten was personally acquainted with Hauptmann and mentions that his son, Otto, published a small *Nachschlage-Heft beim Marmorieren* in 1914 which is very good. My collection includes a copy of this rarity. While its text is slight—merely a three-page outline of the art's method—the many large samples it contains, including some of the "fantasy" type to be described more below, demonstrate that Otto Hauptmann was a very advanced marbler, perhaps one of the best, who experimented with taking the craft to new heights.[14]

The outstanding German bookbinder and teacher Paul Adam (Figure 17) was another leading exponent of the Halferian school of marbling. Adam's main efforts were directed toward teaching bookbinding at Düsseldorf, but he contributed significantly to the literature of marbling as well, even before the Halferian method came into vogue. In the years 1882–1885, on the very eve of the appearance of Josef Halfer's revolutionary manual, Adam edited and published a book of essays on bookbinding

FIGURE 17. Josef Halfer and Paul Adam (*left*); Paul Kersten and Franz Weisse (*right*).

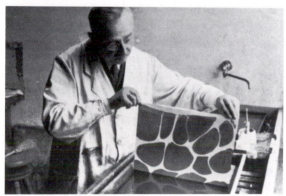

(written by himself and by Baum of Frankfurt, Blankenburg of Berlin, Philipp Dessauer of Aschaffenburg, and Fritzsche of Leipzig) which contained an important section on marbling. This work, *Systematisches Lehr- und Handbuch der Buchbinderei und der Damit Zusammenhängenden der Fächer in Theorie und Praxis,* came out in twenty-one parts, making up three volumes in all. The third volume contains an essay on the mechanics of marbling, followed by another on its theoretical aspects. There is also a plate containing eight long, thin marbled samples of patterns then popular: Italian or hair vein, large comb, nonpareil, and even bouquet, the latter a design then coming into vogue that would be highly exploited under the Halferian system, which permitted its delicate features to be more beautifully effected.[15]

In addition, Paul Adam published a bookbinding manual (translated into English in 1903) which contained a number of pages on Halferian marbling and its techniques.[16] Of greater importance to the subject at hand, however, is his first (1906) edition of a marbling manual, *Das Marmorieren des Buchbinders auf Schleimgrund und in Kleisterverfahren,* reissued in a second edition in 1923.[17] This manual is quite informative, covering all the basics of Halfer's method, which had gained general acceptance by 1906 in Germany and many other countries as well; it also contained many pages on the making of "Kleistermarmorpapiere," or paste papers. In the historical section of the manual, Adam refers to the upswing in marbling and the growing interest in bookbinding, for which he credits Halfer: "Er selbst hat die mehr oder weniger Handgriffe und Künste des Marmorierens in ein festes System gebracht, und im wesentlichen nach seinen Angaben wird heute überall marmoriert."

Another leading figure of this period who deserves the highest praise is Paul Kersten (Figure 17). He is distinguished as a craftsman, teacher, historian, innovator and producer of an important manual on the subject: in short, scarcely anyone has been more active on behalf of bookbinding and paper decoration than Kersten. Born in 1865 and trained as a bookbinder, he worked chiefly as an art binder and teacher in Berlin, embuing many pupils with the highest principles and techniques of his craft. Kersten learned to marble early, and in 1898–1901 worked as artistic advisor in the colored-paper factory at Aschaffenburg, developing patterns and becoming familiar not only with all aspects of Buntpapier manufacture but with its history as well. So significant were his contributions to the literature of marbling and colored paper that a list of his publications on these subjects takes up the equivalent of nearly an entire page of Easton's bibliography.[18] Included in this list are numerous articles on colored paper, its use in bookbinding, and the production of several marbled types, as well as marbling with oil colors, the making of paste papers, and similar topics.

In 1922 Kersten published *Die Marmorierkunst,* which he wrote to introduce the marbling methods of Josef Halfer and Josef Hauptmann. This little manual was translated into Norwegian and issued at Oslo three years later,[19] constituting the only piece of marbling literature that I know of in that language. (I translated the German edition into English in the early 1960s and used it to teach myself to marble on Halferian principles; I found Kersten's little manual to be an excellent introduction to this subject.) In 1930 Kersten supplemented his manual with the pamphlet *Anleitung zur Herstellung von Buntpapier für den Eigenen Gebrauch:* it consists of a rather good set of general instructions intended to assist bookbinders in the production of all sorts of colored papers, including marbled ones, and it was reissued in 1939.[20] From 1916 Kersten served as co-editor and then full editor of *L. Brade's Illustriertes Buchbinderbuch*; this publication included plates of samples made at the trade school for bookbinders (conducted by Hans Bauer at Gera in Saxony) and patterns produced through Halferian methods of marbling.[21]

The importance of the Gera bookbinding school in spreading the Halferian system in Germany has not been sufficiently appreciated. Opening in 1880, it soon established a course on marbling based on the methods that Josef Halfer had introduced within a few years of its founding. In 1900, Paul Hüttich published an account of the Gera school's progress and activities that recorded the names of all of its graduates,[22] among them Josef Hauptmann, Halfer's protégé; following page 12 of this account is a two-page layout with eight samples that show that Halferian marbling was being taught at the school (Plate XXII).

Also worthy of note is Kersten's original bookbinding manual, which he called *Der Exakte Bucheinband.* This work went through a total of five editions, all illustrated with samples of colored and marbled paper.[23] The several editions in my collection contain marbled samples that were made by Wilhelm Leo's Nachfolger at Stuttgart. The capstone of Kersten's career came in 1938 with the publication of his important study on the history of colored paper, "Die Geschichte des Buntpapiers." This contributed enormously to our understanding of the colored paper industry in Germany and the role of marbling in its nineteenth-century colored paper factories.

Franz Weisse (1878–1943) was the last of the great German marbling masters to follow in the footsteps of Halfer, Hauptmann, Adam, and Kersten (Figure 17). Like some of his predecessors, he was exposed to marbling while attending bookbinding school; he carried on the craft, developed his technique, and taught the subject throughout his professional life. After working for several years as a journeyman bookbinder, Weisse in 1905 began a career as a teacher of bookbinding and allied subjects, settling finally at the Kunstgewerbschule at Hamburg two years later and attaining the rank of full professor in 1925. Collections of modern Buntpapier in European museums and libraries attest to Weisse's great influence in promoting the art along the lines laid down by Halfer. He was especially interested in the development and manufacture of what may be termed "fantasy patterns," that is, marbled papers with flowers and other artistic designs, somewhat reminiscent of those developed in Turkey at an earlier time. In wartime Germany of 1940, Weisse produced *Die Kunst des Marmorierens,* which takes its place among the great marbling manuals of Halfer, Hauptmann, Adam, and Kersten. This work devotes much space to the elucidation of fantasy marbling, and does so through the use of pictures—nearly a hundred of them; it is the first marbling manual to rely heavily on photography to illustrate the various methods, stages, and patterns of the craft. Weisse's *Die Kunst des Marmorierens* (in English, *The Art of Marbling*) is by any standard one of the most significant pieces of marbling literature ever produced.

The Koninklijke Bibliotheek at the Hague (which acquired the large collection of Buntpapier literature formerly owned by the Aschaffenburg company after it was dissolved in the early 1970s) has a copy of an artistic volume completed and issued by Franz Weisse in 1931 under the title *Getropfelte Gälle auf Buchblättern*—"Gall Dropped on Book Pages" might be a rough translation. Limited to an edition of fifty copies produced "in der Klasse für Buchdruck der Landeskunstschule zu Hamburg," this imaginative work was printed entirely on marbled paper that shows many of the fantasy patterns illustrated in Weisse's *Die Kunst des Marmorierens.* Several years later, Weisse wryly recounted some of the ups and downs of his marbling career in an article entitled "Mein Kampf mit der Ochsengalle"—"My Struggle with Ox-Gall."[24]

Several other marbling manuals were published in Europe in the early decades of the twentieth century. Two were produced in 1908, one by a marbler who identified himself only as Bohniert[25] and another by Johann Bönisch.[26] Other ambitious manuals devoted to marbling and paper coloring—some of which incorporated information on the new type of oil marbling—were compiled by N. L. Weigner (1909),[27] Herman Nitz (1922),[28] and Mariann Finckh-Haelsig (1926).[29] Then, of course, there was the Dutch manual of Halferian principles produced early in this century by J. Van Wenderden and discussed in Chapter 5 in our survey of marbling in Holland.

Halfer, Adam, Kersten, and Weisse occupy center stage in the modern history of marbling not only because of the literature they produced and the students they influenced but also because they revitalized the art and gave it continuity. Examination of extensive collections of colored paper at the Koninklijke Bibliotheek at the Hague, the Kunstgewerbemuseum in Berlin, the Deutsches Museum von Meisterwerken der Naturwissenschaft und Technik in Munich, the Deutsche Bücherei in Leipzig, and museums and libraries at other locations throughout Europe, however, indicate that a number of other individuals, some of them pupils or colleagues of the great masters, were hard at work making marbled paper from about 1890 to the 1920s and 1930s. If some of these ar-

tisans or craftspeople who have left us a sampling of their work can be judged as amateurish or mediocre, or even poor, in their marbling achievements, others like Johann Rudel (d. 1955)—a colleague of Weisse's who worked at Elberfeld early in this century and whose fantasy patterns are illustrated on Plate XXII here—were very good.[30]

Examples of papers I have examined in these collections from both individual makers and small workshops indicate a strong revival of interest in marbling in the post-Halferian era, and its practice by a great many people. Among others, I have seen examples of the work of the following makers: Anker Kyster of Copenhagen (co-author of the history of Danish eighteenth-century bookbinding mentioned earlier), who reintroduced the art of marbling into Denmark in the period after 1892, imitated old Turkish patterns and did fantasy work as well;[31] Carl Ernst Poeschel, probably of Leipzig, whose work does not show high attainment; Auguste Geber, of Hamburg, a student of Franz Weisse; Wilhelm Rauch, also of Hamburg, who executed mostly fantasy patterns earlier in this century (a collection of ten specimens of his work, showing marbled motifs such as goldfish, a cornfield, blackthorns, and thistles, is preserved in Hamburg's Museum für Kunst und Gewerbe); Frau Margarete Rumpf of Potsdam, who executed oil marbling rather badly;[32] Andreas Hausmann of Konstanz;[33] A. and P. Renner of Munich; Laura Langa of Munich; Walter Ziegler, probably also of Munich, who employed marbling as a background for his artwork; Georg Trepplin of Berlin; W. Valentin, also of Berlin and active around 1914; Heinrich Niebler of Stuttgart; F. Svoboda of Prague; Hans Dannhorn of Leipzig; Ernst Leistikov, whose papers show oil marbling or very poorly executed Turkish marbling, made with only one or two colors;[34] Heinrich Wahle of Leipzig, who did much fantasy work of mediocre quality; Ch. v. Wahl of Berlin, who used oil colors and did not achieve good control; A. Köllner of Leipzig, whose colors are splotchy and uncontrolled; the Buchbinderei Luderitz und Bauer of Berlin, where sunshine marbling was executed around 1909; Giuseppe Rizzi of Varese, who imitated Turkish and French patterns rather well, and whose work shows good control; H. Ochman of Leipzig; and Anna Plate and Eduard Gabelsberger, whose work locales have not been ascertained.

The craft was carried on also at the Wiener Werkstätte (the Vienna craft studio), founded in 1903 by Josef Hoffmann and Karl Moser for the purpose of combining utilitarianism and aesthetic quality in the creation of decorative art. Eight sheets of paper marbled by Hoffmann and Moser can be found at the Deutsche Bücherei; these contain large fantasy patterns and show techniques that are no more than mediocre. Hoffmann's own marbling work is represented in the Kunstgewerbemuseum collection in Berlin, showing fantasy patterns on a Turkish background, with birds and other images. Others of the Wiener Werkstätte represented in the Berlin collection are Solomon Moser, Carl Beitel, and Therese Trauthan.[35]

Some of the large collections also contain examples of the work of the masters Paul Kersten and Franz Weisse.

Marbling, especially on Halferian principles, was also taught in many of the bookbinding and craft schools throughout Germany late in the nineteenth century and well into the present one; Weisse's school at Hamburg, the school at Gera, and another at Glauchau—where Weisse first became acquainted with the craft—are but a few of these.

In Denmark, in addition to Kyster, several other marblers were active earlier in this century. Carl Gydesen and Ingeborg Börjesson (née Heckscher) were two who taught and carried on the art there. Trained as a master bookbinder in Paris in the 1920s and 1930s, Börjesson first worked in her native Denmark and, following her marriage to a Swedish violinist, later in Sweden. She produced some charming marbled papers, but is best known for her batik designs as well as for her method of making designed patterns with oil colors. She worked up to a short time before her death in 1976, and has recently been memorialized in a short article in *Ink & Gall*.[36]

Many samples of factory-produced marbled papers of the late nineteenth century and up until the First World War are also represented in the European collections, with both handmade and machine-made papers among them. Some of these firms include the Akt. Gesellschaft für Buntpapier, A. Nees & Co., and Franz Dahlem und Compagne, all of Aschaffenburg; the Luxuspapierfabrik at Goldbach; the Märk Phantasiepapiermanufaktur, Zassen; Spötlin & Zimmerman of Vienna, which produced mostly machine-made papers about 1880; Hagwerk-Buntpapier (Hagener Werkstatt, Bussman & Co., Hagen); Dübn Buntpapiere (Kunstwerkstatt Fr. Pätz, Düsseldorf); and Ibbotson, Ltd., E. Becker, and the Fancy Paper Company, all of London.

England and Cockerell Papers

A revival of interest in hand marbling and marbled papers also occurred in England, where, from the last decades of the nineteenth century, machine marbling or the printing of marbled paper had all but taken over. Renewed interest in the art can be credited once more to the innovative methods of Josef Halfer; the Hostman Printing Ink Company's 1904 second edition of the little pamphlet we have spoken of previously is an indication of this revival. Information on marbling in the several editions of the Zaehnsdorf bookbinding manual and in the bookbinding manuals compiled and issued by Paul Hasluck at London from 1902 and W. J. E. Crane somewhat earlier also made available to bookbinders the necessary details for decorating their books with marbled edges. Moreover, a Halferian marbler by the name of W. C. Doebbelin, who probably had emigrated from Germany, where he had been trained in the craft, was actively teaching and practicing marbling at Orpington, Kent (just outside Lon-

don) from 1910, and issued a manual on the subject in that year. Some years later, Dane and Company, Ltd., which had been in the business of manufacturing printing, lithographic, and other types of inks since 1853, issued the first of two editions of a pamphlet entitled *Instructions for Using Dane and Co.'s Liquid Marbling Inks on Carragheen Moss Size*, in conjunction with their marketing of a line of colors manufactured specifically for marbling purposes.[37]

But it was with the production of marbled papers by Sydney M. Cockerell, beginning about 1930, that British marbling once more began to achieve prominence and even preeminence in the world. The son of a fine hand binder and book restorer who had issued a manual on bookbinding in 1901 (which, however, contained essentially no information on marbling), Sydney Cockerell (1906–1987) grew up in an atmosphere of fine bookbinding and in time became fascinated with the subject and with marbling as well. He began to marble about 1926 at the family home and bindery in Letchworth, Hertfordshire, and eventually erected special quarters for marbling in the garden there. He soon hired William Chapman to attend to the marbling business, and over the years the firm known as Douglas Cockerell and Son became famous worldwide for the production of fine marbled papers used in bookbinding and in the decoration of fine book editions, among other purposes. These were made for the most part by or under the supervision of Chapman who, prior to his retirement in 1984, laid claim to marbling more than half a million sheets of paper.[38]

When I discussed the impact of Josef Halfer in my translation of the Weisse manual, I suggested that a dramatic example of the activity and success his methods engendered is illustrated by the work of the Cockerell group. Cockerell papers were made according to pure Halferian methods, principles, and standards, and their producers in time achieved such a high degree of perfection that for two generations they had practically no rivals among modern marbled papermakers. I also noted in my introduction the irony that this high point in English marbling could be traced to a German progenitor rather than to one of the fine English masters of the pre-Halferian classical style.

Sydney Cockerell and his workers achieved much of their success by executing a limited number of excellently combed patterns based (for the most part) on Halferian methods and traditions. They achieved near-perfect color distribution through the use of a jiglike apparatus, somewhat akin to the "Dutch apparatus" of old. Such a device, mounted on a spring contrivance, took color from receptacles positioned in predetermined configurations and placed it in corresponding locations on the size. Thus, through uncomplicated mechanical means, they achieved in a simpler way what Charles Williams did perhaps seventy-five years earlier. If any criticism can be made of the Cockerell papers it is that they are almost too perfect, appearing mechanically contrived and perhaps lacking in

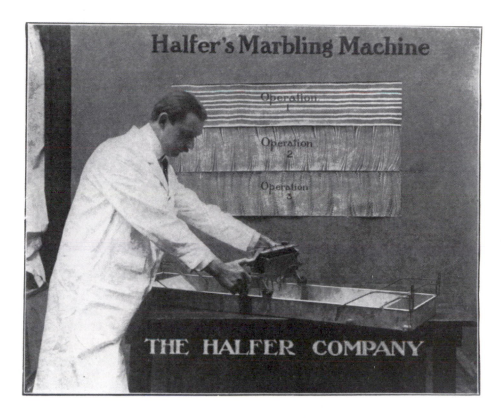

FIGURE 18. Color distribution through the use of Halfer's Marbling Machine. From part four of Pleger's *Bookbinding* (1914).

part the natural charm of the usual hand-produced sheet. The colors are also overly bright and appear too glaring and too precise when used in imitations of ancient patterns.

America

Toward the end of the nineteenth century, Halfer's new wave of marbling crossed the Atlantic to America as well. Through Louis Kinder's publication of a translation of Halfer's treatise, these methods were made directly available to American hand bookbinders who might wish to employ them to effect edge marbling or otherwise. Kinder's publication did much to popularize Halfer's methods in this country, for a number of agencies (including Kinder's) sprang up to supply Halfer's colors and other materials, and carragheen moss began to replace tragacanth and other gums in marbling. As an inducement to secure subscriptions, the *American Bookbinder* magazine in 1894 purchased copies of Halfer's *Progress of the Marbling Art* (issued by Kinder), and offered them as a bonus to subscribers. In this way, Halfer's work was brought to the attention of a wide audience of American binders, and a large number of copies are extant today. Kinder also included advice on marbling in his 1905 *Formulas for Bookbinders* (see note 8).

In 1914 John J. Pleger, a master binder in Chicago, issued a work on bookbinding in four parts, the last of

which contains excellent details on gilt edging, gauffered edging, marbling, hand tooling, and the care of books.[39] Pleger, whose background is obscure, had somehow become acquainted with the Halferian system of marbling and evidently became quite proficient in it. The instructions provided in his manual are purely Halferian and serve as a guide to the rudiments of Halfer's system. Pleger's intent was to enable bookbinders to execute their own edge decoration, and the illustrations on two color plates show edge marbling alone. His decoration looks almost identical to the type of marbling in original samples mounted in Halfer's own manuals and those of some of his distinguished students. Pleger's use of sprinkling water and other Halferian innovations is further evidence that he clearly belonged to Halfer's school.

In his 1914 manual, Pleger reproduced a scene showing a recently invented apparatus, called a "color dropping machine," which consisted of a four-part reservoir with tubes connected to each compartment. As the machine was moved along the rim of the marbling trough and over the size, colors were released by depressing levers so that they fell in an orderly fashion for even distribution on the size. The scene in Pleger's manual shows a marbler doing just that and is captioned "Halfer's Marbling Machine," with the legend "The Halfer Company" below (Figure 18). Pleger's work appeared in four separately bound parts in its 1914 edition, but on reissue by the *Inland Printer* company in 1924[40] it was packaged in a single volume. In the later issue, the scene showing the mechanical distribution of colors was retained but the original titles were cropped off and the legend below read "Halfer's Marbling Machine. The Halfer Co., New York, N.Y."[41]

Another exponent of the Halferian system of marbling in the United States was W. C. Doebbelin. Doebbelin, whom we previously encountered in London, had migrated to America some time before 1926 and settled in the North Shore area of Boston, and the same marbling manual that he had issued while in London in 1910 under the title *The Art of Marbling* was being advertised from a Middleton (near Salem) address.[42] Doebbelin went on to publish a number of articles on marbling and its various techniques and patterns in the *Bookbinding Magazine* in 1926 and 1927, and he issued price lists of supplies and advertising literature as late as 1933, under his firm's name, "The Halfer Marbleizing Company."[43]

The Rosamond B. Loring collection of books on decorated paper in the Houghton Library at Harvard University contains a copy of Doebbelin's rare 1910 manual, the only one that I have ever seen, with both the Orpington imprint on its title page and a Massachusetts address stamped on its red covers, identifying it as a product of the "Halfer Marbling Company, Inc., Salem, Mass., Middleton, Mass." According to this work and to advertising literature inserted into the Loring copy, Doebbelin was the inventor of a device for marbling paper called "Doebbelin's Dutch Apparatus." He claimed that the Dutch marble could only be made satisfactorily using this mechanism and his directions. First the size was prepared exactly as for comb marbling, with four colors being used. These were put in separate tins so arranged as to receive the teeth of a large wooden comb. After ox-gall had been added to the colors and they were tested and adjusted to insure correct expansion, the rake was plunged into the first of the colors in the tins and then moved to touch the size. After the four colors had been applied, the pattern was drawn and taken off in the usual manner.

Doebbelin also advertised a marbling machine called "Doebbelin's Marbling Machine," but the illustration in his manual is labeled "Halfer's Marbling Machine." This device and his Dutch apparatus are illustrated in two scenes in the advertising section at the middle of his manual and are reproduced as Figure 19 here. The second of these scenes shows a marbler, possibly Doebbelin himself, in the process of operating the marbling machine; the machine is identical, as is the scene itself, to the one appearing in Pleger's 1914 manual, but here "London E. C." is printed below the name of the Halfer Company. Doebbelin claimed that his machine applied the comb, double-comb, peacock and bouquet patterns to the size simultaneously, in a single operation for each. His device, he explained, was composed chiefly of a color reservoir divided into four compartments, each of which held one of the four working colors. A system of tubes was connected with the reservoirs to serve as outlets for the colors and distribute them evenly on the surface of the size. The two principal colors were dispensed by five and three outlets respectively; two apiece served for the secondary ones. Two levers forming part of the handles of the machine opened the outlets under slight pressure and freed the colors so that they could run out. The operator had only to move the machine along the marbling trough so that the teeth of its comb penetrated one inch into the size. The ends of the tubes, however, could not be allowed to come into contact with the size. The four compartments of the reservoir were filled about two-thirds full with the colors, which had been treated with ox-gall beforehand and tested on the size to insure equal or adequate expansion.

Doebbelin contended that "Halfer's marbling colors" were the only ones suitable for use with this machine; notwithstanding their intensity, they were lighter in body than the other, thicker colors which tended to obstruct the tubes and generally interfered with the success of the marbling. To complement this machine Doebbelin recommended the use of a special trough with the irregular proportions of either 14 × 48 inches or 14 × 60 inches. This elongated bath can be seen in Figure 19.

Doebbelin was still in business in 1933, when he advertised his manual and other literature in the *Bookbinding Magazine*, but little else is known of his activities. The samples mounted in the Loring copy of his work denote a high proficiency in making Halferian patterns including peacock, American, bouquet, and comb, but two samples showing oil marbling are not so well done. It seems reasonable to postulate that Doebbelin trained in Germany in the Halferian marbling method, emigrated first to England and then to America, where he taught marbling, sold its supplies, promoted his machine, with which he is pictured, and published and advertised on its behalf. He probably allowed the re-use of the pictures of him and his marbling invention in Pleger's 1914 manual for such advertising purposes. They also associate him with Pleger in some unexplained way; perhaps his London period was followed by an interlude in the American Midwest.

Rosamond Bowditch Loring (1889–1950), pictured in Figure 20, who began to marble in the mid-1920s, made an important contribution to the art by serving as its publicist (as also did Olga Hirsch, first in Germany and later in England). Mrs. Loring's influence was spread in America and abroad, mainly through her book, *Decorated Book Papers*. Today, the work is somewhat dated and must be used with caution, for it is not without errors, but at the time of its publication in 1942, it served admirably as a source at a time when the art was at one of its lowest ebbs. The examples I have seen of her marbling do not reveal an overly advanced technique, and although she was more proficient in the making of paste papers, she was not on par with Veronica Ruzicka, Nancy Storm, and others, working in that genre. There can be no doubt, however, that Rosamond Loring made a lasting contri-

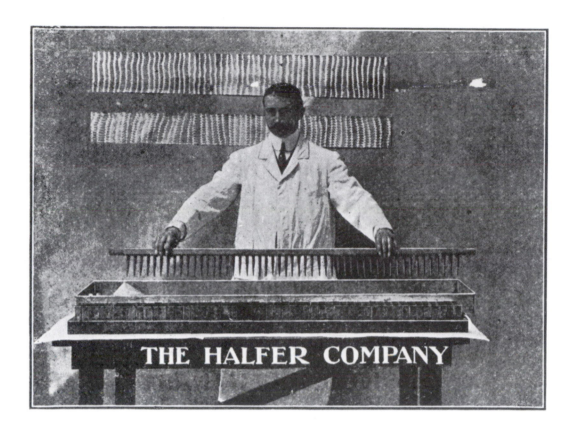

FIGURE 19. Illustrations from W. C. Doebbelin's *The Art of Marbling*.

FIGURE 20. Rosamond Loring demonstrating the marbling process to a group of service men and women at the Bay State Club, U.S.O. in May 1944.

bution to the field of paper decoration by assembling one of the most outstanding collections of its literature and a superb collection of some of its original examples. Now in the Houghton Library at Harvard, this collection remains the best of its kind in America and one of the most outstanding in the world.

In her first publishing effort in the realm of paper decoration—a little work entitled *Marbled Papers* which was based on a lecture and demonstration she delivered before the Club of Odd Volumes in Boston on November 16, 1932—Mrs. Loring described the incident that had led up to her initiation into the art. Between 1927 and 1928 she had tried her hand at marbling and later put on a demonstration at a crafts show in Boston:

My work fascinated the crowd, among whom was an old man who stood beside me for nearly an hour. As he interested me, I asked him if there was anything I could do for him. He turned and, with the nicest smile, said, "Mrs. Loring, I like what you do, but you don't do it right." I asked him if he were a professional marbler, and he said that he was and that it would give him great pleasure to show me what he knew about marbling. So he came to my studio twice a week for part of one winter and gave me lessons.[44]

In her article devoted to making paste papers, Mrs. Loring identified her teacher as Charles V. Safland of Fitchburg, Massachusetts.[45]

It seems that afterward Mrs. Loring wanted to improve her technique, for laid into her copy of the Doebbelin marbling manual in 1980 was a letter from Doebbelin to her husband, Augustus P. Loring. Doebbelin was responding to an inquiry from Loring, whose wife wanted to receive instructions from him in the craft. Doebbelin suggested that he put on a practical demonstration for a fee of ten dollars. This letter subsequently became misplaced or lost, and its date is now unknown; it is likely, however, that this episode took place around 1932 or 1933. The outcome of Loring's inquiry is not known.[46]

Marbling with Oil Colors

Early in the twentieth century, several artisans and craftspeople began to marble with oil colors in place of the traditional water-colors. Paul Kersten credits Ernst Leistikov and his sister Gertrude in Breslau for inventing the process,[47] but he acknowledges that as far back as 1855 an English marbler named Tucker had written about oil color techniques, and, furthermore, that Tucker's method had been discussed in W. F. Exner's 1869 treatise on the wallpaper and colored-paper industry.[48]

Kersten also observes that the firm of Pelzer & Co. of Düren had been putting such papers on the market for thirty-five years, or since about 1904 or 1905. Kersten cites as his source an article in "Dinglers Polyt. Journal" and attributes it to the year 1869. Actually, the article appeared in 1856 and was a reprint of one published a year earlier.[49] Hiram Tucker's own description of this process was printed in the second, 1879 edition of the British Commissioner of Patents' *Abridgements of Specifications Relating to Cutting, Folding, and Ornamenting Paper, &c.*[50] Tucker asserted that his invention consisted of "marbling" paper and other substances in a "water bath" by means of "oil colours." In order to overcome the "fluent" property of the linseed or drying oil used, or to alter it so that the colors mixed with the oil would remain broken up and not combine with other colors thrown onto the surface of the bath, gum resin from the "damara australis or pinus kuari," mixed with essential oil of turpentine or another suitable vehicle, was combined with the oils in a proportion of about two or three pounds of gum to one gallon of essential oil, and about two quarts of the mixture to one quart of the drying oil. The various colors were added to some of this preparation until the required consistency was achieved. These then were deposited on a water bath in the usual manner, with veining accomplished with a thin spatula.

Tucker's method may not have been so easily accomplished as he claimed; nor could the results have been acceptable to many consumers at that time, when traditional marbles of reasonably good quality were still available. Indeed, I have not observed (or recognized) any English imprints of the second half of the nineteenth century bound with such papers in or on them, and there is no other mention of Tucker or his method in the English marbling literature of this or a later period. The method subsequently developed by artists and amateurs in Germany was simpler, although its limited results are not competitive with those achieved by classical marbling. Modern oil marbling is effected by thinning down the marbling size, or simply using plain water, and dropping or sprinkling oil colors—the type used by artists—onto it. Printing inks and other light or thinned-down oil base paints also can be employed.

Oil marbling is actually a bastardized form of marbling, for it does not allow control; patterns cannot be produced seriatim in a regular and continuous way. Colors move about as they please, and the oil marbler simply obtains a pattern that has formed itself. Yet despite these drawbacks, the method became popular, and it remains so even today; it produces quick and easy results, and now and then some really interesting effects can be achieved. Oil marbling, in essence, is the choice of those craftspeople unwilling to take the time and trouble to undergo the rigid training and tribulations of the legitimate marbling art. Many of the artisans and craftspeople

whose specimens are preserved in the collections of Buntpapier in museums and libraries in Europe worked in this medium, with more or less success.

Paul Kersten published an article on oil marbling according to Tucker's process as early as 1904,[51] and Haemmerle's bibliography takes notice of a 1905 article by an individual named Wolf entitled "Marmorieren auf Wasser," which I have not had an opportunity to examine.[52] In addition, other articles on this method have appeared in bookbinding and allied literature from the 1920s on and are cited in the bibliographies compiled by Hunter, Haemmerle, Easton, and Grünebaum. The only manual I know of devoted exclusively to this method of paper decoration was produced in 1945 by Tim Thrift at his Lucky Dog Press in Winchester, Massachusetts; interestingly, it is the first native American marbling manual. Entitled *Modern Methods of Marbling Paper*, this small work was printed, bound, and illustrated (with original marbled samples) by its author.[53] Thrift intended it as an instruction book for the amateur marbler who wanted decorated paper that could be quickly and simply produced. He advocated the use of thinned-down gum size, water alone, or water slightly stiffened with melted flexible glue, with artists' oil colors serving as the coloring medium.

Flickering Embers

In Europe, the flaming resurgence marbling enjoyed during the early years of this century—provoked by Halfer and his superior methods, and their propagation by his pupils and the German bookbinding schools—was partially smothered by the ashes of the First World War. When the flame flickered again during the 1920s and 1930s throughout Germany and in Switzerland and other European locations, it did not regain its former strength and was kept alive by fewer and fewer devotees. Postwar inflation and recovery followed by a worldwide depression and the disastrous political events that led up to the Second World War contributed to a sombre outlook.

By the 1930s in America, most decorated paper was imported from abroad. Virtually no marbling was being done at home; the limited range of decorated papers offered by American craftspeople consisted mainly of paste papers made by Veronica Ruzicka, Rosamond Loring, and a few other semi-professionals or amateurs. The major importer and distributor of decorated paper was the firm of Andrews, Stevens, Nelson, Whitehead, Inc. of New York, which furnished hand bookbinders and publishers of special and deluxe editions with all the fancy and colored papers they required. A sizable collection of sample books in my possession displays papers being distributed to binders and publishers in the 1920s and 1930s and indicates just how limited the range and supply actually were.

In the marbling line, dealers could offer only Cockerell

papers, the *ne plus ultra* of this class; Turkish-style papers made by Ingeborg Börjesson, now of Enskede, Sweden (though her batik papers were much preferred); and marbled papers made in France by the Putois firm and a few other unidentified craftspeople. The latter group, while showing a few classical patterns, consisted mainly of papers marbled through the oil process. Other decorated papers offered by Andrews, Stevens, Nelson, Whitehead were printed ones, such as St. Albans papers from England and Bertini and Rizzi papers from Italy, as well as some types from other sources.

In spite of the fact that the amount of decorated paper made in Europe at this time obviously was limited, there was a little more activity going on there than initially meets the eye. To take an example, in my collection of pattern books are two containing swatches of an oil type of marbling that was done at Barcelona, Spain, in the 1930s by Vincente Villaplana Gadea. Again, a marbler by the name of Hesse established a one-person workshop in Leipzig in 1924; both he and his son, Gerhard, who joined him in 1949 and succeeded him in 1959, annually turned out paste papers, classically marbled papers, and oil marbles by the thousands.[54] Also active in Germany were Franze Weisse and his group, as well as others.

World War II and its aftermath had another quenching effect on this craft, especially in Germany and adjacent regions of Europe, which had formed the traditional home of marbling in the Western world. In the last two decades, however, a resurgence of interest and activity in this fascinating art has occurred in Europe, America, and other regions of the world, with a simultaneous rebirth of interest in hand bookbinding. For the purposes of this survey, however, these recent developments qualify more as current events than as history, and will be more properly worthy of comment in the future rather than now. Suffice it to say that a long view of this marbling business shows that it has endured a great many ups and downs over a lengthy period of time. The fire has at times burned brightly, and at times it has sputtered irregularly or smoldered. But the most important lesson we can learn from reviewing the history of this ancient and venerable craft is that the fire has never burned out.

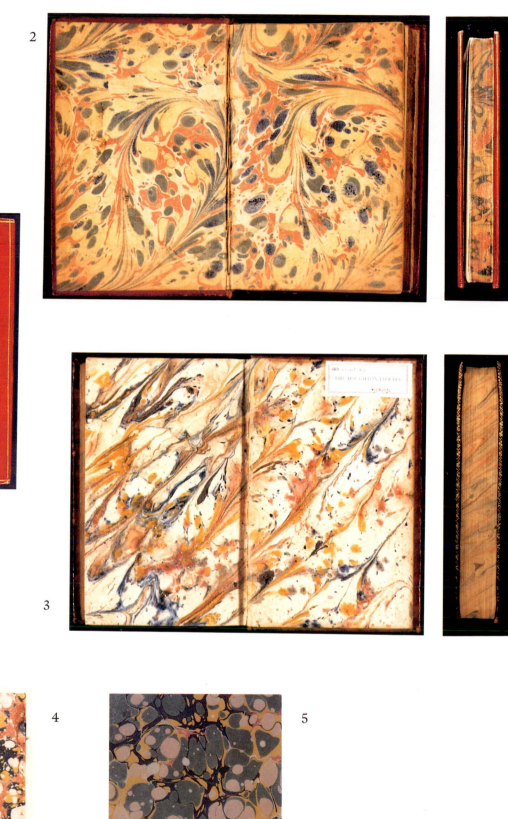

PLATE XVII

1

2

3

4

5

6

PLATE XVIII

1

2

3

4

5

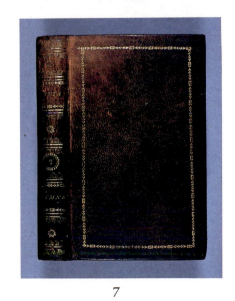

6

7

PLATE XIX

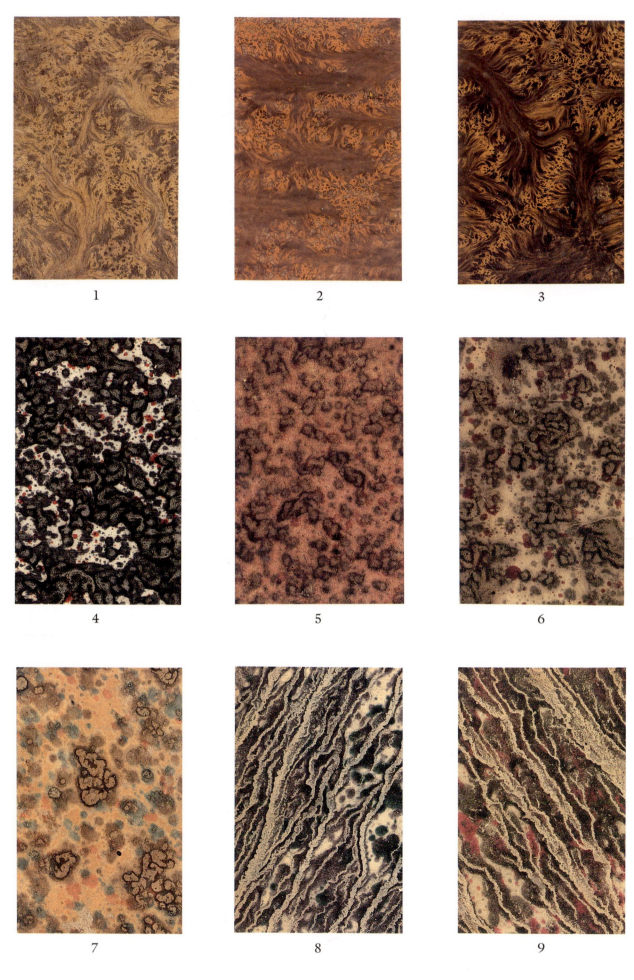

1

2

3

4

5

6

7

8

9

PLATE XX

Captions for Plates XVII–XXII

PLATE XVII: 1. Front cover on one of two copies of Thomas Sheppard's *England's Balme* presented to Harvard College by Thomas Hollis. These were bound for Hollis by Mathewman of London in 1761–1764 and imprinted in gilt with Hollis's liberty stamps which were destroyed by fire in 1764. Houghton Library, Harvard University; 2. English-made endpapers and fore-edge decoration on the same work, showing the sort of marbling that was being done in Britain at this time; 3. Another example of British marbling from its formative period. Marbled endpapers and marbled fore edge on one of two volumes of Milton's *Poetical Works* printed by John Baskerville in 1758 and afterward bound and marbled in his shop. Richardson bookbinding collection, Houghton Library, Harvard University; 4. Inserted sheet of marbled paper, marbled on both sides with a stencil to show a white border around its edges, in the first edition of Laurence Sterne's *Tristram Shandy*. Houghton Library, Harvard University; 5. Marbled paper inserted in the edition of *Tristram Shandy* issued by Harrison & Co., London, in 1781, after a dozen or more editions, including some pirated ones, had been published. The same pattern appears on both sides of the sheet. Author's collection.

PLATE XVIII: 1–4. Documents and paper currency marbled to attest to their authenticity, all in some way connected with Benjamin Franklin: 1. Promissory note, Paris, 4 December 1781, signed by Franklin, representing one of the several loans advanced by the French to help finance the American Revolution. The note is one of a series printed by Franklin at the private press he set up at Passy to serve the needs of the American mission to France. The marbling, undoubtedly executed in France, was added to one side only. This copy is now in a private collection, but others are in the American Philosophical Society in Philadelphia (courtesy of Joseph Rubinfine, West Palm Beach, Florida); 2. Marbled Continental currency, 1775; a $20.00 note issued on paper supplied by Benjamin Franklin (courtesy of Leonard H. Finn, West Roxbury, Massachusetts); 3. Front side of a three-pence note, printed by Benjamin Franklin Bache, Benjamin Franklin's grandson, for the Bank of North America and dated 6 August 1789 (courtesy of Leonard H. Finn of West Roxbury, Massachusetts); 4. Verso of the Bank of North America's 1789 three-pence note, polychromed through the marbling process; 5. Gilt morocco binding, executed in the Boston area, containing the Protestant Episcopal Church's *Book of Common Prayer* (1794) and a copy of *Hymns, Selected from the Most Approved Authors, for the Use of the Trinity Church, Boston* (1808). Bryn Mawr College Library; 6. Endpapers in the same binding, showing marbling over printed text of the *Monthly Anthology*, published at Boston in 1804. The marbling was executed in Boston after 1808, and the binding dates after that time.

PLATE XIX: 1. Overmarbled endpapers and spine of a volume of David Longworth's two-volume edition (New York, 1814) of Washington Irving's *Salmagundi*. The marbling on the endpapers was applied over printed waste sheets of an edition of *The New and Complete Book of Martyrs* printed at New York in 1798. Author's collection; 2. Overmarbling by the Mann family on a printed waste sheet from Oliver Shaw, Amos Albee, and Herman Mann's *The Columbian Sacred Harmony,* printed by Mann at Dedham in 1808. Part of one of the overmarbled waste sheets was later used as cover paper on a copy of Elias Smith's *The Age of Enquiry,* issued by Abel Brown at Exeter, N.H., in 1825. Author's collection; 3. Overmarbling by the Mann family on a printed waste sheet from the Dedham 1815 edition of the *Militia Laws of the United States and the Commonwealth of Massachusetts.* Author's collection; 4. Overmarbled text of "Fanny Hill" on a sheet disbound from a volume in the American Antiquarian Society. The marbling undoubtedly was executed by a member of the Mann family; 5. Overmarbled "Fanny Hill" sheet on a binding on a periodical in the American Antiquarian Society; 6. Endpapers in a copy of Isaac Watts's *Hymns and Spiritual Songs* that Herman Mann printed at Dedham in 1811 and undoubtedly also bound. American Antiquarian Society; 7. Binding on Watts's *Hymns and Spiritual Songs* of 1811.

PLATE XX. Imitation and "pseudo-marbled" papers: 1–3. Maroquin or morocco or Saffian papers, the first, French, 1830 period, the others German, 1840 and 1850 periods; (4–9— Papiers d'Annonay) 4–6. Of the "papier tourniquet" variety, France, 1830 and 1840 decades. 7. American papier tourniquet, made by Charles Williams of Philadelphia, 1862–1864; 8–9. Of the "papier coulé" variety, France, 1830 and 1850 period respectively.

PLATE XXI. More imitation and pseudo-marbled papers: 1–3. Papiers d'Annonay, of the "papier croisé" variety, France, 1830s to 1850s; (4–7. Agathe, "Achat," or "agate" papers) 4. France, 1840 period 5. France, mid-19th century; 6–7. Germany, later 19th century; 8–9. "Gustav Marmor," Germany, later 19th century.

PLATE XXII. Halferian and fantasy marbling: (1–3. Reproductions of samples in Josef Halfer's *Die Fortschritte der Marmorierkunst,* 1891 edition. Author's collection.) 1. Combed patterns; 2. Peacock and bouquet patterns; 3. Hair-vein patterns; 4. Two-page illustration of original mounted samples of marbled paper (made at the Gera bookbinding and gilding school) in Paul Hüttich's *Lehrplan und Ausführlicher Bericht der Geraer Vergolde Schule und Buch Binderei,* 1900. Koninklijke Bibliotheek, The Hague; (5–6. Fantasy patterns executed by Johann Rudel of Eberfeld, Germany, between 1900 and 1910. Rudel was a colleague of Franz Weisse. Koninklijke Bibliotheek, The Hague.) 5. Frog design; 6. Penguin design.

12

Technical Aspects of the Craft, I: Marbling Process, Equipment, and Tools

WE now turn our attention to some of the technical aspects of marbling in order to further elucidate this unique craft. While the account in this and the next two chapters does not purport to be a definitive explanation of the art or of the chemical and physical forces underlying it, it will attempt to show how and why these forces operate as they do, what the craft's limitations are, why it produces the particular effects that it does, and what equipment and supplies are necessary to bring everything into operation.[1] In order to interpret these constituents along historical lines, as well as to illustrate them, I will relate my descriptions and analyses to illustrations in the literature—particularly the two well-known scenes of the eighteenth-century marbler's atelier that accompany the discussion of marbling in the Diderot-D'Alembert *Encyclopédie* of 1765.

Marbling consists of dropping, throwing, or otherwise depositing mineral and vegetable colors upon a watery surface that has been "stiffened" or made slightly thick through the addition of a starchy substance. This additive produces a viscous, less fluid medium which under proper conditions is conducive to the support of colors on its surface. A chemical substance of one sort or another is added to the colors beforehand to help sustain them on the surface by causing them to expand into thin films, and to keep them from commingling with one another. Finally, the resulting color pattern is absorbed onto paper.

Marbling is, in theory and in essence, no more than these few basic steps, and—as I suggested in Chapter 1—initially probably arose by accident. In its simplest form it has come down to us over the ages as the pattern designated as "Turkish." This design is made up of plain color spots, with naturally formed white veins between, where one color was antagonistic toward another and drew back from it, causing the paper to show white where that interstice had been. We shall now observe how this process was carried on in private workshops and in factories,

and how it developed more sophisticated forms. We shall also see the kinds of ingredients and tools marblers, over time, found necessary to make it all work.

1. The Marbling Process

The first operation with which the marbler must concern himself is making his size or gum medium, for this is the key element in the whole process, and more than any other determines success or failure. For this purpose, gum tragacanth (sometimes referred to in the early literature as gum dragon), an exudate of various Asiatic or East European shrubs, was universally employed until recent times; in the lower right hand corner of the first Diderot print (Figure 21) a workman can be seen straining a supply of this all-important ingredient into his marbling trough. Tragacanth was purchased dry, in lump

FIGURE 21. A workman strains gum tragacanth into the marbling trough.

form, and converted into size by mixing it with water, which caused it to swell. It was gradually brought to the proper consistency or viscous state through the addition of more water, and the mixture was strained through a sieve, hair search, or straining cloth.[2] The workman pictured in Figure 21 is stirring the gum water through a horsehair sieve to complete the final state of this process.

The opposite side of the same Diderot plate shows another important step in the setting-up operation: the grinding of colors (Figure 22). In earlier times, colors were obtained in dried, cake form; they had to be pulverized and brought to the proper consistency for use. This was achieved by grinding the colors with a muller on a marble slab or stone, all the while adding water and perhaps brandy and ox-gall, and then transferring them to individual color pots for storage. Several of the early commentators—Dossie and G. Smith among them—call for grinding the colors with spirits or wine or brandy alone. The flat plate or object lying upright against the grinding slab was known as a "collector." This was a flat piece of metal or strong leather, measuring about 4×3 inches, with which the workman scraped up bits of diffuse color into the center pile, thereby saving every fragment of the often costly ingredient. The Diderot article advised the operator to retrieve the color remaining on the stone by taking some water into his mouth, spraying it onto the muller and stone, and then placing this washed mixture into another pot: "It is necessary not to neglect these small economies in all matters which occur again and again. They often mean the difference between loss and gain."

In the very center of the Diderot scene (Figure 23), we can observe the actual marbling process being carried on, now reduced to three individual operations by the artist. The first step, the sprinkling of colors onto the size, is depicted in the center of the scene, and slightly to the rear. The marbler, brush in hand (but using a separate brush for each color), deposits successive colors onto the size in the marbling trough, tapping the brush full of paint on his wrist or forearm to diffuse spots of color throughout the surface of the bath. If desired, the design could be lifted off onto paper after all the colors had been thrown down, forming the ancient and venerable "Turkish"—or "stone" or "spot"—pattern in the process. The marbler could go a step further and fashion a "combed" pattern, as the workman to his right is doing. This would entail passing a comb through the color spots, from one end of the trough to the other, causing them to break into even rows, in a straight, symmetrical fashion. He might or might not rake the colors beforehand with a pointed instrument, using a back and forth motion in a crosswise fashion; this would distribute them in straight lines and result eventually in an evenly combed configuration that in older times was referred to as "Dutch."

Notice the position of the trough on one side of the table. This may simply seem the trough's logical place, but it is more significant. By placing the trough at one of

FIGURE 22. Grinding the colors.

the far sides of the table (depending on whether the operator was left- or right-handed), and not at its center, the marbler could comb in two directions more easily, allowing him to form his pattern according to the direction of the grain of the paper—a major consideration for the bookbinder who would eventually use it for endpapers. (This is also an especially important consideration in Halferian marbling, where double and sometimes triple combing in transverse directions is called for.)

The marbling process was completed when the operator, as seen on the far left of this triad, laid a sheet of paper onto the pattern floating on the surface of the size to absorb it. Today, the usual way to lay the sheet is to hold it by opposite corners. This practice is necessary when working with especially large sheets of paper; otherwise, the paper may buckle or slip, causing unseemly lines, air bubbles, or other defects to ruin the pattern. Notice, however, that the workman in the Diderot print is holding the paper by the middle of its narrow edge— the method in fact advocated in its accompanying text.

Before leaving these operations, we can observe in Figure 24 a French marbler of the Putois firm sprinkling colors onto a bath in the 1930s, approximately 175 years after the action depicted in the Diderot scene.[3]

After it was removed from the size, the marbled sheet was suspended over cords to dry, as shown in the background of the Diderot picture (Figure 25). When each sheet was finished, the size was skimmed free of all remaining color and the process begun anew, with a fresh application of colors, new combing, and the laying on of another clean sheet of paper.

Turning now to the second Diderot print, which is less

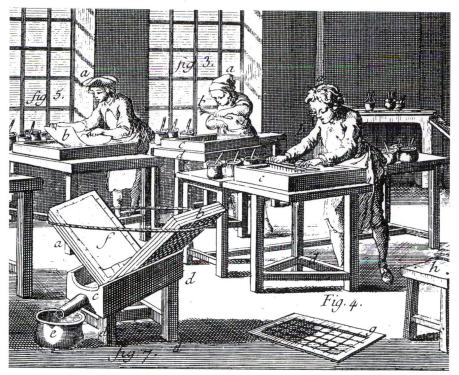

FIGURE 23. Three steps in the marbling process: sprinkling the colors (*center*); combining the size (*right*); laying a sheet of paper (*left*).

FIGURE 24. A modern French marbler sprinkles colors onto a bath.

FIGURE 25. Marbled sheets being suspended for drying.

known today because it has been reproduced less often, we observe the subsidiary operations required to bring the sheets to final, marketable form. But first, observe two other marbling operations depicted at the far left of the scene for the marbling of book edges (Figure 26). In the background a workman is using a stylus to complete a pattern, while in front another workman is decorating book edges by dipping them—several at a time, as was the custom—onto the color-covered size. The marbler simply clamped the books together and dipped them straight onto the size, first the fore edges and later the upper and lower edges. To the side sit a row of books waiting to be decorated. Whether this operation was effected by more than one workman, as depicted by the Diderot artist, is unknown. A single marbler could, of course, perform these operations alone; however, in a large shop, where rapid production was called for, the individual steps may have been carried out as shown. It should be pointed out that the workman to the rear, shown perfecting the design to be transformed to the edges of these books, in all likelihood was drawing the well-known pattern that the English later would call "snail" or "French curl," and that the French themselves referred to as "commun."

To contrast this scene, I now reproduce a woodcut from the second, 1868 edition of Ludwig Brade's *Illustriertes Buchbinderbuch* (Figure 27). This shows a German bookbinder carrying out the same operation a little more than a century after the Diderot scene. By the middle of the nineteenth century, large workshops such as the one depicted in the French print were no longer in existence or were being phased out, and bookbinders were more and more forced to perform edge marbling themselves, with the aid of a support literature that had been appearing from early in the nineteenth century. (Edge marbling can also be observed in Figure 13.)

The workman on the far right of the second Diderot print (Figure 28) is rubbing wax onto marbled sheets of paper. Sometimes a small amount of wax was added to the colors during their preparation in order to heighten their sheen under polishing. Adding wax to colors was not easily accomplished, however, for wax is hard and must be softened or made friable beforehand. It was easier to wax sheets directly, as is shown here. After the sheets had been rubbed over with a piece of white or yellow wax, or with a rag saturated with wax, they were subjected to burnishing, which we can see being done on the immediate left. Sometimes white soap was employed in place of wax. The application of wax or soap closed the pores of this early handmade paper, bound the colors more closely to it, and kept them from rubbing off. Waxing and burnishing also gave the pattern an overall luster, deepening and heightening the brilliancy of the colors and making them more appealing.

Glazing or burnishing was accomplished either by hand or using an apparatus of the type depicted here. If effected manually, the operator rubbed a highly polished flint stone, an agate stone, a piece of granite marble, or a piece of thick glass finely ground to the shape of an egg, over the sheet (which had been placed on a marble slab), thereby polishing it brightly. Here in the Diderot print we see the operation being done mechanically, as would be expected in a workshop of these large proportions. The mechanical device consisted of a shaft attached to a movable flange in the ceiling, which could be moved about at its lower extremity within a restricted radius. The lower end of the shaft contained a case or bed—with a highly polished agate stone embedded in it—and had handles at its sides to permit the operator to move it about easily and control its movement. Newly decorated paper was placed on the marble slab, seen on the center table in Figure 28 here, and the stone was moved over the paper's surface, to lend it a fine gloss.

The Germans were especially known for the superior glossy or glazed finish of their sheets, which were apparently held in high esteem in earlier times. On the floor to the operator's right can be seen a pile of burnished papers, and on the far left of the picture we can observe a concluding operation. Though this workman appears to be carrying out an alternative method of glazing, more likely he was using his knife to scrape off the excess wax and color that had bunched up or rubbed into small clumps during the polishing process. The occurrence of this residue is not unusual in this process, as I have learned when burnishing many hundreds of sheets containing early patterns. It happened then, just as it did during my recent experience, for red and other color stains from the waxing and burnishing process are still to be seen on the white parts of French sheets that are 250 years old.

These then constitute the major steps in marbling paper. Although they have been made to seem simple, that appearance is deceptive, for the actual process is fraught with difficulties mainly because of the unstable and antagonistic nature of the chemicals and ingredients employed. Before going further into this matter, it would be well to consider what sort of equipment came to be used over the centuries to carry out the various marbling operations.

2. Equipment and Tools

The equipment and tools needed for marbling paper appear to be the simplest and most ordinary imaginable—an illusion that, I believe, has contributed to the misconception that marbling is an easy craft to master. A few specialized materials are required, but many, if not most, of the necessary implements fall into the class of general or ordinary household supplies. Our objective now is to review the paraphernalia required and to determine, insofar as the old manuals as well as current experi-

FIGURE 26. Marbling book edges in eighteenth-century France.

FIGURE 27. Marbling book edges in nineteenth-century Germany.

FIGURE 28. Waxing, burnishing, and finishing marbled sheets.

ence will allow, how these needs have been met from earlier times up to the present.

From the previous literature, we rely especially on the Diderot-D'Alembert article on marbling, the slender advice advanced by Robert Dossie, the recommendations and descriptions of Charles Woolnough and Fichtenberg, the manual of C. F. G. Thon, and similar sources. For the modern period, best represented by the methods of Josef Halfer and his disciples, we have the manual of that master himself as well as those of his adherents, most importantly the works of Josef Hauptmann, Paul Adam, Paul Kersten, and Franz Weisse. Especially useful for our purposes, some of these manuals contain illustrations to supplement their descriptive texts.

THE MARBLING TROUGH

Earlier in this work I likened the gum size to the stage on which the marbling play is enacted. If this metaphor may be extended further, we might consider the marbling trough to be the theater that contains the stage—it is the vessel that holds the size whereon the scenario is played out. The earliest marbling literature in the Western world, such as Athanasius Kircher's *Ars Magna Lucis et Umbrae* of 1646, simply refers to the marbling receptacle as a trough, indicating that it should be the size of a full sheet of paper and two or three fingers deep. John Evelyn, however, in his presentation to the Royal Society in 1662, was somewhat more to the point, advising that this "may bee made of lead, or wood well ioynted, pitched or primed so as to containe the liquor," and "let it bee deepe about foure fingers."

From Evelyn's description, as well as later accounts by Dossie and others, we learn that the early marbling trough was most often made of wood and was rectangular in shape, measuring slightly in excess of 13 × 17 inches, the size of a sheet of foolscap paper of that period. Its dimensions may have been greater to accommodate larger formats, say 15 × 19 inches, the earlier dimensions of a sheet of paper called demy. The depth of two or three or

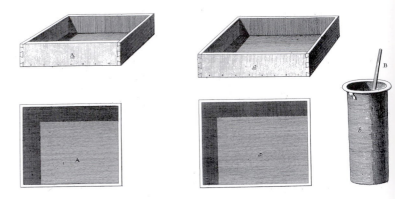

FIGURE 30. The Diderot-D'Alembert trough assembly.

four fingers was probably equivalent to two to four inches. Furthermore, it is likely that the trough was made watertight through the application of pitch or tar at its seams.

The anonymous author of the article in the Diderot-D'Alembert encyclopedia told his readers merely to ready a trough of oak wood of a depth of about half a foot, and exceeding by about one inch in every direction the dimensions of either demy paper or a larger paper variety called *montfaucon*.[4] The trough should be supported, of course, by a table or workbench. Such an assembly was depicted in one of the Diderot plates (Figure 29). It should be pointed out that although the two marbling scenes in the 1765 *Encyclopédie* have been reproduced many times, their lower parts, showing the various tools and implements of the trade, have been virtually ignored. By examining these areas of the illustrations, we can see more clearly how the eighteenth-century marbling trough was fashioned and secured by mortises or tenons (Figure 30).

Charles Woolnough in his classic manuals of 1853 and 1881 marks that the troughs of those times were generally made of wood. They had to be watertight, and perfectly flat and smooth at the bottom inside, because when bottom combs were used, any unevenness would injure them and distort the patterns. "Sometimes," he states, "they are made of slate, which is better; but they are very heavy, if you have to shift them, and are more expensive."[5] Some, he added, were made to take a single sheet and others two sheets; but they should be larger than the papers to be marbled, otherwise the edges of the paper would be imperfect. Woolnough went on to describe the classic marbling trough, worked out or evolved through much labor and experience:

> There should be a small partition on the right-hand side, about three inches wide, made by letting in a narrow piece of wood or slate, about a quarter of an inch in thickness, and so placed in a sloping position,—the top being about the eighth of an inch below the sides,—as to allow of the waste being skimmed over it, without running over the sides. A hole about the size

FIGURE 29. The Diderot-D'Alembert trough and workbench.

of a wine cork should be made in one corner, to run the contents out whenever you want to do so.[6]

Josef Halfer described the trough as a long, flat oblong box about 20 inches in length, 10 inches wide, and 1-1/4 inches deep. He advised that its interior be painted with white oil paint so that the size would appear light and the colors more discernible on its surface. This result could be obtained, one manual states,[7] by placing a piece of milk glass on the bottom of the trough, or, according to another source,[8] by positioning on the bottom of the bath a sheet of lacquered white writing paper. Halfer, like Woolnough, calls for a sloping partition on one side, but made of sheet zinc (assumedly the material of the trough he used), so that waste could be skimmed over it. While he mentions no outlet or drain to remove the spoiled colors and size, he does recommend that a smaller trough or basin, 10 inches in width and 1-1/4 inches in depth, be placed to the left of the first so that such wastes could be skimmed into it.

Paul Kersten, a disciple of Halfer, advises that the trough or bath be made of sheet zinc, and positioned on a wooden base having two crosspieces or trestles on its underside. Kersten also recommends that the trough have a sloping partition to facilitate the removal of residual color and a round hole and cork for draining it or stopping it up (Figure 31). He particularly liked Szigrist's marbling bath (Figure 31), which is constructed so that one of its narrow sides slants down obliquely and curves, hooklike, into a small receptacle that receives the waste color and size. The advantage here is that the smaller pan can easily be removed—without draining the bath—to discard waste colors that have been skimmed off. Today all sorts of pans are used—galvanized, porcelainized metal, even stainless steel, which probably is the most durable of all, although slightly heavier and more expensive. For beginners, any rectangular pan of proper proportions will suffice. I myself use a modification of the two types described by Kersten, with either a sloping partition or a separate receptable at one end and a drain plug at the other. My troughs are made to order by local tinsmiths from sheets of zinc-coated tin or stainless steel, the former lasting five or more years and the latter indefinitely.

In his marbling manual J. P. Boeck illustrated his own variation on a marbling trough, one fastened into the side of another (Figure 31). This device, it seems to me, would be difficult to drain and clean, and even to comb.

COLOR CONTAINERS

Almost any container can be used for holding the colors. As we see in the illustration in G. Smith's *The Laboratory: or, School of Arts* (Figure 8), and from the Diderot-D'Alembert illustration of the marbling table and trough (Figure 29), the receptacles in the eighteenth century were earthen pots with wide mouths. The term "pot"

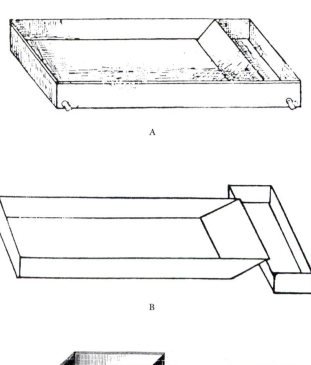

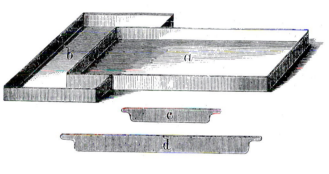

FIGURE 31. Marbling troughs of *a*, Kersten; *b*, Szigrist; and *c*, Boeck.

was most frequently used for color containers in the English literature on marbling, although sometimes "jar" or "pipkin" (an earthen pot with a handle) was employed. For my work, glass custard cups of varying sizes serve very well; they are especially suitable when made of Pyrex, which allows them to withstand the pressures of an automatic dishwasher, for the process requires cleanliness.

BRUSHES

The early literature of marbling, including the reports of Athanasius Kircher (1646), John Evelyn (1662), and others, dictates that colors be sprinkled onto the size with brushes, and Evelyn specifically alludes to "a reasonable large brush with hoggs haire (such as Painters use)." However, in the first known illustration of marbling, published by G. Smith in 1738 and in later editions, the color pots are pictured containing quills or some similar device. Additionally, Robert Dossie, in 1758, directs that the colors be put onto the size by means of a pencil or quill. From these accounts we may conclude that early marblers applied their colors in either of these ways. Brushes permit the colors to be put down in concentrated form, but in irregular configurations—that is, falling where they may—while the quill, pencil, stylus, or drop point achieves the same purpose in a more controlled manner, though the colors are more thinly distributed. (The pointed instrument allows the operator to place colors wherever he pleases, but they spread out in thin films and do not show as brightly on the paper.) The 1765 Diderot article mentions brushes as the tool for distributing color, and illustrates an assortment of them on one of its plates reproduced here as Figure 32. These brushes, the article notes, were made by attaching pig's bristles to a stick.

Charles Woolnough in 1853 advocated two types of brushes to allow the colors to be either beaten or sprinkled onto the size (thus "beating" brushes or "sprinkling" brushes). The beating was done by slapping the brush against the finger (or forearm, as in the Diderot scene) or against a metal rod, while sprinkling was accomplished by freely shaking the brush. James Sumner, whose manual followed close on the heels of Woolnough's, recommended dropping colors by means of a quill, half of which was slit away and the remaining portion rounded to a point. This configuration channeled color onto the size in crosswise stripes or lines and helped achieve better color distribution. Sumner also mentioned that pieces of wood, about the thickness of a penholder and tapered to a point, could serve the same purpose. He wrote that "the colours must be laid on the size in equal stripes. There should be properly as much space between each two colours as the space occupied by each colour."

In his *Progress of the Marbling Art*, Josef Halfer devoted a few paragraphs to the brushes employed in his style of marbling. Stating that it was practically impossible to distribute the colors equally around the size by using a common brush, particularly for drawn patterns, he advised the use of brushes with bent bristles. He particularly advocated the "bristle brush" which had bristles 3 inches long and from 2 to 2 1/2 inches thick and bound to a handle by well-waxed packing thread, about 1 1/4 inches from the lower end, so that they were open for a length of 1 3/4 inches. This instrument, in Halfer's opinion, was very well adapted for distributing the color drops. He also mentioned the "broom corn whisk," a small brush or broom made of soft broomcorn 1 to 2 inches thick. The whisks were bound in the same manner as the bristle brushes, but about 5 inches of straw was allowed to protrude.

Paul Kersten's useful manual, *Die Marmorierkunst* (1922), tells us that long-handled brushes of hog's bristles, about one centimeter thick and about six centimeters long, are required for laying colors onto the marbling size. These bristles should be tied up with a thread and placed for a time in boiling water, then cooled off in cold water. In this way the bristles are given their required

shape, shown in Figure 33: on the left, the drop brush is being made to bend and on the right is finally bent and ready for use. A disciple of the Halferian system of marbling, Kersten undoubtedly was explaining making the bent instrument that Halfer had advocated but not otherwise described.

Kersten also recommended the use of three other brushes: the rice straw brush, the beating brush, and the large beating broom (Figure 34): modifications, designed for special purposes, of the broom used by Halfer.

Kersten advocated the rice straw brush for laying on the ground or final predominating color in Turkish, stone, or spot marbling. The brush was, of course, made of rice straw, about 2 or 3 inches thick. The beating brush, also made of rice straw, was a larger version, designed to achieve the same purpose but in a bigger and better way. The large beating broom, made of the same material, was used to prepare hair-vein patterns; its straw was bound together to allow it to be held comfortably in the hand, with the bristles on its lower end having a spread of 25 to 30 centimeters.

Every marbler has his or her favorite tools. For myself, I have found small artist's brushes—inexpensive ones with moderately long, soft bristles—to be the best for dropping colors. These serve quite well for achieving good control, that is, for laying colors down in reasonably even rows. The more expensive sable brushes are not well adapted to this purpose, for their bristles are too stiff and do not release color freely. For Turkish or spot patterns, a slightly larger brush is required—thicker, with longer bristles, so it can be loaded with a larger amount of color. When this is tapped against the finger, or held about a foot above the size and shaken in a quick, abrupt way, it deposits color spots evenly throughout the size. The rice straw brush or beating broom is useful for making hair-vein patterns and for throwing down the ground color to achieve the shell design. I make these brushes myself, using broom straw obtained from a supplier to the broom-making trade. One can take a large bunch or patch of broom straw, being careful not to use the ends that are too thick, and glue the straw evenly around a small stick or dowel, afterward binding it tightly with a cord and gluing it further. The ends can be trimmed evenly with a paper cutter.

Colors can be laid on with a drop point or stylus, as we have observed before. This is a slower process, suitable mainly for using a needle stuck in a cork to emulate some of the old French patterns or for fantasy work, such as putting down successive color spots to be worked into the shape of flowers and other objects of nature. Some marblers today lay down colors by means of a drop bottle. This is a small bottle fitting into the palm of the hand; its cap allows color to flow through, drop by drop, when the bottle is turned upside down and its stopper is depressed.

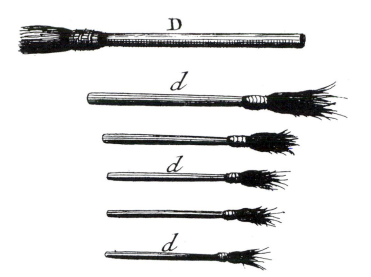

FIGURE 32. Assorted brushes for distributing color, as pictured in the Diderot-D'Alembert *Encyclopédie*.

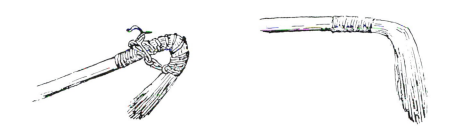

FIGURE 33. *Left*, the drop brush is being made to bend; *right*, the brush finally bent and ready for use.

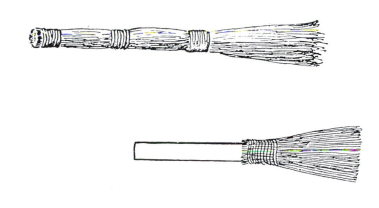

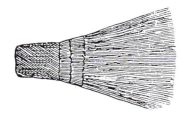

FIGURE 34. *Top*, the rice straw brush; *middle*, the beating brush; *bottom*, the large beating broom.

THE DUTCH APPARATUS AND THE MECHANICAL DISTRIBUTION OF COLOR

Without question, the even distribution of color is one of the greatest challenges to the marbler. It is difficult, when using brushes, to effect an even arrangement of colors on the surface of the size. For one thing, colors put down initially on one side of the trough will have expanded in the interval more than those put down later on the other. For another, colors fall from the brushes freely and indiscriminately, and too much of one here or another there can spoil the symmetry of the pattern. To circumvent this obstacle, makers sometimes employed special devices for distributing colors evenly, particularly for the pattern that came to be termed "Dutch" or "old Dutch." When discussing this pattern, Charles Woolnough advised that the colors not be scattered about indiscriminately but follow each other in a regular succession across the whole sheet of paper; to achieve this regularity, he recommended the use of a device he called the "Dutch apparatus."

The Dutch apparatus consists of a frame the size of the paper to be marbled; for making the Dutch or old Dutch pattern, two of these were required. Into each frame were inserted a number of wooden pegs, about 3/8 inch thick, fixed at equal distances about 2 1/2 or 3 inches apart. Small color pots or receptacles were assembled and arranged to correspond in location with the points on the frame, so that each point would drop easily into its respective color pot. With this device colors could be put down evenly and in a systematic and predetermined way to make the Dutch pattern (and a few others). The initial color, red, was put down with a brush. Then, the first frame was taken up and its points placed into color pots containing white only. The frame was positioned over the size and carefully let down until the tip of each peg touched the surface, leaving an even arrangement of white spots on the red. The other frame was taken up and its points placed into color pots containing blue, yellow, and green in staggered configurations, so that these colors were put down on the previously deposited white spots. The pattern then was completed by raking and combing, its proper definition having been achieved through the orderly placement of colors. The placard pattern discussed in the Diderot-D'Alembert article of 1765 similarly required an orderly and fixed arrangement of colors, but no mention is made there of depositing them in any way other than by brushes. A comb somewhat equivalent in form to the Dutch apparatus and pictured on one of the Diderot plates (Figure 36) was employed only for effecting curls in the pattern called "commun."

In his *Progress of the Marbling Art,* Josef Halfer discussed a similar apparatus for laying down colors evenly. His device, pictured in an advertisement at the end of the 1891 edition of his *Fortschritte der Marmorierkunst* (Figure 35), consisted of a frame from which four rows of needles protruded at regular intervals. The frame construction corresponded to a four-channel color receptacle so that

FIGURE 35. An 1891 advertisement for Halfer's apparatus for even color distribution.

each row of needles picked up a different color; in this way, large drops of color were put onto the size in a controlled and orderly fashion. A row of needles was positioned at the back of the device so that final combing could be achieved as well. Halfer observed that this device was especially effective for large-scale production of comb-marbles; it saved much time.

Besides the devices developed by Halfer and W. C. Doebbelin (pictured in Figure 19), and the attempt by Charles Williams of Philadelphia after the middle of the nineteenth century to accomplish color distribution mechanically (Figure 11), many others developed techniques and devices to achieve color symmetry in their patterns. More than a decade ago I visited a professional gilder and neophyte marbler who had devised such a machine. It had tracks, pulleys, gears, gear levers, and a complex set of contraptions designed to enable him to distribute color evenly on the size, and its weight was enormous. In spite of this—or perhaps because of it—his efforts to overcome the pitfalls of the process failed, and he became an enthusiast rather than a successful practicing craftsman. An engineer rather than an artist, he took great pride in his useless contraption because it was a mechanical marvel.

In reality, perfection is not the ultimate goal of the marbling process and usually is not even consistent with it. In those instances when perfection is achieved, the end product often appears mechanical and contrived. It is through the use of brushes and by acute observation, the maintenance of high standards, and self-discipline that one can better replicate the patterns of old and better uphold this ancient tradition. When we examine marbled papers in books that are 150 to 250 years old or more, we can readily discern that they are full of blemishes and imperfections. But these imperfections, as well as their harsh tones and original bright appearance, have been transposed and muted by the passage of time. It may even be said that the original imperfections add a certain charm to the present appearance of these old sheets, a condition difficult to emulate when attempting to reproduce the older patterns. On the other hand, sheets that have achieved perfection mechanically often look artificial and unnatural by comparison and have little of the innate charm of the hand-produced design. Marbling is a hand process developed long before sophisticated machinery came into existence, and if we accept it on these terms, we will realize that its imperfections contribute to rather than detract from its overall appeal.

COMBS

In his report on marbling to the Royal Society in 1662, John Evelyn spoke of "combing the liquor." Combing, a very old step in a very old process, was in all probability transferred to the West from the Near East, along with marbling itself, for combed designs can be seen on ancient Persian and Turkish sheets that survive today. Evelyn described the comb as an instrument "made with a straite stick, about the bignesse of the little finger, and as far as amounts to the bredth of the Trough, inserted with small pinns (such as Women use) at the distance of a quarter of an inch, but let the ends of the stick unpinn'd extend a little beyond the dimensions of the Trough's bredth for the better managing them of when you are to Comb the liquor." He also noted that "the finer the Comb is, the closer the teeth, the more curious and minute will bee your worke." The elaborate device depicted in the marbling scene in G. Smith's 1738 *The Laboratory; or, School of Arts* gives us an idea of what one early marbling comb looked like (Figure 8).

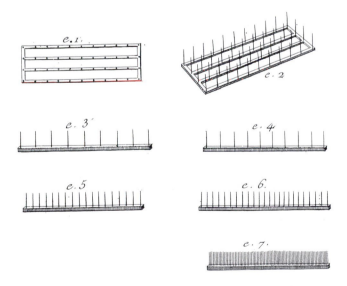

FIGURE 36. Combs illustrated in the Diderot-D'Alembert *Encyclopédie*.

The 1765 Diderot-D'Alembert encyclopedia article mentions several combs and their use in making various patterns then in production. The comb was described as a wooden bar with teeth, the bar being the thickness of a finger and the width (or length, depending upon the direction of combing) of the trough. The teeth—sharp pieces of iron 2 inches high, of the same shape and strength of an ordinary nail or pin—were positioned at equal distances throughout the bar or stick. The account's anonymous author called for the use of a number of these instruments, ranging from the "large" combs that had as few as nine teeth over a distance of a foot or more, to combs carrying as many as 104 teeth over the same distance. The latter were the instruments used in making the pattern known as "small comb" or "small Dutch."

The Diderot-D'Alembert work also described and depicted (the two drawings at the top of Figure 36) a combing apparatus for making "commun" or ordinary paper; it imparted a series of curl or snail-like configurations into the pattern. The device was an assembly of four of the larger combs, parallel and joined together with cross pieces; the combs contained eleven teeth on each bar. As I pointed out before, this instrument could also have been employed as a Dutch apparatus, for the makeup of the two is nearly identical, except that Woolnough's Dutch apparatus had wooden pegs rather than metal teeth. However, since the Diderot article says nothing about laying down colors with such a device, we must conclude that the French did not use the Dutch apparatus at this early time. This conclusion is reinforced by the fact that in describing patterns requiring color symmetry, such as the placard, for which color placement had to be exact, the Diderot author calls for placing colors on the size through the use of brushes alone.

In his 1758 *Handmaid to the Arts*, Robert Dossie noted that "the comb may be also of wood, and five inches in length: but should have brass teeth, which may be about two inches long, and placed at about a quarter of an inch distance from each other." Charles Woolnough's combs of about a century later were much more representative of those of a professional maker—which, indeed, he was. Their importance in contemporary English patterns (it should be remembered that the English, along with the Germans, excelled in combed patterns) is corroborated by the fact that Woolnough devoted nearly four full pages to these simple instruments and their use.

Woolnough divided the combs employed in his type of marbling into two types: top combs and bottom combs. The former was drawn along the surface of the size so that the teeth just touched the floating colors; the latter was positioned so that the points of its longer teeth dragged along the bottom of the trough as it was propelled through the size. According to Woolnough, the bottom combs (Figure 37) generally were made by a reed-maker, that is, by one who manufactured the peculiarly fine and uniformly regular wire apparatus used by silk weavers. These "they can divide with the nicest precision and exactness into any number of teeth to the inch; but twelve or thirteen to the inch is fine enough for any Nonpareil comb, if finer it is apt to drag."[9] He recommended that the teeth of the combs be made of brass wire, the smaller the pattern, the finer the wire.

Top combs (Figure 38) generally were crafted by the marblers themselves, since their construction was relatively simple. Pins, needles, and wire were used for the teeth, and paper, cardboard, and similar materials formed the frame. The quality of the final product depended on the skill of the individual attempting the task. The greatest difficulty in making such combs was (and still is) maintaining a uniform distance between the teeth, especially for a fine-toothed comb. It was necessary also to keep the points of the needles exactly straight and level so that they touched the surface of the size uniformly and at equal distances.

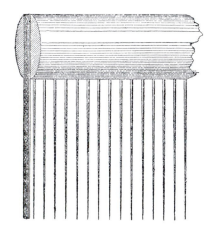

FIGURE 37. A section of Woolnough's bottom comb.

Woolnough's manual illustrated two other instruments of this genre (Figure 39). One, called a peg-rake, was a comb fashioned of wood that was as long as the entire length of the trough. In all probability, its bar was thicker than those of the fine combs used to complete patterns, and its teeth were wooden pegs. The marbler used this coarse instrument to draw through the spots of color deposited on the size, first in one direction and then in the other, back through the middle of the configurations previously drawn. This process distributed colors in long, thin lines so that they could be combed through afterward. The device was especially useful for making fine patterns such as nonpareil.[10] The second instrument was a comb or combination of two combs used to produce the pattern Woolnough referred to as "zigzag" or "antique zigzag." The two combs were attached together so that there was space of an inch or two between the teeth, with the teeth of one comb placed so that they were centered exactly between the teeth on the other. More will be said about this instrument later, for it can be employed to produce peacock and bouquet patterns, as well as for variations in shell designs.

In his *Mysterious Marbler* of 1854, James Sumner devoted just over one page to "The Combs We Use." His instruments were made of pieces of wood or millboard of the required length. The ends of the wires were filed smooth in order not to drag the size and colors. Josef Halfer's combs were made of pasteboard, and the teeth consisted of fine steel pearl needles or pins. Paul Kersten also used pasteboard for the frames, but covered it with asphalt sealer to enable it to withstand dampness. The only unusual comb used by these authorities was the so-called peacock comb. This device was made up of two identical combs mounted together inside a frame and attached in such a way that they moved sideways about 1/4

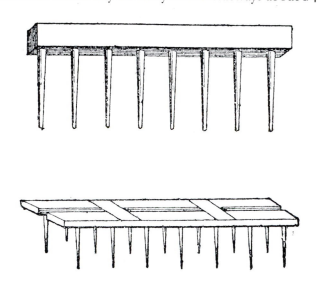

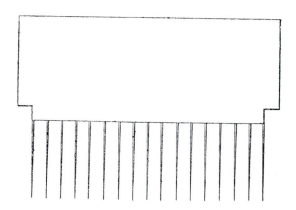

FIGURE 38. Woolnough's diagram of a top comb.

FIGURE 39. Woolnough's peg-rake and zigzag device.

inch in opposite directions; they could then be pushed or pulled back again to travel the other way. The operator pulled the ends apart and then pushed them together several times while passing the comb through the size, thus bringing the pattern together and then pulling it apart. When combed beforehand, the design that the Germans called "bouquet" resulted; when the size was dragged but left uncombed, the plainer peacock design resulted.

Although Halfer failed to illustrate the peacock comb, Paul Kersten did so in his *Marmorierkunst*, as Figure 40 shows. Like Halfer's device, Kersten's was made from pasteboard, lacquered to prevent water and moisture damage. Kersten advised the use of "insect pins" or steel pearl pins for the teeth. As he noted, combs of any size, with their needles or pins set in any number of configurations, may be used to produce various types of drawn patterns. Moreover, combs can be employed in crosswise fashion—that is, drawn across patterns that previously had been combed—to produce additional effects and patterns. This practice, in fact, is one of the center points of Halferian marbling. One of the earliest of the crosswise designs that arose out of the Halferian system was called the "American" pattern (no. 174 on Plate XXXVII).

THE SKIMMER

Marbling is a process which, like engraving on metal plates, requires a new and separate application of color for each sheet of paper treated or produced, so the medium—in marbling, the size—must be cleaned between operations. After the colors are thrown or laid onto the size, worked into patterns, and absorbed onto paper, residue color on the sides has to be removed so that the process can be repeated on a clean surface. This cleaning was done in earlier times by means of an instrument known as a skimmer, and the operation was known as "skimming the size." By the same token, each time marbling is commenced, or any time the size has been left standing for more than a few minutes, it has to be skimmed before colors can be thrown down, for during such intervals a skin builds up on its surface which impedes normal color expansion. (Franz Weisse likened this buildup on the size surface to the skin that forms on soup that has been left standing; in his *Art of Marbling* he describes how this situation can be turned to advantage to produce novel effects and specialty papers, showing jagged stars and other irregular shapes where the dropped color tore through this covering and spread out in odd ways.) [11] The device shown in Figure 41, reproduced from one of the plates in the Diderot encyclopedia, was described in the accompanying text as a thin piece of wood, about two inches deep and as wide as the narrow side of the trough, with somewhat beveled edges. It was fastened to a long stick, three or four feet long, which allowed the operator to extend it over the size and move it back and forth to skim off color in the process.

Because skimming is such an easy, uncomplicated operation, the literature says little about it or about any special skimming implement. Paul Kersten devotes a few sentences to the skimming board, noting in his *Marmorierkunst* that it was used in lieu of paper for cleaning residue color from the surface of the size. As he suggests, pieces of paper do the job just as well. One need only cut strips of newspaper the width of the trough and about two inches thick to accomplish this task. In the second, 1896 edition of his *Marmorierkunst*, J. C. Boeck illustrated the two implements shown here in Figure 42; he did not explain their use, but their obvious function was to skim off adulterated size.

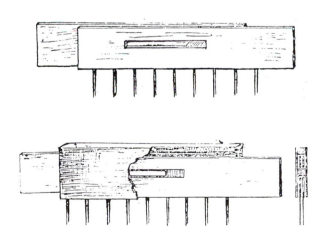

FIGURE 41. The French eighteenth-century skimmer.

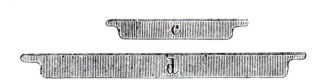

FIGURE 40. Diagrams of the peacock comb, reproduced from Paul Kersten's *Marmorierkunst*.

FIGURE 42. Skimmers used by the German marbler J. P. Boeck in the late nineteenth century.

DRYING OPERATIONS

The author of the Diderot-D'Alembert article describes the draining and drying of the sheets as two separate and distinct operations. One of these, it will be remembered, involved suspending the sheets over cords strung along the ceiling of the workshop in areas that did not interfere with other operations. If this were done immediately after marbling, however, mucilaginous size would drain off onto the floor, making it slippery and coating it with color that could be tracked about. Such undesirable results were averted by draining the sheets before they were hung. Prior to their suspension, marbled sheets were placed in frames set in a chase that was inclined to drain off any surplus gum and color into an accompanying receptacle.

Two methods of draining can be seen in the Diderot plate; they used approximately the same type of frames and differed only in the method of suspension and the types of receptacles employed to support them. The frames were a rectangular assembly of four pieces of lathing (sometimes five, with the fifth serving as a cross-piece to give additional strength and support) arranged with sufficient space between them to accommodate the largest sheet of paper to be marbled. Strings or cords were affixed to the sides of the frame in a crisscross fashion, thirty-six in each direction. A number of these frames could be stacked together. After a sheet had been marbled, it was laid on the network of strings on a frame, and another empty frame placed on top of it for the next sheet. The Diderot instructions indicate that the frames could be fixed to face one another and kept in an open and inclined position by roping them, as seen in the inset portion of Figure 43 and in enlarged form in Figure 44. Alternatively, they could be inclined in a large tub, one on top of the other, after fifty sheets had been decorated (Figure 43). A similar draining system is described in Fichtenberg's manual of 1852, so it seems likely that this was a standard operation in French marbling (although Fichtenberg may have derived such information from the Diderot description).

Our anonymous Diderot author relates that it took about fifteen minutes for the sheets to discharge their surplus gum and color, after which they were lifted from the frames, one by one, and hung over cords stretched in the rear of the workshop. After drying, they were waxed (if wax had not been added to the colors previously), burnished or glazed, sorted, packed, and shipped. According to Hugh Sinclair's manual, some marblers omitted the draining operation and suspended their sheets directly after marbling. Woolnough specified that a stick wider than the trough be placed on the sheet laying on the bath after marbling took place. The paper was doubled over it and lifted from the size, and placed on a rack to dry—what sort of rack, he does not say. In his manual on making colored papers, Fichtenberg also spoke of fashioning a drying frame by nailing strips of lath to upright

FIGURE 43. Two methods for draining size from the sheet after marbling.

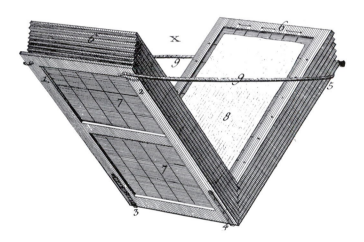

FIGURE 44. Frames or chases into which marbled sheets were placed for draining.

and crosssections of boards; the sheets then could be suspended from the laths. He further advocated setting a network of wooden trenches beneath the frame to collect the surplus gum and water that drained from the sheets as they dried.

MISCELLANEOUS EQUIPMENT

Apart from the foregoing materials and supplies, a number of other implements and utensils (frequently of the common, household variety) were and still are useful for carrying out the marbling process. Several of them were depicted on one or the other of the Diderot plates. For example, the Diderot description called for a large butter crock (Figure 45a) for mixing the size and a horsehair sieve (Figure 45b) for straining it. A large iron needle, set into a wooden handle (Figure 45c), was used to draw patterns on the size and for some of the specialized designs. A marble slab and pestle for grinding colors were also il-lustrated (Figure 45d), as was a knife for mixing them (Figure 45e). Other tools in the Diderot illustrations that are worthy of special notice are the lower portion of the apparatus—its bed and stone and handles—used for burnishing or polishing the decorated sheets and the flint or marbled slab on which the polishing took place (Figure 46).

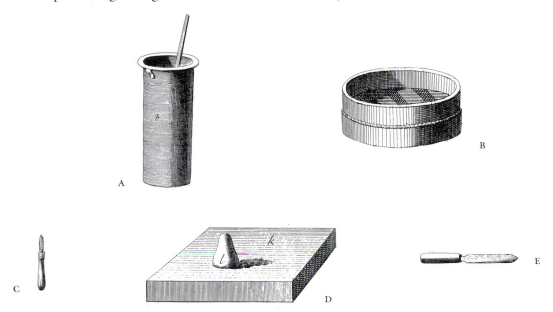

FIGURE 45. Common marbling tools: *a*, a large butter crock; *b*, a horsehair sieve; *c*, a large iron needle; *d*, a marble slab and pestle; *e*, a knife.

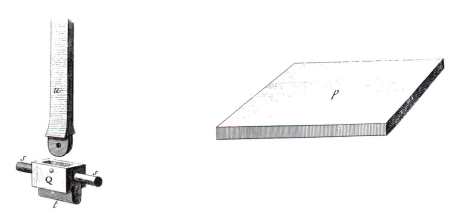

FIGURE 46. *Left*, an apparatus for burnishing or polishing; *right*, a slab on which marbled sheets were placed for polishing.

To end this review of the marbling process, and its equipment and tools, we note that one of the workmen in the Diderot scene is dipping book edges. He appears to be gripping them between boards, or binder's board, or a strong piece of leather. Pictured below (Figure 47) is a gripping device which Josef Halfer devised and advocated for this process. His method called for the use of C-clamps made of strong iron and eccentric in their movement, and were clamped around protective boards. They could be swung around so that all three edges of the book could be marbled easily.

As I pointed out in Chapter 10, by the late nineteenth century book edges also could be decorated mechanically, through the use of rollers invented by Wilhelm Leo and others. Two of "Leo's Mechanical Marblers" are shown in Figure 48. Any binder could use rollers to decorate the edges of his books without resorting to the messy, capricious, and tedious marbling technique—which required a great deal of trouble, effort, and costly and perishable supplies in exchange for limited results. The device usually consisted of two rollers mounted on a frame equipped with a handle. One roller was smooth and designed to accept and hold color, which it distributed to the other roller; this second roller contained a marbled design in relief on its surface. When the entire apparatus was passed over the edges of books that were held in a finishing or other type of press, the pattern was transferred simply and mechanically. Various colors were deposited into a pan or other receptacle and worked into configurations so that the pattern imparted to the book edges would approximate in coloration an actual marbled design.

FIGURE 47. Halfer's device for clamping and dipping book edges. Advertised at the end of the 1891 edition of his *Fortschritte der Marmorierkunst*.

FIGURE 48. "Leo's Mechanical Marblers," reproduced from the second, 1890 edition of J. W. Zaehndorf's *The Art of Bookbinding*.

13

Technical Aspects of the Craft, II: Chemical and Physical Bases and Basic Constituents and Ingredients

I F, as we have observed, the equipment needed to marble is in almost every respect the simplest imaginable, the ingredients that are necessary to the process are not. These mainly organic materials are far more complicated chemically and physically than they initially appear. Their individual chemical actions are quite specific, but the interplay between the chemical and physical factors that govern the process is critical for a system that has to be perfectly balanced. Thus, while the craft outwardly appears to be simplicity itself, it is in fact one of the most difficult to control and execute properly.

The U.S. Government Printing Office's Joint Research Bulletin, *The Process of Marbling Paper,* states that the whole marbling operation depends on a balance of relations between the chemical character and particle size of the color pigments and the viscosity and surface-tension phenomena of the mucilaginous bath on which the colors are suspended.[1] Further, the pigment particles must be surrounded by a film of a substance such as ox-gall in order to remain in suspension and not sink beneath the surface, for their weight exceeds the buoyant power of the gum solution. It is necessary for the operator to establish a proper balance between the viscosity of the gum bath and the buoyant power and dispersion properties of the pigments so that the colors may expand in thin films that can float on the surface of the size. Finally, the nature of the water employed and the absorbent quality of the paper used, among other factors, also have some influence on the successful execution of the process.

It is the interplay of these various elements and their judicious application and control by the operator (that is, his or her knowledge and ability to employ exactly the right materials at the right time and in the proper amounts and consistencies) that are critical to success or failure in achieving the charming and sometimes exquisite patterns that this process can produce. Before going on to consider the materials themselves, let us examine some of the

chemical and physical forces inherent in the process. This overview will better enable us to understand just how and why these materials come together to make this delicately balanced system work.

1. Underlying Principles of Colloidality and Surface Tension

Colloid science relates to micro-heterogeneous systems, that is, systems containing large molecules and/or small particles.[2] There are many types of colloidal systems, made up of mixtures of liquids, solids, and gases, they include aerosols, cement, dyestuffs, emulsions, ink, paint, paper, plastics, rubber, soil and many other materials. Processes relying heavily on colloidal surface phenomena and which are of interest to us here include detergency, emulsion polymerization, ion exchange, and wetting, to name a few. The factors that contribute most to the general nature of a colloidal system are particle size, shape, and flexibility; surface (including electrical) properties; particle-particle interaction; and particle-solvent interaction.

Particles in a colloidal dispersion are sufficiently large for definite surfaces of separation to exist between the particles and the medium in which they are dispersed. Thus, simple colloidal systems are two-phase systems. The phases are distinguished by the terms *dispersed phase* (for the phase forming particles) and *dispersion medium* (for the medium in which the particles are dispersed). Basically, colloidal systems are formed either through the degradation of bulk material usually by grinding (for example, the marbling pigments and colors) or through the aggregation of a molecularly dispersed supersaturated solution (for example, the marbling bath) from which the material in question precipitates in a suitably divided form. Since the particles of a dispersion usually have a density somewhat different from that of the dispersion medium, they will tend to accumulate, due to gravity, at the bottom or at the surface, with particle aggregation enhancing sedimentation.

If sedimentation takes place, the volume in the final sediment depends upon the extent of aggregation. When the particles aggregate to form a continuous network structure extending through the available volume and immobilizing the dispersion medium, the resulting semisolid or solid system is called a gel, the rigidity of which depends upon the number and strength of the interparticle links in the continuous structure. Hence, the material solvated in a gel becomes, to some extent, trapped and mechanically immobilized—wholly, in the case of a solid gel, or partially, in the case of a semi-solid one. The marbling medium, then, because of its semi-glutinous or mucilaginous nature, may be characterized as being a highly liquid gel. Marbling actually involves the interplay of two colloidal systems: one, consisting of a solid in the form of a pigment in water that is enclosed within the pores of a gel, interacts with the other made up of mucilaginous particles in water forming a highly hydrated gel.

In the absence of external forces, all suspended particles, regardless of size, have the same average translational kinetic energy. The motion of the individual particles of the suspending medium continuously changes direction as the result of random collisions with molecules, pursuing an irregular zigzag path. This random motion is called Brownian movement, so named for Robert Brown, the Scottish botanist who, in 1727, first observed the phenomenon with pollen grains in water.

The short-range forces of attraction existing between molecules are responsible for the existence of the liquid state. An examination of the surface-tension phenomena involved in liquid colloidal systems—for surface science is closely linked to colloidal science—shows that the fundamental property of liquid surfaces is its tendency to contract to the smallest area possible; the simplest properties of molecules in liquids account for this tendency. Molecules, for the most part, consist of unions of two or more atoms, which possess definite size and shape in all states of matter. In gases they are free to move relative to one another, but in liquids they are kept close to each other by the cohesional forces between them. In the interior of a liquid, each molecule is surrounded by others on every side and therefore is subject to attraction in all directions; that attraction is, on the average, uniform.

At the surface, on the other hand, conditions are entirely different. While molecules located within the bulk of the liquid are subjected to equal forces of attraction in all directions, those located at the surface experience unbalanced attractive forces resulting in a net inward pull. This occurs because the outward attraction is weak, limited to only the outside air and vapor pressure. Therefore, as many molecules as possible leave the surface for the interior of the liquid, and the surface tends to contract. This in turn causes the surface to diminish in area, for surface molecules are continually pulled inward more rapidly than others move outward to take their places. All the while the number of molecules at the surface is diminishing, and the contraction of the surface continues until the maximum number of molecules are in the interior. At that point, the surface is the smallest possible for a given volume.

The view that featured prominently in most of the older theories of capillarity held that the surface of a liquid had a special structure resembling a skin in tension, such as a stretched string or rubber membrane. This belief gradually gave way in this century to the idea that, while surface tension has physical reality, it is actually the equivalent of free surface energy. If a liquid surface contracts spontaneously, there is free energy associated with it, and work must be done to extend the surface; in molecular terms, when the surface is extended, molecules must be brought from the interior to counter the inward attractive forces. This results, when equilibrium is reached between the surface and the interior of a liquid mass, in a slightly smaller density of molecules at the surface than in the interior.

The modern view of surface tension is based on a statistical model, which defines it as the force acting at right angles to any line of unit length on the liquid surface. The theory states that in the interior of a liquid the spacing of molecules is such that the attractive and repulsive forces exactly balance. At the surface, however, the spacing is slightly greater, so that an attraction between neighboring molecules results in a tension there. This statistical model proposes that the tension does not depend on the degree of extension of the surface, but remains constant. There is, however, a continual interchange of molecules between the interior and the surface because, as we have seen, molecules in a fluid are free to move relative to one another. As a result, surface tension can no longer be properly characterized by the old analogy of the tension of a stretched string or rubber sheet, since either substance would break if any particle left them.

What happens when two substances that do not mix come into contact with one another, as happens in marbling? When a quantity of a practically insoluble and nonvolatile substance is placed on the surface of a liquid, it may behave in one of two ways: it may remain as a compact drop, leaving the rest of the surface clean, or it may spread over the surface. In order for the substance to spread, its molecules must attract those of the liquid on which it has been placed more than they attract each other; that is, the work of adhesion between the two substances must be greater than the cohesion of the substance itself. Provided that these energy requirements for spreading are fulfilled, as many possible of the molecules of the spreading substance move into direct contact with the underlying liquid, forming a surface film one molecule thick.

In marbling, when a drop of fluid color—consisting of a pigment and a binding agent suspended in a liquid—is placed on the surface of the size, its weight will cause it to fall to the bottom of the trough. It is the surface tensions between the two liquids and the interfacial tension between them that determine whether or not the color spreads. A lipid substance (that is, a fat or an analogous ester), in the form of bile salts or a saponaceous material or some other substance having a close chemical affinity to bile salts, must be added to the color preparation to alter its particular surface tension and allow it to spread. Its molecules will then attract the fluid size more than they attract each other and they will adhere to the size rather than to themselves, spreading out as much as they are able and forming the necessary thin film of color.

The marbling system, it will be remembered, constitutes a solid-in-liquid dispersion, with the size a glutinous polysaccharide (i.e., a carbohydrate decomposed by hydrolysis into two or more molecules of simple sugars) forming a highly hydrated gel. The terms "hydrophilic" (water-loving) and "hydrophobic" (water-fearing) are employed to describe the tendency of a liquid medium to become wetted. The molecules of surface-active materials have a strong affinity to interfaces because they contain both hydrophilic and lipophilic (oil-loving) regions. When bile salts, which have a strong hydrophilic tendency and are partially lipid as well, are added to the color solution, it becomes motivated to spread out in this semiliquid dispersion after being deposited in spots there. What we have, in effect, is a solid-liquid (gel) suspension (rather like toothpaste), which, when brought into contact with paper, penetrates its pores and dries, thereby resulting in a solid-solid suspension on the order of a pigmented plastic.

With this general scheme of the underlying chemical and physical nature of the process in mind, we now can examine some of the constituents used to create the colloidal mass that supports the entire system.

2. Marbling Size

The marbling size, or mucilaginous or gelatinous bath, is obtained by boiling various plants or vegetable matter with water. As they cook, they absorb the water and expand by the rupture of their cellular structures, releasing their gum and mucilage. Mucilage, along with gum, starch, and sugar, is found in many plants but especially in the outer skins of seeds and in many roots, barks, stems, and leaves. A variety of vegetable and other materials have been recognized over the ages as providing suitable substances for marbling size (that is, for making up the dispersed phase of the suspension medium or the colloidal particles of the gel), and we shall examine the most important of these shortly. But first a few general observations concerning the size.

The density of the size depends on the quantity of water in which it is dissolved. Its consistency is also affected by changes in temperature, since the surface tension of most liquids decreases with increasing temperatures: the warmer the size, the more mobile it is; the colder, the more rigid. The consistency of the size is also affected by aging. As gravity pulls its molecules downward, particles tend to accumulate on the bottom when the size has been left standing, with the part above becoming thinner. In addition, its sugars and starches are transformed chemically over a period of time into lactic and other organic acids; the process can only be slowed down by the addition of "preserving fluid" and other agents that are added to protect the size against bacterial degradation. Many other elements—humidity and contamination of the size with color, for example—can influence the operation of this process, and novices graduate to the status of seasoned marblers when they can not only recognize and even anticipate these pitfalls but learn to control them and turn them to their advantage.

At the instigation of Franz Weisse and Fräulein Kollenkark[3] of the Landeskunstschule in Hamburg, F. V. von Hahn conducted numerous chemical experiments with marbling sizes and published his findings in two articles in the *Kolloid-Zeitschrift* in 1932.[4] After briefly reviewing the basic steps of this handcraft method, Hahn commented, "we have formed the view that there is scarcely any work method that is beset with so many colloidal problems as this."[5] He related that there were several important physical and chemical factors involved in marbling: (1) the viscosity of the size; (2) the extent of dispersion of the coloring matter; (3) the surface activity of the admixture to the coloring matter (i.e., the bile fluid or other dispersing agents); (4) the loading phenomena during the maceration of the paper to which the colors would be transferred; (5) the surface orientation according to Langmuir's precepts.[6] Hahn defined the size as a primary film and the extended coloring matter as a secondary film. In all, he tested ten or more materials as marbling sizes, of which we shall discuss six; for all intents and purposes, however, the two most important are gum tragacanth and carragheen moss.

GUM TRAGACANTH

We have already seen that, up to perhaps a century ago, gum tragacanth was the staple ingredient for making marbling size (it still remains in use in the Near East). All contemporary literature on this subject (and it is extensive, although often brief and of a limited or derivative nature) from the seventeenth century until after the middle of the nineteenth attests to its primacy, to the exclusion of almost all other types of material. Charles Woolnough emphasized gum tragacanth's importance in 1853, and even as late as 1881 in the reissue of his important manual, when he stated that "of all of the varieties of gum, there is but one that is of any use for the purpose of marbling, and that is called gum tragacanth, or gum dragon—called by some druggists gum elect."[7] The use of this commodity in Europe for other purposes was undoubtedly ancient, for gum tragacanth appears on old drug lists and in the early literature of materia medica and pharmacy, where its use was advocated to increase the viscosity of solutions and as a demulcent (that is, as a remedy for soothing an irritated or inflamed mucous membrane). Woolnough advised that, for the purpose of marbling, one could not be too particular in the choice of this article, "for it is like the foundation of a building: if that be faulty, the whole fabric will fall to the ground."[8]

Gum tragacanth is the product of various species of *Astragalus* found in Greece and Turkey. According to one source, the name tragacanth means goat thorn,[9] and the best gum comes in the form of hard, flat, ribbonlike pieces that have a hornlike appearance. Its mucilaginous consistency is thicker than that of carragheen moss and it is more durable, but it is not so delicate in its reactions to colors and, consequently, does not need quite as much care in its preparation as does Irish moss.

According to directions given in the Diderot-D'Alembert article—as well as in other early literature—tragacanth size is prepared by soaking about a pound of the gum for three days. This same source advises, as do Woolnough and other authorities, that the gum should be large, white, hard, and flaky and that the water in which it is mixed should be rain or river water. The material swells when mixed with water and becomes semifluid; it is then diluted with more water until the proper consistency is achieved, after which it is strained for use as marbling size. Size is usually made overly thick, and thinned down to the proper consistency when finally used. If made too thin at this final stage, it can be brought to the proper viscosity through the addition of some of the stiffer size.

The proper strength or weakness of the size (that is, its higher or lower viscosity or fluidity) has to be altered to accommodate the requirements of different patterns to be made; the success or failure depends on this factor alone. Its proper consistency is determined in a number of ways, as there is no reliable instrument, even today, to assure accuracy on this point.[10] By and large, this task is performed visually or through trial and error. An experienced marbler will know immediately after dropping the initial colors and assessing their expansive characteristics whether the size is too thick or too thin. The Diderot-D'Alembert article mentions several alternative methods for testing the size, for example, to stir it and observe how quickly it foams or moves about in circles. Franz Weisse's advice was more precise: in the event that the dropped colors did not spread out to 12 to 15 centimeters, the size was adjudged too thick and was thinned down either with water or a thinner gum solution (or vice versa, depending on the circumstances). It is my experience that a seasoned marbler can determine the propriety

of the size simply by running his or her fingers through it and stirring it about. As Weisse advised, this is also a good preparation for the marbling which follows for the size seems to take on the bodily warmth of the operator and becomes livelier and more relaxed in the process.[11]

In Woolnough's time, marbling size was prepared in approximately the way advocated in the French article a century before. By the middle of the nineteenth century, however, other materials had been introduced, although they seem to have served chiefly to supplement the tragacanth size, to obtain a stronger and more balanced solution according to the requirements of specific patterns. Three additional materials mentioned by Woolnough as sources of marbling size were plantago (flea seed), linseed (flax seed), and carragheen (Irish moss).

PLANTAGO, OR FLEA SEED

Of the three, plantago was by far the most highly recommended in Woolnough's time, being particularly useful, he advised, when employed in combination with tragacanth size, for making Spanish and French patterns. *Plantago psyllium* (fleabane or flea seed), a short-stemmed shrub widely distributed throughout much of Europe, contains a large amount of plant mucilage. Marbling size was prepared from it merely by saturating it with boiling water and stirring. This shrub yielded a powerful mucilage that remained stable and usable for a number of days; because it is quite viscous, it was not used for comb or drawn patterns since, as Halfer later remarked, the colors would be drawn along by the stylus or rake or draw point without being cut. Plantago was, however, a useful adjunct to tragacanth for stiffening for Spanish and other patterns requiring a stouter and more gripping size.

LINSEED, OR FLAX SEED

Linseed, or flax seed, was prepared in about the same way as flea seed; it was deemed less useful by Woolnough because it quickly decomposed and turned to water. Halfer noted that linseed mucilage is as viscous as that of fleabane. In spite of this, the marbling directions John Hannett supplied in his *Bibliopegia* (1835 and later editions), which were intended only for the decoration of book edges, called for linseed as the size material. It is easily obtainable in health food stores today.

CARRAGHEEN, OR IRISH MOSS

In Woolnough's day, carragheen or Irish moss (sometimes referred to as Icelandic moss) was utilized essentially as an additive to tragacanth size, especially for the nonpareil pattern, although he notes that it could be employed alone. Woolnough undoubtedly called for its use in drawn patterns because, in view of its delicate nature, it enabled finer combing. My own experience has indicated that carragheen size is probably the best medium for producing finely combed and drawn patterns; it allows the most delicate forms to be created. Woolnough directed that the moss be soaked, then boiled for an hour or two; after cooling, it was strained and well beaten with tragacanth size before being put into the trough. Later authorities claimed that carragheen size decomposed too quickly and became watery and useless, but Woolnough remained silent on this point. His manual and Hannett's work on bookbinding are the only sources I have noticed that refer to sizes other than tragacanth before the modern era of marbling that commenced with the work of Josef Halfer.

Halfer's investigations, carried on in the later decades of the nineteenth century, resulted in the adoption—first by himself, later by exponents of his system, and ultimately by almost every marbler in the Western world—of carragheen as the staple for making marbling size. When reading Halfer's manual, one cannot but be impressed with the scientific manner and curiosity with which he approached the problem of marbling size—and, for that matter, all of the ingredients and methods of this art. He not only investigated a great number of plants and vegetables in order to determine their mucilage content, but also made extensive researches concerning the gum, starch, and sugar content of each and their homogeneity and viscosity. His researches over a period of time proved to him that carragheen moss surpasses all other glutinous materials in the quantity and quality of the mucilage it contains, although he approved a number of other products for marbling, such as tragacanth, plantago, salep, linseed, and even quince seed. His decided preference, however, was for carragheen.

Centuries ago, the people of the southern counties along the coast of Ireland began harvesting an abundant red seaweed that today is known most familiarly as Irish moss. In Gaelic they called it *carraghéen,* and mixed it with milk to form a sort of pudding.[12] This red lichen or alga, *Chondus crispus,* grows in abundant quantities on the cliffs of the Atlantic Ocean and North Sea and off the coasts of Ireland and Iceland as well. It also grows abundantly off the coast of New England and in the Maritime Provinces of Canada, where it may be found in the intertidal waters along four thousand miles of jagged Nova Scotia coastline and around Prince Edward Island. Varieties also thrive in oceans off the islands of the Philippines and Indonesia, off the coasts of Chile, Mexico, and Korea, and in still other regions. It takes approximately sixty days for fronds to attach themselves to reefs and rocks and grow to maturity; they grow at the rate of about three percent a day.

The starch and mucilage this seaweed yields have become an important and profitable staple in the modern food industries, where it is used as food thickeners and for many other purposes. It has served in the making of toothpaste, drugs, and even air fresheners; in industry it has been employed, for example, in the glazing of metal, where it has been found useful for suspending pigmented frits. At least four large American companies now harvest

carragheen and prepare it by drying and cleaning it and subjecting it to a series of chemical procedures in which the starch and mucilage are extracted through an alcohol process. After reduction, the material is supplied to food processors and other manufacturers in fine, powdered form, under a variety of trade names.

We have seen that probably the major factor that prevented the greater use of carragheen as a marbling size in former times was its tendency to spoil rapidly. When boiled with water, its sugar and starch quickly fermented and turned to lactic acid, and the size soon became watery-thin and useless. Halfer remedied this problem by adding borax, a natural salt with strong antiseptic qualities, which delayed fermentation and decomposition for a long time. Paul Kersten explained in his *Marmorierkunst,* with regard to the spoilage of carragheen size:

The indefatigable investigations of Josef Halfer succeeded after years of toil in overcoming this drawback, for he found the means to make it usable for months at a time, up to a duration of sixty days. This is the so-called "Halfer Preservation of Carragheen Size." This universal size is the most ideal base that one can think of and to it alone is thanks due for the popularity which the art of marbling has enjoyed in recent years. The size can be prepared as little as one day before use.[13]

In his *Formulas for Bookbinders,* Louis Kinder (who espoused the Halferian system of marbling and sold Halfer's marbling colors and other supplies) advised that half an ounce of powdered borax and two teaspoonfuls of beech wood creosote be added to twelve ounces of good, dried carragheen and twenty-seven quarts of water; this proportion he said, would be sufficient to hold it fast. In recent times, formaldehyde and formalin, a dilute solution of formaldehyde (about 37% by the Merck index), have been used as preservatives of carragheen size. Franz Weisse observed in his 1940 *Die Kunst des Marmorierens* that a thimbleful of formalin was sufficient to preserve about five gallons of the size, although I have found that it takes four ounces to preserve twenty gallons for six weeks to two months.

There are many recipes for preparing carragheen size, all of them useful and legitimate. Importantly, the muci-late content differs in various mosses, and the considerations of stiffness and other factors have to be determined in each case by trial and error. My own formula calls for the addition of a given quantity of dried moss (the fine-limbed sort is best)—say, five ounces to six quarts of clean water; soft water must be used as lime or calcium carbonate and other harsh mineral salts inhibit the action of the colors on the size. In regions where hard water predominates, this problem can be surmounted by using distilled water (or rainwater, as called for in the early literature and in the manuals by Woolnough, Sumner, and others in the nineteenth century) or by adding a few pinches of borax or baking soda to the water. After a small quantity of formalin has been added, the mixture is cooked slowly for an hour and then brought to a boil. A galvanized bucket or pail is an adequate container for this purpose, and a gas flame is recommended, for it can best be controlled to bring the preparation to a boil in the prescribed time. At the end of an hour, a brown crust will appear at the top, but soon begins to break up under boiling and is supplanted by a white foam. The mixture should boil for three minutes more (stirred all the while), and be removed from the flame, whereupon three quarts of cold water are added. This preparation is then allowed to stand for twenty-four hours, after which it is strained and restrained. This method yields two gallons of a thickish, high quality size that can be thinned down according to need. If the moss is of high quality, this formula yields the best size obtainable.

Several of the American companies that harvest and process carragheen moss for industrial and technological purposes will supply marblers with their product in powdered form. One has only to add a predetermined amount of water to ready the size for use, which usually takes from 24 to 48 hours, with another week's rest needed to allow the powder to dissolve fully. Unfortunately, the powdered product can only be obtained in large quantities; fifty pounds is the minimum usually sold at one time. Not only does cost present a problem for occasional marblers, but the powder retains its maximum potency for only about two years, after which it begins to lose some of its thickening and gripping ability. I have used powdered carragheen from a single lot for up to five years, but it became less potent after two, and sometimes I had to double the amount of powder to obtain the proper consistency. When fresh, 16 to 18 ounces of powder will produce 20 gallons of size, which, I have noted, can be preserved for several months by the addition of four ounces of formaldehyde.

Dried carragheen moss can be obtained from health stores and other sources and, while not so easily prepared, yields a slightly better size than does the powder. With formaldehyde as a preservative, it holds for a very long time if tightly capped. I once stored a few gallons for five years and found it as good as newly prepared size, for a skin had formed on top and kept it airtight.

It is well known that, when marbling on carragheen size, one must first apply a coat of alum to the paper so that the colors will hold fast, just as in textile dyeing a mordant is added to the dyestuff to form an insoluble compound to fix the color in the fiber. On the other hand, none of the old manuals, when discussing the use of tragacanth size, mention the need to apply such a mordant beforehand. This discrepancy can be attributed to several factors. First, earlier marblers almost always used soft, unsized paper, not today's harder, sized sheets. Second, the more viscous nature of tragacanth size and its particular colloidal properties may have held the colors

better and helped them to transfer to these older papers. Finally, as we shall see in the next chapter, earth and lake colors were employed in marbling through the middle of the nineteenth century; when these pigments were made, they were bonded to a metallic oxide, with alum or potassium mainly being used, so that a mordant was infused right into them, obviating the need to apply another to the paper. Halfer remarks succinctly that when earth colors are used on tragacanth size they can be transferred onto paper not prepared with alum.

SALEP

The U.S. Government Printing Office pamphlet, *The Process of Marbling Paper,* informs us that (like plantago-psyllium or fleabane) radix salep, the dried tubers of several species of orchids, will provide an excellent marbling size. Salep comes in round pieces, quite flat, yellowish white, horn-like, semidiaphanous, very hard, and without taste or smell. Salep formerly was imported from Iran, but the same species now grown elsewhere will furnish a good quality gum. It is chiefly used today for finishing silks and for medicinal purposes, and can be purchased in powdered form in drugstores. As a marbling size, radix salep possesses fine qualities similar to that of carragheen moss, but it is more expensive. Two and a half ounces boiled in six quarts of water until the powder is fully dissolved yields a good size.

GUM HOG

Gum hog or hog gum (also known as karaya gum) is another product used for marbling size at the professional level. This gum resin is obtained from a West Indian tree or from similar varieties of tropical American timber trees. Like tragacanth, it comes in dry lump form, and is soaked in water overnight; later, it is boiled with additional water until the proper consistency is obtained, and some borax is added to preserve it. This resin offers a good source of mucilage, and, because of its low cost and general availability, was commonly used in recent times for commercial marbling. Edward Artesani has informed me that this was the material employed for many years in the Riverside Press's bindery for marbling the edges of *Webster's New International Dictionary of the English Language* and other works; *The Process of Marbling Paper* reports that this preparation was adopted also by the Government Printing Office for marbling book edges. Gum hog neither possesses the fine properties nor produces the excellent detail of most of the other gums employed for marbling, and so is not well adapted to fine pattern work; yet under skillful manipulation it can yield good results. According to the recipe provided in *The Process of Marbling Paper,* twelve ounces will produce ten gallons of size. The same source also cautions that one pint of oxalic acid must be added to that preparation if the colors are to expand on the size, and also to prevent the sudden and uncontrolled spread of pigments on the surface of the bath.

OTHER PREPARATIONS

Any starchy or glutinous material may be employed as a medium for marbling paper or book edges. In his studies of the colloidality of marbling size, F. V. von Hahn experimented with several others, including potato starch, quince seeds, arrowroot, peptone, ithyphallus, and peridium. According to Halfer, the leaves of mallows, coltsfoot, and marshmallows yield gum—although in lesser amounts—that can be used for marbling purposes. And in his 1940 marbling manual, Franz Weisse noted that fresh and thinly cooked wheat starches had been employed for marbling; in particular, a contemporary glue product with the trade name of "Glutofix." Tim Thrift observed in his *Modern Methods of Marbling Paper* that a satisfactory base for supporting the colors could be obtained by melting bookbinder's flexible glue (made of hide glue, glycerol, and water) and thinning it with water. Thrift's size, however, was intended only to be used in combination with oil colors in the "modern" method of marbling with which he was specifically concerned.

3. Bile Salts and Other Dispersing Agents

Along with the mucilaginous size and colors, bile fluid (or a similar constituent) makes up the third essential ingredient for marbling: this component alters the surface tension of the color solution and permits it to spread out on the size and come into full play. Over the ages, ox-gall has been the agent usually employed for this purpose: James Sumner described this substance in his *Mysterious Marbler* as "that which imparts life to the colours, making them spread and float upon the surface of the size." Indeed, without the addition of gall, the colors would sink to the bottom of the size. "But," Sumner counseled his readers, "only impart a few drops of gall, as the case may require, and you impart the lifegiving power, and put in motion the otherwise motionless color."[14] Franz Weisse went even further in extolling the magical qualities of this liquid. Referring to ox-gall as the method's sustaining and driving force, he observed, "whoever it was who had the notion to employ the gall of oxen for this purpose must have stood in compact with the Devil."[15]

Ox-gall (or sometimes the bile fluid of fish) was mentioned as an essential ingredient in the very earliest marbling literature; it continues to be as important an additive to the colors as it was centuries ago, although soap compounds, which act physicochemically in the same way as gall, have at times been used instead or as a supplement. Bile fluid was also an essential element in making tempera and watercolor paints in earlier times: a natural wetting agent, it alters the surface properties of the pigments and plays an important part in any colloidal system in which

pigments are involved. When ground to a certain point, individual particles of color tend to agglomerate rather than reduce further under pressure. Consequently (as Marjorie Cohn points out in her *Wash and Gouache*),[16] John Bates recommended in his 1634 treatise on *The Mysteryes of Nature and Art* and, specifically, in *The Third Booke of Drawing, Limning, Colouring, Painting, and Graving,* that the colors be ground with the "gall of a neat." This gall—because part of the bile salts it contains are soluble in water—promotes the penetration of particle clumps with water. Similarly, the Diderot-D'Alembert marbling article advised that gall be added to the colors, along with water and a little gum tragacanth (the latter to make the mass more cohesive).

Gall, or bile fluid, is a yellowish, yellowish-brown, or green secretion produced in the liver of all animals, in that organ's role as an exicrene gland.[17] It is a solution of detergent-like molecules that regulates intracellular lipid metabolism; it disperses and transports a number of intracellular membrane lipids into bile, and removes unwanted molecules, especially excess cholesterol. Thus, bile plays a major role in promoting fat digestion and absorption. In man and some other primates, half the hepatic bile remains in the biliary region or gut undergoing continuous recycling there; the other half enters the gallbladder for concentration and storage. In response to hormonal influences during eating, the gallbladder contracts over a fifteen to forty-five minute interval, and eighty percent of its contents discharge into the duodenum. The gallbladder, therefore, acts as a holding tank and mechanical pump for the enterohepatic circulation.

Bile salts, a major component of bile fluid, are the soluble sodium and potassium salts of a family of hydroxyl-substituted cholanic acids ultimately deriving from the hepatic catabolism of cholesterol. The primary ones are cholic acid and chenodeoxycholic acid. The action of intestinal bacteria on these produces secondary (deoxycholic and lithocholic acids) and tertiary bile acids. The bile salts are detergent or soaplike molecules that are very soluble in water because they form micelles, or polymolecular aggregates; the micelles are so arranged that the hydrophobic or water-fearing parts of the molecules are directed toward the center of the aggregates while the hydrophilic or water-loving groups project into the bulk water phase. In addition to salts, bile contains phospholipids (primary lecithin), unesterified cholesterol, pigments, and a mixture of proteins, all dissolved with electrolytes in water.[18] Lecithin and cholesterol molecules are insoluble fatty molecules principally found in cell membranes. In bile, they are brought into aqueous solution by the bile salts, which form mixed micelles with these otherwise insoluble molecules. The mixed micelles contain all the fatty (or hydrophobic) parts of the molecules in their interiors and all the water-loving (hydrophilic) groups remain on the outside, interacting with water molecules. The other molecules of bile—bile pigments and proteins—are water-soluble and hence do not require a "micellar sink" to be transported in a fluid that is between eighty-five and ninety-seven percent water. Bile salts, then, cause fat molecules to become mixed with water by means of mixed micelle formation, a process that is termed "micellar solubilization" today, or "hydrotropy" in the older literature.

Besides true micellar solubilization induced by bile salts, bile can disperse otherwise insoluble solid particles in a colloidal suspension or dispersion. If the soluble pigment used in marbling is ground sufficiently fine, molecules of bile salts and lecithin will adhere to the pigment particles by hydrophobic interaction, and confer a net charge on them. The surface charge will prevent the particles from agglomerating, the polar groups of the amphiphiles (i.e., both the hydrophilic and hydrophobic micelles) will induce "wetting," and the Brownian movement—that is, the rapid vibratory movement exhibited by the particles in suspension—will prevent sinking. Soap molecules and the molecules of synthetic detergents will act in the same way. Like bile salts, they are water-soluble and are capable of forming micelles in water, although the structures of their molecules are different.

The major bile salt in fish bile is usually taurocholate. Because fish bile contains alcohol sulfates, which are capable of inducing particle dispersion, taurocholate's action may not be so different from mammalian bile salts; its low protein and lecithin content makes it cleaner and less subject to oxidative destruction.[19] The use of fish bile is recommended in some of the earliest Western literature on marbling, for example, in the *Kunst- und Werck-Schul* of 1707 and in Robert Dossie's classic account of 1758; however, the majority of accounts called for the use of ox-gall, possibly because it was much easier to acquire, and, as time went on, fish gall was only mentioned as a secondary and alternative dispersing agent.

Though the use of ox-gall is advocated in marbling literature from early on, it was not until the publication of Charles Woolnough's manual in 1853 that an exact method was outlined for obtaining this essential product. According to Woolnough, the surest way of getting the genuine article was by procuring it just as it came from the bladder of an animal, that is, by first acquiring, from a butcher or slaughterhouse, one or more gallbladders and then draining the fluid from them. Woolnough advised his readers to be careful not to obtain a diluted product, for some butchers in his day were not above watering down the fluid. He further observed that, though the gall of some animals was thick and ropy, its consistency would thin if it was kept a while and it would lose none of its properties: "In fact, gall is all the better for being kept some time, and is none the worse for stinking, excepting the disagreeableness of the odour to those using it."[20]

Josef Halfer states in his manual that the preparation of ox-gall for marbling is a simple process. He directs the marbler to take a quart of fresh ox or fish bile and put it in a bottle approximately one and a half to two times its volume. After one half bottle of absolute alcohol has been added, the bottle is shaken and left to stand for two to three weeks. During this interval, all particles of gum and fatty substances will fall to the bottom of the jar, with the separated bile fluid left floating at the top in the form of a thin, pure, and diaphanous liquid—brownish-yellow or greenish in color, depending on the diet of the creature from which it was obtained. In comparing the various galls, Halfer noted that fish gall, if it could be obtained in sufficient quantities, would be the most useful of all. He also observed that the addition of alcohol causes the precipitation of glutinous and fatty substances and prevents the gall from decomposing, adding that it can be kept for years without spoiling. The addition of alcohol to bile prevents putrefaction through bacterial and fungal infection (for native bile is a superior culture medium that encourages the growth of organisms). Alcohol will precipitate all bile proteins and it may precipitate some lecithin. It also breaks micelle formation, thereby producing a true monomeric solution of the major bile components and making this product more suitable for marbling purposes.

I have found Paul Kersten's method of preparing ox-gall outlined in his *Marmorierkunst* to be eminently satisfactory. One can procure the bladders of cows or steers from a slaughterhouse or from any person who attends to the slaughter of animals. The charge is usually slight, and sometimes there is no charge at all. Merely have a pail or bucket on hand and most butchers will gladly accommodate you, for this organ is a waste product in their estimation. After a day or two, a few gallbladders taken from recently slaughtered beasts will release a great amount of fluid to fill your bucket or pail. Afterward, discard the gallbladders but retain the fluid, and add to each quart of ox-gall one-fourth quart of alcohol. This bottle preparation should be tightly capped and shaken, then left standing, undisturbed, in a cool room for six to eight weeks. During this interval, its fatty and proteinaceous content will settle to the bottom and form a white, solid mass. The clear liquid on top should be transferred into a second, clean bottle, with care taken to ensure that the fatty sediment does not run out. The gall is now ready for use.

Kersten does not specify the kind of alcohol to use. The common drugstore variety of isopropyl rubbing alcohol, which usually is about 70 percent by volume, has worked well for me. It preserves bile fluid so that several gallons can last ten years or more—after all, it is dispensed drop by drop—and it seems to improve with age. The alcohol also has the advantage of imparting a sweetish smell to the preparation that is not at all objectionable and distinguishes it from other preparations in drop bottles and similar containers.

4. Alum

Most authorities consider size, colors, and bile fluid the essential elements in paper marbling, but the more one looks into the dynamics and mechanics of this craft, the more one is impressed with the crucial role that alum plays, either directly or indirectly. Alum, I would venture to say, is as much an essential constituent of the process as the other three.

Alum, a double sulfate of aluminum and potassium, was widely used in marbling in early times, for it made up the metallic base to which pigments were bonded to create the lake colors, the ones, according to Paul Adam and others, best suited to this particular medium. Additionally, alum, potassium, or a combination of the two was naturally present in earth and metallic colors. Today, however, when entirely different colors are in use that do not contain such agents, alum serves as the principal mordant that combines with the dyestuffs and forms an insoluble compound to fix the color to the paper.

Insofar as I have been able to determine, alum was not mentioned in the marbling literature issued before the publication of Josef Halfer's *Fortschritte der Marmorierkunst* in 1885. The sole exception occurs toward the end of the Diderot-D'Alembert encyclopedia article, as the second of nineteen observations on the ways of making marbled paper. We are told that "there are some who claim that it is necessary to add alum to the gum tragacanth solution at the time when you grind the colors."[21] Halfer devoted a few pages to the subject in his manual, remarking that in order to achieve beautiful results from his colors, one must wet the book edges or the paper to be marbled with concentrated alum water or the colors would not take but run or wash off.[22]

Halfer's recipe is relatively easy to follow. He directed that thirteen ounces of alum be added to two quarts of water and the preparation heated until the alum had entirely dissolved. After cooling, the solution was bottled and tightly capped. (Because, as Halfer observed, alum is only sparingly soluble when used directly with cold water, it would be too weak if not prepared in this way.) Prior to marbling, the book edges or papers were sponged over with the cold concentrated alum solution and allowed to partially dry for five to eight minutes: then the marbling could commence.

While Halfer said nothing about the quality and source of the alum he used, he undoubtedly used whatever was readily available, for this is a product of common household use. Today, alum can be purchased over-the-counter in drugstores, as it still has medicinal uses, being employed internally as an emetic and locally as an astringent and styptic. Acquiring alum in this way, however, is expensive because drugstores stock it in its purest, most refined, and costliest form. Franz Weisse observed that any alum intended for industrial purposes will serve well; I

have found that the item sold in craft shops supplying textile dyers is relatively cheap and very satisfactory, and it can be procured in large quantities—say, thirty or fifty pounds at a time. In a solution prepared in advance, it separates when cold and sinks to the bottom of the container in the form of small particles; Weisse recommended that fresh alum always be used and that it be applied to the paper in as warm a state as possible. While he indicated that alum frequently is applied to the sheets by sponging, he advocated soaking the sheets in the solution while it was hot.

Alum is recognized today as a major cause of the acidic embrittlement and deterioration of paper. This sorry state has evolved not because of alum's inherent characteristics but rather through an essential change in the way it is used in papermaking. Alum is only weakly acidic; when the amount used is carefully controlled, it is relatively harmless. When combined with rosin, however, it can become destructive. Late in the nineteenth century, alum came to be overused as a hardener for gelatin in sizing sheets of paper. By 1870, alum resinate was precipitated into the paper fibers in the pulp stage, leaving a residue of sodium sulfate and free sulfuric acid that ultimately resulted in the sheet's deterioration. Marjorie Cohn has commented on the unfortunate attraction that the resin/alum process had for papermakers then, mainly because the alternative, gelatin tub sizing necessitated an additional process in papermaking, and because gelatin, being an excellent medium for culturing or promoting bacteria, is difficult to maintain in optimum condition. Rosin/alum sizing employs stable, dry chemicals which may be incorporated directly into the paper pulp, thus saving a step in the total process.[23]

The fact that so many millions of marbled papers remain in good or at least fair condition within or on book covers that are up to 250 years old offers reliable evidence that their alum content is relatively harmless. Nonetheless, as an added safeguard, I recommend that when using marbled papers as endpapers, binders should place acid-free flyleaves between them and the pages of the book to keep even the slightest amount of acid from leaching through. I have attempted to marble on paper that has been made acid-free, but these sheets (such as the one under the brand name Permalife) have been so highly buffered against accepting anything even slightly acidic that they will not accept marbled decoration.

5. Water

As mentioned previously in discussions of color and other materials, most if not all the old recipes called for the use of river or rainwater for marbling. "Soft or rain water," Charles Woolnough tells us in his manual, "where it can be procured, is best adapted for all the preparations of marbling, but hard water will do, especially if a small quantity of soda or pearlash be dissolved in it. Water that has been boiled, and allowed to cool, answers every purpose."[24]

James Sumner, who, in 1854, parodied the secret and restrictive practices of the contemporary marbler by labeling them "mysterious," revealed that the "elixir" of the craftsman in that period, the all-powerful agent which endowed him with his special powers and gave him his air of mystery, was nothing more than clean rainwater— "nature's own elixir," he termed it. Accordingly, Sumner advised future marblers to collect clean rainwater, for which one had only to keep rain barrels handy.[25]

Halfer makes only a few passing references to the water used in marbling, commenting that soft water or rainwater formerly was used exclusively for preparing the size in order to achieve greater durability. However, he found that by adding sodium or potassium (probably potassium chloride) to hard water, the carbonate of lime present would be precipitated as a white or yellowish powder (depending on the amount of iron contained in the water), and a soft water would remain. In this manner, he claimed, even spring and pump water could be used without danger.

6. Paper

It seems to me, in my conversations and correspondence with young marblers, that they consider paper to be perhaps the master key to success in this art. Is it not, after all, they ask, the material that is being decorated, the bearer of the colors, and the object that ultimately shows off the talent and ability of the craftsperson? Young marblers appear to reason that if they discover the "right" paper, they will immediately be transformed into virtuoso marblers.

There is no denying that paper plays an important part in the overall expression of some arts, but with regard to marbling, it is doubtless one of the lesser constituents, for paper neither presents marblers with the difficult problems and challenges that are inherent in the chemical and physical aspects of the craft, nor does it possess any of those "magical" qualities imputed to the process itself. The fact of the matter is that it is a combination of innate talent and training, tempered with a measure of experience and good intuitive qualities that makes virtuosos in this art, as in any other. Paper is merely the medium through which the marbler-artist can better express the sum total of his or her ability.

Little or nothing was said about paper in the early literature of marbling. Most of the manuals (the extensive German literature on marbling from the 1880s on excepted) were produced before the so-called "bad paper era" began, when chemical sizing at the pulp stage was introduced and subsequent paper deterioration along with it. Apparently, there was no need to talk about a

component which, being entirely satisfactory, was taken for granted. In the era before 1800, virtually all paper was made from rags or from materials that went into the making of cloths of various sorts, and its constituents were long-fibered and high in vegetable content. Much later in the nineteenth century, short-fibered materials, especially wood pulp, were introduced to papermaking on a large scale, and paper quality began to deteriorate.

Since its fabrication before the early nineteenth century was essentially a hand process, paper came in relatively small sizes: the rectangular molds for making it had to be extended at arm's length, and their weight and bulk severely restricted the size of sheets that could be produced. Before 1800, the paper employed in marbling usually measured about 15 × 20 inches at most. However, after the papermaking machine came into use in the third and fourth decades of the next century, paper came to be produced on large rolls and individual sheets were cut to larger proportions.

In the Diderot-D'Alembert account of marbling, paper is described as demy (*quarré*) size, which, in general, measures about 14 × 18 inches, with another size called montfaucon only slightly exceeding the proportions of demy. The smallness of the sheets produced in the eighteenth century is proved by old folio volumes covered with marbled paper. Because of the large format of folios and the limited size of papers made in early times, several marbled sheets had to be pieced together to entirely cover such volumes.

Another aspect of the paper used in marbling in these times was that it was invariably of a cheaper or lesser grade. I have soaked marbled paper from seemingly thousands of old covers but seldom have I encountered any that were watermarked or of high quality. Marbling is a chancy business, and much spoilage or indifferent effects can result. It would be folly to risk spoiling expensive paper on a slip of the hand, an air bubble, or some other element that might ruin the sheet. Even today, though I exercise the utmost care, I dislike using handmade papers that cost several dollars per sheet. In any event, the paper becomes submerged beneath a covering of paint and its quality does not show through. A good quality machine-made paper is perfectly adequate. It should be without or low in acid content and not too highly sized or calendered. In fact, the Diderot description calls for paper that had been only half sized at the paper mill.

A dry sheet of paper should not be laid onto the size, for air bubbles and other defects can easily result. In his discussion of marbling in *The Handmaid to the Arts*, Robert Dossie recommended that "the paper should be previously prepared for receiving the colours, by dipping it over night in water; and laying the sheets on each other with a weight on them, in the same manner as was before described . . . in the case of papers to be imprinted by copper plates." He suggested that five or six sheets at one time be dipped into a copper trough or tray half filled with water. The dipping was to be done two or three times, depending on the strength of the paper and the amount of gum size within it, the operator taking care that the sheets be kept exactly even, for in a wet state they were fragile and their ends easily could be torn. The sheets were then deposited on a large, flat piece of wood, the procedure repeated until all the sheets had been dipped and placed together in a pile. When all the sheets had been soaked, a second flat piece of wood was set on top, enclosing the sheets between the two boards. A large weight was placed on last so that water would be forced into all the sheets equally and any surplus pressed out. The sheets could be maintained in a damp state for marbling, and in this condition were all the more easily laid on the size. In copperplate printing this wetting task was performed the night before the sheets were to be used. If it happened that they were not used on the following day, the sheets were subjected to the same treatment all over again.[26] An exception to this practice occurs in the making of the Spanish pattern, where a dry or almost dry sheet is required for the proper waving.

The marbling description in the Diderot-D'Alembert work says nothing about dampening sheets prior to marbling; in the workshop depicted there, sheets presumably were laid onto the size in dry condition (which may account for the unusual manner advocated for laying them down). Nothing is said about paper in the manuals of Charles Woolnough and Josef Halfer, nor, so far as I have ascertained, in most of the succeeding literature. Such omissions substantiate the observation made previously that paper did not appear to present much of a problem.

It is not necessary to wet or soak the sheets prior to marbling in the manner Robert Dossie advocated in 1758 if they have undergone the alum process. However, once alum is applied to them, usually by sponging on the solution, it is necessary to place the sheets between pieces of felt or paper (or under some sort of covering) and to weight them. This process holds them in the damp state and maintains them in a flat, uniform condition; they would otherwise pucker, curl, or dry unevenly, all of which would make it difficult to lay them properly and result in poor or uneven marbling.

Franz Weisse advocated that careful attention be given to the selection and preparation of the paper. His discussion may be summarized as follows: paper utilized for this purpose should have as high a rag content as possible and also be the best quality available, with long fibers that will hold it together when it is subjected to water during the various stages of marbling. Weisse tells how paper may be analyzed for acid content and, in general, gives other advice that accords with common sense and is compatible with the trial-and-error method of investigation.[27]

In my experience, any fairly absorbent paper meets the requirements of the craft. I found that inexpensive mimeograph paper of the standard letter size provided a good sheet to work with at the beginning stage. I sponged this paper with alum water, laid it between pages of the *New York Times Magazine* or any magazine or newspaper of similar format, and, by weighting it with a large book or similar object, maintained the sheets in proper condition for marbling.

As one progresses and begins to turn out better work, one must, as Weisse suggested, visit paper-supply companies and ask for samples or purchase various sheets in small quantities to try out as many varieties as possible and determine which are best suited to the process and one's needs. Some suppliers welcome marblers into their domain, being intrigued with the unusual end to which their product is being directed. Correspondingly, art stores and other outlets for good quality paper offer similar possibilities, although they are not the cheapest sources for acquiring this commodity. With a little ingenuity and effort, it is not difficult to procure a reliable supply of paper suited to marbling.

7. Miscellaneous Materials

Throughout the history of marbling, various ingredients have been introduced to vary and enlarge the range of patterns possible or to stabilize or improve the method in every possible way. While some of these will be discussed in the final chapter, which deals with the patterns themselves and their evolution and use over the ages, a brief summary and explanation of the materials is in order here.

Around 1800, or perhaps a little earlier, the shell (or French shell or merely "French") pattern came into use, assumedly in the country from which it derived its name, but soon afterward in Germany, England, and elsewhere, and remained in the repertory for most of the nineteenth century, being produced in large quantities for cheap work. The shell pattern, we have seen, was achieved by adding an oily substance to the final or ground color. It was characterized by spots in ringlike configurations, with more color in the centers of the rings and less at their edges; the ground color drove other colors that previously had been thrown down into narrow veins, creating, overall, a very pleasant effect. Linseed and olive oil were the additives most often employed to bring about this effect, although any greasy substance would do; indeed, Hugh Sinclair obtained his oil by toasting salmon, or salmon kipper cut in slices, before the fire and preserving the fine oils that ran from it.[28]

In Woolnough's view, the best oil in general use for making this pattern was "Florence" or olive oil, an ingredient that I employ today for the shell design. Three or four drops in a cupful of color is sufficient to bring about the desired results.[29] Sumner, for his part, advocated the use of linseed or boiled linseed oil and directed that it be soaked into a clean linen rag. Placed in a safe location, it was set afire and the oily fluid running from it was caught in a basin. Burning the oil in this way, he reasoned, took away part of its greasy nature; he added that a penny-worth of oil will last for years, and, when treated in this way, it never failed.[30]

Turpentine is another ingredient that came into use in marbling either at the beginning of the nineteenth century or in the final decade of the preceding one. In fact, it was introduced to bring about the Stormont pattern at about the same time as olive or linseed oil was in order to bring about the shell pattern. One can easily imagine contemporary marblers scurrying about, attempting to find other additives with which they might create new effects and vary and enlarge their repertoire. The introduction of turpentine into the process may also perhaps be credited to the French, for this pattern sometimes was first known as the "French marble." The French or, as it later came to be known, "Stormont" pattern is distinguished for having a network of fine, lacelike holes in the predominating or ground color—the last to be thrown on. This effect was brought about through the addition of turpentine to that ground color. Woolnough and others called for "spirits of turpentine," though we know it today as plain turpentine. As these authorities caution, it is a very active ingredient that must be carefully controlled lest overly large holes and blotches occur and spoil the total effect; furthermore, the addition of turpentine to color will cause it to expand uncontrollably and shoot all over the size. There is a special knack to handling color impregnated with turpentine, but it can take an extremely long time to learn.

Some of the old manuals call for the addition of wine, spirits of wine, and even beer to the colors. Speaking of spirits of wine (in modern terminology, alcohol, rectified alcohol, brandy, or other alcoholic preparations),[31] Sumner in 1854 cited it as an essential ingredient: "Without this, the colours are slow in their movements, and rough in their appearance, they seem to want some greater propelling force than gall." Then, he unashamedly punned, "in fact, they have no *spirits* to move on."[32] A few drops of wine, spirits of alcohol, or stale beer are called for in other old manuals. These additives seem to have been a staple of the marbling practices of yesteryear, and, undoubtedly, alcohol also had a preservative or inhibitory effect on the development of bacteria and molds in colors which had been mixed with gall and kept over a period of time. Such additives also aided in the reduction of the colors.

In his 1885 manual, Josef Halfer spoke of sprinkling water (*Sprengwasser*) as the newest discovery in the art of marbling. It was prepared by adding Venetian soap to water. (Venetian or castile soap was prepared from olive oil and caustic soda, that is, sodium hydroxide.) Like gall, this preparation worked as an expanding agent, and

it has continued to be employed in the Halferian system of marbling for making certain patterns such as hair-vein and Turkish. It was prepared, in accordance with Halfer's instructions, by boiling shavings of Venetian soap with alcohol and water. Halfer found that sprinkling water produced fine oval and circular forms of color on the size and had a greater expanding power than did ox-gall, and, in my experience, both observations hold true. Instead of sprinkling water, however, I employ a preparation of tincture of green soap (which is made of an oil—frequently linseed oil—and sodium hydroxide, to which alcohol has been added). I prefer using this preparation in combination with gall, when making Turkish or spot patterns—in particular, the "Italian" pattern, which shows very small spots. The dimensions and evenness of the spots in these patterns can best be controlled through the use of gall combined with a soap compound, for the spots grow more slowly and are more uniformly round. Once one gains experience in handling these two expanding agents, their combined use becomes an indispensable aid.

Although Halfer referred to sprinkling water as a recent innovation in the 1880s, the fact that soap marbling was accomplished as early in 1811, as shown by the Oswestry bookbinding manual, indicates that the gall-like expanding qualities of soap compounds had been recognized long before. Most of the patterns outlined in the Berlin master bookbinder J. A. F. Schade's 1845 *Marmorir-Kunst* called for Venetian soap in their making, but it must be recognized that the use of soap in Schade's marbling was intended more to bring about visual effects in the pattern than for the dispersal of colors.

During the first half of the nineteenth century, many kinds of chemicals and compounds were introduced, with a number of new patterns resulting, such as the sunshine design, the Schroëtel (Scrôtel, Schrötel, Schrottel, schroffel, as it was variantly termed), and the one called "romantic." Additives to the colors included, besides Venetian and castile soap, potassium hydroxide and the others previously mentioned: rosin, hydrochloric acid, nitric acid, powdered alum, borax, lime water, and so on. Schade also called for the use of white shellac, usually in combination with Venetian soap and sometimes with rosin as well, to form what he called his "special solution." This compound was added to both the size and the colors in the making of certain patterns. Halfer discusses in his manual a number of substances that act in a manner similar to gall, and cites shellac as one of these, to be used in combination with rosin and ammonia. Shellac undoubtedly had a place in the marbling that took place in the transitional period between the old marbling and the new—between, roughly, 1840 and 1880.

14

Technical Aspects of the Craft, III: The Colors Used

MARBLING, in final analysis, is a color process: colors constitute the basic element of this art's ultimate expression. Admittedly, a great deal has been written about colors in the literature of this craft that has been produced over the last three centuries, but attention has focused essentially on the choice of available colors for making specific patterns. With the exception of Josef Halfer's manual and a few others deriving from it, little if any consideration has been given to the underlying nature of the colors or how they work. We shall now attempt to gain a more detailed view of this subject, not only considering the various colors that have been and can be employed in paper marbling, but also examining their chemical and physical constituents to determine what makes them work.

What Is Color?

It must be understood, first of all, that color does not itself constitute an object or physical entity. Color is actually a quality of visible phenomena, distinct from form—a sensation produced in a variety of ways but predominantly by the action of light on the retina of the eye. Visible objects produce vibrations or waves that impinge on the fibers of the optic nerve, and in their transmission to the brain these vibrations or waves are translated into the sensation we call light and color. Hence, color differs from individual to individual, depending on his or her anatomical and physiological make-up, that is, the individual's particular optical system and its ability to perceive sensations.

Colors are produced by several different phenomena of light. By and large, however, they are determined by the manner in which light is absorbed or reflected by various objects. What we know as color and pigment are examples of selected absorption of certain rays of light and the reflection or transmission of others. For instance, the blue pigment known as ultramarine reflects to the eye nearly 40 percent of the green-blue, blue, and blue-violet

rays, while the remaining rays, consisting of red, orange, and yellow, are absorbed within the pigment. This color is thus due to its quenching those rays from red to yellow, and reflecting the remainder, from green to violet, which combine within the eye to give the sensation of ultramarine blue. A second example is the brilliant pigment of emerald green. This color reflects to the eye nearly 70 percent of the pure yellow-green, green, and blue-green rays of the spectrum as well as 25 percent of the blue and violet, while the red, orange-red, and orange are completely extinguished. Yet another example is furnished by the brilliant red pigment known as vermillion. This color absorbs all the violet, blue, green-blue, and green rays, leaving only the yellow, orange, and red rays to be reflected. The light reflected from vermillion consists of 90 percent of the orange and red rays, from which it derives its characteristic scarlet color.

The absorption of certain rays and the reflection of others produce the innumerable shades commonly found in nature to give the artist, dyer, and marbler their many varieties of color. Other factors, such as diffraction (or interference), dispersion, and fluorescence of light waves also influence how colors are perceived or sensed, but to a lesser extent. In general, it should be remembered that bodies give off a sensation of color according to the amount of light they absorb or reflect, which, of course, is determined by the nature of the specific materials within them. These materials are called pigments.

The Composition of Artists' Colors

The colors employed by watercolor artists, dyers, marblers, and others, for the most part are tripartite in nature and makeup. In order to be useful for such artistic and practical purposes, colors normally require three constituents: a pigment; a carrier or binder or vehicle; and an extender or dispersant, which often fulfills the role of a wetting agent as well. Pigment is a quantity of vegetable or mineral matter (or, more likely today, a synthetic material) which causes the color sensation itself by the amount of light it reflects, absorbs, refracts, and so forth. The second constituent, the carrier, is some glutinous matter which gives body to the pigment and makes it cohesive, that is, holds it together and provides it with some of its essential capacity to stick to paper or to another surface. The extender or dispersant alters the surface qualities of the first two constituents so that they flow smoothly or spread out evenly and adhere to another surface instead of sticking together. In essence, the paints or colors we use in marbling are still another colloidal mass or suspension or system, in and of itself. The foregoing mixture is known as a watercolor, and in this form it is useful to watercolorists, marblers, and others. By mixing a pigment with varnish and turpentine, one obtains an oil color of the type useful to oil painters, house painters, sign painters, and others working with oil media.

One hears today of the term "inks" to describe marbling colors. Inks are a matter altogether different and have little resemblance to marbling colors. Though inks also are coloring matter in solution or suspension, they consisted, in olden time (in the case of writing ink) of a mixture made from a decoction of nutgalls[1] or another source of tannic acid, and a solution of copperas (i.e., crystallized ferrous sulfate), to which was added color and a little gum. Inks needed for printing were obtained by mixing a dye, such as lampblack, to an oil, usually linseed oil. Since neither writing nor printing ink bears any resemblance to the colors required for marbling, ink should not be identified with the process. Indeed, none of the old marbling manuals use the term—they refer only to colors or paints. In the marbling literature of today, particularly the literature on oil marbling, we see the term "inks" employed, and I think incorrectly. Such usage only exposes an imperfect knowledge of marbling on the part of those using such a term and an even poorer grasp of its history.

When a pigment is ground and mixed with water, and afterward dropped or thrown onto marbling size, it disperses and floats about randomly in its ground-up form or falls to the bottom of the marbling size, depending upon the specific gravity of the material used. If ox-gall is added beforehand, the pigment will expand into a round disc which, upon close examination, will be found to contain innumerable dots of color. If, to go a step further, a carrier or a binder or a vehicle is then added—in the form of some type of gum—the color drop will spread out in an even-appearing, homogeneous circle, for now the particles of color are united and bound together by the glutinous matter in which they are suspended.

The pigments employed in oil and watercolors until late in the nineteenth century were usually obtained from vegetable and mineral matter. When minerals were used, these pigments were known as earth colors. The binder (or carrier or vehicle) consisted of a mucilaginous or glutinous material such as gum tragacanth, gum arabic, gum mastic, gum Senegal, carragheen size, or some similar preparation. Gum arabic was considered the best for water-borne pigments from the sixteenth century or even before, and it continues to be the best available today. Ox-gall served then, as it does now, as the most frequently used dispersant. A soap compound or synthetic detergent is also employed, especially in many of the water and paste colors that are sold on today's art-supply market for general purposes; in cheap colors, a super-abundance of such material can render them useless for marbling because they have too much expansive power incorporated in them at the manufacturing stage.

Old-Time Marbling Colors: The Earths and the Lakes

All the early literature of marbling—from Neri, Kunckel, Evelyn, and the rest to the information supplied by Robert Dossie in his *Handmaid to the Arts* and by the anonymous writer on marbling in the Diderot-D'Alembert *Encyclopédie*—recounts that colors were prepared for the specific purpose of marbling by taking ready-made color, grinding it with water and ox-gall, adding a little gum, and, sometimes, a little wine or spirits as well. Such directions indicate that the colors were obtained by the marbler in prepared form, normally in hard, dry cakes, the usual manner of putting up colors in those days. Furthermore, we may infer (with confidence, I believe), that in many if not all cases the color cakes to be employed for marbling colors contained, in addition to their pigment, a carrier or binder—that is, some glutinous agent such as gum arabic that would give them cohesiveness and bind them together. If they had been ground up previously, as earth colors were, they probably had a dispersant or wetting agent such as ox-gall in them as well, for such a material was useful to grind them finely. Finally, as we shall soon see, these pigments were prepared with alum, potassium, or a similar metallic oxide which was either incorporated or naturally present in them. Such constituents endowed them with a built-in mordant and gave them the power to grip paper well. Thus, all the essential elements were already in the prepared color cakes which the marbler obtained from the color suppliers. He had only to adjust them to his specific requirements during the grinding process by adding water, more gall, and, perhaps, a little more gum binder and some wine or spirits, as experience dictated.

The earliest marblers worked with just a few of these ready-made colors, adjusting them in shade and intensity to their specific needs by mixing them together; through this process of "color mixing," they created a number of additional colors. This is confirmed by the many recipes provided in the literature, of which the best and the fullest appear in the Diderot-D'Alembert article of 1765 in a section devoted to the preparation of colors. Here we are told that for blue one took indigo and ground it up finely on a grinding stone with a muller, adding water and gall the while. For red, the marbler took a cake of red lake and obtained the final color by grinding it and adding another red color preparation, along with ox-gall and a very small quantity of gum tragacanth (about a hazelnut's worth). (The red coloring preparation added to the red lake was obtained by boiling a quantity of brazilwood with quicklime.) Yellow was prepared with ocher, a mineral earth; green with a mixture of indigo and ocher; black with indigo and lampblack; violet with red, indigo, and lampblack; and so on. These materials contained all the ingredients necessary to insure good coloring matter for marbling.

The manner in which the cakes of color were prepared and put up in the eighteenth century, and probably in earlier times as well, is best determined by consulting Robert Dossie's *The Handmaid to the Arts,* which first appeared in 1758. Additional material on making marbling colors and other commercial watercolors may be found in Fichtenberg's *Nouveau manuel complet du fabricant de papiers de fantaisie,* issued in 1852; in Christian Friedrich Gottlieb Thon's *Der Fabrikant Bunter Papier,* which appeared in several editions from 1826; and in similar works directly concerned with our subject. Still other information on early pigments and dyes used for this purpose derives from the literature of dye making, which was fairly extensive at this time and of which James Haigh's *The Dyer's Assistant* of 1778 is one source that has been helpful.[2] Another work which should be mentioned in the context of fabric dyeing, but which contains substantial information on those dyes that were useful to calico printers and colorers of paper alike, is Edward Bancroft's *Experimental Researches Concerning the Philosophy of Permanent Colors.*[3] In the literature of commercial color making, C. H. Schmidt's *Vollständiges Farben-Laboratorium* of 1841 is an important resource.[4] Finally, two anonymous publications, one entitled *Die Zeichnungs- und Mahlerkunst* (1756)[5] and the other *The Artist's Assistant; or, School of Science* (early nineteenth century),[6] can be cited from among the large corpus of literature issued to assist fine artists in preparing their colors. (This literature includes Dossie's *Handmaid to the Arts* and several other titles previously mentioned.)

At the very beginning of his manual, Dossie makes it clear that colors or pigments must be mixed with a fluid vehicle before they can be employed as paints for almost any purpose. After characterizing them as oil colors, watercolors, enamel colors, and so forth, and discussing their qualities such as brightness, purity, and durability, he enters into a long and detailed discussion of the manufacture of the pigments and the coloring matter for them.

According to Dossie, the pigments for colors of all types are made in several ways: sublimation, calcination, solution, precipitation, filtration, evaporation, and levigation. Sublimation is the process of raising solid bodies in fumes that afterward are collected by condensation, ei-

ther in the upper part of the same vessel in which they are raised, or in others properly adapted for this purpose. Calcination involves operating on substances by means of heat so as to produce some change in their texture or color (that is, the substances were reduced to powder, or to a friable state, by burning). Solution refers to the reduction of any solid body to a liquid state by means of another fluid, by melting, "dissolving," or other action. Precipitation, the most important of the methods and the one most frequently used, is the separating of a solid body from any fluid in which it is dissolved or melted, by the addition of a third body capable of producing that effect. Filtration is used to free fluids from solid bodies; though very simple, this operation had to be done with the utmost care in order to succeed. Evaporation is the reduction of moist bodies to dry ones by the action of artificial heat. Finally, levigation is the washing over of bodies in order to reduce them to a degree of fineness, such as powders. Use of one or more of these methods to prepare given colors depended on the constituents from which each was made, and different methods were applicable or preferable accordingly.

Dossie's treatment of the marbling method (which appears to have been added as an afterthought in an appendix near the end of his second volume) relates that the colors employed were the following. For red, carmine, lake, rose pink, vermillion, and red lead (the last two, hard and glaring ones, had to be softened with rose pink or lake, and the carmine and lake were too expensive for common purposes); for blue, Prussian blue and verditer; for yellow, Dutch pink and yellow ocher; for green, verdigris (a mixture of Dutch pink and Prussian blue) or verditer; for orange, orange lake or a mixture of vermillion or red lead with Dutch pink; for purple, a combination of rose pink and Prussian blue. Clearly, only a few basic colors were needed, for still others could be produced through color mixing.

At the beginning of his first volume, Dossie relates in detail how all the colors that were deemed useful at the middle of the eighteenth century for painting and for other artistic purposes were made. While these were prepared through one and sometimes several of the above procedures, the majority were produced through the process of precipitation, with mineral and metallic earths employed as the precipitating agent; therefore, they were bonded to a metallic oxide. Colors, or more correctly, pigments or coloring matter produced in this way, were known as lakes or lake colors.

In principle, precipitation occurs when two or more substances in the state of solution are mixed together and a reaction (what the chemist calls double decomposition) occurs, with new products formed in the process. One of these, being insoluble, is thrown down in the form of a fine powder. For example, when a solution of potassium chromate is added to a solution of lead nitrate a yellow powder falls to the bottom of the container; on examination, this will be found to be lead chromate, while the liquor contains potassium nitrate in solution.

The two most commonly used red colors in the eighteenth and well into the nineteenth century were manufactured through precipitation. To make lake, Dossie observes, a quantity of the best pearl ashes (potash, or potassium carbonate) was put into water and purified by filtering the solution through paper. Then more water was added, together with shreds of scarlet cloth obtained from a tailor. After boiling, the first red shreds were replaced with a fresh batch, and the process was repeated up to four times. Meanwhile, a quantity of cuttlebone (composed mainly of the mineral calcium) had been dissolved in aquafortis (dilute nitric acid) (to produce calcium nitrate) and, after straining, poured into the initial preparation. When properly managed, the fluid became clear and colorless, for the third body—the cuttlebone and acid—had precipitated the pigmenting particles to the bottom of the vessel in the form of solid particles. The residue, or lake, afterward was separated from the fluid through filtration, and was washed up to five times (that is, put through the process of levigation) to reduce it to a fine powder. The powder was then pressed into cakes and dried for use.

A better grade of lake was made by using alum instead of potash as the basis; cochineal then would be employed as the coloring or pigmenting matter in place of the scarlet shreds. The ancient dyes, such as Tyrian purple (which came from a species of snail) and others that had come down from classical times, began to disappear early in the sixteenth century as the discovery of the New World and the establishment of trade routes to the Americas led to the introduction of new mordant dyes such as brazilwood, logwood (campeachy wood, from Mexico), and cochineal into Europe. Cochineal, which produced a beautiful scarlet, was made from the dried female insect *Dactylopus coccus* (or to use its synonym) *Coccus cacti* which lives and propagates on certain varieties of cactus that grow in Mexico, principally the nopal.[7]

An even more beautiful lake could be prepared by using alum and brazilwood, with potash serving as the precipitating agent.[8] This preparation approximates one called for in the Diderot-D'Alembert article in a discussion on making red color. According to Dossie, lake was obtained by boiling a quantity of brazilwood in a solution of three gallons of water and three pounds of common salt. A prepared, filtered solution of five pounds of alum in three gallons of water was added. A filtered solution of three pounds of pearl ashes or potash in a gallon and a half of water was added next, until all the coloring matter had been precipitated to the bottom of the vessel.

To obtain the coloring matter known as rose pink, or rose lake, the earth or basis of the pigment employed was principally chalk (calcium or soft limestone), and the tingeing substance was extracted from brazilwood or from campeachy (commonly called peachy) wood, a logwood from the Campeche region (and present-day state) of Mexico. In order to prepare the tingeing substance, brazilwood alone or in equal combination with campeachy wood was put into water with alum and boiled for an hour. The resulting liquid was purified by straining it through flannel. The wood was put back into the boiling vessel with the same quantity of alum, and the process was repeated, and again a third time. The three tinctures were mixed together and allowed to evaporate until only two quarts of fluid remained. In the meantime, a large quantity of chalk was prepared by covering it with water to which alum had been added. Afterward, the initial solution was poured off and a fresh quantity of chalk was supplied, until the chalk was freed from the salt formed by the alum; it then was dried to the consistency of a stiff clay. The chalk and the red mixture were next mixed together and subsequently dried.

Lake and rose pink were the principal reds employed in marbling both during and after Dossie's time. Because carmine (a bright crimson color) of superior quality was not then made in England and consequently had to be imported from France at great cost, it was used only for the best work. Vermillion and red lead were less frequently used, for both colors were considered too glaring and had to be toned down with rose pink. According to Dossie, the carmine color, which he rated the best of the reds (an opinion reiterated by Woolnough a century later), was made by tingeing cochineal with weak nitric acid. The best carmine came from France where its manufacture was kept a secret, accounting for its high price. The product later made in England, while equally beautiful, was less durable, being subject to color change.

Vermillion, a bright scarlet pigment, was mentioned in some of the early marbling manuals, such as Hugh Sinclair's and Charles Woolnough's, as an alternate red color or one used in combination with other reds. Dossie notes that it was formed from common sulfur and quicksilver, or mercury. A quantity of sulfur was melted and gradually poured into quicksilver, which had been gently warmed; when stirred, the mixture effervesced. Care had to be taken lest the combined materials caught fire; if this happened, a wet cloth, held in readiness, was thrown over the vessel to extinguish the flames. When cold, the combination was reduced to powder by grinding. It then was placed in an oval glass container and hung in a furnace and sublimed. The resultant mass was finally levigated to produce a fine vermillion powder. To make the color less expensive, and to cut down on its glaring brightness, vermillion often was mixed with red lead—that is, lead that had been calcined. This mixing tended to adulterate the color by turning it black. For this reason, vermillion was sparingly used, and red lead was of limited use as well because of its tendency to turn black.

Dossie defined Prussian blue as the "fixt sulphur of animal or vegitable coal, combined with the earth of alum."[9]

He says that it was prepared by adding three parts of dried blood (of any animal) to one part of pearl ashes and mixing them in a large crucible or earthen pot. Next, the mixture was put into a furnace and calcined. After the vessel was removed from the fire, its contents were emptied into water and, after soaking, transferred to a tin vessel and boiled further. The preparation was filtered and set aside. Then a quantity of alum and green vitriol or copperas (ferrous sulfate) was put into water, and this solution was added to the first preparation, resulting in an effervescence that precipitated a green powder. When the precipitate was washed with a double quantity of spirit of salt (hydrochloric acid), the green matter quickly turned to blue. Prussian blue, supposedly discovered in 1710 by a Berlin color maker named Diesbach, is sometimes designated in the literature as Diesbach or Berlin blue (or alternately as Parisian blue).[10]

The other blue recommended by Dossie for marbling was verditer, prepared by adding the proper proportion of chalk to a solution of copper nitrate. The copper solution was a by-product of the refining of silver by precipitation from a nitric acid solution, in the operation called parting. As a result, verditer was relatively cheap. Washed chalk gradually was added to the copper solution, and in the ensuing effervescence the fluid lost its green tinge and became colorless, while a blue sediment, the verditer pigment, formed at the bottom of the vessel. This sediment later was freed from the fluid by filtering.[11]

Although Dossie says nothing about the use of indigo as a marbling color, he does refer to *indico* when discussing colors in general, relating that it was brought from the East and West Indies (whence the name) and was formerly almost the only blue color used in painting other than ultramarine. Because of its high price, however, indigo could be used only for special purposes. After the invention of Prussian blue, and because of the poor qualities of the indigo brought from the French or British plantations (which was inferior to that made in the Spanish West Indies), indigo fell into disuse as a color for all but the grossest work, such as paperhangings. When it was possible to procure the best Spanish indigo, it was preferable, in many cases, to Prussian blue.

Indigo was used as a dye in India and Egypt long before the Christian era; indeed, ancient Egyptian mummies have been found with blue wrappings dyed with indigo. The Romans too were acquainted with indigo but used it only as a pigment, for they did not know how to render it soluble and could not avail themselves of it for dyeing. Beginning in the sixteenth century, after the discovery of the passage to India around the Cape of Good Hope, indigo became generally known in Europe, but it met with great opposition by the woad cultivators, who induced the English, French, and German governments to promulgate laws and edicts against its use. (Woad, a biennial plant of the cruciferous family, had been used previously for a blue dye and was cultivated

extensively in England and on the Continent.) According to one source, it was only in 1737 that French dyers were given the right to use indigo without restriction.[12] Nevertheless, reference to "Indigo" in the Witgeest *Naturlyk Tover-Boek* of 1684 and afterwards, and the use of the word "Indig" in the marbling directions in the 1707 *Kunst- und Werck-Schul* indicate that use of this dye had already become somewhat standard in some parts of Europe by the late seventeenth century.

We know from the Diderot-D'Alembert marbling description of 1765, as well as from later literature on this subject, that indigo had become the principal material for producing a blue marbling color from the mid-eighteenth century on. Even before, its use had been called for in the *Kunst- und Werck-Schul* of 1707 and in the *Grund-Mässige und Sehr Deutliche Anweisung zu der Schönen Laccir- und Schildkrotten-Arbeit* of the same year. In fact, it was not only a color popularly employed in the marbling craft, but became one of its staples.

Indigo is a vegetable color that occurs in considerable quantities in a number of different plants, of the genus *Indigofera*, cultivated in India, Java, China, and other regions of the Far East and introduced into the West Indies and South America by the Spaniards. When the macerated leaves gathered at flowering time are allowed to ferment in vats of water, a colorless form of indigo is liberated; stirring the liquid causes oxidation of the colorless material to form a blue sediment, indigo. This natural dye produces a strong blue color of great permanence, though it is less brilliant than Prussian or some of the other blues; extenders such as chalk and clay frequently were added in its manufacture to make the product less costly. We shall have more to say later about this important dyestuff and its use in marbling.[13]

The two yellows called for by Dossie were yellow ocher and Dutch pink. Yellow ocher is a mineral earth found in many places, but with differing degrees of purity. When freed of other earths and heterogeneous matter, it is a true yellow of moderate brightness, well suited to painting and other artistic purposes; the only preparation required is levigation. Dutch pink is a pigment formed from chalk colored by the tingeing particles of French berries or other vegetables (the berries were most often used). French berries, or Avignon berries, as they were also called, were dried, unripe fruit of various species of the buckthorn shrub (of the genus *Rhamnus*). The powder extracted from them was commonly used in former times to dye textiles and for other purposes. There were many ways of preparing Dutch pink, but Dossie recommended the following as an easy and cheap method. French berries were boiled with tumeric root (or turmeric, itself a yellow dye and best known as an ingredient in the condiment curry), and the tincture was strained and reboiled with a small quantity of alum until it had evaporated considerably. Afterward, a large quantity of washed chalk was mixed into this tincture, and the mixture was ground and dried. Dutch pink had many uses as a color, being very bright and easily preserved. By mixing it with Prussian blue, the marbler obtained the green color he needed. Sometimes, in place of French berries, Persian berries, a Near Eastern species of buckthorn, were used for the coloring matter.

Quercitron was another valuable yellow coloring agent. It was obtained from the inner bark of a particular species of oak, *Quercus velutina* (called in the older literature *Quercus nigra*), or *tinctoria,* a tree indigenous to the United States found especially in the forests of Pennsylvania, Georgia, and North and South Carolina. The physician-chemist Edward Bancroft first introduced quercitron to English dyers, and in 1785 obtained, by Act of Parliament, the exclusive rights to import this wood into Great Britain.[14] After removal from the tree, the bark was dried and ground to a very fine powder. The yellow coloring matter obtained from quercitron was sometimes referred to as English pink.

Still another yellow mentioned by Dossie (but not as a marbling color) was king's yellow, or arsenic trisulfide, made by powdering orpiment, which occurred naturally as a yellow crystalline mineral. The use of king's yellow was called for, along with yellow ocher, in the Diderot-D'Alembert marbling article for making the placard pattern, and Hugh Sinclair also mentioned it, along with Dutch pink, yellow ocher, and English pink, in his *Whole Process of Marbling Paper* early in the nineteenth century.

The last color described by Dossie specifically for the purpose of marbling was orange lake, produced by precipitating annatto (a reddish or yellowish-red dyestuff prepared from the pulp surrounding the seeds of the annatto tree) with alum. Orange lake was a very bright color that worked well as either an oil or watercolor. To obtain it, several ounces of annatto were added to a pound of pearl ashes, put into water, and boiled. After straining, an alum solution was added, which precipitated the coloring matter to the bottom of the vessel. The resultant sediment formed an orange lake (hence the name of the color); afterward it was dried for use. As Dossie points out, a substitute orange could be obtained by combining the colors vermillion and Dutch pink. Later manuals, such as Sinclair's, called for the use of orange lead, a pigment of the same composition as red lead but lighter, or orange orpiment.

These then were the major colors recommended by Robert Dossie in 1758 for the purpose of marbling paper. Black, which he failed to mention, was obtained from lampblack, a soot or oil collected as it was formed during burning. Oil was burned in a number of large lamps in a confined place, and the soot formed by the trapped fumes was collected from the top or sides of the room. As lampblack is a brownish-black, it was brought to a fuller and deeper color through the addition of indigo, a combination that was recommended in the Diderot-D'Alembert article.

More on the Lake Colors—And Fichtenberg's Method for Making Them

In the second, 1923 edition of his marbling manual, *Das Marmorieren des Buchbinders auf Schleimgrund und im Öl- und Kleisterverfahren,* Paul Adam says that the most suitable colors for marbling are the so-called lake colors— "am geeignetsten sind die sogenannten Lackfarben." In these, he tells us, the specific coloring matter is bound to a metallic oxide. As we have observed in the discussion of early marbling colors, the lake colors were formed by precipitating a coloring matter by means of a metallic earth, principally aluminum or potassium. Other colors that were used, while not prepared in precisely this way, were mostly metallic in nature, being pigments obtained from earths and minerals, which especially suited them to the marbling process. Such colors often are grouped together with the lakes in marbling and other literature; sometimes all such colors, including the lakes, are called by the general designation "earth colors." Small wonder, then, that Halfer could remark with impunity that aluming the paper was not necessary when such colors were used, for we can see that they were endowed with mordantlike qualities by their very nature. As Edward Bancroft has noted:[15]

> Earthy and metallic bases . . . serve not only as a bond of union, between the colouring matter, and the dyed substance, but they also *modify* (as well as fix) the colours; some of them, particularly the oxide of tin, and the earth of alum, *exalting* and *giving lustre* to most of the coloring matters, with which they are united.

Thus, we see that the lake colors are somewhat similar to the metallic colors, being bound to an element such as aluminum, potassium, or tin.

Alum is the name commonly applied to a hydrated double salt, usually consisting of aluminum sulfate and the sulfate of another element. The alum of greatest commercial importance today is aluminum potassium sulfate, also known as potassium alum. A compound of aluminum, the most abundant metallic element on earth, alum has a wide range of uses in the production of medicines, textiles, hides, sugar, paper, paints, matches, and other articles. It is also used in baking powder, as a flocculating (aggregating) agent in water purification, for waterproofing paper, and, as I have pointed out several times, as a binder or mordant in dyeing.

Potash, or potassium carbonate, is obtained by washing wood ashes and evaporating the resulting solution to dryness. Potassium belongs to the alkali metal group; it is the seventh most abundant element on earth, comprising 2.6 percent of the igneous rocks of the earth's crust. In addition to being necessary to sustain human and other animal life, potassium and its compounds are important for making fertilizers, explosives, chemical reagents, medicines, and for many other industrial purposes.

Why, it may be asked, can some colors (such as indigo) derived from non-metallic materials, seemingly be employed without the use of a mordant? The answer can only be advanced in stages. To begin with, indigo, like the lake colors, which it resembles in several ways, has a low specific gravity. Secondly, it is likely that in its earlier, unsynthesized state, indigo contained minerals and metallic traces. There is good reason to suspect that somewhere during its manufacturing process or final preparation, alum was added, because earths, presumably containing alum and mineral salts, such as chalk, were often added as extenders to cut costs. But most of all, indigo (like a few other dye-bearing plants) was insoluble in water, and had the ability to fix itself to an organic fiber without the aid of a mordant (see p. 177).

Although Robert Dossie's extensive description of the making of artist's colors in his *Handmaid to the Arts* is probably the longest and most detailed treatment in the early literature, the information he provided was of a general nature and not intended specifically for use in marbling and coloring paper. And yet, since many of the colors he discussed had applications to marbling, his manual provides us with the best and earliest account not only of the makeup of the colors used in early marbling, but also of how they interacted in this process. Dossie, it will be remembered, was one of the outstanding industrial chemists of the eighteenth century, a fact that accounts for the validity of the information he provides as well as its uncommon detail. Similar information on these same colors at a later date and on a number of others that came into use after Dossie's time (such as Brunswick green and Cassel earth) can be found in C. F. G. Thon's *Der Fabrikant Bunter Papier.*[16]

Another excellent source on the make-up and manufacture of colors used in marbling before its modern era is M. Fichtenberg's 1852 *Nouveau manuel complet du fabricant de papiers de fantaisie.*[17] It is evident that Fichtenberg had considerable experience in the making of colored and fancy papers, including marbled ones. As we observed earlier, he may well have acquired his knowledge while working in one of the large German factories or French workshops devoted to their production before setting up his business in Paris early in the nineteenth century. His information dates to a time when the classical or traditional form of marbling had begun to wane and was being replaced by a mechanical or imitative kind, but the colors Fichtenberg employed were still the basic ones that had been in use for a very long time. Only in the ensuing decades would they be replaced by modern synthetic dyes.

Fichtenberg began his account with directions for making two preparations, salts of aluminum and tin. These were the two metallic bases employed in his time to precipitate the colors and at the same time provide them with body. (Again we note the use, for marbling and

paper-coloring purposes, of lake and mineral or earth colors and another instance in which the pigment was metallic or bound to a metallic salt.) To produce the first of these constituents, the salts of aluminum, Fichtenberg directed that alum be dissolved in a copper boiler with ten parts of river water. When the alum was completely dissolved, the solution was transferred to a deep wooden vessel, potassium was added, and effervescence resulted. The copper boiler was rinsed free of alum, and after potassium or pearl ashes in half the quantity of the alum had been added, together with eight or ten parts of water, it was put over a fire. After boiling, the preparation was removed from the fire and allowed to settle. Next, it was transferred to the vessel containing the alum, very gently and in slender threads, and stirred constantly with a stick to control effervescence and prevent overflow. The mixture was then left to settle for six to twelve hours; in the interval, the liquid clarified and the salts of aluminum were precipitated to the bottom of the wooden vessel. After the water had drained off, the precipitates were washed up to six times and the preparation was stored until needed.

The tin preparation was made by mixing three parts of muriatic acid and two parts of nitric acid in a bottle into which pure tin wire was dropped, little by little, until the acids no longer dissolved the metal. One part of ammonia salts, dissolved in eight parts of water, was then added and the preparation was allowed to settle.

The tin preparation and the aluminum salts were the two bases which Fichtenberg directed be used to make most of the lake and metallic colors needed for professional paper decoration at mid-nineteenth century; one customarily served as the base and the other as the precipitating agent, depending on the specific materials and methods employed. For example, to make carmine, the finest red color, one part of crushed cochineal was put over a fire in a copper boiler, to which had been added fifteen parts of filtered water. After boiling, the mixture was removed, and cream of tartar, amounting to one-third the weight of the cochineal, was added. When the color had settled, it was strained through a sieve and a quantity of the aluminum salts added. This preparation was precipitated with the tin solution, and a beautiful carmine lake settled at the bottom of the vessel. Again, red lake (often referred to simply as "lake") could be made by using Pernambuco or brazilwood as the coloring agent. Here twelve parts of chopped wood were put into a copper boiler with fifty parts of river water and two parts of alum. These were boiled for half an hour and then strained into a large vessel. The aluminum salts and then the tin preparation were added, after which the red lake appeared as a precipitate at the bottom of the container. A similar red lake could be procured by combining water, alum, and Pernambuco in a boiler and then, after these had been boiled and strained, precipitating the solution with potassium. Violet was made in the same way, with campeachy wood substituted for Pernambuco as the coloring agent.

A good yellow lake was obtained by boiling two parts of Avignon berries in twenty to twenty-four parts of water. After straining, the preparation was returned to the fire and four parts of potassium and two parts of pure soda (sodium carbonate) were added. The solution afterward was precipitated with alum. Another yellow was made by boiling quercitron with alum, and precipitating it with potassium. Canary yellow, lemon yellow, and gold were made in the same manner, using different coloring agents with either potassium or alum as the base or precipitating agent.

While Fichtenberg mentions that Prussian or Berlin blue, which he describes as very beautiful, is prepared in cakes in special factories on a grand scale, he relates that for the last twenty to forty years a salt called "prussiate of potash" has come to be prepared as a substitute color; this is adequate for making a blue paste, a form of color more suitable to the fabrication of colored papers than colors put up in cakes.

For preparing this one puts into a large stoneware pot three parts of nitric acid and two parts of muriatic acid, tosses in copperas (iron oxide) in very small doses, and stirs the preparation from time to time with an iron rod until it gives off no more fumes. It is then allowed to rest and is bottled and put aside until needed. For making the blue color, two or three kilos of potassium cyanide are added to from fifty to sixty kilos of water in a large wooden vessel, after which the previously prepared solution of acids and iron oxide is poured in, drop by drop, being stirred with a spatula all the while. This operation causes the precipitate to take on a green color that soon turns to blue. The preparation is then washed twice, the second time with dilute muriatic acid, which makes it brighter. He also describes the making of several other types of blues, which he calls "mineral blue," "Paris blue or ash blue," and another, "new-style blue," which is an imitation of ash blue.

Fichtenberg reported that the green colors generally were formed from blues and yellows. Two other greens (and fine ones, too), Schweinfurt green and Scheele's green, were made by using arsenic, which caused their fabrication to be extremely dangerous (wallpaper manufactured with these colors caused arsenic poisoning in the inhabitants of homes where it was hung, somewhat akin to the problem of lead poisoning from paint in homes today).[18] In order to make Schweinfurt green, verdigris (a green or blue-green poisonous pigment obtained by the action of arsenic acid on copper) was boiled in water until it became pasty, then washed with vinegar. When the remaining liquid had been strained into another receptacle, river water and arsenic were added and the vessel placed over a fire. After this preparation had come to a boil, the verdigris solution was poured in, little by little, and the preparation boiled further until the remaining

color was pure and clean. Copper sulfate could be used in place of verdigris, with the arsenic acid being dissolved in an equal part of potash. Scheele's green was made in this manner too, but with verdigris, and a little more potash than arsenic, and no vinegar.

Some of the other colors used in the paper decoration of Fichtenberg's period, such as yellow ocher, Cassel earth, Italian red (burnt sienna), and Italian yellow (raw sienna), were natural or earth colors that could be purchased raw, while still others, such as vermillion, orange lead, ceruse, and the like, were manufactured commercially and could best be obtained on the market. Fichtenberg concluded his discussion by stating that, as a rule, it is better to grind the colors yourself, or have one of your assistants attend to the matter. He advocated the use of a grinding mill, such as was used for grinding mustard, although he observed that in small establishments the grinding had to be done on a stone with a muller. His final piece of advice related to the preparation of the earth colors, which, he said, had to be levigated before use.

And so we have, through the works of Dossie and Fichtenberg, the most detailed information available on the colors used in marbling in the eighteenth and nineteenth centuries and, to some extent, even before. Although synthetic colors came into use within a few decades after the publication of Fichtenberg's manual, the lake and earth colors were employed in marbling for as long as they continued to be produced and could be procured, for they constituted the best colors adapted to this process.

Charles Woolnough's Colors

In his 1853 manual, *The Art of Marbling,* and specifically in the revised edition issued in 1881 under the title *The Whole Art of Marbling,* Charles Woolnough says practically nothing about the preparation of colors. He merely notes that they are the same as those ordinarily used for painting in either oil or distemper, and that they may be procured just as they are produced or manufactured—whether in lump, powder, or pulp form—and then ground by their user. With regard to contemporary English practice, they could be obtained in London at most of the respectable oil and color shops, in provincial towns at the druggists, or wholesale at the principal manufacturers throughout the kingdom. For making the various marbled patterns of his day, Woolnough asserted that the following colors would suffice, although others could be brought into use to please the fancy:

REDS

Carmine

Drop Lake

Peach Wood Lake (a pulp, made expressly for marbling)[19]

Vermillion

Rose Pink

Burnt Oxford Ocher[20]

BLUES
Indigo
Chinese Blue
Prussian Blue
Ultramarine

YELLOWS
Chrome
Dutch Pink
Raw Oxford Ocher
Yellow Lake (pulp)
English Pink

GREENS
Chrome Green[21]
Green Lake
Emerald Green[22]
Brunswick Green

BLACKS
Vegetable Lampblack
Common Lampblack
Drop Ivory Black[23]
Blue Black

BROWNS
Burnt Turkey Umber[24]
Burnt Sienna

ORANGES
Orange Lead
Orange Chrome[25]

WHITES
China Clay
Pipe Clay
Flake White
Paris White[26]

What little discussion Woolnough provides on marbling colors relates to their use in various patterns rather than to the technical aspects of their composition and manufacture. It is obvious from his brief treatment, however, that he recommended the older lake and mineral or earth colors rather than the new synthetic colors that were being introduced at the time he issued his 1881 manual. Woolnough tells us that he obtained his colors readymade and was little concerned with the exact methods of their manufacture or the underlying principles that governed how and why they worked. It merely interested him that they did work, that this one or that one was useful, and for what particular pattern each was best adapted. He cautioned that the colors be well-ground and recommended the use of a color mill when working with large quantities. His method of color preparation called for the addition of a bit of beeswax in its native state, to be mixed with the colors while they were being ground. The wax had been combined with a small amount of white soap and water and cooked beforehand to make it friable; one ounce of wax was added to one pound of color. The wax, we know, was intended to better allow the finished papers to be burnished or glazed and hold their colors.

We may ask why Woolnough recommended so many alternates for each color—six reds, four blues, five yellows, and so on. The answer is simple, for some colors, by their very nature, are more brilliant than others and thus are usually preferable. Colors of the same family differ among themselves in degree of brilliance, with brilliance being defined as the degree of resemblance to black or to white; the greater the amount of darkening material in them,

the less brilliant they are. (The tone of the paper can, to some degree, also affect brilliancy; the darker the paper, the more likely that it will diminish the brightness of the colors applied to it.) Woolnough also rated colors according to their beauty and ease of use, among other factors. The large number he discussed in each family gave readers a wider range of choices depending on availability and the patterns or effects desired.

Josef Halfer's Colors

Josef Halfer, who eventually engaged in the commercial manufacture of marbling colors, confessed in his *Progress of the Marbling Art* that his lack of precise knowledge of colors gave him his greatest trouble when he began to make them; moreover, he had to conduct numerous experiments before he could unlock the puzzle of their nature and manufacture. His breakthrough came when he realized that the true value of color for marbling purposes is its body, and that the color itself, which is bound to the body either naturally or chemically, is of less importance.

Halfer claimed that "the [marbling] size and the technical application of the colors demand great attention and practice; on the other hand, the preparation of colors [demand] but labor."[27] He divided colors into two groups: mineral and lake. In the lakes, the coloring matter is bound to the metallic oxides, and its weight is equal to one half of the whole weight of the color. Therefore, he said, the lakes can be prepared and successfully used as marbling colors without the addition of anything but gall. The mineral colors, on the other hand, which in a natural or chemical way are bound to bodies that weigh much more than the coloring substance, require some glutinous matter to unite their particles and make them useful for this purpose. The best glutinous material is a preparation of dissolved isinglass[28] or parchment glue with gum tragacanth. As the first two ingredients are expensive, Halfer felt that they could be replaced by fine gum arabic. Halfer said no more about the technical aspects of making marbling colors—after all, he was in that business himself and did not wish to divulge too many trade secrets.

The colors sold on the market in Halfer's time came either in the form of little cones or as powder. When formed into cones, they had to be ground or reduced to powder in a dry state and then mixed with water and a few drops of ox-gall to produce a thick paste. If the coloring matter was a mineral, glutinous matter, about a nut's worth, had to be added. If the color was a lake, the addition of water and gall was fully sufficient to bring it to usable form. Halfer advised that rainwater be used for diluting the color, and he recommended that the grinding be done by an apprentice, for the time of a journeyman would be too valuable for this task. He cautioned, however, that this aspect of the work be done carefully and that the colors be ground uniformly fine to avoid problems.

The essence of Halfer's discussion of colors, to which he devotes eight pages of his manual, lies in just a few sentences—namely, that the best marbling colors are those of the lake group where the coloring matter is bound to a metallic oxide (and is, in effect, a pigment united to a mordant). Also preeminent as marbling colors are the mineral or earth colors, which contain a mordant in them in the form of metallic salts, but which, because of their heavy weight, require the addition of a body or vehicle in the form of a glutinous material to carry them and make them cohere. And, of course, ox-gall or a similar substitute must be used in all cases as a dispersant and as an agent to alter the colors' surface tension so that they can carry out their role properly.

This, then, was the secret behind Halfer's marbling colors, which he marketed in Germany, throughout Europe, and in England, America, and elsewhere, mainly through agents. In reality, there is no secret to them at all, although they were little understood by their users before his time. In fact, Halfer believed that the earlier lack of understanding of colors was the reason marbling had failed to become a popular art or craft. Its progress in workshops and on an individual basis, he related, advanced greatly after he had entered into the manufacture of proper marbling colors and other materials.

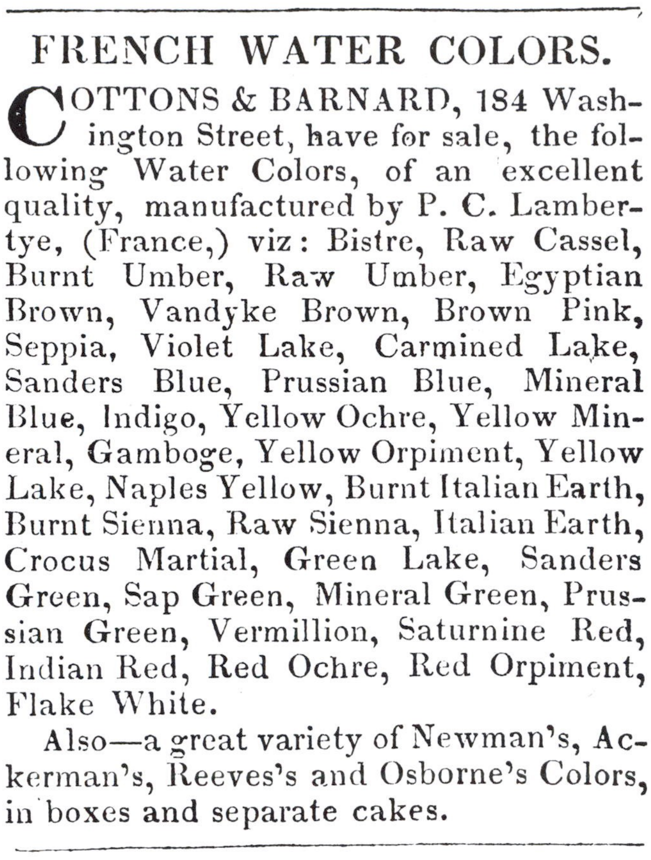

How Colors Were Put Up

I have emphasized several times before that in the eighteenth and early nineteenth centuries, colors came onto the market mostly in the form of compressed cakes. The lake color precipitates were put up in this way while still wet, as were the mineral colors, which first had to have a small amount of gum binder added, and possibly a few drops of ox-gall as well. This format required that the marbler or his assistants perform the tedious task of grinding and mixing individual colors before any marbling could take place. The color cakes often were hard and gritty, of varying quality, and apt to crumble with age. A number of color manufacturers and colormen experimented, from the early nineteenth century on, with preparing colors ready for use, in moist form rather than in cakes, directing their attention, as Marjorie Cohn notes, "particularly to the addition of hygroscopic agents, which, attracting and holding atmospheric water within the color cake, would predispose it to softening and dissolving more readily."[29]

Sugar had long been a secondary ingredient of the gum binders of watercolors—indeed, Robert Dossie mentions it in this regard in his 1758 *Handmaid to the Arts*.[30] Early in the nineteenth century, French manufacturers substituted honey for sugar, and their *couleurs de miel* were quickly copied by English manufacturers, who

FRENCH WATER COLORS.

COTTONS & BARNARD, 184 Washington Street, have for sale, the following Water Colors, of an excellent quality, manufactured by P. C. Lambertye, (France,) viz: Bistre, Raw Cassel, Burnt Umber, Raw Umber, Egyptian Brown, Vandyke Brown, Brown Pink, Seppia, Violet Lake, Carmined Lake, Sanders Blue, Prussian Blue, Mineral Blue, Indigo, Yellow Ochre, Yellow Mineral, Gamboge, Yellow Orpiment, Yellow Lake, Naples Yellow, Burnt Italian Earth, Burnt Sienna, Raw Sienna, Italian Earth, Crocus Martial, Green Lake, Sanders Green, Sap Green, Mineral Green, Prussian Green, Vermillion, Saturnine Red, Indian Red, Red Ochre, Red Orpiment, Flake White.

Also—a great variety of Newman's, Ackerman's, Reeves's and Osborne's Colors, in boxes and separate cakes.

FIGURE 49. Advertisements for the sale of watercolors, early and mid-nineteenth century: *Left,* "French Water Colors," in the *Bosto Medical and Surgical Journal* of 23 June 1829 (v. 2, no. 19, advertising section at end); *right,* page 5 of *Panorama of Industry; or, The Merchants' and Shippers' Guide . . . Published under the Direction of Messrs. Brunswick and Dollingen . . .* (London, Brewster and West, 1845).

in the 1830s substituted glycerine, a strongly hygroscopic, syrupy form of alcohol, for some or all of the honey. Such colors were christened "moist colors"; while not wet to the touch, they were perceptibly sticky compared to dry cakes. Mrs. Cohn has likened their binder to the consistency of a gumdrop. By 1841, shortly after the development of moist colors packed in porcelain pans, the metal tube container was introduced for oil paints, and five years later the English manufacturers Winsor & Newton Co. adapted their moist watercolors to tubes; tube color must be more moist than color in a pan so that it may be squeezed out. By mid-century, the English watercolor artist, or, for that matter, any person who had need for watercolors, could procure them in at least three consistencies (see Figure 49). Thus Charles Woolnough, speaking of colors for marbling in the period around 1853 and after, could report that they were produced in lump, powder, and pulp form.

ARTIST'S COLOURMAN. 5

C. BARBE,
60, REGENT'S QUADRANT, LONDON.

All the articles sold at this house are warranted of superior quality.

Any article found defective, purchasers are at liberty to exchange, or should they not find anything to suit them, the money will be returned.

All Brushes are warranted, so that if any should be found defective, they will be exchanged or the money returned, even though they should have been dipped in colours.

Artists residing in the country may have their orders executed by sending the address of some person in town authorised to pay on delivery; or sending an order for the amount on the post-office or a banker.

The most conscientious dealing may be relied upon in the selection of articles.

A list of prices may be obtained GRATIS *on application as above, or will be sent per post. The following List shows the leading articles contained therein.*

Colours in powder.	Drawing papers.
Laques de Smyrne.	Turnbull's boards.
Mars colours.　Carmine.	Sketch book and blocks.
Crimson cakes.	Drawing boards.
Bronze in powder.	Earthenware.
Colours in shells & cakes.	Miscellaneous.
Moist colours.	Mathematical instruments.
Japanned tin boxes.	Drawing pencils.
Colours in tubes.	T squares.　Flat rulers.
Oils and varnishes.	Set squares.
Lay figures.	Mathematical curves.
Palettes and palette knives.	French prints.
Glass slabs and mullars.	Wax painting.
Eazles.	Round and flat Hog's hair
Sketching boxes, &c.	brushes in ferules.
Prepared cloths and ticken.	Round & flat Sable brushes
Prepared millboards.	in ferules.
Prepared cloths on frames.	Quill pencils.
Prepared panels. [boards.	Swan-quill pencils.
Oil paper and Academy	Flat Hog's hair varnish
Ivories for miniatures.	brushes.
Miniature glasses.	Badger softeners.
Crayons, pastels.	Bear's hair ditto.
Stumps, portecrayons.	Fitch ditto.　[string.
Portfolios, India rubber.	Hog's hair bound with

Binders and Carriers

In any discussion of marbling colors, some attention must be given to the binding agents or carriers employed to hold them together. Even though the true lake colors did not require the addition of such a material, the Diderot-D'Alembert *Encyclopédie* article shows that it was customary to add a small amount of glutinous material even to these; and, of course, the greater weight of the earth and mineral colors required that a binder be added to them to extend and support them and make their particles stick to paper.

Robert Dossie devoted a small section of his book to "the substances used for rendering water a proper vehicle for colours,"[31] in which he mentions gum arabic as probably the best material for the purpose. This transparent gum was collected from the sap of several species of the acacia bush or tree, and was dried and ground for use. In Dossie's day, as at the present time, the gum was brought to Europe from Africa and the Levant. It is easily soluble in water and dries with a considerable degree of tenacity. Gum arabic was considered the best ingredient for making an aqueous vehicle for colors, and its use in Europe for this and other purposes, particularly medicinal ones, dates from at least 1598.

Dossie also discussed several other substances employed as binders or vehicles for watercolors, among them gum Senegal, and sizes concocted from leather, sugar and sugar candy, starch, and isinglass. Gum Senegal, as its name implies, is a vegetable exudate much like gum arabic (but comes from the Senegal region of West Africa) and is applicable in the same way. Dossie believed it was apt to retain some moisture which rendered it soft and clammy and made it a less fit vehicle for watercolors than gum arabic. Nonetheless, it was used as a substitute or sometimes in combination with gum arabic, and it was cheaper. Size, Dossie continued, was made by boiling leather in water until it melted and the solution became viscid. Size commonly was prepared in bulk from the refuse pieces of leather and skins of beasts by those who specialized in the making of glue; when cold, it had the consistency of jelly. Sugar and white sugar candy also were used for rendering water a suitable vehicle for colors, but one suspects that the application of this material was mainly in miniature painting where, when mixed with gum arabic, it helped to keep the colors from cracking. Isinglass, formed from the bladders and cartilage of large fish, was also used in miniature painting to give the colors good spreading power; it was especially helpful for binding pigments of an earthy nature. Starches were used as substitutes for both sugar and isinglass.

Synthetic Colors: The Colors We Use Today

Early in the nineteenth century, a chain of chemical discoveries resulted in the development of a long series of synthetic dyes which made obsolete the lake and mineral colors that had been used for dyeing textiles and other materials for so long a time. The first of these was the aniline group. In 1826 Otto Unverdorben obtained an organic base through the destructive distillation of indigo, to which he gave the name "crystallin" because of its tendency to form crystalline compounds with various acids. In 1834 F. F. Runge extracted a substance from coal tar, which gave a blue color when combined with hypochlorite of lime and which he called "kyanol." In 1840 Julius Fritzsche obtained a base oil by distilling indigo with caustic potash; he called it "aniline," which derives from the specific name of the indigo plant, *Indigofera anil*. In 1842 N. Zinin prepared a base, "benzisam," from nitrobenzene by the action of ammonium sulfhydrate. Years later, A. W. Hofmann showed that all these substances, obtained in different ways from various sources, were identical.

We can look to the year 1856, however, as marking the beginning of the production of synthetic dyestuffs. At that time, William Henry Perkins, then a student and assistant to August Wilhelm von Hofmann at the Royal College of Science in London, discovered a purple coloring matter that had dyeing properties in a product he had obtained through the chemical treatment of aniline from coal tar. Coal tar was produced in those times from coal gas by condensation, and later on through the destruction of coal; it yielded in the process many by-products, of which the principal one, for our purposes, was nitrobenzene, which afterward was reduced to aniline. Perkins patented his purple dye, and in 1857 established a factory to manufacture it, first calling his color "aniline purple" or "Tyrian purple," but subsequently renaming it "mauve" (or mauvine), a French word for a mallow plant with a purplish flower.[32]

Mauve was an immediate success, and the general method of its preparation, the oxidation of aniline, was adapted and elaborated on by other investigators who succeeded in producing new dyestuffs. In 1858 Hoffman observed a beautiful red coloration while studying the action of tetrachloride of carbon on aniline; however, credit is due to the French chemist Verguin for preparing the color on a large scale. The following year, Verguin took out a patent in conjunction with M. M. Renard frères of Lyon for the manufacture of a red dye derived from the action of bichloride of tin on aniline. The process then became the property of the Fuchsine Company, which had been established to produce this dye; and the dye was called magenta (or fuchsin or fuchsine). Further discoveries followed with astonishing rapidity, and soon magenta (or fuchsine) itself was converted by chemists into "imperial violet," "Lyon blue," "Paris violet," and other commercial colors.

The formulation of August Kekule's theory of the benzene ring in 1865 gave great impetus to synthesis in the field of dyestuffs.[33] With the subsequent adoption of the theories of valency and radicals, and hence the structural formulae by which the characteristic properties of carbon compounds were diagrammatically represented by simple symbols, organic chemistry began to pass through a period of rapid development almost unparalleled in the history of science. In 1868 a team of German chemists showed that alizarin, the coloring matter of madder root, a Eurasian plant that had been widely used for dyeing purposes, derives from the chemical compound anthraquinone. Their synthesis of alizarin from anthraquinone was the first preparation of a natural dyestuff by purely chemical means. Being very stable, it subsequently replaced natural madder root for these purposes.[34]

Despite the marvelous advances being made, the complex mechanism of the reactions that gave rise to these new products was not then perfectly understood—the percentage of composition and the exact arrangement of the molecular structure of these dyestuffs was unknown. An important contribution to the understanding of the relationship between color and structure was made by the German chemist Otto N. Witt, who, in 1876, proposed the so-called "chromophore theory." In every dye, Witt identified a chromophoric (color-bearing) group and one or more "auxochromes," or associated groups, whose function it was to intensify the color. And in 1888 the English chemist Henry Edward Armstrong showed that the chromophores generally could be depicted as quinones, oxidized structures derived from the benzene ring.

Almost simultaneously, the azo dyes, the largest group of synthetic dyestuffs and the ones most used today, were being developed. In 1858 Johann Peter Griese, a young German working in the laboratory of an English brewery, discovered the diazonium compounds. Diazotization is brought about by the action of nitrous acid on aromatic amines (nitrogen-containing benzene compounds). Diazonium salts readily combine with aromatic amines or phenols to produce deeply colored substances containing the azo group (involving two nitrogen atoms). Griese's discovery was not exploited until the 1870s, however, when the development of the azo dyestuffs occurred, stimulated by the discovery that the addition of sulfonic acid groups produce highly water-soluble materials of great intensity and adhering power. By treating naphthalene derivatives with sulfuric acid, various sulfonated aminonaphthalenes and hydroxynaphthalenes were formed, from which the new azo dyestuffs could be prepared in a range of shades from orange to black. Yellow azo dyestuffs could be produced as well by substituting derivatives of pyrazolone for naphthalene.

It was not until 1883 that any azo dyestuff was capable of dyeing cotton or other vegetable colors without mordanting. In that year, Böttiger discovered that by tetra-azotizing benzidine and combining it with naphthionic acid, a red was obtained that acted directly upon cotton. Known as Congo red, this preparation was the forerunner of a long series of successful colors, still used today, called "direct-cotton" or "direct" dyestuffs, which can dye cotton without a mordant.

In 1880 Adolf von Baeyer accomplished the first synthesis of indigo, although artificial indigo did not become commercially important until many years later. Significant discoveries continued to be made in the field of dye chemistry into the present century, with the disperse or nonionic dyestuffs being discovered in 1923, the phthalocyanine dyestuffs and pigments in the late 1920s, and reactive dyestuffs in the 1950s—all of these synthetically derived. And so it came about that the older lake and earth colors were replaced by new, synthetic colors. The latter remain in use today for providing the coloring or pigmenting matter used in commercial and industrial paints and dyes of all sorts.

Using Synthetic Colors in Marbling Today

Unless, as Halfer did, the modern marbler chooses to make his or her own lakes or uses pure mineral colors, he or she must contend with colors in which the pigmenting matter is a synthetic product that requires a binder or carrier to hold the color particles together and make them cohere; a dispersing agent is required as well to allow the mass to spread out and be worked easily. Color chemists and other knowledgeable people have informed me that the high-quality tempera and watercolors on today's art market continue to contain gum arabic as their binder, which contributes to their high cost. A chemical of the soap family is used as a dispersant, with the commercial product Darvan most frequently mentioned. Cheaper paints use less expensive and often synthetic materials that make them less adaptable to marbling and even, at times, useless; not only are their pigments inferior, but they contain heavy substances for binders, such as latex, cellulose, and even vinyl. To make such color masses spread out, dispersants must be added to them in large quantities; when such colors are thrown onto the marbling size, they immediately extend to the whole area of the trough or pan and thus are uncontrollable and unusable.

When marbling, it is necessary to start off with a color which, when thrown onto the size, extends only slightly or initially sinks. Its buoyancy and spreading power is carefully developed and brought under control through the addition of ox-gall or another acceptable dispersing agent, so that the operator can make each color interact properly with the others to make the whole system work. There are colors sold as tempera, water, or poster colors which are in the water-soluble class having acrylic (a plastic) or casein (a phosphoprotein) binders. While some marblers claim to use these, I have found them unsuited to the marbling process and have done little with them beyond experimentation. In any event, acrylic paints are far too glaring for use in marbled decoration.

One last word about today's synthetic paints and dyeing materials: it is necessary to treat the paper with a mordant beforehand; alum is still acknowledged to be the best product.

Mordanting

While I have touched on the subject of mordants and mordanting and particularly alum, in prior discussions of color, it is desirable to add a few more words here. A mordant, in dyeing or coloring of any sort, denotes a body which, having a twofold attraction for organic fi-

bers and color particles, serves as a bond between them to give fixity to the dyes. In order properly to appreciate the utility and true function of mordants, it is well to bear in mind that coloring matters are peculiar compounds that have certain affinities, their distinctive characteristics being neither acid nor alkaline and yet capable of combining with many bodies, especially with salifiable bases, and of receiving from each of them modifications in their color, solubility, and alterability.

Some organic coloring substances, when pure, have a strong attraction for certain bodies, while others have only a weak attraction, and still others none at all. Again, as the products of animal and vegetable life, some colors are soluble in pure water, while others become so only through the action of specific agents. A number of pigments used in textile and other dyeing in earlier times, such as indigo, safflower and annatto, are insoluble in water and thus can fix themselves to fibers without the intervention of mordants. Because those products are soluble in alkalis (safflower or annatto, when dissolved in weak lye solutions; indigo, naturally soluble in alkalis) they have, when applied to fibers, their tinctorial substances precipitated within their pores by attracting their solvent alkali with an acid. As a result, the coloring matter, in the instant that it comes into contact with organic fibers for which it has a certain affinity, unites with them; being naturally insoluble in water (that is, having no affinity for this vehicle), it remains fixed so that subsequent washings have no effect on the dye. For dyes or colors that are soluble in water, however, it is the reverse: they possess no affinity for the organic fibers which can counterbalance their affinity for water, and, under the circumstances, intermediate bodies must be added to them. Such agents add their affinity for the coloring matter to that possessed by the particles of the stuff; by this twofold action, they increase the intimacy and the stability of the combination. These intermediate bodies are true mordants.

As a rule, mordants are found among the metallic bases or oxides. Because they must meet the twofold condition of possessing a strong affinity for both the coloring matter and the organic fiber to be dyed, however, mordanting substances are not so common as might be supposed. Of all the bases that serve as mordants, aluminum, potassium, and tin succeed best. Over and again, we have observed that the old-time lake colors, having been precipitated with these nonferrous metals, contained a metal base; earth and mineral colors possessed this quality through their very nature; and still others, such as indigo, could attach themselves to fibers without mordants by virtue of their chemical nature. With regard to modern water-soluble colors, which are made up of synthetic dyes and pure vegetable matter and hence do not possess natural mordanting powers, a mordant must be added to the material to be dyed in order for the colors to become permanently fixed—that is, in order that they may become insoluble.

Color Mixing

To conclude this treatment of colors, a brief note on color mixing is in order. A century or more ago, as the manuals of Sinclair, Woolnough, Sumner, and Halfer inform us, the marbler had available earth and mineral colors that had their own distinct coloration. Modern colors, which are synthetically contrived and are more brilliant and wider ranging, serve well when one wishes to marble according to modern standards; that is, when doing pure Halferian marbling. But if one attempts today to reproduce the patterns of old—perhaps for the use of book restorers or when reissuing old literature illustrated with newly marbled samples, one faces the problem of approximating the appearance of old colors by means of modern ones.

In such cases, colors have to be modified through the process of color mixing, that is, by mixing two or more colors together and reducing their brilliancy through the addition of black, brown, or some other darkening material. As I remarked in my introduction to *Three Early French Essays on Paper Marbling,*[35] color mixing is a hazardous undertaking, for it is difficult to predict at the outset whether combined colors will turn darker or lighter upon drying. Furthermore, strong colors tend to dominate and submerge weaker ones, creating undesirable results—another matter that cannot be predicted. Color mixing is a process of trial and error that often must be repeated a number of times before successful results can be achieved. When the correct pattern finally does result, however, all else pales, and one finds that the experience has provided an unparalleled insight into the marbling of the past.

15

The Evolution of Marbled Patterns

I T has been no simple task to attempt to create some semblance of order out of the jumble of marbled patterns that were developed in Europe and the Western world during the past four hundred years. This undertaking has required the detailed examination and translation of most of the existing literature on marbling, and constant examination of marbled papers in original bindings in libraries over a period of more than a quarter of a century. Several trips to Europe were required to inspect bindings containing these materials in the places where they were created and where they had remained relatively undisturbed; for, as we now know, the early export of French and German (and, later, English) papers and the migration of books worldwide has scattered such materials widely—thereby contributing to the problems of identification that sometimes seemed difficult and even impossible to solve.

In spite of the many advances made in our knowledge of how and where various patterns came into being and into manufacture, it is still difficult in some cases to state with surety whether this paper is German, that one French, or another English. The simultaneous employment of identical or near-identical colors and practices in Germany and France in early times, the extensive manufacture of the same patterns in a number of regions simultaneously, the export of papers far and wide, the intermixture of designs, the later recopying of earlier patterns, and the fading and subtle alteration of designs over the years due to light, dirt, and the fugitive aspects of the colors themselves—all of these have combined to confuse our efforts and, in some cases, still make positive identification tenuous or even impossible. Another factor contributing to this difficulty has been the spate of marbling articles and literature published by young artisans and enthusiasts throughout this century and particularly in recent times. Possessing little or no actual knowledge of the history and evolution of this craft, they have made many specious and contradictory pattern attributions derived from the error-laden literature of the past or, worse yet, have jumped to far-fetched conclusions that have little basis of fact.

Even in cases where certainty is assured, it is difficult—and in some cases impossible, given the wide range of forms and colors—to present all of the facts in a clear and convincing manner. Nuances of coloration and subtle variations in technique, along with other minuscule factors, cannot easily be put into words—it is no mean feat to convey intuitive judgment, instinct, and a priori knowledge descriptively. And even a generous allotment of color reproductions, as we have here in the nearly 200 examples illustrated on the plates that follow, can never be enough to serve as more than a mere outline or guide to the most common patterns produced in Europe and America during the first four centuries when this art came to be practiced in the West. It is hoped, nonetheless, that these will be sufficient and representative enough to allow librarians, book restorers, antiquarian book dealers, book collectors, and other interested parties to determine what designs evolved in particular regions at given times. Furthermore, with respect to binding, bibliographical and collateral criteria, the information should enable the user to judge, in many cases, whether the marbled papers and binding in a particular instance are contemporary with the volume containing them or if these were added at a later date.

I considered several alternative ways of presenting pattern origin and development. For instance, all Turkish, shell, and other generic designs could have been grouped together, with French and German and other nationalistic productions appearing within each group in chronological order. After giving the matter serious thought, I elected to discuss and arrange the following patterns by country and period—according to their development and manufacture in various geographical locations. Although this arrangement scatters some of the designs, I believe it will allow for a better evolutionary understanding of the subject as well as provide a better understanding of marbling practices in general. That said, we may now begin with a discussion of the French and German productions of the seventeenth and eighteenth centuries.

French Patterns in the Seventeenth and Eighteenth Centuries

By far the largest number of marbled patterns extant in books today, particularly for the seventeenth century, evolved in France. The French, we know, were the first to employ marbled paper for book and bookbinding decoration. Early French tomes have survived in considerable numbers due, in large part, to the high quality of their bindings and because they were executed for the libraries of royalty and the nobility who had come to prize books for their ornamental coverings as well as for their texts.

Examples of some of the earliest marbled designs in French books can be found on the first five plates (numbers 3–29) of Mme. Guilleminot-Chrétien's *Papiers marbrés Français,* of which the earliest and most important ones are reproduced here on Plates XIV and XV. During most of the seventeenth century, the craft in France was in the hands of a limited number of bookbinders and prototype marbling specialists who experimented widely, making a great many designs, but especially combed ones and more especially the type which later would become popularly known as "small-comb." This design was a finely combed pattern—that is, the needles on the comb used were spaced very closely together—with red or black sometimes comprising the predominating color. These artisans worked apparently with small sheets of paper, mainly of the foolscap variety, whose dimensions at that time measured approximately 13 × 16 inches. Many of these papers were added to very small volumes such as those of the duodecimo format, a favorite French format then and at later times as well.

Mme. Guilleminot-Chrétien has told me about a volume now preserved in the manuscript collections of the Bibliothèque Nationale that contains a large number of marbled papers from that early time showing almost every conceivable design then known. This volume indicates that, during the cradle period of French marbling, makers gave vent to their curiosity and imagination.[1] For the most part, however, one is more likely to encounter the combed designs in early French books, with the "small-comb" predominating into the 1680s. One may also see examples of such papers in English bindings from about the 1660s onward, which indicates that a sufficient quantity of marbled paper was then being made in France for export.

By the end of the seventeenth century, the small-comb and other patterns representative of the initial period of French marbling are seen in books less and less and finally not at all. Beginning with the 1680s, apparently, individuals who had deserted bookbinding and had come to specialize in decorating paper ushered in a new era of marbling in France. They introduced other types of patterns into production, some of them, one suspects, copied from German examples that had recently been developed. By this time, marbling had achieved sizable proportions in Germany as well, and bookbinders there were beginning to follow the example of the French in employing marbled paper for book decoration. To further complicate matters, from the standpoint of identifying the papers made in these countries at this time, German colored paper was also being exported to France. The 1698 letters of M. Collinet to M. Colbart de Villermont that were described in Chapter 2 are indicative of such exportation, though the designs they specifically discussed deal with a quite different type of decorated paper.

The patterns introduced beginning in about the 1680s were representative of the second era of French marbling and would remain in force into the 1730s and 1740s and, for one or two of these designs, even longer (these are the patterns discussed in the Diderot-D'Alembert article). Inasmuch as marbled papers came to be produced so beautifully and in such large numbers, we may look upon this as the golden age of French marbling. Indeed, the papers created at this time surpass anything that came before or after, and they are a delight to behold today, centuries after their making, when one comes upon them between the covers of old books. Mme. Guilleminot-Chrétien refers to the expansion in the manufacture and use of marbled paper in France at this time as "la vulgarisation du papier marbré"; but we must interpret the French "vulgarisation" not in a negative sense but as meaning popularization and common usage.[2] Many of the patterns developed in this period bear large configurations to correspond to the larger paper being used, for now binders were adding marbled decoration to larger volumes as well as smaller ones. Samples 1–12 on Plate XXIII and 13 on Plate XXIV are representative of the patterns made in France in 1680–1740.

By this time, the curl, or snail, design had become a rather common feature of French marbling; indeed, so frequently was the pattern made that the Diderot-D'Alembert author referred to papers with curls in them as "commun," or ordinary, papers. It is obvious from the pattern numbered 12 in Mme. Guilleminot-Chrétien's catalog (reproduced as the fourth illustration on Plate XV here) that the curl had been introduced into French marbling as early as the 1630s; in time, its production and use became very large, for curling is a quick and easy way to vary a pattern and cover up imperfections at the same time—and, with larger and quicker production, imperfections undoubtedly multiplied.

Also representative of the golden era of French marbling are the colors that came to be employed. These were, for the most part, four in number: red, yellow, blue, and green, with red invariably predominating. The patterns that evolved to exploit the beauty of this combination of colors were rather formal ones, designated by the Diderot-D'Alembert author as "placard" (samples 1–4); "persillé" (samples 5–6); "commun," small-comb, or "Dutch," (both with and without curls); and Turkish designs (although such spot designs were often curled, moving them into the "commun" category). All of these are shown on Plate XXIII.[3]

The later alteration of the curl or snail pattern is interesting to follow, for it is representative of the decline in French marbling that occurred as the eighteenth century progressed. During the early decades of the golden era, the colors employed in making this pattern were the four described above. Initially, the curls usually were large, as were the patterns overall, and they were irregularly made— that is, the curls were randomly placed throughout the pattern. As time went on, however, the curls not only became smaller but were also dispersed at regular intervals throughout the design. It is evident that in the early eighteenth century French makers had come to employ the "Dutch apparatus" for quicker and more regular manufacture. In addition, the colors typical of this second era of French marbling—red, yellow, blue, and green— gave way, in the curl or snail pattern, to red, yellow, and blue only, with the red often being vermillion or rust and the blue a darker and sometimes even a muddy color.

By the 1730s or 1740s, when the placard, persillé, and some of the other patterns representative of this golden era ceased to be made, the small and regularly curled "commun" paper continued in force as the principal marbled paper produced in France for the next fifty years or so; this is the design most frequently seen in French volumes dating from the 1720s or 1730s and throughout the remainder of the century. Examples of the "commun" or curled designs made in the late seventeenth century can be seen on Plate XXIII and in the first illustration on Plate XXIV; the second through sixth illustrations on Plate XXIV (samples 14–17) show its later forms, where its curling was regular and its colors varied from those employed previously.

Around the middle of the eighteenth century, the Turkish or spot design came into vogue again in France. It was produced in large quantities from then until late in the century, not in the colors representative of the initial era (which were copied after original Turkish designs), but with the ground or predominating color blue, brown, green, purple, or orange, usually with black, red, and yellow veins (which became the standard vein colors in marbling everywhere from that time). Such Turkish or spot patterns are depicted in the final six illustrations on Plate XXIV (samples 19–24). This design and the small curl pattern were essentially the only ones produced in France in the later eighteenth century, although every now and then one sees French papers of this period that indicate that makers sometimes imitated ancient designs, chiefly the curl pattern, that were colored red, yellow, blue, and green earlier in the century—albeit in a modified, more organized way.

The rather lowly state to which French marbling fell after mid-century is evidenced by the 1758 article on the making of marbled paper published in the *Journal Oeconomique*. Only the Turkish design—sometimes with variations accomplished through curling or drawing other figures into it with the point of a feather or a stylus—is discussed there. Mme. Guilleminot-Chrétien alludes to a new taste and a new motif entering French marbling about 1780 and continuing to about 1815, basing her belief on the beautiful, predominantly green, Turkish papers

made by Nicolas-Denis Derome (Derome *le jeune*) that decorate many extant bindings in the library of King Louis XVI.[4] In my opinion, Derome's beautiful papers do not mark the beginning of a new era of French marbling at this time but merely an extraordinary high point in an otherwise lackluster period. I ascribe the next era of French marbling as beginning *after* the French Revolution had run its initial course—perhaps in the late 1790s but certainly not before. We shall have more to say on this matter later, when we take up the early nineteenth-century revival of French marbling. As for Derome's productions, it should be noted further that he brought nothing novel or new to the French marbling of the 1780s but produced outstanding forms during an otherwise mediocre state of the art.

German Patterns in the Seventeenth and Eighteenth Centuries

The marbled paper produced initially in Germany in the seventeenth century, it will be remembered, was employed mainly for artistic and everyday purposes rather than for bookbinding. As a result, few early specimens have survived the ravages of time to aid us in reconstructing what was happening in this land for most of the seventeenth century. We have only the German marbled papers in some of the Album Amicorum, such as the first two illustrations on Plate VII and the later seventeenth-century collage appearing with them, and a few other examples of early German marbling to indicate what was happening during this early and formative period.

Because marbled paper did not find its way into German bindings nearly as early as it did in France, we are at a great disadvantage when attempting to assess the early state of the German art. We could jump to the conclusion that the French outproduced the Germans at this time, but this assumption probably would be incorrect. Conversely, we might infer from their slight priority in this field and their well-known penchant for industry that the Germans early achieved considerable production of marbled paper—although, admittedly, production before the middle and later years of the seventeenth century was low by later standards. As in France, it would not be until the final decades of the century, when considerable numbers of artisans were attracted to it, that the German craft began to assume the identity of a sizable and recognizable industry.

Some indication of the production and appearance of German marbles in the late seventeenth and early eighteenth centuries is afforded by the examples surviving in the outstanding Buntpapier collection now preserved in the Germanisches Nationalmuseum in Nürnberg. (If only there existed a corresponding collection at Augsburg, where the craft assumedly first took root in Germany and the West!) Reproduced on Plates XXV and XXVI are six of the early marbled papers found there (samples 25, 26, 29, 31, 37, and 39), which date from the latter years of the seventeenth century and the first part of the eighteenth. Looking at these and some of the other samples accompanying them, one is struck with the feeling of déjà vu—of having already seen them. And indeed we have, for they closely resemble the placard, persillé, small-comb (or Dutch), and double-combed patterns reproduced among the French marbles on Plate XXIII. The fact that the author of the Diderot-D'Alembert article acknowledged the small-comb pattern (in its later form) to be a German invention (whence its alternate name) and spoke of the superior quality of German marbling in general is significant. When contemplating the telltale red, yellow, blue, and green colors and the very precise, superior technique of the German placard, persillé, and small-comb patterns illustrated on Plate XXV, one is led to suspect that it was the Germans who initiated or developed these patterns, and that the second phase of French marbling commenced when French marblers adopted and began copying the German designs.

Clearly, the Germans also did a great deal of experimenting and developed a wide range of patterns early in their exploitation of this art. For example, the first design on Plate XXV (sample 25) was effected by raking the red, yellow, and blue color spots that had been laid upon the size, and then passing through them a comb similar to Charles Woolnough's "zigzag device," to produce—at this very early time—the very peacock design that would become popular in Germany late in the nineteenth century and that would be especially identified with Halferian marbling. (A late nineteenth-century machine-made imitation appears as sample 172 on Plate XXXVII.)

In marbling, as in many other fields of endeavor (*viz.* printing and bookbinding), the early productions mark a high point of artistic achievement. In its formative phase, early marblers devoted great attention to overcoming initial difficulties. As a result, greater care and curiosity and other factors inherent in experimentation led to the development of some of the art's finest forms. Later on, when initial problems had been solved, difficulties overcome, and continuing production achieved, the exquisite forms that exemplify the initial two stages of French and German marbling gave way to a pedestrianism that represents the practical but humdrum exploitation of this craft. Afterward, high points were achieved only occasionally, when extraordinary artisans came along, such as Derome *le jeune* or some of the outstanding English masters who, arriving late to the craft, conducted it with the enthusiasm and curiosity of the early French and German marblers. Because they came into contact with the craft at a later stage in its development, English masters reproduced the forms of old with renewed vigor, and thus were able to sustain the art at a time when it was waning and losing ground elsewhere.

"Progress" in marbling, as in most other fields, has been marked by a continual search for cheaper and quicker methods. The production of such intricate combed patterns as appeared in France and Germany in the seventeenth and early eighteenth centuries, and the wide experimentation that occurred simultaneously, could be tolerated so long as the papers were made and used by the few advanced bookbinders who catered to a wealthy and sophisticated clientele that would pay a high price for them. As time passed and the use of marbled paper spread, however, a greater demand for it arose on the part of ordinary binders and less sophisticated book collectors as well. As a result, a new group of professionals, who abandoned the intricate and time-consuming patterns in favor of simpler ones that could be more quickly, more easily, and more cheaply produced, entered the field. Thereafter in Germany, as in France, only a few traditional designs remained in production from the third or fourth decade of the eighteenth century; of these, the small-comb, or Dutch pattern, predominant early in the century, and the Turkish pattern continued in production at later times. The marbled samples on the pattern cards of Johann Christoph Stoy (reproduced on Plate IX) and the evidence of marbled papers in authentic German bookbindings are proof of this conclusion. The simpler patterns shown on Plate XXVI are indicative of the designs that were produced in Germany from about the 1730s on, although, as noted above, the Dutch pattern continued in force for many decades afterward.

Once again, I must emphasize that it is often difficult and sometimes impossible to distinguish German and French productions of a given design (such as the small-comb, double-comb, placard, or persillé). It is evident that marblers in both lands were aware of events going on in the other, for as Plates XXIII and XXV show, several patterns produced in both Germany and France from around 1680 to 1730 are curiously similar and show nearly identical colors and configurations. Only imprints and binding evidence can assist us in final identification of such materials or, in some cases, allow us to speculate that a given paper originated in one place or the other.

Eighteenth-Century Marbled Patterns of Spain, Italy, and Other European Countries

Marbling, as we have seen, did not migrate beyond the borders of France and Germany until around the middle of the eighteenth century. Accordingly, the simple spot patterns which by this time had become typical of German and French marbling came to be reproduced elsewhere—though there were exceptions. In Italy, Spain, and Portugal, the spot design alone came into production, but in Spain a unique and identifiable variation was introduced in the form of the waved effect. Spot patterns were produced in Denmark and Sweden as well, but makers there also turned out papers that imitated the placard and a few other French and German papers of an earlier time that were no longer being made in their original locales.

Samples 49 through 54 on Plate XXVII show typical spot patterns that came to be manufactured in Italy during the second half of the eighteenth century; the Remondini papers reproduced on Plate XVI show Italian marbles of the early nineteenth century. Only spot patterns have ever been associated with early marbling in Italy, with the spots of these designs being customarily rather small. These configurations, as well as their characteristic pale colors, make identification of Italian papers rather easy.

The six Spanish patterns appearing as samples 55–60 on Plate XXVII are also easy to identify by their distinctive coloration and the irregular waving that came to be added to the majority of them. The first Spanish design exhibited there, made at about mid-century, contains no waved effect and indicates that waving was introduced a decade or more afterward. I am especially partial to authentic Spanish papers, which constitute, in my opinion, the "royalty" of marbling. They have a charm about them that is unrivaled by other marbled papers and designs, no matter how beautiful. Waving is sometimes absent from authentic Spanish papers of the late eighteenth and early nineteenth centuries (at which time the pattern was still in production), but so strongly did the waved effect become part of the marbling of this nation that one automatically looks twice or thrice when encountering in an ancient Spanish book a Spanish paper that had not been waved.

The Portuguese patterns (numbers 61–63) on Plate XXVIII were removed from Portuguese pamphlets of the late eighteenth and early nineteenth centuries and display the distinctive colors that a small number of Portuguese marblers or binders came to employ. It is apparent from the poor techniques displayed that Portuguese marblers were not highly advanced, even when making the simple Turkish design. Portuguese marblers, and their Spanish brethren, began to make the shell pattern, which was introduced early in the nineteenth century, and the Turkish and shell remained the staple designs in the marbling that went on in these two lands. Additionally, I have noticed that the design that came to be known in England in the later nineteenth century as "Stormont" also came into production in Portugal early in the nineteenth century.

The Danish marbling that appears as the final illustration on Plate XVI shows the spot pattern that Georg Julius Liebe came to apply to both paper and book edges in the 1750s and early 1760s. It is an obvious imitation of the German design—with spots of black, red, yellow, and green—that is illustrated in two variant forms on Plate XXVI (samples 41–42). Liebe also imitated the German or French placard design, as did August Heinrich Helmuth, who trained and worked with him. Helmuth,

for the most part, restricted his efforts to producing the older French and German patterns with softer colors and less technical skill. In the period before 1750 only imported French and German marbles had been used to decorate the best productions of the leading Danish binders; it was a few of these early types that were later imitated by Liebe and Helmuth and by an unknown maker who succeeded Helmuth and continued to marble until about the end of the century.

I have noted before that Swedish binders, particularly Lorns Walter Rothof, who appears to have been a professional paper decorator, also came to produce the placard, Dutch, and other early French and German patterns. But this did not occur until the 1750s, 1760s, and 1770s, at which time they were no longer being made in France and Germany. Understandably, these works show somewhat different colors and forms than do the original French and German productions; not only are their colors softer and lighter, but the distribution of colors and the combing appears different as well. The spot patterns attributed to the bookbinder Fredrik Wilhelm Statlander late in the eighteenth century and early in the nineteenth are patently imitations of designs that had come to be made in England.

English Eighteenth-Century Marbled Patterns

English binders and others who tried their hands at marbling after the middle of the eighteenth century undoubtedly attempted to imitate the imported small-comb or Dutch design that long had been popular in English book decoration. We have already seen that Richard Dymott, in his 1766 advertisement, boasted of having brought to perfection the making of Dutch marbled paper in England. Many times over I have observed, in English bindings of the later eighteenth century, small-comb designs that might well qualify as English rather than German or French productions—especially those showing only red, blue, and white stripes, irregularly disposed. Since I have never been able to prove conclusively that any of these actually were made in Britain, I have not included Dutch designs among the early English marbles illustrated here. For the most part, those who attempted to marble in England during the craft's cradle period there produced spot patterns—as did most protomarblers elsewhere—for these are the easiest to make and produce immediate success. In fact, not until the 1820s, when the English began to marble the nonpareil pattern in great numbers, would they become famous for combed designs.

Essentially, there are only two kinds of marbled patterns: spot or thrown designs and combed ones; indeed, all marbled designs, including the combed ones, are merely modifications and refinements of the initial spot pattern. This is true also of the patterns developed around the beginning of the nineteenth century and produced in great numbers in France, Germany, England, and elsewhere; these marblers would merely vary the spot design by adding oil, turpentine, or chemicals to the final color deposited on the size to alter the general effect of the pattern and allow the papers to be produced very quickly.

The nine English patterns illustrated on Plate XXVIII show Turkish or spot designs of the late eighteenth and early nineteenth centuries. The constant development of technique and mastery of the art that they reveal leaves little room for doubt that, by the first quarter of the new century, the English deserved to be counted along with the Germans and French as the Western world's great marblers. English marblers turned out the kinds of patterns that are shown here in great numbers, and sent them to all parts of the realm as well as to Portugal, America, and other nations with whom they traded. The first of our illustrations (sample 64), showing yellow, red, and pale grayish-blue colors, is a design often seen in edge decoration as well as on endpapers in English books of the 1760s and early 1770s; it seems reasonable to conclude that it was one of the earliest patterns to be made in quantity in England. Despite the fact that its overall appearance is suggestive of later and even modern marbling, the early "laid" type of paper on which this decoration appears and other factors corroborate its true eighteenth-century origin.[5]

The yellow color predominant in the earliest English spot patterns soon gave way to green, and better color distribution was achieved as well. The pattern most frequently made in the period that followed called for throwing down red, yellow, and black, and then the dominant green color. Afterward, pink spots and sometimes additional white spots were added to complete the pattern. The pink color, thrown down last or next to last, often looks muddy; sometimes it appears as light purple or even gray.[6] At times, the initial red, yellow, and black colors were raked into linear configurations before the green and pink were laid down, thus creating variation in the pattern. Occasionally, as sample 69 shows, marblers would draw serpentine lines in the final pattern to accomplish still another variation. Or again, the green color could be replaced by or wander over into blue, as is shown on the final two patterns on Plate XXVIII (samples 71 and 72).

When Hugh Sinclair issued his manual on *The Whole Process of Marbling Paper* in the second decade of the nineteenth century, the pattern I have just described was the only Turkish or spot design he discussed, for it was, in fact, the only one being made. Referring to this pattern as "Common French Marble," Sinclair provided directions on how it could be executed:

Throw on red color till the surface of the solution is pretty well covered; of yellow, not quite so much; black, about the same quantity as yellow; green, what quantity you please. A last colour may be added, to enliven it, by having a pot with red or purple; put a greater quantity of gall and water into this last colour.[7]

Although Sinclair described the predominating English pattern of the 1790–1810 period, the two copies of his manual I have seen are illustrated with the later form of this design—that is, one with blue rather than green spots as the dominant ground color. This matter presented me with a nice problem when I was about to marble samples for the 1987 reissue of Sinclair's manual: should I marble according to the samples I had seen, or should I follow Sinclair's directions for what I knew to be the original form of this pattern? I opted for the latter on the ground of authenticity and to help the reader better visualize what he or she was reading about. Sinclair's reference to this as the "common French marble" is indicative of the probable origin of this pattern: the beautiful green pattern made by Nicolas-Denis Derome at Paris in the 1780 period. (An example of Derome's green pattern, which, I believe, served as the basis for the English marblers' green spot design, can be seen as Illustration 34 in Mme. Guilleminot-Chrétien's catalog; the similarity between the two is striking and surely more than coincidental.) We soon shall see that most of the marbled patterns that the English became famous for were constructed not along original lines but by imitating in their own particular way the classic marbled designs that had been developed in Europe during the preceding centuries.

To recapitulate, the progress of the marbler's art in Europe during its first two hundred years may be divided into three distinct phases. The first occurred in Germany and France from the early 1600s until late in the century and was characterized by experimentation and slow improvement. The second, a golden age in Germany as well as in France, ran from the 1680s into the 1730s or 1740s and is noteworthy for the production of a large quantity of beautiful, rather formal, patterns. (This period also represents, in all probability, the high point of the art's achievement in the Western world.) The third phase is distinguished by an overall decline, with a marked decrease in the number and range of patterns attempted and with the simple Turkish or spot pattern becoming dominant by the middle of the eighteenth century (although in France the curled design and in Germany the small-comb or Dutch pattern continued). During this third phase the art began to wander away from Germany and France, becoming associated with a number of other European countries and with England as well. In these lands, however, as in Germany and France, the spot design was mainly produced.

Revival in the Early Nineteenth Century:
The "French," "Empire," or "Stormont" Pattern
and the "Shell"

About the turn of the nineteenth century, a time when marbling had attained full production in England and begun what would prove to be a long and active existence there, the craft entered into a fourth phase. New life was pumped into this form of paper decoration in Europe through the creation of two new patterns, the one referred to by Hugh Sinclair and James Sumner as the "French marble"[8] and later by Charles Woolnough as "Stormont," and the pattern which universally was known as "shell." (Woolnough referred to the latter as "French or shell marble.") All evidence points toward France as the region where these designs arose and where the marbling revival originated, but the matter is moot. While both patterns appear to have been developed at approximately the same time, the shell probably came in a little after the other.

According to Mme. Guilleminot-Chrétien, Alexis Bradel (called "l'aîné," successor to Derome) abandoned around 1803 the green and reddish-brown stone patterns hitherto used abundantly in favor of a pattern which soon became characteristic of French bookbinding in the early nineteenth century. This she refers to as "marbré Empire," although its manufacture and use in France extended slightly beyond the chronological limits of that historical period (i.e., beyond 1814).[9] Initially, this pattern showed only a dark blue color, so that its veins were white where the blue spots avoided coming together. Over time, however, marblers came to put down red prior to laying on the blue, so that the red was driven into veins; afterward, they also began to employ other colors such as yellow, green, blue, or black—alone or in combination—as vein colors. The principal characteristic of this pattern is its continuous system of small, even, pin-sized holes throughout the blue ground, which gives it the appearance of a network of fine lace. Mme. Guilleminot-Chrétien attributes this effect to the greater admixture of gall, but it was actually brought about through the addition of turpentine or "spirits of turpentine" to the blue (usually indigo) ground color.

This variously named pattern (Plate XXIX) appears on a great quantity of French, German, English, American, and other imprints of the late 1790s and the first two decades of the nineteenth century; it became the dominant pattern in France and England before 1820, although Turkish designs continued to be turned out concurrently and the shell was just coming into fashion. Hugh Sinclair sums up the English marbling of this period by giving directions for making three patterns only: the Turkish or spot design (which he refers to as "common French marble"), the turpentined pattern, and the shell. He describes making the turpentined design in various colors, with the ground or predominating color showing pink, purple, green, or orange instead of blue. In America, the turpentined pattern's vogue extended even longer; the Mann family continued producing it throughout the 1820s. Actually, the pattern never completely went out of production as it was made now and again by advanced marblers throughout much of the nineteenth century; it is also described by Charles Woolnough and James Sumner in the 1850s. The pattern's manufacture and use, however, became severely limited because of the difficulty of doing it well, and it eventually gave way to the shell pattern and others that were far easier to make.

As Charles Woolnough pointed out in his manual, this pattern, which he called "Stormont," is most difficult to keep in working order,[10] mainly because of the rapid evaporation of the turpentine and the continuous action among the ingredients with which the color is mixed. Turpentine makes the ground color spread uncontrollably, and it is not easy to keep the holes small, fine, and even—large, unseemly white spots tend to burst forth here and there. "It requires acute observation and great quickness of manipulation on the part of the operator to keep it anything like uniform in appearance," Woolnough observed.[11] I have noted previously that there is a special trick to making this pattern properly, and, once learned, its production becomes commonplace. But, compared to the shell pattern, which took me six months to learn to execute well, overcoming the tribulations involved in acquiring total mastery of the "Stormont" pattern required a full ten years.

It has always puzzled me that information on new marbling techniques could spread rapidly in olden times, when literature was mostly wanting or severely limited and restricted. But such information did spread, for after the turpentined pattern had been introduced, assumedly in France, its manufacture soon commenced in Germany, England, and in other locations, including even America. French, German, and English examples of this pattern, all dating to the first quarter of the nineteenth century, appear on Plate XXIX, while two early American patterns and a later nineteenth-century one can be viewed on Plate XXX.

The shell pattern arose, assumedly, in the first years of the nineteenth century, soon after the introduction of the turpentined one, when an enterprising maker substituted oil for turpentine in the ground color. To create this pattern, one simply adds a few drops of olive or linseed oil, or another oily substance, to a moderately thinned color and, after thorough mixing, throws the color onto the size, usually with a rice straw brush or a broom whisk. The color can be applied singly or after one or several colors for veins have been laid down. The ground color drives these latter into thin veins and itself shows a predominating network of spots that have a ringed appearance, with color gradations in the rings. The spots will be large when the brush is held high, or small if the brush is set just above the size and the color beaten on with a rod.

Despite its ease of construction, the shell pattern requires a certain amount of skill to keep the spots evenly colored and proportioned throughout the pattern. A slip of the hand can result in smaller spots here and larger ones there.

Once mastered, the shell design is probably the quickest and easiest of all marbled patterns to make—including even the spot designs—and sometimes its effects are startlingly beautiful. In a given period of time, a seasoned maker can turn out twice as many shell papers as most other patterns, especially combed ones. This accounts to a great extent for its popularity and extensive manufacture in England, Germany, and America throughout the nineteenth century, and, to a slightly lesser extent, in France as well. In Spain and Portugal, where only the spot design had been produced previously, the shell soon became the principal pattern made during the early nineteenth century. The illustrations on Plate XXX (numbers 88–96) depict nine early shell designs made in Great Britain and Germany (and with regard to number 92, Portugal) during the nineteenth century; number 89, showing blue and black veins amid bright orange ringed spots, was a common British design of the early years of the century, used on the best and cheapest work alike.

Eventually marblers began to intermix the shell and the turpentined patterns—that is, to produce them in combination. For example, they might deposit throughout a completed shell pattern, as a novel and final touch, a shower of spots in a contrasting color with turpentine. Conversely, they might sprinkle a color with oil onto a completed Stormont design. Laying the shell onto the other patterns almost always drives the turpentined spots into veins, so that one obtains a shell pattern with Stormont veins. On the other hand, a turpentined pattern dropped onto a shell design tends to have limited expansive power, so that it usually appears distinctly as small, scattered, lacy spots amid an overall shell design. In other words, one can better control the application of a color with turpentine when laying it onto one with oil than vice versa. Both of these variant patterns are illustrated on Plate XXXI—"Stormont on shell" and "shell on Stormont"—along with patterns showing "shell on shell" (that is, patterns having several colors with oil in them dropped on consecutively). Some early makers added a drop or two of turpentine to the shell color, to give the appearance of just a few fine holes in each of the shell rings (normally, the power of the turpentine was severely compromised by the oily substance). However, when too little oil or too much turpentine was used, a shell pattern having a great many holes resulted, making it sometimes difficult to state unequivocally whether a pattern is basically a Stormont or a shell.

Finally, some makers varied the shell pattern by working designs into it. Sample 130 on Plate XXXIII shows how the French sometimes drew the point of a quill, a draw point, or a needle through the design indiscrimi-

nately, while sample 132 illustrates how in America the Manns varied the pattern in a more orderly way by drawing through it the "antique zigzag" device described by Charles Woolnough.

German Patterns of the Nineteenth Century

As the factory system developed in Germany toward the end of the eighteenth century, and especially with the founding of the Dessauer-Aschaffenburg empire early in the nineteenth, German marbling took on new aspects and proportions. Along with the continuous expansion of the industry a great many marbled patterns were put into production, for we must remember that hand marbling continued in force in Germany throughout most of the nineteenth century and would diminish sharply only towards the century's end. The output included most of the traditional patterns so beloved by hand binders: the Turkish and curl, the recently introduced shell and Stormont designs, and combinations of them. In addition, in the 1840s and 50s makers introduced other totally novel designs. Three sources—the Dessauer pattern books, the Fichtenberg manual (both dating to the early 1850s), and the Schade manual of 1845—give us a pretty fair indication of just what was going on.

The pattern book[12] shows, among the many marbled patterns grouped at its front, a large number of Turkish or stone designs, in great variety and in combinations of colors. Also grouped under the category "Fein Turkisch Marmor" are the turpentined and shell designs, and combinations of the two. Then follow two pages of curled designs, called "Fein Pfauen Marmor" (fine peacock marbles), nearly two pages of "Fluss Marmor" (shell patterns that have been curled and swirled), and three and a half pages of "Fein Griechisch Marmor," which is the German designation of the Spanish design. (This last pattern, reintroduced in about the 1820s and by now made in England, Germany, and America with very straight and precise waves, will be discussed separately.) Included within the Turkish category, or displayed separately, are several new patterns developed from the 1830s: called "Tieger Marmor," "Schrottel Marmor," and "Polnisch Marmor," with a fourth, unnamed pattern (grouped here among the Turkish designs but alluded to in other sources as "broken" or "romantic"). All four of these appear here on Plate XXXII.

In his *Die Geschichte des Buntpapieres*, Paul Kersten sets the date of the origin of the Gustav pattern (the pseudo-marbled paper referred to in Chapter 10) at 1855 and that of the "Tiger" (or "Sonnen-Marmor," as it also is known) at 1867.[3] While his date for the Gustav pattern likely is accurate, he appears to be far off target with regard to the other pattern, for the Tiger is among the new patterns discussed in Fichtenberg's 1852 manual and even earlier in the Schade work of 1845.

1

2

3

4

5

6

7

8

9

10

11

12

PLATE XXIII

13 14 15

16 17 18

19 20 21

22 23 24

PLATE XXIV

25 26 27

28 29 30

31 32 33

34 35 36

PLATE XXV

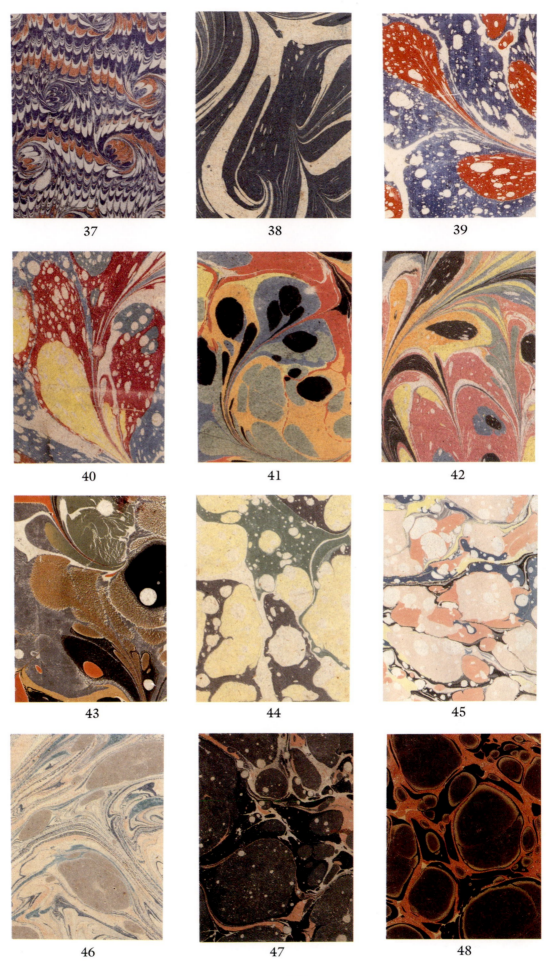

37   38   39

40   41   42

43   44   45

46   47   48

PLATE XXVI

49   50   51

52   53   54

55   56   57

58   59   60

PLATE XXVII

61

62

63

64

65

66

67

68

69

70

71

72

PLATE XXVIII

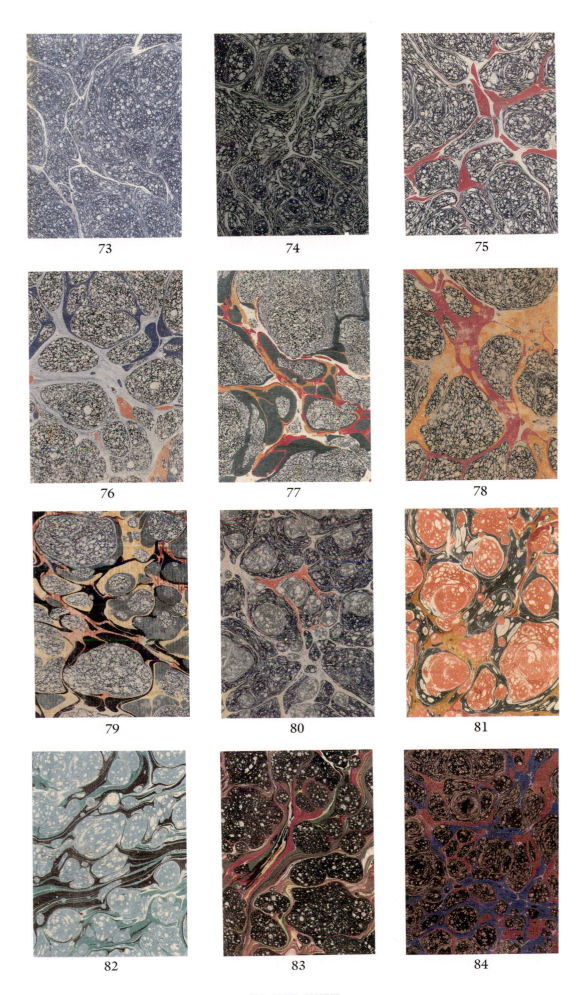

73   74   75

76   77   78

79   80   81

82   83   84

PLATE XXIX

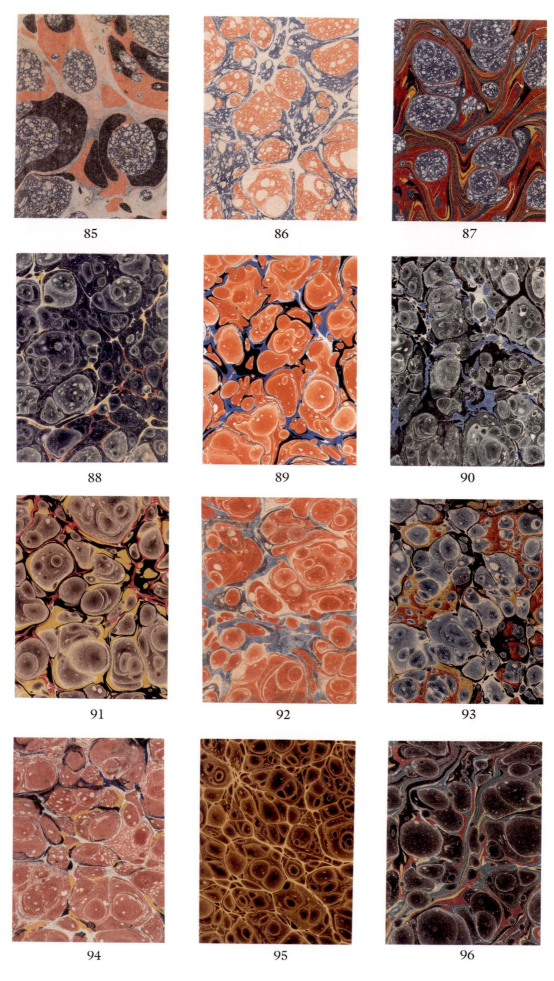

85

86

87

88

89

90

91

92

93

94

95

96

PLATE XXX

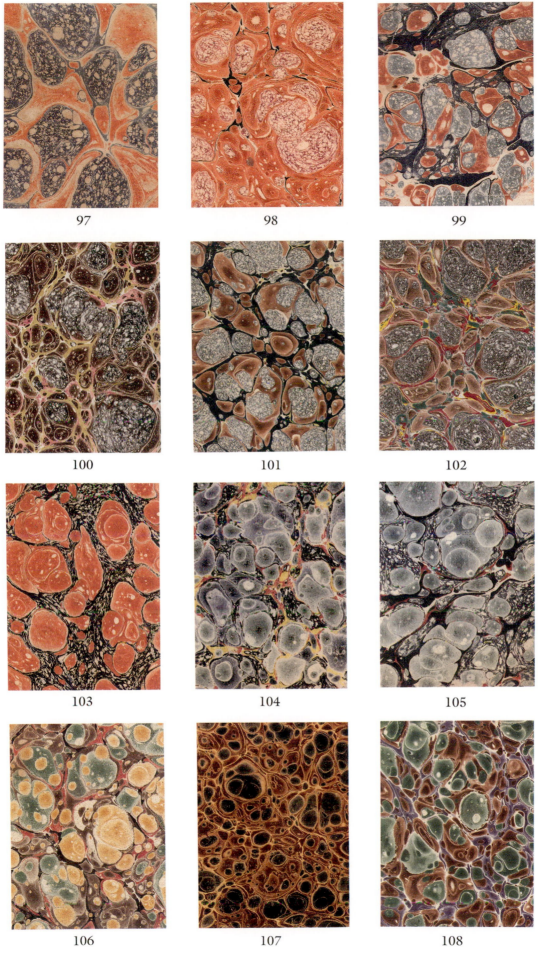

97   98   99

100   101   102

103   104   105

106   107   108

PLATE XXXI

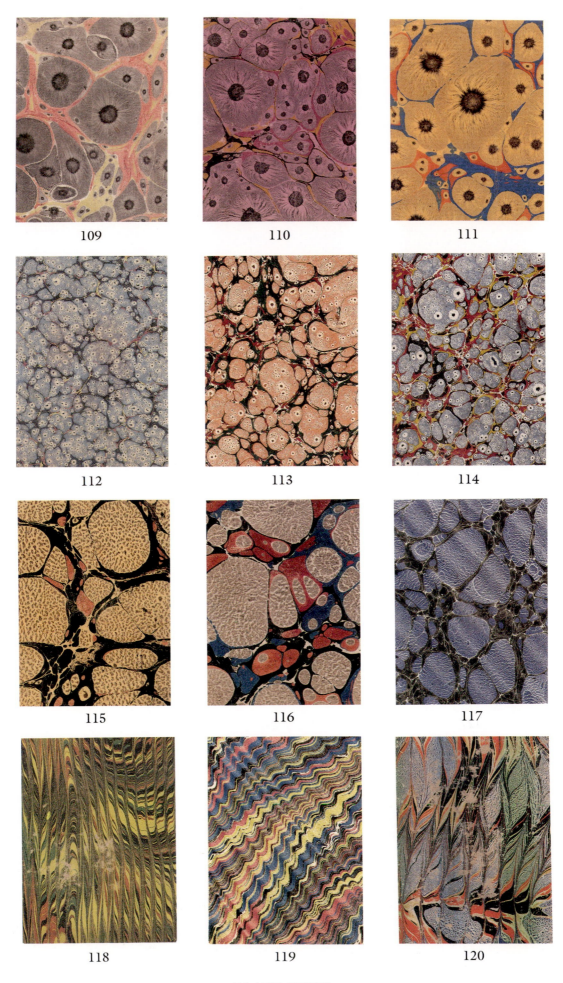

109   110   111

112   113   114

115   116   117

118   119   120

PLATE XXXII

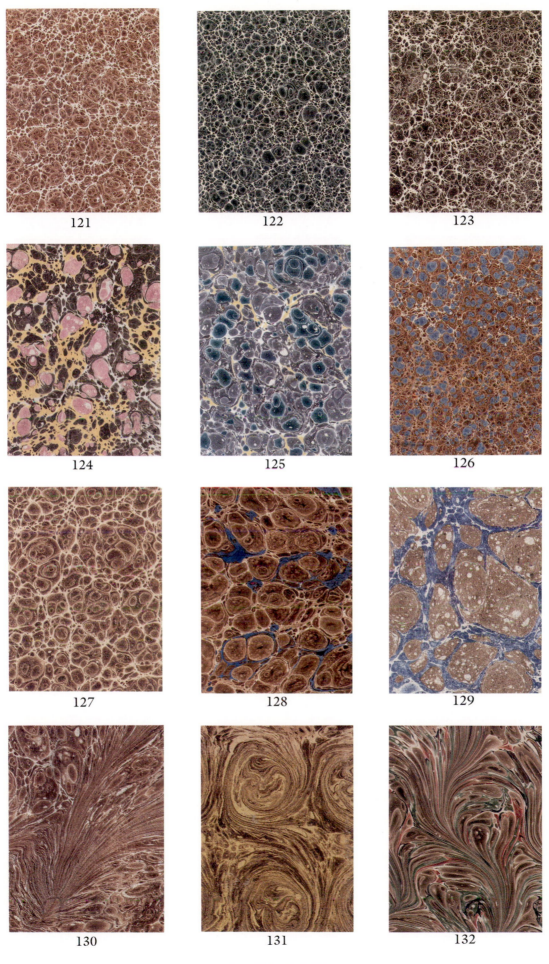

121   122   123

124   125   126

127   128   129

130   131   132

PLATE XXXIII

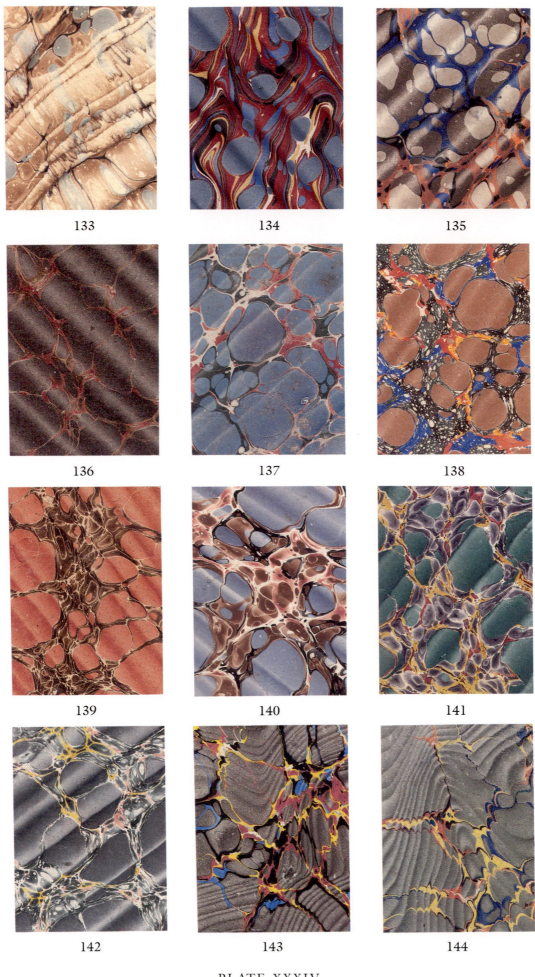

133   134   135

136   137   138

139   140   141

142   143   144

PLATE XXXIV

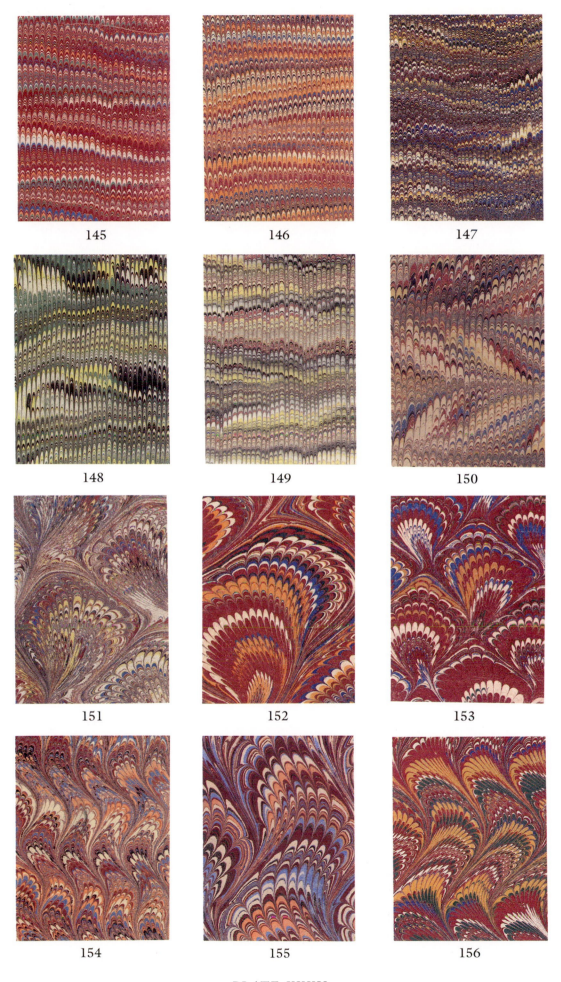

145   146   147

148   149   150

151   152   153

154   155   156

PLATE XXXV

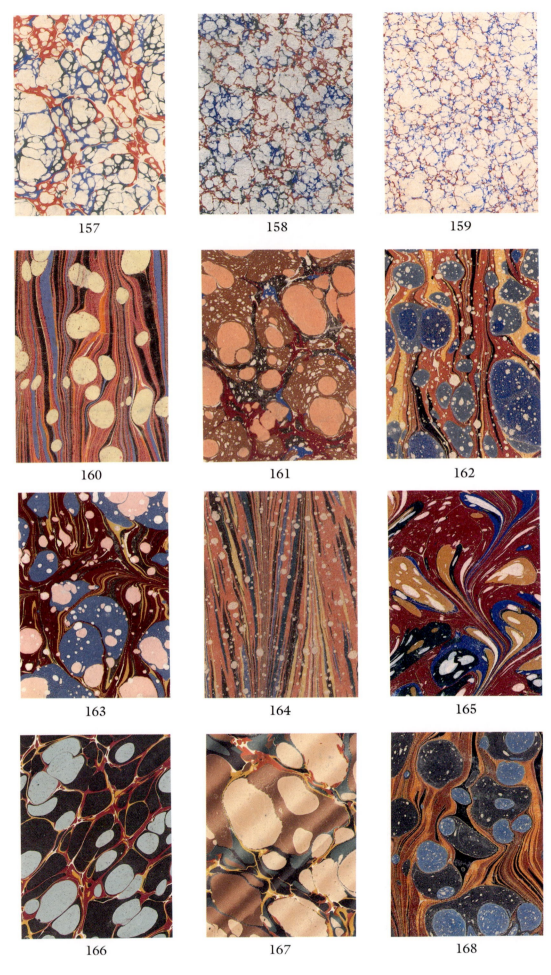

157 158 159

160 161 162

163 164 165

166 167 168

PLATE XXXVI

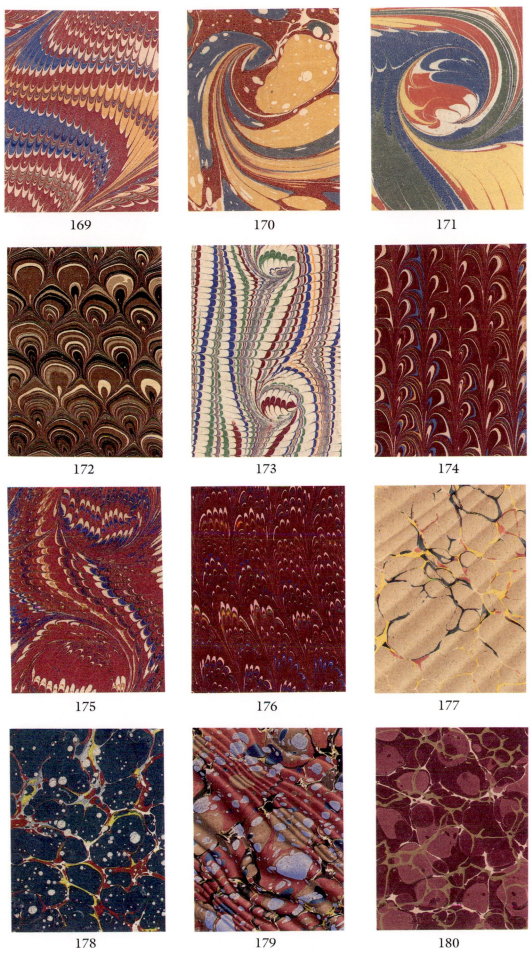

169   170   171

172   173   174

175   176   177

178   179   180

PLATE XXXVII

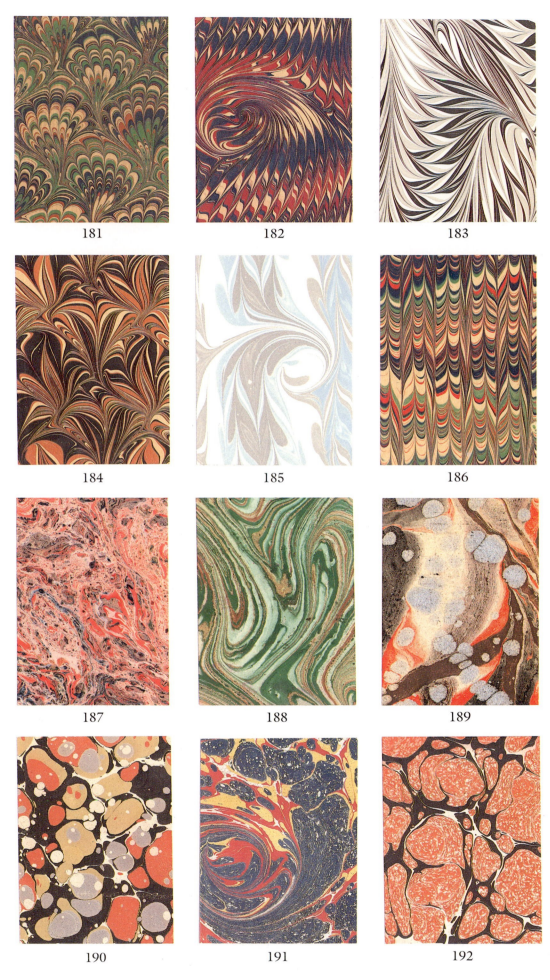

181   182   183

184   185   186

187   188   189

190   191   192

PLATE XXXVIII

Captions for Plates XXIII–XXXVIII

Samples of the most common marbled patterns. Samples 25, 26, 29, 31, 37 and 39 are reproduced from papers in the Germanisches Nationalmuseum, Nürnberg; all others are reproduced from papers in the author's collection.

PLATE XXIII, French patterns, late 17th and first half of the 18th centuries: 1. Placard pattern; 2. Placard pattern, combed; 3. Placard or spot pattern, swirled; 4. Placard or spot pattern, curled; 5. Persillé (parsley) pattern; 6. Persillé pattern, curled; 7. Turkish pattern, swirled; 8. Double-comb pattern, made with small and medium combs; 9. Double-comb pattern, made with small and wide combs; 10. Wide comb pattern; 11. Dutch pattern; 12. Dutch pattern, curled.

PLATE XXIV, French curl and spot patterns, 18th century: 13. Curl pattern, late 17th or early 18th century; 14–16. Curl patterns, early 18th century; 17–18. Curl patterns, late 18th century; 19–24. Turkish or spot patterns, mid- to late 18th century.

PLATE XXV, German patterns, late 17th and early to mid-18th century: 25. Combed pattern with antique zigzag or peacock design; 26. Placard pattern; 27. Placard pattern, combed with medium-small comb; 28. Placard or spot pattern, combed with wide comb; 29. Persillé or parsley pattern; 30. Large Turkish or spot design; 31. Double-comb pattern, made with small and medium combs; 32. Double-comb pattern, made with medium small and wide combs; 33. Dutch pattern; 34–35. Dutch patterns, curled; 36. Medium-comb pattern, swirled.

PLATE XXVI, German combed and Turkish or spot patterns, curled, swirled, or left plain: 37. Medium-small comb pattern, curled, early to mid-18th century; 38. Spot pattern, curled and swirled, early to mid-18th century; 39–43. Turkish or spot patterns, swirled, 1730s to 1780s; 44–46. Turkish patterns, late 18th century; 47–48. Turkish patterns, very late 18th and early 19th centuries.

PLATE XXVII: (49–54—Italian patterns) 49. Plain rose spot pattern, middle to late 18th century; 50–53. Small spot or Italian patterns, late 18th century; 54. Larger spot pattern, very late 18th or early 19th century; (55–60—Spanish patterns) 55. Spot pattern, unwaved, middle 18th century; 56–58. Spot patterns, waved (typical Spanish patterns), 1760s to 1780s; 59–60. Spot patterns, waved, 1790's and early 1800s.

PLATE XXVIII, Portuguese and English spot patterns: 61–63. Portuguese spot patterns, late 18th and early 19th centuries; (64–72—English spot patterns, late 18th and early 19th centuries) 64. Spot pattern, 1760 period; 65–68. Spot patterns with green predominating color, 1770s to 1790s; 69. Spot pattern, combed in a serpentine manner; 70. Spot pattern, with vein colors raked beforehand; 71–72. Spot patterns with blue instead of green spots predominating, 1790s and early 1800s.

PLATE XXIX, "French" or "Empire" or "Stormont" patterns: 73–74. France, 1800–1815 period; 75–82. Britain, 1805–1825 period; 83–84. Germany, 1810–1825 period.

PLATE XXX, "Stormont" and "shell" patterns: 85. Stormont, made in Boston, Massachusetts, before 1810; 86. Stormont, made by Samuel Mann, Dedham, Massachusetts, early 1820s; 87. Stormont, British, 1860 period; (88–96—Shell patterns) 88–91. Britain, 1805–1825 period; 92. Portugal, early 19th century; 93–96. Germany, 1810–1825 period.

PLATE XXXI, Stormont and shell patterns, mixed: 97–99. Stormont on shell, Britain, first decade of the 19th century; 100. Stormont on shell, Germany, 1820 period; 101–102. Stormont on shell, Britain or America, later 19th century; 103–105. Shell on Stormont, Britain, 1830s and 1840s; 106–108. Shell on shell, Britain, Germany, and America respectively, 1820–1840 period. No. 108 was made by Samuel Mann of Boston and Dedham, Massachusetts.

PLATE XXXII, new German patterns of the 19th century: 109–111. Tiger (or Tieger or tigré) or Sonnen-Marmor, 1830–1860 period; 112–114. Schrottel or Schröetel or Schroffel, later 19th century; 115–117. Romantic or broken or "marbres cassés" patterns, 1840–1860 period; 118–120. Polnisch (Polish) pattern, 1840–1860 period.

PLATE XXXIII, French patterns of the 19th century; German and American curled and swirled patterns: 121–123. Small Turkish pattern, France, early 19th century; 124–126. Small shell design, France, early to mid-19th century; 127–128. Larger shell patterns, France, 1830–1850 period; 129. Empire or Stormont pattern, France, 1830 period; 130. Shell pattern, swirled, France, 1840 period; 131. Shell design, curled, Germany, 1830 period; 132. Shell design, combed through with the antique zigzag comb; made by Samuel and Edward Mann, Boston and Dedham, Massachusetts, 1830s.

PLATE XXXIV, "Spanish" or "neo-Spanish" designs of the 19th century: 133. England, late 1820s, probably one of the early Spanish papers produced in that country; 134–135. Britain, 1840–1860 period; 136. Germany, end of the first half of the 19th century; 137. America, 1840–1860 period; possibly made by Charles E. Williams at Philadelphia; 138. Spanish with Stormont veins, America, second half of 19th century; 139–140. Spanish with shell veins ("shell-veined Spanish"), Britain or America, second half of the 19th century; 141–142. Fancy Spanish or Lace pattern, Britain, second half of the 19th century; 143–144. Spanish pattern with a moiré or crimpled effect, Britain, 1850–1870 period.

PLATE XXXV, nonpareil and other combed patterns of the 19th century: 145–150. Nonpareil patterns, Britain and America, 1840s–1870s; 151. Peacock design, Britain, 1850 period; 152–153. Peacock designs, Britain and Germany, 1860–1880 period; 154–155. Double-comb, waved, Britain, 1870s; 156. Double-comb, waved, Germany, 1880s.

PLATE XXXVI, patterns of the mid-19th century and later: 157–159. "Italian" or "neo-Italian" (158 is German, the others English or American); 160. Zebra, Britain, 1850s; 161. West end, Britain, 1850s. 162–163. Antique spots, Britain, 1840s and 1850s; 164. Antique straight, Britain, 1850s; 165. Antique zigzag, Britain, 1850s; 166–167. Extra and Spanish drag, Britain, 1850s and 1860s; 168. Gloucester, England, 1850s.

PLATE XXXVII: 169–171. British-made "Dutch" and "old Dutch" patterns of the later 19th century; (172–180—mechanically and photographically reproduced patterns of the later 19th and early 20th centuries) 172. "Pfauen" or peacock design, Germany, late 19th century; 173. Combed design, Germany or England, late 19th century; 174. "American" design, Germany, late 18th or early 20th century; 175–176. Curled and double-combed designs, Germany, late 19th century; 177. Spanish, made probably in France, late 19th century; 178. Turkish pattern, Britain or America, early 20th century; 179. Spanish pattern of the moiré type, Britain, late 19th or early 20th century; 180. Turkish pattern, with gold veins overprinted, Britain, late 19th or early 20th century.

PLATE XXXVIII, 20th-century patterns: 181–186. Cockerell papers, 1930 period; (187–189—oil marbling) 187. Made by Vincent Villaplana Gadea, Barcelona, 1920s or 1930s; 188. France, 1930s; 189. Made by Ingeborg Börjesson (Börgesson), Enskede, Sweden, 1930s; (190–192—Modern French patterns) 190. Turkish design; 191. Empire or Stormont pattern, curled; 192. Empire or Stormont pattern.

Fichtenberg refers to the four patterns noted above as German designs "tigré," "Schroëtel," "marbres cassés," and "papiers Polonais." When we examine Fichtenberg's instructions to determine how these specific patterns were made, we find that all but the Polish papers were effected through the use of caustic and other chemicals; a more complicated version of the Polish design could be produced in this way as well. For the tigré (Plate XXXII, samples 109–111) and Schroëtel (samples 112–114) patterns, old size was used[14] with the vein colors laid down in the usual way. The special effect for which the tigré (in Germany, "Tiger," and later "Sonnen-Marmor") was known—spots with black dots at their centers and rays emanating from them—was produced by grinding a cake of fine black color with ox-gall and adding a little water and caustic potash (potassium hydroxide). The mixture then was dropped on as the final ground color or combined with another color, and the spots with rays appeared. The Schroëtel pattern was achieved in a similar manner, but a mixture of Marseilles, Venetian, or castile soap, water, gall, red prussiate of potash (ferricyanide), and a little alum, was added to the ground color bringing about its special appearance.

The broken effect of the "marbres cassés" (Plate XXXII, samples 115–117) was produced by adding to the ground color (an earth color such as Italian yellow or sienna, Cassel earth, Italian yellow mixed with indigo, or indigo alone) a compound that Fichtenberg referred to as "glazing paste"[15] and soap made from soda. For this pattern two troughs, both containing tragacanth size, were employed in tandem. After the vein colors had been sprinkled on and the ground color laid onto one trough, the operator shifted to the second trough and repeated the same operation, by which time the pattern on the first trough had broken up, for a brief interval was required for this reaction to take place. As sample 117 indicates, the "broken" or "cassés" or romantic pattern could also be waved.

Fichtenberg says that the Polonais (Polish) paper was considered a fantasy paper; it was an elegant design, especially when shaded (sample 119) to form what was called "trocadero." This paper could be made in two ways. A simple pattern was produced without chemical additives. After a variety of colors had been sprinkled onto the size—usually yellow, red, blue, green, and black—they were worked into long, thin, straight lines of intermixed color by careful raking through the trough, backward and forward along its entire length. The pattern's special appearance depended on the manner that the paper was laid down, not smoothly and in one continuous motion in the usual way, but by drawing the paper back and forth with small hand movements. A more complicated version was effected by adding a mixture of lacquer or shellac, "glazing paste," soap, and potash to the last color laid on, which caused the color to open up. The paper was then put down as before (sample 120).

The master bookbinder and amateur marbler J. A. F. Schade discusses the "Schroffel" (or, as he called it, "broken") pattern and also the one with rays in his *Marmorir-Kunst*. To make Schroffel—we can only surmise that this was the "Schrottel" or "Schroëtel" design, since he provides no original samples—Schade calls for the addition to the ground color of his "special solution," a mixture of shellac, resin and Venetian soap. But he indicates that this can also be made in still another way.[16] For the other pattern, described as having dark spots the size of peas, with rays emanating from each of the spots, he calls for the addition of his special solution to the final or black color. Gall is added to give the color sufficient driving power, and it is tempered little by little with drops of hydrochloric acid until the proper effect—that is, the expansion of rays—is achieved. I have made this pattern many times, following Schade's directions, and have found his method excellent for obtaining beautiful, root-like emanations.[17]

The German repertoire of marbled papers through most of the early and second half of the nineteenth century was fairly extensive, including Turkish, turpentined, shell, curled, swirled, shaded, and other classical patterns as well as the special designs described above. Furthermore, Annonay papers (referred to in the Dessauer pattern book as "Margrafen Papier"), agate papers, paste papers, a huge variety of printed, stamped, and embossed papers, and papers that imitated the grained surface of leather also were produced. Throughout much if not most of the century, the majority of these papers, as well as the marbled types, were produced by hand. Many of these German papers are scattered about the colored plates accompanying this survey; others can be seen on pages of the Dessauer pattern book illustrated on Plates XII and XIII.

French Patterns of the Nineteenth Century

During the first two decades of the nineteenth century, the French produced mostly the Empire and shell patterns, although the standard Turkish design still continued to be made. But the introduction of the agate, Annonay, and other pseudo-marbled papers in the 1820s and 1830s delivered a staggering blow to traditional marbling in France. Soon makers restricted their output to the few types of designs illustrated on Plate XXXII, which consisted mainly of a monochrome Turkish pattern with very small spots (samples 121–123), a shell design usually showing very small spots (samples 124–126), and a rather poorly constructed Stormont or Empire pattern (sample 129). It is possible that the monochrome Turkish design with very small spots (one sometimes sees it with a black vein color) was achieved by blowing on the color with a mouth atomizer (my own method for producing it), although a similar effect can be obtained by holding a rice straw brush full of color directly above the size and beating the color on with a metal rod. The small shell spots were produced in a similar manner, being added sometimes to a previous shell pattern of another color and sometimes to the small Turkish design previously described. Other shell patterns were made with larger spots (samples 127 and 128), frequently without veins or with black and blue veins only; sometimes they were swirled (sample 130).

As the range of French marbled patterns was diminishing, Annonay and other pseudo-marbled papers were made and used in increasing numbers. These were employed as cover papers only, never as endpapers; if decorated endpapers were desired, the marbled variety invariably filled this role. Quite often, the small, plain Turkish paper appeared as a cover paper with the shell design as the endpaper, or vice versa. Despite the vastly diminishing repertoire, a handful of French marblers continued to fulfill the needs of the best hand bookbinders with a fairly wide array of patterns, including many of the old designs and even imitations of some of the newer German designs as well. At least, this is what the pattern books of the Chagniat-Putois firm and other later nineteenth-century French makers that are preserved in the Musée des Arts Décoratifs seem to tell us. Except for these few makers, who probably numbered only in the handfuls, by the latter decades of the nineteenth century the French industry of old was all but gone.

Nonpareil and Spanish Designs of the Nineteenth Century

At some point in the 1820s, English makers revived the waved pattern that had been popular in Spain at the end of the eighteenth century, introducing it into their own repertoire and produced it more precisely, with very even waves. Not long after, the small-combed pattern that came to be termed "nonpareil" was introduced as well. These two designs, together with the shell pattern, were the stock-in-trade of British marbling throughout the nineteenth century. By the time that John Hannett published his *Bibliopegia: or, The Art of Bookbinding* in 1835, the shell, Spanish, and small-combed (now termed "Anglo-Dutch") patterns were the only ones mentioned, although the Turkish and Stormont patterns were turned out by a maker every now and then. So adept did British marblers become in producing the Spanish and small-combed designs that in 1852 Fichtenberg referred to these two patterns as typifying "marbres Anglais." We know, too, that the Germans made the Spanish pattern in quantity under the designation "Griechisch,"[18] and that American marblers like the Manns and Charles Williams produced rather good versions of the Spanish, shell, and nonpareil patterns in large numbers. (The Germans, for some reason unknown to us, never bothered to produce the non-pareil pattern at all, although they did turn out larger combed designs.)

The Spanish, or, as I refer to it, the "neo-Spanish" pattern that came to be waved in a very precise manner in the nineteenth century was made by first laying down a Turkish or spot or stone design. The waving was accomplished by the manner in which the sheet of paper was laid onto the size, the marbler holding the paper by its two opposite corners and keeping it upright and nearly vertical. The right, front corner was held so that the paper barely touched the size and it was let down in abrupt but regular movements—shaken, and moved to and fro until the whole sheet came to rest on the surface of the size. The agitation could be enhanced by tapping the sheet with the middle finger of the right hand while the sheet was being laid down, and the narrowness and regularity of the waves could be controlled by the regularity in which the sheet was deposited onto the bath. To make the Spanish pattern, a thickish size—usually, a mixture of gum tragacanth and flea seed—was employed, for this combination had a grasping power that helped bring about proper shading of the waves.

The Spanish pattern was quickly produced, and it presented a pleasing appearance to the nineteenth-century eye. Then, too, it could be varied in a number of simple ways. For instance, throwing a ground color impregnated with a sizable amount of gall onto a Stormont pattern previously laid down, and then waving the final design, resulted in a Spanish pattern having Stormont veins (Plate XIV, sample 138). Shell-veined Spanish paper could be made by carrying out the same process on a shell pattern, as samples 139 and 140 indicate. "Fancy Spanish" or "Lace Pattern" (according to Woolnough's designations) was made by first throwing down vein colors and then driving them up into lacy veins by water, strongly saturated with gall, tincture of green soap, or the so-called sprinkling solution. After a colored ground was laid on, waving took place in the usual manner (samples 141–142). An even fancier Spanish—Woolnough did not name this pattern, but the Manns called it "Spanish crimpled"—could be produced by first folding the paper into small squares, unfolding it, and then laying it onto the pattern on the size in the usual Spanish manner. The resultant pattern showed irregular waves in uneven and varying configurations that approximated the appearance of watered silk or moiré cloth. The small squares caught the color spots in uneven undulations as the paper was laid down, resulting in the configurations in samples 143 and 144. A Spanish pattern made in this manner approximates the lushness and charm of the original Spanish paper and is equally beautiful. This pattern was not discussed in the first, 1853 edition of Charles Woolnough's manual; undoubtedly, it came into production between then and the 1881 edition, where he devoted a page and a half to it and illustrated it with an original sample.

Woolnough, when discussing the nonpareil pattern

(Plate XXXV, samples 145–150) in the 1881 edition of his manual, declared, "perhaps no pattern that ever was produced has had such an extensive and prolonged life as this,"

> and although it has now become so common as to be used on almost every description of work, it still holds its place in the favour of the public. About forty-five years ago it was sold at the extraordinary price of six shillings per quire for demy size, and that was very inferior to what may now be obtained for half-a-crown or three shillings.[19]

The nonpareil pattern is formed by laying down three, four, or five colors in spots, raking them crosswise, and then combing through the stripes with a comb with many teeth spaced very closely together. Some marblers used a peg-rake to rake the colors twice—once across the trough and then back again through the middles of the streaks just created; this thinned the lines and better distributed the colors, resulting in a superior pattern.

The nonpareil design appears to have come into production and vogue in Britain in the late 1820s; its origins may well be in the closely combed papers made in France in the early and middle decades of the seventeenth century. British marblers, it seems certain, were rarely originators, but developed most of the patterns they became famous for by imitating designs of earlier times. There can be little doubt that they chose as their examples papers in early French and German books that were being restored or rebound; or perhaps they sought out examples in seventeenth-century French bindings in the British Museum and other libraries. Interestingly, the French seem not to have done much with combing after their initial experience with it in the seventeenth century, except to imitate the German small combed pattern called "Dutch;" otherwise, combing formed no part of the French marbler's repertoire.

Because the nonpareil became such a popular pattern and was so extensively made, I have collected hundreds of examples, in a large variety of colors. Nonpareil was normally made with four or five colors, but now and then one encounters papers made with two and, infrequently, only one. Occasionally, a marbler tried to vary the pattern by combing it in the same direction a second time with a wider comb, producing the double-comb pattern in the process (as the French and Germans did a century before); or, he might decide to move the comb back and forth in a sideways motion (Plate XXXV, samples 154–156). Although the time of the peacock pattern had not yet come, some makers after mid-century nonetheless produced early, imperfect examples by combing through a completed nonpareil design with the antique zigzag device, moving the comb to and fro during the combing process (pattern 151).

A peacock pattern can be accomplished in three ways: by using the antique zigzag device (Figure 39); by combing through a nonpareil pattern on thin size with a wide comb (moving the colors from side to side while at the same time moving them apart and then bringing them together again); and, lastly, by using the special movable comb introduced along with Halferian marbling (Figure 40). Several patterns on Plate XXXV show early examples of peacocking, and the Boeck manual of 1880 proves that by then peacocking had already come into fashion, but the peacock design gained its fame and became one of the most striking patterns only with the introduction of Halferian marbling and the wide use of carragheen size. Peacocking requires the fineness of carragheen size for its delicate yet brilliant forms. Tragacanth size scarcely allowed the pattern to appear in its full glory, so it was only infrequently attempted in earlier times, even though some marblers were aware of it, as these samples indicate. British refer to this design as "peacock"; the Germans call it "Boukett" using the term peacock ("Pfauenmarmor") for the same pattern formed into shell-like configurations without the thin lines. This latter pattern was made by raking the colors and then using the antique zigzag device or the movable comb to complete the pattern. Seemingly an innovation of Halferian marbling, sample 25 on Plate XXV shows that it was accomplished long before Halfer's time, even as early as the seventeenth century.

British Marbling at Mid-Nineteenth Century

British marbling in Woolnough's, Sumner's, and Corfield's time represents the last blossoming in the craft's fading existence. As one carefully peruses Woolnough's manual, it becomes obvious that all the patterns he discusses fit into the classical or neoclassical mold. Aside from the shell, Stormont, Spanish (including its fancy veined forms), and nonpareil designs, almost all the other patterns he describes, while having new names, are merely attempts to reproduce the older designs, sometimes faithfully but now and then in varied ways. The pattern Woolnough called "Italian" (or, in his 1881 edition, "Italian Four Vein"), for example, was a recreation of the small spot design that had appeared in Italy in the last decades of the eighteenth and early decades of the nineteenth centuries. His "Antique Spot," "Antique Straight," "Antique Zigzag," and "Old Dutch" patterns were anachronistic reproductions of French and German designs of the late seventeenth and early eighteenth centuries, snatched out of the golden age of marbling and dressed in modern colors and forms. Even Woolnough's "West End" pattern, despite its contemporary-sounding title, was a copy of an old design—the Turkish pattern made in Europe in the late eighteenth century and copied by the British when they began to marble in a large way—but with different colors that gave it a somewhat modern appearance. Woolnough claimed to introduce a few new patterns, such as "Zebra," "British," "Gloucester," and "Drag," but these too were merely variations on familiar themes or new combinations of old designs.

The Italian pattern (Plate XXXVI, samples 157–159), also made by the Germans in the later nineteenth century and which Halfer would perfect and call "Ader-Marmor" (translated as "hair-vein"), was executed by throwing down vein colors, then applying a white color containing a large amount of gall. The spots were kept small by using a large brush or broom, held just over the size, and beating or knocking the final color on. Water with a good deal of gall in it could also be used for producing this final effect, for the paper would show white where the gall-impregnated water had fallen on the size. And the pattern could be given more depth and character by using white with a tint of gray or blue in it. Josef Halfer's improvements were to substitute sprinkling water for gall in the final color and, of course, to execute the pattern on carragheen size. The greater driving force of the sprinkling water and the fineness of the size gave the veins hairlike configurations and imparted to the entire pattern an appearance of delicacy and great beauty (Plate XXII).

Woolnough's "Curl" patterns were copies of the large French curled designs of old, but their modern colors imparted a flatness that little approximated the charm and beauty of the late seventeenth- and early eighteenth-century articles. "Zebra" (Plate XXXVI, sample 160) was a very simple pattern, made quickly by throwing a combination of red, yellow, black and blue spots onto the size, raking or combing the colors into straight lines, and finally throwing on a shower of cream or pink spots. Woolnough describes and illustrates how it sometimes was varied by adding the Spanish wave and shading. James Sumner's directions for making Zebra called for laying the four Dutch colors lengthwise on the size, then raking them up and down the trough in the manner of the small Dutch pattern, but without the final small combing. Sumner also omitted the final shower of spots, so that the pattern was actually a small Dutch one left uncombed. "The small Dutch and Zebra answer well for small and fancy stationary, octavos, and quartos," he advised. "Small Dutch is generally used for a better class of work, and Zebra for common, with the red used sparingly."[20]

Woolnough's "West End" pattern (Plate XXXVI, sample 161) was similar to the Spanish, but it was left unwaved and unshaded. It was made with two prominent ground colors, usually brown, the dominant one being dark and the other showing as lighter brown spots upon it. The "Antique Spots" pattern (samples 162 and 163) had raked or swirled veins of red, yellow, and black (the colors most commoly used for vein colors in all marbling since they are the best adapted to this purpose) with two spot colors thrown on them, such as blue and pink or dark and light blue. The pattern was completed by beating on a shower of white spots. The veins, reduced to fine,

straight lines by raking them first in one direction and then in the other, could be left straight or subsequently curled. The "Antique Straight" design (sample 164) was produced by simply raking the vein colors in two directions, as before, and then beating on a shower of fine white spots. The "Antique Curl" pattern resulted when curls were imparted to the streaks before the shower of white spots was applied. The "Antique Zigzag" pattern was accomplished by first completing an Italian pattern, adding less gall to the final white color before it was beat on so that the other colors would be more prominent. The marbler then passed the antique zigzag device through the pattern, moving it from side to side, to give a shell-shaped effect to the colors. This pattern could be varied in many ways; for example, the zigzag combing could be accomplished on spot and other patterns (sample 165).

Woolnough also gave directions for making the old Dutch patterns, relating how such patterns could be finely combed, curled, and constructed to imitate the old *placard* pattern (Plate XXXVII, samples 169–171). In addition, he described the "Extra" or "Spanish Drag" pattern (Plate XXXVI, samples 166–167), noted in his 1881 manual as a pattern that stands out quite distinctly from the others and was at one time in great demand. This was a spot pattern with elongated spots, and was accomplished by using a trough double the length of the paper. After the pattern had been laid down, the sheet was let down onto the size about an inch at a time and dragged in stages from one side of the trough to the other, until the other end of the trough had been reached. Although not a true Spanish paper, it was so named because of the unusual manner in which the paper was laid down. In both editions of his manual, Woolnough discussed a pattern he called "British" which was similarly produced. Made with or without vein colors, this pattern also was marbled on a double trough so that the paper could be dragged. In essence, the same ground color—black or blue—was put down twice; the second color had more gall in it so that it would expand further and show in a lighter and variant black or blue tone. The paper then was laid down in the drag fashion. The final pattern that Woolnough described was "Gloucester" (Plate XXXVI, sample 168). This was merely the "Antique Spots" design to which a blue Stormont color was applied in place of the second spot color, and the final shower of fine white spots was omitted.[21]

With the passing of Woolnough, Sumner, Corfield, and other British marblers of the later nineteenth century, the art as it existed for the prior three centuries all but came to an end. This situation had already come to pass in France and it occurred in the German factories at about the same time as in England. As previously noted, machine marbling (introduced into the German factories in the last decades of the nineteenth century) and greater production of Achat, Gustav, and other pseudo-marbled papers continued to make inroads on what was left of the marbling trade, so that very little high quality paper was produced any more. Even though Halferian marbling brought about an upswing in the quality of original marbling, the output was relatively limited; it attempted to meet the needs of a highly reduced class of hand bookbinders who employed such decoration on a small scale, compared with the extensive usage of the past. Indeed, many Halferian marblers were themselves bookbinders who made paper mainly for their own use and for comrades and a restricted clientele.

The patterns on Plate XXXVII (samples 172–180) are indicative of this dismal trend: more and more machine marbling or patterns photographically produced and less and less of the authentic product. As the twentieth century commenced, few craftsmen remained who could execute real marbling, and the First World War and its consequences brought about further deterioration. By the 1930s, only a handful of professional marblers were active in the entire Western world; they produced papers solely for the use of a restricted number of hand bookbinders and restorers. Moreover, some of their product came in the form of oil marbling (samples 187–189 on Plate XXXVIII), which could be effected more easily, quickly, and cheaply.

The Cockerell papers of the 1930s displayed on Plate XXXVIII (samples 181–186) are proof that it was still possible to attain high quality and substantial production in an otherwise lackluster era, though they were achieved through Halferian rather than ancient methods. The bright colors used by Cockerell and his staff, however, made their papers better suited for decorating new art bindings or binding limited editions of specialty books than for the restoration of ancient ones; in fact, they found equally wide use in artistic and decorative work outside the field of the book arts. With the diminution of hand bookbinding over the previous seventy-five years or so, book restoration was also at a low ebb in the first half of the twentieth century, so that there was little call for ancient patterns to fulfill its requirements. The final three samples on Plate XXXVIII show, however, that in the 1930s attempts still were being made to produce a few of the familiar, comfortable designs of old.

American marblers, who have been mostly omitted from this survey, followed their British counterparts in the production and styles of marbled paper throughout the nineteenth century. The British literature, available to Americans mainly in the form of Woolnough's manual reprinted in the Nicholson bookbinding work, was highly influential for Charles Williams and others who tried their hands at the craft. Earlier, the Manns were undoubtedly influenced by instruction from the itinerant London marbler and paper decorator R. C. Mitton; before his arrival, the family had restricted their type of marbling mainly to Stormont designs, but once they received instructions from him, shell, Spanish, nonpareil, and the other "modern" British patterns literally poured from their hands. Virtually no pseudo-marbled papers appear to have been made in America—although Charles Williams offered an exception to this rule, as the sample of his Annonay paper on Plate XX and as Edwin Freedley's discussion of him indicates. British binders seem not to have been attracted to this bastard form of decorated paper either, directing all of their affection to the marbled kind.

Concluding Remarks

At the present time, and for some years past, marbling has again attained popularity among craftspeople in America and abroad, especially among those engaged in or interested in the book arts. Artistic bookbinding has once more become a respectable occupation or avocation, and a new class of professionals and amateurs are being drawn to the use of marbled paper so that their books will emulate and stand up to the finest productions of the past. Equally important, with the decreasing availability of fine old books on the antiquarian book market and the deterioration of our research libraries, the need for skillful restoration has become critical. Libraries must keep their precious rarities in good condition in order to assure their existence well into the future; antiquarian booksellers, faced with shrinking resources and supplies, are more and more forced to restore whatever copies of ancient tomes are available to them in order to sell them and realize the highest possible return on their sales. In order to achieve an "authentic" appearance when repairing such materials, and make them more desirable and salable, binders and book restorers are more and more seeking and requiring marbled papers that bear ancient patterns. A properly copied paper can, in the hands of an accomplished restorer, not only impart the correct appearance to a binding and to the ancient work it contains but, by replacing damaged or deteriorated materials with new ones, contribute to its preservation for the future. This is especially true as librarians and others have become aware of problems with acid in paper and leather and have begun to take steps to deal with them.

If a new era seems to be upon us, it nevertheless remains a stark fact that few binders and restorers today are able or willing to pay a high price for quality marbleized paper. These craftsmen also have a bottom line that has been forced upon them by booksellers' profit margins and library budgets alike, so that marbling hardly exists today as an economically viable business but struggles along as a marginal trade at best. This situation, however, is neither new nor recent. We have repeatedly observed in this survey of the craft during the past few hundred years that, due to the increasing industrialization of society and the simultaneous, continuous increase in the cost of living, there has occurred a continuous quest for quicker and cheaper methods of production. Industrialization makes life today neither simple nor affordable, and marbling has been but one of the many casualties resulting from its relentless advance.

Thus, the pitfalls that have accompanied the accomplishment of this craft during the past several hundred years remain constant, despite the present surge of interest and vitality. Notwithstanding these drawbacks, it seems certain that the charm and allure that marbled papers offer and the challenge and mesmerizing qualities the craft presents will always entice artisans and other interested parties to try their hands at it; and, undoubtedly, some of these people will persist until they have overcome its initial difficulties and will carry it on. Somewhat paradoxically, the very problems that are inherent in marbling and which have discouraged its practice on a wider scale seem responsible for having kept it alive these past hundred years or more.

We may conclude on a positive note that these circumstances—coupled with the fact that some hand bookbinders, art binders, and book restorers will always insist on endowing their work with the traditional and authentic appearance of old—will insure that this venerable art will in one way or another be perpetuated into the future. Undoubtedly, just so long as there is a literature available, there will always be marbled paper and marbling. To this end I have endeavored over the years to provide future generations with the important marbling literature in English translation or at least an important segment of it which, due to its existence in only a few recorded copies, has been severely restricted. I have added original marbled samples to most of these works not only to serve as instructive illustrations, but also to prove that through persistence, all problems can be overcome and that this difficult and challenging art can be accomplished.

NOTES

CHAPTER I

1. I have previously pointed this out in my book on *The Role of the Mann Family of Dedham, Massachusetts in the Marbling of Paper in Nineteenth-Century America and in the Printing of Music, the Making of Cards, and Other Booktrade Activities* (Newton Centre, Mass.: 1981), [1]–2.

2. Various kinds of decorated paper have served since the seventeenth century to adorn the outsides and insides of books, and as wrappers on pamphlets, theses, and other ephemeral publications. However, the marbled papers were without doubt the most popular and enduring, probably due to the small size of their patterns and the bookbinding traditions that became associated with them. Other types of colored papers employed to decorate books over the ages have included paste papers, pattern papers, stained or monochrome papers, and some additional kinds, all of which will be described in the chapters following.

3. The Papier-Historische Afdeling of the Museum Meermanno-Westreenianum of the Koninklijke Bibliotheek at 's Gravenhage (the Royal Dutch Library at the Hague) contains a piece of marbled paper that reportedly was removed from the wall of the poet Goethe's study (Plate I). Pattern papers, printed from both wooden and metal blocks in a variety of colors and designs, were more suited to wall covering, and marbled paper, when so used, probably was restricted to covering only panels and parts of walls. That this custom probably persisted into the mid-nineteenth century is suggested by Henry W. Cleaveland, William Backus, and Samuel D. Backus's *Village and Farm Cottages; the Requirements of American Village Homes Considered and Suggested; with Designs for Such Houses of Moderate Cost* (New York: D. Appleton and Co., 1856; also reissued in 1869); on p. 125, discussing the choice of paper for covering interior walls of houses, it advised that "All grained and marbled papers, and imitations of stone blocks, mouldings, etc., are so clearly contrary to what we regard as a cannon of true art, that we need but name them." For references to the production of marbled paper for wall coverings in late eighteenth-century Germany see Chapter 3 of this work, pp. 23–24.

4. On p. 89 is reprinted an 1832 advertisement of Samuel C. and Edward Mann (see note 1), who were marbling in the Boston area at that time. It mentions a type of "Mottled" paper they offered for sale which they considered suitable for lining trunks and for covering fancy boxes. Their "mottled" pattern was probably the well-known "shell" type often employed for this purpose in early America. See also Plates I and XXX.

5. Page 129 of the second part of *The Court and Country Cook Book: Giving New and Plain Directions How to Order All Manner of Entertainments,* issued at London by W. Olney, for A. & J. Churchill, and M. Gillyflower in 1702, discusses the arrangement of the table and, specifically, the placing of wicker baskets and pyramids of fruit on separate oval tables at either side of the main table; it directs that the board of these smaller tables "ought to be cover'd with marbled or painted Paper, and always set out with Leaves and Flowers, or other ornaments, according to the season." *The Court and Country Cook Book* was a translation by one J. K. (otherwise unidentified) of *Le Cuisinier roial et bourgeois* and the *Nouvelle instruction pour les confitures, les liquors et les fruits,* attributed to François Massialot. For details on the arrangement of the pyramid of fruit in early table decoration, see Georgiana Reynolds Smith, *Table Decoration, Yesterday, Today, & Tomorrow* (Rutland, Vt: C. E. Tuttle Co., [1968]), Chapter 5. The use of marbled paper for table ornamentation is undoubtedly but one example of the many common household purposes for which this commodity was used in earlier times.

6. The literature of marbling, while fairly extensive, is printed in a variety of languages and is difficult to obtain, as some works have survived only in a handful of copies. (The inclusion of original marbled samples in some of these often severely limited the size of their editions.) Furthermore, while the directions in some of these books are derivative and repetitive, in others they are quite contrary, because each marbler customarily solved his problems in his own particular way. Now and then one even encounters a book containing directions that are entirely wrong; one such work is an anonymous collection of recipes entitled *Valuable Secrets Concerning the Arts and Trades,* printed at Dublin by James Williams in 1778. The directions this book provides for marbling paper go contrary to accepted practice and would be sure to result in failure. We are told (p. 160) that after colors are deposited on the surface of the marbling bath they fall to the bottom; a substance then is added to make them rise and swim on top of the water, after which they are removed onto paper. Anyone experienced in marbling knows that such directions amount to sheer nonsense.

7. Much confusion has arisen also from marblers' long-enduring practice of bestowing fanciful names on the patterns they produce and develop. There is no standard nomenclature, and because of the custom of intermixing designs, it probably would be difficult to develop a practical one. Some of these matters will be discussed in the final section of this work.

8. Charles W. Woolnough, *The Art of Marbling, As Applied to Book Edges and Paper, Containing Full Instructions for Executing British, French, Spanish, Italian, Nonpareil, Etc., Etc. . . . With a Brief Notice of Its Recent Application to Textile Fabrics, and Particularly to the Cloths So Extensively Used by Bookbinders* (London: Alexander Heylin, 1853), [1]–2. This volume was reissued in 1854, and a new edition, somewhat revised and with an important Preface, appeared in 1881 under the title *The Whole Art of Marbling* (London: George Bell and Sons). The 1853 and 1854 editions contained at the end a small section dealing with the marbling of cloth, as well as several samples of marbled cloth. Woolnough had been trying to promote his marbled cloth for bookbinding purposes, and exhibited several samples of it at the famous Crystal Palace Exhibition of 1851.

9. James B. Nicholson, *A Manual of the Art of Bookbinding: Containing Full Instructions in the Different Branches of Forwarding, Gilding, and Finishing. Also, The Art of Marbling Book-Edges*

and Paper. The Whole Designed for the Practical Workman, the Amateur, and the Book Collector (Philadelphia: Henry Carey Baird, 1856), 82. Stereotype plates were made from the type of the original edition and were reemployed by the Baird firm in 1871, 1882, 1887, and 1902 to reissue this work in the same form.

10. Phoebe Jane Easton, "Suminagashi: The Japanese Way with Marbled Paper," *Coranto, Journal of the Friends of the Libraries, University of Southern California* 8, no. 1 (1972): 3–17.

11. The chemical and physical laws and principles underlying this craft are discussed in detail in Chapter 13.

12. August Weichelt has admirably expressed this in the section "Marmorpapiere" of his *Buntpapier-Fabrikation*, 3d ed. (Berlin: Verlag der Papier-Zeitung, [1927]), 309: "Es gibt kaum ein Handwerk, welches so leicht erscheint und so einfach auszuüben ist, wie das Marmorieren. Die Hilfsmittel sind die denkbar einfachsten. Aber es gibt wiederum kein Handwerk, welches von äusseren Einflüssen so abhängig ist, wie dieses; es ist mit solch ausserordentlichen Zufälligkeiten verbunden, dass es die meisten, die as zu erlernen versuchten, nach kurzer Zeit wieder aufgegeben haben. Es ist eine Tatsache, dass es zu wenig Marmorierer, d. h. gute Marmorierer gibt."

13. Franz Weisse, *The Art of Marbling: Translated from the German with an Introduction and Fourteen Original Marbled Specimens, by Richard J. Wolfe* (North Hills, Pa.: Bird & Bull Press, 1980), 28. The original German edition, *Die Kunst des Marmorierens, oder die Herstellung von Buchbinder-Buntpapieren mit Wasserfarben auf Schleimhaltigem Grund*, was issued by the Max Hettler Verlag at Stuttgart in 1940. A large part of the edition is said to have been destroyed in an Allied bombing raid during World War II.

14. Various authorities have attributed Belon's account to the year 1555, using as their source the Avignon edition of his *Les observations du plusieurs singulairez et choses memorabiles trouvées en Grêce, Asie, Judée, Egypte, Arabie et autre pays estranges*. However, the first edition of this work was published at Paris by Gilles Corrozet in 1553, and Belon's reference appears in it (on folio 75^r). This pertinent passage also appears on folios 73^v–74^r of Corrozet's subsequent editions (issued at Paris in 1554 and 1555) and in an edition published at Paris in 1554 by Guillaume Cavellat. All of these appear to be identical printings, following the same setting of type. The Avignon edition of 1555 was published by Christofle Plantin. Belon's reference is very slight, merely an allusion to how the Turks completed the preparation of their unusual (to European eyes of that time) paper by polishing it.

15. George Sandys, *A Relation of a Journey Begun An. Dom. 1610* (London: W. Barren, 1615), 72. Sandys related that the Turks "curiously sleeke their paper, which is thick; much of it being coloured and dappled like chamolets; done by a trick they have of dipping it in water."

16. Herbert made his journey to Persia and adjacent regions in the years 1627–1629, but an account of his travels did not appear until 1634, when its first edition was printed at London. A second edition was published in 1638, a third in 1665, and a final, seventeenth-century edition in 1677. (Meanwhile, Dutch and French translations from the second edition had appeared in 1658 and 1663.) There was no mention of marbling in any of the first three editions. It was not until the 1677 edition—almost fifty years after his visit to the Near East—that Herbert first made any allusions to marbling. The first of these relates, with reference to the Persian king, that his name is "usually writ with gold upon paper of a curious gloss and fineness varied into several fancies, effected by taking oiled colours and dropping them severally upon water, whereby the paper becomes sleek and chamleted, or veined, in such sort as it resembles agate or porphyry." Herbert later repeated essentially the same observation in slightly abbreviated form. The 1677 edition, entitled *Some*

Years Travels into Divers Parts of Asie and Afrique, was issued at London (Printed by R. Everingham, for R. Scot, T. Basset, J. Wright, and R. Chiswell). One is tempted to conclude that Herbert was prompted to insert information on the technique (first observed approximately fifty years earlier) in this final account of his travels to Persia because of the popularity that marbled paper had attained in Europe and England in the last quarter of the seventeenth century. The 1677 edition was abridged and edited by Sir William Foster, and was reissued as part of the Broadway Travellers series by George Routledge & Sons, London, in 1928 under the title *Thomas Herbert, Travels in Persia, 1627–1629*. The passages on marbling appear on pp. 228 and 234 in that edition.

17. Athanasius Kircher, *Ars Magna Lucis et Umbrae in Decem Libros Digesta* (Rome: Hermann Scheus, 1646). The first printed description of the marbling process in Western literature appeared on pp. 814–815 under the title "Chartae Turcico More Pingendae Ratio." An English translation of this passage appears in Charles M. Adams, "Some Notes on the Art of Marbling Paper in the Seventeenth Century," *Bulletin of The New York Public Library* 51, no. 7 (July 1947): 411–417; a German translation, taken from a 1671 edition that had appeared at Amsterdam, is printed as front matter in Emil Kretz's *Dreihundert Jahre Marmorpapier* (Basel: Tagenfachklassen für Buchdruck und Buchbinden der Allgemeinen Gewerbschule, 1960).

18. Such accounts are summed up and discussed in the following chapter.

19. Max Rosenheim, "The Album Amicorum," *Archaeologica or Miscellaneous Tracts Relating to Antiquity Published by the Society of Antiquaries of London* 62 [2d ser. 12, pt. 1] (1910): 251–308. Mr. Rosenheim based his researches on information from 40 albums and approximately 500 loose leaves in his own collection, from about 400 other albums in the Manuscript Department of the British Museum, from an exhibition held at Leipzig in connection with the university's jubilee, and from contacts with European collectors of such materials and their catalogs. Although he had learned of a specimen dating from 1548, the earliest example he had seen dated to the year 1554: a bound book with thirteen blank leaves at its beginning and ten at its end. Rosenheim relates that while the Album Amicorum was chiefly in use among the students at the universities, the custom spread and owners could be found among princes and nobles, high officials, ecclesiastics, soldiers, physicians, lawyers, painters, musicians, merchants, and artisans. Illuminations included in most of them were done by professionals, and the signatory or person writing an inscription in them afterward paid to have a scene or his coat of arms added.

20. Robert and Richard Keil, *Die Deutschen Stammbücher des Sechzehnten bis Neuzehnten Jahrhunderts; Ernst und Schertz, Weisheit und Schwank in Original Mittheilungen zur Deutschen Kultur-Geschichte* (Berlin: G. Grote'sche Verlagsbuchhandlung, 1893). Another useful discussion of this subject, with particular reference to Swiss albums, is Wolfgang Klose, "Frühe Stammbücher (Alba Amicorum)," *Librarium, Zeitschrift der Schweizerischen Bibliophilen-Gesellschaft* 26 (June 1983): 150–164.

21. Albert Haemmerle's *Buntpapier: Herkommen, Geschichte, Techniken; Beziehungen zur Kunst* (Munich: Georg D. W. Callewey, [1961]) shows several examples (pp. 40–43) and cites additional examples in German and other libraries. A splendid specimen, reproduced in color and showing an album opened to expose a marbled paper and a silhouette paper side by side, appears on p. 40 of Marie-Ange Doizy and Stéphane Ipert's *Le Papier marbré, son histoire et sa fabrication* (Paris: Éditions Technorama, 1985). This particular album is French and dates to the year 1586. It is preserved in the Bibliothèque Nationale. There are more of these Album Amicorum scattered around Europe and in America than might be supposed. In his "Frühe Bunt-

papiere" *Jahrbuch der Einbandkunst* 4 (1937): 65–91, Adolf Rhein cites two fine specimens: one, assembled for Emperor Maximilian II in 1572, was then in the city library at Erfurt; the other, owned by the Baron von Haymb zu Reichenstein in 1575, was located at the Royal Library in Copenhagen. Reference to these and a number of other examples can be found in the "Bibliographie der Buntpapier-Literatur" of Gabriele Grünebaum's *Buntpapier, Geschichte, Herstellung, Verwendung* (Cologne: DuMont Buchverlag, 1982, 211, under "Stammbuch." A welcome addition to the limited literature on this subject is M. A. E. Nickson's *Early Autograph Albums in the British Museum* (London: The British Museum, 1970), a slender volume containing in its bibliography references to most of the principal articles and books. Evidently, Nickson was much influenced by Rosenheim's report and by the Keils' book, and he gives an entertaining survey of much that they covered in a more technical way. Nickson mentions only one volume containing marbled papers: an album known to have been kept by a sovereign prince, Charles Lewis Elector Palatine. Entries in this album, which date between the years 1622 and 1633, were all contributed by fellow princes and members of noble families. Among these are the signatures of Charles I of England and his queen.

22. To my knowledge, Haemmerle has been the only historian of Buntpapier to discuss silhouette papers in detail and to explain the methods of their making. His treatment of them appears on pp. 39–41 of his *Buntpapier*.

23. That such costume books and similar manuscripts containing silhouette papers were copied or reissued (perhaps time and time again) and made available to more than one collector or purchaser is suggested by the recent sale of what appears to be a near-identical copy of the book to which Haemmerle refers. I first examined this volume in 1966 or 1967 when, on a trip to New York City, it was shown to me by the late Otto H. Ranschburg. Ranschburg, along with the late Douglas G. Parsonage, had just assumed control of the long-standing antiquarian bookselling firm of Lathrop C. Harper, Inc. About a year later, in their Harper catalogue 197, issued in the autumn of 1968, Messrs. Ranschburg and Parsonage offered this item for sale (no. 3, entitled *16th Century Watercolors of Turkish Costumes, etc. Interleaved with "Silhouette Papers"*). Their description indicates that the album contains 43 single leaves and two folding leaves depicting natives of the city of Constantinople in their various costumes, and 44 interleaves of Turkish silhouette paper. They date this volume "1587." Its first leaf contains a portrait of Sultan Murad III (1574–1595) on horseback (captioned at the bottom in a manuscript hand "Il Gran Signore") that is almost identical to the illustration Haemmerle reproduces from another such work. The caption indicates that this copy came early into the hands of an Italian owner. Mr. Ranschburg subsequently informed me that this volume was sold to a German purchaser.

24. Albert Haemmerle, *Buntpapier*, p. 41.

25. Tsuen-hsuin Tsien, *Paper and Printing*, comprising v. 5, pt. I, ("Chemistry and Chemical Technology") of Joseph Needham's *Science and Civilization in China* (Cambridge: Cambridge University Press, 1985). References to colored and marbled papers are scattered throughout the book: on pp. 23, 74–77, and 90–95. I have Stéphane Ipert to thank for pointing out Dr. Tsien's recent research. His book was available in Europe earlier than it was in America, and Doizy and Ipert were able to make brief mention of it in their *Le Papier marbré*, published the same year (p. 13).

26. Tsuen-hsuin Tsien, *Paper and Printing*, 94.

27. Ibid. The *Wen Fang Ssu Phu* is described on p. 13 of Tsien's book.

28. In an attempt to determine if any marbled paper from this early period exists in China today, I wrote, on the advice of Dr. Tsien, to Professor Yixing Pan at the Institute for the History of Natural Science of the Academia Sinica in Beijing. In his reply of April 8, 1987 (preserved in the author's files), Pan reported that though he had visited museums and other institutions throughout China, he had never seen any sort of decorated paper approximating the European variety. Knowledge of marbling in China in this early period, he related, derives entirely from Su-I-Chien's *Wang Fang Ssu Phu*.

29. Tsien cites, as the basis for this fact, E. J. Labarre's *Dictionary of Paper and Papermaking Terms* (Amsterdam: Swetts and Zeitlinger, 1937), 260, and Dard Hunter's *Papermaking: The History and Technique of an Ancient Craft,* 2d ed. (New York: A. A. Knopf, 1947), 479. However, I have not been able to confirm his reference in the Labarre dictionary, or in the second edition of it published in 1947.

30. Kiofusa Narita, *Japanese Paper-making* (Tokyo: Hokuseido Press, 1954), 55–60.

31. Kiofusa Narita, "Suminagashi," *The Paper Maker* 24, no. 1 (1955): 27–31.

32. The first of these was Phoebe Jane Easton's article "Suminagashi: The Japanese Way with Marbled Paper," cited in note 10. Mrs. Easton later incorporated much of her material into the first chapter (having the same title) of her recent book, *Marbling: A History and a Bibliography* (Los Angeles: Dawson's Book Shop, 1983). Another descriptive account of the exercise of Suminagashi marbling, especially today, is Karo Thom's article "Suminagashi: Ink Floating," *Fine Print* 7, no. 3 (July 1983): 79–81, 107.

33. References to marbling in areas east of Persia at a very early time appear in several works on Persian art. Furthermore, discussing the types of patterns that developed in Turkey and the East, Mehmed Ali Kâğitçi related (in his article, "Turkish Marbled Papers" published in the Swiss magazine *Palette* in 1968 (no. 30, pp. 14–20), related that one of these, Akkâse-Ebrû (white dish marble), was created in Samarkand and Herat at the instigation of the King of Khorasan, Hussein Baykara (1438–1506). Haemmerle also advanced the belief (*Buntpapier*, p. 41) that knowledge of marbling on a tank or bath traveled from the Orient over the silk trade routes through Turkestan and into Persia and Turkey. Finally, in a recent book on Turkish marbling, *Türk Sanatinda Ebrû* (Nisan: Ak Yayinlari Ltd., 1977), M. Uğur Derman notes that the art set out from Bukhara in Turkestan, the Turks' ancient homeland, picked up its name (ebrû) in Persia, and came over the silk road to Anatolia, where it settled.

34. M. Uğur Derman, *Türk Sanatinda Ebrû*, 8.

35. On pages 15–16 of his "Turkish Marbled Papers," Kâğitçi gives a fairly detailed description of Aher paper and its making. He reports that the paper used in Turkey for manuscripts was either made locally or was imported, but that invariably it was bought in an untreated condition. It was the task of the calligrapher to prepare it for writing: he either burnished it with a burnishing stone or coated it with a liquid called "Aher." Kâğitçi describes both the making and consistency of this liquid and indicates how it was used. He also tells us that paper for official documents had to be glazed only and that Aher paper was used for writing. Haemmerle (*Buntpapier*, 37) states that Aher solution was made in two ways, through the application of either egg white or starches. Another authority, Fredrik Robert Martin, writes in his *The Miniature Painting and Painters of Persia, India and Turkey from the 8th to the 18th Century* (London: Bernard Quaritch, 1912), 108, that "before using paper the Orientals polished it in the following manner:—A plank of chestnut-wood of even grain having been obtained, the paper was placed on it and rubbed with a crystal egg weighing about half-a-pound. The paper, after the process of rubbing and polishing, became as shining and glossy as glass. At times, the

paper was rubbed with soap or the white of an egg to render it more easy to write on."

36. Mehmed Ali Kâğitçi, "Turkish Marbled Papers," 15.

37. One of the governing principles of Islamic art was aniconism, or the religious prohibition of figurization and representation of living creatures. Underlying this prohibition was the assumption that God was the sole giver of life, and that a person who produced a likeness of a living thing sought to rival God. Another tradition, ascribed to the Prophet Muhammad, specified that a person who made a picture of a living thing would be asked on the Day of Judgment to infuse life into it. Finally, Islamic religion rejected all things that might become idols.

38. M. Uğur Derman, *Türk Sanatinda Ebrû* (see note 33).

39. Işik Yazan, "Ebru Sanati," *Antika; the Turkish Journal of Collectable Art* 2, no. 14 (May 1986): 40–46.

40. A recent Turkish publication on Islamic calligraphy, Mahmud Bedreddin Yazir's *Medeniyen Âleminde Yãzi Ve Islam Medeniyetinde Kalem Güzeli*, 2d ed. (Ankara: Ayyildiz Matbaasi A.S., 1981), discusses the use of marbled paper as a background for Arabic script (pp. 162–165). This account also contains color illustrations of papers marbled by Mecmeddin Okyay and Mustaffa Düzgünman, two of Turkey's modern marbling masters.

41. Celal Esad Arsevan, *Les Arts Decoratifs Turcs* (Istanbul: Milli Eğitim Basimevi [1953?]). Arseven devotes several pages (320–321) and colored plates to marbled paper and illustrates an early volume containing paintings with marbled découpage.

42. Mehmed Ali Kâğitçi, "Turkish Marbled Papers," 16–17.

43. As Kâğitçi points out in his *Historical Study of Paper Industry in Turkey*, (Istanbul; Grafik Sanatlar Matbaasi, 1976), page 22, in the work cited in the preceding note, in an article entitled "Beitrag zur Türkischen Papiergeschichte" (*Papier Geschichte* 13, no. 4 (November 1963): 37–44), and in another article also titled and closely resembling "Turkish Marbled Papers," (but without its colored plates: published in *Pulp & Paper International* (March 1971): 41–43), there is so much variation in Turkish marbled papers and patterns that, like those that later evolved in Europe and the West, making sense out of them and cataloging them becomes quite difficult. However, he does provide lists and brief descriptions of some of them in these sources. The "battal-ebrû" or large spot pattern probably was the most common and the one that formed the background for later floral designs. "Tarakli-ebrû" designated marbling made with a comb, and "gitgel-ebrû" described the pattern later European marblers would call "comb-return." In making this pattern, a comb with somewhat widely spaced needles was used and then drawn backwards through the centers of the channels that initially had been effected. "Somaki-ebrû" denoted marbling imitating the design of porphyry, and had spots smaller than "battal-ebrû." "Hafif-ebrû" designated very light marbling with very pale coloring, and so on. Many Turkish patterns were named after the masters who developed them. "Necmeddin-ebrû," which showed flowers and floral designs laid down on the "battal-ebrû," bore the name of Necmeddin Okyay, who invented and developed it. And "Hatip-ebrusu" described a pattern with floral petals or corollas and was named after the eighteenth-century preacher of Aya Sofya mosque, Hatip Mehmed Efendi, who invented it. See Plate V.

44. The greater part of Derman's *Türk Sanatinda Ebrû*, 29–52, is devoted to a discussion (in chronological order) of the known Turkish masters and includes many of their papers reproduced in color as well as portraits of later makers. Lists and descriptions of some of these marblers also appear in Kâğitçi's *Historical Study of Paper Industry in Turkey*, 20, 23, and in his other articles cited above, and in Mrs. Easton's *Marbling, A History and a Bibliography*, 18–24.

45. My research has uncovered the existence of three other pertinent articles which I have not been able to locate. These are Mehmed Ali Kâğitçi, "Les Colorants utilisés dans le temps par les artisans Turcs," *I P F Information* new ser. 4, no. 3 (1970): 50–54; Sevim Eti, "Soyut Resim Ve Ebrû," *Turkiyemiz* 8, no. 23 (1977): 987–993; and U. Ehrensvärd and L. Stenius, "Marmoreat Papper, *Ebru*, fràn Äldre Tider," *Meddelanden fràn den Svenska Forskingsinstitut i Istanbul* 5 (1980): 49–82.

46. Mehmed Ali Kâğitçi, "Turkish Marbled Papers," 19.

47. When Kâğitçi published his article "Turkish Marbled Papers" in 1968, he reported that only three marbling masters remained in Turkey at that time: Necmeddin Okyay (born 1883), his son, Sacid Okyay (born 1915), and Mustaffa Düzgünman (born 1920). The elder Okyay died in 1976, according to Derman, but in 1970 or 1971, according to information supplied to me by Norma Rubovits of Chicago (personal communication of 21 December 1987, author's files), and his son is not mentioned in recent Turkish marbling literature. In an early book on the paper arts of Turkey, *Kâğitçilik Tarihçesi* (Istanbul: "Kader" Basimevi, 1936), Kâğitçi reviewed the history of marbling there (pp. 221–229) and included five original samples of marbled paper made by Necmeddin Okyay, including one with the floral pattern, "Necmeddin-ebrusu," which bears his name. In his "Turkish Marbled Papers" article, Kâğitçi devotes much space to Düzgünman, as does most subsequent literature on marbling in Turkey. One such example is Robert Arndt's beautifully illustrated account of his work in an article entitled "Ebru: the Cloud Art," *Aramco World Magazine* 24, no. 3, (May–June 1973): 26–32, from which two illustrations on Plate IV are reproduced. Much attention is also paid to Düzgünman in Derman's *Türk Sanatinda Ebrû*, which contains many pictures of him at work as well as beautiful color illustrations of some of his patterns. As note 40 indicates, he is pictured and described also in M. B. Yazir's book on Turkish calligraphy, along with Necmeddin Okyay. Mustafaf Düzgünman is universally acknowledged to be the greatest Turkish marbling master of the present time and was recently the subject of a Turkish television program. I had the pleasure of meeting one of Düzgünman's pupils, Niyazi Sayin, during Sayin's visit to Boston in 1986, at which time I demonstrated European (or Western) methods of marbling and exchanged marbled papers with him.

48. Frederick Robert Martin, *The Miniature Painting and Painters of Persia, India and Turkey from the 8th to the 18th Century*, text, v. 1, 91, 93, but especially 107–108; illustrations, v. 2, Plate 231.

49. The last mentioned is cataloged as no. 105, "un cheval étique, Turquie, fin du XVIᵉ siècle," and illustrated on Plate 65 of Ananda K. Coomaraswamy's *Les Miniatures orientales de la collection Goloubew au Museum of Fine Arts de Boston* (Paris & Brussels: Les Éditions G. Van Oest, 1929; no. XIII of the series *Ars Asiatica*). Another marbled miniature, "un évèque, papier marbré, vers 1600," is cataloged as no. 106 and is also illustrated on Plate 65.

50. The catalogs issuing from these exhibits are: *Indian Miniature Paintings from the Collection of Edward Binney, 3rd: Mughal and Deccani Schools* (Portland, Ore.: Portland Art Museum, 1973); *Turkish Miniatures Paintings and Manuscripts in the Collection of Edward Binney, 3rd.* (New York and Los Angeles: Metropolitan Museum of Art and Los Angeles County Museum of Art, 1973); and *Other Treasures from the Binney Collection* (Los Angeles: Los Angeles County Museum of Art, 1974). Mr. Binney discussed these partly marbled paintings in his Sir George Birdwood Memorial Lecture of 3 May 1979, "Indian Paintings from the Deccan," *Journal of The Royal Society for the Encouragement of the Arts, Manufactures and Commerce* 127 (1979): 784–804.

51. Basil W. Robinson, *Persian Paintings in the India Office Library, a Descriptive Catalogue* (London: Sotheby Parke Bernet, 1976), entry no. 142. (Mrs. Easton cites Robinson's entry as a plate, but this miniature is not illustrated in the catalog.) Robinson describes this piece as a tinted drawing, showing two

oxen locking horns; they are silhouetted in marbled paper upon which a number of other animals are drawn; one ox is outlined in black, and the other in gold. He further describes this as "Qazwin style (or possibly Turkish); second half of sixteenth century." It is contained within a marbled frame, with owner's seal of Hajji (?) Muhammad Mu'min.

52. The catalog of this exhibit, produced by Stuart Cary Welch and entitled *Indian Drawings and Painted Sketches, 16th Through 19th Centuries* (New York: The Asian Society, in Association with John Weatherhill, Inc. [1976]) reproduces one of these marbleized drawings in black and white and another in color (plates 34 and 35).

53. Phoebe Jane Easton, *Marbling: a History and a Bibliography,* 17–18; Christopher Weimann, "Techniques of Marbling in Early Indian Paintings," *Fine Print* 9, no. 4 (October 1983): 134–137, 164–166.

54. Weimann's checklist located two at the Fogg Art Museum of Harvard University; and in 1986, Woodman L. Taylor, then with the Islamic Department in the Harvard University Museums, showed me half a dozen or more of these, all of them in the Museum's collection. While these marbled paintings admittedly are rare, clearly there may be more of these than has been accounted for in the past.

55. Toby Falk and Mildred Archer, *Indian Miniatures in the India Office Library* (London: Sotheby Parke Bernet; Dehli, Karachi; Oxford University Press, 1981).

56. Mark Zebrowski, *Deccani Painting* (London: Sotheby Publications; Berkeley and Los Angeles: University of California Press, 1983), 135–138, illustrates five marbled paintings and locates several additional ones. His doctoral dissertation at Harvard, "Indian Painting at the Courts of the Deccani Sultans" (1977), contained no reference to marbling. Dr. Zebrowski learned about these marbled miniatures after the completion of his dissertation, for which reason he added the chapter on "Marbled Drawings" to his book in the form of an appendix.

57. Stuart Cary Welch, *Indian Drawings and Painted Sketches, 16th Through 19th Centuries,* 74.

58. One piece of evidence in support of this view is an eighteenth-century Indian manuscript account of marbling that Stéphane Ipert recently brought to my attention and sent to me in both photocopy form and translation. This account, found in the Indian Office Library in London, was written entirely in Persian, thus suggesting an especially strong Persian connection with marbling in India. Mr. Ipert did not inform me of the manuscript's present location, but this has recently been reported in an article entitled "A Marbler's Quest," by Pam Smith published in *Ink & Gall* 1, no. 4 (Spring 1988): 5. A translation of this manuscript, which is contained in a deteriorated Western binding in the Persian collection at the India Office, has recently been made by Salim Quraishi and published with commentary by William Bull as "An 18th Century Indian Manuscript on Marbling," *Ink & Gall* 2, no. 1 (Summer 1988): 5–7. Entitled *Khulasat-Almujarrabat* ("the quintessence of prescriptions") and dating to the year 1767, this is classed as Persian MSS Ethe 2346. It is reputed to be the only known text on Indian marbling.

59. Basil W. Robinson, *Persian Paintings in the India Office Library,* 43.

60. Stéphane Ipert, who has traveled the world to examine many of these early Eastern papers, has, in conversation, agreed with me completely on this point.

CHAPTER 2

1. Haemmerle's discussion of the introduction of the art into Germany and of these early albums and reproductions of several marbled pages in them appear on pp. 49–52 of his *Buntpapier*. Another page from the 1604 album, not reproduced by him, is illustrated in Olga Hirsch's article "Decorated Papers," published in *The Penrose Annual* 51 (1957), Illustration 3.

2. Mirjam M. Foot, "The Olga Hirsch Collection of Decorated Papers," *The British Library Journal* 7, no. 1 (Spring 1981): 12–38. Mrs. Foot describes the 1604 and 1618 albums on p. 22 and illustrates two of the stenciled sheets from the latter volume as her figures 6 and 7. In the illustrations from the 1618 album that are reproduced in her article, it can be noted that the pattern was blocked out with the cut-out of the stencil before marbling took place, and the same process can be noted in the two other reproductions from that same album on Plate VII here.

3. Paul Kersten, *Die Marmorierkunst; Anleitung zum Marmorieren nach Josef Halfer und Josef Hauptmann* (Halle a. S.: Wilhelm Knapp, 1922), 1.

4. Denis Diderot and Jean L. D'Alembert, *Encyclopédie, ou Dictionnaire raisonné des sciences, des arts et des métiers, par un société de gens de lettres* (Paris, 1751–1772). The *Encyclopédie* was reprinted and reissued in pirated editions several times; thus, the location of the description of marbling differs with each edition. It is found in all of them under the entry "Marbreur," in alphabetical sequence.

5. Graham Pollard, "Changes in the Style of Bookbinding, 1550–1830," *The Library,* 5th ser. 11, no. 2 (June 1956): 79.

6. Charles M. Adams, "Some Notes on the Art of Marbling Paper in the Seventeenth Century," 13. Adams was quoting from the *Diary of Samuel Sewall, 1674–1729,* issued initially in the *Collections of the Massachusetts Historical Society,* 5th ser. 5–7 (Boston: 1878–1882). The above references are from v. 1, pp. 58 and 96, entries for 23 March 1682/3 and 15 September 1685.

7. Hannah D. French, "Early American Bookbinding by Hand," in Hellmut Lehmann-Haupt, *Bookbinding in America; Three Essays* (Portland, Me.: Southworth-Anthoensen Press, 1941), [3]–127; her reference to Sewall in on p. 13.

8. Collinet's references in his letters to these early German imported papers are discussed by Marie-Ange Doizy and Stéphane Ipert, *Le Papier marbré,* 50–51, 75. Collinet's letters to de Villermont are in the Bibliothèque Nationale's Collection Dangeau, Ms. Français 22806. Ipert has informed me in private conversation that they contain many references to decorated papers.

9. For a description of brocade or "Dutch gilt" paper, which probably was a novelty at that time in Germany as well as in France, see Chapter 3.

10. Rosamond B. Loring, *Decorated Book Papers, Being an Account of Their Designs and Fashions* (Cambridge, Mass.: Department of Printing and Graphic Arts, Harvard College Library, 1942), 18. Second and third editions of Mrs. Loring's pioneering book were issued in facsimile by the Harvard University Press in 1952 and 1973, but without the original samples included in the first edition. Therefore, references are identical in all editions.

11. Charles W. Woolnough, *The Art of Marbling,* 11. Woolnough's assertion was repeated several times, the first being in the 1881 edition of this work, *The Whole Art of Marbling,* 14. Joseph W. Zaehnsdorf iterated it in his popular bookbinding manual, *The Art of Bookbinding* (London: George Bell & Sons, 1880), 29, and in subsequent editions. Mrs. Loring repeats the story as well in *Decorated Book Papers,* 19, using Zaehnsdorf as her source.

12. Rosamond B. Loring, *Decorated Book Papers,* 18–19.

13. In an unpublished article entitled "The Dutch Gilt Papers in the Collection of the Royal Library in the Hague," Henck Voorn, formerly curator of that library's paper collections, had this to say (p. [1]):

Of course, Mrs. Loring knew very well that Dutch gilt papers were not Dutch, but chiefly German. She assumed that this German paper was chiefly exported by Dutch traders, which seems rather doubtful to me. Perhaps the usual confusion between the Dutch word "Duits", which means German, and the English word "Dutch", which means Netherlandish, has given birth to this misnomer.

Mr. Voorn presented this paper at the 16th Congress of the International Association of Paper Historians (I.P.F.) in Boston in late September of 1982, and a copy of it is on file in the Paper Section of the Royal Dutch Library in the Hague.

14. "Some Notes on the Art of Marbling Paper in the Seventeenth Century," cited fully in note 17 of Chapter 1.

15. Nürnberg. In Verlegung Wolffgang Moritz Endter und Johann Andreáe Endters se. Erben, 1677, 523–524. The first volume or part of Harsdorfers collection had been published in 1651. The German text of his description of marbling has been reprinted as front matter in Emil Kretz's *Dreihundert Jahre Marmorpapier.*

16. Adams refers to H. Taherzade Behzad's article on "Marbleized or *Abri* Papers" in the *Survey of Persian Art,* published under the auspices of the American Institute of Iranian Art and Archaeology, edited by A. U. Pope and P. Ackerman (New York: Oxford University Press, 1939), v. 5: 1924–1926.

17. Evelyn's diary was not actually published until 1818, when G. Newnes of London issued it in a volume of more than 800 pages. It was subsequently edited by William Bray and published in 1850, and it has been reissued in this form in a great many editions. I have used the Bray edition of 1879, a popular one which is frequently found. This was published in 4 volumes at London by Bickes and Son, with a biographical sketch of Evelyn by Sir Henry Wheatly. Reference to Evelyn's 1644 visit to Kircher in Rome appears on p. 125 of its v. 1.

18. Note that Englishman's use of the term "Dutch" in this case to connote not a Hollander or a Netherlander but a German.

19. Houghton's collection was initially published in weekly folio numbers, and it was in numbers 360 and 361, issued on Friday, June 16 and June 23, 1699, that Evelyn's lecture, entitled "An Exact Account of the Making of Marbled Paper," appeared. Houghton's *Husbandry and Trade Improv'd* was issued in collected form at London in 1727, with the Evelyn lecture appearing on pp. 418–428.

20. Francis Bacon, *Sylva Sylvarum: or A Natural History, in Ten Centuries* (London: W. Lee, 1627), 192. This work went through many editions by 1700. Bacon merely noted that "The Turks have a pretty art of *chamoletting* of *paper,* which is not with us in use. They take divers *oyled colours,* and put them severally (in drops) upon *water,* and stirre the *water* lightly; and then wet their *Paper* (being of some thicknesse) with it; and the *Paper* will be waved and veined like *Chamolet,* or *Marble.*"

21. Schott's work was printed by H. Pigrin "at the expense of the heirs of Johann G. Schönwetter," a bookseller of Frankfurt. It came out in four volumes, the last in 1659, with the marbling description printed on pp. 237–239 of volume one. Later editions appeared at Bamberg and Frankfurt in the 1670s.

22. Boyle devoted a paragraph to marbling in his essay "On Doing By Physicall Knowledge What Is Wont to Require Manual Skill," the fifth appearing in his publication *Some Considerations Touching the Usefulnesse of Experimental Natural Philosophy.* This appears on p. 10 of the second edition, which was issued by R. Davis at Oxford in 1664. I have not had an opportunity to examine the first edition published a year earlier, where, assumedly, it appeared earlier. Boyle's reference to marbling also was republished in the several editions of his *Works,* of which Adams cites the third edition of 1772 (v. 3, p. 461).

23. Johann Kunckel von Löwenstein, *Ars Vitraria Experimentalis, oder die Vollkommene Glasmacher Kunst* (Frankfurt and Leipzig: the author, 1679). In the second part of the third book, pp. 86–88, appears "Ausführliche Beschreibung, das schönste Türkische Pappier zu machen." Kunckel's treatise is basically a rendering into German of the Neri work, with Kunckel's notes

and augmentations, and it usually is cataloged in libraries under Neri's name. Charles M. Adams, "Some Notes on the Art of Marbling Paper in the Seventeenth Century," footnote 9, and Phoebe Jane Easton, *Marbling, a History and a Bibliography,* p. 164, provide reference to twentieth-century bookbinding articles which reprint Kunckel's passage on marbling. In addition, it was reprinted on pp. 20–21 of Hans Enderli's *Buntpapier Geschichte und Rezepte des Buntpapiers mit 205* Original-Buntpapier-Mustern, (Winterthur: Alex Scheebal, 1971).

24. Antonio Neri, *De Arte Vitraria Libri VII. & in Eosdem Christophori Merretti, M.D. & Societatis Regiae Socii, Observationes & Notae in Quibus Omne Gemmarum Artificialium, Encaustorum & Lacassarum Artificium Explicatur* (Amsterdam: H. Westenium, 1686). The reference to marbling appears in Merrett's notes and comments on pp. 359–360.

25. This has a lengthy title which reads, *Modern Curiosities of Art & Nature. Extracted out of the Cabinets of the Most Eminent Personages of the French Court. Together with the Choicest Secrets in Mechanicks: Communicated by the Most Approved Artists of France. Composed and Experimented by the Sieur Lemery, Apothecary to the French King. Made English from the Original French.* It was printed at London for Matthew Gilliflower, at the Spread Eagle in Westminster-Hall, and James Partridge, at the Post-house between Charing Cross and White-hall, in 1685, and provided a description of marbling on pp. 234–235. This work was reissued in two editions in 1711 with altered titles.

26. Salmon's *Polygraphice* was reissued in 1672, 1673, 1675, 1678, 1681, 1685, and 1701.

27. The initial edition of White's work was printed at London for W. Whitwood and Mrs. Feltham. It usually was reprinted without the year of issue on imprint, making the dating of later editions difficult. Four editions had appeared by 1695, and a fifth about 1710, but then its printing slowed down dramatically, for the final editions did not appear until 1761 and 1773 respectively.

28. The earliest edition of *Het Natuurlyk Tover-Boek* that I have been able to check for inclusion of material on marbling is the one issued in 1684, a copy of which is in the Cleveland Public Library. This was issued by Jan ten Hoorn at Amsterdam, and the description "Om Turksofte gemarmelt Papier te maken" appears on its pp. 17–20. The Cleveland library also holds a copy of the 1698 edition, which likewise was published by ten Hoorn; the description can be found on pp. 214–216 there. Of the many German editions, which appeared under the title *Natürliches Zauber-Buch,* I have had occasion to check only the 1718 Nürnberg edition, issued by the Hoffmanischen Buchladen, and the 1766 edition, which was published at Nürnberg also, by Wolfgang Schwarzkopf (both editions are at Harvard). The recipe "Türckische Papier zu machen" is printed on pp. 703–704 of the 1718 issue and on pp. 557–558 of the 1766 edition.

29. Zahn's *Oculis Artificialis Teledioptricus Sive Telescopium* was published by Q. Heyl. The pertinent description appears on pp. 158–160 of the third volume. A second edition was issued in a single volume at Nürnberg by J. C. Lochner in 1702.

30. This reference derives from Emil Kretz's *Dreihundert Jahre Marmorpapier,* 10. It also is noted in the "Bibliographie der Buntpapier-Literatur" (p. 214) of Gabriele Grünebaum's *Buntpapier, Geschichte, Herstellung, Verwendung.* The bibliographical details of this work, which are troublesome, will be reviewed in the following chapter.

CHAPTER 3

1. Haemmerle discusses Trorbach's petition and privilege on pp. 62–64 of his *Buntpapier.* This document was first published and discussed in an article entitled "Das Druckprivileg für Heinrich Trorbach," *Wochenblatt für Papierfabrikation* 29, no. 38 (1898): 2875–2876 and signed at the end "Colatta." The opening paragraph related that its existence was first made known by

Herr Kirchner, which accounts for the fact that it is entered under Kirchner in the bibliography of Buntpapier literature in Haemmerle's history, under Colatta in Grünebaum's work, and under both Colatta and Kirchner in Mrs. Easton's book. The Karlsruhe document was also reprinted and discussed by Alfred Schulte, "Die Anfänge der Buntpapierherstellung in Deutschland," *Archiv für Buchgewerbe und Gebrauchsgraphik* 6 (1941): 162–165, and Mrs. Easton mentions having seen it in typescript form in the Olga Hirsch collection now in the British Library.

2. Gabriel Magnien, "L'Exotisme dans les vieux papiers dominos; notes à propos d'un album de gravures et papiers coloriés du XVIᵉ siècle," *Albums du Corcodile*, Lyon (1946): 3–12. Reference to the Dürer album is made on p. 5. Stéphane Ipert basing his information on an interview with Magnien's widow, has told me that this album now is in the possession of a private owner in the Lyon area. Discussing marbled paper in his *Bookbindings and Rubbings of Bindings in the Victoria and Albert Museum* (London, 1898; reprint ed., London: The Holland Press 1962), W. H. James Weale noted, in reference to an Album Amicorum of 1616 and other marbled papers (p. xx of reprint ed.), "Since this note was in type I have seen a fine set of Duerer's *Little Passion*, interleaved with very fine marbled paper, in an Oriental binding of the end of the sixteenth century." It may well be that Weale viewed the very same volume that Magnien discussed, long before it came to the latter's attention. Unfortunately, Weale did not divulge its location in 1898.

3. Gabriel Magnien, "Vieux papiers de garde et de couverture de livres," *Le Vieux Papier; Bulletin de la Société Archéologique, Historique et Artistique* 22, nos. 188–190 (July 1959, January 1960): 209–215, 242–244, 281–286. Mrs. Easton has also taken notice of Magnien's work, discussing the Fuggers on pp. 33–34 of *Marbling, a History and a Bibliography*, but not extensively, and not with as much understanding as this subject deserves. She relates in her bibliography, which does not contain the above reference, that her information is taken from a 7-page typescript in the Olga Hirsch collection in the British Library, where also can be found a reprinting of Magnien's above-cited articles in the journal *La Reliure* 71, no. 6 (June 1961): 4–5, 7; no. 7 (July 1961): 6–7; no. 8 (August 1961): 8–11; no. 9 (September 1961): 6–10; 72, no. 2 (February 1962): 5–7. She notes that these are similar to the typescript in the Hirsch collection, but it appears that all of the above references, in fact, are one and the same article. I have also been shown a copy of Magnien's typescript by M. Toulet of the Département des Imprimés Réserve at the Bibliothèque Nationale in Paris.

4. One can obtain some perspective of the use of the angel watermark in early times from C. M. Briquet's *Les Filigranes: Dictionnaire Historique des Marques du Papier dès Leur Apparition Vers 1282 Jusqu'en 1600*. I have used the facsimile reprinted from the original 1907 edition, issued at Amsterdam in 1968 by the Paper Publications Society in four volumes. The textual account of the angel mark, and references to its reproductions in this dictionary, appear in v. 1, pp. 44–48, with reproductions of the mark appearing as entries 594–684 in v. 3. As is noted on pp. 44–45 of v. 1, the mark was used in Italy and France from about 1331 until about the 1590s, and during the last half of the sixteenth century in Germany, with most marks found in the fifteenth and sixteenth centuries. The mark, indeed an early one, was little used after the beginning of the seventeenth century.

5. "Fondaco" mainly referred to a draper's shop, a warehouse, or a store, and was used to describe a foreigner's (especially a foreign trader's or merchant's) quarters of a town.

6. Albert Haemmerle, *Buntpapier*, 22.

7. Albert Haemmerle, "Augsburger Buntpapier," *Viertel Jahreshefte zur Kunst und Geschichte Augsburg* 3 (1937–1938): 133–179. Haemmerle was editor and publisher of this esoteric journal, which was reproduced from typescript.

8. Graham Pollard, in his *Early Bookbinding Manuals, an Annotated List of Technical Accounts of Bookbinding to 1840* (Oxford, Oxford Bibliographical Society, 1984; this was continued by Esther Potter after Pollard's death and published as the Society's Occasional Publication No. 18), no. 109, assigns to this series of prints the cumulative title of *Assemblage Nouveau des Manouvriers Havillés. Neueröffnete Sammlung der mit Ihrer Eigenen Arbeiten und Werckzeugen Eingekleideten Künstlern, Handwerckern und Professionen* . . . , deriving this possibly from a half-title or series title on them, and dating them to "c. 1730." The Library of Congress holds a bound collection of nearly 160 of these quaint depictions, with the binder's title "Trades and Occupations." In all likelihood, Engelbrecht published these mainly to be sold separately, but they obviously were collected and perhaps even issued in collections. The prints showing the *dominotier* and the *dominotière* are numbered 52 and 53 in this series. While many of these loose prints can be found today with early coloring, such as those reproduced on Plate VIII, those in the Library of Congress volume were left uncolored. Engelbrecht's depictions of these colored-paper makers have been reproduced many times in this century. One or the other, and sometimes both, appear in just about every modern work dealing with the historical aspects of marbling or colored-paper making. For example, the print showing the dominotière appeared as the frontispiece in Paul Adam's *Das Marmorieren des Buchbinders auf Schleimgrund und im Kleisterverfahren* (Halle a. S.: Wilhelm Knapp, 1906; 2d ed., 1923), and both prints are shown in color in H. Clouzot and C. Follot's *Histoire du papier peint en France* (Paris: C. Moreau, 1935), 5. Gabriel Magnien provides identifications in French and German of all of the papers and materials appearing in them in his "Répertoire des principaux dominotiers fabriquant spécialement des papiers d'ornament pour la reliure en France, en Allemagne et en Italie aux XVIIᵉ, XVIIIᵉ siècles et au début du XIXᵉ siècle," *La Vieux Papier; Bulletin de la Société Archéologique, Historique et Artistique* 19 (1946–1949): 258. In issuing this underappreciated series, Engelbrecht was fifty years or more ahead of his time, for late in the eighteenth century and the middle of the nineteenth, a number of books were published depicting and describing the trades and professions that then flourished (referred to by booksellers, librarians, and collectors as "books of trades"). These were intended to inform young men of the possibilities open to them when searching for an occupation in that earlier time.

9. The distinction between the German use of the terms "marbled" and "Turkish" at this time has not been duly appreciated by many prior commentators on early colored and marbled papers, and thus confusion and misinterpretations have resulted. However, there is such a distinction made in just about every contemporary German publication that touches on the subject of decorated paper. One example is Johann Hübner's *Curieuses und Reales Natur-, Kunst-, Berg-, Gewerck-, und Handlungs Lexikon*, issued initially at Leipzig by J. F. Gleditsch und Sohn in 1712 and reissued by Gleditsch in 1746, 1766, and 1792. In her bibliographical notice of this work, (*Buntpapier*, 207) Gabriele Grünebaum tells us that Hübner's dictionary contains a description of gilt paper, which indeed it does. In addition, it has under the entry "Türckisches Paper" a short but reasonably good account of true paper marbling, which she failed to notice. (This appears in column 1566 of the 1712 edition, in column 2160 of the 1746 edition and in column 2351 of the 1776 edition; I have not had an opportunity to verify its location in the issue of 1792.)

Further examples are afforded by Johann Theodor Jablonski's *Allgemeines Lexicon der Künste und Wissenschaften*, which appeared early in the eighteenth century, and by Johann Christoph Adelung's *Kurtze Gegriff Menschlicher Fertigkeiten und Kenntnisse So Fern Sie auf Erwerbung des Unterhalts, auf Vergnügen, auf Wissenschaft, und auf Regierung der Gesellschaft Abzielen*, published later in the century. Jablonski's dictionary of the arts and sciences went through three editions: the first, which appeared anonymously, was issued at Leipzig by Thomas Fritschen in 1721; the second at Königsburg and Leipzig by Johann Heinrich Hartung in 1748; and the final one at the same locations by the widow of the printer Zeisen and by Hartung's heirs in 1767. A description of "Türkisch Papier, *papier marbré*," appeared in all three editions (p. 803 of the 1721 edition, p. 1245 of the 1758 edition, and p. 1602 of the final edition of 1767). The description is brief and remained unchanged in all editions. Adelung's work was issued initially at Leipzig in four volumes between the years 1778 and 1781 by C. G. Hertel, with a second edition coming out at Leipzig in 1783. This work also was published anonymously, "von dem Verfasser der Unterweisung in Künsten und Wissenschaften," and its aim was to describe most of the trades and professions then being practiced. On pp. 487–490 in the first volume, under the section-title "Türkisches Papier und Papiertapeten" (Turkish paper and wall hangings), Adelung first devoted a few sentences—about only forty words—to the "sogennanten Türkischen Papiers" (the "so-called Turkish papers," that is, truly marbled), while the remainder of his article discussed the types that were printed by means of wood blocks, stencils, and stamping devices, which he referred to as wall hangings. He devoted some space to the colors used in these processes and likened their production to the color printing of cotton fabrics. With regard to marbled papers, Adelung related (p. 490, section 1196) that the manufacture of Turkish paper, as well as paper hangings, was an open trade, that is, it was unconnected with any guild, and that it could be practiced by anybody who had the ability to execute it; also, it was carried on in many places and at factory production levels.

10. Haemmerle included toward the end of his *Buntpapier* (pp. 197–[245]) a "Verzeichnis von Brokat-Papieren," in which he described pattern papers that could be identified with the various makers who had stamped their names on the borders. And on pp. 120–130 of *Buntpapier* he provided a biographical register of such makers. Georg Christoph Stoy may be found in both sections, and, because of his importance, he is discussed in Haemmerle's main text as well (p. 20). Furthermore, his patent or privilege to manufacture colored paper is reproduced on p. 19. Stoy is also described in Haemmerle's "Augsburger Buntpapier," p. 174.

11. Hans Enderli, *Buntpapier, Geschichte und Rezepte des Bunt papiers mit 205 Original-Buntpapier-Mustern*, 7–8.

12. It is of interest to note that on p. 149 of Haemmerle's "Augsburger Buntpapier" one Johann Jakob Bechdolf is described as a "Cottonpapiermacher," the older term for Kattunpapiermacher. The use of the terms Kattunpapier and Damaskpapier to denote calico and damask papers appears to be a carryover from the beginnings of the German decorated paper industry and is evidence of its origins in the textile industry. Damask paper, which contained large designs, was used mainly for wall decoration.

13. Henck Voorn, "The Dutch Gilt Papers in the Collection of the Royal Library in the Hague," 1–4.

14. Voorn notes in his article on Dutch gilt paper that "Mrs. Lorings [sic] book does not mention the origin of the usual denomination 'Dutch gilt paper'. A fairly identical term was used in a note, dated 1865, on the 'gilt books' of Mr. Newbery, which books were described as 'strange and fairylike in their gaudy Dutch paper bindings'." Voorn's information is derived from an 1865 review of *Alice's Adventures in Wonderland*, reprinted in Robert Phillips, ed., *Aspects of Alice* (London: Penguin Books, 1971), 117.

15. Two works published in Germany early in the eighteenth century, the books of Hübner and Jablonski (see note 9) described the making of gilt papers only through the use of metal

impregnated varnishes, which indicates that the method of making it through the use of gold and silver leaf was not well known outside of the workshops of professional makers before the 1720 period.

16. Albert Haemmerle, *Buntpapier*, 126; "Augsburger Buntpapier," 167.

17. Stetten's book, published at Augsburg by L. H. Stage in 1779, contains a discussion of colored paper on pp. 257–258 of v. 1. Stetten began his account, "Das gedruckte und gefärbte Papier is eine Erfindung, welche mit dem Kottonfärben und Malen eine Aehnlichkeit hat, und vermutlich hat dieses zu jenem die erste Gelegenheit gegeben."

18. Albert Haemmerle, *Buntpapier*, 112.

19. In 1935 Arno Knapp of Leipzig first reported Liscovius's petition in an article entitled "Die Errichtung einer Buntpapierfabrik in Leipzug zu Beginn des 18. Jahrhunderts," *Allgemeiner Anzeiger für Buchbinder* 50 (June 28, 1935): 366–368). Knapp was correcting a reference made to colored paper making in Leipzig in an earlier article by Paul Kersten, "Historisches über Türkisches Papier und Marmorierkunst," which had appeared in the same journal the preceding May 10 (pp. 272–273). Kersten iterated Knapp's account in a later and extremely valuable article on the history of colored paper, "Geschichte des Buntpapiers," which appeared in the *Wochenblatt für Papierfabrikation* 69 (1938): 953–955, 976–979. (This also was issued as a separate, 10-page pamphlet by Güntter-Steib Verlag at Biberach an der Riss in 1938.) The Knapp and later Kersten articles make several references to the spread of colored paper making in Germany, as does an article on Turkish paper in Johann Georg Krünitz's *Ökonomisch-technologisches Encyklopädie, oder Allgemeines System der Staats-, Stadt-, Haus- und Landwirtschaft, Wie Auch der Erdbeschreibung, Kunst- und Naturgeschichte in Alphabetischer Ordnung* (Brünn: J. G. Tressler, 1818), v. 160: 730–743).

20. Arno Knapp, "Die Errichtung einer Buntpapierfabrik in Leipzig zu Beginn des 18. Jahrhunderts," 367.

21. Albert Haemmerle, *Buntpapier*, 23. The Olga Hirsch collection in the British Library contains a copy of a little book in two parts that Gottlieb Immanuel Breitkopf published at Leipzig in 1784 on the subject of playing cards, *Versuch den Ursprung der Speilkarten, die Einführung des Leinenpapiers, den Anfang der Holzschneidekunst in Europa zu Erforschen*.

22. Johann Beckmann, *Beyträge zur Oekonomie, Technologie, Polizey- und Cameralwissenschaft* (Göttingen: Verlag der Wittwe Vanderboek, 1780), pt. 3: 464–472. Beckmann referred to the making of marbled paper in still another of his publications, *Beyträge zur Geschichte der Erfindungen*, issued at Leipzig by Paul Gotthelf Kummer in five volumes between 1786 and 1805, and in English translations in 1797, 1814, and 1817, with a concise, abbreviated version appearing at London also in 1823. In the fourth volume of this work, Beckmann devoted chapter 4 to the subject of "Türkisches Papier." Mainly a résumé of the discovery and early history of this craft as it was understood in his time, it includes references to some of the articles and reports that were mentioned in Chapter 2 above, such as those of Francis Bacon, John Houghton, the Diderot-D'Alembert *Encyclopédie* article, etc. While it is incomplete and sometimes inaccurate, Beckmann's account constitutes one of the earliest attempts to discuss the origin and early conduct of this craft in Europe.

23. Information on the activity of Graul and Gräff comes from the sources cited here in notes 19 and 24. Krünitz refers (p. 733) to a notice of Gräff's factory that appeared in the *Journal für Fabrik*, January 1801, but as the following note indicates, this actually was published in 1804.

24. "Die Gräffische Bunt-Papier-Fabrik in Leipzig," *Journal für Fabrik, Manufaktur, Handlung und Mode* 26 (January–June 1804): 45–48.

25. "Tapeten von Marmor-Papier, in Architektonischem Geschmecke," *Journal des Luxus und der Moden* (September 1787): 326–329, with the marbled samples appearing with the plates at the end of this issue.

26. This appears in the "Intelligenz-Blatt" of the *Journal des Luxus und der Moden* (June 1788): L–LIII.

27. Wilisch's information was published as a supplement, entitled "Erganzung," at the conclusion of a separate printing of Paul Kersten's article on the history of colored paper that appeared originally in the *Wochenblatt für Papierfabrikation* in 1938 (cited in note 19).

28. Albert Haemmerle, *Buntpapier*, 137.

29. Otto Uttendörfer, in his *Wirtschaftsgeist und Wirtschaftsorganisaton Herrnhuts in der Brüdergemeine von 1743 bis zum Ende des Jahrhunderts*, which forms the second part of his *Alt-Herrnhut, Wirtschaftsgeschichte und Religions Soziologie Herrnhuts Während Seiner Ersten Zwanzig Jahre (1722–1742)*, relates (p. 280) that on 18 November 1764, the motion was made to establish the manufacture of colored paper, as proposed for some time by a number of unemployed women and as desired by the tradespeople with whom the community dealt. Uttendörfer's classic work on Herrnhut was published initially by the Verlag der Missionsbuchhandlung Herrnhut in 1925–1926; I have used the facsimile reprint, issued in 1984 by the Georg Olms Verlag of Hildesheim, Zürich and New York under the collective title *Schlesien und Herrnhut* (volume 22 of its *Nikolaus Ludwig von Zinzendorff, Materialien und Dokumente*).

30. Christian Gottlieb Frohberger, pastor at Rennserdorff, passed on this bit of information in his *Briefe über Herrnhut und die Evangelische Brüdergemeine; Nebst einem Anhange* (Budissen: George Gotthold Monse, [1796]), when discussing the various arts and crafts that were being carried on in that Moravian community.

31. I have in my files a 1964 letter from the late Dard Hunter in which that doyen of American paper historians wrote, "At one time we had a plan for doing a book on the early woodblock and paste-papers used by German printers in Pennsylvania and we have a very comprehensive collection of these papers, ranging from about 1720 to 1830 or 40." Hunter died a few years later and his son, Dard Hunter, Jr., subsequently informed me that this collection had been sold. Thus, hopes for such a book were never realized. A rare Pennsylvania Dutch imprint containing information on Herrnhut papers came into my possession not long ago—Johann Krauss's *Oeconomisches Haus- und Kunst-Buch, oder Sammlung Ausgesuchter Vorschriften, zum Nutzen und Gebrauch für Landund Hauswirthe, Handwerker, Künstler und Kunst Liebhaber* (Allentown: Henrich Ebner, 1819). This contains, in addition to excellent instructions on the preparation of colors, two sections (340, 341, pp. 488–489) devoted to the making of paste papers. One is entitled "Einfärbiges Marmorpapier zu machen" (although it has nothing to do with true paper marbling) and the other "Wie das Herrnhuter bunte Papier gemacht wird." Both are concerned with the making of paste papers alone. The first description tells of coating them with colored flour and then pressing their colored sides together and pulling them apart. The latter section discusses their stamping with woodblocks onto which patterns had been cut—that is, the Herrnhut way. I cannot recall ever seeing directions for making paste papers in any other book of recipes or secrets. I have observed few such German collections, however, in which such information would most likely be found in earlier times, since paste papers were a German invention and method.

32. While the making of paste papers is described in detail in the manuals of Paul Adam and Paul Kersten as well as in other German literature, the only detailed technical information in English that I am aware of appeared in two articles, one by Rosamond B. Loring, "Colored Paste Papers," *The New Colo-*

phon 2 (January 1949): 33–40, and the other by Nancy Storm (an excellent maker herself), "Paste Papers," *The Guild of Book Workers Journal* 18, no. 1 (1979–1980): 24-31. And recently Henry Morris has contributed to the literature by advocating a semi-mechanical method for producing this particular type of paper decoration in his *Roller Printed Paste Papers for Bookbinding* (North Hills, Pa.: Bird & Bull Press, 1975). In addition to relating her own interests and experiences in learning this craft, Mrs. Loring (as does Mrs. Storm) provides recipes, mentions tools needed, and discusses six types of paste paper that she made. The slight information she could find on this technique previously, she reports, appeared in Joseph W. Zaehnsdorf's *The Art of Bookbinding*, which was first published in London in 1880 and then in numerous editions early in this century.

33. Kersten devotes the final section of this small but important manual to "Die Technik des Marmorierens mit Kleisterfarben" (pp. 21–26); the reference to his grandfather appears in the second paragraph. He also relates that a little later (while Kersten served an apprenticeship with him), his grandfather desisted from making paste papers because craftspeople had begun to mass-produce and market them, making individual production unnecessary.

34. Number 94 (April 7, 1820): columns 1017–1020.

35. L. W. Schertel, *Ueber den Zustand der Bayerischen Gewerbsindustrie, inbesondere seit dem Segenreichen Regierungs-Antritte Seiner Majestät Königs Ludwig I* (Munich: the author, 1836), 54–56.

36. Hans Enderli, *Buntpapier, Geschichte und Rezepte des Buntpapiers mit 205 Original-Buntpapier-Muster*, 10.

37. Doubtlessly, many of these pattern books were issued over the years, but only a small number have survived the ravages of time. The examples preserved in the Loring collection at Harvard, at the Dutch Royal Library in The Hague, and by Enderli appear to be among the earliest that the Aschaffenburg firm issued. (As far as I can determine, the Loring example was issued around the year 1850, or perhaps slightly later, and it appears to be similar to the copy at the Hague.) A large collection of the firm's pattern books is reported to be in the local museum at Aschaffenburg but I was unable to confirm this, as the museum was closed at the time of my visit. In subsequent searches in libraries and museums around Europe, I located many more Aschaffenburg sample books, most dating from a later time. The largest collection I encountered was in the Dutch Royal Library at the Hague, as might be expected, since that institution recently acquired many of the books, papers, and other materials owned by the Aschaffenburg firm. In addition to the important one noted above, I found there sample books issued in 1902, 1910, 1913, and many later years. The Museum für Kunst und Gewerbe in Hamburg contains a copy of the 1881 issue, bound in two volumes. The Olga Hirsch collection in the British Library also has a copy of the 1881 issue and other examples dating to 1906 and 1926. Finally, the Deutsche Bücherei in Leipzig has a volume put out in 1927. This is a very large volume, containing thousands of samples, including some marbled ones.

38. There are a great many sources of information on the history and activities of the Dessauer-Aschaffenburg firm, of which Albert Haemmerle's *Buntpapier* is the most comprehensive. (This volume exists in two forms, with one containing special material on this firm; the other is described in note 39.) Excellent material is also provided in Hans Enderli's *Buntpapier*, the 1820 article in the *Allgemeiner Anzeiger der Deutschen* (cited before), and, in particular, a file on this firm that includes newspaper clippings and is maintained in the municipal archives in Aschaffenburg. Also useful is a lecture by Philipp Dessauer, Alois Dessauer's grandson, entitled "Entstehung und Entwicklung der Buntpapier-Industrie," issued in 1881 as a separate printing from *Der Papierhandel*, the organ of the Papierzwischen- und

Kleinhandel at Dresden-Blasewitz. Mr. Dessauer delivered this lecture before the Verein der Papier- und Schreibwaarenhändler on 12 January 1881. The article on Wilisch's involvement in helping Alois Dessauer reorganize the Aschaffenburg plant (note 27) is especially useful, as are brief accounts of Buntpapier and analogous subjects in L. W. Schertel's history of the Bavarian trades and industries (note 35). Finally, the history of the Dessauer enterprise, particularly in the later nineteenth and early twentieth centuries, is detailed in a thesis compiled by Albert Stadelmann of Aschaffenburg, "Die Buntpapierindustrie in Aschaffenburg," which was submitted for the doctorate degree to the Julius-Maximilians-Universität at Würzburg in 1922. I located and examined a copy of this thesis in the university's new library. It relates that the firm was founded in 180 by Johann Daniel Knode, and taken over by Dessauer in 1811. Stadelmann also published a pertinent article that is helpful, "Die Buntpapierfabrikation," *Archiv für Buchbinderei* 28 (1928): 115–118.

39. Haemmerle's *Buntpapier* actually exists in two forms. One includes at its end a twenty-three-page section entitled "150 Jahre Buntpapierfabrik AG Aschaffenburg"; the other lacks this section. It apparently was added for presentation purposes, for the copy that came into my possession was given to me by the late eminent anesthesiologist Henry Knowles Beecher, who had been presented with it on the occasion of receiving an honorary degree at the University of Munich.

40. Henry Knowles Beecher, personal communication, November 17, 1971.

41. This information was transmitted to me by Henck Voorn of the Koninklijke Bibliotheek in the Hague in several letters and in personal conversation. Among the materials sent to the Royal Library are six handwritten recipe books or manuals, the earliest being dated 1836. These contain hundreds of recipes for the making of marbled and other types of colored paper, and some even have original samples. Unfortunately, the handwriting is in old German longhand or script, which makes reading extremely difficult, even for present-day Germans, few of whom are acquainted with it.

42. Albert Haemmerle compiled an inventory of the colored and decorated papers in the Aschaffenburg collection, of which typescripts are in the Dutch Royal Library and the Olga Hirsch collection of the British Library. Entitled "Die Buntpapiersammlung Guido Dessauer, Aschaffenburg," this inventory extends to 41 pages and groups the various papers according to their pertinent classes.

43. Issued by La Librairie Encyclopédique de Roret as one of its "Manuels-Roret."

44. A copy of what I believe to be the first, 1696 part of this work, but lacking its title page, has been traced to the University of Michigan Library in Ann Arbor, which has supplied me with reproductions of pertinent pages. This appears to be of the utmost rarity, for I have not been able to locate other copies of it anywhere; Kretz's citation seems to be the only such reference. The second, 1707 part, however, is noticed in the "Schrifttumsverzeichnis zum Buntpapier" in Albert Haemmerle's *Buntpapier* (p. 190, under the entry "I. K."), and Grünebaum's *Buntpapier* picks it up also (p. 204); she undoubtedly derived her information from Haemmerle. On the other hand, Mrs. Easton omits notice of the title entirely. The University of Michigan copy of Part 1 is printed in different type than is the second, 1707 part, and both contain different head pieces and ornamental initials as well; but this is to be expected of two parts of the same work that were published a decade apart. I have compared the two as best I could, and they definitely appear to be the first and second parts of the same work, and probably of the same edition, too. Michigan has cataloged its first part to the year 1784, most likely following the reference that is given in the next note.

45. Christian Gottlob Kayser, *Vollständiges Bücher-Lexicon* (Leipzig: L. Schumann, 1835), pt. 3: 448 cites a "Kunst- u. Werkschule, oder Samml. auserlef. Kunste. 2 Thle. 8. Nurnb. 5e A[ufl.], [1]784. Bauer u. Raspe." What appears to be an earlier eighteenth-century edition is noted in Wilhelm Hensius's *Bücher Lexikon* (Leipzig: J. F. Gleditsch, 1812), v. 2: 687.

46. Issued at Nürnberg by Benjamin Schillern im Dohnt, this anonymous work has a title or subtitle that is nearly as long as that of the second part of Johann Zieger's *Kunst- und Werck-Schul* published the same year.

47. The first part of this work contains another of those prolix titles so favored by German authors and publishers of this period. Its imprint told that it had been printed at Nürnberg by Christian Sigm. Froberg and could be purchased from Johann Christoph Lochner. The second part, which contains an additional section title that is nearly as long as the title page itself, commences *Der Selbst-Lehrenden Laccir- u. Furniss-Kunst Anderer Theil;* after it enumerates the five subjects with which it is concerned, it ends with the imprint specifying that it was sold by Lochner, but that it had been printed by Melchior Gottfried Hein in 1707.

48. This dictionary or lexicon has still another of those period title pages that is tortured and long; its title encompasses thirty-four lines, most of them crammed with information. The work is comprised of sixty-four volumes and four supplemental volumes. Information on the making of Turkish paper appears in v. 45, columns 1715–1716; on gilded paper in v. 11, column 133; and on edge coloring in supplemental v. 4, column 861.

49. [Johann Friedrich Pfeiffer] *Die Manufacturen und Fabriken Deutschlands nach Ihrer Heutigen Lage Betrachtet und mit Allgemeinen Vorschlägen zu Ihren Vorzüglichsten Verbesserungs Mitteln Begleitet* (Frankfurt am Mayn: Varrentrapp Sohn und Wenner, 1780), v. 1: 483–484. This occurs in an extensive section on papermaking, and particularly on the use of alternate materials for rags in the making of paper, such as wood and straw. The section extends from p. 456 to 524.

50. Carl Gottlieb Roessig, *Lehrbuch der Technologie für den Angehenden Staatswirth und den Sich Bildenden oder Reisenden Technologen* (Jena: In der Akademischen Buchhandlung, 1790), 25–26.

51. The initial edition of Prediger's work, with a lengthy title commencing *Der in Aller Heut zu Tag Üblichen Arbeit Wohl Anweisende Accurate Buchbinder und Futteralmacher,* was issued in four volumes between 1741 and 1753, and, according to its imprint, could be found in Anspach, Frankfurt, and Leipzig. The section on edge marbling appears on pp. 85–88 of volume 1. Prediger (1702–1768), the son of a bookbinder, was trained in that craft in his father's workshop, and received a broad cultural education as well. After his apprenticeship, he traveled widely and acquired a wide experience. Upon his father's death, he returned to Anspach and passed his master's examination, subsequently entering into the life of a bookbinder. He not only transformed his father's business into a large-scale workshop, but he engaged in publishing as well. His work on bookbinding and slip-case making is considered the oldest German technical manual on bookbinding and the first really important such work worldwide. It was unusual for an artisan in his day to engage in writing and especially to divulge professional secrets; indeed, when his first volume came out he was reproached by his fellow binders, who wanted to force him from the trade and forbid other publications of this kind. Despite it all, Prediger went on writing and published everything he knew about this craft before his death at Anspach. Any edition of his manual is rare. It was recently reissued in Germany in facsimile, with a commentary volume by Adolf Rhein, Albert Haemmerle, and Heinz Petersen.

52. Christian Gottlieb Kayser, *Vollständiges Bücher Lexicon,*

v. 5, 168. Kayser's reference subsequently was picked up by Haemmerle, Grünebaum, Easton, and other observers of the literature of Buntpapier. For a number of years I tried to locate a copy in Germany, and as late as 1987 was informed that no copy of it was on record (Dr. Wolfgang Schleider, Leiter der Papierhistorischen Sammlung der Deutsche Bücherei, Leipzig, to Richard J. Wolfe, February 2, 1987).

53. Johann Georg Krünitz, *Oekonomisch-Technisches Encyklopädie,* v. 84, 784–789.

54. Ibid. v. 106, 730–743

55. J. J. H. Bücking, *Die Kunst des Buchbinders; Mit Weglassung der für Gegenwärtige Zeiten Nicht Mehr Passenden Sachen Neu Verbessert und Vermehrt; Herausgegeben von I. M. D. B.* (Stadtamhof: In der Daisenberger'schen Buchhandlung, 1807). Its marbling instructions appear in section 144, pp. 208–209. Bücking's manual was reissued in facsimile in 1978 by the Zentralantiquariat der Deutsche Demokratischen Republik, Leipzig.

56. Christian Friedrich Gottlieb Thon, *Die Kunst Bücher zu Binden. für Buchbinder und Freunde dieser Kunst, Welche Bücher Aller Art Selbst Binden, Marmorieren, Vergolden und Lackiren Wollen, Nebst einem Anhange, Das So Genannte Tücrkische Papier auf das Vollkommenste zu Verfertigen; Zeichnungen, Kupfer, Landkarten u. auf Pappe oder Leinwant zu Ziehen, und Allerhand Runde, Ovale und Eckige Gegenstände, Sowohl mit Untersatz und Deckel, Als Auch Schrauden, Geschmackvoll aus Pappe zu Arbeiten und zu Lackiren* (Sondershausen und Nordhausen: Bei Bernard Friedrich Voigt, 1820), 127–135.

57. Ernst Wilhelm Greve, *Hand- und Lehrbuch der Buchbinde- und Futteralmache-Kunst. In Briefen an einen Jungen Kunstverwandten nach Vieljährigen eigenen Erfahrungen gründlich und möglichst vollständig Ausgearbeitet* (Berlin: In Commission der Mauerschen Buchhandlung, 1822–1823), 2 volumes. Information on colored paper making, including marbling, appears on pp. 500–508 of v. 1, with all of it repeated on pp. 344–348 of v. 2.

58. As Graham Pollard and Esther Potter's *Early Bookbinding Manuals* indicates (pp. 9–11), a few German works devoted to bookbinding did appear subsequently in the eighteenth century, but these seem not to have paid attention to marbling, possibly because edge marbling had really not yet come into vogue there and because marbled paper was abundant— produced in large quantity by specialists.

CHAPTER 4

1. Richard J. Wolfe, *Three Early French Essays on Paper Marbling, 1642–1765* (Newtown, Pa.: Bird & Bull Press, 1987), 17.

2. Jean-Michel Papillon, *Traité historique et pratique de la Gravure en bois* (Paris: P. G. Simon, 1766).

3. Haemmerle attributes its manufacture to south France, ca. 1570. Another early *domino* paper is reproduced as figure 19 in Alan V. Sugden and John L. Edmundson's *A History of English Wallpaper, 1509–1914* (New York and London: Charles Scribner's Sons, 1926).

4. Philadelphia and London: J. B. Lippincott Company, 1924, 27–28.

5. *Decorated Book Papers,* 38–39.

6. Mrs. Loring relates that because of this and subsequent legislation in 1618 and 1649, the *dominotiers* gave up making pictures from woodblocks, with names and descriptive legends, and concentrated on making marbled papers, which did not involve them with the guilds. Mrs. Loring's conclusion does not stand up under close scrutiny, at least with regard to marbled paper.

7. *Le Grand Robert de la Langue Français* (2d ed., Paris: Le Robert, 1985), v. 3; 623 provides the following descriptions of a *domino,* in addition to its meaning as a decorated paper: a black shoulder covering with a hood, which the clergy wear in winter; a costume for a masked ball, consisting of a robe flowing into a hood; a person dressed in a *domino.* Nearly the same meanings appear in seventeenth- and eighteenth-century French dictionaries, of which the *Abregé du Dictionnaire universel François et Latin, vulgairement appellé dictionnaire de trévoux* (Paris: Les Libraires Associés, 1762), v. 1: 738 is but one example. Nowhere have I noticed such a costume imputed to marblers or dominotiers.

8. Charles M. Adams, "Some Notes on the Art of Marbling Paper in the Seventeenth Century," 411. Mrs. Loring also discusses L'Estoile's interest in marbled papers, in her *Decorated Book Papers,* 24. Adams provides the French text for the second entry in L'Estoile's diary, and Mrs. Loring provides an English translation of passages in 1608 and 1609 discussing marbled paper. Haemmerle illustrates L'Estoile's original diary entry for May 13, 1609 on page 49 of his *Buntpapier.* The original manuscript of L'Estoile's "Mémoires Journaux" is in the Bibliothèque Nationale. Adams cites from a printed edition, published in twelve volumes at Paris by the Libraire des Bibliophiles in 1875–1883.

9. The two exhibitions evolving from Mme. Guilleminot-Chrétien's research—they actually amounted to a single exhibition held in two locations—took place at the Dutch Royal Library in The Hague from May 22 to July 11, 1987 and at the Bibliothèque Nationale in Paris from December 9, 1987 to early 1988. A single catalog was prepared for both showings, in Dutch translation for the initial one and in French for the latter one, with the same illustrations appearing in both. The Dutch catalog bears the title *Franse Marmerpapieren in Vorstelijke Boekbanden, Uit de Collectie van de Bibliothèque Nationale te Parijs* while the French one is entitled *Papiers marbrés Français reliures princières et créations contemporaines.*

10. As I noted in note 21 of Chapter 1, on pages [40] and [41] of that work are described and illustrated an Album Amicorum, now preserved in the Bibliothèque Nationale, which belonged to Jean Huenich of Anvers (MSS., Latin 18596) and which is dated 1586. This contains both marbled and silhouette papers, which are pictured side by side in the illustration on p. [40] there.

11. Jean La Caille, *Histoire de l'imprimérie et de la librairie, où l'on voit son origine & son progrès jusqu'en 1689* (Paris: J. de La Caille, 1689). Rosamond Loring cites this in her *Decorated Book Papers,* page 16, stating that La Caille asserts that "Macé Ruette, a Parisian stationer and bookbinder of about 1606, invented the art of marbling and used marbled paper for end-papers." More recently, Roger Devauchelle, in his *La Reliure on France de ses origines à nos jours* (Paris: Jean Rousseau-Gerard, 1959), v. 1: 119 relates that its invention is attributed to Macé Ruette, successor to Clovis Eve, royal binder from 1635 to 1644, but it has been proved that marbling, which is also called *dominotérie,* was already known in Germany at the end of the sixteenth century.

12. For example, the work of the Le Bretons, père et fils, are mentioned in the Diderot-D'Alembert *Encyclopédie* of 1765 and in Johann Beckmann's *Beyträge zur Geschichte der Erfindungen* of 1799, which derives some information from the Diderot article.

13. Mrs. Loring, in *Decorated Book Papers,* [23], tells us that "La Caille asserts that marbled papers were used in several bindings by Le Gascon between 1617 and 1630. One of these books, now in the British Museum, has end-papers of the fine combed type." Le Gascon, she asserts, was probably the first to use the leather doublure, employing marbled papers for the contrasting flyleaves.

14. Phoebe Jane Easton, *Marbling: a History and a Bibliography,* 39–40. Typically, Mrs. Easton does not cite her source of this information.

15. Roger Devauchelle, *Le Relieure en France,* v. 2: 37–45, 247.

16. Ibid., v. 2: 53–58, 229–230.

17. This was reported to me in conversation and repeated later in a letter of 20 March 1986.

18. In the article "Marbreur de Papier," found in v. 10, p. 72 of the edition issued at Neuchâtel by Samuel Faulche & Compagnie in 1765.

19. *Decorated Book Papers*, 24, citing as her source Papillon's 1766 treatise on wood engraving.

20. Roger Devauchelle, *La Reliure en France*, v. 1: 119.

21. Octave Uzanne, *The French Bookbinders of the Eighteenth Century* (Chicago, Caxton Club, 1904), 91.

22. In *The Role of the Mann Family of Dedham, Massachusetts in the Marbling of Paper in Nineteenth Century America* I have related (p. 98) how Samuel and Edward Mann, after suffering business reversals in Boston and moving back to their point of origin in nearby Dedham, set up an order box at the store of Charles A. Wells in Boston where, bookbinders could leave uncovered books to be collected and have their edges marbled by the Manns. The books were then transported back to Wells for pick-up by the binders; boarding-in and finishing followed.

23. The initial edition was published at Paris by Louis Vendosme.

24. The Lyon edition of 1684 was issued by Pierre Vander Aa, and the Paris edition of 1686 by P. Trabouiller. P. Vander Aa also issued his 1684 edition with two title pages, the second reading *Nouveau recueil des curiositez rares*, etc., and in copies where the original title is absent, this serves as a variant title. Vander Aa also published an edition at Lyon with its title beginning with the word *Nouveau* in 1688, 1697, and again early in the next century. P. Mortier issued another edition with this title at Amsterdam early in the eighteenth century, as did Estienne Roger of Amsterdam in 1709. The last French edition that I have been able to locate was published at Paris by Ribou in 1737.

25. In 1711, J. King and J. Morphew had printed and put on sale a second edition of this work, retitled *New Curiosities in Art and Nature: or, a Collection of the Most Valuable Secrets in All Sorts of Arts and Sciences,* and at about the same time there was issued another London edition, undated and retitled *Curiosa Arcana: Being Curious Secrets, Artificial and Natural,* with its imprint indicating that it had been printed for J. N.

26. The article on Nicolas Lemery, written by Owen Hannaway, appeared in the *Dictionary of Scientific Biography* (New York: Charles Scribner's Sons, 1973), v. 8: 172–175.

27. This collection of early French marbling literature is fully cited in the first note of this chapter. My translation of this early manuscript account appears on pp. 25–31, with the facsimiles on pp. [33]–40.

28. University of Glasgow Library, MS. Ferguson 150. It was acquired by Prof. Ferguson, compiler of the *Bibliotheca Chemica,* on 4 May 1881, as recorded on its front endpaper, with the name "Ellis White," presumably the previous owner of the volume or the bookseller who offered it to him. The volume is of small octavo format, measuring 15 × 10 centimeters, and is bound in early vellum, probably of the period.

29. *Sécrets concernant les arts et métiers* was first issued at Paris by C. Jombert in a single volume in 1716; it had a short discussion of the method of marbling paper that amounted to about 150 words, on pp. 161–162 ("Sécret pour marbre & jasper le papier"). Later editions, some multivolumed, were issued in 1721 (Nancy); 1724 (Rouen); 1755, 1762, 1767 (all three at Brussels); 1781 (Caen); 1791, 1792, 1801 (all three at Paris); and 1810 (Avignon), and there may have been others. This work was indeed a true "book of secrets," and was evidently popular and much used. Besides the first edition, I have also examined the Rouen, 1724 edition, where the brief passage on marbling appears on pp. 254–256 of v. 1.

30. Jacques Savary des Bruslon's *Dictionnaire Universal de Commerce* appeared in many editions (and in several translations) from 1720, when it was initially issued, into the later eighteenth century—so many, in fact, that it would be of little use to cite them all here; they can be found described in a number of large library and bibliographical catalogs. I have examined the 1723–1732 Amsterdam edition and the 1741 Paris edition in the Kress Library of the Harvard Business School. The passage on marbling is not extensive; when an English translation was made by Malachy Postlethwayt and issued at London by Paul Knapton in 1751 under the title *The Universal Dictionary of Trade and Commerce,* the original short marbling description was replaced by two longer accounts from other sources (see my discussion in the chapter dealing with marbling in England).

31. Jacques Gautier d'Agoty, *Observations sur l'histoire naturelle, sur la physique et sur la peinture* (Paris: Chez Delaguette, 1752–1755), 6 volumes. The marbling account appears on pp. 63–64 of the second part of volume 1, issued in 1752.

32. "De la Meilleure manière de faire le papier marbré," *Journal Oeconomique* (March 1758): 112–116; a translation appears on pp. 43–53 of my *Three Early French Essays on Paper Marbling, 1642–1765.*

33. This other translation was made by Anne Renault and student helpers and published under the title *The Art of the Paper Marbler, a Mechanical Art* (Camberwell, England: Camberwell School of Arts and Crafts, 1980). The edition was limited to 75 copies, tastefully printed on Van Gelder mold-made paper.

34. The translator and her helpers noted that "a few technical terms are marked in the present text by an asterisk: they might well have been understood by a knowledgeable reader in the eighteenth century, but they have remained obscure and insufficient information is given by their context to allow the translator or editor to identify them with confidence."

35. Since the marbling trough called for in the Diderot-D'Alembert article measured approximately 18 × 20 or 21 inches (almost the same size as the pan I use today), and since the combing was probably done crosswise, along the shorter dimensions of the trough, we may presume that the needles or pins on the comb were spaced about an inch and a half, or slightly less, apart. As I noted in my *Three Early Essays on French Marbling,* the exact meaning of "montfaucon" remains obscure. The term was associated with a French city, and several individuals also carried that name. The only earlier reference I could find appeared in François Raymond's *Dictionnaire général de la langue Françoise et vocabulaire universel des sciences, des arts et des métiers* (Paris: 1835), which stated that the term described the size of a sheet of one sort of paper, but gave no measurements or size or other details.

36. Franz Weisse, *Die Kunst des Marmorierens,* 12. This passage appears on p. 12 of my translation.

37. Henri Gabriel Duchesne's work appeared anonymously under the title *Dictionnaire de l'industrie, ou collection raisonnée des procédés utiles dans les Sciences et dans les arts; contenant nombre de sécrets curieux & intéressans pour l'économie & les besoins de la vie; l'indication de différentes expériences à faire; la description de plusieurs jeux très singuliers & très amusants; les notices des découvertes & inventions nouvelles; les détails nécessaires pour se mettre à l'abri des fraudes & falsifications dans plusieurs objets de commerce & de fabrique. ouvráge également propre aux artistes, aux négocians & aux gens du monde. par une société de gens de lettres.* The first edition was issued by Lacombe, the second by Rémont, and the third by Pougnee, with the marbling description appearing in the third volume of the 1776 edition and in the fifth volume of the latter two. The Italian edition is reported by Pollard and Potter (*Early Bookbinding Manuals,* 19); I have not had an opportunity to examine a copy of this work. They report that the section on marbling occurs on pp. 256–258 of volume 1, under "Carta marmorizzata."

38. John Grand-Carteret, *Papeterie & papetiers de l'ancien*

temps; les corporations, les boutiques, les marchandises, notices sur envelopes, l'encre, les encriers, les plumes, les crayons, le papier à lettres, la cire, les pains à cacheter, les portefeuilles, copies d'écritures, bibliographie, enseignes, étiquettes et addresses des marchands-papetiers d'autrefois (Paris: Georges Putois, 1913).

39. The *Rapport sur les papiers peints, papiers de fantaisie et stores,* Groupe III, Classe 22, prepared by M. Isidore Leroy and issued by the French Ministère de l'Agriculture et du Commerce following the Exposition Universelle Internationale held at Paris in 1878 (Paris: Imprimerie Nationale, 1880), reports (p. 22) on the various colored papers made by the firm of Chagniat and Son of Paris, among which is named marbled paper. Thus, it is almost certain that Chagniat included this item in his overall manufacture, probably from the very beginning of his activity in 1838.

40. Gabriel Magnien, "Répertoire des Principaux dominotiers fabriquant spécialement des papiers d'ornement pour la reliure en France, en Allemagne et en Italie aux XVIIᵉ, XVIIIᵉ siècles et au debut du XIXᵉ siècle," *Le Vieux Papier; Bulletin de la Société Archéologique, Historique et Artistique* 19 (1946–1949): 154–258.

41. Musée des Arts Décoratifs, *Trois siècles de papiers peints* (Paris: Musée des Arts Décoratifs, 1967). The exhibition ran from June 22 to October 15, 1967.

42. Mme. Guilleminot-Chrétien, in her recent exhibition catalog, speaks of "the 'new style' in marbling: 1780–1815," which I have referred to before as a revival of interest in the art in France through the introduction of new patterns. She postulates that this occurred about 1780, nearly a decade before the French Revolution broke out, basing her estimate of its beginning on the beautiful papers that Nicolas-Denis Derome the younger produced at this time. Derome, his binder's tickets indicate, worked in this period and in the next century, and his papers embellish many bindings in the library of King Louis XVI. While Derome admittedly did produce beautifully marbled paper, mainly with either a brown-red or a clear, bright green predominating, these actually are designs of the standard Turkish pattern. There is nothing new or innovative about them, although they show more refinement and vigor than is representative of most other contemporary French marbles. Mme. Guilleminot-Chrétien relates that his was the only marbled paper made during the early years of the Revolution, a period of austerity and a lessening of taste and manners, when the use of marbled paper was mainly abandoned in French binding circles in favor of papers coated with paste colors (and used primarily for cover papers). She relates that Derome's successor, Pierre-Alexis Bradel, (called l'âiné) abandoned Derome's green marble in 1803 for another which in France came to be termed "marbré Empire." This pattern showed an overall predominance of blue spots, with the spots broken into networks of fine, lacy holes, with red or black sometimes appearing as vein colors but often with blue appearing alone. In England, where marblers soon came to imitate it, (with the veins made in a different way), this pattern came to be called "French marble," and later, at mid-century, Charles Woolnough would refer to it as "Stormont." It was the introduction of this pattern, the "marbre Empire," along with another called "shell" or "French shell," (which all evidence indicates was introduced at about the same time—in the late 1790s), that I believe ushered in the new era that pumped new life into this art in France, at least for a few decades more. Mme. Guilleminot-Chrétien does not refer to the shell pattern at all, which came to be one of the two or three most popularly made in the nineteenth century.

43. Maroquin or morocco paper is discussed on pages 51–52 of *Der Vollkommene Papierfärber,* alluded to in Chapter 3, which I believe to be the long-lost or long-unrecognized Schuder work of 1808. It also is discussed in several of the early nineteenth-century manuals devoted to the decorating of paper that will be

mentioned later: Louis Sébastien LeNormand's *Manuel du fabricant d'étoffes imprimées et du fabricant de papiers peints* (1830) and Christian F. G. Thon's *Der Fabrikant bunter Papier* (1826), for example. LeNormand, who devotes a great deal of space to the making of this type, states that Fortin in Paris brought this pattern very far. Grand-Carteret identifies the stationer Fortin, who had a very considerable business, as active in Paris from 1802.

44. This statement is made in the introduction (Einleitung) of *Der Vollkommene Papierfärber,* cited in the previous note.

CHAPTER 5

1. I have noticed marbled papers of possible Italian manufacture in bindings on Italian imprints dating from the 1720s, but one cannot be sure that these bindings were executed that early; evidence, and reasoning, point toward later rather than earlier execution in most of these cases. Papers in bindings on such imprints usually are the simplest imaginable, consisting of a single color—rose or blue—with white veins (i.e., the paper showing through where the color did not entirely cover the size and eventually the sheet). If such marbling actually was executed in Italy in the beginning decades of the eighteenth century, it undoubtedly represented early and sporadic attempts by Italian bookbinders and others to produce the sheets of colored paper that were required or desired for occasional use; they should not be thought of as the product of any long-continuing industry.

2. *Decorated Book Papers,* 42–45. The Remondini enterprise, which had a long and interesting existence, has not until recently been afforded the historical treatment it deserves. In addition to the various sources referred to here, discussions of its activities have been published by Gabriel Magnien, "Imagiers Vénetiens au XVIIIᵉ siècle: la famille Remondini de Bassano-Venuto," *Le Vieux papier; Bulletin de la Société Archéologique, Historique et Artistique* 22 (1958–1960): 29–35; and by Gino Barioli, *Mostra dei Remondini, Calografi Stampatori Bassanese* (Bassano: Stamperia Vincenzi, 1958). Barioli's small monograph was issued by the Museo Civico of Bassano del Grapa. He also produced two other works that relate to the activities of this firm, *Centi Legni Remondini* (Bassano: 1959) and *Stampe Populari Venete dal Secolo XVII al Secolo XIX* (Venice: Pozza, 1959), the latter being a catalog of an exhibition held at the Verona Galleria d'Arte Modena in March 1959.

The most complete study to date of the Remondinis and their activities is Mario Infelise's *I Remondini di Bassano; Stampa e Industria nel Venuto del Settacento* (Bassano: Tassotti Editore, con la Collaborazione della Libreria Scrimin, 1980). Infelise reproduces in color a few of the decorated papers the Remondinis produced—pattern papers, and one of the morocco kind, but none of the marbled variety. He devotes only 3 of his 210 pages to the subject of decorated paper (pp. 62–64, "Le Carte Lavorate"), although he does allude to decorated papers on the pages following (pp. 65–69) when discussing governmental protection granted to the Remondinis by the Venetian Republic. While he also makes reference to marbled paper, he does not say much about it and does not specify when it came to be made in Bassano. One of Infelise's tables indicates that in 1798 the Remondinis obtained about 3 ½ percent of their total income from the sale of "stampe e carte dorati."

3. Notice of this legislation of 1738 is recorded in a manuscript in the Venetian state archives, as follows:

Fabbriche di Bassano.	Remondini Carte
Fabbrica della Dita Fratelli	
Remondini di	
Bassano.	

La Term:ne 1738 Rj. Luglio, esecutiva del Decreto 4 Giugno anteded.te, et approvata dal sasseg.te Bj. Luglio lore concesse il jus privativo nella Dom.te, e nello Stato per tutto il corso di loro vita naturale per la Fabrica delle Immagini, Iconj &c. carta dorata, colorata, ed all'Inglese, coll esenzion pel tempo del privativo dai Dazj di Terra Ferma sulla carta dorata, e colorata per successiva Terminaz.ne 1739. RB. Gen.:ro, esecutiva del Decreto jB. detto.

4. This large broadside commences *Terminazione Degl' Illustrissimi, & Eccelentissimi Signori Deputati, et Aggionti alla Regolazione del Commercio. Intorno alla Nuova Fabbrica Remondini di Bassano di Carte Demascate, e Velutate;* after a number of paragraphs, it is signed at the end, "Alessandro Bernardo, Segr., Adi 29. Settembre 1755. Approvata con Decreto dell'Eccellentissimo Senato." Finally, its imprint at the bottom related that it was printed "per le Figiuoli del qu: Z. Antonio Pinelli Stamporati Ducali." A copy is preserved in the Venetian state archives in Venice.

5. This large broadside, depicted in Figure 7, measures about 18 inches in height and 16 inches in width and commences *Terminazione degl' Illustrissimi, et Eccellentissimi Signori Cinque Savj alla Mercanzia Esecutiva di Decreto dell' Eccellentissimo Senato de Di 9. Febbraro 1764 Concernente la Fabbrica delle Carte Dorate, Miniate, ed in Varie Altre Maniere Configurate, della Dita Giuseppe Remondini, e Figli di Bassano;* its lengthy text deals with the taxing of papers and other materials manufactured by the Remondinis and the placing of excise duties upon them, modifying earlier decrees of 13 January 1739 and 7 April 1763. The decree is dated the first day of March 1765. Another copy is reportedly in the Venetian state archives. All evidence that has come to my attention, including general information provided by Mario Infelise in his *I Remondini di Bassano,* tends to establish the manufacture of marbled paper by the Remondinis around the year 1764, concurrent with this proclamation.

6. Phoebe Jane Easton, *Marbling: a History and a Bibliography,* 170.

7. Estrellita Karsh, who at my request researched the Venetian state archives for materials on the Remondinis, reported that a series of their pattern books are preserved in that repository.

8. Mrs. [Mary Philadelphia] Merrifield, *Original Treatises, Dating from the XIIth to the XVIIIth Centuries in the Arts of Painting, Oil, Miniature, Mosaic, and on Glass; of Gilding, Dyeing, and the Preparation of Colours and Artificial Gems; Preceded by a General Introduction; with Translations, Prefaces, and Notes* (London: John Murray, 1849), 2 volumes. This compilation is a veritable gold mine of information for anyone interested in the nature and composition of colors and analogous materials during the late Middle Ages and Renaissance. The Padua manuscript under discussion, titled "Ricette per Far Ogni Sorte di Colori," appears on pp. [641]–717 of volume 2, including Mrs. Merrifield's "Preliminary Observations," with English and Italian texts on parallel pages.

9. In a letter postmarked December 14, 1987 M. Ipert wrote to me about this manuscript, relating that "a friend who is a paleograph[er] just told me that it could be beginning of XVIIᵉ century."

10. A reasonable index of the approximate dates of the transfer of these dyestuffs from the New World to the old is afforded by their definitions in the *Oxford English Dictionary,* which cites examples of their use from the earliest times. Cochineal was introduced into Europe from Mexico, where it had been used as a dyestuff long before the coming of the Spaniards; it first appeared in English literature in 1582 and reappeared frequently thereafter. Campeachy wood first appeared in 1652, while brazilwood, or Braziletto as the *OED* cites it, first entered there in 1656. Certainly, words and descriptions are used in everyday language long before they appear in printed literature, but the first appearance of the names of these two dyewoods in printed

form after the middle of the seventeenth century provides a reasonably fair indication that this Italian manuscript containing them also dates to the second half of the seventeenth century.

11. William Osmun, in his introduction to a catalog entitled *Decorated Book Papers, Seventeenth to Twentieth Century,* issued to accompany an exhibition of such materials at the Cooper Union Museum for the Arts of Decoration in New York City in 1954, states (p. 5) that "Spanish marbled papers (no. 91, Fig. 5) originated in the seventeenth century." And Mrs. Loring (*Decorated Book Papers,* 27) reports that "Spanish marbled papers are a type which was very much identified with one country. They were used in Spanish books from the early seventeenth century and were a most harmonious blend of soft colors." Osmun's Figure 5, a paper he describes as "Spain (?). Probably second half of the nineteenth century," and attributes to the Rosamond B. Loring Collection, The Harvard College Library, is not a true Spanish paper at all, but one made in Europe in the nineteenth century, and probably in England, being of the specific variety that Woolnough designates as "Fancy Spanish or lace pattern" and dating after the middle of the nineteenth century.

12. A case illustrating this point indicates how important a knowledge of bookbinding history and practice is to this game. A book that came to my attention a number of years ago (now in the Countway Library in Boston), while lacking a title page, could be identified as the Paris, 1583 edition of the *Opera* of the surgeon Ambroise Paré. It was rebound and restored late in the eighteenth century, at which time its original French backstrip (tooled in gilt in a diaper pattern of small ovals), dating probably to about the time of its issue, was laid back on the spine and new, tree marbled sheepskin was put down on its covers. Tree marbling of leather, Bernard Middleton indicates (*A History of English Craft Bookbinding Technique,* 191) came into style about 1775 and continued in vogue in the early decades of the nineteenth century. (I pointed out earlier that the maroquin or morocco paper, introduced about 1800, appears to be decorated in imitation of tree marbled leather.) Our restored French binding also contains marbled endpapers of the authentic Spanish design, with red and black making up the veins and with large green spots predominating, onto which some light brown ones finally were thrown (see sample 57 on Plate XXVII). This pattern was popularly produced in the 1770 or 1780 period. The book also contains some marginal notes in Spanish, and a loose note is laid in, also in Spanish, apparently belonging to a later owner, for the manuscript date "1830" appears on it. From all of this evidence a fairly clear binding history unfolds. Originally bound in France at about the time it was printed, the book fell into disrepair—it is badly worm holed, as well as imperfect. It was eventually acquired by a Spanish physician who had it restored in his native land in the 1770s or 1780s, in the fashion that was popular at that time. Not only was the original backstrip then laid down, together with the original red leather label containing the legend in gilt, "Ambrosii Pare Opera,'" but newly marbled endpapers of Spanish manufacture were added also at this time to give it the most up-to-date appearance.

13. Charles W. Woolnough, *The Whole Art of Marbling, as Applied to Book-Edges, Paper, &c.,* 50–51.

14. Rosamond B. Loring, *Decorated End Papers,* 27–28.

15. A great deal of the marbled paper that I have soaked off of endpapers provided to me by restorers is thin paper that has been pasted onto another, reinforcing sheet. Lightweight paper was often employed in this form of paper decoration.

16. Louis Sébastien LeNormand, *Manual del Encuadernador, Teórico y Práctica, al Gusto del Dia* (Barcelona: Manuel Saurí, 1840; 2d ed., 1846).

17. Rosamond B. Loring, *Decorated Book Papers,* 19.

18. William Henry James Weale, *Bookbindings and Rubbings of Bindings in the Victoria and Albert Museum,* xx, xxi.

19. Phoebe Jane Easton, *Marbling: a History and a Bibliography*, 64.

20. In a letter of November 4, 1987 Albert J. Elen, who succeeded Henck Voorn as curator of the Department of Paper History at the Dutch Royal Library in the Hague told me that his collection contains a transcript of the document in the Gemeente Archief (Municipal Archives) of Amsterdam that concerns Visscher. Dated 19 April 1657, this reports that Sijmon Egbertsz Visscher, marbled papermaker living on the southside of the Elandsgracht (Amsterdam, AE), son and heir of Machtelt Rijcke, procreated by Edgert Sijmonsz Visscher also living there, confesses to have received his mother's possessons as only heir. He thanks his father and discharges him. Mr. Voorn had previously shown me a photocopy of this document during my visit to The Hague in the fall of 1982.

21. "The Art of Marbling," *Journal of Arts and of the Institutions in Union* 2 (1853–1854): 249–250.

22. This eighteenth-century Dutch imprint with marbling on its edges is a copy of the Amsterdam, 1739 edition of Lorenz Heister's *Institutiones Chirurgicae*, issued in two volumes, now in the collections of the Boston Medical Library in the Francis A. Countway Library of Medicine. The work, bound in two separate volumes, is covered with contemporary sheepskin, with plain covers, except for a blind rule around their outer edges. The spines are divided into six compartments by binder's bands, with five containing gilt ornamental stamping in the Dutch style, and a red leather label on the sixth giving title information. Both volumes contain marbled endpapers of the "Dutch" or combed variety (but without swirls), which appear to be German in origin, for they are bright and extremely well made. The edges are decorated with a blue color that gives every indication that it was deposited onto a bath and afterward absorbed onto these edges, but the marbling is very crude. The blue spots are few and they do not cover much area on the edges, leaving more white showing than blue and indicating that the marbler had difficulty making his color expand. They were combed through and swirled about with a draw point before they were taken off the bath and onto the volumes' edges. They indicate, overall, extremely poor technique on the part of their marbler.

23. This work appears as item 61 in Pollard and Potter's *Early Bookbinding Manuals*. They record that its full title is *Volkomen Handleiding tot de Boekbindkonst. Uit de Beste Schrijvers Bijeen Versameld en met de Nodige Ophelderingen en Verbeteringen Verrijkt*. They indicate that this work is in octavo format and contains three parts, citing the *Catalogus der Bibliotheek van de Vereeniging ter Bevordering van de Belangen des Boekhandels te Amsterdam* 1 (1920): 69, as their source.

There is actually on the record an earlier significant piece of Dutch bookbinding literature: a manuscript account dating to about the year 1658 by Dirk de Bray. This is now preserved in the Gemeente Archief of the city of Haarlem and was reproduced in facsimile in 1977 by Nico Israel of Amsterdam, with an English translation by H. S. Lake and an introduction by K. van der Horst and C. de Wolf. The introduction points out that De Bray was apprenticed to the bookbinder Passchier van Wesbusch and that his manuscript records only the simplest instructions he was given in the step-by-step methods of how to bind a book in the most common kind of vellum and leather, the binding in which the vast majority of seventeenth-century books were placed and which "remained standard until far into the eighteenth century." At the very end of De Bray's manuscript, however, there appears a brief explanation of "How you gild the edges" of books; this section was placed there by Ambrosius Vermerck in 1677, about nine years later. The manuscript contains no reference whatsoever to marbled paper or marbling.

24. Hendrik de Haas, *De Boekbinder; of Volledige Beschrijving*

van Al het Gene Wat Tot Deze Konst Betrekking Heeft. Met Platen (Dordrecht: A. Blussé en Zoon, 1806). A facsimile edition of this rare work was issued by the publishers "H & S" of Utrecht in 1984, with an introduction by Jan Storm van Leeuwen.

25. Pollard and Potter supply the title (entry 64) as *Over de Noodzakelijke Kundigheden der Boekbinders in Betrekking Tot Alle Technisch-chemische Proceduren en Voortbrengselen Zoowel, Als Van Alle Natuurlijke Kleuren*. They do not assign to this a place or date of issue, but proposed Middleburg at the beginning of the nineteenth century.

26. This small work is devoted mainly to the finishing aspects of bookbinding: the gilding of leather, paper, silk, velvet, and book edges; the marbling of book edges; and the coloring of leather—subjects to which the Dutch had paid only infrequent attention in earlier times. It has a somewhat lengthy title: *Geheim der Boekbinderij, of Handleiding voor Bookbinders, en voor Allen, die Zich in dit Vak Wenschen Te Bekwamen. Bevattende eene Beknopte Doch Volledige Beschrijving van het Vergulden op Alle Soorten van Leder, Fluweel, Zijde en Papier, Benevens het Vergulden van Marmeren op Snede, en Eindelkjk het Marmeren en Verwen van het Kalfs- en Schapenleder*. Its imprint relates that it could be obtained in Amsterdam from Ipenbuir and van Seldam.

27. Louis Sébastien LeNormand, *Handboek voor den Boekbinder, Bijzonder, met Betrekking to de Nieuwste Englische en Fransche Verbeteringen. Met een Aantal Afbeeldingen. Naar de Nieuwste Uitgave uit het Fransch* (Amsterdam: Gebroeders Diedrichs, 1843). This Dutch translation and edition is referred to in Pollard and Potter's list (no. 53) and in Mrs. Easton's bibliography (p. 164); her entry is derived from Dard Hunter's original listing.

28. Ludwig Brade and E. Winkler, *Het Geillustreerde Boekbinderboek. Volledig Onderright in het Boekbinden. Waarin Beschreven Worden de Nieuwste Fransche, Engelsche en Duitsche Verbeteringen in dit Vak, met Uitvoerig Onderright in het Vervaadigen van de Verschillende Marmeren Andere Sneden en het Vergulden, over het Gebruik van de Nieuwste Machinerien. Met een Aanhangsel Bevattende 76 Bijzonder Goede Recepten. Met Vele Houtgravuren* (Leyden: A. W. Sijthoff, 1861). This work went through seven German editions by 1930.

29. *The Art of Marbling and Treatment of the New Bronze Colours. A Practical Guide to Marbling by Halfer's Method. With 26 Specimens of Marbling, Some of Which are Gelatinised; also Illustrations. Second Improved and Enlarged Edition* (London: Hostmann Printing Ink Co., 1904). This is usually attributed to Josef Halfer and is a compilation of many instructions to assist purchasers in the use of the Halfer marbling colors which the Hostmann company produced early in this century.

30. Josef Hauptmann, *De Marmerkunst, Tot Versiering der Boeksnede. Eene Handleiding Tot de Practische Beofening* (Dordrecht: T. Van Buul, 1899). Mrs. Easton notes in her *Marbling: a History and a Bibliography* (p. 159) that a copy she examined contains the date "1900" on its printed wrappers.

31. J. Van Wingerden, *Geschiedenis der Marmerkunst*. This small pamphlet of 23 pages is undated, and its imprint reads, "Drukkerij 'Didot' Avereest."

32. Paul Kersten, *Die Geschichte des Buntpapiers*, separate Nachdruck, 2.

33. *Le Papier Marbré*, 85–86.

34. H. Dubois D'Enghien, *La Reliure en Belgique au dix-neuvième siècle; essai historique suivi d'un dictionnaire des relieurs* (Brussels: Alex. Leclercq & Paul Van der Perre, 1954). References to marbling and marbled papers are scattered about by period, but generally can be found on the following pages: 15–17, 23–24, 49–50, 69–70, 84–86.

35. Henck Voorn, in his unpublished "The Dutch Gilt Papers in the Collection of the Royal Library in The Hague" (cited in Chapter 3, reports that brocade or Dutch gilt papers were made at Turnhout from 1796 onward. Turnhout appears to have been

a center for the printing of playing cards as well as colored paper, from the early 1800s on. See Eugene Van Autenboer, *L'Industrie des cartes à jouer de Turnhout, 1826–1976; synthèse précedée d'un histoire de la carte à jouer Belge de 1379 à 1862, par Louis Tummers avec la collaboration de Jan Bauwens* (Brussels: Ministère des Affairs Étrangères, du Commerce Extérieur et de la Co-opération au Développement, 1976).

36. Sofus Larsen and Anker Kyster, *Danish Eighteenth Century Bindings, 1730–1780* (Copenhagen: Levin & Munksgaard, 1930). Marbling on the edges of Danish bindings is discussed especially on pp. 17–20.

37. Avarvid Hedberg, *Stockholms Bokbindare, 1460–1880* (Stockholm: Nordiska Museet, 1960), 2 volumes. It is only volume 2, which covers the period from 1770 to 1880, that we are concerned with here. These volumes were issued as the Nordiska Museet's Handlingar 36 and 37.

38. Sten G. Lindberg, *Mästarband, Bokbindarmästareforeningen i Stockholm 350 År* (Stockholm: [1980]).

39. Sten G. Lindberg to Richard J. Wolfe, undated, but written in late 1982. Mr. Lindberg typed his letter on the blank side of a piece of Ingeborg Börjeson's well-known batik paper.

40. The title of this work commences *Actiengesellschaft der k. k. priv. W. Knepper'schen Buntpapier und Oberwaltersdorfer Maschinen Papier Fabriken, Wien.*

CHAPTER 6

1. Great Britain, Commissioner of Patents. *Abridgements of Specifications Relating to Printing, Etc.* (London, 1859), 85–86; reprinted by the Printing Historical Society, London, in 1969. Mrs. Easton reprints Pope's petition on p. 47 of *Marbling: a History and a Bibliography.*

2. Various dictionaries, including the *Oxford English Dictionary*, define the word "margent" as a margin and nothing more. Therefore, it is difficult to know exactly what Pope meant in his use of this word. He could have meant a marbling trough, an edged container, but more likely he meant a stencil which would be used to marble only the edges or parts of the notes (a method later practiced in America, we shall see) and thus reduce his work. In this event, a stencil or margent would have been placed over a whole sheet containing many copies of notes printed on it, with cut-outs on the stencil so arranged as to allow only one of the edges of each note to show through and thus be marbled.

3. Phoebe Jane Easton, *Marbling: a History and a Bibliography*, 47–48. Mrs. Easton, in turn, bases her information on a treatment of the subject in Dard Hunter's *Papermaking, The History and Technique of an Ancient Craft*, 2d ed., 281ff.

4. Geoffrey Wakeman, *English Marbled Papers, a Documentary History* (Loughborough, Leicestershire: The Plough Press, 1978), 11–12.

5. Barrow's work was issued by C. Hitch, D. Davis, and S. Austin at London. The pertinent definition appeared in volume 2 under "Marble."

6. The full title of this book reads, *The Gentleman's Companion; or, Tradesman's Delight. Containing, The Mystery of Dyeing in All Its Branches. The Manner of Preparing Colours. The Method of Cleaning and Taking Out Stains from Silks, Woolen or Linnen. To Clean Gold or Silver Lace, and Plate. To Prepare a Cement for China, or Glass. The Art of Drawing, Limning, Painting, Etching, Engraving. Carving, Gild-Enamelling, and Refreshing Pictures. Likewise the Quality of Natural and Artificial Metals. How to Harden or Soften Them. The Art of Soldering, Burnishing and Guilding Metals. To Make All Sorts of Ink. To Prepare Gold and Silver for Writing. To Make Sealing Wax, or Wafers. To know the Purity of Gold or Silver, and Detect Counterfeit Coins. The Great Mr. Bayle's Method of Writing in Such a Manner as Cannot Be Discovered without the Help of Fire, Water, &c. To Take Blots out of Paper. The Art of Dressing, Cleaning, and Perfuming Gloves and Ribbons; and Washing All Sorts of Lace. To which Is Added, the Method for Curing and Preserving All Sorts of Wines in the Best Manner. Also, Some Excellent Receipts in Cookery, Physick, and Surgery. Observations on Silk-Worms, with Directions How to Manage to Keep Them to Advantage. With Many Other Useful Things Never Before Printed.* Its imprint relates that this volume was printed for J. Stone and sold by G. Strahan, W. Mears, J. Jackson, and C. Corbet in the year 1735.

7. When James and John Knapton first published Ephraim Chambers's *Cyclopaedia* at London in 1728, the work contained only the slightest reference to marbling. Under "Marbling of Books" in volume 2 (p. 449), a sentence or two reported how marblers sprinkled the covers of their books with black by tapping a pencil or rod containing the color gently against their fingers. The section concluded by noting that they also marble books on the edges, but for this marbling function blue and red are used in lieu of black.

8. Chambers's *Cyclopaedia*, issued in a number of editions at London and Dublin throughout the eighteenth century, sometimes with supplements, has a complicated bibliographical history. The first edition, which contained really no definition of marbling, appeared in 1728; by 1751 at least seven editions had been published. After Abraham Rees took it over and revised it between 1778 and 1786, it continued to have a somewhat complicated and tortured history.

9. Its title page reads, *The Laboratory, or School or Arts: In which Are Faithfully Exhibited and Fully Explain'd, I. A Variety of Curious and Valuable Experiments in Refining, Calcining, Melting, Assaying, and Toughening, of Gold; with Several Other Curiosities Relating to Gold and Silver. II. Choice Secrets for Jewellers in the Management of Gold; in Enamelling, and the Preparation of Enamel Colours, with the Art of Copying Precious Stones; of Preparing Colours for Doublets; of Colouring Foyles for Jewels, Together with Other Rare Secrets. III. Several Uncommon Experiments for Casting in Silver, Copper, Brass, Tin, Steel, and Other Metals; Likewise, in Wax, Plaster of Paris, Wood, Horn, &c. With the Management of the Respective Moulds. IV. The Art of Making Glass: Exhibiting Withal the Art of Painting and Making Impressions upon Glass: and of Laying Thereon Gold or Silver; Together with the Method of Preparing the Colours for Potters-Work or Delft-Ware. V. A Collection of Very Valuable Secrets, for the Use of Cutlers, Pewterers, Grafters, Joiners, Turners, Japanners, Bookbinders, Distillers, Lapidaries, Limners, &c. VI. A Dissertation on the Nature of Saltpetre; Also, Several Other Choice and Uncommon Experiments.* The first edition was published at London by T. Cox in 1738.

10. Cox's first edition of 1738 was followed by a reprinting at London by J. James in 1739, and an edition of 1740 that was printed by J. Hodges, J. James, and T. Cooper. Hodges issued editions in 1750, 1755, and 1756. Another edition issued in 1756 was printed for C. Hitch and L. Hawes, R. Baldwin, S. Crowder, and W. Woodgate; the edition of 1770 was printed for Stanley Crowder and B. Collins; the edition of 1799 carried the imprint, "Printed by C. Whittingham for H. Symonds" (and others); an edition was issued in Manchester in 1800 by J. Seddon and others; and, finally, the 1810 edition, called the seventh, was published at London by Sherwood, Neely, Jones, and others. The second and later editions contained additional material on dyeing silks and other cloths, the making of fireworks, and other subjects.

11. For example, the British Library catalog lists him as editor of a collection of German academic publications and theses which appeared in England under the title *Acta Germanica. The National Union Catalogue of Pre-1956 Imprints* (volume 551 [1978]), 85–86, lists the author of *The Laboratory* as George Smith, 18th cent.; it also lists under that name works on distilling and

surgery. Whether these two "George Smiths" were the same person, and whether George was actually Godfrey, remains unknown.

12. Malachy Postlethwayt, *The Universal Dictionary of Trade and Commerce, Translated from the French of the Celebrated Monsieur Savary, Inspector-General of the Manufactures for the Kind, at the Custom-House of Paris: With Large Additions and Improvements, Incorporated throughout the Whole Work; Which More Particularly Accomodates the Same to the Trade and Navigation of these Kingdoms, and the Laws, Customs, and Usages to Which All Traders Are Subject.*

13. *Jacques Savary des Bruslon's Dictionnaire Universel de Commerce* appeared in a number of French editions from 1723 on, and was enlarged with each successive issue. I have examined several in the Kress Library of the Baker Library, Harvard Business School.

14. Robert Dossie, *Memoirs of Agriculture & Other Oeconomical Arts* (London: J. Nourse, 1768), v. 1: 122.

15. F. W. Gibbs, "Robert Dossie (1717–1777) and the Society of Arts," *Annals of Science, a Quarterly Review of the History of Science Since the Renaissance* 7 (1951): 154. Gibbs's article appears on pp. 149–172 and is the fullest and best account of Dossie yet published. He followed it up two years later with a further note, published in the same journal (v. 9, pp. 191–193); it dealt mainly with Dossie's translations of works from Latin and French into English. These included a number of medical works (translations of Storck's essays on the medical nature of hemlock, works on midwifery and gynecology), and Gibbs states that "his right to practice medicine or to call himself a physician was presumably based on nothing more than his training as an apothecary and his knowledge of midwifery."

16. This work, entitled *The Handmaid to the Arts*, has a subtitle equally as long, if not longer, than G. Smith's *The Laboratory, or School of Arts*. The second edition, claiming considerable additions and improvements, was also issued by Nourse in two volumes of the same format, and likewise omitted Dossie's name from its title page. Dossie commenced both editions with a letter "To the Noblemen and Gentlemen, members of the Society for the Encouragement of Arts, Manufactures, and Commerce," dedicating the book to their efforts. A subsequent or third (called "new" on its title page) edition was issued in 1796 in two volumes by A. Millar, W. Law, and R. Cater of London, and by Wilson, Spence, and Mawman of York. The marbling instructions appear on pp. 377–381 of volume 2 of the first edition; on pp. 413–417 of volume 2 of the 1764 edition; and on pp. [283]–286 of volume 2 of the 1796 reprinting.

17. According to Gibbs (pp. 159–161), while Franklin resided in London in the 1760–1762 period, he took an active interest in the affairs of the Society, attending its committee meetings the while. The value of Dossie's presence during this time is perhaps best shown by the fact that either Franklin or Dossie occupied the chair on nearly every occasion when both were present. On December 16, 1760, with Franklin in the chair, it was decided that the committee on trade and colonies should consider the question of offering a premium for the manufacture of potash, a subject which interested both Dossie and Franklin. Gibbs devotes several pages to the developments that followed.

18. Royal Society of Arts, London. "Guard Books," v. 4, no. 106. The late Hans Schmoller of Windsor, to whom I owe a special debt of gratitude, brought some of these materials to my attention and copied entries from the Society's "Guard Books" for me. Schmoller's transcriptions, as well as his letter of February 17, 1980, are in my files.

19. Royal Society of Arts, London. "Minutes of Committees," 1758–1860, 4th series, p. 91. I am grateful to Dr. William H. Bond, formerly librarian of the Houghton Library of Harvard, who came upon the above reference while examining the society's manuscript minutes in London and kindly sent a transcript to me (William H. Bond to Richard J. Wolfe, May 19, 1983, author's files).

20. Baskerville's initial success as a printer and type designer was based on his printing of an edition of Virgil in 1757. This encouraged him to print Milton's poetical works in 1758 and another edition of Milton in 1759, the typography, paper and ink of both equal to, if not excelling, those of the Virgil. The marbled papers and edge decoration illustrated here appear on a copy of the 1759 edition in the Houghton Library.

21. Royal Society of Arts, London. "Minutes of Committees," 1758–1760, 4th series, p. 181.

22. Joseph Collyer, *The Parent's and Guardian's Directory, and the Youth's Guide, in the Choice of a Profession or Trade. Containing, I. An Essay on the Education of the Tradesman and Mechanic. II. The Qualifications Necessary for Those Designed for the Three Learned Professions. III. An Account of the Serveral Trades and Mechanic Arts. IV. Advice to an Apprentice on His Behaviour While Subject to His Master* (London: R. Griffiths, 1761). The description of the paper marbler appears on pp. 185–186.

23. This figure appears on p. 122 of his *Memoirs of Agriculture, & Other Oeconomical Arts*. It would appear likely that the committee's figure of £100 was subsequently reduced to £50.

24. Ibid., 123.

25. William Bailey, *The Advancement of Arts, Manufactures, and Commerce; or, Descriptions of the Useful Machines and Models Contained in the Repository of the Society for the Encouragement of Arts, Manufactures, and Commerce: Illustrated by Designs of Fifty-five Copperplates. Together with an Account of the Several Discoveries and Improvements Promoted by the Society, in Agriculture, Manufactures, Mechanics, Chemistry, and the Polite Arts; and Also in the British Colonies in America* (London: Printed by William Adlard, and sold by the author; also by R. Dodsley, and G. Peach, 1772), 219.

26. *English Marbled Papers, a Documentary History*, 11.

27. There is another letter of this early period that indicates how much interest and activity had been stirred up by the premiums. It is undated, but appears as no. 127 in volume 8 of the society's "Guard Books," covering the years 1762–1769. In view of the society's alleged abandonment of its program for the promotion of the manufacture of marbled paper in Great Britain in 1763, we can assume that this letter was written before that time. Its author, apparently a paper stainer, wanted to know if his particular product would be counted in the "marbled" category and thus earn him one of the society's premiums:

Gentlemen,
    the Dutch Marble paper as well known has been for a long time of very great use to ye Stationers and Book binders, and my Dealing with them in Plain Coullour paper gave me to Understand of ye Encouragement giving by you honble Gentlemen for any foreign Art, that could be Occupy'd in England, for which in hopes, not Only to Gain ye Encouragement, but to get the good name & Will of my Country for my Art, as many Statoners has been pleasd to call it, I have been at A Great expense to bring it to bear thus far, and of which I am certain Several Stationers & Book binders are Ready & willing to testifie ye Many Reams has been Used for their Uses Not only the mock Dutch Marble but the blue marble which never was seen or Used by any till my first bringing it out, which, Gentlemen my customers, using so much of it which is at least five hundred Ream from ye beginning, and their still encouraging encouragement, Gentlemen, to bring [bottom of sheet missing]. . . . Sorts of paper for ye Stationers Use, and of which I am sure they will Agree had been of Very Great Service to them, it being so far Cheaper

than the foreign paper, as from Thirty Shillings pr Ream to Sixteen and yet has equally pleas & yet Gentlemen tho' it has been so far pleas'd ye Town, I am persaded [sic] if I was impowered by an Encouragement to Enable me to go on, I Could still bring to A Greater perfection, of which Gentlemen I am in hopes you will consider and

am Sir, Your humble Sert.
to Command
Wm Garnett

28. Derek Hudson and Kenneth W. Luckhurst, *The Royal Society of Arts, 1754–1954* (London: Murray, 1954), 136.

29. *Transactions of the Society Instituted at London for the Encouragement of Arts, Manufactures, and Commerce; with the Premiums Offered in the Year 1789* 7 (1789): 117–119.

30. Geoffrey Wakeman, *English Marbled Papers, a Documentary History*, 12–13.

31. Rosamond B. Loring, *Decorated Book Papers*, 26.

32. Geoffrey Wakeman, *English Marbled Papers, a Documentary History*, 12.

33. From the viewpoint of its bibliography, *The Life and Opinions of Tristram Shandy, Gentleman*, is a very complicated book, for its instantaneous success brought about reprintings of early volumes even before later ones had been written and published. For further details, see Kenneth Monkman's "The Bibliography of the Early Editions of *Tristram Shandy*," *The Library* 5th ser. 25, no. 1 (March 1970): 11–39.

34. Pesonal communication, Diana Patterson of Toronto to the author, 1984. For the past several years Ms. Patterson, who has been attempting to reissue a deluxe facsimile edition of the first edition of *Tristram Shandy*, corresponded with me not only in reference to the sheet of marbled paper that had been inserted into volume 3, but also in regard to how the pattern in the original edition might be duplicated with a hand-marbled sheet in the facsimile. My files contain a fat folder of letters on this subject, and in an attempt to assist Ms. Patterson, I have examined a number of copies of the first edition of *Tristram Shandy* in the Houghton Library at Harvard and in the Beinecke Library at Yale. Furthermore, I have marbled sheets in imitation of the leaf in Sterne's novel.

35. For a description of the earlier Thomas Hollis's Harvard benefactions, which began in 1723 and continued for a number of years after, see Alfred C. Potter, "The Harvard College Library, 1723–1735," *Publications of The Colonial Society of Massachusetts* 25 (1924): [1]–13.

36. Details of the later Thomas Hollis's benefactions to Harvard are recorded in Caroline Robbins's "Library of Liberty—Assembled for Harvard College by Thomas Hollis of Lincoln's Inn," *Harvard Library Bulletin* 5 (1951): 5–23, 181–196.

37. The diary and the *Memoirs of Thomas Hollis, Esq.*, (the latter compiled by Archdeacon Blackburne and privately printed in two volumes at London in 1780), give ample information about the nature of Hollis's scheme and the extent of his benefactions. For an account of Hollis's unpublished diary of 1759–70, the Hollis plan, and Hollis's life and background in general, see Caroline Robbins, "The Strenuous Whig, Thomas Hollis of Lincoln's Inn," *William and Mary Quarterly*, 3rd ser. 7 (1950): 406–453.

38. What scant details we have of these binders comes from Hollis's *Memoirs;* Ellic Howe's *A List of London Bookbinders, 1648–1815* (London: The Bibliographical Society, 1950), 67, 85; and a few miscellaneous sources. One of the latter, J. Basil Oldham's *Shrewsbury School Library Bindings; Catalogue Raisonné* (Oxford, 1945), 159, states that Mathewman was the binder whom Hollis habitually used, but nothing seemed to be known about him. It was Oldham who related that Mathewman's

house was burnt down while he had there a number of Hollis's books dealing with government from a liberal position, the implication being that it was set afire because of this. Apparently Hollis expressed the opinion that his binder "is got in link with popish priests and bad people, and is at this time little different from them." Oldham's other crumb of information is that Hollis's emblematic tools were engraved by the artist Thomas Pingo.

39. Dr. Bond has been collecting material on the bibliographical aspects of Thomas Hollis's Harvard benefactions for many years now, especially on Hollis's relations with his bookbinders, and the latters' activities. Bond, in fact, while serving as Sandars Reader in Bibliography at Cambridge University in 1981–82, delivered a lecture on the subject. He is at present editing and preparing that material for eventual publication by the Cambridge University Press under the tentative title "Thomas Hollis of Lincoln's Inn."

40. James B. Loudon, *James Scott and William Scott, Bookbinders* (London: Scolar Press, in Association with the National Library of Scotland, 1980).

41. Crocker's dictionary was issued in three volumes. The description of marbling appears on folio 83 of volume 2. It apparently went through several reissued editions within a decade of its initial appearance.

42. *The New Royal and Universal Dictionary of Arts and Sciences*, which was printed in two volumes for J. Cooke in 1771 and 1772 (volume 2 in 1771), is unpaged. The pertinent definition appeared in volume 2 under "marbling," and marbling illustrations appear on plates 63 and 64.

43. Erasmus Middleton, William Turnbull, Thomas Ellis, and John Davison, *The New Complete Dictionary of Arts and Sciences; or, An Universal System of Useful Knowledge* (London: printed and sold by Alexr. Hogg and S. Leacroft, 1778), 2 volumes. This also has a huge descriptive subtitle, too lengthy to reprint here. The appropriate definition appears in v. 2 under "Marbling," and the marbling illustrations are reproduced on plates liv and lv.

44. The definition of paper marbling that appeared in the first edition of the *Encyclopaedia Britannica* (1771, v. 3, p. 25) is insignificant and disappointing, amounting to less than 200 words.

45. George Selby Howard, *The New Royal Encyclopaedia and Cyclopaedia; or, Complete Modern and Universal Dictionary of Arts and Sciences*, in three volumes printed at London by Alex. Hogg in 1788. The marbling definition appears on p. 1332 of v. 3. This work also has one of those wordy title pages that does not warrant complete inclusion here.

46. I have in my files a photocopy made many years ago of pp. 580 and 581 of an unidentified dictionary containing another reprinting of Dossie's marbling description; unfortunately the title page was lost over the years and various attempts to correlate these pages with those in many early dictionaries have proved unsuccessful. Not from any of the works noted before, it is eighteenth-century and English without doubt. The size and format of the page approximates that of the later Rees *Cyclopaedia*, but it is not from that work, either, which contains a completely different description of the process.

47. Abraham Rees (1743–1825), an independent minister, began work as a cyclopedist in the mid-1770s, when he undertook to improve the cyclopedia of Ephraim Chambers, which had been published originally in 1728 and in several subsequent editions. Encouraged by the success of this undertaking, he projected a similar but far more comprehensive work, *The New Cyclopaedia; or Universal Dictionary of Arts and Sciences*, to which we refer here. This appeared in a total of forty-five volumes (including six volumes of plates and an atlas), between 1802 and 1820; the whole was issued over the intervening years in parts,

two parts to each volume (or approximately ninety parts in all, each of them large and thick). The Rees work was reprinted at Philadelphia by Samuel F. Bradford and sold by his agents throughout the eastern United States. The Philadelphia edition contains no imprint dates on the volumes, which I estimate could have been issued between 1816 and 1825, though that matter is unclear. I have not had an opportunity to examine the English original edition, but in the American reprinting the definition of marbling appears in Part 1 of volume 27, under "Paper."

48. A great deal of confusion exists with regard to these English eighteenth-century books of secrets, and the matter seemingly defies a definitive unraveling. The earliest edition I have noted in library catalogs was printed by and for J. Barker at London in 1758 as *Valuable Secrets of Arts and Trades*, but its title related that it was a new and improved edition. Many other English editions followed with slightly variant titles: 1775, printed and sold at London by W. Hay; 1778, printed and sold by J. Williams at Dublin; 1780, printed by W. Hay at London (with the notation "second edition"); 1791, printed for J. Barker, J. Cattermoul, and J. Parsons; and 1800 and 1801, issued by Barker and J. Scarcherd in London. And it is likely that there were others.

49. This was published at London by J. Johnson, Darton, and Harvey in 1798. The material quoted appeared on pages 132–133.

CHAPTER 7

1. Geoffrey Wakeman, *English Marbled Papers, a Documentary History*, 13.

2. *The Whole Art of Bookbinding. The Whole Art of Marbling Paper. Reprinted from the Original Editions, with a Foreword by Bernard C. Middleton and Twelve Specimens of Marbled Paper and Notes by Richard J. Wolfe* (Austin, Texas: W. Thomas Taylor, 1987).

3. Graham Pollard and Esther Potter, *Early Bookbinding Manuals*, 35.

4. The title page of this early American reprint reads: *The Whole Art of Book-Binding, Containing Valuable Receipts for Sprinkling, Marbling, Colouring, &c. The First American, from the Third London edition, with Considerable Additions. Richmond, Published by Peter Cotton, and For Sale at His Law and Miscellaneous Book-Store, 1824.* English editions, other than the first, do not seem to be recorded in catalogs, bibliographies, or other literature.

5. Those without a title page are at the University of Texas and the Rochester Institute of Technology (the latter being Bernard Middleton's copy, to which a facsimile title page of the 1820 edition has been added). One of the two with the 1820 title is in the British Library; the other was sold in London at Bloomsbury auctions in September of 1986 and is now in private hands. Bernard Middleton has recently informed me that a fifth copy has been located at the United States Patent Office. My inquiry there, however, has determined that this copy, although listed in its library's catalog, cannot now be physically located. Inasmuch as it is listed under Sinclair's name, and its title is given, it seems likely that this copy has its title page intact.

6. On the other hand, one must concede that Middleton's conclusions could be correct. However, inasmuch as the work was printed on wove paper, there is no actual way of proving that an earlier or original title page, assumedly printed earlier in Scotland, had been canceled or removed and that a substitute, with the London imprint, had been added in its place. In the one copy that I have examined carefully, the imposition and printing of the title appears identical to the text that follows.

7. I owe thanks to Dr. C. Helen Brock, formerly with the

Department of the History of Science, University of Glasgow, for searching out directory listings of Hugh Sinclair. These are summarized in a letter from Dr. Brock of 12 November 1980 (author's files).

8. Middleton cites as his source, "Reports from Assistant Hand-loom Weavers' Commissioners; J. C. Symons on the South of Scotland; P. P. 1839, vol. XLII, p. 51."

9. Middleton's source here was the *Bookbinding Trades Journal* 1, (1905): 122.

10. Bernard C. Middleton, *A History of English Craft Bookbinding Technique* (New York and London: Hafner Publishing Company, 1963), 260–262.

11. "French Marbled Paper," *Portfolio, the Annual of the Graphic Arts* (Cincinnati: Zebra Press, 1951). This publication is unpaged; the article appears before its midpoint.

12. Phoebe Jane Easton, *Marbling: a History and a Bibliography*, 169.

13. Geoffrey Wakeman, *English Marbled Papers, a Documentary History*, 13. Pollard and Potter's *Early Bookbinding Manuals*, p. 39, indicates that the text was a reprint of John Farey's *The Circle of Mechanical Arts* of 1813, issued under the pseudonym Thomas Martin, which is noted hereafter.

14. Materials on marbling in Cowie's *Bookbinder's Manual* appear on pp. 86–96.

15. The first edition of 1828 bore no date on its imprint. It was reissued in 1829; by 1832 a fourth edition had been printed and in about 1835 a fifth, with a seventh appearing circa 1852.

16. Hannett issued in 1837 an accompanying work, which he entitled *The Bookbinder's School of Design*, and incorporated this into the sixth edition of his *Bibliopegia*. Hannett also wrote and published in 1837 a history of bookbinding.

17. Thomas Martin, *The Circle of the Mechanical Arts, Containing Practical Treatises on the Various Manual Arts and Manufactures* (London: Richard Rees, 1813), 83. Thomas Martin was the pseudonym of John Farey, a civil engineer and illustrator. A second edition appeared in 1815.

18. Alexander Jamieson, *A Dictionary of Mechanical Sciences, Arts, Manufactures and Miscellaneous Knowledge* (London: H. Fisher, Son & Co., 1827), 622, 762–763.

19. "On Improvements in Marbling the Edges of Books and Paper" appeared in *Gill's Technological Repository; or, Discoveries and Improvements in the Useful Arts, Being a Continuation of His Technical Repository* 4 (1829): 27–33. The translation was signed at the end "L*****R" and noted that the French original had appeared in the *Dictionnaire Technologique*. This identical translation was, in turn, reprinted in the *Journal of the Franklin Institute of the State of Pennsylvania* 3 (1829): 246–249, and, more recently, by me, with an explanatory introduction and fourteen original marbled samples, in a little volume entitled *On Improvements in Marbling the Edges of Books and Paper; a Nineteenth Century Marbling Account Explained* (Newtown, Pa.: Bird & Bull Press, 1983).

20. A review, or more correctly, an abstract of Woolnough's *The Art of Marbling* appeared in the *Journal of the [Royal] Society of Arts* 2 (1853–1854): 249–250 under the title "Art of Marbling."

21. This was published in the *Journal of the [Royal] Society of Arts*, (January 28, 1878): 154–157.

22. Geoffrey Wakeman, *English Marbled Papers, a Documentary History*, 17.

23. The collections of the British Library contain a number of London directories which are very useful. For the early 1820s I searched the *Triennial Directory* (11th edition, issued in 1822) covering the years 1822, 1823, and 1824, and various issues of the *Post Office London Directory*. For later periods I employed the *Post Office London Directory* and as many issues of *Robson's London Directory, Street Key and Conveyance List* as I could locate.

24. S. Woolnough appears in the directories through 1840,

but in the number for 1842 his name is omitted, and in its place and at his address the name "Mary Woolnough" appears.

25. Edward Graham Woolnough's name appears in the *London Medical Directory* for 1846 and 1847, the first of these issued, but is dropped thereafter, for some unknown reason. Listed at 15, St. Thomas's Street, Southwark, as a surgeon-accoucheur, his brief description tells that he had qualified M.R.C.S. on June 25, 1842, and was made a member of the London Surgical Society on March 2, 1843. The only other information given was that he was an Assistant-Accoucheur to St. Thomas's Hospital and that he was a member of the Hunterian Society. My letter to the Royal College of Surgeons of England brought a reply from E. Allen, Quist Curator (October 15, 1987), reporting that the College had no detailed record of this member, or of his place and date of birth. Its "Examination Book" merely recorded the names and dates of qualification. We can only conjecture from this evidence that he was born about 1816 or slightly later and may have been the younger brother of our marbling master.

26. As another example of marbled cloth on a contemporary British imprint, I can cite the *Manual of Artistic Anatomy, for the Use of Sculptors, Painters and Amateurs* of the ill-fated Scottish anatomist Robert Knox; it was issued at London by H. Renshaw in 1852, and is bound in red cloth that is veined in black.

27. I first came into contact with Woolnough's great-granddaughter, Mrs. R. Conklin, of Hawthorne, New Jersey, in March of 1963, and my files contain a letter she wrote to me on November 23, 1964, which mentions her great-grandfather, the marbling master.

28. James Sumner, *The Mysterious Marbler; With an Historical Introduction, Notes and Eleven Original Marbled Samples by Richard J. Wolfe* (North Hills, Pa.: Bird & Bull Press, 1976).

29. *The British Bookmaker* published two sets of samples of Berry & Roberts marbled papers, with short descriptions of them. The first description, entitled "End Papers," appeared on p. 15 of no. 39 (in volume 4), for September 1890, with the leaf containing the mounted samples tipped in before it; the second description, headed "Best English Extra Antiques," appeared on p. 12 of no. 61 (in volume 6), for July 1892, with the page of samples following.

30. "A Machine for Marbling Paper," *The British Bookmaker* 4, no. 44 (February 1891): 7.

31. The pertinent advertisement appeared in no. 49 (of volume 5) and can be found on p. XIII of the advertising section that forms a supplement at its end. This told that the firm's works were located at 12 Baches Street, Hoxton, and its warehouse was at 21 St. Bride's Street, London, with another at 33 Hope Street in Glasgow.

32. In addition to checking the London postal and other directories in the British Library, I also had recourse to a good run of the postal directory—from the late 1840s on—in the Harvard College Library. There seems to be some confusion in the postal directories in the 1850s with regard to Corfield's Christian name and the name of his son. The "Joseph William Corfield" entered in some of these appears to be a mixing up of his name, Joseph, with that of his son, William (actually, William Henry). Thus, such entries should read instead Corfield, Joseph & William, or Corfield, Joseph & Son William; or something to that effect. The son is entered in later directories alone, as a gilder, and as William Henry Corfield. Joseph Corfield, who established himself as a gilder in 1832, was probably his early or mid-twenties at the time and probably would have been born about 1810; he would thus be nearly a contemporary of Charles Woolnough. It should be pointed out that, in 1904, the auction gallery of Sotheby, Wilkinson & Hodge disposed of, in a two-day sale, a large collection of William Henry Corfield's

books in valuable bindings. This, however, was not our gilder and sometimes marbler, but the distinguished professor of hygiene and public health of the same name (1843–1903), who, in addition to his medical feats, was a collector of rare books and a connoisseur of bindings. It does not seem likely that there was a direct relationship between these two William Henry Corfields, in spite of the coincidence that both of these identically named individuals had a connection with bookbinding.

33. H. Dubois D'Enghien, *Le Reliure en Belgique au dix-neuvième siècle*, 70.

34. Two such works were the multivolumed *British Manufacturing Industries* and Charles Booth's *Life and Labour of the People of London*. In volume 8 of the fourth edition of the former, published at London by E. Stanford in 1892, appeared an account of contemporary British bookbinding by H. Freeman Wood, in which gilding and marbling were discussed (pp. 77–78). Booth also mentioned marbling and edge gilding (pp. 240–241) in a larger discussion of bookbinding printed in the sixth volume of his *Life and Labour of the People of London*, issued by Macmillan at London in 1895. With regard to book-edge gilding and marbling, Booth wrote that these are distinct but small trades, the work usually being given out to a number of small employers, known as gilders or marblers to the trade.

35. Charles Tomlinson, *Cyclopaedia of Useful Arts, Mechanical and Chemical, Manufactures, Mining and Engineering* (London: George Virtue & Co., 1854), v. 2, 233–235.

36. Dard Hunter, "A Bibliography of Marbled Paper," *Paper Trade Journal* 72 (1921): 52–58. Hunter's bibliography is reprinted on pp. 8–10 of Morris S. Kantrowitz and Ernest S. Spencer's *The Process of Marbling Paper* (Washington, D.C.: U.S. Government Printing Office, 1953), issued as GPO-PIA Joint Research Bulletin, Bindery Series No. 1.

37. Phoebe Jane Easton, *Marbling: a History and a Bibliography*, 170.

38. *Prepared Papers and How to Make Them: A Collection of Principal Receipts for the Production of All Kinds of Papers Used for Artistic, Medical and General Purposes* (London: Groombridge & Son, 1873). Marbling is discussed on its pp. 10–12.

39. Joseph W. Zaehnsdorf, *The Art of Bookbinding* (London: George Bell & Sons, 1880). "Marbled Edges" appears on pp. 66–68 in a chapter on "Colouring of Edges"; the other allusions to marbled paper are printed on p. 29.

40. Chapter 16, "Colouring of the Edges," of this and succeeding editions contains a much more extensive treatment of marbling and shows, on pp. 76–77, the Smith cut and the illustration of Leo's marbling outfit.

41. W. J. E. Crane, *Bookbinding for Amateurs: Being Descriptions of the Various Tools and Appliances Required for Minute Instruction for Their Effective Use* (London: L. Upcott Gill, circa 1891; reprint edition, L. Upcott Gill; and New York: Charles Scribner's Sons, 1903). Although the initial English edition of this work is undated, publisher's advertising at the end is marked "91," and indicates that this work appeared at or about 1891, although it could have been issued initially several years earlier. I have seen innumerable copies in booksellers' catalogs, in antiquarian and out-of-print bookstores, which indicates to me that it was a popular and continuously available work.

42. Paul N. Hasluck, *Bookbinding, with Numerous Engravings and Diagrams* (London: Cassell & Company, 1902). This treatise went through thirteen editions in the thirty-eight years before 1941.

CHAPTER 8

1. Rita Susswein Gottesman, *The Arts and Crafts in New York, 1726–1776; Advertisements and News Items from New York City Newspapers* (New York: The New-York Historical Society, 1938), 243. Mrs. Gottesman compiled two additional volumes,

covering the years 1777–1799 and 1800–1804 respectively, before her untimely death in an automobile accident. These three lists comprise volumes 69, 81, and 82 of the Society's *Collections*. The first two of Anderton's three-paragraph advertisement read, according to Mrs. Gottesman's entry:

T. ANDERTON.—Lately arrived from England . . . T. Anderton, Book-Binder, Letter Case, and Pocket Book-Maker; Makes and sells wholesale and retail, all sorts of letter cases, desk cases, travelling cases and travelling boxes either with or without shaving equipages; Ladies travelling writing desks, fishing cases, solo cases . . .

The said T. Anderton, performs book-binding in its full perfection, in all sorts of plain and rich bindings; marbles and gilds the edge of books, gilds and letters libraries, or parcels of books, journals and leidgers [sic], &c. (as exact to any pattern) but with greater ellegancy than if taken from copper plate, and binds in parchment, or vellum, either with or without Russia bands. Gentlemen and Ladies who please to try his abilities may always depend on being well used on the very lowest terms. New pocket books, made to old instruments.

Anderton's final paragraph concerned a curious black writing ink he manufactured as well.

2. George L. McKay, *A Register of Artists, Engravers, Booksellers, Bookbinders, Printers & Publishers in New York City, 1633–1820* (New York: The New York Public Library, 1942), 8.

3. Hannah D. French, "Early American Bookbindings by Hand, 1636–1820," 36, 110.

4. Rita Susswein Gottesman, *The Arts and Crafts in New York, 1726–1776*, 246. Leedell's notice also provides much of the flavor of the craftsman of that time and requires reprinting:

GEORGE LEEDELL, Book-Binder, late of London, Begs leave to return his thanks to his friends and customers, and the publick in general, for their past favours, and hopes for the future continuance of them, which he will endeavour to deserve. He has removed to Peck's-Slip, next door to Mr. White Matlack's, watch-maker, where he proposes to continue to carry on his business in all its different branches, as neat as can be done in London. Merchants and others, may be supplied at a very short notice, with all kinds of books (such as ledgers, journals, and waste books) as cheap as they can be imported. Where may also be had his much admired Black and Red Ink, and Hundon's Bay Quills, so long wanted in this country; spelling books and primers, books marbled on the edges, as in London; and paper gilt and blackt.

5. Franklin's involvement in the design of early American currency is discussed in *The Papers of Benjamin Franklin*, edited by William B. Willcox (New Haven, Conn.: Yale University Press, 1982), v. 22 (March 23, 1775–October 27, 1776), 357–358, and accompanying plate.

6. The background of the printing of this initial Continental Currency is explained in Eric P. Newman's *The Early Paper Money of America; an Illustrated, Historical and Descriptive Compilation of Data Relating to American Paper Currency from Its Inception in 1686 to the Year 1800* (Racine, Wis.: Western Publishing Company, 1976), 34.

7. The illustration here appeared on the cover of List 74, issued by Joseph Rubinfine, a dealer in autographs and manuscripts of Pleasantville, New Jersey (now located in Florida), in the early 1980s and was described on the initial printed page of this catalog. It was sold to a private collector.

8. Eric P. Newman, *The Early Paper Money of America*, 314.

9. Despite Anderton's and Leedell's advertising, edge marbling does not appear to have enjoyed the vogue in early America that it did at a corresponding time in Great Britain. Two recent catalogs of early American bookbindings, *The Early American Bookbindings from the Collection of Michael Papantonio* (New York: The Pierpont Morgan Library, 1972; 2d ed., American Antiquarian Society, 1985) and *Bookbinding in America, 1680–1910 from the Collection of Frederick E. Maser* (Bryn Mawr, Pa.: Bryn Mawr College Library, 1983) bring this point home dramatically, for neither lists or illustrates an American bookbinding containing edge marbling before the year 1820, although a few pre-1820 American bindings with marbled edges are known in other collections. The author's collection relating to marbling and marbled paper contains a beautiful example, on a two-volume set of Robert Bisset's *The History of the Reign of George III. to the Termination of the Late War*, issued at Albany by B. D. Packard in 1816. This was apparently bound in New York City in 1819, for in the lower spines of each volume appear in gilt, "New York, 1819." The volumes are encased in diced Russia skins, with gilt-edge rules and edge rolls and with black leather labels and gilt panel stamps on their spines. The marbling on all edges is a simple blue and black spot design, displaying poor or at best fair execution. These volumes contain marbled endpapers as well, showing a plain blue shell design onto which some red lacy or Stormont spots had afterward been thrown. Willman Spawn, who contributed an essay on the evolution of American binding styles in the eighteenth century to the Bryn Mawr catalog, has informed me that he knows of no American bookbindings with marbled decoration on their edges before the year 1804, and that the practice was uncommon in America for many years later. The sprinkling and staining of edges was effected in America from the late seventeenth century, and edge gilding before the end of the eighteenth, but marbling seems not to have been done much, Anderton and Leedell notwithstanding.

10. This information is printed on p. 52 of Miss French's "Early American Bookbinding by Hand." Some confusion exists as to the Burbanks' relationship with Isaiah Thomas. In his biography of this eminent early American printer, *Isaiah Thomas, Printer, Patriot and Philanthropist, 1749–1831* (Rochester, N.Y.: Leo Hart, 1948), Clifford K. Shipton relates (p. 63) that in 1793 Thomas set up a paper mill; on a preceding plate he illustrates a ream wrapper from "The Thomas Paper Mill" on which is printed "Sold by Elijah Burbank, Worcester, Mass." Shipton also relates (p. 66) that Thomas in 1798 sold his paper mill to Caleb and Elijah Burbank. Thomas was then establishing a self-sufficient printing and publishing empire, employing many bookbinders as well, and it is not impossible that he had someone in his employ who was marbling.

11. H. Glenn and Maude O. Brown, *A Dictionary of the Book-Arts and Book Trade in Philadelphia, Including Painters and Engravers* (New York: The New York Public Library, 1950).

12. The material on the Manns presented here is extracted from my book, *The Role of the Mann Family of Dedham, Massachusetts in the Marbling of Paper in Nineteenth Century America*, and additional facts uncovered since its publication.

13. It is not beyond the realm of possibility that he may have been an English emigrant binder or paper colorer who worked in the Boston area from about 1800, and later in the decade sold his knowledge and equipment and supplies to Herman Mann and moved on, or returned home.

14. Herman Mann, Jr., *Historical Annals of Dedham, from Its Settlement in 1635, to 1847* (Dedham, Mass.: Herman Mann, 1847), 74.

15. *First Exhibition and Fair of the Massachusetts Charitable Mechanic Association, at Faneuil Hall, in the City of Boston, September 18, 1837* (Boston: Dutton and Wentworth, 1837), 58. The

silver medal has recently been found among the Mann family possessions in the Dedham Historical Society.

16. The shortage of paper in late eighteenth-century America is pointed out in Nancy McClelland's *Historic Wall-papers, from Their Inception to the Introduction of Machinery*, 237. Here it is related that when the French revolutionist and journalist J. P. Brissot de Warville visited the United States in 1788, he made a report on its commerce with Europe, which was translated and published in New York in 1795. After citing the various American exports, such as indigo, tobacco, rice, flax, foodstuffs and timber for ships, he went into detail about articles imported from France for America's needs. The American people, he observed, were unable to produce wines, cloth, linens, silk stockings, jewelry, and "different sorts of paper, stained paper, etc." Brissot de Warville also notes that

If there be an object of commerce for which Europeans need not fear a reciprocal competition, if there be an article which offers to all European manufacturers a certain and lucrative employ, it is that of paper.

The Americans cannot enjoy this advantage for a long time to come; besides the dearness of workmanship, their population cannot furnish them old rags in quantities sufficient to establish paper-mills whose production would be equal to the consumption of the inhabitants.

Rags are excessively dear in America; but the time is arriving when by an increase of population they will become plenty. In Pennsylvania they already have made very good paper.

See further Richard J. Wolfe, *Early American Music Engraving and Printing; a History of Music Publishing in America from 1787 to 1825, with Commentary on Earlier and Later Practices* (Urbana: University of Illinois Press, 1980). Chapter VIII specifically relates to paper, and the shortages are fully discussed on pp. 150–153 there. While I stated, based on the evidence of paper used in issuing sheet music, that the situation ameliorated by 1810, Rollo Silver, in his *The American Printer, 1787–1825* (Charlottesville: Bibliographical Society of the University of Virginia, 1967), notes (p. 37) that shortages continued, and that the search for rags to make into paper became so exasperating that in 1810 they were imported from Europe. Mr. Silver has informed me in private conversation that even while the War of 1812 was being waged, a transatlantic trade in rags for this purpose was being carried on.

17. I have observed books covered with paper that had been marbled over printed text in English collections, and I have in my own collection papers containing English or Scottish printings on one of their sides and what appears to be British marbling on the other side that had been left unprinted. Furthermore, Bernard Middleton has informed me that he, too, has noticed overmarbling on British printed sheets of the early 1800s, always employing the Stormont pattern because this was the pattern predominantly made in the period when overmarbling was carried on.

18. This practice was apparently rare in Germany, for during the past twenty-five years I can recall noticing only one or two German imprints containing papers with marbling over printed text. Unfortunately, this occurred early on in my research and I did not record title pages or locations. On a recent trip to Leipzig, I observed in the Deutsche Bücherei a volume containing marbled decoration where the marbling had been applied only to the blank verso of a printed sheet. The imprint of this work (its shelf listing was BU I, 3312, 1983, 769) dated to 1745, and its marbled pattern was clearly an eighteenth-century design of the Turkish type, showing black, green, red, blue, yellow, and orange spots that had been combed and swirled

about (as in samples 41–42 on Plate XXVI). It is evident that the practice of employing waste sheets for marbling, although seemingly rarer there, occurred in Germany at a much earlier time than elsewhere. I do not recall ever seeing such overmarbling on French volumes or marbled papers.

19. This periodical was published in ten volumes between the years 1803 and 1811. I have Willman Spawn to thank for bringing this particular instance of overmarbling to my attention.

20. I have matched up the printed and overmarbled end papers in the *Salmagundi* volume with pages in a copy of the Durrell printing of *The New and Complete Book of Martyrs* in the Houghton Library at Harvard, the latter contained in a fine American "gilt extra" binding. This work was published on a subscription basis, and it was printed and usually is found bound in a somewhat lavish manner.

21. The pattern on James Mann's medical text is a blue Stormont with red and black veins. The Manns had published on the front page of the Boston *Independent Chronicle* of 1 August 1816 and for some weeks afterward a proposal for issuing this work. Their stated conditions were that it would be printed in long primer type on fine wove paper and delivered to subscribers in boards at two dollars per copy, with copies bound in sheepskin and lettered priced additionally. The work was scheduled to be out of press four weeks later.

22. Other sheets in my collection containing overmarbling of this Durrell printing, removed from discarded bindings, show the plain Stormont pattern, without colored veins.

23. Advertisements requesting subscriptions for this work appeared in the *Dedham Gazette* in January 1815, and publication was announced on August 15 of that year.

24. Ralph Thompson, "Deathless Lady," *The Colophon* n. s. 1 (Autumn 1935): 207–220.

25. Marcus A. McCorison, "Two Unrecorded American Printings of 'Fanny Hill'," *Vermont History* 40, no. 1 (Winter 1972): 64–66, 174; "Fanny Hill," *Proceedings of the American Antiquarian Society* 82 (1972): 65–66; "Memoirs of a Woman of Pleasure or Fanny Hill in New England," *American Book Collector* (May–June 1980): 29–30.

26. John Alden to Marcus A. McCorison, 8 December 1980, American Antiquarian Society (copy in the author's files).

27. Marcus A. McCorison, "Memoirs of a Woman of Pleasure or Fanny Hill in New England," 30.

28. A few of Isaiah Thomas's manuscript books make reference to marbled paper, but there appears to be nothing in them referring to the purchase of these overmarbled "Fanny Hill" sheets. Thomas's "Account of Stock left with Cheever Kelch to be sold on commission," dated November 17, 1809, and now in the American Antiquarian Society, for example, shows that Thomas had on hand large amounts of marbled paper that he wished to dispose of, some at cheaper prices:

Bookbinding stock:
8 Reams whole marbled paper
    6.00 per ream   48.—
5 do & 3 Qrs. do do
    4.00 do do   20.60

29. "Books and Newspapers Bound in Sheets from Fanny Hill," 2-page typescript, American Antiquarian Society, together with a folder of fragments of overmarbled sheets of this work removed from bindings being restored.

30. In the *Dedham Gazette* of Friday, December 24, 1813 (p. 3, col. 4) appeared the announcement that "a quantity of new and elegant type had just been received from Philadelphia, and a farther supply is expected daily." And on February 4, 1814 it announced (p. 3, col. 5) that a complete assortment of new and elegant type had just been received from Philadelphia. Approxi-

mately two years later, in the issue of the *Gazette* of February 23, 1816, and in subsequent issues, Samuel Hall, then its owner, gave notice to printers that, due to professional and other avocations, he was offering his establishment for sale. Among its contents he listed one of Adam Ramage's presses, almost new, and fonts of long primer, pica, great primer, double English, cannon and fine-line pica type from the Binny & Ronaldson foundry, likewise new, and two other fonts with which the paper was printed. Dedham lacked a newspaper between late 1809, when Herman Mann ceased publishing his, and August of 1813, when the *Gazette* commenced publication and reportedly was being printed by Abel D. Alleyne (although the Mann boys may have assisted in its printing, especially after the family's return from Providence in the spring of 1815). Thus, fonts of the Binny & Ronaldson types were available to them in Dedham; indeed, James Mann's *Medical Sketches of the Campaigns of 1812, 13, 14* appears to have been printed by them in the Binny & Ronaldson long primer face.

31. I pointed out in my book of the Mann famiily (p. 9) that in as early as 1800 Herman Mann advertised that "bookbinding is carried on at the Minerva *Office.*-Second hand books rebound, as reasonably as in Boston, or elsewhere." And I recently noticed, while reading through the Dedham newspapers to monitor various Mann family activities, the following advertisement that appeared in the *Norfolk Repository,* Herman Mann's newspaper, on 19 July 1808 (volume II, no. 36, p. 290):

Book-Binding
H. Mann

At his Book-Store in Dedham, carries on Book-Binding in its several branches, and on the most reasonable terms.-Old books *rebound.* Blank-Books ruled and bound to any pattern and size.

Calf and sheep-skins, well tanned (white oak is best) whole grain, and shaved thin for the above business, will at any time be received in pay for books, bookbinding, &c.

It is well known that printers and stationers in Mann's day had to be jacks-of-all-trades to survive, and Herman was as versatile as any. As this book goes to press, I have submitted an article on the alleged Herman Mann binding on Isaac Watts's *Hymns and Spiritual Songs* and other Herman Mann bindings to the American Antiquarian Society for publication in its *Proceedings.*

32. It is no accident that many of the examples we have today of fine bookbindings executed in America in prior times appear on Bibles, prayer books and hymnbooks, for they were the most personal possessions of a religious and spiritual folk of an earlier era. If a person, or one intending a present for a loved one, would choose one book to put into a fine and expensive binding, it likely would be a prayer book, a hymnbook, or a Bible; these were one's most cherished and intimate objects; not only were they frequently used, but they were part of one's personal communication with one's God.

33. Mr. Spawn and I have had many discussions on this matter and are fully in accord on it.

34. This pattern book, which could not be located earlier, but which turned up in a recent reorganization of the Mann Papers in the Dedman Historical Society, was, according to an accession note penciled onto it, presented by Mrs. A. M. Pickford of Lynn, Massachusetts, in May of 1903. Anna Maria Tolman Pickford, Herman Mann's granddaughter, served as the family genealogist, contributing an important article on "The Dedham Branch of the Mann Family" to the *Dedham Historical Record* in 1895 and 1896. Some loose samples of papers marbled by the Manns have recently been found at the Dedham Historical Society as well.

35. If such a printing was begun, or if such an article appeared in a contemporary periodical, it probably would have been in the period around 1815 or 1816. Robert Walsh was a prominent American journalist and litterateur, and I have checked a number of periodicals of that era which he founded or edited in an attempt to see if he had published the "Strictures" article in them, but without success. I have also examined a run of *The Rhode-Island Literary Repository,* a monthly literary and political magazine which Herman Mann printed at Providence from April 1814 until March 1815, for the same purpose and with the same results.

36. This, of course, is among the Mann Family Papers in the Dedham Historical Society. This document is discussed on pp. 90–94 of *The Role of the Mann Family of Dedham, Massachusetts in the Marbling of Paper in Nineteenth Century America.*

37. The most complete documentation of the initial printing of Cleland's *Memoirs of a Woman of Pleasure,* and of the legal and other incidents that resulted from it, appears in David Foxon's *Libertine Literature in England, 1660–1745; with an Appendix on the Publication of John Cleland's* Memoirs of a Woman of Pleasure, *commonly called* Fanny Hill (London: The Book Collector, 1964), 52–63. This was reprinted as a separate monograph from *The Book Collector* issues of Spring, Summer, Autumn, Winter, 1963. Foxon's main focus was to identify the true first edition of this work, but he publishes here the most complete information on the incidents attending its publication. William B. Ober, in his *Bottoms Up! A Pathologist's Essays on Medicine and the Humanities* (Carbondale: Southern Illinois University Press, 1987), specifically in the chapter, "The Iconography of Fanny Hill: How to Illustrate a Dirty Book," relates that Cleland wrote "Fanny Hill" while in prison and sold the manuscript for twenty pounds to Ralph Griffiths in order to get enough money to settle his debts and get out of prison. He also notes that Fenton Griffiths, presumably Ralph's brother, was a shadowy figure and may have been an invention. Ober relates as well that throughout the book's checkered career only two people have actually been convicted for publishing or selling it, and although both Cleland and Griffiths, as well as Thomas Parker, who printed it, were brought before Lovel Stanhope, Law Clerk to the Secretary of State, no one seems to have been punished for his role in this episode.

38. Because of the clandestine nature of its printings, "Fanny Hill" is difficult to assess bibliographically. A number of catalogs and literary works report editions, but the picture is nonetheless confused, at times unclear, and incomplete. Catalogs and other works providing listings of various editions include *The British Library General Catalogue of Printed Books to 1975* (London: Clive Bindley, 1980), v. 64 under Cleland; *The National Union Catalog of Pre-1956 Imprint* (London, Mansell Information/Publishing, 1969), v. 112, 82–83; Patrick J. Kearney, *The Private Case; an Annotated Bibliography of the Private Case Erotica Collection in the British (Museum) Library* (London: Jay Landesman, 1981), 132–164; and *John Cleland's Memoirs of a Woman of Pleasure; with an Introduction for Modern Readers by Peter Quennell* (New York: G. P. Putnam's Sons, 1963), 300–319. Useful for background information is William H. Epstein's *John Cleland, Images of a Life* (New York: Columbia University Press, 1974), as is the Foxon work cited in the prior note. None of these works mention a British edition after 1784, and for three or four decades afterward, although many French translations and editions appeared subsequently.

39. Brigham's memorandum is a two-page typescript, now filed in the folder of disbound "Fanny Hill" overmarbled sheets which is housed in the Print Department at the American Antiquarian Society. Undated and untitled, and signed at end, "C. S. B.," it commences: "Isaiah Thomas received a letter from Thomas Evans, dated July 29, 1786, in which Evans replied to

Thomas's request for a copy of the *Memoirs of a Woman of Pleasure.*" Brigham relates that in 1814 Thomas had a hundred or more volumes of newspapers bound in these overmarbled sheets. Although Thomas invariably bound all of his books at one of his binderies, and presumably these oversheets came from his surplus paper stock, in one of the volumes of the *National Aegis* for 1812 Thomas noted that he had "Paid Rich'd Gross for 11 volumes, bound in 5 vols. $18.00." Brigham questioned whether Gross bound for Thomas regularly or was an independent binder. The memorandum concludes with a reference to Thompson's 1935 article, indicating that Brigham wrote his memorandum subsequently.

40. These possible Vermont printings form the gist of McCorison's "Two Unrecorded American Printings of 'Fanny Hill'" article. McCorison also refers to these in his "Memoirs of a Woman of Pleasure or Fanny Hill in New England."

41. *A Specimen of Metal Ornaments Cast at the Letter Foundery of Binny & Ronaldson. Philadelphia, Printed by Fry and Kammerer, 1809.*

42. *Specimen of Printing Types, from the Foundery of Binny & Ronaldson, Philadelphia. Fry and Kammerer, printers, 1812.*

43. *The Specimen Books of Binny and Ronaldson, 1809–1812, in facsimile; with an introduction by Carl Purington Rollins and facsimiles of some early American Types* (Connecticut: The Columbiad Club, 1936).

44. The imprint on this reads, "H. Mann, printer, Providence, 1813." It was the second edition of this work that Herman Mann printed at Providence in 1813, probably soon after moving his main operation from Dedham. The printer of the earlier edition, which contains an almost identical title page, is unknown—the imprint simply says, "Providence: Printed for the Author, 1812." The 1812 edition is set in old style types, which contain the medial "s" and ligatures. Overall, it is aesthetically inferior to Mann's edition, composed in Binny & Ronaldson types, and the layout of the title page on the 1813 edition is much more pleasing and tasteful. The name "Sylvan" is treated in library and bibliographical catalogs as a pseudonym, but Sylvan may have been this author's real surname, or assumed name at least, for in a letter written from Providence on 11 November 1814, to his wife in Dedham, Herman Mann related, "Dr. Sylvan is to be the bearer of this. I could not accomplish our business so as to accompany him." Dr. Sylvan is not mentioned, so far as I have been able to determine, in the medical literature of Rhode Island at this time, and he may have been an irregular physician; in fact, it is almost certain that he was.

45. Daniel Mann's schemes to make a fortune and his uneven nature form Chapter IV, "Daniel Mann and the Making of Cards," of *The Role of the Mann Family of Dedham, Massachusetts in the Marbling of Paper in Nineteenth Century America.* Some of Daniel's financial and legal problems are noted on pp. 60–62 there.

46. Its title page reads, "Memoirs of a Woman of Pleasure. Written by Herself. Seventeenth edition. With plates designed and engraved by a Member of the Royal Academy. London: Printed for G. Felton, in the Strand. 1813." Its classification number or class mark is Im C589 749md. It runs to 299 pages in all, but pages 123–154 are lacking from this copy.

47. It is not possible to determine who was responsible for producing these illustrations. In his "Two Unrecorded American Printings of 'Fanny Hill'," Marcus McCorison relates, with regard to the alleged Brattleboro edition, that the engraver was Isaac Eddy (1777–1847), whose lack of skill is demonstrated in the Bible that Preston Merrifield and James Cochran published at Windsor in 1812. There has been little written on the iconography of "Fanny Hill" editions. Dr. Ober devotes his small seventh chapter to this subject, "The Iconography of Fanny Hill: How to Illustrate a Dirty Book," in his *Bottoms Up!* The surface of this subject, however, has barely been scratched.

48. Marcus McCorison, in his "Memoirs of a Woman of Pleasure or Fanny Hill in New England," also takes notice of this alleged 1813 printing in the Beinecke Library and has stated, "I have inspected this edition and concur with David Foxon's opinion that it is an American edition." In his earlier "Fanny Hill" article, McCorison related that Foxon had informed him of the existence of the Beinecke copy and obviously had examined it as well.

CHAPTER 9

1. *Letter from the Secretary of the Treasury, Transmitting, in Obedience to a Resolution of the House of the 29th of June Last, Information in Relation to Steam Engines, &c.* (Washington, D.C.: 1839). This is Document No. 21, House of Representatives, 25th Congress, 3rd Session, being volume 345 of the Serial Set. My thanks to Rollo Silver of Boston for bringing this important piece of information to my attention.

2. Charles W. Woolnough, *The Whole Art of Marbling, As Applied to Paper, Book-Edges, &c.*, 8–9.

3. Edwin T. Freedley, *Philadelphia and Its Manufactures: a Hand-Book Exhibiting the Development, Variety, and Statistics of the Manufacturing Industry of Philadelphia in 1857. Together with Sketches of Remarkable Manufactories; and a List of Articles Now made in Philadelphia* (Philadelphia: Edward Young, 1859), 178–179.

4. No catalog or literature relating to this exhibition was published. Information on this subject derives mainly from a letter from Mrs. Hamblett to the travel editor of *The New York Times*, which was published in the section entitled "Letters on Travel" on 31 January 1988, and from a subsequent telephone conversation with her. Mrs. Hamblett wrote to the *Times* in response to an article by Susan Lumsden on "Marbled Papers from Florence" that that newspaper had published. She concluded her letter by noting that "New Yorkers can see a marbleized-slate side altar honoring St. Paul at the Church of St. Paul the Apostle on 59th Street."

5. "Report of the Committee on Marbled Paper." Franklin Institute of Pennsylvania, Archives. Exhibition, 1852.

6. Franklin Institute of Pennsylvania, Archives. Exhibition, 1874.

7. *United States Patent Office. Charles Williams, of Philadelphia, Pennsylvania. Apparatus for Coloring Paper, &c. Specifications of Letters Patent No. 21,584, Dated September 21, 1858.*

8. Rita Susswein Gottesman, *The Arts and Crafts in New York, 1800–1804*, 306–307. According to McKay's *Register*, several other Jansens—George Jansen, J. B. Jansen, Lewis Jansen— were bookbinders or stationers and booksellers in New York at this same time.

9. Richard J. Wolfe, *The Role of the Mann Family of Dedham, Massachusetts in the Marbling of Paper in Nineteenth Century America*, 64. Chapter 5 discusses Daniel's slight marbling activities.

10. Ibid., 68–69.

11. In Philadelphia, similar processes were taking place. Carey & Lea was building on the earlier successes of the printer Henry Carey, which firm continued through Henry Carey Baird; and Joshua Lippincott established a similar firm. By the mid-1830s, however, Philadelphia had relinquished its earlier bookmaking supremacy to New York.

12. A description of this catastrophe can still be found in *The New York Times*, but, alas, only on microfilm in most libraries.

13. In his "Epistle Dedicatory" to a facsimile reprinting of the work cited in the following note. This facsimile edition was issued in 1956 by the Shoestring Press of Hamden, Connecticut.

14. Jacob Abbott, *The Harper Establishment; or, How the Story Books Are Made* (New York: Harper & Brothers, 1855).

15. *The Art of Book-Binding, Its Rise and Progress; Including*

a Descriptive Account of the New York Book-Bindery (New York: E. Walker & Sons, 1850).

16. My collection contains two such broadside advertisements of the Walker firm, both undated. One, probably printed in the late 1840s, commences "New York Book-Bindery, 112 and 114 Fulton Street, New York," and is followed by a view of the interior of the Walker Bindery, reproduced at the bottom of Figure 13 here. The woodblock for that illustration was employed to print the frontispiece in the Walkers' *The Art of Book-Binding* of 1850, and it is possible that the broadside and the book were published at about the same time. The other, also headed "New York Book-Bindery," is followed by the note "(Established 1836.-Burned down January 2d, 1852.-Rebuilt May 1st, 1852)," and shows the exterior of the newly reconstructed establishment (Figure 13, top). A lengthy text follows, advertising the firm's activities and wares. It is signed at end, "E. Walker & Sons," and obviously dates after May 1852. Paul Koda points out in his introduction to the recent facsimile edition of this work, cited in note 18, that Walker did not hesitate to borrow from other publications to complete his *The Art of Bookbinding,* for he relates that Walker borrowed heavily from materials published as early as 1842 in Charles Knight's London *Penny Magazine,* including the very scene of the interior of a bookbindery that appears in Figure 9 here; furthermore, Bernard Middleton has informed me that this scene had also appeared in the interim in George Dodd's *Days at the Factories,* issued at London in 1843.

17. This appeared in *The New York Times* on January 13, 1879, page 5, column 4, and noted that Walker had died the prior Saturday, "at the ripe age of 75."

18. A facsimile edition of the original, 1850 *The Art of Book-Binding* was issued by Oak Knoll Books of New Castle, Delaware in 1984. This contains an introduction by Paul S. Koda, who corroborated many of the facts I had gathered about the Walker firm and added a few others as well. Koda relates that Edward Walker was born in London in 1804 and trained as a bookbinder there, coming to the United States in 1832 or 1833, but maintaining English ties throughout his life. Walker and his wife spent some time in London at the time of the Great Exhibition of 1851 and made another trip there in 1867. Koda devotes space to an altercation between Walker and his son Joseph over the disposition of the Walker bindery, stating that the bindery finally went out of business in 1892, and he discusses Walker's foray into publishing as well as his binding activities.

19. Walker's advertisement appeared on page 3, column 5 of the edition of that day.

20. Sue Allen provides a brief account of the Walker firm in her "Machine-Stamped Bookbindings, 1834–1860," *Antiques* 115, no. 3 (March 1979): 564–572, reproducing the cut of the firm's building from *The Art of Book-Binding.* She notes from that source that the bindery employed from sixty to one hundred workers in 1850 and could bind up to a thousand books a day. She also mentions that Walker was a publisher as well as a binder.

21. Richard J. Wolfe, *The Role of the Mann Family of Dedham, Massachusetts in the Marbling of Paper in Nineteenth Century America.* Chapter VIII reviews the career of Franklin Mann. A few facts, discovered since its publication in 1981, are incorporated here.

22. It was probably Franklin who was reponsible for the abundance of marbled paper that E. Walker had on hand and for sale in October 1855.

23. The background of marbling in Houghton's Riverside plant is discussed in the chapter on Franklin Mann in my Mann family book.

24. Publishing at the Riverside Press was discussed by Emily C. Pearson in her book *Gutenberg and the Art of Printing* (Boston: Noyes, Holmes and Co., 1871), 229ff. R. R. Bowker used

the Harper establishment to contrast modern methods of book publishing with earlier ones in "A Printed Book," *Harper's New Monthly Magazine* 75 (1887): [165]–188, the seventh of a series of articles on "Great American Industries."

25. *United States Patent Office. Thomas Carson, of Brooklyn, New York. Letters Patent No. 112,544, dated March 14, 1871. Improvement in Marbleizing Paper.*

26. Richard J. Wolfe, *The Role of the Mann Family of Dedham, Massachusetts in the Marbling of Paper in Nineteenth Century America,* 39–40.

27. Kendall's various locations and some of his advertising as a bookseller in Providence are outlined in H. Glenn and Maude O. Brown's *A Directory of Printing, Publishing, Bookselling & Allied Trades in Rhode Island to 1865* (New York: The New York Public Library, 1958), 94. The only biographical discussion of him that I could locate appears in a genealogy compiled by his son, Oliver Kendall (born 1813), *Memorial of Josiah Kendall, One of the First Settlers of Sterling, Mass, and of Some of His Ancestors, and of His Descendants* (Providence, R.I.: author, 1884), 95–99.

28. Oliver Kendall's papers in the Rhode Island Historical Society contain three account books relative to his binding and bookselling activities. The first, in a brown wrapper, contains the marbling recipe; the second, with a blue cover, continues recording the work which Kendall did for Wilkinson between 1814 and 1817; and the third records the paper, binding equipment, and other materials that Kendall bought from Wilkinson when he took over the business in 1817.

29. Francis Gagliardi, "The Babcocks of New Haven, Connecticut: Printers, Publishers, Booksellers; with a Bibliographical Checklist of Their Publications," Master's Thesis, Southern Connecticut State University Library School, 1971.

30. *Reports of the First Exhibition of the Worcester County Mechanics Association, at the Nashua Halls, in the City of Worcester, September 1848* (Worcester, Mass.: H. H. Howland, 1848), 74.

31. *Springfield Directory for 1853–1854* (Springfield, Mass.: M. Bessey, 1853). Wilson's advertising occupies eight pages at its back, and is dated June 1853.

32. Samuel N. Dickinson was one of the first successful job printers in Boston until his premature death in 1848. The only complete and detailed account of his life and activities is Rollo G. Silver's "Flash of the Comet: The Typographical Career of Samuel N. Dickinson," *Studies in Bibliography* 21 (1978): 68–89.

33. *The Great Industries of the United States: Being an Historical Summary of the Origin, Growth, and Perfection of the Chief Industrial Arts of This Country,* by Horace Greeley, Leon Case, and others (Hartford: J. B. Burr & Hyde, 1872), 187–188. The description of marbling appears on p. 187, in the section in "Processes in Bookbinding," which is accompanied by several interior scenes of a bindery at work and one showing the exterior of Case, Lockwood & Brainard's printing office and bookbindery.

34. *A Sketch Descriptive of the Printing-Office and Book-Bindery of the Case, Lockwood & Brainard Co. With Illustrations* (Hartford, Conn.: 1877). The firm opened its doors in 1836 when Newton Case and two others began printing in Hartford, and by 1838 they were running the largest printing office in the state; they were equipped with five power and nine hand presses, a large amount of type (for those days), and a steam engine. In 1850 the firm erected a five-story structure, and in 1867, it moved to yet another new building, of which the bookbindery comprised the entire third story and part of the fourth as well.

35. Richard J. Wolfe, *The Role of the Mann Family of Dedham, Massachusetts in the Marbling of Paper in Nineteenth Century America,* 97–98.

36. John R. Gannett to Richard J. Wolfe, August 27, 1975; in the author's files. In the bibliographical section of her *Marbling: a History and a Bibliography,* Mrs. Easton cites (p. 165) a descriptive account of "marbling at the George D. Barnard Co." which appeared in the Gravure Pictorial Section of the *St. Louis Globe*

Democrat on May 9, 1948. I have not seen this article, which reportedly contains illustrations in color and shows Benjamin Bohn marbling.

37. The episode of Franklin Mann and the Webster *Unabridged Dictionary* is reported on pp. 115–117 of my book on the Mann family.

38. On August 31, 1974 I interviewed Artesani at his home in Wellesley Hills, Massachusetts, and taped our conversation. My files contain the audiotape and a 40-page transcription, into which I mounted a few of the samples of his work that he had given me. As indicated on page 148 of Mrs. Easton's *Marbling: a History and a Bibliography*, Artesani also told about his experiences in a brief article entitled "Marbling Magic," which appeared in the *Bookbinding and Book Production Magazine*, (May 1953): 51–52.

39. According to Charles Evan's *American Bibliography* (no. 29243), this had been printed by W. W. Woodward. The section on marbling appears on its pp. 139–140.

40. Most of these editions differ as to the wording of their lengthy subtitles, depending on what their publishers and printers wanted to emphasize in order to help sell them. Some were slightly rearranged internally as well, and at times they contained variant information and recipes. It would be an absorbing (and probably mind-wrenching) task to research them all, including the British editions, and try to determine how they differ; it might also prove frustrating to try to untangle the sources and editions whence their information derived. Some of these apparently were altered by printers along the way according to their own wishes and inclinations. It was customary for the short description of paper marbling to appear in the fourth or sixth chapter of these works.

41. A. F. M. Willich's *The Domestic Encyclopaedia; or, A Dictionary of Facts and Useful Knowledge, Comprehending a Concise View of the Latest Discoveries, Inventions, and Improvements, Chiefly Applicable to Rural and Domestic Economy*, was first issued at London by Murral and Highle in four volumes in 1802. It was reissued in its "First American Edition; with Additions, Applicable to the Present Situation of the United States, by James Mease," in five volumes by W. Y. Birch and Abraham Small of Philadelphia in 1803 and 1804, with the article on marbling appearing on pp. 40–41 of volume 4. A second American edition was issued by Small in three volumes in 1821.

42. James Cutbush, *The American Artist's Manual, or Dictionary of Practical Knowledge in the Application of Philosophy to the Arts and Manufactures. Selected from the Most Complete European Systems, with Original Improvements and Appropriate Engravings Adapted to the Use of the Manufacturers of the United States* (Philadelphia: Johnson & Warner, and R. Fisher, 1814), 2 volumes. "The Marbling of Books and Paper" appears alphabetically in v. 2.

43. See note 47, Chapter 6.

44. See note 4, Chapter 7.

45. Richard J. Wolfe, *On Improvements in Marbling the Edges of Books and Paper; a Nineteenth Century Marbling Account Explained and Illustrated with Fourteen Original Marbled Samples* (Newtown, Pa.: Bird & Bull Press, 1983).

46. According to its title page, this was republished from the latest London edition and contained numerous and important additions, with the medical part carefully revised and adapted to the climate of the United States by an American physician. This work went through four or more American editions, and its imprint told that it could be had by John I. Kay and Company in Pittsburgh. Marbling is discussed on p. 94.

47. Its subtitle related that it was designed for senior scholars in schools and for young persons in general, and that this first American edition had been reissued from the ninth London edition, which was enlarged and extensively improved. Marbling is discussed on p. 215.

48. Mrs. Sarah Josepha Hale, *Mrs. Hale's Receipts for the Millions. Containing Four Thousand Five Hundred and Forty-five Receipts, Facts, Directions, Etc. in the Useful, Ornamental, and Domestic Arts, and in the Conduct of Life* (Philadelphia: T. B. Peterson, 1857). "To Marble Books or Paper" is recipe 1383, on p. 382.

49. M. LaFayette Byrn, *The Artist's and Tradesman's Companion; Embracing the Manufacture and Application of Varnishes to Painting and Other Branches of the Arts; Instructions for Working Enamel, Foil Etc.; The Art of Glazing, Imitation of Gold Color, Tortoise-Shell, Marble, and Art of Staining Wood and Metal; Imitation of Fancy Woods, Granite, Precious Stones, Silver, Brass and Copper; House-painting, Carriage-painting, Etc., with Everything Relating to the Fine Arts, Etc., Etc., Entirely Simplified* (New York: Stringer & Townsend, 1855). Byrn's instructions, extending over more than four pages (134–139), are very good and detailed for that time.

50. R. Moore, *The Universal Assistant, and Complete Mechanic, Containing Over One Million Industrial Facts, Calculations, Receipts, Processes, Trade Secrets, Rules, Business Forms, Legal Items, Etc., in Every Occupation from the Household to the Manufactory* (New York: R. Moore, 1881), "To marble Books or Paper," pp. 247–248.

CHAPTER 10

1. M. Fichtenberg, in his *Nouveau Manuel complet du fabricant des papiers de fantaisie*, relates (p. 50) that the French paper called *agathe* was made at Strasbourg.

2. Most of the information on Montgolfier and his papers is from Fichtenberg's manual, but some scraps of information derive from other sources. In 1981 Marie-Hélène Reynaud published a work on the family's papermaking activities, *Les Moulins à papier d'Annonay à l'ère pre-industrielle* (Annonay: Editions Vivarais), but it does not extend much beyond the year 1800 or explore the subject of colored paper.

3. Fichtenberg reports (pp. 71–77) that there were three types of papier d'Annonay, and he gives directions for the making of each: *papier croisé*, *papier coulé*, and *papier tourniquet*. All were made with potash or potassium hydroxide, and the manner of laying on the colors resulted in the varied configurations that differentiated them and which can be observed on Plates XX and XXI.

4. For more information on the Putois firm, see René Bouvier's *Le Voyage du Papier Autour du Monde* (Bar-le-Duc: Edmond Jolibois, 1931), 95–97. The article entitled "French Marbled Papers," which appeared in *Portfolio, the Annual of the Graphic Arts* in 1951, contains three illustrations of marbling done at the firm of Putois Frères (misspelled Patois Frères). This included a full-page sample of its marbled paper, which had been obtained from the Stevens-Nelson firm. The Doizy-Ipert book *Le Papier Marbré* contains another reference (p. 227) to this firm, an essay by Georges Degaase entitled "Le Livre" in *Le Monde et la Science* (1945, pp. 1248–1251), with black and white illustrations, which I have not seen.

5. These early editions were issued by Bernard Friedrich Voigt as volume 25 of the "Neuer Schauplatz der Künste und Handwerke. Mit Berücksichtigung der Neuesten Erfindungen. Herausgegben von einer Gesellschaft von Künstlern, Technologen und Professionisten," and I have examined copies of all of them. Mrs. Easton's *Marbling: a History and a Bibliography* reports (p. 175) later editions that I have not seen: an undated 5th edition, issued at Ilmanau; a 6th edition, revised, put out at Weimar by Krehan in 1865; a 7th revised edition, also issued at Weimar, but by Bauer; and an 8th revised edition which A. Franke published at Leipzig in 1903.

6. Gum Senegal, or Senegal gum, as it is better known, is in fact gum arabic that comes from the region of Senegal.

7. The full citation for this edition of LeNormand's book is *Manuel du fabricant d'étoffes imprimées et du fabricant de papiers peints, contenant les precédés les plus nouveau pour imprimer les étoffes de coton, de lin, de laine et de coie, et pour coleur de toutes sortes de papiers* (Paris: À la Librairie Encyclopédique de Roret, 1830). The work is a large one, extending to 342 pages, and it contains two folding plates. In Chapter III of the second part, from pp. 263 to 269, there is a description of the atelier of the marbler, with a discussion of his utensils and supplies (including gum, ox-gall, etc.) and directions on the application of colors and the making of patterns. The copy I examined is at the Deutsche Bücherei in Leipzig. In 1831, a German translation appeared bearing the title *Gründliche Anleitung zu Verfertigen Aller Gattungen von Papier-Tapeten und Gefärbtem Papier* (Ulm: In der J. Ebner'schen Buchhandlung), a copy of which I located at the Württemburgische Landesbibliothek in Stuttgart and obtained in microfilm form. I have not seen a copy of the French 1856 edition, cited in the Grünebaum bibliography.

8. Philipp Dessauer, *Entstenung und Entwickelung der Buntpapier-Industrie*, 4.

9. Johann Roehberg, *Die Papierfarbekunst in Allen Ihrer Theilen. Ein Lehrbuch für Angehende Papier- und Tapetenfarbikanten, Buchbinder, Papparbeiter, u.s.w.* (Leipzig: Wilhelm Lauffer, 1839). Roehberg is described on the title page as "Fabrikant Bunter Papier," maker of colored paper. The copy I examined in the Deutsche Bücherei contains descriptions of all manner of colored papers and their making, such as monochrome papers, flower papers, satin and atlas papers, gauffered papers, morocco papers, "Kattunpapiere," paste papers, and, on pp. 121–127, those of the true marbled variety. Haemmerle's *Buntpapier* (p. 193) erroneously dates the first edition to 1838, and it refers to a second issued in 1851.

10. This was printed "In Commission in der Nicolaischen Buchhandlung." The original edition contains no samples of marbling. According to Easton (p. 172) and Grünebaum (p. 209), a new edition, undoubtedly a photofacsimile, appeared at Berlin in 1975. I have located copies of the original edition in the Houghton Library at Harvard and in four libraries in Europe.

11. For reasons which I cannot satisfactorily explain, German manuals and pattern books of the nineteenth century refer to the old Spanish pattern as the "Greek" one. Indeed, the Dessauer pattern books describe it so.

12. I have translated and am in the process of publishing Schade's manual, which deserves to be brought to the attention of a larger audience and which should have marbled patterns to illustrate it. In making these, I have followed Schade's directions exactly when executing the sunshine design. By adding what Schade calls the "special solution"—a combination of shellac and Venetian soap—to black color, and adding hydrochloric acid, drop by drop, until the proper result is attained, a beautiful pattern results. This shows a circle having dark spots in its middle, with rays emanating out of each of them. By following Schade's directions, beautiful results can be obtained, with delicate variations in the form of the rays. Schade ended his booklet by relating that flea seed, carragheen moss, tragacanth, some of the colors, and some of the new materials such as shellac, resin, and Venetian soap, could be obtained in Berlin at Lampe, Kaufman & Co., or at Grabow's.

13. Both titles are cited by Haemmerle, Easton and Grünebaum. Seemingly, the first appeared in two editions or printings in 1853, or at least with two variant title pages, or in a single edition with a double imprint, for Easton notes that it was published by its author at Rochlitz and also by Kollman at Leipzig in 1853. She also notes that it was twenty-nine pages in length and contained five samples of combed marbles in both printings. The second title, according to Easton, was issued at Rochlitz-Leipzig by Kollman.

14. Haemmerle indicates that this contained only fifteen pages. Easton and apparently Grünebaum took the citation from his *Buntpapier*.

15. Boeck's contribution to the literature of marbling, entitled *Die Marmorierkunst. Eine Lehr-, Hand-, und Musterbuch Buchbindereien, Buntpapierfabriken und Verwandte Geschäfte*, carried the imprint "Wien, Pest, Leipzig, Hartleben's Verlag, 1880," and, according to its title page, contained thirty marbled samples. When first published, it was a modest pamphlet of eighty pages, including the advertisements at the back. This work was reprinted in 1896, without samples of original marbling, but with more information, particularly with regard to the mechanical methods of marbling then being introduced. (It also contained a section on the making of combed patterns according to the new precepts of Josef Halfer.) Haemmerle indicates that the first edition contained sixty samples, and it seems likely that he encountered an "extra illustrated" copy with additional samples added by an interested marbler or binder. In the Württemburgische Staatsbibliothek in Stuttgart I examined a copy of the second edition, which did not have samples included in it on publication, but there contains fourteen samples at its back—two to a page, cut long and thin, being almost as tall as the pages themselves—undoubtedly added by an owner. The publisher, Th. Shafer of Hannover reissued the second edition in facsimile in 1987, with a brief introduction by Olaf Meussling and the thirty samples of the first edition reproduced photographically as color illustrations.

16. Haemmerle cites (p. 195 of *Buntpapier*) only the "2. Auflage Leipzig (1880)," noting that it contained sixteen pages. It was the first volume of a tripartite work, the second and third ones being devoted to the decoration of book edges and gilding. Easton indicates (p. 178) that another edition appeared in 1882.

17. Easton takes notice of this (p. 174), citing Paul Kersten as her source; it is also cited in Otto Gurbat's *Einbandbuntpapiere, Techniken und Rezepte zur Herrstellung* (N.p.: Meister der Einbandkunst, 1971), 30.

18. Haemmerle and Easton cite the fourth edition of 1884, but earlier ones are not recorded. Wilhelm Leo, who became identified with Josef Halfer's "new marbling," manufactured and marketed his colors and his marbling materials early in the present century.

19. W. F. Exner, *Die Tapeten- und Buntpapiere-Industrie für Fabrikanten und Gewerbtriebence, Sowie für Technische Institute* (Weimar: Bernhard Friedrich Voigt, 1869), text volume pp. 332–341. This work has an accompanying atlas containing eight tables of drawings of machinery and seven tables with samples of patterns.

20. Theodor Seeman, *Die Tapete, Ihre Ästhetische Bedeutung und Technische Darstellung, Sowie Kurze Beschreibung der Buntpapierfabrikation. Zum Gebrauche für Musterzeichner, Tapeten-Fabrikanten und Buntpapier-Drucker* (Vienna, Budapest, Leipzig: A. Hartleben's Verlag, 1882). Pages 126–131 are devoted to classical marbling.

21. Gabriele Grünebaum, *Buntpapier*, 198.

22. François Ambrose Mairet, *Notice sur la lithographie, deuxième édition suivie d'un essai sur la reliure et le blanchiment des livres et gravures* (Chatillon-sur-Seine: C. Cornillac, 1824). The essay "Tranche Marbrée" appears on pp. 125–133.

23. Louis Sébastien LeNormand, *Manuel de relieur, dans toutes ses parties. Précédé des arts de l'assembleur, de la plieuse, de la brocheuse, et suivi des arts du marbreur sur tranches, du doreur sur tranches et sur cuir, et du satineur* (Paris: Roret, 1827). The second edition came out in 1831, with subsequent ones appearing in 1840, 1853, 1867, 1879, 1890, 1910, 1921, and 1923; German, Dutch, and Spanish translations were issued as well. From 1840, it appeared under the title *Nouveau Manuel Complet de Relieur, dans Toutes Ses partes*.

24. Graham Pollard and Esther Potter, *Early Bookbinding*

Manuals, 21. Most likely, it was Esther Potter who made this observation. She continued and completed this work left unfinished at the time of his death; Bernard Middleton has informed me that most of the comments in the published work are hers, but that it is impossible to separate her observations from Pollard's.

25. Marie-Ange Doizy and Stéphane Ipert, *Le Papier marbré, son histoire et sa fabrication,* 233. The appears under its title alone, *Manuel de marchand papetier* (Paris: Audot, 1828), as part of the series "Collection Encyclopédie Populaire." Doizy and Ipert note that there are "quelques pages sur la marbrure, technique classique," specifying these as pp. 125–131. In his *Papeterie & Papetiers de l'ancien temps,* John Grand-Carteret cites its title in full as *Manuel du marchand Papetier. Dans la préparation des plumes à écrire, des encres noires, de coleurs, de la chine, de celles propres à marquer le linge, etc.; des cires et pains à cacheter, des colles à bouche et autres; des crayons, de la sandaraque, des sables de coleur, du papier glacé et des différentes papiers à calquer; des papiers glacés, huilés, à dérouiller, suivi d'un tableau de tous les formats de papier, avec leurs mésures.* He relates that it was published at Paris by Audot in 1828 "in-18," which indicates a very small book, probably one that could comfortably fit into the hand and into the pocket.

26. Jean Sébastien Julia de Fontenelle and P. Poisson, *Nouveau manuel complet du marchand papetier et du régleur* (Paris: Roret, 1853; nouvelle édition, 1854). On pp. 68–71 of both editions is a section on "Papiers Marbrés." This, like the Fichtenberg manual, was issued in the Collection Encyclopédie-Roret.

27. Edmond Pelouze, *Sécrets modernes des arts et des métiers* (Paris: Audin, 1831–1840), 3 vols. In the first part of v. 2, on pp. 224–232, appears the essay "Papier (Marbrure, Jaspure et Granttage du)." The copy that I have examined is of the third edition, the only one referred to in catalogs and bibliographies. Indeed, I have noted or found no others.

28. Henri Bouchet, *De la Reliure* (Paris: Rouveyre, 1891).

29. H.-L. Alphonse Blanchon, *L'Art et pratique en reliure* (Paris: J. Hetzel et Cie., 1898). This is undated, but a copy in the Boston Public Library carries the note "received November 15, 1898." The work exists in two editions, apparently produced from the same setting of type or from stereotype plates, but with variant title pages. The one received in 1898 and undated has an added section at its end (pp. [167]–172), "Assurances contre les accidents du travail, rapport presenté par M.-J. Lemale . . . 11 Fevrier 1898," and carries at the head of its title the series note "Bibliothèque des Professions Industrielles, Commerciales, Agricoles et Libérales, J. Hetzel Éditeur. Arts et Métiers: Series G." The other edition has similar information within the imprint. A large section, entitled "Ornamentation des Tranches," forms chapter IV, pp. [61]–86. In what appears to be the true first edition, the one received on November 15, 1898, five marbled samples are mounted on both sides of one sheet inserted between pp. 76 and 77. In the apparent reprinting, the samples, which are on two sheets and seem to have been made by the Putois firm, show the Schroetel, Italian or hair vein, Turkish and imitations of ancient patterns.

30. Émile Bosquet, *Guide manuel théoretique et pratique de l'ouvrier ou praticien doreur sur cuir et sus tissus à la main et au balancier . . .* (Paris: Ch. Béranger, 1903). A detailed account of "Marbrure sur Tranches et sur Papiers" appears on pp. 156–173; a description of gilding the edges of a book after it has been marbled is provided on p. 141.

31. Paul Kersten, *Die Geschichte des Buntpapieres,* p. 3 of Nachdruck.

32. Philipp Dessauer, *Entstehung und Entwickelung der Buntpapier-industrie,* 5–6.

33. Mrs. Easton relates in two places (pp. 41, 121) of her *Marbling: a History and a Bibliography* that a Frenchman named Meuglin invented a marbling machine introduced at Aschaffenburg in 1810, and in another place (p. 58) ascribes the event to 1820. I rather suspect that Meuglin's supposed invention was not a bona fide marbling machine but a polishing device that Alois Dessauer installed in 1820. The facts do not support the invention of a marbling machine before the last decades of the nineteenth century.

34. Louis Edgar Andés, *Papier-Specialitäten. Anleitung zur Herstellung von den Verschiedenen Zwecken Dienenden Papierfabrikaten* (Vienna: A. Hartleben, 1896; 2d ed., 1922).

35. Louis Edgar Andés, *The Treatment of Paper for Special Purposes. A Practical Introduction to the Preparation of Paper Products for a Great Variety of Purposes Such as Parchment Paper, Transfer Papers, Preservative Papers, Grained Transfer Papers, Fireproof and Antifalsification Papers, Polishing Papers, Tracing and Copying Papers, Chalk and Litho Transfer Papers, Leather Papers, Luminous Papers, Tortoiseshell and Ivory Papers, Metal Papers, Colored Papers, Etc., Etc., and Paper Articles. Translated from the German by Chas. Salter* (London: Scott, Greenwood & Son, 1907; 2d ed., 1923), chapter 13.

36. Egbert Hoyer, *Die Fabrikcation des Papiers nebst Gewinnung der Fasern aus Ersatzsstoffen, Inbesonders aus Holz, Stroh und Alfa, Sowie Fabrikation der Pappe. des Buntpapiers, des Pergamentpapiers, der Tapeten, u.s.w., und Anseitung zur Prufung des Papiers auf Seine Eigenschaften und Zusammensetzung* (Braunschweig: Friedrich Vieweg und Sohn, 1887). "Gesprengtes und Gezogenes Buntpapier" is discussed on pp. 448–454. This work forms volume 8 of the "Handbuch der chemischen Technologie" series, edited by P. A. Bolley and K. Birnbaum.

37. August Weichelt, *Buntpapier-Fabrikation* (Berlin: Carl Hofmann, 1903; 2d ed., undated, but probably in the next decade; 3rd ed., 1927; 4th ed., 1932). All were published by Hofmann in Berlin.

38. The presence of these mechanically produced samples as extra illustrations in some copies of the Woolnough manual of 1881 indicate that copies of it were around for a decade or more after its publication and that these may be copies remaindered after Woolnough's death.

39. R. S. Bracewell, "Marbled Papers," in Robert H. Mosher, ed., *Specialty Papers* (New York: Ramsen Press, 1950), 187–193.

40. "Leo's Mechanical Marbler" is pictured on p. 75 of this and later editions.

41. *Abridgements of Specifications Relating to Cutting, Folding and Ornamenting Paper, &c.; Including the General Treatment of Paper After Its Manufacture. A.D. 1636–1866.* 2d ed. (London: The Commissioners of Patents' Sale Department, 1879). The Patents of Thomas Kersay (no. 1476, p. 288), Robert Smith and Jabez Booth (no. 2025, p. 351), and Thomas Titterington (no. 3330, p. 424), issued in 1860, 1863, and 1866 respectively, all have reference to the use of rollers for the printing, graining, painting, or marbling of paper. Kersay's patent, it notes, is an improvement of the one for which Edmund Barber obtained letters patent No. 10,880 in 1846.

42. J. W. Zaehnsdorf, *The Art of Bookbinding,* 2d ed., 74. This attributes the prior publication of the transfer method under discussion to the *English Mechanic* of March 17, 1871. The description is repeated in the same place in subsequent editions.

CHAPTER II

1. I first became aware of Josef Halfer's great contribution to marbling approximately twenty-five years ago when translating Paul Kersten's *Die Marmorierkunst; Anleitung zum Marmorieren nach Josef Halfer and Josef Hauptmann*—"The Art of Marbling; an Introduction to Marbling According to the Methods of Josef Halfer and Josef Hauptmann—and teaching myself to marble. Kersten reviewed briefly the important roles that Halfer and Hauptmann played in reviving and revitalizing the art after it

had fallen into decay. The paragraph he devoted to the efforts of Halfer is very important; as an accomplished marbler and historian of the art, Kersten was in a position to know better than anyone else the background of this matter.

2. In his *Marmorierkunst*, Kersten remarked (p. 1) that while Halfer's manual was the first really comprehensive one, it was needlessly burdened down with a description of the preparation of colors.

3. Charles Woolnough, for example, discusses it in his *The Whole Art of Marbling* (p. 29), devoting but a short paragraph to it. Woolnough suggested that Irish or carragheen moss may be used alone or in combination with other sizes. He reported that some marblers like to use a little of it mixed with gum tragacanth for making the nonpareil pattern (undoubtedly because nonpareil was a finely combed pattern, and carragheen size permitted finer and more delicate combing); he also said that it is possible to marble on this size alone.

4. Szigrist's colors were noticed and extolled in a brief unsigned article entitled "Neue Marmorierfarben von Paul Szigrist," which was published in the *Archiv für Buchbinderei* in 1911 (v. 11, pp. 167–168). They also were highly advertised in the contemporary marbling literature.

5. Josef Halfer, *Die Fortschritte der Marmorierkunst. Ein Praktisches Handbuch für Buchbinder und Papierfabrikanten* (Budapest: Im Selbstverlage des Verfassers, 1885). This initial edition contained no original samples or marbled paper.

6. Josef Halfer, *Die Fortschritte der Marmorierkunst. Ein Praktisches Handbuch für Buchbinder und Buntpapierfabrikanten. Nach Technisch-Wissenschaftlichen Grundlagen Bearbeitet* (Stuttgart: Wilhelm Leo, 1891). This edition contained thirty-five original samples.

7. Josef Halfer, *L'Art de la Marbrure. Guide pratique basé sur des données techniques et scientifiques pour relieurs et fabricants de papiers marbrés. Traduction Française autorisée par Joseph Grillet et Émile Schultze* (Genève: Th. Grossman, 1894).

8. Joseph Halfer, *The Progress of the Marbling Art from Technical Scientific Principles; with a Supplement on the Decoration of Book Edges. Translated by Herman Dieck, Philadelphia* (Buffalo, N.Y.: Louis H. Kinder, 1893). Dard Hunter, in his "Bibliography of Marbled Paper," states, in citing a second, undated edition, that "of this edition of 1,000 copies, all but 100 were destroyed by fire, in October, 1904." I have never seen a copy of the alleged second edition.

9. As I noted in my recent appraisal and appreciation of Kinder's work, *Louis Herman Kinder and Fine Bookbinding in America; a Chapter in the History of the Roycroft Shop* (Newtown, Pa.: Bird & Bull Press, 1985), "the Leipzig binder," as Hubbard often referred to Kinder, in 1901 began publishing a magazine called *The Whisper*. He intended to publish in this all sorts of recipes and advice for bookbinders, based on what he had learned over the years. The magazine was not a financial success and concluded publishing before Kinder had exhausted all of his information. To fulfill his goal, Kinder in 1905 had the Roycroft Press issue his monograph entitled *Formulas for Bookbinders*. About a third of this work is devoted to marbling—no information on this subject had appeared in *The Whisper*—mainly information on gums appropriate for sizes, a binder for colors, and edge marbling. Kinder indicated that he hoped one day to publish his own marbling manual, but it seems certain that he never advanced far toward that goal. While a neat, efficient worker, Kinder, his extant marbled papers indicate, was not a highly advanced craftsman, particularly in the Halferian system of marbling; as a bookbinder, and particularly as an art binder, however, he was among the best.

10. In his *Marmorierkunst*, Paul Kersten relates (p. 2) that Halfer contributed an important essay on the subject of a new marbling size, an integral part of his revolution in marbling, to

the *Allgemeiner Anzeiger für Buchbindereien* in 1901, under the title "Charrangenmoos oder Gummi Tragant?" In 1901 also appeared the first of a series of little pamphlets he issued on marbling subjects. These came out at irregular intervals afterward, as Kersten reports, unfortunately without dates or numbers, so that their actual time of issue and sequence cannot now be determined. It may only be said that each new part rejected the recipe of a previous one, based upon some new experience or investigation, right up to the perfection of a really well-established recipe for the preparation of a permanent size from carragheen moss (which Halfer called his "Universalgrund") and reliable marbling colors. The larger of these little publications, Kersten noted, were entitled *Die Rekonstruktion des Universalgrundes; Die Konservierung des Karagheengrundes für eine Lange Haltbarkeit; Das Beste der Drei Konservierungsmittel; Der Universalgrund; Zwei Neue Erfindungen; Für den Marmorierer; Neue Technische Fortschritte;* and *Die Echten Marmorierfarben, Ihre Behandlung und Pflege*. Most of these pamphlets are headed "Für den Marmorierer." Mrs. Easton reports in her *Marbling: a History and a Bibliography* (p. 158) that the Huntington Library owns a volume containing seven of them under that title, and most of them can be found in the Royal Library at the Hague. This series constitutes a veritable bibliographical nightmare. The Huntington Library purchased part of Paul Kersten's bookbinding literature in 1932, the seven Halfer pamphlets in it, and The New York Public Library subsequently obtained another part.

11. Paul Kersten, *Die Marmorierkunst*, in its Preface. Hauptmann is also referred to as the greatest exponent of Halferian marbling in an anonymous article, "Neue Marmoriermuster von Jos. Hauptmann, Gera," in the *Archiv für Buchbinderei* 4 (1904–1905): [129]–131. This illustrates six of his patterns in black and white. Mrs. Easton, in her *Marbling: a History and a Bibliography* (p. 159), cites this as one of Hauptmann's own writings, but my examination of this article indicates that it was written about him by someone else.

12. Josef Hauptmann, *Die Marmorierkunst. Ein Leitfaden zum Praktischen Erlernen des Marmorierens nach Halfer'schen Methode* (Gera Reuss: Selbstverlag des Verfassers, 1895). This initial edition was printed in small octavo format and contains 34 samples of original marbling. A second edition, undated and in larger octavo format, was issued by Englert & Ruckdeschel at Gera in 1901 and contains 31 samples. A third edition, issued by these same publishers in 1906, also contains thirty-one samples of marbling.

13. Josef Hauptmann, *De Marmerkunst, Tot Versiering der Boeksnede. Eene Handleiding Tot de Practische Beofening.* This contains twenty specimens of marbling, as well as a portrait of Josef Halfer.

14. Otto Hauptmann, *Nachschlage-Heft beim Marmorieren, mit 30 Verschiedene Beispielen von Otto Hauptmann, Gera-Reuss* (n.p., n.d., but Kersten says 1914). On its third and final page, at the bottom, appears the notice that if one wants to work without difficulty, one should use only the true Halferian colors, which can be obtained from J. Hauptmann, Berlin S.W. 11, neben Theater in Königgrätzerstr. 56bI.

15. *Systematisches Lehr- und Handbuch der Buchbinderei und der Damit Zusammenhängenden der Fächer in Theorie und Praxis. Unten Bewährter Mitwirkung der Herren Baum, Frankfurt a. M., Blankenburg, Berlin, Phil. Dessauer, Aschaffenburg, Fritzsche, Leipzig, Etc. . . . Bearbeitet und Herausgegeben von Paul Adam, Buchbindermeister* (Dresden-Blasewitz: Löwenstein'sche Verlagshandlung, [1882–1885]). The marbling essays appear on pp. 119–216 and 217–233 of volume 3, with the plate following p. 213.

16. Paul Adam, *Die Praktische Arbeiten des Buchbinders* (Vienna: A. Hartleben, 1898). This was translated by Thomas E.

Maw and published under the title *Practical Bookbinding* (London: Scott Greenwood & Co., 1903). Marbling techniques are reviewed on pp. 62–73.

17. Both editions were published by Wilhelm Knapp at Halle a. Saale. The title of the second edition states that it also contains an introduction to linoleum printing, silhouette processes, and similar methods.

18. Phoebe Jane Easton, *Marbling: a History and a Bibliography*, 162–163.

19. Paul Kersten, *Marmorerkunsten; Oversatt ved Arne Paasche Aasen* (Oslo: Utgitt av Bokbinderforbundene i Skandinavien, 1925).

20. The 1930 edition was issued at Stuttgart by the Allgemeiner Anzeiger für Buchbindereien; the 1939 edition was published by Wilhelm Knapp at Halle.

21. Hans Bauer and Paul Kersten, *L. Brade's Illustriertes Buchbinderbuch, ein Lehr- und Handbuch der Gesamten Buchbinderei und Aller dieses Fach Einschlagenden Kunsttechniken* (Halle a. Salle: Wilhelm Knapp, 1916). This was the sixth edition. By the eighth edition, issued in 1930, it had come to be titled *Brade-Kersten Illustriertes Buchbinderbuch*.

22. Paul Hüttich, *Lehrplan und Ausführlicher Bericht der Gerauer Vergolde-Schule und Buch Binderei; Kunst Gewerbliche Anstalt* (Gera: Konigl. Preuss. Amt. für Handel und Gewerbe, 1900).

23. Editions of this work were issued in 1909, 1912, 1920, 1923, and 1929, all published by Wilhelm Knapp in Halle.

24. Franz Weisse, "Mein Kampf mit der Ochsengalle," *Das Buchbinderhandwerk*, no. 6, 1938, and a separate reprinting from it.

25. Bohniert, *Marmorieren* (Vienna: 1908), I have seen several copies of this little work, which gives good instruction according to Halferian principles, but contains no samples. Bohniert's first or Christian name is unknown.

26. Johann Bönisch, *Über Technik und Neuheiten im Marmorieren: Vortrag Gehalten im k. k. Gewerbeförderungsamte in Wien am 12. Dezember, 1907* (Vienna: O. Maas & Sohne, 1908).

27. Napsal L. Weigner, *Baravné a Pestré. Papíry Jich Vyroba a Upontřebení* (Praze: Náklad Vlastní, Tiskem Politiky, 1909). In a section titled "Technika Mramorovaci," pp. 21–36, there is a résumé of Halferian methods, with the same equipment, patterns and other subject matter of the classic Halferian manuals of this and an earlier period. There also appears a section on the making of paste papers and another on oil marbling, with mounted samples included; the classical types of marbling were executed by J. Šubert and Jindrich Kloubek of Prague and the four samples of oil marbling by G. Trepplin of Berlin-Rixdorf. A copy of this manual can be found in the Royal Library at The Hague.

28. Herman Nitz, *Buntpapiere. Ihre Herstellung und Vorwendung* (Leipzig: Spamer, 1922). A copy of this fifteen-page pamphlet with some original samples is preserved in the Deutsche Bücherei in Leipzig.

29. Mariann Finckh-Haelsig, *Die Herstellung Buntpapier. Eine Anleitung zur Selbstherstellung von Kleisterpapieren, Stempel-, Tusch-, Tunk-, Oel- und Schlabonenpapieren* (Ravensburg: Otto Maier, [1926]). Chapter 4, "Die Tunk- oder Marmorpapiere," is devoted to marbling. Classic marbling on carragheen size is described on pp. 46–49; oil marbling on water on pp. [41]–44, and oil marbling on a paste made from potato flour on pp. 44–46. This manual also discusses many other types of colored papers, such as paste papers, and in some respects it resembles Paul Kersten's *Die Herstellung Aller Arten von Buntpapieren*. There are 16 original samples mounted at its end, but only one, no. 14, is of the marbled variety, and then only of oil marbling in one color. The remainder show paste paper and other designs.

30. Rudel's bookbinding accomplishments were reported in a brief article, "Arbeiten von Johann Rudel, Elberfeld," that appeared in the *Archiv für Buchbinderei* in 1911 (vol. 11, pp. 166–

167). He was described as a fine hand bookbinder, but nothing was said about his attainments in marbling paper.

31. Kyster also specialized in the making of paste papers. Large collections of his decorated papers can be found in the Kunstgewerbmuseum in Berlin, the Deutsches Museum von Meisterwerken der Naturwissenschaft und Technik in Munich, the Deutsche Bücherei in Leipzig, and, as would be expected, in the Kunst Industrie Museets in Copenhagen. Kyster's earliest work appears to date to the 1892–1898 period. See V. Brunn's "Der Erdog Dansk Opfindelse. Anker Kyster Marmorede Papier," *Saertryk af Tidsskrift for Kunstindustri*, 1898, pp. 114–118.

32. A résumé of oil marbling appears in the section "Marbling with Oil Colors," later in this chapter.

33. A report on the marbling activities and production of Georg Kowash of Budapest, in "Buchbinder-Buntpapier," *Archiv für Buchbinderei* 3 (1903–1904): [153]–156, is followed by eight illustrations that show marbled patterns executed on water by Andreas Hausmann of Konstanz. A fairly large collection of his papers is in the Deutsche Bücherei in Leipzig. These show that he executed oil marbling rather poorly.

34. In his article, "Moderne Buntpapier und Ihre Verwendung," *Archiv für Buchgewerbe* 44 (1907): 354–358, Dr. Hans Sachs of Berlin devoted a paragraph (p. 356) to the colored papers of Ernst Leistikov (or, in its Germanized form, Leistigow) of Bromberg, relating that he worked with oil colors, using them in the same manner as a classical marbler would use his watercolors and ox-gall, although Leistikov lacked any knowledge of how the normal marbling technique was executed. While Sachs found Leistikov's papers to appear somewhat unruly and agitated, he nonetheless thought that they provided delightful signs of renewed interest in individual craft techniques.

35. Sachs, *ibid.*, also devotes a paragraph to the colored-paper productions of the Wiener Werkstätte, and especially to the work of Karl Moser and Josef Hoffmann. The activities of the Wiener Werkstätte have recently begun to attract the attention and interest of art historians, and two books have been published on it. In 1982 appeared Werner J. Schweiger's *Wiener Werkstaette; Kunst und Handwerk, 1903–1932* (Vienna: C. Brandstaetter), issued in English translation in 1984 as *Wiener Werkstaette; Design in Vienna, 1903–1932* (New York: Abbeville Press). Two years after that appeared Jane Kallir's *Viennese Design and the Wiener Werkstätte* (New York: C. Braziller, 1986). Both these works devote short sections to the shop's book designs, but mention decorated papers only in passing.

36. Jan-Olov Nyström, "Remembering Ingeborg Börjesson, *Ink & Gall* 2, no. 1 (Summer 1988), 10–11.

37. Dane & Co., Ltd., *Instructions for Using Dane & Co.'s Liquid Marbling Inks on Carragheen Moss Size* (London: 1928; reissued in 1937 and 1952).

38. Information on the Cockerell marbling effort derives from a number of sources, of which the following are the most informative: Geraldine Cashin, "The Cockerell Bindery," *Crafts (U.K.)*, no. 49 (March/April 1981): 40–44; Sydney M. Cockerell, "Marbling Paper," *Craft Horizens* 12 (1952): 32–35; Aylmer Vallance, "Marbled Ends," *New Statesman and Nation, Weekend Review* 54 (August 23 1950): 206, 208.

39. John J. Pleger, *Bookbinding and Its Auxiliary Branches; Part Four, Gilt Edging, Goffered Edging, Marbling, Hand Tooling and the Care of Books* (Chicago: Inland Printer Company, 1914).

40. John J. Pleger, *Bookbinding: Blank, Edition and Job Forwarding; Loose Leaf Binders; Pamphlet Bindings, Etc.; Finishing, Hand Tooling, Stamping, Embossing, Gilt Edging, Goffered Edging, Marbling, the Care of Books, Some Inconsistencies in Bookbinding, Incongruity of Bookbinding Styles* (Chicago: Inland Printer Company, 1924).

41. According to Frank E. Comparato, *Books for the Millions; A History of the Men Whose Methods and Machines Packaged the*

Printed Word (Harrisburg, Pa.: The Stackpole Company, 1971), Pleger, after advising the Philippine government on setting up its bindery, formed a company in Chicago in 1926 to make industrial bookbinding machinery, including a roller-backer, a back gluer, and a round-corner turning-in machine. The John J. Pleger Company was in 1953 acquired by Gane Brothers & Lane, a bookbinding supply house. Thus, after starting as a hand binder, Pleger contributed significantly to the industrialization of book work and assisted the collapse of old values, which he had lamented earlier in the 1924 reprinting of his *Bookbinding* (p. 421).

42. W. C. Doebbelin, *The Art of Marbling* (London, 1910); reissued as *The Art of Marbling, A Practical Guide to Marbling, Doebbelin's Simplified Method* (Middleton, Mass.: The Halfer Marbleizing Company, 1927).

43. W. C. Doebbelin, "The Art of Marbling," *Bookbinding Magazine* 4 (October 1926): 14; 6 (January 1927): 34; 6 (March 1927): 24; 6 (April 1927): 28; 6 (June 1927): 44, 50; 7 (July 1927): 28. Also, *Price List of "Halfer" Marbling Gums and Directions How to Marble. Doebbelin's Simplified Process* (Middleton, Mass.: Halfer Marbling Company, 1927).

44. Rosamond B. Loring, *Marbled Papers; an Address Delivered before the Members of the Club of Odd Volumes, November 16, 1932* (Boston: Club of Odd Volumes, 1933), vi.

45. Rosamond B. Loring, "Colored Paste Papers," 33–34.

46. I came across this letter laid into the Loring copy in the early 1980s, but when reexamining Doebbelin's manual about six years later, it was no longer present, nor has it since been located.

47. Paul Kersten, *Die Herrstellung Aller Arten von Buntpapier für Bucheinbände, Mappen und Kästen nach Bewährten Verfahren*, 2d ed., 1939, 26.

48. W. F. Exner, *Die Tapeten- und Buntpapierindustrie*, 339.

49. The full citation of this is "Neues Verfahren in der Fabrication Marmorierter Papier; von Tucker," *Polytechnisches Journal, Herausgeben von Dr. Emil Maximilian Dingler* (142 (1856): 229–231. (It notes that this information had previously been published in the *Deutsche Gewerbzeitung*, 1855, p. 404.) This article reported that the reason for using a gum bath in marbling was that it not only supported colors on its surface, but allowed them to spread out and ultimately be absorbed onto paper. When attempts had been made in the past to use oil colors in marbling, it was found that the colors ran into one another or formed drops; that they would not transfer properly to paper; and, finally, that they would not dry satisfactorily. Tucker's method reportedly eliminated all of these problems and objections, and, additionally, could be conducted on a bath of clear water instead of the usual tragacanth size, which was prone to spoiling when left standing for a long time.

50. Hiram Tucker's patent is no. 2203 and appears on p. 131 of the compilation.

51. Paul Kersten, "Ölmarmor mit Tucherischem Verfahren," *Papierzeitung* (1904): 3749.

52. Albert Haemmerle, *Buntpapier*, 195. Haemmerle records that this had appeared in the *Deutsche Buchbinder-Zeitung*, Barmen, 1905.

53. Tim [Timothy Burr] Thrift, *Modern Methods in Marbling Paper; a Treatise for the Layman on the Art of Marbling Paper for Bookbinding and Other Decorative Uses, Including a Description of Several Practical Methods, with Illustrative Samples of Marbled Effects* (Winchester, Mass.: Lucky Dog Press, 1945).

54. Information on the Hesses came from the son, Gerhard, with whom I had carried on a correspondence from 1973. The younger Hesse died in January of 1983. An article on him, "Der Regen Bogen Papier Macher," by Horst Drescher, illustrated with scenes of Hesse at work and with color reproductions of some of his papers, appeared in the *Leipziger Blätter* no. 10

(Frühjahr 1987): 25–30. Mr. Hesse's marbling activities are being continued by his daughter, Ilona Ruckriegel-Hesse, who now lives in nearby Liebertwolkwitz.

CHAPTER 12

1. I am aware of only a single attempt to investigate and explain marbling in relation to its chemistry and technology, a small work issued by the Institute voor Grafische Technique of Amsterdam in April of 1946 as its Publicatie 7, *Marmeren, Theorie en Toopassing*. However, the fact that it is written in Dutch, a language not widely used outside of Holland, has made it accessible to only a few. Josef Halfer, we have observed, attempted many times to understand the technology of this craft and explain it in his excellent manual and other publications. More recently, the U.S. Government Printing Office had similar studies carried on by Morris S. Kantrowitz and Ernest W. Spencer; their findings were issued in a small pamphlet entitled *The Process of Marbling Paper*, which formed their GPO-PIA Joint Research Bulletin, Bindery Series No. 1. This was issued in 1948, and it has been reprinted recently by the TALAS bookbinder's supply company of New York. While containing a good deal of useful information on sizes and the like, it is overly dependent on Halfer's explanations for much of its technical data.

2. Hugh Sinclair and other English marblers employed the term "hair search" for the straining apparatus through which the size was passed prior to marbling to remove lumps and foreign matter. The hair search was a sieve with finely woven hair at its bottom and served well for this purpose.

3. This scene has been reproduced from the article "French Marbled Papers" which was published in *Portfolio, the Annual of the Graphic Arts* in 1951.

4. I noted in *Three Early French Essays on Paper Marbling, 1642–1765* (p. 106) and on p. 133 here that the term "montfaucon" is obscure. While one dictionary pointed out that this term denoted the size of a sheet of one sort of paper, it did not indicate what that size was, nor did any other of the many sources I checked. As the usual demy sheet was about 15 × 20 inches, a sheet of montfaucon paper obviously exceeded those proportions.

5. Charles W. Woolnough, *The Whole Art of Marbling Paper, as Applied to Paper, Book-Edges, &c.*, 35.

6. Ibid.

7. Franz Weisse, *Die Kunst des Marmorierens*, 18; *The Art of Marbling*, 39.

8. Paul Kersten, *Die Marmorierkunst*, 3.

9. Charles W. Woolnough, *The Whole Art of Marbling, as Applied to Paper, Book-Edges, &c.*, 36.

10. In the letter that Franklin Mann sent from New York to his brother Samuel in Dedham on 22 February 1847, now in the Dedham Historical Society, and written on the reverse side of a piece of nonpareil marbled paper he had made, he told Samuel of just such a rake:

> You will see that I have remedied the evil of having bad ends on the sheet in combing the first time. It is done by having a comb the whole length of the trough, made of common size wire, teeth 1 3/4 inches apart, and they are drawn forwards through the colors once and then back in the intermediate spaces. It has the effect of making a more perfect sheet and the colors are brighter, as it does not mix them up so much, and which I consider a great improvement.

11. The making of such patterns is discussed on pp. 72, 75 of my translation of Weisse's manual. I have experimented a bit in this area and can attest to Weisse's assertion that some interesting results can be obtained. However, it is slow work.

CHAPTER 13

1. U.S. Government Printing Office, GPO-PIA Joint Research Bulletin, Bindery Series, No. 1, *The Process of Marbling Paper*, 3.

2. Several modern works dealing with surface chemistry can be useful in understanding the chemical and physical problems of marbling. Among these are Neil Kensington Adam's *The Physics and Chemistry of Surfaces* (Oxford: Oxford University Press, 1930, of which a 3rd ed. was printed by Dover in 1941); Albert Ernest Alexander's *Surface Chemistry* (London: Longman's, Green, 1951); and Duncan J. Shaw's *Introduction to Colloid and Surface Science*, 3rd ed. (London: Butterworths, 1980).

3. Fräulein Kollenkark is the marbler who appears in the illustrations along with Franz Weisse in his *Die Kunst des Marmorierens*.

4. F. V. von Hahn, "Studien über Schleimoberflächen, I.," *Kolloid-Zeitschrift* 59 (1932): 130–135; "Studien über Schleimoberflächen II," *Kolloid-Zeitschrift* 60 (1932): 247–253.

5. F. V. von Hahn, "Studien über Schleimoberfläche, I," 130. "Nach Kenntnisnahme dieser kunstgewerblichen Methodik waren wir den Ansicht, das kaum eine Arbeitsart so viele kolloid-chemische Probleme umfasst, wie gerade die Marmoriertechnik."

6. Reference here is to work on the kinetics of surface films by Irving Langmuir, whose studies of the molecular orientation and detailed structure of films on solid and liquid surfaces earned him the Nobel Prize for chemistry in 1932. Important studies in this area were conducted earlier by the English physical scientist John William Strutt, Lord Rayleigh; by Agnes Pockels, a German amateur physicist; and, interestingly enough, by Benjamin Franklin, who may actually have been the first to conduct scientific investigations on the effect of oil on water. Franklin's curiosity was aroused during a transatlantic voyage in 1757, when he noticed two ships sailing remarkably smoothly in a choppy sea while others were ruffled in the wind. He was told by the captain that this was probably due to cooks emptying their greasy water through the scuppers, thereby greasing the sides of the ships a little; and Franklin remembered reading Pliny's account of a practice among seamen in ancient times to still the waves by pouring oil into the sea. In subsequent years in England, Franklin conducted several researches into the effect of oil on water, and especially the pouring of oil on water to calm waves. See further Nathan G. Goodman, ed., *The Ingenious Dr. Franklin* (Philadelphia: University of Pennsylvania Press, 1931), 188–197; C. H. Giles, "Franklin's Teaspoon of Oil; Studies in the Early History of Surface Chemistry, Part I," *Chemical Industries*, London (1969), 1616–1624; Martin C. Carey, "Benjamin Franklin, Lord Rayleigh, Agnes Pockels, and the Origins of Surface Chemistry," in G. Paumgartner, ed., *Enterohepatic Circulation of Bile Acids and Sterol Metabolism* (Lancaster: MTP Press, Ltd., 1985), 5–26.

7. Charles W. Woolnough, *The Whole Art of Marbling, as Applied to Paper, Book-Edges*, &c., 26.

8. Ibid.

9. U.S. Government Printing Office, GPO-PIA Joint Research Bulletin, Bindery Series, No. 1, *The Process of Marbling Paper*, 5.

10. A good many years ago it occurred to me that if I could measure the viscosity of the size accurately I would be able to solve most of the problems inherent in marbling and make the process slavishly obey my will. But when I asked a friend with advanced training in chemistry—in fact, the head of research of a large paint company—where I could obtain a viscometer (or viscosimeter), he advised me not to bother, saying that a reliable instrument of the type I needed did not exist.

11. Franz Weisse, *Die Kunst des Marmorierens*, 17; *The Art of Marbling*, 39.

12. With reference to its nutritive qualities, Albert J. Bellows, M.D., who described himself as "late professor of chemistry, physiology, and hygiene," had this to say about Irish moss in his *The Philosophy of Eating* (New York, Hurd and Houghton; Boston; E. P. Dutton and Company, 1867), p. 67:

> A sea-weed known under the names of carragheen moss, pearl moss, and Irish moss, grown on the rocky sea-shores of Europe, especially those of Ireland and the north of England and Scotland. It contains but little nutriment, but is used in England, and sometimes in this country, perhaps with advantage, with our too concentrated nourishment; but alone it can sustain life but for a short time. It is, however, resorted to by the poorer classes on the sea-shores of Ireland when the ordinary crops of corn and potatoes have failed, and for a time will keep them from actual starvation.

13. In my experience, it is best to allow the size to rest for a week or even two after making it, as this allows all particles to attain their finest consistency. While it can be used immediately after being made, the resulting marbled patterns, especially combed ones, will show jagged and uneven lines and have a certain "tension" about them that is not pleasing. It needs further rest before optimal results are obtained: the resting time allows the solution to reach complete dissolution, which is necessary to produce the more delicate forms.

14. James Sumner, *The Mysterious Marbler*, 8; reprint ed., 1976, 22.

15. Franz Weisse, *Die Kunst des Marmorierens*, 19; *The Art of Marbling*, 40.

16. Marjorie B. Cohn, *Wash and Gouache, a Study of the Development of the Materials of Watercolor* (Cambridge, Mass.: Fogg Art Museum, 1977), 33, 76.

17. This outline of the nature and action of bile fluid has been aided greatly through discussions with Dr. Martin C. Carey of the Brigham and Women's Hospital in Boston, an acknowledged expert on this subject. Information has also been obtained from the following printed sources: Martin C. Carey, "The Enterohepatic Circulation," in I. Arias, ed., *The Liver: Biology and Pathology* (New York: Raven Press, 1982), 429–465; Martin C. Carey and Donald M. Small, "The Characteristics of Mixed Micellar Solutions with Particular Reference to Bile," *American Journal of Medicine* 49 (1970): 590–603; Martin C. Carey to Richard J. Wolfe, Memorandum of June 22, 1987, author's files.

18. One of the functions of the enterohepatic circulation is to eliminate excess cholesterol in the adult organism. Cholesterol is synthesized in all cells of vertebrates and is vital to their function and growth. Excessive synthesis and retention of cholesterol may be lethal and characterizes the lesions of atherosclerosis and most gall stones. Bile secretion provides the only significant mechanism for its removal; not only are cholesterol molecules converted into bile salts continually to balance fecal loss, but conjugated bile salts, by their detergent action, solubilize cholesterol in macromolecular aggregates called micelles. These micelles promote excretion of cholesterol from the liver and its eventual loss in the feces. Moreover, intestinal conservation of bile salt molecules permits them to mediate continuously hepatic cholesterol excretion by recycling repeatedly through the parenchymal cells of the liver. Furthermore, bile salts indirectly regulate cholesteral synthesis in these organs.

19. Fish bile differs significantly from mammalian bile in that it contains bile alcohol. The bile of fish also contains much less lecithin, protein, and cholesterol.

20. Charles W. Woolnough, *The Whole Art of Marbling, as Applied to Paper, Book-Edges, &c.*, 32–33.

21. Richard J. Wolfe, *Three Early French Essays on Paper Marbling*, 78.

22. I have experimentally marbled without alum, using modern colors, and have watched a beautifully formed pattern suddenly "break" and flow off the paper, particularly under washing. Similarly, when using coated papers and papers that are treated so as not to accept alum or any other acidic material, the pattern—sometimes exceedingly beautiful in its initial perfection—simply disintegrates and fades or washes away.

23. Marjorie B. Cohn, *Wash and Gouache*, 21.

24. Charles W. Woolnough, *The Whole Art of Marbling, as Applied to Paper, Book-Edges, &c.*, 32–33.

25. James Sumner, *The Mysterious Marbler*, 9–10; reprint ed., 1976, 23–24.

26. Robert Dossie, *The Handmaid to the Arts*, 1758 ed., v. 2, 380; his method of damping the paper is described on pp. 194–195.

27. Franz Weisse, *Die Kunst des Marmorierens*, 14; *The Art of Marbling*, 32–33.

28. Hugh Sinclair, *The Whole Process of Marbling Paper*, 21; reprint ed., 1987, 67.

29. Charles W. Woolnough, *The Whole Art of Marbling, as Applied to Paper, Book-Edges, &c.*, 30–31.

30. James Sumner, *The Mysterious Marbler*, 20–21; reprint ed., 1976, 48.

31. The British Spirits Act of 1880 defined this as rectified spirits of the strength of not less than 43 degrees above proof.

32. James Sumner, *The Mysterious Marbler*, 11; reprint ed., 1976, 26–27.

CHAPTER 14

1. Nutgalls are not to be confused with ox-gall or bile fluid, two totally dissimilar materials. A swelling or excrescence on plants (often oak trees), this gall is produced by vegetable organisms, such as fungi, bacteria, and slime molds, as well as by various insects such as mites, aphids, and some worms which lay their eggs in punctures they made in plant or tree bark. The resultant growth is a rich store of tannic acid and was important in commerce, particularly in ink making, with the galls of oaks being especially potent.

2. James Haigh, *The Dyer's Assistant in the Art of Dying Wool and Woolen Goods. Extracting from the Philosophical and Chymical Works of Those Most Eminent Authors, Mess. Ferguson, Dufay, Hellot, Goeffery, Colbert, and that Reputable French-Dyer, Mons. De Julienne. Translated from the French. With additions and Practical Experiments. By James Haigh, Silk and Muslin-Dyer, Leeds* (Leeds: Printed by J. Bowling; and Sold by Mess. Rivington and Son, London, and R. Spence, York, 1778). A second edition was issued in 1800.

3. Bancroft's work was first issued by T. Caddell at London, with the notation "Volume I." A second edition, incorporating a second volume, appeared under the London imprint of Cadell and W. Davies in 1813. The reprinting of this edition at Philadelphia by Thomas Dobson in 1814 serves as my source hereafter.

4. C. H. Schmidt, *Vollständiges Farben-Laboratorium, oder Ausführliche Anweisung zur Bereitung der in der Malerei, Staffirmalerei, Illumination, Fabrication Bunter Papier und Tapeten Gebrauchlichen Farben, und Namentlich der Erd- und Metall- oder Oxydfarben, Lackfarben, Saftfarben, Pastellfarben und Tuschfarben* (Weimar: Verlag, Druck und Lithographie von B. J. Voigt, 1841). This forms the 170th volume of the "Neuer Schauplatz der Künste und Handwerke" (cited above in note 5 of Chapter 10).

5. *Die Zeichnungs- und Mahlerkunst* (Frankfurt und Leipzig: 1756). The greater part of this little work of 120 pages relates to the preparation and uses of various types of pigments used by artists, including water, oil, and dry based paints; it provides formulas for making the colors.

6. *The Artist's Assistant; or, School of Science. Being an Introduction to Painting in Oil, Water, and Crayons, with Biographical Accounts of Some of the Principal Artists; the Arts of Drawing; Designing, Colouring, and Engraving, in All Its Different Modes, on Copper and Wood; or Enamelling, Gilding on Metal, Wood, Glass, and Leather; Japanning, Dying, Casting, &c. With a Great Variety of Miscellaneous Information Relative to Arts and Manufactures* (London: printed for Thomas Ostell, by Swinney and Ferrall, Birmingham, 1807).

7. Edward Bancroft, *Experimental Researches Concerning the Philosophy of Permanent Colors*, gives a fascinating account of the discovery of the dyeing power of this insect by the Spanish conquerors of Mexico and of attempts to propagate it later in the West Indies, as well as the special properties of cochineal as a pigmenting and dyeing material. See further v. 1, pt. 2, especially chapters 3 and 4.

8. Bancroft again (op. cit.) gives good information on the brazilwood and logwoods of the New World that were used for making red coloring material in these early times. See his v. 2, pt. 2, chapters 5 and 6.

9. Robert Dossie, *The Handmaid to the Arts*, 1758 ed., v. 1, p. 77.

10. Edward Bancroft, *Experimental Researches*, v. 2, p. 45 is the source of this information. He also gives a good account of the making of Prussian blue. Andrew Ure's *Dictionary of Arts, Manufactures, and Mines*, which first appeared at London in 1839 (I refer to the fourth edition issued at Boston by Little, Brown in 1853), tells us (v. 2, pp. 499–504) that Prussian or Berliner blue is a chemical compound of iron and cyanogen made by first burning animal matter rich in nitrogen, such as dried blood, horns, hair, skin, or hoofs, with potash. This resulted in a preparation that was referred to as *lixivium sanguinis*, or blood-lye which, in addition to its use for producing this coloring matter, served as an excellent reagent for distinguishing metals from one another. When the precipitating solution, obtained from a green sulphate of iron (which was very cheap) was added to the lixivium, with which alum previously had been mixed, it precipitated a greenish-gray material that gradually became blue by absorption of oxygen from the air. The Ure dictionary explains the process in detail and mentions a new process introduced in 1837 for manufacturing the color in quantity.

11. Verditer, also referred to as Bremen blue, was very easy to make, as the article in Ure's dictionary (see previous note) indicates. A quantity of blue vitriol and an almost exact quantity of sea salt, both free of iron, were ground together to make a paste. An amount of old copper, equal to half their combined weight, was cut into inch squares and agitated in a wooden tub containing sulfuric acid diluted with a little water. This was done in order to separate any impurities, and the copper was thereupon washed in revolving casks. The bits of copper then were placed in oxidation chests, along with the salt and vitriol, and left for some time for their mutual reaction.

12. See further F. Crace-Calvert, *Dyeing and Calico Printing: Including an Account of the Most Recent Improvements in the Manufacture and Use of Aniline Colors* (Manchester: Palmer & Howe, 1876), [140]. The severity of some of these restrictions may be judged by the fact that Henry IV of France issued an edict condemning to death anyone who used that pernicious drug called the "devil's food."

13. James Haigh, in his *The Dyer's Assistant*, devotes Chapter VII to "Of the Method of Dying Blue" and provides a fairly detailed account of the reduction of indigo dye from the *Anil* plant of the East and West Indies.

14. As would be expected, Bancroft devotes a longish chapter, number 2 of volume 2 of his *Experimental Researches*, to "Of the Properties and Uses of Quercitron Bark."

15. Edward Bancroft, *Experimental Researches*, v. 1, p. 87.

16. Christian Friedrich Gottlieb Thon, *Der Fabrikant Bunter Papier*, 2d ed., 24–57.

17. M. Fichtenberg, *Nouveau Manuel complet du fabricant de papiers de fantaisie*, [6]–26.

18. A great many articles appeared in the American medical literature during the last three decades of the nineteenth century concerning poisonous substances, mostly arsenic in wallpapers. One of the earliest and most complete, published by Frank W. Draper, "On the Evil Effects of the Use of Arsenic in Certain Green Colors," in the *Third Annual Report of the State Board of Health of Massachusetts, January, 1872* (Boston: Wright & Potter, 1872), [17]–57, reported several local cases of arsenic poisoning occasioned by green-colored wallpaper. Draper pointed out that as early as 1740, the employment of arsenic as a pigment in certain manufactures had been forbidden in France, although such bans were not always effective. He noted the specific toxicity of such greens as Schweinfurt and Scheele's green, which were known among workmen as emerald green, mineral green, Brunswick green or Vienna green; in France the color was called *Vert Anglais* or English green. In 1885, Edward S. Wood, Professor of Chemistry at the Harvard Medical School, issued a similar report, "Arsenic as a Domestic Poison," which appeared as a supplement to the *Fifth Annual Report of the Massachusetts State Board of Health, Lunacy and Charity,* and was issued separately.

19. This was a lake color manufactured through the use of peachwood or Niagara wood, or hypernic, a dye obtained from a tropical American logwood somewhat akin to brazilwood. Bancroft discusses it on pp. 249–250 of volume 2 of his *Experimental Researches*.

20. Oxford ocher (or ochre) was a superior yellow ocher found near Oxford, England, and in this case calcined, as was sienna earth, to bring about its red color. Woolnough pointed out that the addition of a little black made a good brown; or adding a little blue or indigo made a good olive. By itself, it produced a bright fawn color.

21. The chrome colors, which consisted usually of potassium or sodium dichromate, varied in shade from lemon-yellow to orange. Chrome green frequently was made by tingeing chrome yellow with Prussian blue. Woolnough observed that most of the greens used in marbling were obtained by mixing Dutch pink or yellow lake with blue, according to the shade desired.

22. Woolnough says nothing about this color. Most likely, it was an arsenous color (see note 18).

23. Ivory black was made by calcining ivory or bone. Woolnough observed, and I wholeheartedly concur from experience, that it must be combined with lampblack or indigo to get it to work properly as a black.

24. Umber is a brown earth, highly valued by artists as a pigment, which is used either in the raw state or calcined, or burnt, which gives it a slightly reddish hue. The best variety comes from Cyprus and is called Turkey umber. Woolnough commented that it was infrequently needed, for it required a great deal of grinding.

25. Orange chrome was one of the natural chromes of orange color (see note 21).

26. China clay was kaolin; pipe clay was a highly plastic and fairly pure clay of a grayish-white color, used in pipe making; flake white was white lead; Paris white, a good grade of whiting, was similar to China clay, but harder. Woolnough related that China clay was most often used in the marbling of his day. Kaolin is a hydrous silicate of aluminum, derived from the decomposition of aluminous minerals, especially feldspar.

27. Josef Halfer, *The Progress of the Marbling Art*, 87.

28. Isinglass is a semitransparent, whitish, and very pure form of gelatin, largely made from the bladders of fishes such as cod, ling, catfish, carp, and others.

29. Marjorie B. Cohn, *Wash and Gouache*, 54.

30. In his *Handmaid to the Arts* (1758 ed., v. 1, p. 136), Dossie comments that waters added to color must be given an "incohering" texture, which is done "by adding gums, size, sugar, or such other bodies as tend to inspissate and impart to the waters a more clammy and thick consistence." This matter will be discussed in the section "Binders and Carriers" that follows.

31. Robert Dossie, *Handmaid to the Arts*, Chapter 8, Section 3.

32. Perkins reviewed the discovery and early history of aniline colors in three Cantor lectures delivered to the Royal Society of Arts early in 1869. These were titled "On the Aniline or Coal Tar Colours," and appeared in the Society's *Journal* 17 (January 8, 15, 1869): 99–105, 109–114, 121–126. The part relating to his discovery is reprinted and discussed in F. Crace-Calvert's *Dyeing and Calico Printing*, 384–387.

33. It is interesting to observe how prior experiences can influence one's career. Intending to be an architect, Kekule (1829–1896) entered the University of Giessen but came under the influence of Justus von Liebig and switched to chemistry. His early training in architecture may have helped him conceive his structural theories. The story goes that one night in 1865 Kekule dreamed of the benzene molecules as a snake biting its tail while whirling in motion. From that vision was born the concept of the six-carbon benzene ring, and the facts of organic chemistry known to that time fell into place.

34. Although apparently not much or not at all used in early marbling, madder was an important source of red color for textile dyeing, as it producing the Turkey reds. A Eurasian herb of the Rubiciae family, specifically *Rubia tinctorum*, its root was employed in dyeing in India, Persia, and Egypt from antiquity, spreading to Asia minor in the tenth century and to Europe in the sixteenth. In his *Dyer's Assistant*, James Haigh devotes a chapter (the fourteenth) to "Of the Red of Madder;" and in 1800, John Arbuthnot, who is best known for producing at London in 1773 a publication entitled *An Enquiry into the Connection between the Present Price of Provisions and the Size of Farms*, had printed at Dublin by Graisberry and Campbell a pamphlet *On the Culture and Curing of Madder,* in which he provided details on the culture and curing of madder. Its coloring agent, alizarin, was isolated and purified in 1827, and laboratory methods of preparing it from anthracene were discovered in 1868, with the commercial introduction of the synthetic dye following in 1871; thereafter, the natural product quickly disappeared from the market. Philip Dessauer, it will be remembered, in 1881 extolled the virtues of the synthetic color for decorating paper, principally wallpaper.

35. Richard J. Wolfe, *Three Early French Essays on Paper Marbling*, 22.

CHAPTER 15

1. Mme. Guilleminot-Chrétien and I discussed this subject at length during one of my visits to the Bibliothèque Nationale in September of 1987. We are in total agreement on this matter.

2. Geneviève Guilleminot-Chrétien, *Papiers marbrés Français*, 27.

3. The methods and materials employed in the making of such papers are described in the Diderot-D'Alembert article on the maker of marbled paper and can be found in English translation in my *Three Early French Essays on Paper Marbling, 1642–1765.*

4. Genevieve Guilleminot-Chrétien, *Papiers marbrés français*, 30–31 ("Le goût nouveau: 1780–1815").

5. "Laid" paper is, as all book people know, paper made originally on a frame or mold having both widely and narrowly spaced wires making up the mesh of the mold. Although it is generally thought that before about 1800 all paper was laid, and all paper was "wove" thereafter, the situation differs from country to country and sometimes even from region to region

within a given country. "Wove" paper, or paper showing an even, granulated texture, began appearing in England in quantity from the 1780s, and by 1800 little of the laid kind was being made or used there. In Germany, in contrast, laid paper continued in use longer, as the example I noted earlier regarding the German 1808 *Vollkommene Papierfarben* indicates.

6. When imitating this pattern, I have noticed that the longer one retains a quantity of pink color (which normally is chalk white tinted with a little red), sometimes even over a number of weeks and marbling sessions, the dirtier the color becomes; subtle changes occur in it that eventually make it appear gray. Under these circumstances, the pink seems to go out of it. One has to continually refresh it with more red.

7. Hugh Sinclair, *The Whole Process of Marbling Paper and Book Edges*, 17–18; reprint edition, 1987, 57–58.

8. While Sinclair appears to refer mainly to the first spot pattern he discusses, to the one I have pointed out just before, as the "French" marble, it is my belief that he is placing all three of the patterns he discusses—the spot, turpentined, and "shell" designs—in the category of "French."

9. Genevieve Guilleminot-Chrétien, *Papiers marbrés Français*, 30–31.

10. The pattern with turpentine in it is generally known in English-speaking countries as "Stormont" because Charles Woolnough referred to it by that name. Mme. Guilleminot-Chrétien, we have noticed, called it "Empire" and James Sumner and probably Hugh Sinclair referred to it as "French." So far as I know, Woolnough is the only marbler to denominate this pattern as "Stormont," and I am at a loss to say why. Following my delivery of the second Rosenbach lecture on marbling in 1981—at which time I had, when reviewing some of the early marbled patterns, confessed my ignorance as to the origin of the name "Stormont" for one of them—I received a letter from Howell J. Heaney, then Rare Book Librarian at the Free Library of Philadelphia, who had attended this lecture, offering a possible explanation. Heaney speculated that the pattern may have been named for David Murray, first Earl of Mansfield and sixth Viscount Stormont, the British ambassador to Paris during the time of the American Revolution. Actually, the *Dictionary of National Biography* refers to several Murrays who succeeded to the Stormont title and after whom the pattern could have been named. David Murray was chosen possibly because he was a book collector. Howell J. Heaney to Richard J. Wolfe, 14 November 1981, author's files.

As an example of how much unjustified speculation has gone on in marbling literature, and how erroneous conclusions are picked up and republished by later commentators, I cite a recent discussion of the Stormont pattern by Iris Nevins, a self-taught marbler. Writing about this design in an article entitled "The Nineteenth Century Marbler " published in the Spring 1988 issue of *Ink and Gall* (1, no. 4: 6–7), Ms. Nevins relates (basing her information on Rosamond Loring's *Decorated Book Papers*, p. 28, but at the same time, omitting to cite Mrs. Loring as her source) that it is believed that the Stormont pattern originated in Ireland, the earliest example of it found being in *A Book of Common Prayer*, printed in Dublin in 1750 (which Mrs. Loring locates in the Boston Public Library, in its Benton Collection); furthermore, that it was named for the Irish House of Parliament. All evidence that I have mustered over a very long time (and which is corroborated by Mme. Guilleminot-Chrétien's observations, based on French archival records) indicates that this design arose in the very last years of the 1790s or in the very early 1800s; that it does not have an Irish origin or ancestry; and that it probably was not named for the Irish Parliament, which has been based at buildings (at Stormont, a site four miles east of Belfast in Northern Ireland) that were erected in 1928. One can only surmise that the copy of the *Book*

of Common Prayer which she and Mrs. Loring refer to received its binding—probably a new one, replacing an original or older one—in the nineteenth century, long after this pattern had been introduced.

11. Charles Woolnough, *The Whole Art of Marbling, as Applied to Paper and Book-Edges, &c.*, 68.

12. I refer to the copy in the Houghton Library at Harvard University, which was most conveniently available for my use.

13. Paul Kersten, *Die Geschichte des Buntpapieres*, separate Nachdruck, 5.

14. For making the tigré design, Fichtenberg called for an old tragacanth size that had been thinned down with water. For the Schroëtel, he noted that an old size was required also, consisting of gum psyllium (fleawort) and gum tragancanth mixed together. Fichtenberg may have advocated the use of old size because of the detrimental or destructive effect that the use of chemicals caused on size in general.

15. Glazing paste was a mixture of wax and tartar salts. It was employed mainly to prepare the paper for taking a fine gloss under glazing, by rubbing it onto the marbled paper before glazing or burnishing took place.

16. According to Schade, a good gradation of color could be achieved by combining caustic potash, linseed oil, nitric acid, turpentine and whiskey; after the ground color had attained sufficient driving force, that is, after enough gall had been supplied, ten drops or more of this preparation were added. One had to take care when blending the turpentine to the nitric acid, as they were volatile in combination and fire could easily result.

17. Another major source for directions on making the Tiger or Sonnen-Marmor is Paul Kersten's *Marmorierkunst*. Here are provided no less than four variant recipes. One calls for the combination of alum, soda, and potash; another for the addition of a solution of creolin (i.e., creosol and resin soap) to the ground color, a solution of caustic lime, and a ten-percent potassium solution. A third recipe, used by the Berlin marbler Hartmann, calls for the combining of potash, lime solution, and pulverized alum, with creolin added just before use. Another recipe derived from Hartmann directs that alum and borax be combined in hot water, bottled, and allowed to cool. This preparation is thrown onto the size, and the preparation in the third recipe is added to the color. Kersten relates that the method for making the sunbeam pattern in the factories had always been kept secret; it was Josef Hauptmann who first made it known, and Halfer afterward marketed a made-up solution as a commercial preparation.

18. There is no rational explanation for the use of the term "Griechisch" by German marblers to designate the newly revived and altered Spanish pattern. Neither marbling, nor any marbled patterns, have ever been imputed to Greece. I suspect that, as was the case with the Polish pattern, it received this name for "romantic" reasons, perhaps because "Griechisch" seemed an exotic name for it; Greece conjured up an exotic and romantic image in the German mind—at least, more than Spain did.

19. Charles W. Woolnough, *The Whole Art of Marbling, as Applied to Paper, Book-Edges, &c.*, 53.

20. James Sumner, *The Mysterious Marbler*, 15; reprint edition, 1976, 35.

21. In the 1853 edition of his manual, Woolnough discussed a pattern which he omitted when reprinting it nearly thirty years later. Called "Reverse Comb," this design was made by first laying down a variety of colors, raking them, and combing them with a somewhat wide comb; the needles of the comb were then placed in the centers of the channels created during the first combing, and a second combing was accomplished in reverse, with a sort of herringbone pattern resulting. (This is the Western equivalent of the Turkish "gitgel-ebrû" pattern dis-

cussed in note 43 of Chapter 1.) I have observed few British papers of the nineteenth century with this pattern; the design is more associated with Halferian marbling, and was much used by the Cockerells in Britain in this century. It can better be produced on carragheen size than on the tragacanth size of Woolnough's day. It is not so simple to make good examples of this design as might be supposed, either, for although it is easy to effect from the standpoint of mechanics or technique, it is difficult to produce papers that show straight designs and which do not appear trite.

INDEX